But Still,
Like Air, I'll Rise

In the series

Asian American History and Culture

edited by
Sucheng Chan, David Palumbo-Liu,
and Michael Omi

A list of books in the series appears
at the back of this volume

But Still, Like Air, I'll Rise

New Asian American Plays

Edited by

VELINA HASU HOUSTON

Foreword by

Roberta Uno

TEMPLE UNIVERSITY PRESS   PHILADELPHIA

For Kiyoshi, Kuniko-Leilani, and Steven

Temple University Press, Philadelphia 19122
Copyright © 1997 by Temple University
All rights reserved
Published 1997
Printed in the United States of America

♾ The paper used in this publication meets the requirements of the American
National Standard for Information Sciences—Permanence of Paper for Printed Library
Materials, ANSI Z39.48-1984

TEXT DESIGN BY KATE NICHOLS

Library of Congress Cataloging-in-Publication Data
But still, like air, I'll rise : new Asian American plays / Velina
    Hasu Houston, editor ; foreword by Roberta Uno.
        p.   cm.—(Asian American history and culture)
    Includes bibliographical references (p.   ).
    ISBN 1-56639-537-2 (cloth : alk. paper).—ISBN 1-56639-538-0
(pbk. : alk. paper)
    1. American drama—Asian American authors.   2. American
drama—20th century.   3. Asian Americans—Drama.   I. Houston,
Velina Hasu.   II. Series.
PS628.A85S75   1997
812'.54080895073—DC21   96–48729

ISBN 13: 978-1-56639-538-0 (pbk. : alk. paper)

072309P-4

Just like moons and like suns,
With the certainty of tides,
Just like hopes springing high,
Still I'll rise . . .
But still, like air, I'll rise . . .

—FROM "STILL I RISE"
BY MAYA ANGELOU

Contents

Foreword

by Roberta Uno

Velina and I never formally decided to have an annual conversation; it is something that evolved out of our "bicoastal" friendship as we have followed the lines of our separate paths—lives that defy geometry, running simultaneously parallel, divergent, and intersecting. The conversation insists on beginning somewhere in the middle of where it last ended. It is continuous and looping, always breaking with news, and yet echoed in memory. It is a conversation about new projects, ideas, our children, our passions, the latest play, politics, our mothers, health, the distance traveled.

This particular conversation, Velina maintains her good humor while I am spewing about a phone call I received from an Asian American woman journalist who called me to clarify some dates regarding the plays of an early Asian American playwright. She tells me she is writing a chapter on Asian American theater for an encyclopedic reference on Asian America. Her approach to the subject is to focus on what she terms "major figures." When I ask her to define "major," her response is, "those writers who have achieved visibility." I ask her to define "visibility" and she says, "those whose work have been reviewed in major publications."

We debate the issue of visibility. *Whose* vision determines an Asian American playwright's work is major? Is the work invisible unless a (white, probably male) reviewer at a "major" (white) publication notices it? What if a thousand Asian Americans see it somewhere a white reviewer will not even go?—is it less significant? Why does her list only include those playwrights who have had productions at Asian American and/or mainstream theaters? What about those Asian American artists who are self-produced, particularly those in solo performance? What about those who collaborate with other artists of color? What about those whose work is community-based? We end up talking for quite some time; I want her to understand that while it is important to look at the individual achievements of specific writers, it is essential to provide a context for their writing and to look at the major work that has *not* been validated by the mainstream.

Velina quips astutely, "Another casualty of graduate school," and indeed I tell her that at the conclusion of the phone call the woman explained apologetically that she is a victim of her training, stating that her entry into this literature is as an academic and that she is an Asian American who did not grow up "Asian American," part of an Asian American community. That conversation left me feeling both angry and sad—angered toward an academic power structure that has the ability to grant credentials and legitimacy; saddened by the perception that Asian America is one, definable and exclusive, entity, so monolithic that an Asian American can feel locked out.

When Velina first sent me the manuscript for this book, I could not help but reflect on these two conversations. This collection, in its conception, defies the narrow and reductionist categorization that is frequently imposed on our dramatic work by those seeking a convenient way to place it as literature or market it to an audience. The eyes through which Velina sees these plays are first and foremost those of a working artist and creator. The prevailing sensibility is that of someone who has felt constricted by the lines of the box demanding to be checked; someone who, with courage, joy, and honesty, has always drawn outside the lines. As an artist, Velina has naturally sought to recognize and embrace the sources of creativity and vision; thus her discerning eye has been drawn to and beyond the traditional centers of theatrical production. As an Asian American who was raised in Kansas, shaped by a rich and complex Asian America emanating from within the walls of her home, Velina understands that our art is being created everywhere we are and have been— Hawaii and the mainland, urban centers and the suburbs, both coasts and the heartland, within and beyond our borders.

Velina's metaphor for her own multiracial, multicultural, and binational identity is that of a "double," a concept that at once subverts and obliterates historical notions of fragmentation, impurity, and displacement. As a double one is able to occupy simultaneously more than one cultural space; so too, an added lens sharpens, expands, and deepens vision. This sense of "doubleness" permeates the construction of this anthology. It is clearly a source for theater production as much as it is an academic resource, challenging and redefining the dramatic literary canon and the frameworks used for its analysis and interpretation. Even in its title it interrupts the thought that Asian American theater exists in a bipolar relationship exclusively to a Eurocentric, mainstream theater. The titular tribute asserts an acknowledgment of connected experiences, a multiplicity of themes, an expansion of aesthetic sensibilities.

During our next annual phone call, I want to remember to tell Velina about a graduate student I know who is doing some extraordinary and groundbreaking research on Filipino American Theater. Ironically, this student was told by an advisor that she may not want to limit herself to such a narrow research subject. The lack of knowledge of the topic presumes either that there is little to know or that what exists may not be worth knowing. It is with a sense of mission and urgency, then, that this volume appears before you. It takes its place among a small but growing number of texts that enable theater artists to expand their vision and repertoire and allow scholars to consider theater from a place of immersion and practice.

Acknowledgments

I would like to express my gratitude to the people and organizations that helped bring this book to life with their trust, encouragement, counsel, assistance in research, and direct and indirect support: Sucheng Chan, Janet Francendese, Juli Thompson Burk, Roberta Uno, Endesha Ida Mae Holland, James Day Wilson, Lily Ling Wong, Oliver Mayer, Chay Yew, Angela Pao, Kiyoshi Sean Shannen Kamehanaokala Houston, Kuniko-Leilani Marie Houston, Steven Kent Brauer, Setsuko Perry, Donna Marie Carolan, Theatre of Yugen, Playwrights Preview Productions, Japan Society (New York), Odyssey Theatre Ensemble, and A Contemporary Theatre.

In addition, I extend special thanks to Yuriko Doi, Tina Chen, Peggy Shannon, Jan Lewis, and Akira Wakabayashi for their insights into *Kokoro*.

Velina Hasu Houston

Introduction

by Velina Hasu Houston

To be marginalized in the United States is (especially for those marginalized because of their ethnicity) to have much of one's experience inadvertently or conveniently omitted from the nation's "history." Written from the heterosexual, patriarchal, Eurocentric perspective, this incomplete history presents itself as unchallengeable, immortal, and righteous; any examination of it meets cries of indignation. Drama has long been a means for the voices marginalized by the dominant society to document their own histories.

Yearning to be free from the limitations imposed on the exotic or the marginal, the soul of color wants to be valued as an individual and to function in society in an unburdened fashion. As created and perpetuated by Eurocentrism and its power structures, the essentialized nature of people of color is imagined to be exotic, entwined solely with ethnic roots and an inability to function "appropriately" in society. These manifestations of colonialism in our society sustain an "ethnicist" view of nation and individual that strangles our ability to heal the ethnic disparities and wounds; and they prevent us from recording our history in a more inclusive way.

In her essays "Can the Subaltern Speak?" and "Subaltern Studies: Deconstructing Historiography," South Asian intellectual Gayatri Chakravorty Spivak speaks of the lower strata of the marginalized within the context of colonized India as being "subaltern."[1] She notes that, under capitalism, the colonized become politicized. In keeping with the view that internalized colonialism exists in the United States with ethnicities of color being the colonized within the Eurocentric patriarchy that writes a history that only genuinely and fully represents its *own* history and that rules sociopolitically in exclusionary ways, I see parallels between U.S. citizens of color and Spivak's subalterns. The politicization of these citizens forms an educated consciousness on the part of people of color, a consciousness that can no longer sit still and wait for The Great White Hope to deliver the progress and agency that the subaltern's latter-day twentieth-century consciousness knows are long overdue.

However, Spivak notes that the elite believe that the current political expression of people of color will dissipate because it eventually must defer or succumb to the will and concentrated energies of the Eurocentric powers that be; that subaltern progress is discourse and discourse alone, without agency, and therefore limited. I think not. The dramatic voices contained in this volume are too eclectic, intense, powerful, and rich not to leave a permanent mark on the American psyche, and perhaps beyond the boundaries of this continent. *That* is agency. These voices extend from the mainland United States to Hawaii to the South Pacific Islands, Southeast Asia, and the Far East. They include heritages of Japan, China, Korea, Singapore, Taiwan, the Philippines, Africa, Samoa, Native America, Scotland, the United Kingdom, Vietnam, and Hawaii and the rest of the United States.

We are fortunate to have these unique playwrights of Asian descent—and often Asian dissent—residing here in the United States. They lift stereotypes to the wind, broaden the perspectives of ethnic identities of color, and flood people's understanding, in the hope of greater ethnic tolerance.

From my peculiar point of view as a multiethnic, multicultural, and binational female, I believe that this agency is the future, with perspectives on truths of history that must and will be combined with European–European-American truth. For change, as we all know, is inevitable. Myths must crumble, societies must shift . . . evolve or die, as the saying goes.

For my first anthology, *The Politics of Life: Four Plays by Asian American Women*, my editors requested that the Introduction be a personal essay on surviving in the American theater as a multiethnic and multicultural female. Many people were uncomfortable with this personal view, wanting my approach to dramatic literature perhaps to align with that of the European-American tradition. My traditions, however, are different (though inclusive of the European-American tradition because that heritage is a part of the American context in which I was reared). My traditions are born of a culturally hybrid aesthetic and sociopolitical vision. In that vein, I am merely a conduit to bring stories to you that emerge vibrantly from America's diverse ethnocultural landscape and to reveal to you American persons of Asian descent who are bringing unexpected weather to that landscape that alters how we live and think and how we will trip or glide into the future. No matter what, the climate is permanently changed—and it will change again and again and again.

As an activist, I would be remiss if I did not examine this meteorology and its relationship to the American theater. The closest thing that we have to a national theater, our network of regional theaters, remains the "bastion of white male representation," as *Los Angeles Times* journalist Jan Breslauer diagnosed it in 1991.[2] Regardless of which European-American males may be getting left out of the national production picture (which is unfortunate, because I am absolutely certain from personal exposure that many of them have rich and significant stories to tell), their stories *are* being represented by members of their group and in a generous fashion. As the status quo, they need not fear colored or female encroachment upon the representation of their world. While the predicted demographics of this nation may engender some stress for that dominant faction of our society in the future, it continues to recuperate its standing within the persistent (intentionally or otherwise) European–European-American patriarchal protectionism of mainstream American theater, not to mention film, television, and other empowered media. This protectionism is becoming more and more prevalent in U.S. society at large.

Roger Boesche, a professor of politics at Occidental College, suggested in the *Los Angeles Times* that European Americans work "silently, almost invisibly, albeit painfully" to assure their dominance in America. They do it by reducing the representation of communities of color via sociopolitical means because they can—because they are "the powerful elites who control decisions." By controlling who gets heard, what gets seen, and who gets what, the dominant European-American patriarchy can continue to rule without ever raising a fist—at least not one that we can see. Boesche discusses an "unease" the country is recognizing with regard to "just how gaping . . . the chasm" is that separates ethnic groups in America. That unease fuels a great deal of backlash protectionism, and it appears that it is only beginning.[3]

Noted playwrights publicly challenge the Eurocentric idea that affirmative action has increased opportunities for people of color in the arts and the academies of this nation. To many of them, it is myth. In the view of African American playwright Cheryl West, "The whole multicultural drive in theater—with theaters getting grants to do more culturally diverse work and to try to bring in more diverse audiences—still means, at best, only one play by a person of color getting done a season." While West noted that producers often state economics as the reason for this imbalance, a reason that West finds legitimate, she also posited that "racism and sexism play a larger, more insidious role than most producers care to admit." Many theaters have told her that they "couldn't do more than one black play a season," the assumption being that "the black audience for a theater . . . could only afford to go to one play." "The larger question should be," West suggests, "are the play seasons offering diverse enough work to attract a diverse and appreciative audience?"[4] She doesn't think so.

George C. Wolfe, artistic director of the Joseph Papp Public Theater, hates the word diversity: "The need to come up with a term to express the inclusion of people is based on the absurd fact that in America, European culture is held up as the only true legitimate culture." Rather than theaters deciding to invite people of color "to the party," Wolfe says, the whole scenario should be reversed; theaters "should be forced to explain why they are excluding people." Speaking in a writers and diversity forum sponsored by the Non-Traditional Casting Project, Wolfe wondered how American theaters can rationalize their not presenting stories of people of color from the United States, even though they have presented works of people "from somewhere else" (perhaps alluding to the widely produced works of Athol Fugard that depict the lives of black Africans). "If you are not telling . . . the stories of all the different people in this country, then you can't call yourself an American theater," Wolfe noted. "You are an elitist white institution and should hang a banner outside calling yourself that." While Wolfe acknowledged that most people working in theaters are liberal, he said there is a refusal to share power, despite "a long history of white artists extolling the cultures of non-whites." Echoing Spivak and my notion of internalized U.S. colonialism, Wolfe called the situation in theater "cultural colonization." "Until the people from those [nonwhite] cultures are involved in making decisions as directors, writers, producers, artistic directors—and there are very few of them—there will be no substantial change." He sees himself as a "rare creature," being a person of color with power in the American theater. He views his rarity as "a reflection of how rigid the systems are and how much more rigid they are becoming." Despite his success, however, being an African American male, he "still can't get a cab in New York."[5]

The rigidity of the systems—and white society's inability or lack of desire to recognize this rigidity as a big part of the race equation in the United States—may be a point of departure for beginning to ease the race war in America. Peggy McIntosh, Associate Director of the Wellesley College Center for Research on Women, discusses over-entitlement as an aspect of systematic oppression in her 1988 working paper, "White Privilege and Male Privilege: A Personal Account of Coming to See Correspondences Through Work in Women's Studies." First of all, McIntosh makes it clear that she is a white woman. (Some might argue that this gives her point of view extra validity because when whites talk about race it is often perceived as ordered and balanced, but when people of color talk about race it is perceived as grousing.) That careful distinction in place, McIntosh presents a metaphor for systems that ensure the sustenance of privilege, stating that she as a white woman possesses an invisible, weightless knapsack of "unearned assets" that she can take advantage of on a daily basis, but about which she is "meant" to remain oblivious.

Noting the extent to which white men work from a base of unacknowledged privilege, McIntosh offers a list of ways in which she experiences white privilege in her own life (in contrast to African American women who live in her building and whose employment differs from her own). She can go shopping without being harassed by store security personnel, see her race meaningfully and favorably represented in media, have teachers assert that her race built civilization, berate the government without being seen (culturally) as an agitator, and get a job "with an affirmative action employer without having coworkers on the job suspect that I got it because of my race, or keep it because of my race, or will be promoted because of my race. . . ." McIntosh posits that if these conditions are real (together with the over 41 others that she names), then the United States isn't the land of equal opportunity that it presents itself to be. McIntosh notes that her whiteness has protected her from hostilities, distresses, and violence that she feels she is "being subtly trained to visit in turn upon people of color." She says that she wrote her paper because she came to see that some of the power that she initially saw as "attendant on being a human being in the U.S. consisted in unearned advantage and conferred dominance."[6] Her solution? Use that advantage to share power.

Her position on the future health of society is not too far from Wolfe's position regarding the future health of culture and arts (particularly theater). Systems of dominance *do* exist, and we have to stop being silent or being in denial about them. Equal access or opportunity are myths manufactured by these systems. Within the bastion of liberalism that the arts are perceived to be, artists of color remain the culturally colonized. Their success is a result of sheer determination, chutzpah, and good fortune—because to survive against such intense systematic odds when you are not allowed to carry an "invisible weightless knapsack" reflects a truly pioneering spirit. Certainly, many with

McIntosh's invisible "knapsacks" may still find themselves, in some situations, empty-handed and without recourse. The reasons for this are clear, because we have to consider not only the racial, ethnic, and cultural aspects of systems of dominance but also the sexual, gender, class, and economic aspects.

The artist of color, ever the anarchist in the eyes of dominant U.S. society, must stand far from Oz's emerald-green curtain—all too painfully aware that the man behind it is nothing but a mythmaker—and state with resolution, "I'll bet that there is nothing in that bag for me." Courage, brains, heart, and the ability to create a home—an ethnic, cultural, racial, and national "home"— are qualities that the artist of color will have to find without the help of the Wizard and his knapsack full of privileges.

I would be equally remiss if I did not acknowledge the efforts of the many non-Asian-descent intellectuals, practitioners of the arts, and professors who do struggle to bring balance to Eurocentrism's near monopoly of the American theater. For example, Dr. Juli Thompson Burk at the University of Hawaii has made great strides in producing and teaching the works of ethnically diverse women playwrights. Professor Edit Villareal at the University of California at Los Angeles and institutions such as Cornell University, the University of California at Berkeley, the University of Kansas, the University of Michigan, the University of Massachusetts at Amherst, and countless others teach diverse drama.

Many leading regional theaters also have sought to present or produce diverse American plays on their primary and secondary stages—regional groups such as the Old Globe Theatre, the Mark Taper Forum, A Contemporary Theatre, La Jolla Playhouse, the Joseph Papp Public Theatre, Manhattan Theatre Club, Berkeley Repertory Theatre, Actors Theatre of Louisville, TheatreWorks, Syracuse Stage, and others. Perhaps the real trailblazers, however, are the small-to-medium-sized theaters in urban centers such as Los Angeles, Washington, D.C., Chicago, San Francisco, Seattle, New York, and San Diego that historically and still today make pioneering efforts to present many different kinds of American plays, not merely those about or by European Americans.

Perhaps the underlying realization of this activity is that ethnic diversity is as American as apple pie.

Nevertheless, many literary managers still suggest that audiences are conditioned to see one thing—to eat meat and potatoes every season, so that the inclusion of an "exotic" item on the menu is always a novelty and, therefore, suspect. Audiences are rarely allowed to get used to the play of color as being part of normal consumption. It is outside of the norm, something special or something deviant, but marginalized—as in that "black play" or that "Asian play" or that "Latino play." The strides being made by key regional theaters and many prominent smaller theaters in urban areas are important contributions to balancing the artistic representation of life in the United States. Change is slow, but perhaps we are approaching a time when a play about people of color is not seen as an exotic anomaly, but is judged (solely) on the basis of its artistic quality.

In this anthology I wanted to represent as wide a spectrum as possible of voices of Asian-descent American playwrights living and working in the United States, to embrace a pan-Asian perspective to as great an extent as possible, even though certain realities placed constraints on my idealistic objectives. For example, the limited periods of time that people of Asian ethnicity have resided in the United States and have been able to move beyond mere survival and cultural collision management to the luxury of artistic expression in the theater arts have resulted in U.S. Asian-descent playwrights who are mostly of Japanese American, Korean American, or Chinese American descent. Another constraint is the availability of material; several "Asian American" anthologies are now in the making, I am happy to report. Furthermore, some playwrights will not allow their work to be published at all or only at certain times for various legitimate reasons. The need to limit the size of an anthology also forces exclusion of certain voices. Another constraint is that in certain Asian ethnic groups new to the United States, the writing of plays is a relatively new experience.

Given these restrictions, I have compiled an anthology that is as pan-Asian as I could make it. It includes a wide spectrum of subject matter and writing styles, some very American, some very Asian, and some a composite of both origins. One thing I can say about all of them is that they are both individualistic and universal in their views of the human condition. Moreover, it is important to note that these are not "ethnic plays," but American plays that should not be relegated to the artistic ghetto of Eurocentrism's manufacture.

Thank you for your support of the theater. I offer special thanks to readers of literature and to people who enter the theater and live the art with us.

NOTES

1. Gayatri Chakravorty Spivak, "Subaltern Studies," *In Other Worlds: Essays in Cultural Politics.* New York: Routledge, 1988.
2. Jan Breslauer, "Hues and Cries," *Los Angeles Times*, July 1991, p. 3.
3. Roger Boesche, "How White People Riot: Quietly, but Lethally, at the Ballot Box," *Los Angeles Times*, October, 11, 1995.

4. Cheryl West, "Writers and Diversity: A Forum (Part 2)," *New Traditions, The NTCP Newsletter,* Non-Traditional Casting Project, New York, Vol. 2 (4), Summer 1995, p. 3.

5. George C. Wolfe, "Writers and Diversity: A Forum (Part 2)," *New Traditions, the NTCP Newsletter,* Non-Traditional Casting Project, New York, Vol. 2 (4), Summer 1995, p. 3.

6. Peggy McIntosh, "White Privilege and Male Privilege: A Personal Account of Coming to See Correspondences Through Work in Women's Studies." Working paper no. 180. Wellesley College Center for Research on Women, 1988. Quoted with permission.

Talk-Story

by
JEANNIE BARROGA

*A Filipina daughter, with a penchant for emulating the heroines of '40s movie
flicks, continues her father's legacy of telling stories to herself and to those
around her. Moving between her world in present-day San Francisco and that of
her father in his '30s world of rural California, she tells her version of dealing
with bigotry much the same way her father told his own heroic tales to her.*

TIME: Pasts and presents of both father and daughter

PLACE: Various: Father's past (told from hotel room): church, stores, Watsonville corner, diner, jungle road.
Present: hotel room, hospital room

Daughter's present: office, cafe, moviehouse, Headlands, Lon's couch, hospital

CHARACTERS (TWO FEMALES, FOUR MALES)

FRANK   Asian (prefer Filipino), Dee's tall-tale father, somewhat
itinerant, 70s, a braggart, endearing, exasperating, lives
in San Francisco hotel (noticeable accent)

| DEE | Asian (prefer Filipina-American), 30s, a 1940s aficionado, fantasizer, storyteller, a columnist |
| CLARA | African-American, 30s, Dee's best friend, account rep, follows Dee's tales, blunt |

IN THEIR STORIES

LON	Caucasian, 30s, Dee's editor, the modern-day liberal
PEDRO	Asian (prefer Filipino), Frank's brother and hero-self, sexy confident (will age)
	Island relative (both roles: noticeable accent)
CHARLIE	Frank and Pedro's World War II buddy
	also CHIEF, BULLY, BOSS, DRUGGIST

═══════════

ACT I

[*In darkness,* SLIDE: "TALK-STORY." *Voice-over of a man teaching song to his young daughter, who half-tries to sing along. It is the English translation of Joey Ayala's* "Walang ganggang Pa'alam" *("Never Ending Good-Bye") repeated in second act:*]

Many times I think of you, many dreams to remember
You haunt all my thoughts, my life
Dreaming brings you close to me, dreaming makes me wonder
When will you return this time?
Although you are so far away I always will remember
Though we are apart the memories still linger
Always smiles with the sighs, always tears with the laughter
Till the day we'll be together . . . come that day
(Tell me you will be returning, tell me no more yearning)

[*Lights up.* DEE *is heard as young girl urging* FRANK, *narrating. Whether 70 years old or younger, he in his costume will never change. Always in baggy pants, button shirt, hat, a man who's been the itinerant, the lettuce picker, the cannery worker. Above all, he is a storyteller.*]

DEE: Okay, daddy, now a story!
FRANK: I thought you wanted to learn this song . . .
DEE: [*oblivious*] The GHOST one! The spooky one! Go on, daddy!
FRANK: [*laughs*] Okay, okay!

SLIDE: LEYTE, THE PHILIPPINES

[*Seen is a makeshift cot, army-issue, behind scrim/filmstrip and sleeping body* (PEDRO). *One cricket heard. The feeling should be a very warm night at guard duty in a hollowed-out church baptismal chamber: World War II, Leyte. Light should suggest haunted feeling, spooky.* FRANK *relishes his story as he tells (audience) his tale:*]

FRANK: [*dramatically*] I was all alone after my brother, your uncle, took off for the base. Me, Frank Abano, far from camp, guarding the movie projector for the company at our makeshift theatre in a baptismal chamber—only one cricket chirping. Can you see it, Dee? Stars overhead at night. And, Clara, you could smell the damp air on that hot, wet island of Leyte. You see, the roof had been bombed off! Yes, the roof! Remember, this is wartime. . . .

[*Moans heard from "body"* (PEDRO).]

[*continues*] I was drunk. I had just stumbled into my cot when I heard . . .

[*Measured footsteps heard.*]

[*continues*] footsteps. [*from where he sits, slurred*] Ano, who'z zair??

[FRANK *does steps with his foot.*]

[*repeats, leans up*] I called again.

SOLDIER: [PEDRO] Who'zout zair?? HALT!!

[*Footsteps stop, then start again. Behind scrim filmstrip.* SOLDIER *with rifle rises groggily from cot and points offstage.*]

[*weaving*] I'm warning you, if you don't identify yourself, I'll shoot!

[*Footsteps hesitate, but continue.* SOLDIER *raises rifle.*]

FRANK: [*to audience*] So, to show I meant business, I shot my rifle—HIGH.

[SOLDIER *shoots wobbily.*]

FRANK: [*continues*] But the steps kept on. So I called, HALT!

[*Footsteps continue.*]

[*continues*] I leveled my rifle. . . .

[SOLDIER *shoots levelly. Silence.* SOLDIER *makes moves toward offstage when footsteps heard again.*]

FRANK: [*amazed*] I should've hit him! He was right in front of me! But there was no one there. No one walking where I heard walking, and from where I could STILL hear walking. Well, I could've grabbed my gear, to hell with the projector, and I could've run out of there! But instead I laughed! Ghosts? HA! I stayed right there, yelling at all the ghosts. . . .

SOLDIER: [*boisterous, drunk*] Come'n get me! I'm not afraid of you! I dare you! I DARE YOU! HA-HA-HA! [*drifts off*] Come on! Come'n try. . . .

FRANK: So drunk, I . . . I fell asleep. [SOLDIER *passes out*] Yep, I stayed put. All alone.

[*Lights down on chamber.* SOLDIER *exits.*]

[*continues*] Later I found out right in front of the chamber was a secret crypt. Former pastors of the church, bones of the elders buried right where I'd been sleeping, disturbed by a soldier, drunk and laughing, on their final resting place. The same place where they whispered vespers and walked in solitude. Dead or alive, you're always alone, braving the elements, animals . . . ghosts. In here [*points to heart*] is the stuff of heroes. Always rely on that. Face the music. Running's not always the answer.

[*Blackout*]

SLIDE: OFFICE—TODAY

[DEE *types furiously.* CLARA *carries chinese food. Surrounded by '40s movie posters,* DEE *emulates its stars.*]

CLARA: Sorry I'm late. Long line at Moon Garden today . . .

DEE: Pass me that white-out.

CLARA: [*peers into bag*] How do you wrap muushu pork again? [*as she nibbles*] Next time when *I* win, it's Filipino food.

DEE: [*still whiting-out*] Lay 'em out, spread some plum sauce, spoon in the stuff, fold and twist the ends.

CLARA: No fair. You were born Oriental.

DEE: Asian. They offer Political Correctness on campus now.

CLARA: [*peers over shoulder*] What are you doing?

DEE: Writing.

CLARA: Thank you, Sherlock!

DEE: An article. Due in two days.

CLARA: I'm still writing those notes from last weekend: The Conference from HELL. Everybody ELSE's group gets first-class treatment. . . . Me, the only

Black female account rep. What do I get? LEFTOVERS! And as top account rep, I stand there, open-mouthed with EGG on my face, and it's not my fault!

DEE: Better hand those notes in.

CLARA: I told you about Murphy.

DEE: It's his format. Nail 'im.

CLARA: He's a CEO! I can't alienate him now.

DEE: Face the music, Clara. Expose the deficiencies of the program. Murphy answers—not you. Don't kowtow, Clara. [*quotes:*] "A career is a curious think . . ."

CLARA: Okay, okay! You know, not everything has to be done in the Sherman-talk way YOU do all the time! [*pouts*] Can't I just hide my head in the sand for awhile?

DEE: Running's not always the answer, Clara. My dad taught me that . . .

CLARA: [*sighs*] I remember . . . the snake story, right?

DEE: No, the ghost one. Damn! White-out again, please?

CLARA: [*hands over*] Stop typing and talk to me!

DEE: Sorry. [*She stopped typing.*] I gotta get this thing done. A prime opportunity. I can't screw it up. [*her Roz Russell delivery:*] "You need timing, an eye for seeing the turning point or recognizing the big chance when it comes along. . . ."

CLARA: Uh-oh. [*like* Poltergeist] "She's ba-ack!"

DEE: "Don't settle for the little dream. Go on to the big one."

CLARA: Just tell your story, Dee. You will, anyway. . . .

SLIDE: AN OFFICE

[CHIEF *enters a busy, fast-paced world of newspapers. A '40s look: The* CHIEF (*like* His Girl Friday), DEE *like tough ace reporter Rosalind Russell. She holds a smart hat.* CLARA *listens.*]

DEE: [*like Roz, to* CLARA] "The chief called me into his office upstairs . . ."

CHIEF: [*ignores her, into phone:*] Get 'em off our backs! We're running a paper here!

DEE: "He'd been watching me and my work and he seemed impressed . . ."

CHIEF: [*pushes button*] Hello, Stan? STAN?? [*pushes another*]

CLARA: [*bit skeptical*] You just walk in and he drops what he's doing, huh?

CHIEF: Hello, anyone there? HELLO??

[*Lights change.*]

DEE: [*her former self, to* CLARA] I'm setting a mood here.

CLARA: Why can't you just tell a story straight?

DEE: [*rolls eyes*] BOR-ING!

CLARA: Amazing how things are all the time happening to you, appearing at a drop of a hat! . . .

DEE: Clara! Let me WALLOW a bit, okay??

CLARA: I know how you are, Dee . . .

DEE: [*quotes* FRANK's *saying:*] "Indulge me! . . . Please?"

CLARA: [*sighs, adjusts hat on* DEE's *head*] And then you said? . . .

DEE: [*eagerly to* CHIEF] I'm Dee Abano . . .

CHIEF: [*inattentive*] Steno pool's down the hall around the corner on your right . . .

DEE: From downstairs? . . .

CHIEF: First door by the cooler. Can't miss it.

DEE: Features! Copy assistant! You sent for me? . . .

CHIEF: [*phone buzzes*] Stan? Stan, where'd you go, okay, where were we? . . . [*turns away*]

[DEE *braces herself, then boldly depresses boss's telephone:*]

DEE: [*again as Roz, kickstarts into fantasy*] "Chief, I came up when I could. Hope you weren't waiting long."

CHIEF: [*hangs up, a complete change*] Well, well, well! Just the person I want to see!

DEE: [*nods to* CLARA *smugly*] Just the reception I want to get.

CLARA: [*dry*] You don't smoke.

[DEE *snuffs cigarette.*]

CHIEF: I'll come to the point. Dee, we got forty-five inches of copy to fill in our series on Oriental groups. . . .

DEE: Which one?

CHIEF: What are YOU?

DEE: You mean, it doesn't make a difference?

CHIEF: [*shifts*] Sure it does! . . . See, there's a quota involved . . .

DEE: Ah.

CHIEF: I mean, you oughta be grateful!

DEE: [*laughs*] Right! [*to* CLARA] And then Lon comes in—Newsroom.

[LON *enters.*]

LON: [*ignores* DEE] Damn it, Chief! You can't cut the meat out of this! We gotta mention the peephole? Secret crypt, video equipment, soundproof room—the whole scenario! Why leave out a peephole??

DEE: [*to* CLARA] We have the same movie poster in our offices. I think he likes me. . . .

LON: [*now sees* DEE] Oh, sorry, didn't see you. Why didn't you say something? [*peers at her*] You sit by that *Casablanca* poster!

DEE: [*eagerly, as* DEE] The one like yours; yes, that's me . . .

LON: [*snaps fingers*] Steno, right?

DEE: [*deflated*] Features.

LON: Right. [*to* CHIEF] Call me when you're done. I want this in, Chief. [*exits*]

DEE: [*to* CLARA] We almost forgot the Chief was there, we talked so long!

[LON *reenters, Cary Grantlike, and resumes former position.*]

[*continues*] Well, I wouldn't say "talked." . . .

LON: [*continues ranting, but as Cary Grant*] "You leave out a peephole, next thing you leave out are the tapes! The pervert TAPED every torture he did! He pops a cyanide pill and his accomplice Chu flits off to Canada! But, no, let's delete that, too! His torture chamber muffles the screams of women, men, AND kids! If he didn't lure them with car ads, he outright KIDNAPPED them! But who CARES about DETAILS like THAT, huh?? As a responsible reporter I want to tell the NEWS, but, NO! Cut this out, cover that up! Keep things LIGHT! Hell, I might as well be writing a KIDDIE magazine! What happened to freedom of the press, huh? CENSORSHIP REIGNS! CENSORSHIP THRIVES! I WANT MY PEEPHOLE! PUT THE PEEPHOLE BACK IN!"

DEE: [*quotes*] "He's dedicated, Chief. . . ."

LON: [*straightens*] Thank you. . . .

DEE: [*still quoting*] "Your solid citizen writes the facts but watches the clock. . . ."

LON: Right, your solid citizen . . . Hey, I know where that comes from! . . .

DEE: [*still quoting*] "When it comes to newspapermen . . ."

DEE/LON: "Give me a reformed LUSH every time."

LON: Cagney . . . [*amused*] I think I just had my hand slapped. . . .

CHIEF: [*introduces*] Lon: Dee, Features. Dee here is an up-and-coming reporter, writer, nose for the news. Keep your eye out for her. She's doing the piece on Oriental groups—with your help, Lon.

LON: An Oriental woman . . . appropriate, I guess.

DEE: [*quotes*] "Lots of things a man can do, and it's all hunky-dory. A woman does the same thing, and she's an outcast."

LON: Katharine Hepburn, *Adam's Rib*. Try another? [*flicks at hat*] Nice hat.

DEE: "This old thing? I wear this when I don't care HOW I look."

LON/DEE: Gloria Grahame.

DEE: Very good. [*holds out unlit cigarette*]

LON: [*pretends to light*] I remember now: you have that, uh, World War II look in your office, don't you?

DEE: [*puffs imaginary smoke*] I like the forties.

LON: Ah, war years. Propaganda. But lots of, uh, love banter.

DEE: Movies today leave nothing to the imagination. I . . .

CHIEF: Excuse me, can we work here?

LON: [*reminded*] I want my column intact, Chief.

DEE: [*buffering*] I hope it'll be as easy for me to keep copy in MY column. Any tips?

LON: Yeah: [*specifically at* CHIEF] Don't kowtow!

CHIEF: God, Lon! . . .

[As LON *and* CHIEF *argue silently:*]

CLARA: So what's the issue?

DEE: The bashings, Clara. Chin's murder in Detroit. Asian gangs in Chinatown. The remark on American workers by that Japanese businessman? Front page news for WEEKS! The country thinks Fu-Manchu rides again. The fear's back, Clara. The takeover by "Orientals." If the paper prints stories about specific Asian groups, it might enlighten the masses, dispel the fear.

CHIEF: [*covers ears*] Okay! Okay, Lon! God, it's only three inches! Cut three inches SOMEWHERE!

LON: I'll shorten the blurb.

CHIEF: It's not the blurb that needs shortening. Lon . . .

DEE: May I? [*takes copy, reads:*] "In these days of electronics and state-of-the-art conveniences, it is chilling to realize that their usage as instruments of torture, as methods to chronicle and preserve murderous events . . ."

LON: [*takes it*] Jesus, did I write that?? [*crosses it out*] Start here. [*crosses out two more sections as well*]

CHIEF: [*relieved*] Thank you. [*to* DEE] And thank YOU. NOW may we proceed, Mr. Quinn?

[*Instead* DEE *takes charge.*]

DEE: Listen, Chief: I've got stories that'll make our readers perk up in their chairs? My dad's! MINE! I kept a journal while I was in the Philippines, the view of an American-Filipino! If this sparks any interest, I could do an ongoing column, nothing big! Forty inches every couple of weeks . . .

LON: Whoa, down girl! Right now, this is a filler! Let's not think ERMA BOMBECK just yet!

DEE: But think of it! No one realizes we're the largest Asian group in California! We're FORGOTTEN! And you—the first kids on the block—prints it up and busts that myth wide open! [earnest] Chief, I'll make you a deal: if I don't come up with something by Wednesday, run whatever copy you have. Put mine on a back page, put it in PERSONALS if you want! But if I get it done by 5 P.M. Wednesday, the column is mine, with more every couple weeks, every month, if you want! Is it a deal?

CHIEF: It's gotta be good, Dee, not just What-I-Did-On-My-Vacation. . . .

DEE: DEAL??

[As CHIEF is shaking DEE's hand, LON also offers his. She takes it. Both men exit. DEE approaches CLARA triumphantly.]

CLARA: A column, huh? And a byline, of course.

DEE: [with a sweep of her hand] "Discoveries" by Dee Abano. Nice ring, huh? It's kinda musical, kinda romantic . . .

CLARA: And what really happened?

DEE: [just looks at her] That IS what happened, Clara . . . really! [silence] Really!!

[CHIEF and LON appear in spot.]

CHIEF: Uh, Miss, uh . . . Abano, is it? Dee, of course. Listen, what ARE you, by the way? Filipino, good. We want a filler on some kind of Oriental group. Can you whip something up, I don't care what. I get to see your work, and you get to fill a quota. Lon here will work with you. Deal?

DEE: [relents] Deal.

[CHIEF and LON exit. Lights change.]

DEE: [continues] What does it matter how I got it? I'm going to write it if it kills me.

CLARA: [sighs] Okay, Dee. I wish you luck.

DEE: Better wish YOURSELF luck. Get those notes in. I'll make you a deal . . .

CLARA: I'm not betting with you!

DEE: You finish your notes and I'll finish my article. . . .

CLARA: No more bets! Lunch was sixteen dollars today!

DEE: Who's ever done last buys dinner Thursday, okay? . . . Okay??

[CLARA *thinks, sighs, then shakes* DEE's *hand. Exit.*]

SLIDE: WATSONVILLE CORNER

[DEE *holds cassette: Spot on* FRANK. *His brother,* PEDRO, *is nattily dressed in early '30s style. Sound cue:* "Birth of the Blues." (*Audience is collectively* DEE.)]

FRANK: [*to* DEE] Your uncle Pedro introduced me to the taxi-dance halls all over California. [*Light cue: Twirling Mirrored Ball*] Ah, yes, ten cents a dance. Dancing all night could use up a whole day's pay!

PEDRO: [*to* FRANK/*audience*] Frank, ss-sst! Don't go out with a white girl by yourself! Naku, I bring you over from the Islands, and already you're looking for trouble! You pass for a man and still think like a boy. . . .

FRANK: When I got to this country I saw right away there were lots of Filipino men here and no women, about 20 to 1. See, the government would not allow as many women as men back then. . . .

PEDRO: Always chasing blondes, chasing white women! Puti! [*shrugs*] Pedro, what choice do we got, eh? Wala!

FRANK: I was young, I knew about girls by then, and I was teaching myself music and singing American songs.

PEDRO: [*sings*] ". . . And they called it The Birth of the Blu-ues!"

FRANK: Girls always like crooners. Men with throats like birds and feet like deer . . .

PEDRO: [*as he dances*] And balls like a bull! HA!

FRANK: Men like me. [*winks*]

[PEDRO *shows steps expertly.*]

[*continues*] Look out for men like me.

PEDRO: You take that white girl to town and damn puti will beat you up! They don't want brown monkeys stealing their women! [*calls again*] Frank! THIS way! Stick with your own kind! Stay away from puti! [*spits*] Hate puti! Hate 'em! HATE 'em!

FRANK: SSSHH!!

PEDRO: [*add Tagalog*] 'Tangina, how many know our language! [*antsy*] I want to dance! [*twirls*] Kammusta, Watsonville! Watch us Pinoys "cut a rug" with those big white girls [*indicates anatomy*]. Frank, sige, sige, the night's getting away from us! Plenty Pinoys waiting at the Club—townsmates! [*dangles keys*]

We even have a car this time—all TEN of us! We'll teach you a new dance! [*rolls out a day's pay of dance tickets*] Plenty brown girls, Frank! Siguro, puti! [*sing song*] They want to meet you! [*bellows belligerently*] FRANK!!

[PEDRO *and* FRANK *laugh, having a good time.* CHARLIE (*as* BULLY) *enters.* DEE *exits here.*]

BULLY: Hey, monkey, what you doing with that white girl?

FRANK: Yeah, I got in trouble all right.

BULLY: Hey, BOY! I'm talking to you.

FRANK: I can't even remember the girl's name. Sige, it was the principle of the thing!

BULLY: We don't like your kind taking over our women. See that sign? "NO FILIPINOS ALLOWED." That's you, monkey. We don't want a bunch of half-breed bastard MONKEYS filling up our town!

FRANK: Five of them. Took them ALL on.

PEDRO: [*approaches* BULLY] Is there a problem here?

BULLY: Yeah, there's a problem. A big brown DIRTY one!

PEDRO: Say that again. I don't quite understand your ignorant English.

BULLY: I got no bone with you . . .

PEDRO: [*not backing down*] Not tonight, eh? But tomorrow, tarantado kang puti, I may be with your sister! [BULLY *throws a punch.* PEDRO *ducks, holds him.*] Run, Frank! Get out of here!

FRANK: I was strong back then—fearless. The girl ran away as soon as the fight started. When you least want it, worlds collide.

BULLY: [*backs off*] I'll be back . . . with MORE! [*Exits.*]

PEDRO: [*to* FRANK]: Come on. Let's warn the Club. There'll be trouble tonight.

[PEDRO *exits.*]

FRANK: Damn puti came into the Club and broke all the windows. Pero we Pinoys banded together. We held our ground and fended them off. It made all the papers. Ano, the Watsonville riot, 1930. The asparagus boycott in Stockton, 1939. All about rights: holding jobs only whites had, wanting better pay, more hours, cleaner hygiene in the barracks. Fighting for less charges, "fines," "FEES!" Oh, there were all kinds of things to keep us down. But you know what it really was? Marrying their women. Sige. We thought marrying white was okay for us—we're alike! But early 1900s maybe, a California law says no marriages between whites and Negros, oh, all the colored back then. In the thirties, they add, guess what? . . . FIL-

IPINOS! Now they say, unconstitutional. But it was law for many, many years. [*shakes head*] Still, not that long ago.

Yes, all riled up in Stockton. Active place, this California, eh? "Little Manila," "fight town." Many Filipino bantam boxers from there. I used to box, did I tell you? [*jabs, uppercuts*] Not long, just enough. It helped me in Seattle, 1936. Oh, there was a cannery strike up there! FIFTY riots nationwide! Rights for Filipinos everywhere. Sige. I was there then, and we're still here now! You kids today dating white now. Easy, isn't it? I paved the way. I didn't care. I went ahead and dated a white girl. [*shrugs*] The past. All in the past . . . [*cassette heard clicking off*] [*Lights change*] FRANK [*continues, shyly*] Tell them like that, diba? . . . Sige.

[*Lights cross-fade.*]

[*Lights change. During set change, FRANK and PEDRO enter opposite and will echo DEE and CLARA's situation. While DEE narrates, PEDRO reenacts scene (tapping foot, waving arms to get druggist's attention) till FRANK takes his place.*]

SLIDE: CAFE

[DEE *and* CLARA *are waiting to be seated.*]

DEE: [*points*] There's a seat. Once we sit we can talk: you know Lon, Newsroom? . . .

CLARA: No. [*hails*] Excuse me!

DEE: Well, last night at the office . . .

CLARA: Come on, let's go. They're ignoring us.

DEE: No, we stay till we're served. Clara, listen . . .

CLARA: Look at her! She seated three other couples before us! What IS this??

DEE: Chill, Clara! Hey, remember my dad in the drugstore? . . .

CLARA: Please, I don't want a parable right now. I want FOOD! [*hails*] Excuse ME!! [*is ignored*] Bitch.

DEE: He was getting cigarettes, and the druggist kept ignoring him, too . . .

[DEE *turns to watch scene.*]

PEDRO/FRANK: [*simultaneously*] HEY!!! [*ad-lib*] "MY story!" "No, it's MINE!"

[PEDRO *relinquishes role to* FRANK.]

PEDRO: Aieee, you go on so long in front of [*indicates* DEE] her! [*exits*]

FRANK: [*waits, then, as John Wayne:*] "Hey . . . HEY!" [*as* FRANK:] I've been waiting five minutes! FIVE MINUTES! Do you want me to time how long five minutes are??

DRUGGIST: I think you're making too much of this. Did you want something or not?

FRANK: Oh no, I'm not done yet! I won't be like the other ones, "accommodating," INVISIBLE!

DRUGGIST: Oh, for God's sake . . .

FRANK: You think I can't PAY, is that it? It's not in my MAKEUP? HUH??

DRUGGIST: I think you're imagining things. . . .

FRANK: Oh, I'm crazy, is that it??

DRUGGIST: I didn't SEE you, okay! I made a mistake!

FRANK: And that's supposed to make it all better, huh?

DRUGGIST: What IS it you want??

FRANK: I want justice! How much?? [throws down dollar bill] That much?

DRUGGIST: Listen here . . .

FRANK: That much?? Huh?? HOW MUCH??

DRUGGIST: I don't KNOW, all right? I don't know how much!

FRANK: How would you like to go through this every time you "make a mistake?" [no answer: Standoff. FRANK looks at watch] Okay, we're even now. You took up five minutes of my life; I took up five of yours. We both made each other's day [chooses dollar bill] over fifteen cents. [orders like John Wayne:] "A pack of Lucky Strikes, Pilgrim." [DRUGGIST hands over pack and change; terse] Thank you. [glances at watch] Three seconds. [exits]

[Lights change. DEE turns back to a very impatient CLARA:]

DEE: When my dad and my uncle told me that story, I sang it on the streets for a week!

CLARA: I know. [not amused] How'd we get on this??

DEE: My dad's tapes. The stories are all coming back to me. . . .

CLARA: This is not getting us service.

DEE: [singsongs] But think of the sce-ene we'll make when it does! [calls] Hey! . . . HEY!

[Lights fade.]

SLIDE: MOVIE THEATRE

[Flickering lights and music indicate the end of movie (Ruby). DEE sits just forward of LON. "House" lights up.]

LON: [leans forward] Hey . . . HEY!

DEE: [*amused*] Following me?

LON: Dee, right? [DEE *moves to leave*] Were you here for the whole movie? I didn't see you. . . .

DEE: [*quips*] I guess I'm easy to miss. No "state-of-the-art conveniences" were trained on ME. . . .

LON [*plays along*] Please! It's "chilling" to think I even WROTE that? Point taken . . . Come here often?

DEE: [*grimaces*] Oooh!

LON: Corny, I know. Knew it as soon as I said it.

[*There's obvious chemistry between them.*]

DEE: I shouldn't even talk to you. At the office . . .

LON: Let's not discuss work right now. What do you like about Barbara Stanwyck? Her toughness, I bet.

DEE: Why do you think that?

LON: A feeling. Strong women, strong women models.

DEE: Shows what YOU know. I like . . . her dreams.

LON: Hmm. Interesting.

DEE: She doesn't want anything for herself, really. She always wants something for her kid, her daughter's future. There's something noble about that.

LON: And poignant.

DEE: Yes.

LON: And futile.

DEE [*raises eyebrow*] Really.

LON: Given her station, you know she can't aspire to much more.

DEE: Do I? Just because she dangles her participles . . .

LON: I hadn't noticed that. Okay, she WON'T, all right? She won't aspire to more because, because . . .

DEE: Because why??

LON: [*finally*] Because it's not in her makeup. (silence) Oh, well, it's just a movie.

DEE: "Who cares?" [*laughs unconvincingly*]

LON: Whoops. Faux pas?

DEE: Walang problema. [*quickly translates*] "No problem."

LON: TAG-alog!

DEE: It's Ta-GAlog. Now THAT'S a faux pas! [*they laugh*]

LON: Listen, have you eaten?

[CLARA *enters; lights change; Sound cue: Doris Day's "It's Magic":*]

LON: How about coffee?

DEE: [*to* CLARA] Then he asked me out . . .

CLARA: Oooh! . . .

LON: [*as Cary Grant*] "No, dinner. By candlelight. On a moonlit night. [*takes her hand*] Amid hugs and banter [*enfolds her*] And later, a romantic ride, a horse, a carriage, clipping slowly by the ocean. [*nuzzles*] Mmm, mmm, and then . . . and then . . ." [*in a clinch*]

CLARA: [*snaps fingers*] Focus . . . FOCUS!

DEE: [*blinks*] Sorry, I got carried away.

[*Lights change back.* LON *resumes former position.*]

LON: Listen, have you eaten?

DEE: I have work to do.

LON: We could talk shop.

DEE: [*laughs*] I already gave at the office!

LON: [*enticingly*] All work and no play . . .

DEE: [*abruptly*] I'll make you a bet . . .

CLARA: He didn't bet with an Abano, did he!? . . .

DEE: You keep my column intact . . .

LON: Whoa, wait a minute! . . .

DEE: And I'll show you a character with LOTS of guts in HER makeup!

LON: Bribery!

DEE: Or I'll front you for next Friday's movie.

LON: Better yet . . . [*moves closer*] You come see it with me.

DEE: [*wags finger knowingly*] Bribery!

LON: [*shrugs*] I tried!

CLARA: [*shakes head*] Mmm-mmm-mmm . . .

LON: [*as they cross*] I tried!

[*Lights change: The office. They banter comfortably:*]

DEE: . . . My favorite? Okay, talk about corny, but I like . . . I like . . . "whistle."

LON: Whistle?

DEE: [*quotes*] "You know how to whistle, don't you, Steve? You just put your lips together and blow."

[*A moment.* DEE *becomes self-conscious.*]

LON: Bacall. *To Have and Have Not.*

DEE: [*embarrassed*] Like life, huh?

LON: The movies? Oh, no, not at ALL like life! Do you believe that?

DEE: Well, I . . .

LON: Ah-ha! THERE's a story! Writes for paper and I bet she even BELIEVES the print!

DEE: "When the legend becomes a fact, print the legend."

LON: Hmm, pretty remote. You got me there.

DEE: [prompts] It's from a Western.

LON: I can't even venture to guess. What about foreign films?

DEE: [laughs] I've got to work now! . . .

LON: So do I! Just five more minutes, okay?

DEE: [relents] I prefer American.

LON: [delaying] But what about, uh, Kurosawa? Jap director?

[DEE becomes remote.]

[continues unaware] Rashomon, Dodes'kaden, Throne of Blood . . .

DEE: I better work now . . .

LON: [still continues] Film noir! German Expressionists! The Cabinet of Doctor Caligari, Nosferatu! . . .

DEE: [moves away] Excuse me, Mr. Quinn . . .

LON: [blinks] MISTER Quinn? What happened to Lon?

DEE: I'm not sure. I think he dove headfirst in a large faux pas.

LON: Oops. What did I say? [silence] Come on, Dee, we were doing so well. That mystique of the Orient disappeared. You didn't clam up! [DEE glares] NOW what??

DEE: That was Number Two!

LON: What? Orient?

DEE: I don't want to discuss this . . .

LON: Oh, I know now. I said . . . I said . . .

DEE: Jap. Jap director.

[Silence]

LON: Yes, I did. Hey, I'm sorry. It just came out. [silence] Oh, come on. It's not like YOU'RE Japanese! Is it?

DEE: [sighs] God, Lon, if you have to ask . . .

LON: I said I'm sorry. . . . I really am.

[Lights change. CLARA again observes.]

DEE: [as Roz; cavalierly] "There was an incident in a pharmacy. I won't go into details, but my father made his point. You don't know what it's like to be ignored. You think: Why can't I be treated like a person! Nobody hears the things going through your mind, wondering WHY? Why am I being treated like this? I take up space, I have skin, blood that will bleed, and tears that will fall! I HAVE FEELINGS, damnit! Know what he told me? My dad said, never take it lying down. Make a point! Take a stand! Don't give in! Be uppity! Get big for your britches! And don't give a goddamn for "your place"! Don't be . . . fools. Don't kiss the ground, and don't yearn for the sky from a place lower than the worms. It's not pretty looking up through dirt. 'Cause then, that's all you are to them."

CLARA: Mmm-mmm-mmm. Academy Award speech.

LON: Okay, I got the point loud and clear.

DEE: [briefly to CLARA] Words to that effect . . . [as DEE to LON] See, when you say Jap or Chink or wetback or any of that, you lump us together. It's you—and us. It doesn't matter who's in the room. Whatever the term is, if we're not white, it's directed at US. It's not fair, Lon. It's not nice and it's not fair. And if you're a friend to someone not white, you'd think twice about using those terms—or anyone else using them. 'Cause friends you support, you stand with—or leave with—or fight for, make a POINT for! As long as you're white, you're protected. The worst you go through because of how you look will never match what those friends experience every day because of of how THEY look. [pointedly] How I look. Okay? Friend?

CLARA: What did he say to that? What'd he say??

LON: I apologize. I didn't think. [ruefully] Is life really all that bad for you, a lot of you?

DEE: For my dad, it was. I don't want to think he went through it just so I have to go through the same thing. [sees his look] I'm just making a point. [changes subject] We're here to work, right?

[DEE turns away to hide tears.]

SLIDE: A DEPARTMENT STORE

[The '30s: FRANK and PEDRO are shopping. DEE holds cassette.]

FRANK: [to DEE/audience] Housing in L.A. [waves hand] We all crowd in together, all us Pinoys. The most gainfully employed—Pedro—got the apartment, and one by one, we move in, sleep on sofas, floors. Around Farmers' Market, one of the first Filipino ghettos . . .

PEDRO: Frank, look at this!

FRANK: When we could, just to get out, we'd shop. Sometimes clerks would follow us all over the store, . . . but we proved we could pay. Sometimes more than we could afford. But we were happy.

PEDRO: Read this: crepe de SHINE. Must be Chinese. [DEE *satisfied with tale, exits.*] And sige, look! This will go good together, eh? [*points to cuff links, tiepin in glass case*]

[CLERK *shadows them, purposely not making eye contact.*]

[*carries shirt*] What do you think of these ties?

FRANK: [*points to his choice*] This. [PEDRO *puts tie to his neck:* FRANK *approves*] Hmph! [*Both move with shirt and tie, with* CLERK *following every move.*]

FRANK: Oy, he's following us.

PEDRO: They always do that. They'll see: we're paying customers. Sige, this is what I want. [*turns to* CLERK] Sir? [*is ignored*] Sir??

CLERK: [*indifferent*] Yes?

PEDRO: I'd like to see the cuff links.

CLERK: [*remote*] And?

PEDRO: [*looks at* FRANK] And buy them if they're right.

CLERK: What's wrong with them?

PEDRO: [*evenly*] I don't know yet. That's why I want to see them WITH the shirt.

CLERK: [*perfunctory key check*] I don't have the key. Can't you just see it through the glass?

PEDRO: [*undaunted*] No, I can't.

FRANK: [*uncomfortable*] Come on, let's go.

PEDRO: I'm not done yet. [*tries again to* CLERK] Listen, I might buy this silk shirt with the cuff links and the tie. . . .

CLERK: You can afford silk?

PEDRO: [*fingers* CLERK's *lapel*] Rayon's not my style.

CLERK: [*holds ground*] My supervisor has the key. . . .

PEDRO: Then get him.

[CLERK *stiffens, turns, returns.*]

CLERK: Maybe I should take these with me. . . .

PEDRO: [*holds on*] I can hold them.

FRANK: [*Tagalog*] Pedro, nagumpisa na naman, you're making too much of this. . . .

PEDRO: No, I'm not! I'm making a point. [*to* CLERK] Are you going to open this glass?

CLERK: I was told only serious paying customers . . .

PEDRO: [*explodes*] What am I?? [*starts to remove jacket*] Here, Frank.

CLERK: [*alarmed*] What are you doing?

PEDRO: [*removes tie*] I'm trying on clothes—like a serious paying customer! [*unbuttons shirt*]

FRANK: Naku, Pedring . . .

PEDRO: Siguro: in the dressing room—where I might pocket something—I try it on out here!

CLERK: [*nervous*] Sir, I wouldn't make a . . .

PEDRO: You already DID. [*loosens cuff links*] You could've gotten the key by now. [*removes shirt, could still have muscle t-shirt*]

FRANK: Pedro, everyone's looking. . . .

PEDRO: Let them! I have nothing to hide. [*unzips pants*]

CLERK: [*panicked*] Wait! WAIT! [*exits*]

[PEDRO *stands there, mischievously, shirtless. Slowly rezips pants.*]

PEDRO: Don't grovel, Frank. Here, you never grovel.

[CLERK *returns with key.*]

CLERK: Here. [*unlocks glass*] Now, please, get dressed. Before we get a crowd.

PEDRO: [*grins*] Three IS a crowd. [*still shirtless, appraises cuff links pompously, holds up to shirt*] What do you think, Frank?

FRANK: [*nervous*] Gwapo. Beautiful. Let's go.

PEDRO: Sige, sige. [*drops links into* CLERK's *hand*] I'll take it. All of it.

CLERK: Don't you want to know how much?

PEDRO: No. [*finishes dressing, picks out silk kerchief*] Throw this in, too.

CLERK: Eighteen dollars and thirty-seven cents.

PEDRO: Eighteen dollars, eh?

CLERK: And thirty-seven cents.

PEDRO: [*hands over bills*] Keep the change.

[FRANK *blanches.* CLERK *exits.*]

[*bursts out laughing*] I showed him, eh?

FRANK: Pedro, that's two weeks' groceries.

PEDRO: So we tighten our belts for awhile.

FRANK: But for a pair of cuff links?

PEDRO: [*pats shoulder*] You make a point, and something costs. [*upturns empty wallet*] It was worth every penny.

[*Lights fade.*]

SLIDE: OFFICE

[*Opposite:* LON *edits final copy.*]

LON: We did it. Forty-five inches. Tight and clean. [*no response*] Don't blend in with the woodwork; come look at this. [*silence*] If you won't be ruthless with your own words, someone else—like me—will. I don't do well with silent treatments. [DEE *finally approaches*] Hello? Anyone there? We speak up or it goes in like this. Is that acceptable?

DEE: [*bites lip*] Okay . . .

LON: Good. [*initials it*] Let's get this in with time to spare, and seeing as it's still early, [*hedges*] may we could, uh . . . [*glances at poster*] if you're not busy, *His Girl Friday*'s on. . . .

DEE: [*distracted*] You know the part about assimilation? . . .

LON: Dee, we've been over this. . . .

DEE: And you took it out and I wanted it back in. . . .

LON: And I took it out again. Dee, come on . . .

[CLARA *enters, gives* DEE *her hat and cigarette, already lit.*]

DEE: [*hints of Roz*] I want it back in.

LON: [*worn out*] I see. . . .

[*Lights change.*]

DEE: [*sits on desk*] Lon, trying to be white, negating one's own culture, THIS is the meat of the matter, the weighty stuff!

LON: [*Cary Grantlike*] "You smoke too much, and I don't mean just cigarettes."

DEE: There's safety in numbers, can't you see? Not sticking out, not drawing attention to yourself . . .

LON: "Like that hat. Sorry: HELMET."

DEE: Lon!

LON: "Ever wonder how many baby turkeys died for that hat."

DEE: I'm being serious. . . .

LON: And I'm being PATIENT! Dee, it's not assimilation, it's sellout! The clothes, the cars, the CONVENIENCES! Hell, they live better than me!

DEE: Anyone with a BROOM could live better than you! Don't you ever clean this place??

LON: "Ho, hit me where it hurts! . . ."

DEE: Lon, could you focus for a moment? I'm trying to say some of them will do anything to look even like YOU—minus the day-old beard!

LON: [*as* LON:] Dee, just don't allude to some kind of takeover!

DEE: Assimilation does not equal takeover! God, Lon . . .

LON: Besides, you ARE like us! From what I see, you've had the easiest transition of all the Asians here in America!

DEE: From a white perspective, of course! Who's writing this article, anyway??

LON: [*indicates papers*] Okay, look at this section: your dad almost got beaten up for dating a white girl. That was in the thirties; that doesn't apply now. There HAS been progress! Awareness!

DEE: That's my point! There's very little progress! Why are there still Asian bashings?? Why is it you know nothing about us? Huh? What do you know? You know Imelda, you know Cory, Subic Bay, and syphilis.

LON: I don't know syphilis.

DEE: Oooh!

LON: YOU'RE the ones with a history of colonization, Spanish THEN American! If you don't like it, change it!

DEE: You took the Philippines over! By some, some divine right "Manifest Destiny"! They didn't want you then, and they certainly don't want you now!

LON: No? Well, for "not assimilating," you sure blend in fast!

DEE: There WAS resistance, Lon! You know about the cannery strikes, Watsonville, Little Manila? . . .

LON: I do now! By reading this NOVEL! . . .

DEE: There's a point I'm making! [*perches on desk*] We've yet to MAKE OUR MARK! We've got to be known for more than being something NOT Chinese or Japanese! For something other than MacArthur, and Marcos, and the color yellow, and a thousand SHOES!

LON: Okay! Okay! Get off the soapbox! AND my desk!

DEE: Run it as is, Lon. Take a chance. LEAVE ME THE PEEPHOLE! Give us a break. Give ME a break. [LON *is amused*] Cut the fat here and there, but . . .

LON/DEE: . . . leave the meat.

LON: Yes, I know! [LON *sighs, takes back paper, marks in big letters, speaks as he writes broadly*] Ess. Tee. Eee. Tee. STET. Okay?

DEE: [*smiles*] Keep it. Yes. [DEE *crosses center, still a distance from* CLARA]

CLARA: And he kept every word, every phrase intact?

LON: [*as* LON, *editing*] Good . . . aah, fair . . . cut that. . . . "Like a seed in a tree . . ." Cut that . . . and that. There! Twenty inches out of sixty-five. Perfect. Now, if you're not busy . . .

DEE: [*points*] Keep this, too.

LON: [*regards her*] Okay, Okay! You win. Talk about light under a bushel. I couldn't get a word out of you before.

DEE: I wasn't sure of my issues before. I guess another "me" came out.

LON: Well, whoever she is that was you then, I like her.

DEE: [*blushes but continues*] It's important, Lon, to have a . . .

LON: PEEPHOLE! [*laughs*] I'll never live that down! Dinner?

DEE: [*taken aback*] What?

LON: After a movie? And oldie goldie: *His Girl Friday*. Art imitates life. Game?

DEE: Okay. The Roxie?

LON: No. [*approaches*] My place.

[DEE *talks to* CLARA *but locks eyes with* LON.]

DEE: Well, there were SOME deletions.

CLARA: That IS his job. Still, it's a big step for you, a good move up the news ladder.

DEE: Speaking of moves . . .

CLARA: Uh-oh.

DEE: I forgot to mention . . .

CLARA: Yeah???

DEE: We're lovers.

[LON *and* DEE *kiss in the background. Lights out. Jazzy, sexy* "Birth of the Blues" *is heard. Lights on* FRANK.]

FRANK: A white woman. She was living with the landlord. Maybe they were married, I don't know. I helped in the kitchen. She bothered me all the time! You know? [*demonstrates*] BOTHERED me. Anyway, one day—I didn't go to the dance hall, so I was, well, anyway, she takes me to her room when the landlord is not home. I think, well, she's nice. I think, well, she's white. I think, well, she can help me . . . I think, well . . . why not? [*stresses*] Just ONCE! It's not a practice! Really, just one time only.

[*Blackout*]

[*Lights up:* LON *and* DEE *have moved to bed. They lie there after making love. Tune:* "Our Love Is Here To Stay."]

DEE: [*purrs*] Mmm, some movie!

LON: Mmm, some MOVES.

DEE: [*embarrassed*] God, my hair!

LON: Don't go.

DEE: [*kisses*] Have to.

LON: [*holding on*] Why?

DEE: Something to do with a participle.

LON: It always follows a PREPOSITION.

DEE: Ooh, good one!

LON: See? We got more conjugating . . .

DEE: [groans] Oh, that word!

LON: [pulls her back] Come on, let's diagram . . .

DEE: [laughs] STOP and I'll come back!

[They kiss.]

LON: Mmm, prettiest PEEN-NEIGH in this whole room.

DEE: [corrects] PEEN-EYE—and that's in your whole LIFE. Bet you never dated MY KIND before, did you?

LON: Always a point, huh? You won't let me forget that, will you?

DEE: [kisses] Never.

LON: "Like father, like daughter."

DEE: "Like a seed . . ."

DEE/LON: "IN A TREE!"

LON: I almost edited that out!

DEE: I know!

LON: [tentative] Was it difficult? Without him?

[FRANK appears in a spot.]

DEE: He left when I was ten . . .

FRANK: Dee, honey? . . .

DEE: . . . wandered about, collecting stories . . .

FRANK: It's just something that has to be, that's all.

DEE: . . . passing them on to me whenever he was in town.

FRANK: Your mother and I, both from the Islands, but like two peas in a pod, the same, but oh, so different.

DEE: Stories that pulled me through rough times.

FRANK: San Francisco's close, lots of hotels for Pinoys like me! [DEE holds back tears] And you'll be fine. 'Cause you have Island sense. Like a bamboo, you'll bend in the wind. When you're older and you can visit me, I'll tell you more stories . . .

DEE: On the nights he left again, I'd dream the images he put in my head . . .

FRANK: And show you City life. And we'll have lots of time together. Okay, Dee?

DEE: Oh, God, did I dream! . . .

FRANK: Dee, look at me . . . Dee, please . . . don't cry. [exits, continues] I still dream.

[DEE *abruptly moves away.*]

LON: [*after a pause*] Poetic.

DEE: [*embarrassed*] Oh, stop.

LON: Now how does this uncle fit in? You must have had SOMEBODY fending for you while he was gone.

[FRANK *joins* PEDRO *and* CHARLIE.]

DEE: Ah, yes: uncle Pedro in Stockton . . .

FRANK: [*calls*] Oy! Sss-sst!

LON: [*as* DEE *enters scene*] What's THAT??

DEE: That's how we hail each other. I could recognize my own family's Sss-sst in a crowd ANYWHERE!

FRANK: Oy! Ssst! Come say hello to your tito!

PEDRO: [*appraises*] She is big now, eh, in the, you know [*indicates anatomy*] . . .

DEE: And my sorta uncle Charlie . . .

CHARLIE: Aw, Pete, leave her alone! She's just a kid! [*to* DEE] Your uncle and women . . . [*makes gesture*]

PEDRO: [*disapproves as* DEE *offers hand*] No, no, no! Ay, naku, you take my hand and touch it to your forehead, like this! [*gruffly demonstrates, clucks tongue, shakes head*]

DEE: [*recalcitrant youth*] Well, I don't know, geez!

PEDRO: [*amazed*] You let her swear like that? To her own uncle?? 'Sus mar y josef!

FRANK: She's American, Pedro. Things are different here.

CHARLIE: [*to* DEE] I learned all of that myself when I married my own little Filipina. [*clears throat, recites:*] "Maraming salamat po." Pretty good, eh?

DEE: The monkeypod Tinikling sculptures hanging on uncle's wall, the bowl of lichee nuts, the homemade altar by every proper Filipino doorway that you kissed coming AND going, these were all foreign to us. There were foods we wouldn't eat, and songs we couldn't sing. . . .

CHARLIE: [*throws coins on floor*] THERE! Go on, get it! [DEE *looks confused*] Gol', Pete, I know more about being Filipino than SHE does! [*to* DEE] See, uncles throw money and kids pick it up as fast as they can! Go on! [*shakes head as* DEE *finally picks up coins*]

PEDRO: [*shakes head*] They don't know, eh? They just don't know.

DEE: [*to* LON] We balked at their ways, hated our own differences. We didn't know what they had been to know what we were supposed to be. [*to* CHARLIE] Are you the snake-poker? The other soldier? . . .

CHARLIE: [*uneasy laugh*] This one's like you, Frank, talk-stories all the time.

[DEE *mocks, staring down "Snake"*:]

PEDRO: Aieee, DOLINGA! That is bad luck! If you cross your eyes at some-one, one day they will stay that way! [*to* FRANK] You should teach her, Frank, send her to the fields to work! She'll see how easy she has it!

FRANK: Some of those things they don't need here, Pedro.

PEDRO/CHARLIE: WHAT KIND OF FILIPINO ARE YOU??

FRANK: What can she know that she hasn't been brought up with??

PEDRO: That's not my fault, 'sus mar y josef, that's YOUR fault! [*to* DEE] You would KNOW what you are in the Islands! In the Islands, you'd see for yourself!

[CHARLIE *exits.* FRANK *watches as* PEDRO *crosses, becomes "Island Rel-ative."*]

DEE: So I went to the Islands. . . .

ISLANDER 1/PEDRO: [*Tagalog*] Aieee! She's too BIG! Too AMERICAN! Look how white she is!

DEE: They laughed when I bought a bag, a memento from the town of my grandfather. . . .

ISLANDER 2/FRANK: [*Tagalog*] Stupid pute'!

[*Both continue to catcall.*]

DEE: [*embarrassed*] They stared at me all the time, till I looked at myself, wondering what made me so different when to me I looked just like they did . . . TAMA NA!

ISLANDER 1/PEDRO: [*Tagalog*] Mestiza! You understand what we say?

DEE: [*flares*] You were talking about my BREASTS, then you made fun of my bag. . . .

ISLANDERS: [*amazed*] Ay, naku! Be careful what you say! This one knows!

[*Both exit.*]

LON: [*sleepily*] Maybe you'd be more accepted if you all would've just stayed where you came from.

DEE: Did you hear a word I said??

LON: I'm just saying [*yawns*] if it's no different here than there, at least you'd be with your own kind, that's all.

DEE: And I'm saying to them: I just couldn't BE more Filipino!

LON: Well, that's their problem, not yours.

DEE: Lon, know what I saw over there? I saw . . . hospitality. And humor. And wit. And sulkiness! I saw where I got all of that from, and where my family did, and where their kids do! I saw . . . [*searches*] my legacy. All those Island Abano's I met, the family plot, the trails my ancestors walked, all part of one nucleus somewhere way back when—the same, but, oh, so different, can't you see? They stayed Island, Lon, and I'm some hybrid planted 10,000 miles away. Because of him, my dad. He's "made" it; I have to, too.

FRANK: [*defending himself*] And there's something to those of us who pick up and move away from roots! In our blood is the stuff of . . .

[Lights fade.]

DEE: Heroes, Lon. That's a legacy I have to carry on. My Dad's coming here has to, to . . . pay off! Understand? . . . Lon? . . .

[LON is fast asleep.]

SLIDE: FRANK'S HOTEL ROOM

[FRANK *and* PEDRO *drinking and playing cards. On* FRANK's *cassette: Bing Crosby's* "Accentuate the Positive."]

FRANK: Ay, naku, sum a gum! You beat me again! Poker not my game today. [*takes a swig*]

PEDRO: [*boasting*] Or any other! You deal.

FRANK: [*as he shuffles*] Remember when Dee first learned to play? I just got back from Seattle, the canneries shut down early . . .

PEDRO: That's not how it goes. You LEFT early! Deal, deal!

FRANK: And she was eight, nine? . . .

PEDRO: [*blunt*] And you were gone eight months that time. And lucky she didn't forget you then. Valentine's Day. And don't cheat. [FRANK *looks innocent*] Oy, see? You dropped your ace. Ah-ha, eh? I know you. Re-shuffle.

FRANK: [*chastised*] I was not cheating.

PEDRO: No, just making sure you win. Play . . . Teaching your own daughter how to bet . . .

FRANK: She's good, too, eh? She says, "Can I play, Daddy? Teach ME to play!" And by God she pulls an ace! In blackjack, remember?

PEDRO: Ay, let me deal. You take too long.

FRANK: So you can beat me again?? Oh, no!

PEDRO: [*abruptly*] She did not want to just play. She wanted to be next to YOU.

[FRANK *is silenced. He deals.*]

FRANK: She wasn't home last night.

PEDRO: [*snorts*] Just like her Daddy . . .

FRANK: But she's a GIRL!

PEDRO: Not no more. I bet two big nickels. [*pause*] Ribada's son is back in town. Hit me.

FRANK: Eh? [*elaborately lays down card*] There, you sum a gum.

PEDRO: Maybe you can FIX THEM UP! I raise you two more buffaloes and one more for good luck!

FRANK: Ay, naku, you clean me out in no time!

PEDRO: [*chortles*] When you hot, you HOT! When you not . . .

FRANK: [*hands over deck*] She won't date Ribada. She hasn't dated brown YET.

PEDRO: That's YOUR fault. You leave her here while you run around, going here, going there. . . .

FRANK: She did fine without me! Look now! She's a writer!

PEDRO: [*still shuffling*] "Copy ASSISTANT"! What kinda writer is that? Copy, copy, anyone can copy. . . .

FRANK: She has her own column! She's been asking me to re-tell my stories for it!

PEDRO: [*surprised*] And print them up??

FRANK: Yes! Might as well, eh? Time does not wait for some of us. She'll be here this afternoon! [*sees look*] Let's play! Why don't you deal?

PEDRO: [*sharp*] 'Cause you'll just LOSE! AGAIN!! 'Sus mar y josef! [*starts to pace*] Why does she have to do this? She has other things she can do! She has that, that class, right? Teaching . . .

FRANK: English-Second-Language! She told me!

PEDRO: Why doesn't she write about that??

FRANK: She WANTS to do this!

PEDRO: For YOU! She wants to get close to YOU!!

FRANK: Let her dream, Pedro. Why do you have to knock down everything she does?

PEDRO: It's not her, Frank, you know that.

FRANK: [*denying*] I'm not doing anything! I'm helping her! After all this time, you should be happy I can help her somehow! . . .

PEDRO: Help her WHAT? Don't do this no more, Frank, stop now. . . .

[DEE *enters, notices atmosphere.*]

DEE: Oh, hi, uncle Pedro. [*attempts perfunctory hand to her forehead*]

PEDRO: [*blunt*] Your daddy says you stayed out last night.

DEE: I'm a big girl now, uncle Pedro. If I want to stay out, I will. If I want to work—which I was—I will, too! Maybe, just maybe, I didn't answer my phone.

FRANK: You hear my voice on your, your, what is it, your MASSAGE machine, and you don't pick it up?

PEDRO: Too many conveniences, eh?

DEE: [*sees coins*] Gambling again, huh?

PEDRO: Don't change the subject! Your daddy is asking you a question! Were you really working? Huh??

DEE: [*pause*] I was with Lon.

PEDRO: [*snorts*] Like father, like daughter . . .

FRANK: Pute'? White?

[*No answer.*]

PEDRO: [*Tagalog*] Talaga! She dates white, divorces white, you'd think she'd KNOW by now! . . .

DEE: If you're going to talk about me in FRONT of me, talk so I'll understand!

PEDRO: Sassy, this one! Always an answer for everything!

FRANK: You two! Like oil and water. Here, sit.

PEDRO: [*to* FRANK] YOU! You're the one . . .

FRANK: Hush now! Sit. [*to ease tension,* FRANK *holds out deck to* DEE] Pick a card . . . Go on!

DEE: [*picks, smiles*] Ah-HA!

FRANK: [*to* PEDRO *proudly*] See? Another ace!

PEDRO: Aaiieee, both the same! One ace won't help you! You need more than that here! Dating white won't get you anywhere! . . .

DEE: Stop lecturing me! Dad, why does he do this all the time??

FRANK: [*shrugs*] He's your uncle.

PEDRO: [*pleads*] Honey, please, I can't have you go through what you're going through ALL THE TIME! . . .

DEE: [*denying*] I haven't much time. Dad, tell the snake story. [*produces cassette and mike*]

PEDRO: [*shakes head*] No one listens to me.

FRANK: [*eager for change, too*] The snake story? The one where I took on a boa this BIG? . . .

PEDRO: You two, I don't know . . .

DEE: "Take the snake." That's what I'm calling it.

FRANK: [*settling in*] Well [*clears throat*] Is this on? [*taps mike, puffs up*] "We were drunk, playing around . . ."

PEDRO: Frank, don't . . .

FRANK: [*continues blithely*] Pedro says, "Did you get a load of the size of that thing?" BIG SNAKE, lying across the width of the road! And Charlie, your uncle Charlie says, "Should we poke it? Can we get around it?'

PEDRO: [*grumpily*] Nagumpisa na naman, not that damn snake again. . . .

DEE: [*shushes him*] Uncle Pedro! Indulge us!

PEDRO: Indulge, indulge, a lifetime he indulges . . .

DEE: [*wheedles*] Please?? [PEDRO *relents*] Go on, Daddy.

FRANK: [*continues*] And I say, "Jungle on both sides? No way!" [*laughs*]

PEDRO: You did not say that!

FRANK: [*waves him off amiably*] Charlie said it, then. And so I say [*puffs up*] "Go pick it up!" And Charlie says, "Hell no!" [*indicates* PEDRO] Grown men afraid of a snake! Hard to believe, eh?

DEE: I would be!

PEDRO: Ay, 'sus mar y josef, that's not the way it goes! . . .

FRANK: I tell your Uncle Pedro here, "Pedring, run over it!" And he says, "No, not me!"

PEDRO: Frank, she's recording this! . . .

FRANK: And me, I'm not afraid! I'm not scared one bit! . . .

PEDRO: [*high-pitched*] Mmm-mmm!

DEE: [*starry-eyed*] Not one bit . . .

[*Lights fade.* DEE *mouthing story as* FRANK *narrates.* PEDRO *shakes head.*]

[*"How Long Has This Been Going On?" is heard.* LON *and* DEE *seated at restaurant and waiter passes many times.* DEE *stands, her Roz side evident, tells off waiter, exits.* LON *looks apologetic. Lights fade.*]

END ACT I

ACT II
SLIDE: FRANK'S HOTEL ROOM

[FRANK *in straw hat (without* DEE *present, this should suggest that this is another taped story, his fondest memory, his lifetime work).*]

FRANK: In the Salinas and Central Valleys were jobs for us Pinoys. We worked alongside the Japanese and the Mexicans. I knew most of the boys, [*laughs*] the MEN now here in this hotel. By day, in sweltering heat like the Islands, we all helped each other. By night, the Pinoys drove into town to spend the money we had left after sending most of it to the Islands. Yes, in the fields we were home again, among the green iceberg lettuce and the red leaf lettuce and butter lettuce and brussels sprouts and tomatoes and even the thorny artichokes! Nut-brown hands under the bluest skies and in the darkest soils—just like in the Islands. But the cities beckoned. And I, for one, answered the Call.

When we weren't in the Central Valley in the spring or in the vegetable fields in the summer, we were in the canneries up north in late fall, and hot Southern California every winter. Life was simple, traveling, working, prowling. But then, after awhile, cities were for me.

The more I saw, the more I wanted. The country boy in me was gone. The boy who swam naked in the streams during hot, white Manila days, climbed coconut trees for their sweet, young fruit, washed the month-old piglet in the yard, walked barefoot through pineapple plantations, trailed his brother from place to place—he was gone. . . . [*Strain heard: "Birth of the Blues." (Honky-Tonk version)* PEDRO *spiffed up, parades as* FRANK *narrates:*] Instead, here was a fresh young man in America: hat-ted, suited, pomaded, perfumed, groomed, BOOTED, shoe-ed, and shod! No more fresh-off-the-boat, no more country bumpkin! I would drink all the liquor and kiss all the girls! I would be sharp and witty and loved. Man-about-town. Twinkling brown eyes, slow, sexy smile. Cigarette between my fingers, brandy on my breath. Gold cuffs, gold tiepin, gold ring, gold watch, gold teeth! [*fantasizes*] Like a . . . a MAYOR! . . .

[PEDRO *exits.*]

But sometimes I miss him, that silly barefoot boy. Cities changed me; now I know only city life in downtown hotels. If you shed enough layers, you won't get them back. Be careful what you let go; be careful what you keep.

[*Strain: "Dahil Sayo" segues into "Love Is a Many-Splendored Thing."*]

SLIDE: MARIN HEADLANDS

[*Spring.* LON *is braced, chest out, wind in his hair, on a windswept cliff (much like the sound cue heard: "Love Is a Many-Splendored Thing"). CLARA watches as DEE is ROZ in love.*]

LON: [*sings last phrase*] "ONCE on a high and windy hill
In the April mist two lovers kissed and the world stood still . . ."

CLARA: Don't tell me he sang. Don't you tell me that!

LON: "Then your fingers touched my silent heart
   And taught it how to SING . . .!"

CLARA: Okay, okay! I get the picture! Windswept cliff, William Holden and
   Jennifer Jones! Give me a BREAK!

DEE: [*enters dramatically*] It's the IMAGE, Clara! I'm creating a mood here!
   [*sweeps into equally dramatic* LON's *arms*] Darling! [*they hug*] Please! People are looking!

LON: Let them look! Let them stare all they want! [*embraces*]

[*Lights, mood changes. Wind howls.*]

DEE: [*calls over wind*] FRIES?? [*offers some to* LON]

LON: [*cranky*] I don't think this is a good idea. The Headlands in February?
   . . . [*sneezes*]

DEE: I thought it would be more romantic.

LON: What time you got? It took me long enough to get here.

DEE: [*deflated*] Aren't you hungry?

LON: I'M COLD! [*sneezes*]

DEE: [*attempts*] I could keep you warm.

LON: [*curt*] Around you, everyone SIZZLES! [*clams up*]

DEE: Maybe this wasn't such a good idea. . . . What's wrong?

LON: Nothing

DEE: [*tries snuggling*] Oh, come on . . .

LON: Not now, Dee.

DEE: [*hurt*] Maybe we should just go back early. . . .

LON: [*blurts out*] Can't we go anywhere with you not getting wigged out about
   something?

DEE: What? I'm not wigged out. . . .

LON: Yesterday! Last week! All the time! You do things one day and then pretend it was nothing the next. Talk about schizoid!

DEE: I'm not schizoid!

LON: No, not really. But you're, you're . . .

DEE: [*pulling away*] And I'm not psychotic! I don't want to talk about this.

LON: Wait. Wait a minute.

DEE: What for?

LON: This. [*just holds her; she softens*]

DEE: Why, Lon?

LON: [*still holding her*] Why what?

DEE: Why don't you understand?

LON: [*sighs*] Just me, I guess. Just my little ol' white genes acting up from time to time. There! An admission.

DEE: Oh, you're just saying that.

LON: [*pointedly*] Yeah, I AM just saying that.

DEE: [*leans away*] It's these articles, isn't it?

LON: [*releases her*] Can I be blunt? [DEE *waits*] Dee, I read this stuff about how people treat other people, and I'm sorry . . . I'm NOT one of them! But somehow I still feel lumped together with them! I don't think that's fair.

DEE: [*to* CLARA, *not confidently*] And then he popped the champagne cork. . . .

LON: The difference is, I'm pretty tolerant. Other people would get tired having to THINK so much! I'd think YOU'D get tired taking EVERYBODY on the way you do!

DEE: Lon, I can't help but think all the time because it HAPPENS all the time!

LON: But you blow up at the littlest of them! It's embarrassing!

DEE: How do you know if it's little? . . . You let one go, then five, then ten, and for all you know, it's number eleven that's the final straw! You don't know! You're not on the side that it happens to!

LON: Dee, listen: this may sound pretty rough . . .

CLARA: [*hearing a different story*] And after champagne? . . .

LON: But I look at you and hear you talk and you seem just as white as I am. All these comments, all these incidents, they're not directed only at you. They can happen to anybody! Even white people! Not everyone thinks Oh, she's colored, I'll pick on her today! You?? Even *I* forget you're Filipino. I don't even think of you as brown.

DEE: [*lamely*] That's because, because . . . [*at a loss*]

LON: I'm saying, Dee, even YOU haven't resisted assimilation. If anybody, YOU'VE bought it, too, hook, line, and sinker.

CLARA: Okay, he held you close to keep you warm, and? . . .

LON: [*holding her shoulders*] Would we even be having this conversation if you ever dated brown guys? [*silence*] No, we wouldn't.

CLARA: [*interrupts*] And then? . . . Dee, what then??

DEE: [*distracted*] What? Oh . . . yeah. We had a great time.

LON: [*releases* DEE] Some of us cope with attitudes like yours, too. Dee, I can't change the world overnight.

DEE: Things start somewhere, Lon. . . .

LON: Well, things take time! Dee: I'm not the problem.

DEE: [*to* CLARA] And, and after we finished lunch, we just sat there on the cliff— [*but voice drifts off*] and we didn't say a word.

CLARA: Then you just stared off at the ocean, right? Then he took your hand . . .

DEE: [*looks at* LON's *back*] Then we didn't say a thing. . . . [*relents*] I—I lied, Clara. We're not doing well. Not at all.

[*Lights up on* FRANK, *opposite.*]

FRANK: Sometimes, hon, everything looks good, everything seems fine. But turn. Stand opposite. Look at the whole picture. It may seem comfortable, but, hon, when one thing's wrong . . . it's all wrong. All wrong.

SLIDE: MOVIE THEATRE

[*Lights flicker on* DEE *and* CLARA. *Sound cue:* "It's a Wonderful Life."]

VOICE-OVER: [*Jimmy Stewart*] "What do you want? You—you want the moon?"

[DEE *repeats quietly.* CLARA, *uneasy, looks around cautiously.*]

VOICE-OVER/DEE: "Just say the word, and I'll throw a lasso around it and pull it down. . . ."

DEE: [*echoes*] Pull it down . . .

VOICE-OVER/DEE: Hey, that's a pretty good idea: I'll give you the moon . . .

DEE: [*sighs*] Wow, the moon.

CLARA: [*looking around*] Could you keep it down, Dee?

DEE: I'm so sappy over this movie.

CLARA: You're just sappy. I want some popcorn.

DEE: [*sighs*] With butter.

CLARA: [*quips*] Whatever you can pay for. [*holds out hand*]

DEE: [*pays*] Why can't life be like this?

CLARA: You paying for snacks? Sounds good to me.

DEE: I mean, in the movies.

CLARA: So far the dude hasn't gotten anything he wants. He could have the girl, but there's no challenge there. . . .

DEE: Sounds familiar.

CLARA: Pop for a soda while you're at it.

DEE: [*pays*] Maybe she's too much of a challenge.

CLARA: "She?" You mean, you . . .

DEE: [*flounces*] If things were perfect, I wouldn't have to always MAKE POINTS! It's a lone crusade out there.

CLARA: Dee, face the music: some of us don't want to make the extra efforts, and some of us [*indicates both of them*] can't help but.

DEE: Sometimes extra efforts wear me down. Oh, I want to be happy, Clara!

CLARA: Oh, come on! [*indicates movie*] Can this be the only thing that makes you happy?

DEE: Well . . . yeah! 'Cause sappy movies are really . . . daydreams! They're so . . .

CLARA/DEE: Perfect.

DEE: Yeah!

CLARA: No. [*sighs*] Sometimes—instead of Academy Award CINEMA-SCOPES—little triumphs are all we can go by. [*rises*] Salt?

DEE: No.

CLARA: Sure?

DEE: Yeah . . . [*as* CLARA *goes*] but maybe I can make my own picture perfect. You think?

CLARA: Straw?

DEE: [*wilts*] No. [CLARA *exits*] Oh, moon! [*repeats*] "Just say the word . . ." [*wishing*] I can make my picture perfect. And everyone lives happily ever after . . . happily ever after . . .

[*Flickering lights fade.*]

SLIDE: DINER

[*Throughout* FRANK'*s narration,* PEDRO, *downstage, strikes three poses, then removes coat, rolls up sleeves for busboy scene. Tune: "Puttin' on the Ritz."*]

FRANK: [*to audience*] We were dandies back then. See this picture? Uncle Pedro. Young, huh? Me, too, even younger! Sassier. He'd been here two years before me. He knew all the "ropes." We'd spend our money on a suit of clothes, the last money we had entered the country with! Then we'd pose for pictures to send back to the Islands. It was this picture of your uncle that brought me here. I would look just like that, I told myself. . . .

[CHARLIE (*as* BOSS) *enters.* DEE *enters with cassette, tapes.*]

I was young, sixteen, seventeen, but I passed for twenty-one. Your Uncle Pedro took me to work with him. . . .

PEDRO: My brother's in town now. Can you give him a job?

BOSS: Looks a little young. How old is he?

PEDRO/FRANK: Twenty-one!

BOSS: Oh, so he knows English, too, huh?

PEDRO: A little.

BOSS: [*loudly*] Wanna wash dishes? [*demonstrates*] You know, wash-ee dish-ee?

PEDRO: [*pointedly in English*] He wants to know if you want to wash dishes.

FRANK: [*gets point*] Certainly!

BOSS: [*missing it*] Okay, then you show up with Pedro here. [*to* PEDRO] You be responsible for him. If he goofs up . . .

PEDRO: No, sir, he'll be fine. I'll watch him.

BOSS: Good. I know your kind are workers; some of my best friends . . .

PEDRO: Yes, sir, we are.

BOSS: Good dishwashers. You DID say this guy's your cousin? They usually are.

PEDRO: Brother.

BOSS: [*not convinced*] Uh-huh. Four bits an hour.

[PEDRO *exits.* BOSS *turns upstage. Tune:* "Lay That Pistol Down."]

FRANK: [*to* DEE] Four bits, fifty cents. That was a lot of money then for ten-to-twelve hours a day. About six bucks a day. In the Islands they paid twenty-five centavos. Two American pennies. I was good at numbers. I was good at other things, too. [*proud*] Girls come in, see me bussing, singing, then smile, eh? Then that owner didn't like me. Because of all the girls, maybe. He didn't like my singing.

BOSS: [*scowls*] Cut the crooning! I didn't pay you to be a bird!

FRANK: [*innocently sassy*] I sing like Bing Crosby . . .

BOSS: You mean, like a lovesick coyote! I want some WORK done around here!

FRANK: [*always the last word*] Music makes work easier. . . .

BOSS: I'm warning you, STOP SINGING!

FRANK: [*pause*] People should not stop other people from singing. . . .

BOSS: Well, I pay the hired hands around here and I FIRE 'em just as fast! So you gonna work here or warble? [*starts to exit*]

FRANK: [*defiantly sings*] "Lay that pistol down, BOY, lay that pistol down . . ."

BOSS: Why, you brown bastard! . . .

FRANK: [*sings*] "Pistol packin' PAPA, lay that pistol down!"

BOSS: [*livid*] You're outa here, you slant-eyed monkey! You hear me?? Get out! GET OUT!

[BOSS *exits.*]

FRANK: [*to* DEE] I got another job, another place. [DEE, *looking satisfied, packs cassette, exits*] I knew no one would stop my song. No one. Don't let anyone stop yours, Dee.

SLIDE: DEE'S OFFICE

[CLARA *observes* LON *and* DEE.]

LON: [*edits*] This goes . . . [*cuts*] And this. And that.
DEE: [*to* CLARA] And then I said: "Lon, I've been thinking . . ."
LON: No comment? [*no response, he cuts again*]
DEE: I said: "I don't think this is working out. . . ."
LON: [*finally puts down pencil*] Dee, I've been thinking. . . .
DEE: "I think we're on different channels. . . .
LON: I'm assigning someone else to edit your work.
DEE: And I don't think outside of work we should see each other anymore.
LON: And outside work, we probably shouldn't see each other anymore.

[*Lights change: Reality.*]

DEE: Please, Lon . . .
LON: Dee, I . . . I just can't work on this every week and deal with you per-
    sonally afterwards. I just can't. Maybe . . . after some time apart . . .
DEE: [*showing desperate card*] Maybe the movie at the Roxie? In two weeks? . . .
LON: [*uncomfortable*] I—I don't know . . .
DEE: Your favorite. Cary Grant . . .
LON: [*anguished*] Don't, Dee.
DEE: [*quickly backs off*] I know: "It's been great fun, but it was just [*starts to
    break*] . . . it was just . . ." [*Resolve breaks.*]

[LON *moves upstage, his back to the audience. Opposite,* FRANK *bids* PEDRO
good-bye, who frowns, shakes his head. Ayala's song (from ACT I) *heard.*]

VOICE-OVER: Although you are so far away I always will remember
Though we are apart the memories still linger . . .

[DEE *approaches* LON, *who exits, not looking back.* DEE, *acting younger,
offers valentine to* FRANK, *who also exits, not looking back.* PEDRO *un-
obtrusively follows.*]

CLARA: [*suspecting more*] Really, Dee? Is that what happened?
DEE: Yes, really, Clara. . . . Really.

[*Song fades.*]

VOICE-OVER:
    Always smiles with the sighs, always tears with the laughter
    Till the day we never part . . . Come that day
    (Tell me you will be returning, tell me no more yearning)

[*Lights cross-fade.*]

SLIDE: FRANK'S HOTEL ROOM

[*Men playing cards*]

FRANK: [*singing*] "You got to accentuate the positive, ee-liminate the nega-
   tive . . ."
PEDRO: Hit me.
CHARLIE: Me, too.
PEDRO: Wait your turn.
CHARLIE: I am. I am.
FRANK: "Latch onto the affirmative, don't mess with . . ."
PEDRO: Play, play! You've been singing that song all day!
CHARLIE: [*jokes*] He's a celebrity now. With those stories . . .
PEDRO: Aah, will they pay your bar bills? Your groceries??
FRANK: [*nudges* CHARLIE] Ay, jealous, eh?
CHARLIE: You guys go through this every time.
PEDRO: [*lays out cards*] There, you sum a gum! Too busy singing you don't pay
   attention!
FRANK: You get more with sugar than salt, so they say. [*pays*]
CHARLIE: I'm not sure that's how it goes.
FRANK: Doesn't matter. The thought is there.
PEDRO: He sounds more and more like those articles, all those wise guy yak-
   yak-yak. Deal.
FRANK: Someone got up on the wrong side of the bed . . .
PEDRO: Tama na!
FRANK: Again!
CHARLIE: [*sees the signs*] Come on, deal. Make Pete happy.
PEDRO: I'M HAPPY! I don't need his singing, playing around to make me
   happy! Putagina!
FRANK: [*frowns*] Oy!
CHARLIE: [*cowers*] That's not nice, Pete.
PEDRO: Knows too much! Everybody thinks they know so much! I know some-
   thing, too!
FRANK: Pedring, what? Why are you like this? You talk "he, him," like we're
   not in the room. You see us; we're here. Say what you mean.
PEDRO: You see me, too! I'm something, too! You heard the things I did! I
   TOLD you!
FRANK: [*to* CHARLIE] What did I do? I don't remember what I did to make
   him mad. . . .

PEDRO: You KNOW who took that snake! You KNOW what snakes are! BAD! Snakes are sneaky, crawling around, getting into things, like LIES do! Lying gets into your life and into your speech, and soon YOU are the snake. No, you're not better than one. Then you are the LIE!

FRANK: [*uncomfortable*] Charlie, get the bottle. Pedro needs a drink.

CHARLIE: Yeah, buddy, let's toast one. [*rises*]

PEDRO: I don't need a drink!

FRANK: Then settle down, Pedro, please. Your high blood pressure . . .

PEDRO: You know that's not it. You KNOW it!

CHARLIE: [*buffering*] I know it, too, Pete. Come on, what's past is past.

PEDRO: Not no more! It's all over the papers!

FRANK: I'm no snake, Pedro. . . .

CHARLIE: Yeah, Pete, let's just play. . . .

PEDRO: What, then, huh? What do you call yourself then??

FRANK: A survivor!

PEDRO: [*scoffs*] Survivor . . .

CHARLIE: YES! Just like you, Pete! . . . Just like you. You both put up with things in different ways, and you're BOTH here. And I'M here. And I want to play. Can we just play??

[*Silence. A standoff.*]

PEDRO: [*relents*] Always the easy way . . .

FRANK: 'Cause you took the hard way. And now you got high blood pressure. And stomach pains. And you're crabby! . . .

PEDRO: And you? What do you have?

FRANK: Dreams, Pedring. That's all I have. And Charlie here. And Dee. And you . . . It's enough for me, Pedro, it always was.

PEDRO: It will catch up with you . . . somehow.

CHARLIE: [*regards both*] Play.

FRANK: [*deals out cards*] Play.

PEDRO: [*after a pause*] Sure. Play.

[*Lights fade.*]

[*Lights change:* FRANK *plays solitaire. Stooped, straining. His cassette plays Crosby tune.* FRANK *sings along:*]

FRANK: [*sings*] "When the blue of the night meets the gold of the day someone waits for me . . ." [*lays down card, winces*] Ah, yes, someone. Always think positive, eh, Frank? A lifetime of being positive. [*winces again*] That's all we can do. . . . Oy, this song is too slow. [*rises slowly, tottering but sings bravely*] "Accentuate the positive, ee-liminate the negative, . . . [*reaches cassette, fast forwards to song*] latch onto the affirmative, . . . [*presses "play"*] don't mess with Mister . . . [*stops, looks surprised, falls heavily*]

[*Song continues to play in blackout.*]

SLIDE: HOSPITAL WAITING ROOM

[DEE *and* CLARA]

CLARA: You gotta eat.

DEE: I'm not hungry right now.

CLARA: How about if I go downstairs and get us a couple soggy sandwiches from the vending machine.

DEE: [*slight smile*] You're not making it any more appealing.

CLARA: There! I got one smile out of you. [DEE *relaxes but is still concerned*] He'll be all right, Dee. That old hickory? Nothing's going to bring HIM down! Why, all his buddies won't have anybody to joke with anymore about his newfound fame! Thanks to you, of course. It would just gall him not to have one more story in print! And another thing . . .

DEE: Clara, please, I realize what you're doing. Stories just . . . aren't priority right now.

CLARA: Whoa, girl. Don't let go of those stories. . . .

DEE: Am I just fooling myself? They kept me going; they put some starch in my spine. Maybe they put a fence around me, too.

CLARA: Dee, if you're talking about Lon, well, he just didn't get it!

DEE: I'm just in some little dreamworld . . .

CLARA: Aw, stop it! THEY'RE the ones who are deluded. You're not overreacting and you're not imagining things! So you call 'em on their delusions and YOU MAKE A DIFFERENCE. WE'LL make a difference. We're the living proof: we're the legacy. "Friends you support, stand with, fight for," remember that? [DEE *begins to match* CLARA's *mood*] The stuff of heroes. The stories are his strength, Dee, and now they're yours. And mine. Hell, I LIKE the stories! . . .

[PEDRO *enters, listens.*]

[*continues*] I don't care WHOSE they are! You know what my favorite is? I like the one about . . . [*sees* PEDRO, *stops*]

[DEE *rises to kiss* PEDRO. CLARA *starts to back out.*]

[*continues*] Well, I guess I'll get those sandwiches now. [*silence*] Uh, Mr. Abano? Would you like anything? . . . [PEDRO *shakes his head no*] What would YOU like, Dee? [*jokes*] Green or brown? [*still silence*] Heh, heh, just kidding . . .

[CLARA *exits. An uncomfortable moment between niece and uncle.*]

PEDRO: [*Clears throat. Tagalog*] Naku, if it's not one thing it's another. Things always happening to both of you. He drinks; you with your puti boyfriends . . .

DEE: Not now, Uncle . . .

PEDRO: [*peers at her*] You're not, uh . . . [*indicates pregnant*] You know, puntes? . . .

DEE: Uncle!

PEDRO: [*matching his niece*] Mmm! Always a mouth on you! Never even return my call when I told you about your daddy . . .

DEE: I've been busy! . . .

PEDRO: Like your daddy, yak-yak-yak, that kind busy.

DEE: Better than complaining all the time. . . .

PEDRO: Don't use that tone with me! I AM YOUR UNCLE, goddamnit! You don't remember when I looked out for you! You only remember his stories! Maybe I should leave! When I'm gone, you'll be sorry! . . .

DEE: [*breaks down*] Uncle, PLEASE! [DEE *cries*]

PEDRO: [*resistant but contrite*] Oy, stop that now . . . sige, sige, stop crying now. [*pushes tissue to her nose*] Here.

DEE: [*also resistant, but complies, wiping nose*] Oh, Uncle, we're too alike . . .

PEDRO: Stubborn, eh, diba?

DEE: Two bulls nose to nose. Like two peas in a . . . [*remembers*] in a pod.

PEDRO: [*relents*] Dee, honey, . . . don't take on everybody, eh? Pick your fights carefully. [*this admission is hard for him*] Or you end up like me . . . a crabby old man, eh?

DEE: [*regards him*] You're so proud, Uncle. You, you hold your head up high. Being with dad.

PEDRO: [*uncomfortable*] Sometimes.

DEE: It was worth it, though, . . . wasn't it?

PEDRO: [*fidgets, coughs*] Sometimes.

DEE: [*wistfully*] I want it all, Uncle. All for one and one for all! And I want things to work not just, . . . just IN MY HEAD anymore! Out there, too! Where I can hold MY head up high!

PEDRO: [*finishes*] And everyone lives happily ever after, eh?

DEE: [*amazed*] Right.

PEDRO: And make your picture perfect. Ah, yes, it's easier, eh? Easier just to . . . get by. [*smiles warmly*] Like peas in a pod, eh? [*sighs*] You see, maybe I am not so different. [*a moment is reached, and passes*] Things not too good now, eh?

DEE: [*sighs*] Things could be better. . . . Someone broke up, I mean, I broke up with someone.

PEDRO: Hmm. [*long pause*] That American? Well . . . if he had been Filipino . . .

DEE: [*angry*] Don't say it, okay?? Please, don't!

PEDRO: Your father should have watched you better. . . . [DEE *give up*] This would not have happened in the Islands. In the Islands . . .

DEE: We're NOT in the Islands! We're HERE, and this is the way I know! And, Uncle? [*braces herself*] Please don't talk about my father. He did the best he could . . .

PEDRO: Dee, honey . . . [*tries again*] Whatever your daddy told you . . . some of it was . . .

DEE: [*flares*] You were always jealous of him. He got to play and travel around and you didn't. He . . .

PEDRO: [*frustrated*] Dee, he was a drifter! And a drunk. And a dreamer who believes his stories so much he thinks they're true! It was easier that way.

DEE: [*shakily*] They ARE true! . . .

PEDRO: [*not easy for him*] Dee: there was no church, no snake, no ghost. (meaningfully) Not for HIM. And he wasn't fired. He quit, like he quit every time things got tough and I had to pull him out. And you . . . just like him. Will you quit, too?

DEE: But those stories . . . his, his legacy . . .

PEDRO: Tangina! "Legacy" to you, lies to me. He could not tell the truth about his failures to you kids, and after awhile, he could not even tell himself. That's the truth.

DEE: Why are you telling me this now?

[CLARA *appears.*]

PEDRO: [*uncomfortable*] "Take the Snake." That's what you called it in the paper. Ask him what it means, why he should take one himself, especially now. Ask him to tell you again. Go on, Dee. I will go speak to him to say you'll be in. Diba?

[PEDRO *squeezes her hand, exits.* CLARA *tentatively enters.*]

CLARA: It doesn't matter, Dee. [DEE *strides by* CLARA] They're yours now, the stories! . . . [DEE *exits, not answering*] Dee??

[*Lights up on* FRANK *in hospital bed.* PEDRO *is patting his shoulder, urges* FRANK *silently to "tell all" and then exits just as* DEE *enters.*]

FRANK: "Take the snake"—I've told you this story many times, eh, diba? Now I will tell you one last time. Because it is important. Because you have made it important in your life. Because it's affected both of us so different. So listen carefully, Dee: Charlie, Pedro, and I, oh, we're always in trouble. This time we drove way out in the jungle looking for adventures, anything to stir things up. Hot, muggy, noises in the night. Or maybe it was quiet. I don't remember. Anyway, this is about snakes, how some of us found different ways to face the music. . . .

[*Screech of wheels.*]

SLIDE: JUNGLE

[*Laughter heard.* S.R. CHARLIE, *dressed as World War II soldier, stands in front of jeep's headlights. When* PEDRO *joins him, both are drunk and unruly. Tune:* "Boogie Woogie Bugle Boy."]

FRANK: [*continues*] See, we were drunk, playing around. . . .
PEDRO: Did you get a load of the size of that thing?
CHARLIE: Should we poke it?
FRANK: No, don't touch it! [*to* DEE] The biggest snake I'd ever seen, lying right across the whole road! We couldn't even see its head!
CHARLIE: Can we get around it?
PEDRO: Jungle on both sides?? No way!
FRANK: [*to* DEE] We were on leave, trying to get back to headquarters. . . .
PEDRO: [*not serious*] Go pick it up.
CHARLIE: Hell, no!
PEDRO: [*playing around*] Frank, run over it.
FRANK: Not me!
CHARLIE: Then you'll just make it mad!
PEDRO: [*with a twinkle*] I bet I can hypnotize it.
CHARLIE: Like that rooster at the cockpit?
PEDRO: Sure! Bet me? Frank? Charlie? Twenty bucks!
CHARLIE: Twenty bucks says you can't even touch it!
PEDRO: Oh, yah? [*quick exit*] THERE! [*he returns*]
FRANK: [*to* DEE] He STROKED it.
CHARLIE: [*admiring*] You're one gutsy son of a . . .
PEDRO: FIFTY says I can hypnotize it while YOU move the tail. . . .

CHARLIE: [*guffaws*] Boy, what a deal! . . .

PEDRO: WithOUT my rifle! We gotta take this snake!

[*Lights could change here: Reality.*]

PEDRO: [*continues*] Frank, remember the ghost? [FRANK *nods*] If I let one thing scare me—something I cannot even touch—it wouldn't take much after that to scare me MORE! This snake you can TOUCH! You can look the big sum a gum right in the eye!

FRANK: [*to* DEE] You see, Dee, the real hero . . .

PEDRO: Come on, where's your BALLS? Sige, the bully, clerk, boss—SAME KIND SNAKE, Frank! Siguro . . . you're running away. . . . Face them head on, anak!

FRANK: All the stories I told you, Dee . . .

PEDRO: If not now, little brother, when, huh? [*Lights change: Storyworld*] Sige, put up fifty; I start hypnotizing, you start moving! Frank, push the tail onto the road with your rifle!

FRANK: [*to* DEE] Peas in a pod, diba . . .

PEDRO: Frank! Frank! Don't daydream!

FRANK: The same, but oh, so . . .

PEDRO: Frank! Come on, clear a path for the jeep! Sige, sige!

FRANK: [*rejoins scene*] But what if the snake don't like it?

PEDRO: Walang problema, eh? I'll be watching his eyes!

FRANK: And so I moved the tail. . . . [*nervously to* PEDRO] Okay, he's now only a foot from the road.

PEDRO: Keep talking nice and easy.

CHARLIE: He's a MONSTER!

PEDRO: Easy, now! He's wary!

FRANK: [*frantic*] I want the light!

PEDRO: NO! I gotta see his eyes!

FRANK: [*resumes story*] All *I* had was my rifle. Pedro had nothing but guts. One wrong move on our parts, and a snake head would go for Pedro's neck! Pedro! Brave, fearless . . . always it was Pedro . . .

PEDRO: Start the engine!

FRANK: And me, I ran like a chicken without a head. . . .

PEDRO: Charlie, get him back in the jeep! Frank, you'll get lost out there! [CHARLIE *runs out;* PEDRO *is alone in that scene*] Okay, snake, it's just you and me now. You and me . . . [*stares "snake" down as lights fade*]

FRANK: I knew Pedro and that snake locked eyes. He saw truth in the lies. He'd stare it down—Pedro. NOT me. HE'S the one that always looked trouble in the eye. HE took that snake.

[*Lights fade.*]

[FRANK *remains in bed.* DEE *nearby.*]

DEE: That's different than before.

FRANK: Because it's the truth.

DEE: Okay, so where WERE you all the time you said you were in the fields or in the canneries or in the RIOTS?? Did you have anything to do with them at all?

FRANK: [*uneasy*] Ay, naku, you sound like the others . . .

DEE: [*brittle laugh*] And after all I told my friends, after all I WROTE! Now there's nothing but LIES! With my byline! An editor that lies!

FRANK: You're no editor. You're a copy assistant.

DEE: [*hurt*] And you're not a hero . . . are you? ARE YOU?? When I was the loud-mouth kid with an armor of brass, singing my stupid lungs out on the street about the HEROES in my life, where WERE you, huh?? [*tearful*] Where was the father to protect me? Where the hell WERE you to help me??

FRANK: [*uncomfortable*] I was nearby! . . .

DEE: You were in a dreamworld! I was out there thinking I could make YOU proud of ME! God, I feel so silly now.

FRANK: Hon, you lived through it, right? I mean, see how proud you are now?

DEE: Proud?? Daddy, I live in dreams, too! My heroine is a saucy, quick-witted woman of the world! She has all the right responses, all the good lines! She's someone "making it," Daddy! I only embellish. My versions start off small and get bigger, just like your snake story! I LIVED by that! I can't tell what's real anymore . . . just like YOU! I take on everybody now, but I can't any-more! Only heroes could, . . . like you, damnit!

FRANK: [*too much for him*] NO, you're FINE! You're all . . . !

DEE: [*anguished*] Daddy! . . . You don't know how lonely I am out there.

[*Her words have affected him deeply.*]

FRANK: I'll make it up to you, I promise. . . .

DEE: [*tearful laugh*] No, you won't!

FRANK: No, hon, I swear. If God permits I come out of this, I'm going to make a big change. . . .

DEE: Just tell me WHY! All those stories, why?? . . .

FRANK: Because things didn't go my way so I told you stories where they DO! The cards are stacked out there, Dee. You have to try three times harder, and hang in there three times longer any way you can. The stories make living a little easier, don't you see? They were meant to be your armor, Dee, in a tough world without a father. I left you strength and hopes and dreams . . .

DEE: Crutches, Daddy. Only crutches . . . I want the truth.

FRANK: And do what with it?

DEE: Something MORE! Something REAL! On MY terms, not that silly world's out there! In my head, things WORK! In real life . . .

FRANK: In your head is all that counts! My head IS my reality! And you HAVE made it, Dee. You HAVE! You hold your head up high in that world out there where, . . . where [*a big admission*] I couldn't . . . You do it, Dee. You do it FOR me, . . . and when I'm out of here, we'll talk. I'll tell you more talk-stories, better ones, about you simple country-boy father and your braver, more courageous uncle. And we'll have time, lots of time. Okay, Dee?

[*It's obvious they won't.*]

DEE: [*tearful*] Why do I always believe you?

FRANK: Because it's easier that way.

DEE: Even now! Even while you're, you're . . .

FRANK: [*deliberately misunderstanding*] I know, diba. I know.

DEE: I can't make it here, can I? You tried, and I'm trying; and all the stories . . . that's what I wasn't hearing. Right?

FRANK: People like me, all of us who've come here and thought we could adjust, how clever we could be, or how strong, or how good we could look, we couldn't change this [*indicates color on forearm*], this: [*points to eyes*] This. [*points to chest*] I burdened you. I know that now. All of us who've come here without this [*indicates chest*], wanting our kids to hold their heads high, we've burdened you. [*wistfully*] Hold up. For me; for us. Ano, here [*points to his chest*], the stuff of heroes. [*tries to rise*] "Throats like birds and feet like deer . . ."

DEE: [*touching his hair*] Till the very end, huh?

FRANK: [*shrugs weakly*] Indulge me.

DEE: But, Dad . . .

FRANK: Hon, please . . .

[FRANK *draws himself up.*]

[*magnanimously*] Got to win back my twenty dollars, play cards at the hotel, go to cockpits . . .

DEE: [*tearful*] Daddy, please . . .

FRANK: See Seattle again . . .

DEE: Daddy, don't . . .

FRANK: [*continues*] Got to sing one more time, my OWN song! Get that gold filling, be Mayor! In my blood, in yours! . . .

DEE: [*relents*] Okay, okay, enough now!

FRANK: Never! Never . . .

DEE: Enough, please! [*tucks him in*] Save your energy . . . for when you're out. [*adds*] God permits.

[*They've reached an understanding. As she watches he gets weaker.* DEE *exits as* PEDRO *and* CHARLIE *(as young memories) surround bed.*]

PEDRO: [*young, virile*] Hey, stop crying! All the ghosts are gone now, all the snakes! Shot down! [*mimes rifle*]

CHARLIE: Petey, the brains, Frankie, the brother . . .

PEDRO: Yak-yak-talk-talk! Talk-stories all the time!

CHARLIE: Pretending, dreaming! Like peas in a pod, but, oh, so . . .

PEDRO: [*indicates heart*] Remember us, okay? Just remember us as heroes. . . .

FRANK: [*smiles weakly*] The stories make dying a little easier, that's all. Your armor, Dee, in a tough world.

[*Lights fade.*]

SLIDE: CAFE

[*Week later:* DEE *and* CLARA.]

CLARA: [*after too long a silence, goads:*] Oy! Ss-sst! [DEE *is unresponsive*] "She was tough . . ." [*No reaction.* DEE *continues to mope.*] [*undaunted*] "She walked like she was . . ." [*sees* DEE *unaffected*]

[CLARA *mimes putting imaginary hat on* DEE, *cranking imaginary camera.*]

CLARA: Say cheese. [DEE *instead rolls her eyes*] Take Two. Again!

[DEE *continues to resist playacting.*]

[*sincerely*] I miss her, girlfriend. [DEE *regards her*] The stuff of heroes. [DEE *begins to straighten*] That's the spirit! [*clearly:*] "She sat on the boss's desk . . ." [*still* DEE *resists*] "She had presence." [*sighs, directs* DEE] WALK, GIRL! . . . [DEE *begins to play along.*] [*cranking camera*] Lookin' good, lookin' good! [*sincerely*] You got his strength, Dee. Don't let it all be for nothing.

[DEE *regards* CLARA, *then the "hat" that had represented her world till now.*]

DEE: Did I ever tell you the one about this girl I knew . . . [CLARA *listens*] with stories in her head? And a friend she had who helped her "indulge" in fantasy, just like some brother let HIS brother indulge in his? . . . [DEE *flings away "hat."*] [*continues*] Did I ever tell you that . . . Friend?

CLARA: Yeah . . . yeah, I think you just did.

DEE:[*with a twinkle*] And there's more . . . lots more. Really . . . REALLY!

[*The women hug briefly, exchanging imaginery hats, start to giggle as lights fade. Song heard:* "It's Only a Paper Moon."]

VOICE-OVER:

> But it wouldn't be make believe
> If you believed in me . . .

CURTAIN

SLIDE: "PAU"

[*Fades, then:*]

SLIDE: GO HOME ALREADY . . .

Day Standing on Its Head

by

PHILIP KAN GOTANDA

Now that my ladder's gone
I must lie down where all the ladders start
In the foul rag and bone shop of the heart

—W. B. YEATS

SET: Should be elemental, spare. For the most part empty. Perhaps a raised up stage area with a scrim. Feeling of the world should be that of a German Expressionist film—moody, black and white. The score, however, is more eclectic and for the most part indicated. Costuming should have an ambiguity of eras—'90s with a comfortable '30s retro quality.

AUTHOR'S NOTE: *In a second production, directed by Marya Mazor and myself, scenic design by Wing Lee, the set was on a steep rake, with a counter rake area built in the center with one lone chair. This level playing area was Harry's world. A trap door provided for Harry's Sinking-into-his-Chair scene and for an entrance for Cream. Upstage was a level playing area that was about 4 feet deep and ran the entire length of the stage where the Man-walking-the-Dog and other actions took place. The look was a loose interpretation of Magritte—large checkerboard patterns on the floor, the upstage wall adorned with columns and drapes, and a painted blue sky full of billowy clouds. Above the stage hung a large ornately framed picture of an anatomically drawn dog. Also the costumes hinted at Magritte, with everyone dressed in the same outfit—black cutaway suits, homburgs, and black high-top tennis shoes. No costumes change but for Peggy Lee's blond wig, fur wrap, and dark glasses. Though the costume design hints at*

Magritte, the original impulse was a picture of my grandfather, newly arrived in America, posing in his "western" garb. Because of the raked stage, movement became integral to the production. Naomi Goldberg created the choreographed scenes in both productions.

TIME: *The present.*

PLACE: *City.*

[*Man lit in pool of light. This is* HARRY KITAMURA. *Glasses, intellectual looking. A bit like Trotsky*]

HARRY: I awoke from a deep sleep . . . I had the strangest feeling. That my arm was disappearing. Becoming invisible . . . I wasn't dreaming, I was awake, or at least I believed so. I turned to my wife. . . . She must have been having a dream because when I touched her arm she whispered a name I had never heard before. . . .

[*Wife appears standing. Eyes closed*]

LILLIAN: "Raoul." . . . [*As she fades to black, opens eyes*]

HARRY: The feeling left. I went back to sleep. [*Lights dip to black, then up again*]The incident was soon forgotten as I was quite busy researching a new paper I was starting to write. However, a week later I had a dream. In this dream, I felt like my arm was disappearing again. Just like I had experienced earlier when I was awake. Only this time, in the dream, a MAN appeared. . . . [MAN #1 *appears. Seedy, dangerous looking*] He didn't say a word. But he knew what was happening to me, my arm. And though he made no move to speak or even acknowledge me, I knew he was somehow connected to this whole affair. That is, what was happening to my arm. But how? Was he going to show me how to get my arm back?

[OLD MAN *lit upstage left, moving very, very slowly across to stage right. Uses a cane and can barely move—moves forward in minute increments. He is walking a* DOG. DOG *played by an actor. This should be done in a non-literal way. Fade to black*]

HARRY: [*getting dressed in front of mirror, adjusting tie*] I'm a law professor at a local institution. It's not one of the more well known ones, and to tell you the truth I'd been a little embarrassed about it. However, I'd recently submitted an idea for an article to a prestigious law journal and they had accepted it. In the early 70s I was part of one of the seminal strikes of the Asian American movement. I hadn't thought about it in a long time. But for some reason I decided to write about it.

[WIFE *enters. Finishing touches on dressing, ear rings. Conservative, business look.*]

LILLIAN: If it bothers you that much just go ahead and color it. Look, you can hardly notice it, I've told you that Harry.

HARRY: I first met my wife during the struggle. When a rival group seized power and co-opted the strike we all scattered. We lost contact. Years later we met again.

LILLIAN: [*trying earrings on*] Do these look better or the other ones? Besides, white hair's better than no hair, believe me . . .

HARRY: I'd also just turned 40 and was having some difficulty accepting it . . .

LILLIAN: I have to work late tonight. The commission wants the report by next week. I'm feeling very insecure about this one . . . [*noticing Harry's reaction*] I don't have to. I can tell Raymond we can do the work over the weekend. You sure? Okay. I'll call you from the office. [LILLIAN *exits.* HARRY *watches her.*]

[HARRY *transitions into lecturing to his class.*]

HARRY: —campus unrest was spreading throughout the country, especially amongst the Third World students. Within the Asian American group there were two competing factions vying for power—the Pro-Maoist Yellow Guard, of which I was a founding member, and the more middle-of-the-road Asian Americans For Action, known as AAFA. It was well known at the time that AAFA was merely an instrument for the Administration while the Yellow Guard truly represented a revolutionary point of view. Infiltration by administration spies and ideological differences eventually led to the Yellow Guard's disbanding . .

[STUDENT *appears. Played by same actor as* MAN #1]

STUDENT: Professor Kitamura?

HARRY: Yes, Mr. . . . Mr. Jozu?

STUDENT: It's fine to tell old war stories about your days as an Asian American radical, but what does this have to do with us? I mean, to students right now, in the 90s. Isn't your idea of a Third World Student Movement a bit of a dinosaur given the trend towards anti-Asian violence in African American and Latino communities?

HARRY: [*flustered*] Well. What I thought was . . . My feeling is that by describing, in some way, in anecdotal form, earlier political activities, it might lay the foundation—

STUDENT: I think we're all aware that the LA Uprisings shattered any remnant of your 60s political model, and I quite frankly find your lecture outdated and irrelevant to our discussion here on "current" political Asian American trends and the legal system. My aunt was also a member of the Yellow Guard. Julie Hong, maybe you remember her? She claims that the group didn't disband because of ideological differences or whatever but because of some stupid boyish prank the male leaders pulled. How do you respond to that Professor Kitamura? Professor? [*The* STUDENT *fades to black.*]

[HARRY *is silent, shaken. Takes off his glasses, cleans them, and puts them back on. Then, takes a homburg and places it on his head.*]

HARRY: My wife and I were leaving a popular restaurant that had just opened. I didn't think we could get a reservation, but my wife knows a lot of people because of her work and managed to get us all in. I normally refuse to go out, but this evening I chose to go. I found the place too noisy and her friends obnoxious. My wife wanted to stay longer but I insisted we leave. [LILLIAN *enters and they leave.*] My wife always says . . .

LILLIAN: —all you ever want to do is stay at home. What's your problem, Harry? Why can't you just relax and enjoy yourself once in a while. There's a world out there, you know; let's have some fun once in awhile.

HARRY: I have a headache. I have to go home and work on the new piece. I'm having a difficult time getting started—

LILLIAN: Now? These are my friends, Harry. This is embarrassing having you do this all the time.

HARRY: No, I don't . . .

LILLIAN: Yes, yes, you do—we're somewhere and suddenly you decide you don't want to be there and it's like if we don't just get up and leave you start pouting like a little boy or something . . .

HARRY: I'm not feeling good, okay? The place was getting to me; I'm sorry, it's just the way I am.

LILLIAN: Where's your heart Harry? Open up. Let go. Live a little, huh? [*pause*] Alright, alright, I'm sorry. Harry? It's okay . . .

HARRY: You stay. Really, you stay and I'll catch a taxi home.

LILLIAN: No, Harry, I don't mind; let's go home.

HARRY: I want to be alone.

LILLIAN: Look, I said I don't mind—

HARRY: I want to be alone, it's okay.

LILLIAN: [*watches him for a beat*] Alright, okay, but you take the car. I'll have Liz give me a ride home.

[LILLIAN *exits. Upstage a night sky slowly evolves. Unusual. Deep bluish-black hue*]

HARRY: Instead of driving right home from the restaurant like I told Lillian I was going to do, I decided to take a walk.

[*A comet streaks across the horizon. In the distance we hear its faint sound.*]

HARRY: I noticed two young women talking to a man.

[*Two women and a man appear. This is* MAN #1, *the same man who appeared in* HARRY's *dream. Night sky fades to black.*]

HARRY: They seemed to be engaged in a lively conversation that quickly turned into a heated argument. It appeared that the man wanted one of the women to go with him and that she did not want to. I thought it might turn violent, when the man abruptly left. As the two women turned and began walking my way, I recognized one of them as a student I had had the semester before. Her name was Lisa.

[*Music: classical, melancholic romanticism*]

LISA: Hello Professor.
HARRY: She was quite beautiful and I had occasionally fantasized about her.
LISA: This is my friend . . . [*Friend ignores* HARRY, *turns slightly away, seemingly preoccupied*]
HARRY: I noticed you were having some trouble over there. [LISA *stares uncomprehending. The other woman looks momentarily at him. Noncommittal look, then turns away. Her face is not visible to* HARRY.]
HARRY: With the young man?
LISA: Excuse me?
HARRY: I found it odd that neither seemed to know or want to acknowledge what I was talking about, but I quickly recovered and the conversation with Lisa became quite pleasant. [*As* HARRY *speaks he moves away, while the other two remain lit in their own light.*] I could tell Lisa was attracted to me. She had made it rather obvious during the course of the year, but I had managed to be good about the whole thing.

[MAN #1 *appears in shadows.*]

MAN #1: Didn't you want to make love to her?

HARRY: [*caught off guard, stares at him*] I remember once she had come by the office . . . [LISA *approaches and stands next to him.*] We were sitting rather close to each other discussing a difficult legal point when I felt her push her leg against mine. For a moment I wasn't sure what to do. . . . She then moved her face so close to mine I could feel her breath on my face. It was sweet, like the smell of fresh peaches . . .

[LISA's *face is quite close to* HARRY's. *He steps away.* MAN #1 *dims to darkness. As he does he motions disgustedly at* HARRY.]

HARRY: As I said, Lisa is quite stunning, but oddly enough during the encounter I found myself drawn to the other woman . . . [HARRY *moves down towards her. She is framed with light.*] She was not that pretty, and in a particular light the severity of her features made her appear almost ugly. I could sense a child-like vulnerability that she covered with an air of sullenness. She was quite unfriendly in my presence and seemed to disapprove of Lisa's flirting with me.

LISA: Would you like to join us for a drink?

HARRY: She never looked directly at me. She always had her face turned slightly away. [*noticing*] She had— [*Pin light on neck of* WOMAN. *We hear* NINA's *musical theme.*] —the most beautiful nape. I had never really noticed this part of a woman before. Something about the way her hair was pulled up so the back of her neck was exposed. Her nape, the soft hairs, the way they . . . It was as if I were looking at some intimate part of a woman, a woman I did not even know. I found myself compelled to stare . . .

WOMAN: We have to meet him. Lisa? I promised him . . .

LISA: Oh, yes.

WOMAN: You know how he can be . . .

LISA: [*looking back at* HARRY] Well . . . [*They turn and exit*]

HARRY: I watched them leave . . . [*We hear moaning. As* HARRY *speaks, lights brought up on* LILLIAN *and* MAN #2 *making love. She's standing backed up against a wall, dress pushed up, with one of her legs wrapped around the man's torso. They're passionately making love.*] That night when Lillian returned from the restaurant we made love several times. We hadn't had sex in several weeks, so it was rather an unusual event. [HARRY *watches them for a beat.*] She had an affair a couple years earlier. [*beat*] I found out in a rather interesting way . . . [LILLIAN *pulls away from the* MAN #2 *and joins* HARRY. *They enact the events as he describes them.* MAN #2 *participates also.*] We were going to her colleague's house for dinner. I remember the one time I met him I was struck by the ease with which he was able to get women to like him. Even Lillian seemed to hang on his every word, laugh at his seemingly insipid jokes. I remember not liking him, yet feeling, against my will, envious of him. That he somehow understood something about women which had eluded me. Lillian said she had never been to his house before, and we had gone through an elaborate discussion of how to get there, with Lillian even looking at a map before we left. I rang the door bell. There was a screen door I pulled on to open, only it was stuck. Lillian, without thinking, reached in, pushed the handle in a peculiar fashion and the screen door popped loose.

[LILLIAN *and* HARRY *exchange looks. Then* HARRY *looks at* MAN #2. MAN #2 *and* LILLIAN *exchange looks. He reaches out to touch her face but she pulls away.* HARRY *watches them.*]

HARRY: We've worked it out. It wasn't easy. That was a while ago. [HARRY *and* LILLIAN *lit in pools of light, looking out*] I'm a bit of a cerebral person. On more than one occasion Lillian has accused me of being . . .
LILLIAN: . . . cold. Sometimes you seem to have no feeling. No heart.
HARRY: I believe too much feeling is a waste of time, gets in the way of logical thinking . . .
LILLIAN: Once when I was in Big Sur I looked up into the night sky and saw moving lights . . .
HARRY: . . . And that at its worst it can make you unsure of yourself, confuse you . . .
LILLIAN: He had these extraordinary eyes . . .

[MAN #2 *lit in half light.* LILLIAN *stares at him.*]

HARRY: Make you do things you wish you hadn't . . .
LILLIAN: . . . eyes that always said "yes" . . .

[MAN #2 *fades to black.*]

HARRY: . . . things you'd rather forget . . .

[*Lighting change. They turn back towards each other.*]

LILLIAN: I'm sorry. I apologize. It will never happen again.
HARRY: It's my fault, too. I realize I'm not the most . . . well, attentive husband. [*Pause. They stare at each other. We hear classical music. They fade to black.*]

[*Upstage the* OLD MAN *and his* DOG *are lit, moving very slowly; now around the middle of the stage. While this action is going on upstage,*

Harry and Lillian lit. A quiet Sunday afternoon. The music continues. Lillian reads a book; Harry sits in a chair watching TV. Harry slowly begins to sink into the seat of the chair. Lillian laughs quietly to herself over a passage she's just read. Life is pleasant, the day peaceful; the sun moves across the sky and begins to set. Lights do a slow fade as Harry continues to sink. We sense that Harry is becoming aware of his situation yet is helpless to do anything about it. He begins to struggle, his middle body being swallowed up into the seat—terrified, trying to signal Lillian. Harry's legs are now sticking out, disappearing into the chair. Lillian takes no notice, turns the page. The music swells.]

[A Dog's Head, suspended in the air above the stage, is flashed up briefly at an odd angle. Harry and Lillian fade to black. The Dog and Old Man continue their very slow walk; Old Man and Dog fade to black.]

[Harry lit]

Harry: I'd begun to feel a little out of sorts. I couldn't write—every time I sat down and tried to recall the events of the strike . . . I decided to visit my mother. She lived alone in a nearby town that I had grown up in . . . [Mother *appears watching a video movie on the TV. Harry puts on his homburg and crosses to her; sits down with his Mother. We can hear the sounds of Japanese voices emanating from the TV.*] She loves to watch Japanese movies . . . [*Japanese samurai movie comes to life. Two* Samurai Warriors *lit in battle. Loud, brutal. In Japanese, one accuses the other.*]

Warrior #1: "INU O KOROSHITA!!" (You killed the dog!) [*He attacks and slashes the other's arm. It is violent and not pretty.*]

Warrior #2: [*gripping his arm*] "AHHH! . . ."

[Mother *switches off the video with her remote and the* Warriors *black out.*]

Mother: [*shaking her head*] Too much violence these days . . .

[*She gets up to switch the video tape.*]

Harry: Hi, Mom.

Mother: [*changing tapes*] Hi, Harry.

Harry: You been okay?

Mother: Un-huh.

Harry: What'd the doctor say?

MOTHER: Said it was nothing. [*beat*] Richard brought more tapes for me. You staying for dinner? I'm cooking a roast. You know how Daddy likes his roast beef. I keep telling him so much red meat's not good for him. "I eat what I want, do what I want" . . . I give up.

[*As* HARRY *watches her, she settles back next to* HARRY *and switches on the video. A Japanese soap opera comes on.* MAN *and* WOMAN *lit, enacting the video. They're speaking in Japanese. It's the actress who plays* NINA *and* MAN #1 *from his dream.*]

WOMAN: "Atashi o tsuketeru no desu ka?" (You've been watching me, haven't you?)
MAN: "Eh?" (What)?
HARRY: I don't speak Japanese, but there were subtitles so I could follow the story . . .

[*The characters transition from speaking Japanese to English.*]

WOMAN: "You've been staring at me."
MAN: "Excuse me?"
WOMAN: "I saw you."
MAN: "I'm sorry, you must be mistaking me for someone else. I don't know—"
WOMAN: "Who are you? What do you want from me?"
MAN: "Really, I don't know what you're talking about . . ."
WOMAN: "If you don't tell me I'm going to call the police."
MAN: [*starting to back away*] "I don't think you need to do—"
WOMAN: "You try and run, I'll scream."
MAN: "Yes, but I'm not doing—"
WOMAN: [*threateningly*] "I'll scream, I will. I'll scream and you'll be found out . . . Thrown in jail. Disgraced. A common criminal."

[MAN *stops.*]

MAN: "What do you want?"

[WOMAN *turns and now begins to address* HARRY *as if he were the soap opera* MAN. *Other* MAN *now watches the action.*]

WOMAN: "What do 'I' want? You're the one, mister. You've been following me. Watching me. Staring at my . . . [*beat*] My neck. [*realizing*] Yes . . . That's it, isn't it? You like the back of my neck . . ." [*She stares at him for a beat. Looks at the* MAN, *then back to* HARRY. *Slowly turns and lifts up her hair for him*] "Go ahead. Touch it." [*Light dim. Pin light on her nape.* HARRY *hesi-*

tates. Looks at his MOTHER, *the* MAN, *then back to the* WOMAN. *Slowly raises his arm, reaching out . . . Stops himself]*
MAN: What's wrong?

[*Before* HARRY *can answer,* SAMURAI #1 *strolls in, stops in front of* HARRY, *wearing trench coat, dark glasses, and hat. Looks Mafioso. We hear the musical tag from the* Godfather's *theme.*]

ITALIAN-SAMURAI: [*Italian accent*] "A gift from the Don . . ."
HARRY: What? Excuse me? . . .

[ITALIAN-SAMURAI *pulls out a shotgun from beneath his coat.*]

ITALIAN-SAMURAI: "You killed the dog. Ciao Harry . . ."

[*Blackout*]

[*Crack of thunder. The sound of rain.* LILLIAN *lit. Dressed in formal black funeral dress, holding a black umbrella*]

LILLIAN: Why don't you like to visit your mother?

[HARRY *lit*]

HARRY: It's not so much her as . . . Something about going back home . . . returning to memories . . .

[LILLIAN *fades to black. Sound cue ends.* MOTHER *lit. Watching a Japanese video movie.*]

MOTHER: I should start the rice. Daddy's going to be home soon.
HARRY: Mama? Mama? Listen to me carefully. Dad's dead. He passed away ten years ago. Okay?
MOTHER: [*stares at him for a beat. Pats him on the head*] Harry? It's alright. It is. You'll be alright.
HARRY: I needed to clear my head out . . . [*Puts on his homburg. Goes for a walk.* MOTHER *fades to black. Fog begins to roll in*] It was very foggy. I could barely see. I began to remember things . . . [*We hear sutra chanting. Casket appears*] My father's funeral. I remember riding in a limousine with my mother and younger brother to the church. It was very hot and the sunlight so bright you had to squint to look outside the windows. This squinting made the outside world shimmer and sparkle. Sitting there with my mother and brother, on the way to Dad's funeral, I suddenly felt like a little boy again passing through some fantastical world . . .

[FISHERMAN *gradually lit in half light, trudging across a river. Same actor who plays the* OLD MAN]

HARRY: I began to remember how he would take me fishing every week. How he knew a secret fishing spot that he would only share with me.

FISHERMAN: [*Moving*] Want a ride?

HARRY: How he would pick me up and let me ride on his back. And we'd forge across the river's current to get to the other side to that special place. At those moments he was huge in my eyes, the bravest of warriors, and I would do anything to make him proud of me.

FISHERMAN: [*Waves, laughing*] Harry . . .

[*Buddhist reverend enters and begins to sutra chant.* FISHERMAN *fades to black.*]

HARRY: It was a Buddhist service—the opulence of gold everywhere, hypnotic chanting and overpowering smells of burning incense filling your head. And amidst it all a minister wrapped in peculiarly restrained black robes. [MOTHER, UNCLES, *and* AUNTS *enter and stand before the casket. Black suits, somber*] I sat with my mother's side of the family. They are all very proper. No one yells, no one ever misbehaves, and they all have professional careers . . .

UNCLE: I'm a pharmacist . . .

AUNT: I'm a dentist . . .

[*trying to top each other*]

UNCLE: My son's a pediatrician . . .

AUNT: My daughter's a brain surgeon . . .

HARRY: Lillian says we're all repressed.

[MOTHER *and two* UNCLES *look at each other curiously. Two of father's* HAWAIIAN RELATIVES *enter. Hawaiian shirts, zoris*]

HARRY: On the other side sat my father's family. They're all Hawaiian—they gamble, they drink . . .

[*Two* HAWAIIANS *argue loudly in thick pidgin*]

HAWAIIAN #1: I pay dis time . . .

HAWAIIAN #2: What you mean? I pay. You went pay last time. You all da time pay.

HAWAIIAN #1: Hey bull lie, my turn for pay brudda . . .

HAWAIIAN #2: No, no, no . . .

HAWAIIAN #1: [*overlapping*] Yeah, yeah, yeah . . .

HARRY: . . . they shout at life, embrace it with their souls. [*beat*] Lillian wanted to sit with them but I ushered her to our side . . .

The service was moving along without a hitch when—

[*A man suddenly bolts past* HARRY *and begins to wail mournfully over the casket.*]

UNCLE ARTY: [*sobbing*] Willie, Willie, I should have gone before you. You were so good to us. I'll miss you Willie, I'll miss you . . . I love you, I love you . . .

HARRY: It was Uncle Arty, Dad's older brother. My mother's side of the family was mortified at his lack of decorum, his raw, unrestrained expression of grief and despair . . .

[ARTY'*s wailing grows. He's now stretched out over the casket, sobbing. The Reverend takes no notice and continues to chant.*]

UNCLE ARTY: DON'T GO, DON'T GO WILLIE . . . LET ME GO IN YOUR PLACE; I'LL GO, I'M THE OLDER BROTHER, I SHOULD'VE GONE BEFORE YOU . . .

HARRY: I found myself feeling a strange mixture of emotions. I was at once shocked, painfully uncomfortable at his overt calling attention to ourselves, the event. And at the very same moment, wanting to join him, to wail, to sob unabashedly, to let a flood of complex feelings pour out of me. [*beat*] But instead . . .

[LILLIAN *and the two* HAWAIIAN RELATIVES *escort* UNCLE ARTY *away.* MOTHER, UNCLES, AUNT, *and Reverend follow them.* HARRY *stands alone, staring at the casket. He starts to approach it. It fades to black. Sutra chanting stops.*]

HARRY: I decided to head back to my mother's house. The fog was getting to me and I started to feel very cold . . .

[HARRY *approached by a shadowy* STREET PERSON. *Filthy. Hat, face is covered with a tattered muffler. Played by the same actor who played* MAN #2]

STREET PERSON: Excuse me sir? Excuse me?

[HARRY *tries to avoid him, but he keeps getting in front of* HARRY. *There's a sense of danger about him, violence just beneath the surface.*]

STREET PERSON: Excuse me sir, but I need some money to eat. I haven't eaten in days and I could sure use some money.

HARRY: [*fumbling through his pockets*] You're not from here are you? Life's been good to you, I can see that. Not me though. You try and serve the people. You do what's right and see what happens. Betrayal, friends abandon you, the world cuts off your legs and leaves you to rot half a man. Who said, "A foolish old man can move a mountain?" Huh? Who said? Better to keep your mouth shut. Go along with everybody else. Then you can have your pretty, pretty wife. Nice fat job at the university. Big fancy house full of fancy wines and expensive jewelry. [HARRY *hands him some change.* STREET PERSON *stares at it.*]

STREET PERSON: What's this? What's this? Fucking Chinamens, fucking Chinamenjaps—the cheapest motherfuckers on the face of the earth! YOU GOT ALL— [*gets right in front of* HARRY's *face*] —THE MONEY AND YOU'RE THE CHEAPEST MOTHERFUCKERS, NEVER GIVE ANY MONEY, TRY TO PRETEND LIKE I'M NOT HERE, LIKE I DON'T EXIST. I'M HERE, I'M HERE, I'M HERE!!! [*Blackout on* STREET PERSON.]

HARRY: [*composes himself*] That night I couldn't sleep. The incident with the street person along with the strange images that had begun to invade my mind at my mother's house had left me rattled and confused. I tossed and turned, alternately sweating and feeling icy cold. Finally I passed into a fitful sleep . . . [HARRY *lies down. Lit in a pool of light.*]

[MOTHER *and* JAPANESE SOAP OPERA WOMAN *lit, strolling through the edges of the light backwards. As they pass,* LILLIAN *lit.*]

LILLIAN: [*eyes closed*] I love you Harry. I love you with all my heart. [LILLIAN *fades to black.*]

[*Sound of birds chirping. Dawn.* FISHERMAN *lit. Mimes pole.* HARRY *looking out. Dreamscape*]

FISHERMAN: [*listening*] Beautiful, huh? I was thinking. Maybe if you recorded the birds—then put the sounds of their chirping down as musical notes. Don't you think it'd make a wonderful song?

HARRY: Sometimes I don't recognize myself anymore. I find myself feeling things I never felt before—thinking the oddest thoughts.

FISHERMAN: I do the same thing. I look in the mirror. Who is this person? I feel like a young man inside, like I could still dive deep, catch fish in my mouth, dance the hula with the wahinis all night long. Then I see this wrinkled, old man staring back at me.

HARRY: Is that what happened? I mean, I always wondered. They just found your boat, nothing disturbed. Everyone assumed it was an accident, but . . . [*Pause.* FISHERMAN *turns and looks at* HARRY.]

FISHERMAN: We all die Harry. That's a given. But you don't have to grow old . . .

[*Blackout. Lights up on* HARRY. *He has only one arm.*]

HARRY: [*stares at his missing arm*] Then the dream changed . . .

[*Loud music, wild, dangerous.* HARRY *moves through an urban night. Music transitions into background, coming from inside a nearby club.*]

HARRY: I find myself wandering through a rough part of town . . . [MAN #1 *and the* JAPANESE SOAP OPERA WOMAN *lit at a table*] I walk into a club and see this person who looks like the man who appeared in my dream. He is sitting with a woman whose back is to me, but I instantly know it's the same woman who was with Lisa. The back of her neck . . . [*We hear* NINA's *theme music.*] . . . I find that I can't help myself. That I have to look. The man notices and seems angry. He glares threateningly at me, and I know I should avert my eyes but I am beyond myself, being pulled along by something within I do not recognize. I must watch her, her nape, the way the hairs on her neck . . .

[MAN #1 *gets up violently, knocking the chair over. At that instant, upstage, three* EXOTIC DANCERS—*two men, one woman—are lit in silhouette. Music becomes very loud. Wild sexual dance.*]

[MAN #1 *strides towards* HARRY. MAN #1 *stands over* HARRY, *pulls out a knife, holds it threateningly, then notices* HARRY *has only one arm. His attitude changes, slowly lowers his knife. Dancers fade to black, music dips*]

MAN #1: Come on.

[HARRY *hesitates.*]

MAN #1: Come on, come on over here. I said come on . . . [*Drags him over to the table and presents him to the* SOAP OPERA WOMAN *who's drinking vodka. A bottle sits in front of her.*] Look who's here Nina. Your friend. [*He tosses the knife on the table in front of her. The* SOAP OPERA WOMAN *glances up at* HARRY *and* MAN #1, *then goes back to drinking.*]

MAN #1: She likes you. You're the man with the disappearing arm.

WOMAN: He's not my friend.

MAN: Ahh, but you're always thinking about him. He's always on your mind— talks about you in her sleep, says your name—

WOMAN: [*upset*] Why do you do this to me, huh? He's not my friend, I've told you that over and over. He's not my friend. I don't think about him. He's old, he's not sexual, and most of all . . . [*She grabs the knife off the table and suddenly drives it into* HARRY's *chest. The music cuts away. Silence. Lights transition into an isolated pool of light on them.* HARRY *stares aghast at the knife sticking out of him.*] . . . he has no heart. No heart. How could I ever be interested in a man who has no feelings, no passion, no fire. The man has no heart. He's already dead and he doesn't even know it.

[MAN #1 *pulls the knife out of* HARRY's *chest.* HARRY *is still in shock. Back to previous lighting*]

MAN #1: Nina, Nina, you're such a . . . Tough woman. That's why I love you so much . . . [*touches her cheek. She knocks his hand away.*] Allow me to introduce myself. Joe. Joe Ozu. And this is Nina—Nina, the Gorgeous—and in a certain light, Nina the Ugly. But, and always, Nina with the mysterious nape, huh?
Don't worry. You can't bleed if you got no heart, Harry. Besides, this is just a dream, right? [*holds out a pill*] A magic pill. Go ahead. Take it. Don't be afraid. If you want to dance you gotta pay the band, Harry.

NINA: Don't.

HARRY: What does it do?

[JOE *puts pill in* HARRY's *hand. He begins to lean in close, talking into* HARRY's *ear.*]

JOE: It makes you dumb. You're too clever, Harry . . .

[NINA *begins to talk into* HARRY's *other ear.*]

NINA: Go home. Back to your quiet, suffocating, inconsequential life, Harry . . .

JOE: You need to have a heart attack. Explode something inside your head. Die. And then live again . . .

NINA: It's safe. No risks. You don't have to worry about someone like me. You don't have to bleed . . .

JOE: Go ahead. Trust me Harry. You have absolutely everything to lose . . .

NINA: You'll live and die and it will all pass like a quiet Sunday afternoon . . .

JOE: And that's what you want, isn't it?

NINA: Your wife reading, you watching TV, sinking, sinking . . . [*beat*] Who cares about some dumb paper?

JOE: Who cares about some dumb strike?

NINA: Just keep it all locked up deep down inside . . .

JOE: And the tiny scream inside your head?

NINA: Just tell it to shut up . . .

[JOE *and* NINA *begin barking and howling like dogs. Dancers brought up. Loud music.* HARRY, *disoriented, stares at the pill in his hand.*]

[*Fade to black*]

[*Lights up.* HARRY *nervously adjusts a tape recorder. A man wanders around, looking at things. He has the feeling of an ex-hippie who never quite left the era. This is* JEFF *from* HARRY's *college days, continuously whacking a pack of cigarettes against his palm in a gesture to pack the tobacco.*]

HARRY: [*notices* JEFF *pulling out a cigarette*] Jeff? I would appreciate it if you wouldn't smoke inside? Lillian doesn't like it. [JEFF *stares for a beat. Puts the cigarette away*] Actually I was about to abandon the idea altogether. The Strike. Writing about it. So when you called out of the blue I was a little—

JEFF: I heard you. In here . . . [*Pointing to his head.* HARRY *stares at him for a beat.*]

HARRY: Now as I explained, I'm doing research on this paper. In particular I'm interested in the factionalism in the Asian American groups, politically what each group stood for . . .

JEFF: [*whispering, overlapping*] Chuckie . . .

HARRY: [*distracted but continuing*] See, if we can trace their roots back to early pre-war Asian communities, to any political, lefty leanings that might have even been brought over from the old countries . . .

JEFF: [*giggling*] Chuckie . . .

HARRY: And then trace those movements into the present to see how they've impacted present-day activism, court litigations—things like the Korematsu case, Vincent Chin, the Soon Ja Du–Latasha Harlins case . . .

JEFF: [*overlapping*] Chuckie, Chuckie . . .

HARRY: That's not my name Jeff. It's Harry.

JEFF: Chuckie, Chuckie . . .

HARRY: [*switches off recorder*] Is there a problem here, Jeff?

JEFF: It's not over.

HARRY: What?

JEFF: [*takes out a cigarette again*] You may think it is. But nothing's forgotten. Everything's remembered. You notice how the music is coming back? I always think about Sam. You heard from him?

HARRY: No, no, I haven't . . .

JEFF: Remember how Sam used to always quote Mao? That parable about the "foolish old man"? I heard a rumor he went underground and was hiding out with the Weathermen. That he was in the Patty Hearst house and got out just before the big shoot out. When I was in— [*continuing*]

HARRY: [*overlapping*] No actually, other than Lillian you're the first person I've contacted . . .

JEFF: —South America I heard he went to Cuba on one of those Venceremos Brigades, stayed on and became one of Fidel's inner circle. [*beat*] Remember how our group was having trouble with that other group, AAFA? During the strike? . . . As to who should represent the Asian component in the negotiations? I mean, we were all fighting the Administration but there was all this infighting going on—

HARRY: Jeff, Jeff, actually I'm not so much interested in anecdotal material as I am in a critical analysis of the social structures of that time and their relationship to present day legal—

JEFF: Asian Americans For Action? AAFA? Remember?

HARRY: Well, yeah, of course I remember them but—

JEFF: No, no, this was a big thing, this was a big thing . . .

HARRY: I wouldn't go that far, it wasn't that big of—

JEFF: Chuckie, Chuckie, how you going to write this paper if you don't remember right? It was a big thing. It was like war, our group against theirs. People doing things, ugly things to each other . . . [JEFF *lights his cigarette,* HARRY *watches him.*]

HARRY: I remember one time I stayed up all night helping Sam write that speech. The one he gave on the steps of the Student Union. He had guts. And I sent that fake memo so they'd set up the microphone for us . . .

JEFF: You disappeared. Where'd you go?

HARRY: My father got sick. I had to go back home . . .

JEFF: You didn't.

HARRY: What?

JEFF: I helped Sam write that speech. You didn't.

HARRY: I did too, Jeff.

JEFF: I sent the memo, you didn't.

HARRY: [*flustered*] I didn't say I did it alone, I meant we—

[OLD MAN *and* DOG *lit upstage, continuing their walk*]

JEFF: [*interrupts*] Lillian took your place after you left. Sam and she worked together, but things weren't quite the same with the group. Everything fell apart, people accusing each other of being spies for the administration . . . [*beat*] Wasn't there this thing about a dog? Remember that? The campus police and some kind of dog incident? . . .

[*The main stage goes to half light.* DOG'S HEAD *lit above.* JEFF *exits.* OLD MAN *becomes the* SCHOOL PRESIDENT *and enters the scene with* HARRY. *He leads* HARRY *to his chair and sits him down. Looks at him for a beat.* PRESIDENT *then moves to edge of the scene and watches.*]

[*A young* SAM *and* JEFF *enter,* SAM *played by same actor who played* MAN #2 *and* STREET PERSON. *Both carry copies of Mao's Little Red Book. In the offices of the Yellow Guard. Early 70s.*]

SAM: The administration has arranged a meeting with Asian Americans For Action to discuss their position on the strike. But if they don't show up, the administration pigs will have to come to us to negotiate. That's why we need you to do this . . .

[HARRY *is silent.*]

JEFF: Chuckie?

[*no response*]

SAM: You know why we call you that? Chuckie? Jeff named you that. Because you never say anything. You're like this worker bee, buzzing around the office—doing this, doing that, but you never talk.

JEFF: Like Charlie Chaplin in one of those silent movies.

HARRY: But why do I have to—

SAM: You have to stop fighting us. The Yellow Guard wants you to be part of the family . . . [*pause.* SAM *watches* HARRY.] They like people like you. You're just like your parents. My parents. We always do what we're told. We do. It's in our blood. Quiet, hardworking, successful—the model minority. Engineers, accountants, maybe even marry Donna Reed. They love saying to our Black and Brown brothers and sisters, "Hey, the Orientals made it on their own, why can't you people?" And secretly our chests well up. Another crumb tossed our way and we lap it up—"Yeah, we raised ourselves up by our boot straps, why can't they?" The "model minority." It's all bullshit. So they accept us for us for now but at what price? To live like a cowardly mouse, never making a peep 'cause we're afraid they'll take it away? Always wearing this silent frozen mask of middle class propriety while inside you want to rage, scream at the injustices all around you? Look at who's getting slaughtered in Southeast Asia, then look in the mirror. It don't lie. One day we'll get too good at what we do. We'll make a little too much money, figure out the game a little too well, and then we'll see middle class America's real face. They'll hate us; they'll hunt us down, kill us in the streets . . . [*pause*]

HARRY: [*quietly*] But AAFA's got a lot more members than we do . . .

SAM: Even a Foolish Old Man can move a mountain, Harry. [*beat*] We have to do something that will let AAFA know we mean business. So they'll get out of the way . . . So the President will have to come to us. He'll hate that. Having to deal with the Yellow Guard.

SAM: These are desperate times Harry.

JEFF: The Panthers being systematically executed. Chicano farmworkers being exploited by our very own kind . . .

SAM: Mylai . . .

JEFF: William Calley . . .

SAM: Cambodia . . .

JEFF: Plain of Jars . . .

SAM: It's the end of the world and the beginning of the world and we're here to usher it in. [*Quickly opens the Red Book to a dog-eared passage and reads*] Mao says, "Political power grows from a barrel of a gun." It must be a statement so single-mindedly committed, so terrifyingly purposeful, AAFA will wilt under the weight of its deed . . . [*beat*] The Yellow Guard wants you to do something for us. Can you Harry? [*pause*] Or is it Chuckie?

HARRY: You've been like. Family to me. Here. With you. I feel. Finally. Like I'm in my house. I can breathe. Finally breathe. Just be who I am.

[*We hear the "Godfather" theme.*]

SAM: We went to see a movie . . . [SAM *and* JEFF *withdraw.*]

[PRESIDENT *enters. Stands before* HARRY]

PRESIDENT: As the school President I have to ask you these things. [*no response*] Harry? [HARRY *is resistant. Threateningly*] Harry?

HARRY: [*relenting, quietly*] Sam. [*beat*] The Yellow Guard . . .

[PRESIDENT *nods. Then withdraws and goes back to being the* OLD MAN *walking the* DOG. *They continue slowly moving across the upstage area. The older* JEFF *enters again. Back in the present*]

JEFF: Wasn't there this thing about a dog? The campus police and some kind of dog—

HARRY: [*interrupts*] There was no dog. [*noticing*] I said not to smoke Jeff, Jesus. [*muttering to himself*] What the hell's wrong with you, can't remember anything. You take too many drugs or something? . . .

JEFF: I'm not crazy Harry. I get the feeling you want me to be but I'm not. I remember everything. Nothing's forgotten. [*stares for a beat*] Chuckie . . . [*withdraws*]

[HARRY *turns upstage and watches the* OLD MAN *and his* DOG *for a beat, then approaches them. The* OLD MAN *stops and turns away to wipe his forehead with his handkerchief, admire the view. As he does,* HARRY *attempts to snatch the* DOG. *Reaches in. The* DOG *resists, knocking his hand away at each attempt.* DOG *is curious but wary of this man's advances. Then* HARRY *grabs its leg.* DOG *is puzzled, then struggles to get away.* HARRY *is pulling on the* DOG's *leg.* DOG *is trying to signal the* OLD MAN, *who is preoccupied blowing his nose.*]

[*Fade to black*]

[LILLIAN *lit. Just finished packing bags.* HARRY *watches.*]

LILLIAN: I'm leaving you, Harry.
HARRY: But I'm just not ready for that kind of responsibility . . .
LILLIAN: It's not just the baby thing, it's—
HARRY: I can't make that kind of commitment right now . . .
LILLIAN: You don't want a baby, that's fine, I can accept that. It's just . . . You're 40 years old Harry; what do you mean, "I can't make that kind of commitment RIGHT NOW?" [HARRY *can't respond.*] I have to go . . .
HARRY: I'll change, I promise.

[*beat*]

LILLIAN: You live on the surface of your life. And you think if you just touch another person's skin, that's living.
HARRY: Is it Raoul?

[*She reaches out and strokes his cheek. Looks at his face*]

LILLIAN: You're pathetic Harry. I love you. [LILLIAN *leaves.* HARRY *watches her exit.*]

[FISHERMAN *lit, fishing with a mimed pole. Wears a homburg. No shoes, bare feet. Creel sits beside him.*]

HARRY: [*approaches the* FISHERMAN] Catch anything?
FISHERMAN: A son's duty is to be greater than his father.

[*beat*]

HARRY: I don't fish anymore. It's not that I don't like it. It's just . . . You have to get everything ready the night before—tackle, poles, reels; prepare food, get your clothes out—then get up, and the sun's not even out yet, and pack it all in the car, then drive all the way up there. Then when you're done, you gotta pack it all back in the car again, drive all the way back, unload the car, throw away all the garbage, wash off all your gear, put your dirty clothes in the hamper; then after all that you still gotta clean all the damn fish. It just seems like too much work, you know. What's the point, huh? What's the point?

FISHERMAN: [*reaches into his creel and pulls out a live flapping fish*] You're my hope Harry.

[*pause*]

HARRY: [*remorseful*] I'm sorry. I failed you.

[FISHERMAN *fades to black.* HARRY *looks down at his hand. There's a pill. He pops it into his mouth.*]

[*Blackout*]

[*Lights up on* JOE. *He has on earphones and is drumming the air with a pair of drum sticks. He has swimmer's goggles pushed up on his forehead. He wears a small parachute pack on his back. A pack sits on the ground.* HARRY *stands next to him.*]

JOE: Here, put these on. [*Hands* HARRY *swimmer's goggles with dark lenses.* HARRY *hesitates.*] What's wrong?

HARRY: It's nighttime.

JOE: [*can't hear. Louder*] I said "What's wrong?"

HARRY: It's dark.

JOE: So?

HARRY: Well, then I can't see . . .

JOE: [*putting them on him*] Whoa, Mr. Uncool. We're talking style here. If you're going to go, you want to go with style right?

HARRY: Where am I going?

JOE: Trust me, I know what I'm doing. What? You don't know what I do?

HARRY: No . . .

JOE: Hey, I just got this tape. Amazing. You ever heard of Ginger Baker? [*louder*] Ginger Baker? Cream? I'd never heard of him. Picked this up in a oldies bin. This guy's nuts. I mean "really" nuts. I can't believe this—everybody thinks he's making music but he's really just going off the deep end, schizo. You can feel his confusion, pain. He's working out his inner torment, trying to organize it so it's manageable but he can't. It's out of control, breaking apart, bits and pieces of his soul flying out through his hands, into the sticks, onto the skins . . .

[*We hear a ginger Baker drum solo from his Cream days over the house speakers, played loudly.*]

JOE: [*talking over the sound*] . . . we get to hear his psychosis. The rhythm of his madness. People paid money for this stuff. Crazy, huh?

[*Loud drumming continues. They speak over the sound.*]

JOE: I arrange things. What I do? I arrange things for people. Services. Actually a very special service. In fact, you could say it's a one-of-a-kind service, to be performed only one time. [*waits for* HARRY *to ask what kind of service.* HARRY *doesn't.*] Don't you want to ask me something? [HARRY *stares.*] Like what kind of service this service is?

HARRY: What kind of service?

JOE: Funny you should ask. I arrange for people's deaths. Most people find planning their own demise a rather distasteful task. Why, I'll never know. I think there's a sort of built in survival mechanism that just resists the idea of killing oneself— [*putting the parachute pack on his back*] —off, even when a big change is in the best interests of all parties involved. So it means not only must I have steely determination but also be tricky and manipulative to get the desired results . . .

HARRY: What are you doing?

JOE: [*grabs his arm*] We're going for a little swim . . .

[*They go to the lip of the stage and jump. Lighting transition. We hear the sound of rushing air. Ginger Baker fades away. They're leaning out at a 60 degree angle, held by cables from behind. Air being blown into their faces. A little smoke to simulate clouds. Bright light shooting up from below at them, illuminating their bodies. Darkness all around them.* JOE *has his arms spread out and is negotiating the air.* HARRY *flails about. Upstage a night sky*]

HARRY: Swimming? Swimming?

JOE: I lied! Spread your arms out! Spread your arms out! Like this! Like this! That's right, that's right. Great, huh? I like to jump at night. That way, you can't tell how far you are from the ground—more of a thrill. Just joking, joking. I can tell by my watch. We have 90 seconds left to pull our rip cords or it's boom, custard pie.

HARRY: [*searching for his rip cord*] Where is it? Where's the rip cord?

JOE: These are special chutes, no rip cords. The chute opens only when you give the right answer. It hears the right answer, and poof—they open up like beautiful, fluffy clouds.

HARRY: Right answer to what? To what?

JOE: Oh-oh, fifty-five seconds. You better hurry up, Harry.

HARRY: To what?! To what, what's the question?!

JOE: Show me your face.

HARRY: What?

JOE: Oh-oh, twenty-five seconds!

HARRY: Show you my face?

JOE: Yes, show me your face!

HARRY: WHAT KIND OF FUCKING QUESTION IS THAT!!!

JOE: Ten seconds!

HARRY: UH, UH—I DON'T KNOW WHAT IT MEANS! WHAT DOES THE QUESTION—HOW'S— [*continue*]

JOE: [*overlapping*] Five! Four! Three!— [*continue*]

HARRY: [*overlapping, making weird, funny facial expressions*] THIS! HOW'S THIS ONE?! HOW ABOUT THIS ONE?!!

JOE: —Two! One! . . .

HARRY: AHHHHH!!!

[*Blackout. Roar of the wind cuts away. Silence.* JOE *and* HARRY *lit. Parachutes are gone.*]

JOE: [*stares at him*] Funny. [*feeling him*] You didn't break apart. Hmmm. You're so tight. I figured the pressure of impending death would force you beyond the threshold, to the other side. Make my work easy. You got tighter and tighter, more and more conflicted, but you didn't break. I figured at least the force of the crash would shatter you, make you see beyond yourself . . . But you're a hard nut Harry. [*Pause.* JOE *thinking*] Something with more flare, more theatricality, more high drama . . .

[*We hear Peggy Lee's "Is That All There Is?" Upstage a Japanese woman is lit, lip-syncing the song. Wears a blond wig, slinky dress, and does a Peggy Lee imitation—played by actress who plays* LISA. *A strikingly handsome* WAITER *walks by with a tray of martinis.* JOE *takes one, then kisses the* WAITER *on the lips, a long, wet one.*]

JOE: Would you like one, too?

[HARRY *quickly shakes his head.* JOE *looks at the* WAITER *and shrugs.*]

WAITER: Pity . . . [*exits*]

JOE: Your song, Harry. Peggy's singing your song. Gosh, you're lucky. It never happens for me. You must be born under a special star. And look. Look who's here . . .

HARRY: Isn't that . . . That's Angela Davis, isn't it?

JOE: Uh-huh . . .

HARRY: And there's, there's, what's his name, what's his name—

JOE: Mario Savio . . .

HARRY: Mario Savio, I'd forgotten all about him. What happened to him?

[JOE *shrugs.*]

HARRY: And there's Joan Baez; what's she doing now?

JOE: Exactly the same thing, I think.

HARRY: Oh my god—S. I. Hayakawa? . . . with his tam–o'–shanter no less.

JOE: Yes, yes, and look who else is here . . .

[JOE *withdraws.* NINA *lit, looking beautiful and cooly reserved. She directs* HARRY *to a bench, where they sit. Night sky is filled with stars. They look out.*]

NINA: I don't want to be here, Harry. I don't.

HARRY: We don't seem to have much choice in the matter. I'm sorry.

NINA: Please don't apologize. It spoils the illusion.

HARRY: I'm sorry . . . [*catches himself*]

[NINA *pulls out a bottle of champagne and two glasses. Begins pouring*]

NINA: I know there is more here than meets the eye. Please don't waste my time, Harry. Especially time taken against my will. Show me your face.

HARRY: What is this face business? I don't know what everyone is talking about . . .

NINA: [*handing him a glass*] Here, maybe this will help you . . . [*downs a glass and pours another for herself*] By the way, how's your arm?

HARRY: What?

NINA: Drink, drink . . . There you go . . . Obviously you refuse to tell me the truth about your face, your arm . . . Drink, go ahead and drink. It'll help the mood. [*They both drink. She pours out more. Both beginning to loosen up*]

HARRY: There are so many things I want to tell you . . .

NINA: Then tell me, Harry. We haven't much time. The pill? The effects wear

off. [*downs another glass. Feeling good. Notices something in the sky*] Look,
that star . . . it's moving . . .

HARRY: I don't know where to begin.

NINA: You wrote a poem for me.

[HARRY *doesn't know what she's talking about.* NINA *reaches into his
pocket and pulls out a sheet of paper and gives it to* HARRY.]

NINA: I'm all ears, Harry. I'm all eyes. I'm all mouth, and we're waiting . . .

[HARRY *looks at the poem. He is hesitant. She watches him while sipping.
He begins to read.*]

HARRY: [*reading*] "In this night. In this night of flight. I hover above your city
. . ."

NINA: Yes, let it go . . .

HARRY: "A web of tears and tiny fires buoyed up on soft hands . . ."

NINA: I like it.

HARRY: ". . . soft hands of wind. I am like a moth, struggling against my nature. Do I willingly die in your mysterious fire? Allow myself to be swallowed
up in eyes, so drunken and wild with fearless wanting that I am as a little
child in the face of new knowledge? How will I make my way home?"

NINA: My hands will guide you . . .

HARRY: "If I were to offer you a rose. Lush, combustable, it's fragrance an angel's scent. Would your eyes say yes? So that I may dream and dream and
dream."

NINA: Good Harry . . .

HARRY: "I long to fall into your breath. Inhale me, deep into your body. I will
ignite, rapturous and howling; I will surrender everything and more to you
. . . [*too much for* HARRY. *Stops. Difficulty breathing. Feeling chest*]

NINA: Harry?

HARRY: I can't take this. It's too much . . .

NINA: I know.

HARRY: I'm afraid I will die.

NINA: That's what love is about. [*She looks at him for a beat, then turns and
offers her nape to him. He bends forward and is about to kiss her.*]

[*Out of nowhere the* STREET PERSON *appears. Same state of agitation.
Pushes his face right in between them*]

STREET PERSON: Excuse me, excuse me, but I haven't eaten for days. I could
sure use some money . . .

HARRY: Look, last time I gave you some change you yelled and said some very insulting things—

[OLD MAN *appears walking the* DOG. *Happy, whistling*]

NINA: [*looking at the* OLD MAN] Don't you recognize him?
STREET PERSON: Don't you know me Harry? Don't you remember me? [*takes off his hat and muffler to reveal who he is*]
HARRY: Sam?
NINA: Our father.
OLD MAN: Hi, Nina.
HARRY: What?
NINA: You see, I'd been having visions . . . Of a Man with a bleeding heart . . . A Man rising into the air. So I decided to enter a convent . . .
SAM: [*to* HARRY] You mean run away.
NINA: But who would take care of my dog, Raymond?
SAM: Ahh, the dog . . .

[DOG *barks playfully*]

OLD MAN: I'll take care of him, Nina. Down Raoul, down boy.
SAM: You ruined my life, Harry. You're responsible for my fate.
HARRY: What are you talking about? You took advantage of me. I believed in you so much, and then you asked me to do that thing to the Old Man's dog . . .
SAM: Aren't you going to do it?

[OLD MAN *becomes the* SCHOOL PRESIDENT]

PRESIDENT: You have a bright future, Mr. Kitamura . . .
SAM: You have to prove your loyalty . . .
PRESIDENT: Law school, medical school . . .
SAM: What are you waiting for?
PRESIDENT: I'd hate to see all that ruined . . .
NINA: Who are you going to listen to? Whose voice are you going to obey?
SAM: Then you ran away like a coward. Abandoned me. What's a leader with no followers?
PRESIDENT: Your father will have to hide his face when other fathers brag about their sons.
SAM: Even Lillian lost confidence in me after that.
PRESIDENT: . . . bow his head in shame, whisper your name like a dirty word.
SAM: How do you think she ended up with you?

PRESIDENT: Maybe even kill himself . . . [PRESIDENT *becomes the* OLD MAN *walking his* DOG *again. Exits*]

HARRY: No, don't say that . . .

SAM: I ended up dying before my time.

HARRY: What, what—you, too?

NINA: Harry?

SAM: I drowned. Didn't you hear the rumor? I sank beneath the surface, the victim of neglect and loveless air.

NINA: What did you do?

[*Lighting shift. Back to the 70s Yellow Guard scene again. Young* SAM. *We hear the "Godfather's" theme tag.* DOG's HEAD *lit*]

SAM: We saw this movie. They were trying to make this point to this Hollywood producer and he was being stubborn, so they delivered the head of his favorite horse to him. Just the head. [*beat*] We'll do the dirty work, Harry. We know how much you prefer to keep your hands clean. We'll do that part. But you get us the dog.

HARRY: What?

SAM: You get the dog. We need a dog. We know an old man who has this mangy mutt.

HARRY: I can't do that . . .

SAM: AAFA needs to know we mean business.

HARRY: Yeah, but . . .

[JEFF *drags the* DOG *in.* SAM *looks at* HARRY.]

SAM: Good, Harry. You did good. [*pulls out a knife. Holds it above the* DOG. *Stops. Looks at* HARRY. *Holds it out to him*]

HARRY: What?

SAM: [*holding the knife out*] Harry.

HARRY: I delivered the dog. That's all you said I had to—

SAM: There's been some talk about you. Rumors . . . about your . . . trustworthiness. Harry?

[HARRY *hesitates.*]

SAM: What are you waiting for? Harry?

[*Blackout*]

[HARRY *lit*]

HARRY: I began to lose myself. What was happening to me? My mind was raging with so many conflicting thoughts. And at night, as soon as I'd close my eyes, all I could see was Nina—her— [*continue*]

[NINA *lit, walking the* DOG]

HARRY: —face, her eyes, the way she smelled . . . I tried to maintain some semblance of normalcy in my life . . .

[LILLIAN *enters, holding* HARRY'*s homburg and scarf. She puts them on him.* NINA *fades to black.*]

LILLIAN: Have a good day. I'm working late again. I'll call from the office. [*Under her breath*] You selfish asshole.
HARRY: What?
LILLIAN: Nothing, nothing dear . . .

[*They kiss. As she turns,* LILLIAN'*s* ATTORNEY *is lit. He carries a briefcase.* LILLIAN *joins him.*]

LILLIAN'S ATTORNEY: As your attorney I have to ask you these things.

[LILLIAN *nods for him to proceed. She puts her arm through his and they speak as they exit.*]

LILLIAN'S ATTORNEY: I understand you wanted a baby and he didn't?
LILLIAN: I wanted to give birth to a child, not marry one . . .

[LILLIAN *and her* ATTORNEY *exit arm in arm.*]

[HARRY *puts on his glasses, opens his notes. He's in the midst of a lecture.*]

HARRY: —thus, the Supreme Court is ultimately not truly free—an objective, unbiased body as we would like to believe. But rather, it is subject to the same cultural and racial biases that the rest of this society . . . [*stops, looks out anxiously*] I was in the middle of a lecture to one of my classes when my mind blanked out . . . I couldn't remember anything. What had I just said? What was I going to say next?
Excuse me. I'm not feeling well. That's all for today . . .
I had to put an end to this, find her one way or another. I hurried back to my office and locked the door. I had an idea . . . [*He picks up a phone and dials.*] I decided to call Lisa. Maybe she would know how to get in touch with her.

[LISA *lit on phone*]

LISA: Who?

HARRY: It's Harry. Professor Kitamura? Harry Kitamura?

[*beat*]

LISA: Oh, yeah . . . What do you want? I'm kind of in a hurry.

HARRY: This will only take a moment. Remember when I ran into you the other day. You were with this woman. This was, oh, about three weeks ago? The two of you were arguing with this man. You asked me if I wanted to join you for drinks. But the woman said—

LISA: I'm sorry I don't remember this. When was this?

HARRY: About three weeks ago? The woman, your friend, said—

LISA: My friend? What was her name?

HARRY: I don't know; that's why I'm calling you. I wonder if you might know how to—

LISA: I don't remember being with any woman. Look, I have to go now. Sorry I can't help you . . .

HARRY: No, no, wait . . .

[LISA *hangs up. Blackout*]

[*Lights up on* HARRY *and a well-dressed young* STUDENT *from the* Law Review *Committee, nervously looking around.*]

HARRY: I don't understand. I thought it was all decided. You said you wanted it for next year's *Law Review*—

LAW STUDENT: Some things came up. I'm not at liberty to say.

HARRY: What kinds of things?

LAW STUDENT: I can't tell you. They asked me not to say.

HARRY: No, no, I want to know—what kinds of things came up?

LAW STUDENT: Look, we all felt it would have been a very good article. Obviously, I mean, we had planned to publish it—

HARRY [*grabs him*] What kinds of things; tell me . . .

[HARRY's *got him by the collar.* STUDENT *is unsure whether to divulge the information. Looking around*]

LAW STUDENT: [*lowering his voice*] Let's just say the article would have been given the okay except for some indiscretions on your part in your college days . . . [*pushing* HARRY's *hands away*] Now excuse me, I've said enough already. If you'd like to re-submit the outline or even the article to next year's selection panel, I'm sure they would be happy to consider it again. [STUDENT *looks around, then hurriedly turns and exits.*]

[HARRY *watches him leave. Pulls out a phone and dials*]

[LISA *lit*]

LISA: [*upset*] I told you I don't know who you're talking about. Now would you please leave me alone. [*turns and starts walking*]

[HARRY *gets an idea.*]

HARRY: I followed her after one of her classes . . . [*starts to follow* LISA] Maybe, just maybe she could lead me—

[LISA *abruptly turns and confronts* HARRY. *This first part should echo the earlier Japanese soap opera scene.*]

LISA: Why are you following me? What do you want from me?
HARRY: Eh? I'm not following—
LISA: Yes, yes you are. I don't know anything about this woman, alright?
HARRY: But I met her with you. If you could just tell me how—
LISA: You keep harassing me, I'm going to tell the school officials on you.
HARRY: You don't understand, its— [*continue*]
LISA: [*overlapping*] I'm going to tell my boyfriend—I'LL SCREAM, I'LL SCREAM, AND YOU'LL BE IN BIG TROUBLE, NOW— [*continue*]
HARRY: [*moving towards her*] —not you, it's the other woman I've got to see . . .
LISA: —LEAVE ME ALONE!
HARRY: Alright, alright . . . [HARRY *backs away as* LISA *runs off.* HARRY *is left alone.*]

[HARRY's ATTORNEY *hurries in and grabs him by the arm, pulling him along to the divorce hearing.* JUDGE *appears, along with* LILLIAN *and* LILLIAN's ATTORNEY]

LILLIAN'S ATTORNEY: . . . the house, her BMW, Harry's Saab, the CD player, the televisions, all the furniture, the IRAs, the T-Bills, the stocks and bonds . . . [*drones on*]
HARRY: [*overlapping, to* LILLIAN] Why are you doing this?

[LILLIAN *refuses to talk to* HARRY.]

LILLIAN'S ATTORNEY: —and most of all, she wants custody of their child Harry . . .
HARRY: [*whispering to his* ATTORNEY] We don't have a child . . .
LILLIAN'S ATTORNEY: . . . by the other woman.

[HARRY *is confused.*]

HARRY'S ATTORNEY: Don't lie to your attorney. Lying to your own attorney is like lying to your god.

JUDGE: Attorney for Harry, what is your response?

HARRY'S ATTORNEY: [to HARRY] Jesus, now I'll have to lie, too . . .

[LILLIAN *is about to answer the* JUDGE *when we hear a phone ringing. The* WAITER *from the dream club walks in, carrying a remote phone on a drink tray. We hear a hint of the club music.*]

WAITER: [enters, calling] Phone call for Harry! Phone call for Harry!

HARRY: [to his ATTORNEY] Wait, wait . . . [to the JUDGE] Excuse me, Your Honor, I just need to . . .

[As HARRY *takes the phone, the* WAITER *grabs him and kisses him hard, then pulls back smiling.*]

[Man *lit with his back to* HARRY *on the phone. He is a university* OFFICIAL. LISA *stands next to him, facing forward and glaring at* HARRY. HARRY *is still dazed by the kiss.*]

LISA: [pointing] There he is!

OFFICIAL: [German accent. Back turned] These are very serious charges, Herr Kitamura. Normally you would be put on indefinite suspension until this could be investigated fully . . . However, since you are a Professor of good standing and it is her word against yours, we will overlook it this time.

LISA: Pigs . . .

[LISA *turns and leaves in disgust.* HARRY *stands, confused.*]

[*Blackout on everyone, but* HARRY *remains lit.*]

HARRY: I began walking home . . .

[A YOUNG MAN *appears.*]

YOUNG MAN: Harry? Harry the Law Professor?

HARRY: Yes?

YOUNG MAN: I'm Lisa's boyfriend . . .

[He suddenly strikes HARRY *in the face, punches him in the stomach, and* HARRY *falls to the ground. The* YOUNG MAN *begins savagely to kick* HARRY. *He continues to kick him, over and over.*]

[Slow fade to black as HARRY *is being repeatedly kicked. We should sense the beating's violence and relentlessness.*]

[*Lights slowly up on* HARRY, *badly beaten*]

HARRY: [*mumbling deleriously*] Nina . . . Nina? What? My arm? Yes? Nina?
Nina the gorgeous . . . Nina the ugly . . . Nina the nape woman . . . Nina the
dog lady . . .

[*Begin to hear Ginger Baker's drum solo gradually brought up.* HARRY *is
lying down. Slow fade to half light. He continues to moan and babble in
the dark. Door opens and a gush of bright light pours through. Drumming
increases in volume. Three dark figures,* MR. BRUCE, DR. BAKER, *and*
MR. CLAPTON, *wearing long lab coats, enter with flashlights. Also have
lights attached to their foreheads, like miners. Looking for something.
Spot* HARRY. *They speak with English working-class accents.*]

MR. BRUCE: Dr. Baker, Dr. Baker there he is!
DR. BAKER: Hurry, check his rhythm, Mr. Bruce.
MR. BRUCE: [*checking* HARRY's *pulse*] My god . . .
DR. BAKER: What?
MR. BRUCE: It's all out of whack. He's beating out a 7/4 over a 13/8 . . . What
do you think, Mr. Clapton?
MR. CLAPTON: [*feeling pulse*] Extraordinary, bloody extraordinary . . .
MR. BRUCE: What shall we do, Dr. Baker?
DR. BAKER: Mr. Bruce, Mr. Clapton, get him up. Get him up and walking . . .
MR. CLAPTON: He seems too weak . . .
DR. BAKER: Harry? Harry can you hear me? Can you get up?
HARRY: [*blinded by the flashlights*] What? Who? Nina? Nina?
DR. BAKER: It looks bad boys. We'll have to carry him . . .

[*They pick him up and carry him above their heads.*]

MR. BRUCE: Dr. Baker, are we going to have to . . .
DR. BAKER: I'm afraid so, Mr. Bruce.
MR. CLAPTON: Poor bloke. I'd hate to be in his shoes . . .

[*They set him down on an operating table. Over head an operation room
light descends. Figures still remain shadowy. They pull out small red saws.*]

HARRY: Wait, wait, what's going on here?
DR. BAKER: We're going to have to amputate, Harry . . .
HARRY: Why?
DR. BAKER: It's starting to rot.
HARRY: My arm?

MR. CLAPTON: Lack of use . . .

HARRY: Say, aren't you Eric—

MR. BRUCE: . . . It's wasting away.

HARRY: Yeah, but I might need it to—

MR. CLAPTON: [*interrupts*] We have to cut it off . . .

MR. BRUCE: . . . before it infects . . .

DR. BAKER: . . . the rest of your soul . . .

[*They grab him. Hold him down.* HARRY *struggles for his life.*]

HARRY: Give me chance! Wait! Please! DON'T, DON'T, I NEED MY ARM! AHHHH!!! . . .

[HARRY *disappears beneath* BAKER, BRUCE, *and* CLAPTON *and their red saws. We hear* HARRY *screaming in pain. Drumming increases in volume.* NINA *appears in shaft of light, watching. Blackout. Silence. We hear the distant strains of "Is That All There Is?" in the background. Peggy Lee lit, silhouetted in the upstage area.*]

[*Lights up, center stage. One should get the sense of a new landscape, a shift in reality.* HARRY *standing, dressed in a trench coat, hat, dark glasses, unmoving. He appears a broken man.* NINA *standing next to him, staring at him. She takes off his trench coat and hat. His one arm hangs limply at his side. Her actions are careful, as if she's trying to not awaken him, that the sudden shock might prove fatal. She then delicately removes his dark glasses. His eyes are closed. She watches him for a beat. He slowly opens his eyes.*]

HARRY: [*wearily*] Nina?

NINA: Yes, Harry, it's me.

HARRY: Nina, I'm lost.

NINA: I know.

HARRY: I'm lost in this dream of you.

NINA: And I in yours. I've been waiting for you.

HARRY: Is there some reason for all of this, why I met you? Or, or, are you just . . . Who are you? What's happening to me? I've given— [*continue*]

NINA: [*overlapping*] Harry?

HARRY: —up everything—career, my standing in the community, personal life . . . It's all gone, taken, ripped from me, destroyed. All I can see is you. All I can think about is being with you. What's happening to me? I'm lost, lost . . . I'm nothing . . . I no longer exist . . .

NINA: Harry? Harry?

[HARRY *stops and listens.*]

NINA: I think you're ready now. [*takes out a pill*] You want to get to know me, don't you Harry? Really know me. You can. But there's a price. A terrible, wondrous, excruciating price that most sane people would never dare to pay.

[HARRY *reaches for the pill, but* NINA *withdraws it, shaking her head.*]

NINA: Tonight you're on your own. [*She takes it.*] Even a dream needs a little help now and then . . . You keep thinking I'm not letting you in. Harry, you're not letting yourself in. In the face of truth I'm always open. It's that simple. You have to live the truth . . . Be the truth . . . Every instant of every heart beat, the truth. Are you ready to do that, Harry? . . . Live the truth, be the truth? If you are, then you're also ready to cross the line. . . . Cross the line Harry? If the moment calls for it, demands it, who will you listen to, whose voice will you obey? . . . What society wants you to do? . . . Or your own? No matter what it says? No matter where it takes you? Are you ready to cross the line? [*noticing*] Look, look, it's the time in between. Two moons and a rogue comet grace the sky. Is it dawn or dusk? Is the sun setting or rising on your life? Your call Harry. The best kept secrets are always right in front of your nose. Whose scent do you smell? Are you ready Harry? Are you ready to take the plunge? . . . To hurl yourself out over the abyss? . . . Leap into the void with no designer clothes, no pinot noirs, no make-up, no credit cards, no excuses, no lies, no history, no mythology, no trickery or deceit—knowing that you will be carried aloft, buoyed up only by, your ass saved only by, the intensity of your realness? . . . [*slaps him lightly*] Harry? Wake up.

HARRY: The dog ran home with its tail between its legs . . .

[NINA *slaps him harder.*]

NINA: Harry, Harry, can you wake up? Or are you already blind to the things that only ghosts, the innocents, and mad men can see?

HARRY: My face, my dog face . . .

[NINA *strikes him very hard.*]

NINA: Wake up Harry. You're dying and the hour is late. The flesh is falling from our bodies. Moments of exquisite perfumed pleasure are slipping away into oblivion. Look, look at this face, this skin; taste my breath—fresh peaches. Harry, you, this divine animal—what an incredibly intricate piece of imagination beating inside of you. Take it out, take it out and share, dream; I give you permission . . .

[NINA *turns around and pushes her backside against* HARRY, *leaning the back of her neck near his face.* HARRY *rubs his face against it, inhales deeply, then begins to smother her nape in kisses.*]

NINA: Bite me. Yes, go on, don't be afraid. Bite me in the back of my neck. Make me feel your eyes . . . Know that you still aren't asleep. [*nibbles*] No, no, I said really bite me . . . [HARRY *bites her hard and holds on.*] Ahhhh . . . [*She pulls free and turns to face him.*] [*Surprised at his ardor*] Harry . . . [*laughing*] Harry, Harry, Harry . . . His arm is waking up. He's getting his muscle back. And now he wants to feel . . . Grab at the world with his heart . . . Did I tell you about my vision . . . Why I was committed to the convent?

HARRY: "Committed?"

NINA: [*Laughing*] I mean, "Why I ENTERED the convent?" [*beat*] Because of what I saw—a man with a bleeding heart. A man rising into the air . . .

HARRY: Fuck the heart; the man rising . . .

NINA: All in due time, all in due time—but for now we mustn't throw out the baby with the bathwater. Remember Harry, my vision's also your dream . . .

HARRY: Harry's unconscious. Harry has no eyes. Harry's orbiting some distant planet with newly grown wings . . . [*begins to falter*]

NINA: Harry?

[HARRY *is struggling, grabbing his chest.*]

NINA: Harry?

HARRY: Better not to . . . better not to feel . . . this kind of thing . . . anything . . . Because if you do, if you do . . . Better to hide . . . Run home, your tail between your legs . . . Be the dog . . . Silent, obedient, dogface . . . Because if you, if you open up, feel, let yourself breathe, howl . . .

NINA: What happens?

HARRY: Because if you do . . .

NINA: What happens? Harry?

HARRY: Then, then . . .

[SAM *enters, dragging in the* DOG (*played by* JOE). *Offers* HARRY *the knife.* DOG'S HEAD *lit.* JEFF *bursts in.*]

JEFF: Julie phoned. They know. The administration goons are on their way.

[SAM *looks at* HARRY *accusingly.*]

HARRY: You betrayed me. The one time I found something. Opened up. My heart . . .

[SAM *slashes the* DOG's *neck.* DOG/JOE *falls to the ground. Silence*]

HARRY: I told them . . . It was me. I told the school officials what we were planning to do. [*beat*] They like people like me. They do. Quiet, hard working . . . the model minority. We always do what we're told; we're always bowing our heads—we're not dangerous, we're not sexual, we're always wearing this silent frozen mask while inside I want to rage and scream . . .

[JOE *gets up, dusts himself off, takes the knife from* SAM *and puts it into* HARRY's *hand.*]

NINA: Don't be afraid.
JOE: We all get a second chance.
NINA: Kill the dog . . .

[JOE *and* NINA *begin to whisper into* HARRY's *ears from both sides while embracing, stroking him.*]

JOE: Kill the dog . . .
NINA: Kill the dog . . .

[*Both keep repeating "kill the dog."* HARRY *has the blade raised. The sound has been building all through this.* HARRY *screams and drives the blade into his chest.*]

[*Loud club music. Exotic dancers lit. They dance for 10 seconds. Erotic, insane. Blackout. Silence. Hold.*]

[*We hear Louis Armstrong singing, "What A Wonderful World." A match is struck. Upstage we see and hear a comet grace the sky.* HARRY *and* JOE *are slowly lit, both dressed identically in sleek, tailored black suits with white t-shirts on underneath, barefoot. They both wear homburgs.* HARRY *is lighting* JOE's *cigarette.* JOE *holds it between his third and fourth fingers. He inhales deeply, then blows out smoke rings.*]

HARRY *notices a growing red stain on the front of his white T-shirt. He is bleeding from the heart.* JOE *begins to slowly rise off the ground. Continues to nonchalantly blow smoke rings.*

NINA *lit, watching the peculiar spectacle. She holds a red umbrella. Dressed normally except for a nun's head covering. She stares in wonder for a beat, then points at her unfolding vision.*]

NINA: [*delighted*] Look, look Raoul!

[*We hear a dog barking happily. NINA begins to laugh like a schoolgirl. She crosses to HARRY, kisses him on the cheek, and softly barks at him. They both laugh. NINA joins JOE and they exit arm and arm. Blackout on scene. HARRY remains lit. Louis Armstrong continues.*]

HARRY: I was at this wine-tasting party. When I saw . . .

[LILLIAN *lit. Next to her stands a man dressed in an expensive dark suit. They hold wine glasses.*]

LILLIAN: [*waving*] Harry?
HARRY: When I went up to talk to her I noticed she was with someone who looked familiar. Then I realized who it was.
MAN: Harry? It's me.
HARRY: I couldn't believe it. It was . . .
MAN: Sam . . .
HARRY: [*overlapping*] Sam . . .
HARRY: For some reason I had thought he was dead . . .
SAM: No, I'm a stock broker.
HARRY: He appeared very conservative and . . .
SAM: Yes, I'm very rich.
HARRY [*staring*] I couldn't get over it—I stared . . .
SAM: [*noticing*] What, I look like some foolish old man now?
HARRY: We both laughed . . .
SAM: Would you like to try this pinot? It's quite good.
HARRY: He wore a Jerry Garcia tie.
LILLIAN: I gave it to him.

[HARRY *turns his attention to* LILLIAN. SAM *withdraws.*]

LILLIAN: [*stares at him for a beat*] You seem different. Your face?
HARRY: My face? Hmmm . . . [HARRY *thinks about it, touching his cheek.*]
LILLIAN: I'm happy now. Are you?

[*Beat.* HARRY *watches her.*]

[LILLIAN *fades to black.* HARRY *remains lit. He turns to look at another part of the stage. Louis Armstrong fades.* HARRY *watches as his* MOTHER *and* FISHERMAN *are lit. They sit side by side, fishing. We hear birds, the river.* MOTHER *reaches into her bag and pulls out a piece of fried chicken, wraps the bottom in a napkin, and hands it to* HARRY's *father. She then holds out a musubi (rice ball) for him to eat, so he doesn't have to use his hands, which hold the imaginary pole. They laugh, and she wipes the corner of his lip.*]

FISHERMAN: Would you like to go to Kauai with me? It's across the river?

[*MOTHER nods. Father then sweeps the MOTHER up in his arms and takes her across the river. MOTHER laughing happily.*]

MOTHER: Harry? You didn't give me a story. You didn't let me really speak.
HARRY: Would you like to?
MOTHER: [*thinking*] No. I'm not finished yet . . .

[*They dim to darkness. We hear their laughter disappearing into the distance.*]

[*HARRY alone in pool of light. The sound of wind blows in the distance. Music—melancholic, mournful, beautiful sadness. HARRY closes his eyes, then slowly opens them again.*]

HARRY: I awoke from a deep sleep. I had the strangest feeling. That I had been asleep for a very long time. [*Looks around, inhales deeply*] Fresh air has a flavor, did you know that? Peaches? And night . . . [*thinking*] Night is . . . [*thought is entering his mind and he's a little surprised at it*] . . . day standing on its head . . . [*begins to quietly laugh at that thought*] I awoke with a sense of fullness. Yes, fullness. And the one thing I knew. Was that I would dance. Yes, dance. Dance any chance I could get . . .

[*"Is That All There Is" begins to play. HARRY sways for a beat, then moves into a brief dance. It should be fun, not taken seriously. PEGGY LEE enters and moves towards HARRY. She holds a red rose.*]

PEGGY LEE: [*hands the rose to HARRY*] Harry . . .
HARRY: I've been expecting you . . .

[*She enters his arms. They begin to slow dance. We see that it is LILLIAN this time beneath the blond wig and dressed as the Japanese Peggy Lee. Lights tighten to a pool of light around them. They stare into each other's eyes. It's a warm, deep exchange. They drink deeply of each other.*

She slowly takes off the blond wig. Their eyes never leave each other. He draws her closer to him. She rests her head on his shoulder. The wig hanging by her side now falls to the ground. HARRY's hand moves up to stroke the nape of her neck. They continue to slow dance.]

[*Very slow fade to black. Music swells, then out.*]

END OF PLAY

Kokoro (True Heart)

by
VELINA HASU HOUSTON

1994 Best Original Script Nomination, San Francisco Bay Area Theatre Critics Circle

"Kokoro" received its world premiere at Theatre of Yugen, San Francisco, in June 1994. The play also received a limited special presentation at Japan Society, New York, in May 1994.

In 1995, it was produced in New York at The 28th Street Theatre by Frances Hill and Margaret Mancinelli-Cahill, directed by Tina Chen.

CAST OF CHARACTERS
(Cast includes five women and one man.)

YASAKO YAMASHITA	A Japanese woman, early 30s
HIRO YAMASHITA	Yasako's husband, a Japanese man, 39
SHIZUKO MIZOGUCHI	A Japanese woman, early 30s
FUYO	A spirit, Yasako's mother
ANGELA ROSSETTI	An attorney
EVELYN LAUDERDALE	A neighbor

TIME AND PLACE: San Diego, California, Japan, and Netherworlds. 1985.

PROLOGUE

[*Ocean sounds fade in and crescendo. In the darkness,* YASAKO *enters as lights fade in low, whirling, shaping a world around her. There is a scrim as backdrop, and ocean waves dress the floor.* YASAKO *comes forward using slow, methodical movements.*]

YASAKO: A tiny rock is cast out to sea by the great Sun Goddess Amaterasu and it grows into an island, strong and unwavering, beautiful and bright. I am a root in this soil. I grow best here, all blossoms, all fruits, always. [*a beat*] But, one day, the gardener comes and I am transplanted. The winds, the rain, the gnawing forces of erosion transform the blossoms, scattering them into the river of time.

[*She removes a silky American flag from her kimono sleeve and billows it about her as the figure of* FUYO *appears as a shadow lit behind the scrim.* FUYO *enters. A spirit, the back of her kimono trails behind her in shredded strands. Her face is snowy white; her hair is wild, long, grey-streaked. She glides beneath a gossamer shroud. The lights on her are shadowy while the lights on* YASAKO *are a bit brighter.*]

YASAKO: Good-bye, Mother. [FUYO *shakes her head.*] But I am his wife. [FUYO *looks downward in sadness.*] And your daughter becomes a mother. [FUYO *beckons to* YASAKO.] Do not fear for my child in America, Mother. Her soul is tied with mine. She will never walk alone.

[FUYO *encircles her daughter as* YASAKO *weaves in and around her.*]

FUYO: Se o hayami iwa ni sekaruru . . .
YASAKO: Our lives like the river's foam split asunder by boulders . . .
FUYO: . . . takigawa no warete mo sue ni awanto zo omou.
YASAKO: In the end,
FUYO: . . . kono yo de . . .
YASAKO: . . . in this world . . .
FUYO and YASAKO: . . . or some other . . .
YASAKO: . . . we will find each other again. [YASAKO *removes her kimono, startling* FUYO. *She gives it to* FUYO. FUYO *kneels to fold it as* YASAKO *kneels to fold the flag.* YASAKO *presents the flag to her mother and bows.*] Doozo, Okaasan. [*a beat*] Wife, mother, and now orphan, I go. [*a beat*] Sayoonara.

[YASAKO *bows again.* FUYO *wipes away imaginary tears and runs off-stage.* YASAKO *rises as the sound of a seven-year-old girl's laughter tinkles, blending with a news bite that marks the year as 1984, i.e., the re-election of Ronald Reagan. The sounds bridge into:*]

ACT I
SCENE ONE

[*The Yamashita home, into which* YASAKO *enters as lights brighten. A hot summer day. Intermittently, sounds of the ocean are heard in the distance.* YASAKO *folds a young girl's dress. She sits and leafs through a journal.*]

YASAKO: August third. Seven to eight: make breakfast. Eight to nine: wash Kuniko's clothing. Nine to ten: piano. My world. America is outside, a place to visit when I take Kuniko to school. My husband buys the groceries, pays the bills. Once I had to take Kuniko to the doctor. That was hard. [*puts book away, calls out*] Kuniko! Kuniko-chan! Come my child. Time for music! [*imagines a girl running in*] Kuniko! You forgot to take your shoes off! What bad manners you've learned! Sit, sit. Kuniko! Keep your dress on! Nice girls do not sing in their panties! Let's sing Japanese songs today. [*plays a few notes on table top*] "Haru ga kita, haru ga kita, doko ni kita. Yama ni kita, sato ni kita, no ni mo kita."

[*Abruptly, the voice of the seven-year-old,* KUNIKO, *emanates seemingly from all around* YASAKO *as she looks around in delight:*]

KUNIKO'S VOICE: [*sings*] "Down the river, oh down the river, oh down the river we go-o-o; down the river, oh down the river, oh down the Ohio! The river is up and the channel is deep, the wind is steady and strong. Oh won't we have a jolly good time as we go sailing along!"

[*Amid this singing,* YASAKO *stands, and lights diminish to a spotlight on her as she looks out at the audience. She begins over the singing:*]

YASAKO: In Japan, your grandmother and I lived by the inland sea. But now there is Coronado and the big Pacific Ocean. Papa found this nice apartment so I can hear the waves. I close my eyes and pretend it is the seashore in Japan. [*a beat*] Kuniko-chan. Did you know there is a world beneath the sea? With mermaids and sapphire fish, coral and sea stars. The mermaids have serious business: they guide lost souls to the next world. [*a beat*] . . . a soul is . . . everything a person feels or dreams, an essence that cannot be touched unless you use your heart, your true heart. Kokoro. Mind, heart, spirit. [*a beat*] You have a soul, too, Kuniko. A seven-year-old soul that has been around the universe many times. And it will never be lost because I will find you easily, wherever there are Japanese peaches. You eat so many that you smell as golden blush and alive as their sweet flesh.

[*Bursts of laughter in* KUNIKO'S *voice are heard in voice-over (V.O.) as the spotlight fades and lights fade up.* YASAKO *resigns herself to this silliness that she finds endearing.*]

YASAKO: [*looks at watch and checks journal*] Okay, silly monkey. Time for homework so you can grow up and go to college like Mommy. Read for an hour, then math. Then we will have lunch and think about O-bon Festival.

KUNIKO'S VOICE: Mommy, when I grow up can I still live with you?

YASAKO: [*overlapping*] Well, I think—

KUNIKO'S VOICE: [*continuous*] Mommy, why can't I ever have friends sleep over like all the American kids?

YASAKO: [*overlapping*] "Sleep over"?

KUNIKO'S VOICE: [*continuous*] Mommy? You ever heard of a group called The Beatles?

YASAKO: [*smiles*] Yes! One of them married a Japanese. But he died. You can say hello to his spirit at O-bon Festival. And Obaachan's spirit. And my father's, too. Festival of the Dead, Kuniko; a happy time to visit with our ancestors and then light lanterns to guide them back to their worlds.

[HIRO YAMASHITA *appears. Lights fade and a spotlight goes up on him and* YASAKO. *Both look out at the audience.*]

HIRO: Good, Yasako. Clothes smell better for my little girl when you wash them by hand.

YASAKO: Kuniko? If I was a kangaroo, I would ride you in my pocket forever.

HIRO: Stop carrying that child! She's too old to be carried!

YASAKO: Kuniko, come. It is time for tea. I made o-manju.

HIRO: I bought you the recipe book. Page 243, how to make apple pie.

YASAKO: Hiro, teach me how to write checks, how to use the "ATM."

HIRO: Last week, lady was robbed at an ATM.

YASAKO: Hiro, teach me how to talk to her teachers.

HIRO: What's so difficult about talking to a teacher? I could talk to President Reagan, if I had to.

YASAKO: One to two: wash floors. Two to three: dusting the furniture.

HIRO: Yasako, make some friends.

YASAKO: I do not know what to say to American women.

HIRO: Go borrow a cup of sugar or something. [*a beat*] Here. I bought you a new dress. With a little style. Try it on.

[*The sound of a child running into a lamp and falling is heard.* YASAKO *screams with suddenness and* HIRO *jumps.*]

YASAKO: Ara, Kuniko! Papa, she fell and hit her head on the lamp!

HIRO: It's just a flesh wound, Yasako. Calm down.

YASAKO: She cut herself twice on that stupid lamp. Poor Kuniko-chan. Get rid of the lamp, Papa.

HIRO: Come here, Kuniko-chan. Papa will make it better. Look at her! She hugs like people in American movie. I love it. Give Papa a great big television kiss, Kuniko.

YASAKO: Mommy tries to kiss, Kuniko, but it feels so strange. Do you remember how my mother taught you how to bow? [*bows*] Bow like this. Very good, Kuniko! [*a beat*] Kuniko-chan, are you ready? Time for O-bon Festival. Put on your yukata.

[*O-bon music begins.*]

YASAKO: We will dance under the lanterns and the moon, and welcome back my mother's spirit.

[FUYO *appears upstage, moving gracefully in O-bon odori (festival dance). O-bon paper lanterns gleam from behind the scrim.* YASAKO *joins her, beckoning to* KUNIKO *and then to the reluctant* HIRO *as a kuro-ko (black-draped figure of traditional Japanese theater who provides on-stage assistance) puts yukata on them. As the dance ends, a bored* HIRO *ceases first, and then* YASAKO. FUYO *continues to weave around them, still dancing:*]

HIRO: [*dismissing culture*] Bon Festival's just old country folktale stuff. An excuse to eat and drink. Your mother's not here. She's ashes and dust.

[FUYO *stamps her foot towards* HIRO *to protest this remark.*]

YASAKO: She is here, listening to all of this; and, when you go to Heaven, she will not make o-manju for you. [*reacting*] Kuniko! No! Do not shake the urn!

[FUYO *reacts as if being shaken and gently tumbles to the ground.*]

YASAKO: Yes, my mother is in the urn. Yes, she is coming to visit you, but in spirit, not like a genie out of the bottle. Oh, Kuniko, bad girl. You spilled Obaachan's cremains all over the floor!

HIRO: [laughs] Let's get out the vacuum cleaner. [FUYO reacts.] Just kidding! Oh, Yasako, all that old Japanese stuff. Nobody cares about Bon Festival or kimono anymore. Not even in Japan. [HIRO removes yukata and drops it to the floor. FUYO looks at it with sadness, picks it up and exits.]

YASAKO: Okay, Kuniko, get ready for bed. [The presence of "KUNIKO" exits.] I care. My mother raised me to care. [a beat] Don't you want Kuniko to learn about Japanese culture?

HIRO: Don't you want her to get along in American culture?

YASAKO: We won't live here forever.

HIRO: Let her be different. A California original.

YASAKO: A place does not change who she is.

HIRO: It does! Even the cherry trees here are bigger and taller. [He sits in the chair and soaks his feet in the basin of water as she hands him a towel.] Why waste your time making homemade o-manju? Just buy it down at Fugetsu-do. My customers at my restaurant never eat it. It just gets hard like rocks. Waitress almost put out my eye when she threw one at me.

YASAKO: What? A waitress threw o-manju at you?

HIRO: Yeah. She could pitch professional baseball.

YASAKO: You must fire her or ask her to resign. After all, what shame she must feel.

HIRO: [laughs] Hardly. Not that one.

YASAKO: But so bold.

HIRO: She says we should put American food on the menu. Strawberry ice cream.

YASAKO: But then it wouldn't be a Japanese restaurant anymore.

HIRO: I mean just change the decoration a little bit; put a small American flag on the counter to make the white people happy.

YASAKO: [She dries his feet. Then, no longer interested, she stops.] We should have moved back to Japan by now.

HIRO: Don't start that again.

YASAKO: It has been six years, Hiro. I thought we were going back before Kuniko started school.

HIRO: Good schools here.

YASAKO: I want her in Japanese schools.

HIRO: There're Japanese schools right here.

YASAKO: One day a week on Saturdays? I want her in real Japanese school.

HIRO: Yes. Of course. [touches her hair] Such beautiful hair. Pull it back, off your face. [*She pulls it away from her face.*] Well, I'd better get to work. Don't wait up for me. [*a beat*] I might have to sleep there if it gets too late.

YASAKO: Oh, don't do that again. You're so grumpy the next day.

HIRO: I need to look at the books. Besides, I don't want to wake you up so late.

YASAKO: You are asleep in the morning when Kuniko gets up and gone to work by the time she comes home from school. You work too hard.

HIRO: We're lucky to have such good business, Yasako. You should see the restaurant. So many customers.

YASAKO: Hiro, if we went home, you could go back into my family's electric company.

HIRO: Yasako, please.

YASAKO: Just promise one day we will go back.

HIRO: Don't worry. Japan isn't going anywhere. And we have a lot to do here.

YASAKO: I'm sorry. You're right. I should be helping you at the restaurant instead of worrying about Japan.

HIRO: You stay home, take care of Kuniko. That's your job. That's how you help me.

YASAKO: But you said there are so many customers.

HIRO: Come here and kiss me, Yasako.

YASAKO: Hiro! Sometimes you sound so American.

HIRO: Good. American men are smart then. Kiss me. [*She looks sad; he kisses her cheek gently.*] I put some tuna in the refrigerator. It's very fresh. Just for you.

YASAKO: Thank you.

[*He suddenly comes into the house with shoes on—which she stares at in shock—and then lifts her up in the air, planting a big kiss on her. She's pleased, but embarrassed.*]

YASAKO: Hiro!

HIRO: To hell with culture, Yasako. When in Rome, do as the Romans do, right?

YASAKO: This is San Diego.

HIRO: Oh, Yasako, it's just a figure of speech.

YASAKO: It's a cliche.

HIRO: [*touches her hair*]My mother told me never marry a girl who was smarter than me or who loved me at first sight.

[*Offstage, the sound of* KUNIKO *calling her mother in Japanese—* "Okaasan! Kite yo!"*—is heard.* YASAKO *reacts.*]

HIRO: Go on. [*begins to exit*]

YASAKO: Hiro? I'm sorry.

HIRO: About what?

YASAKO: If I had friends like in Japan, women to have tea with, it would be different.

[*The girl's voice calls from off stage again: "Mama!"*]

HIRO: Better hurry. Go on, my dear wife.

YASAKO: Hurry home, Papa. [*He exits. Lights cross-fade to a downstage spotlight in which* YASAKO *kneels.*] Here, Kuniko. Drink tea. Ban-cha for good dreams. [*a beat*] No matter what, Kuniko, Mommy will keep you by her side, okay? In Japan, we say mother and child are one until you are a big girl who can live outside of my shadow. Go back to sleep now. Sleep. Good girl.

[*Lights cross-fade to another spotlight in which stands* EVELYN LAUDERDALE, *a faintly exotic-looking, warm, tomboyish woman. She whistles for a pet.*]

EVELYN: Panther? Here, Panther. Here, kitty, kitty. [YASAKO *enters and hands her the "cat."*] You found my cat! Bad cat! Gallivanting all around the neighborhood after sundown! Thank you so much, Mrs. Yamashita.

YASAKO: Glad to help.

EVELYN: Usually, Kuniko rescues her. It's nice that you found her this time. Gives us a chance to talk.

YASAKO: Well, I do not want to bother you. I will be going now.

EVELYN: No, no. It's no bother at all. Ever since you moved in last year, Kuniko's been a bundle of sunshine for me. She's my friend and so you are, too. Okay?

YASAKO: Of course. Thank you. [*mimics handing her another item*] Here. A present. Peaches, my daughter's favorite fruit.

EVELYN: Thank you. To be honest, Kuniko leaves one peach a day on my porch. I made a peach cobbler once and she ate two pieces.

YASAKO: "Cobbler?" [*bows*] I am sorry for the trouble.

EVELYN: Are you kidding? I love it. She's a great kid.

YASAKO: Thank you.

EVELYN: Would you like to come in? Please. Let's have the peaches together.

YASAKO: Actually . . . I came to ask a favor.

EVELYN: Anything. I owe you and Kuniko for saving my cat. I'd lay bets she only has two lives left. What can I do for you?

YASAKO: [*afraid to ask*] Well, I, uh . . . [EVELYN *encourages with a smile*] I, uh, uh . . . I thought I might borrow a cup of sugar.

EVELYN: [*not what she expected*] Sugar? Of course. What are you baking?

YASAKO: Baking? I, uh, well, actually, my favor is a little bigger than that.

EVELYN: Please. Go ahead.

YASAKO: Well, my husband needs me at our restaurant. Just for a short while. Could you stay with my daughter for me? She never wakes up so there shouldn't be any problem.

EVELYN: Don't you worry about a thing, Mrs. Yamashita. I'm happy to help out. Let me get my things. I hope everything's okay.

YASAKO: It's fine. My husband was hinting this evening that he needs help. Things are very busy. Californians really like Japanese food.

EVELYN: And Japanese like American food, too.

YASAKO: Not me. [*They move to the Yamashita home as lights cross-fade.* YASAKO *hands her a long list.*] These are important numbers. Her pediatrician, her allergist, the restaurant, poison control center. But you know you call 1–9–9 first.

EVELYN: [*kindly*] 9–1–1.

YASAKO: Yes, of course.

[EVELYN *gently guides her away.*]

EVELYN: Don't worry, Mrs. Yamashita.

YASAKO: One more thing.

EVELYN: Yes?

YASAKO: The bus.

EVELYN: The bus?

YASAKO: Yes. Could you teach me how to take it?

[EVELYN *smiles and nods. They exit as lights cross-fade.*]

SCENE TWO

[*A small, trendy-elegant Japanese restaurant represented by a table with chairs, linen tablecloth, and flower; contemporary Japanese music in background.* YASAKO *sits at a table perusing a menu. Enter* SHIZUKO MI-ZOGUCHI, *elegant, contemporary, striking. She carries a pad and pen. Her clothing reflects the style of the decor.*]

SHIZUKO: Good evening. Are you ready to order?

YASAKO: Age dashi-dofu and unagi no kabayaki, please.

SHIZUKO: [*smiles broadly*] You made the right choice. The eel is very good. The owner buys his seafood fresh every morning at the fish market.

YASAKO: [*looking at her curiously*] Are you Japanese? You have no accent at all.

SHIZUKO: Yes, I'm Japanese. How long have you been in the States?

YASAKO: Since 1978.

SHIZUKO: Wow. Six years. You seem like the type who'd rather live in Japan. [*smiles genuinely*] Am I right?

YASAKO: [*liking her*] Yes. I married my brother-in-law's cousin and he wanted to live in America. For a while.

SHIZUKO: I see. Well, you'll do okay. Don't worry. Can I get you something to drink?

YASAKO: Hot tea, please.

SHIZUKO: Sure. Let me put your order in. Great dress.

YASAKO: Thank you. My husband gave it to me as a gift. Can you find him for me?

SHIZUKO: Who?

YASAKO: My husband.

SHIZUKO: Are you supposed to meet him here?

YASAKO: Not exactly, but—

SHIZUKO: What does he look like?

YASAKO: [*shy pride*] Well, he's, uh . . . well, you know. Mr. Yamashita.

SHIZUKO: Mr. Yamashita? Hiro Yamashita? You're . . . Mrs. Yamashita?

YASAKO: Yes. And you are?

SHIZUKO: Shizuko Mizoguchi. Have you heard of me?

YASAKO: No. Should I have heard about you?

SHIZUKO: I'm the one who threw o-manju at your husband.

YASAKO: [*surprised*] Oh. I expected someone older and . . . tougher.

SHIZUKO: Tough? Is that what he said? He means assertive. What do you think?

YASAKO: Think? About what?

SHIZUKO: About me throwing o-manju at your husband.

YASAKO: It made me wonder if, well, you know, you were—

SHIZUKO: Crazy? Yeah. Crazy to still be hanging around here after three years.

YASAKO: Well, please be careful. Mr. Yamashita is a patient man, but you must not throw things at your boss.

SHIZUKO: Yeah. My boss. Thanks for the advice, sister.

[HIRO *comes running out and stops short at the sight of the two women.*]

HIRO: Yasako. Hello. What are you doing here?

SHIZUKO: She's a customer, just like everybody else in your life, boss.

YASAKO: Hello, Papa. I took the bus here!

HIRO: Miss Mizoguchi, please bring my wife some tea.

YASAKO: Yes, some tea would be nice, Papa.

SHIZUKO: I have three paying customers to serve.

HIRO: I said bring her some tea. Do it.

SHIZUKO: [*simply*] Yes, Papa. Anything Papa say.

[SHIZUKO *saunters off to get tea.* HIRO *turns to* YASAKO.]

HIRO: Who's watching Kuniko?

YASAKO: Miss Lauderdale.

HIRO: Miss Lauderdale? Who is Miss Lauderdale?

YASAKO: Our neighbor. Kuniko's friend.

HIRO: Oh, yes, yes. When did you learn how to take the bus?

YASAKO: Tonight. Miss Lauderdale explained it. [*a beat*] I came to help you.

HIRO: No, Yasako. Everything's under control here.

YASAKO: Really? Then maybe we can go out. For a walk or—

[SHIZUKO *saunters back in with tea, places it before* YASAKO.]

HIRO: Yasako, I brought you fresh tuna at home. Go home, eat, enjoy.

SHIZUKO: Never enough for me to take home, but enough for sister here, huh?

HIRO: Go back to work, Miss Mizoguchi.

[*But* SHIZUKO *lingers.*]

YASAKO: Papa, take a break. Come walk on the beach with me.

HIRO: You always want to walk on the beach. I don't like sand in my shoes or the smell of dead fish.

YASAKO: Papa, just tonight. There is a full moon and the beach is so beautiful tonight.

HIRO: You drink your tea and go home, all right?

SHIZUKO: Oh go walk on the goddamned beach with her.

HIRO: You have customers, Miss Mizoguchi, remember? Get back to them before they leave you. [*to* YASAKO] Maybe we'll walk on the beach tomorrow, okay?

YASAKO: Okay, Papa.

SHIZUKO: No it isn't okay. Japanese women gotta learn that. When it isn't okay, don't say it is.

YASAKO: You do not talk to my husband like this.

SHIZUKO: [*surprised at* YASAKO's *tone*] I'm not talking to him. I'm talking to you.

HIRO: Miss Mizoguchi.

SHIZUKO: [*to* YASAKO] That was my tea. There's no more left to go around. But I want you to have it. [*exits*]

YASAKO: Why do you let her talk like that?

HIRO: Miss Mizoguchi . . . is a very good waitress. All the customers like her, okay? Now you drink your tea. I'll have dinner packed for you to take home. And we will talk of going to the beach tomorrow, okay?

[*He starts to go, but* YASAKO *summons the courage:*]

YASAKO: No, Papa. It is not okay.

HIRO: Yasako . . .

YASAKO: It is *not* okay.

HIRO: [*exasperated*] Do what you want then. I have work to do.

[*He exits.* YASAKO *isn't at all sure what to do next. But* SHIZUKO's *return helps her decide. She stands quickly to go.*]

SHIZUKO: Sit down.

[*But* YASAKO *still tries to go.*]

SHIZUKO: I said sit down. [*She guides* YASAKO *back into her seat and sits next to her.*] You asked for the tea. Drink it.

YASAKO: My daughter may wake up and ask for me.

[YASAKO *tries to leave.* SHIZUKO *forces her to keep her seat.*]

SHIZUKO: Know what I've got waiting for me at home? A VCR, a color TV, a history worth less than toilet paper. But you, nomi-san, you've had the good life, haven't you? Good and clean. [YASAKO *just stares at her.* SHIZUKO *laughs.*] My bathroom's all cluttered with lipsticks and lotions and eye shadows. But yours is tidy, isn't it? Although you could use a little lipstick. No offense, but you look like you don't have a mouth. And a woman needs it to speak her mind.

YASAKO: I'd better be going now.

SHIZUKO: I've survived America, Mrs. Yamashita. I'm a pioneer. I'm not afraid of the dark. Are you? I think you are. I can tell by the tilt of your chin when you look at me.

YASAKO: What do you want from me?

SHIZUKO: Let me guess: you were raised in the provinces with servants, old-fashioned mama who still wears kimono, women's college, married down, refused to be naturalized, never leave the house, thirty-three. [*a beat*] I was naturalized, married to an American before. Big trouble, but he taught me how to walk six steps in front of him without shuffling. He was looking for Madame Butterfly; he turned out to be Mr. Moth and he's still chasing the golden light. Aren't they all. That's why I have a Japanese lover now. And nothing they say about Japanese men is true. You know: inflexible, no poetry, small penis. Not true. [YASAKO *moves to leave again, but* SHIZUKO *detains her.*] By the way, thanks for the lamp.

YASAKO: Lamp?

SHIZUKO: Hiro gave me a lamp you didn't want. He says you sell all the furniture in the house because you don't want your daughter to fall and get hurt. You know, you can't protect her from the whole world. The world just comes, breathing hard. You gotta breathe back. Like Hiro. He breathes back.

[SHIZUKO *rises to leave. This time,* YASAKO *wants her to stay.* SHIZUKO *relaxes in her seat.*]

YASAKO: What do you mean "he breathes back?"

SHIZUKO: On my . . . neck.

YASAKO: . . . y-your neck?

SHIZUKO: This long, beautiful thing under my chin.

YASAKO: Are you suggesting that—

SHIZUKO: Yes, Mrs. Yamashita. You win the grand prize.

[*Jarred,* YASAKO *drops her tea cup.* SHIZUKO *picks it up and plays with it in the palm of her hand.*]

YASAKO: [*trembling*] How long?

SHIZUKO: [*lights a cigarette*] Too long.

YASAKO: He is my husband.

SHIZUKO: That and a bowl of rice might get you through tomorrow. [*a beat*] And don't think I'm skating on silk. He's a piece of work for me, too.

YASAKO: B-but do you . . . love him?

SHIZUKO: Wow, that's a pretty bold question for a nice Japanese girl to ask. I hold him all night long, Mrs. Yamashita. I dream with him, eat cheeseburgers and strawberry ice cream in bed with him, let him wear his shoes in the house.

YASAKO: Why are you doing this? These are all lies.

SHIZUKO: Are you sure? Can you take that chance? [SHIZUKO *hands* YASAKO *a letter.* YASAKO *doesn't want to take it.*] I've been saving this for a long time. Take it. I said take it. [*She forces the letter into* YASAKO's *hand.* YASAKO *drops it.*] Read it. [*She gives* YASAKO *a business card.* YASAKO *holds it like it has a disease.*]

SHIZUKO: Here's my card: my number and address. When you're ready to talk, come see me.

[YASAKO *looks at the card, tears it in half and drops it at her feet, where the letter lies.*]

SHIZUKO: Fine. Tear it up. Pretend what is isn't, just like most Japanese do. Go on smiling, and when you get tired of smiling, ask your husband where I live. It's our apartment and he's there at least three times a week.

YASAKO: Apartment?

SHIZUKO: In Japan, the tea is always hot. Got home and you won't have to worry about cold tea ever again. Or try coffee some time. [*places the tea cup in front of* YASAKO] Good night, Mrs. Yamashita. Don't drop any more tea cups. Where I come from in Shizuoka, they say it's bad luck.

[YASAKO *stares quietly at* SHIZUKO, *who stares back with discomfort.* SHIZUKO *picks up the two pieces of the business card and tucks them into a pocket on* YASAKO's *purse.* YASAKO *turns and walks away. Lights cross-fade to another spotlight, in which* YASAKO *bows deeply to* EVELYN.]

YASAKO: Thank you so much.

EVELYN: Please, don't mention it. She's sleeping restlessly. You might want to check on her.

[YASAKO *nods as* EVELYN *exits.* YASAKO *kneels as if hovering over her child.* FUYO *appears and anxiously looks from* YASAKO *to the unseen* KUNIKO.]

YASAKO: [*reacts to a waking child*] Go back to sleep, Kuniko. Mommy will sleep right here next to you on the futon.

[HIRO *enters the light.*]

YASAKO: What are you doing here?

HIRO: I live here. Good night, Kuniko. Come, Yasako.

YASAKO: Where are we going?

HIRO: To bed.

YASAKO: I am in bed.

HIRO: My customers would laugh me right out of my restaurant if I told them that my wife prefers to sleep with our daughter.

[*Because he is talking too loud and she fears him waking up the child, she shoos him away from* KUNIKO *and into the main area of the Yamashita home.*]

YASAKO: Americans laugh at taking shoes off in the house, too. So what? The three of us should be sleeping together in the same room, just like we did in Japan.

HIRO: We did that because there was so little room in that house.

YASAKO: My mother said we do it to protect our souls.

HIRO: To hell with your mother and our souls.

[FUYO's *spirit reacts.*]

HIRO: Real life, Yasako. Real life. It just isn't right for me to sleep with Kuniko, especially as she gets older.

YASAKO: Why not?

HIRO: Because Americans would think something else was going on. They don't understand about the Japanese way. They don't understand that our presence protects Kuniko, or even that we leave the room when it is time for us to be together as man and wife.

YASAKO: We are Japanese. If this country is so free, why do we have to give up being who we are to live here? Some things I can change, like learning to shake hands instead of bowing, or going to the bathroom differently than I did in Japan. But you are asking me to change the unchangeable.

HIRO: Yasako, here we can wake up late, sing in the street without being thought a lunatic, challenge the system, speak our minds.

YASAKO: No. You have that freedom.

HIRO: You have it, too. If you want it. Just like all the other Japanese.

YASAKO: Like the ones who work in your restaurant?

HIRO: Come to bed.

YASAKO: For a long time now, I come to bed and you act like you don't want to touch me, but you want me to be there. For what? To keep you warm? Go to bed by yourself.

[*Angered, he leaves abruptly.*]

YASAKO: Hiro? Where are you going?

HIRO: Back to the restaurant.

YASAKO: You just came from the restaurant.

HIRO: If I can't sleep, I'll work. [*an order*] Now go to bed.

YASAKO: [*calmly, a test*] Say hello to Miss Mizoguchi for me.

HIRO: [*agitated*] What? What are you saying?

YASAKO: What are *you* saying?

HIRO: What the hell are you talking about?

YASAKO: I simply ask you to say hello to a waitress and it makes you very . . . agitated.

HIRO: You're being ridiculous.

[*Frustrated and angry,* HIRO *storms out. The distraught* YASAKO *comes face to face with* FUYO, *whose hands caress her from an inch away, never touching. But* YASAKO *refuses the touch and exits.* FUYO *moves urgently through the house as if exorcising evil, the tension she feels demonstrated in the taut pulling and wringing of her kimono sleeves and the wiping away of her own tears, her hands an inch away from her face. She exits as* YASAKO *re-enters and lights widen. A letter flutters from above.* YASAKO *catches it, opens it, and reads it. She sits down, Japanese style. From up-stage center,* SHIZUKO *steps up behind her. Both women look out to audience during the entire scene. The letter is held up in* YASAKO's *hands.*]

YASAKO AND SHIZUKO: "Dear Mrs. Yamashita, . . ."

SHIZUKO: I left Japan behind, and you carry it with you like a dead weight.

YASAKO: "I feel sorry for you,"

YASAKO AND SHIZUKO: But I have to think of myself, too.

SHIZUKO: I have been faithful to your husband for three years, waiting for him to fulfill his promises.

YASAKO: "My patience is wearing thin. You can imaging what this is like, since you have only known about me for a few weeks and already you have lost patience."

SHIZUKO: Mrs. Yamashita, give him a divorce and return to Japan.

YASAKO: "Let him go before he lets you go. It's easier that way."

SHIZUKO: What other choice is there because of this shame Hiro has brought into your life. Into our lives.

YASAKO: "Please forgive me. I didn't go looking for all this trouble."

SHIZUKO: Trouble came to me and I was too lonely to say no. And now I love him.

YASAKO AND SHIZUKO: I have no choice but to prepare a future with him.

SHIZUKO: You will do okay back in Matsuyama.

YASAKO: "Return to the place where you belong."

YASAKO AND SHIZUKO: Don't do anything foolish.

SHIZUKO: America's no place for those who can't take what they want without saying I'm sorry.

YASAKO: "Sincerely yours,"

SHIZUKO: Shizuko Mizoguchi.

[*Blackout as sounds of children playing in a park fade in. Spotlight on* YASAKO. *She writes in the journal.* KUNIKO's *laughter is heard and* YASAKO *waves at the unseen child.*]

YASAKO: Kuniko, be careful! Don't fall in the mud! Don't go so fast on the monkey bars! Oh, Kuniko, silly little monkey. [*reacts as if* KUNIKO *is rushing toward her*] Oh, Kuniko, no, no! Don't jump on Mommy! You'll get mud all over. . . . [*stops as she smiles in defeat and wipes imaginary mud from her clothing*] Kuniko-chan. So cute.

[*The spotlight widens to accommodate* SHIZUKO *as she enters.* YASAKO *stands protectively around the unseen child and tries to keep her as far away as possible from* SHIZUKO.]

[*to* "*child*"] Kuniko-chan, go play please. Go play on the swings. Mommy will watch you. Good girl. [*turns to stare at* SHIZUKO] What do you want?

[SHIZUKO *picks up* YASAKO's *journal and leafs through it.*]

SHIZUKO: Do you write down everything you do? [YASAKO *just stares at her.*] Good idea. Too bad we can't control our men in the same way. Of course, in this situation, it's our man. Just one. Maybe we should just cut him in half. Which half do you want? [YASAKO *grabs her book out of* SHIZUKO's *hands.*] Did you read my letter?

YASAKO: Stop following me, Miss Mizoguchi.

SHIZUKO: Good, you did read it. When are you leaving?

YASAKO: Maybe you better go back to work and mind your own business.

SHIZUKO: Time's running out for me, Mrs. Yamashita. Read the letter again.

YASAKO: I have been married to Hiro for eight years.

SHIZUKO: . . . and I have been fucking him for three years.

YASAKO: You are vulgar.

SHIZUKO: It's a vulgar world, Mrs. Yamashita. [*a beat*] When something is over, it's over. He will come to live with me. Do you want that kind of shame for you and your daughter?

YASAKO: Who are you to talk about shame?

SHIZUKO: Listen, sister, you're no better than me. We're both trying to cut it in this frontier. The difference is I can and you never will. [*a beat*] He wants to get it over by New Year's.

YASAKO: You are lying.

SHIZUKO: Wait and see. Suddenly, he's going to offer you a trip to Japan. As a Christmas present.

YASAKO: Miss Mizoguchi, how is it that you feel free here and I am the cat trapped in a pillowcase?

[*The question surprises* SHIZUKO. *There is a look of compassion on her face for* YASAKO.]

SHIZUKO: Because you don't ask to be more than a cat.

YASAKO: What do you ask to be?

SHIZUKO: Godzilla.

YASAKO: My father's mistress was discreet.

SHIZUKO: I'm not interested in being that stupid.

YASAKO: Is it so stupid?

SHIZUKO: Hiro loves me, Mrs. Yamashita. In a different kind of way than he loves you. And my kind of love is the kind he needs right now. [YASAKO *tries to focus on her child.*] You think I'm evil, don't you? A jealous devil breaking up your family. Well, I'm not. If you want to blame someone, you have to blame Hiro, too.

YASAKO: My husband is not the type to have an affair.

SHIZUKO: Right. He's the type to have a relationship. Which is exactly what he's having—with me. And now we all have to deal with it.

YASAKO: Why do we have to deal with it? Why can't you just go away?

SHIZUKO: For the same reasons you can't.

[YASAKO *reacts as if* KUNIKO *has run up to her. The child's presence silences the women and forces them to be calm.*]

YASAKO: Hi Kuniko-chan. Are you finished? Say good-bye to the . . . nice lady. Papa's . . . friend.

SHIZUKO: Hi, little girl. I'm Shizuko.

[YASAKO *quickly cuts between* SHIZUKO *and the imaginary* KUNIKO *to protect her child from this "evil."*]

YASAKO: [*a warning to back off*] Good evening, Miss Mizoguchi.

SHIZUKO: Good evening.

[SHIZUKO *exits. The sound of* KUNIKO *giggling is heard.* YASAKO *turns suddenly in fear.*]

YASAKO: Kuniko, no! Don't climb up there. It's too high. No, Kuniko! Come down! [*witnesses* KUNIKO'S *fall, which is heard as a thump followed with cries*] Kuniko! [*runs forward and bends over* KUNIKO] Are you all right? Oh, Kuniko, poor thing. Your arm. I think it is broken. Come, Kuniko-chan. Mommy will take you to the hospital. [YASAKO *picks up the unseen* KUNIKO. *She stares straight ahead.*] Uh, hello. I am Yasako Yamashita. My daughter has a broken arm, I think. [*a beat*] Fill out papers? Get in line again? But how can you make her wait out here with all these strangers when she is in pain? [*takes the papers*] Don't you understand? We have to go back to Japan. You have to fix her, make her just like she was, make everything just like it was. [YASAKO *gathers her child and runs out.*]

[*Lights cross-fade to another spotlight, which* YASAKO *enters.*]

YASAKO: Hello. I would like to buy a book for my daughter. She is a second grader, but she reads eighth-grade level. [*surprised that she is not understood*] I am speaking English! [*enunciates s l o w l y, deeply frustrated*] I would like to buy a book for my daughter. Eighth-grade level. [*taken aback*] Excuse me, sir, but I was here first. Sir! Do you hear me? I was here first!

[*Lights cross-fade to another spotlight, which* YASAKO *enters. She's a powder keg.*]

YASAKO: This is Mrs. Yamashita. [*spells out*] Y-a-m-a-s-h-i-t-a. [*spells out again, more slowly*] Y-a-m-a-s-h-i-t-a. Yasako. Yasako. No. Yamashita is my last name. Yamashita.

[*Lights cross-fade to another spotlight, which* YASAKO *enters.*]

YASAKO: He would not take his hands off Kuniko's face? And you did not scold this . . . this bully? No wonder Kuniko pushed him! Miss Nancy, usually I nod and smile at everything you people say and do. I keep my anger inside and quietly walk away. But don't you understand? Kuniko does not want the hands of a child on her face. That boy's hands could have been in dirt, his nose, his pants. [*to audience*] That is what I want to say to this stupid teacher who probably takes a bath only twice a week. [*pain, sadness, shame*] But I just nod my head, smile, and quietly walk away. And Kuniko looks at me like I am not a hero. She says to me, "Mommy, in Japan could you be Super-Mom?"

[*Lights cross-fade.*]

SCENE THREE

[*Twilight. A nervous* YASAKO *paces. A letter and her journal are on the floor. A laundry basket full of folded clothes, a small suitcase, a small basin of water are present. She looks in her journal, writes, puts it down, paces again.*]

YASAKO: [*creating a poem*] "The sea is . . . the sea is a bridge of light, leading back into the warmth of honor, away from its scant reflections in this life, the mere images of honor, those masks of paint and clay." [*Restless, she throws down the journal. She takes several crumpled checks out of her pocket, kneels, and carefully smooths them. She places them by the suitcase.*]

[*Enter* HIRO.]

HIRO: Here you are again. Pacing·at 3 A.M. Are you sure you're okay?

YASAKO: You should know that Kuniko broke her arm. She fell off the monkey bar.

HIRO: What happened?

YASAKO: I was not watching her closely enough.

HIRO: A mother can't afford to be distracted, Yasako.

YASAKO: I am sorry. I won't ever let her get hurt again. [*a beat*] Sit. Let me wash your feet.

HIRO: Go to sleep, Yasako. What's bothering you every single night, walking the floors like a ghost? [*a beat*] It's Japan, right? We'll go back to visit, okay?

YASAKO: We will?

HIRO: [*casually*] Yeah. Maybe for Christmas.

YASAKO: [*devastated*] Christmas? Not Christmas.

HIRO: Yes. A nice present for you. Five months away. Plenty of time to plan.

[*She nervously pulls at her hair. A tuft comes out.*]

HIRO: What—what's the matter with your hair?

YASAKO: . . . everything is falling apart. So much noise.

HIRO: Yasako. Please. Sit down. Let me see your hair. Let me see.

[*She pulls at her hair again and more comes out.*]

HIRO: [*restraining her*] Stop that!

[*She yanks away with a force that surprises him. She grabs the suitcase.*]

YASAKO: [*thrusting suitcase at him*] Here.

HIRO: What is this?

YASAKO: Your necessary things. [*a quick beat*] Go. Please.

HIRO: Come here. Let me hold you.

YASAKO: I SAID TO GO.

HIRO: Yasako, I am not having an affair, okay? I am just trying to manage some problems at the restaurant. Can't you understand?

YASAKO: What I understand is that we have no honor.

HIRO: Who gives a damn about honor?

[*She reaches for the checks.*]

HIRO: What are you doing?

YASAKO: The laundry. [*She shakes them at him, tosses them at his feet.*] Why all the checks to Miss Mizoguchi? What are you buying from her?

HIRO: Nothing.

YASAKO: I packed three trousers, four shirts, and seven underwear. I can mail you the rest.

[HIRO *kicks the suitcase.*]

HIRO: Why don't *you* go? You're the one who can't cut it here.

YASAKO: You have made sure of that.

HIRO: You think it'll be any easier if you run home to Matsuyama? No. Not for you. Not as a divorced woman who lived in America too long. Besides, Kuniko doesn't want to live in Japan.

YASAKO: [*shocked, angry*] You're trying to take my daughter away from me.

HIRO: It wouldn't have been any different in Japan, Yasako. You know that. Even your brother has a mistress. My father had one, too.

YASAKO: Why can't you be different?

HIRO: Why can't *you* be different?

YASAKO: Different from what? A Japanese woman? An American woman? Different from what?

HIRO: You are my wife, Yasako.

YASAKO: That and a bowl of rice might get me through tomorrow.

HIRO: Don't talk like that.

YASAKO: Or maybe just through the next five minutes.

HIRO: Stop, Yasako.

YASAKO: Fire her.

HIRO: What?

YASAKO: If I am your wife, fire her.

HIRO: Surely you aren't suggesting you would divorce me.

YASAKO: Half of American marriages end up that way.

HIRO: If we were in Japan, you would accept this, live with it honorably.

YASAKO: Don't you remember? Honor is what we flush down the toilet. There is no honor in this house, unless you've been to the bathroom lately.

HIRO: Stop talking like that. American women would never act like this. They'd take it in stride.

YASAKO: And then kill you in your sleep.

HIRO: Yasako!

YASAKO: Poison your drink or—

HIRO: Stop it!

YASAKO: Or wait until you were in the deepest sleep and then cut off your penis.

HIRO: Yasako, please! Here. Take some money. Go out tomorrow. To the beach, shopping, buy Kuniko some more books. Something. [*He tries to hand her bills. She takes them, looks at them for a moment, and then lets them flutter to the floor as she stares at him.*] Okay then, get your American divorce. Will that make you happy? Go to Las Vegas and get a 24-hour one. [*He kicks the money on the floor toward her. They stare at each other, at a standoff.*] Business is good now, too good. It has made me busy . . . and crazy. Try to get it through your head that it doesn't mean anything and—

YASAKO: Are you going to fire her or not? [*stares at him intensely*]

HIRO: [*stares back for a few moments and then looks away; sighs with exasperation*] That will solve all your problems?

YASAKO: Yes.

HIRO: [*further exasperation*] Okay. Okay then. [HIRO *sits. She gets the basin of water and sits beside him.*]

YASAKO: The water may be cold. But I will wash your feet—

HIRO: Don't.

[*She persists.*]

HIRO: I SAID TO STOP IT. [*pushes her away*]

YASAKO: Papa.

HIRO: Don't be so ridiculous! Can't you see how ridiculous you are? Don't be so nice to me!

[*He storms out. A letter flutters from above. She stares at it, reluctant to read it, and then picks it up as lights tighten to a spotlight. She begins to read.*]

YASAKO: "Dear Mrs. Yamashita, . . ."

[SHIZUKO *enters and stands on the periphery of the light.*]

SHIZUKO: Dear Mrs. Yamashita.

YASAKO: "Hiro has told me that you are not feeling well."

SHIZUKO: You have a small bald spot on your head where you have picked your hair, your nerves electric, your hands shaking.

YASAKO: "This makes me sad, especially because he speaks of it when he's sleeping in my bed."

SHIZUKO: I know you have discarded your journal.

YASAKO: "As if there is nothing left to record."

SHIZUKO: We Japanese are funny, aren't we? Each struggling to be the one who ends up with the most honor, but the fight gets so ugly that it's all blown to smithereens and nobody ends up with anything. [*a beat*] Yasako?

[YASAKO *looks up and locks eyes with* SHIZUKO *for a moment.*]

YASAKO: Yes?

SHIZUKO: [*embarrassed, frightened*] . . . I am . . . pregnant with your husband's child.

YASAKO: Oh no. No.

SHIZUKO: It will be a boy. Born in January. It's true. I wish it wasn't.

YASAKO: No.

SHIZUKO: I haven't had the courage to tell Hiro.

YASAKO: "Thank you for listening. Sincerely yours, . . ."

SHIZUKO: Shizuko Mizoguchi.

YASAKO: "P.S."

SHIZUKO: Please take care of yourself.

[YASAKO *tears up the letter. Lights dim.*]

SCENE FOUR

[*A* spotlight. EVELYN *enters.* YASAKO, *disheveled and distraught, comes up behind her, startling her.*]

EVELYN: Oh, it's you, Mrs. Yamashita. Good morning. How are you today?

YASAKO: [*eerily calm*] Everything is fine.

EVELYN: Would you like to come in and have a cup of tea? [YASAKO *shakes her head and moves away, as if she's going to leave. Sensing this,* EVELYN *takes her by the arm.*] Are you sure everything's fine?

YASAKO: [*suddenly desperate, urgent*] Miss Lauderdale, I want to go back to Japan.

EVELYN: For good?

YASAKO: Today. I need to go today.

EVELYN: Today?

YASAKO: Yes.

EVELYN: Today. Uh, okay. [*trying to buy time*] Uh, does your husband know about this?

YASAKO: I need to borrow money, Miss Lauderdale. For two tickets.

EVELYN: This is very sudden, Mrs. Yamashita. I'm concerned that you—

YASAKO: Please. I have family there. I can work and send your money back in a few months.

EVELYN: I'm not worried about the money. You just don't seem like yourself.

Maybe you and your husband need to talk about this some more. Maybe I can help in some small—

YASAKO: Never mind.

EVELYN: No, I mean it. Come inside. Let me make you a cup of tea. We'll talk about this. Come on.

YASAKO: How can I expect you to understand.

[Hurt, EVELYN exits as FUYO's spirit enters. YASAKO turns toward her home only to face FUYO's gaze. That gaze holds an answer for YASAKO— the one person who can understand. Lights cross-fade.]

SCENE FIVE

[The Yamashita home. FUYO sits at YASAKO's side. The sounds of the ocean are heard.]

YASAKO: [sad, plaintive] "Haru ga kita, haru ga kita. Doko ni kita . . ." [suddenly she looks up and forces a smile, wiping away her tears] Kuniko-chan! Good morning, little one.

[FUYO's eyes follow the "child" as she emerges.]

YASAKO: Yes, yes, we will go to the beach. Be a good girl and brush your hair. [to FUYO] Is it time to go? [FUYO nods.]

YASAKO: What if Kuniko stayed here? [FUYO stares at her. YASAKO knows the answer. An impatient HIRO enters, put on a tie. FUYO, apprehensive toward him, moves to side stage.]

HIRO: Where are you going?

YASAKO: To walk along the shore, play in the sand.

HIRO: Don't go swimming. Bacteria. Just walk.

YASAKO: She wants to collect sea shells. [a beat] Do you . . . do you want to walk with me? With us?

HIRO: [evasive] Not today.

YASAKO: I see. [He prepares to leave and YASAKO suddenly tries to stop him.] Hiro!

HIRO: What?

YASAKO: Stay today. Come to the beach with us.

HIRO: I have work to do, Yasako. Just work. Another day.

YASAKO: Just today. Stay home.

HIRO: I can't. Besides, you know I hate the beach. You go, enjoy yourself. Papa loves you Kuniko-chan. Bye-bye.

[HIRO *exits.* FUYO *nods her head three times and claps her hands silently once. Ocean sounds intensify as* FUYO *beckons to* YASAKO *to follow, her arms moving like waves as lights darken.*]

YASAKO: We are going on a long journey, ne, Kuniko-chan. To . . . home. Hold my hand.

[*Ocean sounds crescendo. Downstage, enter two kuro-ko, with long stream-ers of ocean-colored silk that they propel from fans repeatedly. Lights re-flect the ocean on the scrim.* YASAKO *faces the audience, the "sea."* FUYO *encircles* YASAKO *and becomes part of the kuro-kos's wave-like movement.*]

YASAKO: Can you see the mermaids waiting? Bow to the mystical sea, Kuniko. Our souls float, our bodies dance.

[YASAKO *and voice-over of* KUNIKO *and* FUYO *chant the earlier poem in unison as* YASAKO *gently pushes forward the "child"*:]

FUYO, YASAKO, AND VOICE: Se o hayami iwa ni sekaruru takigawa no warete mo sue ni awanto zo omou . . . kono yo de . . . ai masho.

[*Crashing waves intensify; lights whirl, drums beat.* YASAKO *sinks beneath the silky, turbulent waters, disappearing in the waves, as lights fade to black.*]

ACT II
SCENE ONE

[*Spotlight center stage on* YASAKO *in plain prison garb, her eyes closed.* FUYO *moves around her in a frenzy as a taiko drum beats.* KUNIKO'S *laughter surrounds her, mixed with ocean sounds.* FUYO *kisses her an inch away from her forehead and then runs out.* YASAKO *sits up and looks around in fear and confusion. And then footsteps are heard, and the sound of a cell door clanging shut. The lights suddenly go to full and glaringly bright, revealing* ANGELA ROSSETTI *standing next to* YASAKO.]

ANGELA: [*extends a hand*] Hello. I'm Angela Rossetti, your attorney. I need to ask you a few questions? [*silence from* YASAKO] Are you okay? Can I get you anything? [*more silence; giving up on the pleasantries,* ANGELA *gets to work*] Do you remember where you went with your daughter yesterday, Mrs. Ya-mashita? [*pronounces it "yama-SHEET-tah"*]

YASAKO: [*distrust, fear*] . . . I-I-I woke up and I was in the hospital and . . . and there was a g-g-guard and I asked him where Kuniko was and . . .

ANGELA: Tell me what happened at the beach.

[YASAKO *remembers and starts to cry.* ANGELA *approaches, pats her gently on the shoulder.*]

ANGELA: You do know that she is . . .

[*simultaneously*]

YASAKO:	ANGELA:
Gone.	Dead.

YASAKO: And you can go now, too. Just tell me when I can go back to the beach.

ANGELA: I'm afraid you won't be going anywhere for a while, Mrs. Yamashita. [*a beat*] First-degree murder. That's what the State of California plans to charge you with.

[YASAKO *registers shock.*]

ANGELA: The court has appointed me to represent you, and I plan to do so to the best of my ability.

YASAKO: Murder?

ANGELA: I plan to fight for a lesser conviction of voluntary manslaughter. [*a beat*] Problem is, Americans don't take too kindly to people killing children, and it'll be Americans staring out at you from the jury. And probably not the kind who eat steamed white rice with their meals. This is a conservative town, full of retired Navy guys whose buddies were killed in World War II. [*a beat*] So we've got a fight on our hands.

YASAKO: You had no right to stop us!

ANGELA: Calm down. I didn't. It was two hotel guests. They thought you were drowning. And now your child is dead and you're alive. Though, to be honest, there are a few people in city hall who wish you weren't.

YASAKO: Is that what you wish?

YASAKO: My wishes are irrelevant.

YASAKO: I did not kill my child.

ANGELA: Let's put it this way, when I take my five-year-old daughter to the beach, we walk along the sand, not into the Pacific Ocean. [YASAKO *is taken aback by this outburst.* ANGELA *wishes she hadn't let it show. She tries to compose herself; she does a good job of it. She comforts* YASAKO.] But, of course, this isn't about me. It's about you. And I'm sorry that I acted like a mother first. Sometimes it just swallows up everything else you are.

YASAKO: Yes, I know. But it is supposed to. That's why you have to let me catch up with Kuniko.

ANGELA: She's gone, Mrs. Yamashita. Her body is in the morgue and you don't want to go there. We're trying to locate your husband.

YASAKO: No. He must not come here.

ANGELA: [*concerned*] What happened, Mrs. Yamashita?

YASAKO: Promise me you won't let him bother me.

ANGELA: I'll try. [*a quick beat*] Now I know this is difficult, but I need you to explain to me what happened as best as you can.

YASAKO: We were . . . traveling.

ANGELA: Traveling?

YASAKO: In a vessel that you cannot begin to understand.

ANGELA: A vessel. Uh huh. [*Exasperated,* ANGELA *addresses an offstage persona.*] Could somebody bring us some coffee, please?

YASAKO: [*urgently*] I need tea. Green tea.

ANGELA: [*to offstage persona, caring*] The lady wants green tea. Can we accommodate her?

[*Lights cross-fade to two spotlights in which* EVELYN *and* HIRO *stand, in mid-conversation on imaginary phones.* HIRO *waits for her to speak as* SHIZUKO *embraces him from behind.* EVELYN *struggles with tears.*]

HIRO: How did you get this number?

EVELYN: Th-th-they tried to call you.

HIRO: [*impatient*] Are you all right?

EVELYN: They couldn't find you. She had them call me.

HIRO: Yasako? What's happened? Where are they?

EVELYN: [*fresh tears*] O-oyako shinju.

HIRO: They're dead? They're both dead?

EVELYN: K-Kuniko. She . . . drowned . . .

[SHIZUKO *studies his distraught state with concern. She pulls away.*]

HIRO: Kuniko is drowned? My daughter is drowned?

[SHIZUKO *gasps and turns away.*]

EVELYN: They saved Yasako.

HIRO: What hospital is she in?

EVELYN: [*pressing him*] She came to me, Mr. Yamashita, very upset. She said she had to go back to Japan.

HIRO: What hospital is she in?

EVELYN: She's not in a hospital. She's in jail.

HIRO: Jail? Why jail? What did she do wrong?

EVELYN: This is America, Mr. Yamashita. They call it murder.

HIRO: No! I must go to her. I must see her.

EVELYN: Mr. Yamashita, what made her think there was no other choice? [*then . . .*] Why was she so distraught? Was something happening between the two of you?

HIRO: That is none of your business.

EVELYN: You're wrong, Mr. Yamashita. And, after today, it's going to be everybody's business.

[*Lights cross-fade to prison.* YASAKO *sits.* EVELYN *arrives with a small box.* YASAKO *is so ashamed that she will not raise her head. She stares down at her hands.*]

EVELYN: When I read the article in the paper and all the horrible things they said about you, I said to myself, "That doesn't sound like my neighbor." So I came to bring you this. [*hands* YASAKO *the box*] They're torn because they had to inspect them.

YASAKO: Thank you. Sorry for the trouble. [*bows*]

EVELYN: You sound just like my mother. [*a beat*] I made them myself.

YASAKO: You made this o-manju? I have never known Americans to even eat these.

EVELYN: My father was American, but my mother was from Japan.

YASAKO: You never told me.

EVELYN: I never told you she was Japanese because, well, it seemed unnecessary to point it out. Unless you had asked.

[YASAKO *leans forward, as does* EVELYN *in response.*]

YASAKO: Do you think what I did was wrong?

EVELYN: [*troubled*] My mother probably wouldn't have thought so.

YASAKO: But what about you?

EVELYN: I don't know. I understand, but then I don't understand. Because I'm not in your situation. Also, I don't look Japanese, so it's easier for me. Sometimes.

YASAKO: Miss Lauderdale, I want you to bring me some . . . special tea. [*looks over her shoulder*] The kind that will allow me to . . . travel.

EVELYN: Mrs. Yamashita, I can't do that.

YASAKO: In the cabinet to the left of the stove, there is a tea cup painted gold and rust. In that tea cup, I wish to drink my tea.

EVELYN: [*overlapping, evading*] I brought you a book. Here. You can rest and read. [*shaken, a pause*] I-it's too late, Mrs. Yamashita.

YASAKO: My family travels the universe now. Before you said you would do anything to help me. Please.

EVELYN: Last year, my mother died. I don't want you to die, too. You're meant to live.

YASAKO: But how? How am I supposed to do that?

EVELYN: Let me help you. Let me be your friend.

YASAKO: You should go now.

EVELYN: I'm sorry.

YASAKO: Just go. Please do not come again.

[EVELYN *fades into the darkness upstage. As lights cross-fade, a* SOUND BITE *cuts in:*]

SOUND BITE: Mrs. Rossetti? We understand that you're a mother. How can you begin to justify your client's actions? How can you even stand to represent the case of an alleged child murderer?

[*Lights cross-fade to downstage as* ANGELA *and* YASAKO *enter the cell.* YASAKO *manipulates a black tea bag with her hands.*]

YASAKO: Those white guards out there. They called me "baby killer."

ANGELA: [*a beat*] Fuck 'em. [*This responses brings a faint smile to* YASAKO'*s lips.*] Okay, Mrs. Yamashita. I'm a white woman on the jury from, say, Topeka, Kansas. I'm Catholic, with balls of iron, and I've got one very precious child. Convince me that what happened was not, according to your system of beliefs, something bad. What'd you call it again?

YASAKO: Oyako-shinju.

ANGELA: Parent-child suicide, right?

YASAKO: Until a certain age, the child is inseparable from the mother. The egg and what it has created are one. If I had taken my life and left my child behind to be raised by substitute mothers, I would have dishonored my family.

ANGELA: I don't buy that. Not in any culture. Let me tell you, Mrs. Yamashita, if anybody tried to harm my child, I'd kill them without a second thought. And probably with my bare hands.

YASAKO: So would I. That is why I took her with me. Bun-shin. "Bun" means divide and "shin" means part of the body. I consider my child bun-shin; my body divides to create the child and we are one. Here you believe that the child is an individual, separate from you.

ANGELA: And Kuniko Yamashita was not an individual in your eyes?

YASAKO: Bun-shin is like a tree. The child is the branch that needs to stay connected to grow. So, if you—the tree—dies, the branch dies.

ANGELA: But if just the branch dies, can't the tree continue to live, grow new branches and leaves?

YASAKO: [*without self-pity*] Who cares about the tree? No one needs the tree.

ANGELA: There was a woman in Kansas City—white; she killed her son and was about to join him when her husband caught her. She went to jail for life. And the American public wouldn't've even flinched if she'd been burned at the stake.

YASAKO: An American woman? You would have killed her for . . . for doing this?

ANGELA: I wouldn't do it. But the People might.

YASAKO: What people?

ANGELA: The People of the United States.

YASAKO: You mean a whole gang? A whole gang of Americans?

ANGELA: It's a phrase, Yasako. The People, capital "P." The government. The good of our society. [*a beat*] I found three cases of Japanese women who ended up with lesser charges of manslaughter. So in arguing for a reduced sentence, I'll use cultural defense to make our case.

YASAKO: Cultural defense?

ANGELA: Laotian man beats up his wife, and when he gets arrested, he looks at the police in surprise—maybe even shock—and says, "What do you mean I'm in trouble because I beat up my wife? I own her. I can do whatever I want with her." To him, see, the wife is as good as a dog. But this is America. He goes to jail and she gets a divorce.

YASAKO: American men do not beat up their wives?

ANGELA: [*looks at her as if to say touché and sighs*] The Laotian man has an easier time of it in the courts because, in Laos, his behavior is within the law. The courts ask him to realize that he must adapt to the American way, but they give him a break.

YASAKO: But then he is no longer Laotian if he exchanges his culture for yours.

ANGELA: . . . I'm still Italian.

YASAKO: . . . and I am still the tree.

[*The women stare at each other over a confounding impasse.*]

YASAKO: What is your daughter's name?

ANGELA: . . . Samantha.

YASAKO: That is a nice name.

ANGELA: Thank you. [*a beat*] I'll bring you some good tea next time.

YASAKO: [*hands her the tea bag with apologetic bow*] Sorry. I do not like American black tea. It is so bitter. Like everything else here, you have to sweeten it or it is impossible to swallow.

ANGELA: So sweeten it. Is that so difficult?

YASAKO: [*nods*] Kuniko means child of the country. I named her that because I wanted her to feel like a child of Japan even though she had to grow up here. [*begins to cry*]

ANGELA: [*with sadness*] She didn't grow up, Mrs. Yamashita. She didn't grow up.

[YASAKO's *tears grow fervent.* ANGELA's *impulse is to comfort her, but she cannot bring herself to do so. Exit* ANGELA. *Lights cross-fade to down-stage.* HIRO *stands to give a speech.* EVELYN *sits nearby, holding a clip-board full of petitions.*]

HIRO: Thank you all for coming to this important community meeting this evening.

[SHIZUKO *appears in an upstage spotlight. She looks exhausted. Her clothes look slept-in.* HIRO *and* EVELYN *continue to function unaware of her presence. She also is unaware of theirs.*]

HIRO: There are many reasons why we are gathered here tonight.

SHIZUKO: The room is cold. He's still here, but not really. Not now.

HIRO: I-I wasn't the best husband or father that my family deserved.

SHIZUKO: . . . Hiro collapses to his knees screaming, "KUNIKO, KUNIKO," and tells me that he killed his child . . .

HIRO: Japanese culture is different from American culture. But what I want to make clear is that my wife, Yasako Yamashita, is not a murderer.

SHIZUKO: Winter in his eyes.

HIRO: Especially considering the incredible bond my wife had with our daughter, Kuniko.

SHIZUKO: Winter . . .

HIRO: All of your ancestors originally came from other lands, and as they struggled to carve a place for themselves in America, they, too, had trouble coming to terms with new cultural views of right and wrong. In this way, we are all the same.

SHIZUKO: I gather all my things and leave without a note.

HIRO: This has been a terrible accident. I hope you will forgive us.

SHIZUKO: I cannot compete with ghosts. [*looks out toward audience*]

HIRO: Please sign this petition asking for leniency for Yasako. Please, for the sake of my child.

SHIZUKO: Yasako?

HIRO: This is our neighbor, Miss Launderdale. She is Japanese and American. She can understand both sides of this. I ask your help, because the media, the public is against us. Ask your friends to sign them as well.

SHIZUKO: Yasako-san? I leave all my secrets to you. Keep them for me, okay? Keep them. [bows all the way to floor]

HIRO: Thank you.

[EVELYN mimics handing out petitions as she exits. Lights fade and SHIZUKO rises. For a brief moment, her eyes and HIRO's meet. Lights cross-fade to prison where ANGELA and YASAKO sit on the cot.]

ANGELA: She said she was Godzilla? Miss Mizoguchi's quite a piece of work. One doesn't often hear of such aggressiveness in Japanese women.

YASAKO: Let me guess. You merely saw "Shogun" on American TV and now you are expert, ne? I saw "Shogun." It was like Gone with the Wind, but Japanese style. Are you Scarlett O'Hara?

ANGELA: I'm sorry. Please, Yasako. I'm here to help you.

YASAKO: Do you believe you possess a soul?

ANGELA: What? Well, yes, I think so.

YASAKO: Then you believe you have lived before and will live again.

ANGELA: I'm not so sure. I'm a recovering Catholic, reinventing my faith. But I know I have a soul.

YASAKO: Where have you lived before?

ANGELA: Cincinnati.

YASAKO: [disappointed in her] I see.

ANGELA: Before that, I lived in Des Moines.

YASAKO: Well, I lived in ninth-century Kyoto.

ANGELA: I see.

YASAKO: Do you?

ANGELA: Yes. I understand. Traveling . . . In a vessel. Is that a Japanese belief?

YASAKO: I don't know. It is my belief.

ANGELA: I guess there are many metaphysical possibilities.

YASAKO: Now I want to . . . live somewhere else.

ANGELA: A life is a precious thing, Yasako. Your life was precious even to a stranger. I want to believe that if this had happened in Japan, a Japanese also would have dragged you from the sea.

YASAKO: I failed as a wife. And now I have failed as a mother, too. [a beat] And all you know of life is that yesterday you lived in Cincinnati and today you live in San Diego.

ANGELA: Yasako, you have to stop wanting to die and start wanting to live.

YASAKO: . . . what happens in San Diego when you are convicted of murder? Is it absolutely certain I would be put to death?

ANGELA: You think it's that easy to get yourself killed? Listen to me very carefully: It means you're admitting guilt. That's like getting up in front of all your Japanese relatives and saying, "I murdered Kuniko."

YASAKO: No! I did not and I will not say that. But I want the death sentence. It's the only way I can catch up with Kuniko.

ANGELA: A guilty sentence doesn't mean you waltz to the gas chamber and join your daughter. It means you *might* get to go. But it also means that, in the eyes of the world—including a lot of Japanese—you are disgraced, you are the cold-blooded killer of the child you brought into this world.

YASAKO: [*momentarily stunned, then draws into herself, stony*] . . . someone once told me that, in America, only soldiers and super-heroes get to die with honor.

[YASAKO *and* ANGELA *stare at one another as lights cross-fade to another spotlight.* EVELYN *sits. She and* ANGELA *are in mid-interview.*]

EVELYN: A few days later, he finally broke down and told me that he'd been having an affair with a Miss Mizoguchi. He said he loved her, but he also loved his wife.

ANGELA: How special.

EVELYN: The woman left abruptly. He hasn't seen her. He wants to see Yasako. Has she changed her mind? [ANGELA *shakes her head.*] Does she know about his efforts to help her?

ANGELA: She doesn't want to be helped, saved, or pitied. She just wants to die. [*With a touch of guilt,* EVELYN *looks away.*] Tell me, Ms. Lauderdale. Mr. Yamashita's Japanese; he's adapted. Why can't Yasako?

EVELYN: She was raised by a woman who grew up before the war. That means old customs, old-fashioned ways.

ANGELA: But I don't get it. Does that mean a lot of Japanese resort to suicide when something goes wrong?

EVELYN: It may surprise you to know that Americans have a higher suicide rate than Japanese, especially American young people.

ANGELA: Okay. Fine. Good point.

EVELYN: So what are you going to do?

ANGELA: The cultural defense isn't enough. To get the jury to be lenient, I have to plead temporary insanity, Ms. Launderdale.

EVELYN: Insanity? Why?

ANGELA: To save my client.

EVELYN: But she's not insane. Why can't we plead not guilty?

ANGELA: Plead that and the jury will grind their heels in her face. In the eyes of that jury, she's psychologically disturbed. They can buy that, maybe even feel sorry for her. I want you to convince her that the insanity plea's the best way to go. I brought it up with her and she asked me to leave.

EVELYN: Is that how it's going to be? If you can't be like everybody else, then let's call you mentally deviant and shove you out of the way? Are you her friend or enemy, Mrs. Rossetti?

ANGELA: Neither. I'm her attorney. Look, if it makes you feel any better, I don't think she was thinking about murdering her child when she walked into the ocean. God help me, I think she was thinking about saving her child.

EVELYN: You mean you really believe she was innocent?

ANGELA: She's not innocent. But she's not guilty either. Here's a riddle for you: is it more crazy for people to expect everyone to behave just like them or for someone like Yasako to expect to behave in another way, but still live among the people? [a beat] What am I saving Yasako for? A lifetime of insomnia as she curses herself for not getting it right? Now that's insane. Good day, Ms. Lauderdale. I think I'll go take my daughter out for a root beer float.

EVELYN: [as ANGELA crosses] I've done some research . . . It's not right for Yasako to be labeled as insane or in any way be painted as a cold-blooded baby-killer. [a beat] So I think we should let the judge decide and plead no contest.

ANGELA: You think I haven't thought of that? Don't you know it's the same thing as a guilty plea to the prosecution?

EVELYN: But it's not the same thing to Yasako. And that's what matters, isn't it?

ANGELA: Thanks for the advice, counselor.

[ANGELA exits and then EVELYN exits. A SOUND BITE of court hallway noises, busy reporters, cuts in:]

SOUND BITE: Mrs. Rossetti! Mrs. Rossetti! We understand that the defendant has lived in this country for six years. Isn't it true that if we let every new immigrant keep their customs and not assimilate that we're asking for trouble for the future of this country?

[ANGELA enters the cell where YASAKO sits, as lights cross-fade.]

YASAKO: Thank you for green tea.

ANGELA: You're welcome. So you wanted to see me. What's up?

YASAKO: I have come up with my own plan, Mrs. Rossetti.

ANGELA: All right. Let's hear it.

YASAKO: . . . I will pretend hysteria. You will say I need special tests. Then they will let me leave to go to a hospital. And you can take me back to the ocean.

[YASAKO *bows to the floor.* ANGELA *gently pulls her up. Overwhelmed,* ANGELA *removes several newspaper articles from a packet and shows them to* YASAKO.]

ANGELA: I think you should see these news stories. You've become a celebrity. Some Americans feel sympathy for you.

YASAKO: [*visibly shaken*] But "Medea?" Why do they call me this "Medea?"

ANGELA: Do you know Medea? Like you, she was a foreigner. Popular myth says Jason brought her back from the East and she helped him obtain a treasure, the Golden Fleece. When Jason deserted her, she killed their children and fed them to him. There're many different versions of the myth. In another case similar to yours, the attorney argued a Medea-like compulsion exists among Japanese women to react to infidelity by killing their children.

YASAKO: Now we are cannibals, too?

ANGELA: No. Although Medea is despised in the West, I believe she killed because she knew Jason's new wife would enslave her children.

YASAKO: The point is to go together. Mrs. Rossetti, please. Help me with this plan.

ANGELA: What about returning to Japan after this, Yasako? Your family would understand.

YASAKO: Maybe, but they will not necessarily forgive. Many may despise me, gossip about me over milk-tea or soda pop—because children are sacred and I have abandoned mine to the afterlife without a mother. You have to understand, Mrs. Rossetti. In Japan, we have no crib death because we sleep with our children from the day they are born. We honor, no, we *worship* our children. In America, you have Mother's Day, Father's Day. We have *Children's* Day.

ANGELA: Yasako, you say the universe is out of balance because your daughter's spirit is fragmented without you. I say this is the only universe we've got. [*a quick beat*] I can't take you to the beach, Yasako. I believe too much in freedom. I believe that people have to live and let live, especially in America. I believe you didn't understand the ramifications of what you were doing, at least not in this cultural context. So don't let me do all this hard work for nothing, Yasako. You said the point is to go together. Well, she's already gone, so you can't have that. Let's concentrate on what you can have. [ANGELA *gathers the articles and returns them to the packet.*

YASAKO *espies one that has a photograph of* KUNIKO *and her, a reprint of a family snapshot. She grabs it, stares at the photo.*] It's a good picture of you and your daughter.

YASAKO: Yes, It is. [YASAKO *hands back the photo.* ANGELA *looks at it, gives it back to her as a gift.* YASAKO *bows deeply in appreciation and looks up at* AN-GELA, *who hesitates and then decides to bow.* ANGELA *exits, acknowledging* HIRO *as she passes him in the "hall."* HIRO *enters the cell.*]

YASAKO: Get out.

HIRO: I know you don't want to see me, but—

YASAKO: Get out or I'll scream.

HIRO: Stop it. Remember. I'm the only one who knows you really aren't crazy.

[*This remark has an impact on her. Her anger subsides momentarily, then:*]

YASAKO: Of course. After all, you celebrate what I am. [HIRO *doesn't understand what she means.*] You celebrate your perfect Japanese wife. You got what you wanted, right? Fine brain, small heart, good sex, clean floors . . . and so traditional that your "perfect" wife is all you have left. [*a beat*] Go. Just go.

HIRO: It's very quiet at home, Yasako. [*no response*] I can't go into the restaurant. Every day someone asks, "How are you doing? Are you okay?" I can't smile anymore and say I'm fine—because it's a lie and there have been too many lies already. So I stay home and clean Kuniko's room. I read her books and take a nap in her bed.

YASAKO: [*quietly*] You must fix it if you sleep in it.

HIRO: [*nods*] I wish . . . I wish none of this would have happened. I'm sorry that I failed you and Kuniko. I should be in jail now, not you.

YASAKO: You should not sleep in her bed.

HIRO: I understand, Yasako. You tried. [*a beat*] You had responsibility for three lives. Now you only have two.

YASAKO: One. And you have to let me go.

HIRO: You look tired, Yasako. But so beautiful. You must sleep and dream again.

YASAKO: Dream of what? What do you want from me? To make you another baby and fix our miserable lives? Forget it. If I could rip my womb out with my bare hands, I would.

HIRO: I just want you. I . . . [*a beat*] I need you.

YASAKO: What for? What could you possibly want me for but to be what I've always been? I'm not willing to live that way again.

HIRO: It's just about you, Yasako. To think I almost lost you.

YASAKO: You did lose me, Hiro. I disappeared that day at the beach and I'm not coming back. . . . you're looking at a ghost.

HIRO: Yasako, listen. We can go back to Japan and—

YASAKO: I don't want to go back to Japan. Not like this.

HIRO: Okay. Then we can stay. We can stay right here and learn to live a new way.

YASAKO: How strange that you are now the dreamer and all I can see is the necessary order of things.

HIRO: Yasako, listen. You can help me at the restaurant. We can be together all the time. And we can talk like we used to when we first met. Who we were is what's dead. Not us. We must go on, learn and repair. [*a beat*] Have I ever needed you before?

[*She looks at him for a beat and then slowly shakes her head.*]

YASAKO: Make certain when you fix the bed that you get the blankets in the right order. She likes the pink-flowered futon on top and the mint one underneath. Make sure you get it right.

HIRO: [*a beat, then:*] Okay.

[*Spotlight out. Spotlight downstage center, into which* YASAKO *enters and stares at the audience as faint ocean sounds are heard.*]

YASAKO: [*recites*]

> She swims so long at sea,
> so strong in the current
> looking for me.
>
> But the web of the net
> detains me as worlds overlap
> and I consider the trap.
>
> Whether to die to live
> or live in death,
> a mother in exile,
> a daughter's last breath.
>
> The sea is she
> and if I do not go,
> then who am I,
> what do I know.

[*Ocean sounds and light fades out. Gavel sound thuds exaggeratedly in the darkness. A* JUDICIAL VOICE *reverberates from the darkness:*]

JUDICIAL VOICE: You have been arraigned in this court on the charges as specified. [*a beat*] Is the defendant ready to enter a plea?

[YASAKO *and* ANGELA *stand in separate spotlights, looking at each other from across the stage.*]

ANGELA:	YASAKO:
She is, Your Honor.	I am, Your Honor.

JUDICIAL VOICE: And how do you plead?

ANGELA: The defendant pleads no contest.

YASAKO: [*haltingly*] . . . no . . . contest.

[*Lights fade out;* ANGELA *and* YASAKO *exit. There is a hubbub of voices, cameras clicking, and footsteps criss-crossing. They crescendo to a pitch and blend with ocean sounds that overwhelm them. Lights fade up on the cell.* YASAKO *crosses to light and sits. A nervous* EVELYN *enters.* YASAKO *is not happy to see her visitor.*]

EVELYN: Hello.

YASAKO: Why do you keep coming to the courtroom every day? I asked you to leave me alone.

EVELYN: You've been handling yourself so well, Yasako. You're going to get through this.

YASAKO: Am I? [*a beat*] When I was returning from the courthouse, an American yelled "murderer" and threw a tomato at me. I didn't wipe it off. She was Japanese American.

EVELYN: Well, their mothers aren't from Japan. They don't look at things the Japanese way. They don't even use chopsticks.

YASAKO: Shame, ne. Even in Japan, children do not want to use chopsticks anymore. I hope you use them.

EVELYN: Before I used a fork.

YASAKO: Your mother was smart to teach you the old ways.

EVELYN: When I have children, I'll teach them, too. [*a beat*] Oh. I'm sorry.

YASAKO: About what?

EVELYN: I shouldn't talk about . . .

YASAKO: Children? Oh, no, it's all right.

EVELYN: We have over five thousand names on the petitions. Mr. Yamashita is very excited about it.

YASAKO: Hiro?

EVELYN: He didn't tell you? He's been the driving force to get signatures on petitions that he's giving to the media and to the court to show that Americans understand your dilemma.

YASAKO: Hiro did that?

EVELYN: It was his idea. The papers have picked up the story, so even the media seem to be more sympathetic towards your case.

YASAKO: But I do not want sympathy.

EVELYN: Yasako . . . what honor is there in dying by someone else subjecting you to gas or the chair?

YASAKO: Please get out. You dishonor me with your persistence. You are so American sometimes.

EVELYN: And sometimes too Japanese for my own good. [*This remark sparks interest, curiosity in* YASAKO. EVELYN *takes from her clothing a small container.*] . . . I brought you tea. Special tea. [EVELYN *passes the tea to* YASAKO *and* YASAKO *stares at the can.*]

YASAKO: A-a-are you sure you want to do this?

EVELYN: No.

YASAKO: You could get in trouble.

EVELYN: I've thought about that.

YASAKO: Thank you.

EVELYN: Yasako-san, is suicide so honorable—when it really isn't about shame, but about running away from facing life . . . without Kuniko?

YASAKO: I'm running *to* her. I think.

EVELYN: Are you sure? Are you certain you're not running away? [*a quick beat*] She's gone, but we have to go on living . . . somehow. Don't you think that's what Kuniko would want?

YASAKO: Kuniko . . .

EVELYN: She would say, "Mommy, don't hurt yourself. Papa needs you." And then she'd sing.

YASAKO: Yes. She would . . .

EVELYN: You know. I think Kuniko came to my yard and took my cat away just so she could be the hero and rescue her. I think that's what she did.

YASAKO: . . . how does one go on living after this?

EVELYN: I don't know, but can't we answer that question together?

[EVELYN *and* YASAKO *stare at each other with clarity and affection.* EVELYN *exits. Lights close to a tight spotlight.* YASAKO *enters the light, kneels, and studies the tea cup as* FUYO *enters and urges her to drink.*]

YASAKO: Who cares about the tree when the branch is gone?

ANGELA'S VOICE: [*offstage*] It must be you who cares. You must start to love yourself, be yourself apart from husband and child. . . .

EVELYN'S VOICE: [*offstage*] We just do it. We just get up in the morning and start walking into the wind.

HIRO'S VOICE: [*offstage*] I can't remember which blanket goes on top of Kuniko's bed. Is it the green one or the flowered one? Help me.

KUNIKO'S VOICE: Mommy?

YASAKO: Kuniko?

KUNIKO'S VOICE: Where's Papa? Make him walk on the beach with you, Mommy. Make him sing like this: [*sings*] "Down the river oh down the river oh down the river we go-o-o!" [*ends singing and giggling*] Come on, Mommy, you can do it. Bye, Mommy!

[YASAKO *stares outward, toward audience, as she struggles with a decision. The wishes of* KUNIKO'S *spirit cause her to contemplate life over death.*]

YASAKO: Bare of branches, the tree in winter forever.
　　But alive, as she would want me to be,
　　breathing her dreams through me.

　　Who cares about the tree when the branch dies?
　　The women say it is I who must rise above
　　this misery that I have wrought,
　　I who must face the future
　　no matter what I've been taught.

　　And so I go, but it will always be cold.
　　And ever with me travels her precious soul.

[YASAKO *picks up the cup, stares at it, turning it around, and then slowly places it on the floor. The placement is not easy, as if a force pushes it upwards, too. She bows to her mother.*]

YASAKO: Mother, do not linger here. Go. Please. Your fate is blessed; mine is cursed. Kuniko needs you.

[*With disappointment,* FUYO *caresses* YASAKO'S *face, her hand coming close but never touching, her face full of longing.* FUYO *exits in defeat as:*]

KUNIKO'S VOICE: [*sings a bit of* "Down the River": "The river is up and the channel is deep, the wind is steady and strong . . ."* [*song fades out as* FUYO *disappears and* YASAKO *turns toward* KUNIKO'S *fading voice.*]

YASAKO: [*slow cadence*] "The river is up and the channel is deep, the wind is steady and strong. Oh won't we have a jolly good time as we go sailing along. Down the river, oh down the river, oh down the river we go-o-o, Down the river, oh down the river, oh down the Ohio."

[*The exaggeratedly loud slamming of a gavel startles* YASAKO *as a* JUDICIAL VOICE *reverberates from the darkness. Lights begin a slow tightening, ending up as a small spot, lighting* YASAKO's *face.*]

JUDICIAL VOICE: [*voice-over*] Yasako Yamashita. The Superior Court of the County of San Diego, State of California, has found you guilty of one count of voluntary manslaughter. [*a beat*] You will be sentenced to five years' probation with psychiatric treatment and a year in County Jail. [*a beat*] Do you understand the gravity of what has happened to you, and, indeed, to us all, Mrs. Yamashita?

[*She does. Her eyes reveal. Extremely slow fade on* YASAKO's *resolute face.*]

THE END

Dance of the Wandering Souls

by
HUYNH QUANG NHUONG

NOTICE: *With the use of multiple roles, only ten actors and actresses are needed to produce the show. The full-length drama, including five dances, lasts about 90 minutes. Simple props can keep the cost of production at a minimum. The play can be done with a purely American cast.*

This is not the Vietnamese version of Romeo and Juliet. *The play focuses on war and peace.*

ACTION AND SCENES: The action occurs in long-ago Vietnam and China. The scenes, oriental in mood, are achieved through costumes and simple props. A bell or gong helps indicate changes of place and time.

CAST OF CHARACTERS

PRINCE TRONG THUY:	The Chinese Emperor's only son. Age 20.
PRINCESS MY CHAU:	The Vietnamese Queen's only daughter. Age 18.
PRINCE DAI LAN:	The Vietnamese Queen's son.
QUEEN AU CO:	The Vietnamese Queen. Age 60.

GENERAL TRAN CAN: A Vietnamese general. Age 60.
ADVISOR HOANG DAO: The chief advisor to the Vietnamese Queen. Age 65.
EMPEROR LIU HAN: The Chinese Emperor. Age 65.
ADVISOR TRUONG LUONG: The chief advisor to the Chinese Emperor. Age 60.
A GROUP of CO HON: Players playing Co Hon (Wandering Souls) have their faces painted white and wear black pajamas with very long sleeves that allow them to hold artificial hands. Thus, their arms look much longer than normal people's.
A GROUP of VIETNAMESE SOLDIERS, a GOLDEN TURTLE, GUARD

———

ACT I
SCENE ONE

SETTING: A battlefield. Fire caused by burning camps and outposts lights up the whole area. Loud war cries mingle with the sounds of musket fire.

AT RISE: QUEEN AU CO and her army are in retreat, carrying with them their dead and wounded. Moments later PRINCE DAI LAN, the commander of the Vietnamese rearguard, appears with his two last fighters. Suddenly one gets hit and falls down. The PRINCE picks up the wounded soldier and carries him along. Shortly afterward he also gets hit, fatally. The Chinese are closing in. The last Vietnamese warrior wants to drag his wounded friend away, but he soon realizes that his comrade has just died and he gives up the idea. He fires his musket at the Chinese and disappears. [*Blackout*]

[END OF SCENE ONE]

SCENE TWO

SETTING: The Royal Palace.

AT RISE: QUEEN AU CO, GENERAL TRAN CAN, and ADVISOR HOANG DAO are onstage.

QUEEN: Glad that we don't have to fight these days! But what a price we had to pay! [*She sighs.*] What a painful loss, the death of your only son, General! I intended to make him my son-in-law. What a painful loss for the two of us!

GENERAL: Thanks, Your Majesty!

QUEEN: How about your relatives, Advisor?

ADVISOR HOANG DAO: I have no relatives, Your Majesty. I have no family.

QUEEN: Oh, I forget all about that!

ADVISOR HOANG DAO: But the loss of General Tran Can's son as well as the King, the three Princes, and the other warriors has hurt me just as much.

QUEEN: A pain grips my heart every time the King and the three Princes are mentioned. The King's face still appears clearly to me as if I just saw him yesterday. As for the three Princes, from the time they left their cradles to the moments they died, not a single day did they know peace. After all, I've lived my life. But theirs had just begun. One of them wasn't even properly buried. Oh my son, my son! You passed away at a very young age, and you didn't have a decent burial! [*Tears come into the* QUEEN'*s eyes.*]

ADVISOR HOANG DAO: Prince Dai Lan made a crucial sacrifice. The Prince was a great leader. Long afterward captured Chinese soldiers still asked who'd led the rearguard that night. Prince Dai Lan inspired all of us.

QUEEN: I know! That made his death all the more difficult for me. As a mother, the loss of all my three sons hurt me equally. But as a ruler, I put all my hope in Prince Dai Lan as my successor.

[*A messenger comes in and kowtows to the* QUEEN.]

MESSENGER: There are unusual movements of the enemy troops along the border, Your Majesty!

QUEEN: [*to the* MESSENGER] Dismissed! [*to the* GENERAL *and* ADVISOR HOANG DAO] It looks like they're coming back soon. [*She wipes her tears.*] What should we do next?

ADVISOR HOANG DAO: Should we find some way to let the Chinese know that we respect them and wish to establish some sort of friendly relationship or alliance?

QUEEN: A very good idea, Advisor! However, an early offer of peace may be interpreted by them as a lack of will to defend ourselves. We'll explore the idea in detail and try it when the right time comes. What do you think, General?

GENERAL: Maybe we should strengthen our defense while trying to promote a better relationship with China.

QUEEN: What is your plan for improving our defense?

GENERAL: To discourage the Chinese from invading our country again, a fort at the single pass between China and Vietnam may help.

QUEEN: A splendid idea!

GENERAL: Thanks! If Your Majesty wishes, I'll supervise the construction of the fort.

QUEEN: You are a very dedicated soldier! I didn't expect you to volunteer for the job. The three of us need a good rest after such a long struggle.

GENERAL: It'll be a great honor for me. In reality architects and workers are the ones who'll do the actual planning and building.

QUEEN: Your presence will help complete the project quickly. You'll be there to solve the problems on the spot.

GENERAL: I'll do my best.

QUEEN: I am happy that we've come up with an excellent idea! The two of you never fail me. Tomorrow we'll inspect the pass to choose the proper location for the fort. Until tomorrow then!

GENERAL AND ADVISOR HOANG DAO: Yes, Your Majesty!

[*Blackout*]

END OF SCENE TWO

SCENE THREE

SETTING: The fort. A group of Vietnamese soldiers guard the site.

AT RISE: The Vietnamese soldiers suddenly fall down and sleep. Eerie wailing is heard. CO HON appear and perform a ritual dance while continuing to wail, before systematically destroying the fort. When the construction is totally demolished, CO HON disappear. Moments later the Vietnamese soldiers wake up. They look at the ruins of the construction, bewildered. GENERAL TRAN CAN appears and talks to the soldiers. [*Blackout*]

END OF SCENE THREE

SCENE FOUR

SETTING: The seashore near the Royal Palace.

AT RISE: The QUEEN and the PRINCESS are onstage.

QUEEN: The fort is almost finished. We'll move there soon, daughter.

PRINCESS: Why, mother?

QUEEN: Because I want to let our fighters go home for a visit. The war was too long for them.

PRINCESS: You can do that by simply staying here.

QUEEN: If we stay here, we need soldiers to guard both places. Staying at the stronghold, we can let more of our men go home. They deserve it.

PRINCESS: Here I hardly see a guard all day. At the fort I shall have to meet a great number of soldiers carrying guns and swords, day in and day out. The sight of weapons turns my stomach, mother!

QUEEN: You seem to forget that you are the offspring of a soldier-king. Your father was a great military leader. Together, he and I, we fought side by side for years, until the day he perished from an enemy's arrow.

PRINCESS: You are brave, and father was brave! Not afraid of anything! I am not brave!

QUEEN: Oh Heavens! What did I do wrong? [pause] Now listen! No matter how you feel, sooner or later you must replace me. The people of this nation will depend on you for their happiness, or at least their survival. We won the latest battle, but the war may resume anytime. I won't live forever. You ought to prepare yourself to lead our warriors. The best way is to live close to them to be familiar with their customs and understand their needs.

PRINCESS: I am willing to work hard as a nurse or a cook to support our army.

QUEEN: We have enough nurses and cooks. What we need from you is to lead our men when I am not here any more.

PRINCESS: I don't think I can make it as a military leader.

QUEEN: Women have successfully led men to battles.

[The PRINCESS wants to say something, but stops short upon seeing GENERAL TRAN CAN.]

GENERAL: [bows to the QUEEN and the PRINCESS] Your Majesty, I am sorry to bring you bad news about the fort.

QUEEN: What happened, General?

GENERAL: The almost-finished fort collapsed last night.

QUEEN: Did you find the exact cause?

GENERAL: Yes! Last night I led a heavily armed contingent to ambush possible saboteurs. We hid carefully near the construction site. Around midnight all the sentinels and the group of soldiers guarding the fort suddenly fell asleep. The Co Hon came out of the ground and systematically demolished the building. I am sorry!

QUEEN: Don't feel bad. You did what you could. You look a bit tired. Go ahead and get a good rest. [*pause*] Daughter, go back to the palace with General Tran Can.

PRINCESS: I would like to stay here with you, mother. I don't want you to be alone at a time like this.

QUEEN: You go back to the palace with General Tran Can. I need to be alone to think about this turn of events.

PRINCESS: Yes, mother.

[*The* PRINCESS *and the* GENERAL *exit.*]

QUEEN: Oh heavens! Human force against human force, I can perhaps contain the Chinese. But what chance do I have against Co Hon?

[*A giant* GOLDEN TURTLE *comes out of the sea and greets the* QUEEN.]

GOLDEN TURTLE: Dear Queen, I give you this claw, my own. [*The* TURTLE *hands the* QUEEN *the claw.*] Affix the claw to the tip of an arrow. When Co Hon appear to destroy your fort, shoot at them with the special arrow. They won't return. The claw can also be used to immobilize enemy troops. No matter how many times you shoot, it will return to your quiver by itself. One thing you should keep in mind, keep the secret of the claw to yourself.

QUEEN: Will Vietnam be free of the Chinese threat from now on?

GOLDEN TURTLE: That depends on your ability to keep the claw a secret. I have to go now.

[*The* TURTLE *disappears into the sea before the* QUEEN *can ask another question.*]

QUEEN: Oh I hope this gift will solve all the trouble! I am tired of fighting! I am miserable to see young men on both sides die! The threat of another Chinese invasion gives me no rest. [*The* QUEEN *looks in the direction of the palace.*] General Tran Can and Advisor Hoang Dao are coming. What should I do next? [*pause*] I'll rebuild the fort and test the claw.

[ADVISOR HOANG DAO *and* GENERAL TRAN CAN *come in.*]

ADVISOR HOANG DAO: It's almost dark, Your Majesty. And you are alone. We came to keep you company.

QUEEN: I wasn't alone. I had a visit from a talking turtle.

GENERAL: Do you really mean a turtle that can talk?

QUEEN: Of course! It spoke Vietnamese fluently.

GENERAL: Amazing! There are talking birds around here, but I've never heard of a talking turtle.

QUEEN: Can you see its footprints in the sand?

GENERAL: [*looks at the sand*] Yes! They are still wet!

ADVISOR HOANG DAO: It must be a good omen. Turtles always bring good luck.

QUEEN: I think so. As a matter of fact, the talk with the turtle helped me reach an important decision.

ADVISOR HOANG DAO: What did it say, Your Majesty?

QUEEN: It urged me to resume the construction project. And I'll do it.

ADVISOR HOANG DAO: Should we move the site of the construction to another place, Your Majesty? This present one must be right on an old battlefield where bodies of fallen fighters on both sides were hastily buried to avoid scavengers. As a result, Co Hon were disturbed and came out of the ground to prevent the completion of the fort.

QUEEN: I understand your sympathy for Wandering Souls, Advisor. *One of my sons must be a Co Hon, too, since we couldn't bury his body.* But we have no other choice. The present site is the only strategic vantage point. A new location will be of little use. We should rebuild the stronghold at the same place or not at all. What do you think, General?

GENERAL: True! There is no use to build the fort if it doesn't straddle the pass. But how are we going to fight Co Hon, Your Majesty?

QUEEN: When the fort is almost finished, tell the members of the ambushing unit to put aside their muskets and provide themselves with bows and fire arrows. Tell them to cover the tips of their arrows with old rags and dip them in coconut oil. If the tips are set on fire, the arrows will carry the fire to the targets. The turtle said that the Co Hon were afraid of fire, and the fire arrows would scare them away forever by their sudden impact.

GENERAL: Your order will be carefully carried out, Your Majesty!

QUEEN: Good! Let's go back to the palace and have some tea. Such an eventful day!

[*Blackout*]

END OF SCENE FOUR

SCENE FIVE

SETTING: The fort. A hiding place nearby. A group of Vietnamese soldiers guard the site. Another group of soldiers, led by GENERAL TRAN CAN, lie in ambush close by.

AT RISE: QUEEN AU CO and ADVISOR HOANG DAO appear at the hiding place.

QUEEN: You're trembling, Advisor. Are you frightened of the Co Hon?

ADVISOR HOANG DAO: I am not fearful, especially in your company, Your Majesty. The chilly northern wind is a little too much for me.

QUEEN: Sorry! Those endless years of fighting have finally taken their toll on you. Here is my coat. Put it on!

ADVISOR HOANG DAO: I can't do that! You'll get cold yourself.

QUEEN: Don't worry! I am fine. After all, you are a scholar who has given up books and accompanied my husband and me on various campaigns. You are more vulnerable to the elements than I.

ADVISOR HOANG DAO: Thanks! [*He puts the coat on.*]

[GENERAL TRAN CAN *appears.*]

GENERAL: All our men are ready with their fire arrows, Your Majesty. I came to see if Your Majesty has any new orders.

QUEEN: Just send me a soldier with good eyes. We can't see the construction site from here.

GENERAL: Then I'll rejoin our ambushing unit. The soldier will be here shortly. [*He exits.*]

QUEEN: [*looks into the sky*] I don't know as much about those heavenly bodies as you do, Advisor. But one thing I am sure of is that they exist in harmony with each other. Their very existence makes me feel so insignificant. Why should not we humans live peacefully with each other? Those stars last forever, but they don't strike against each other. And mortal humans consume their short lives in senseless quarrels.

ADVISOR HOANG DAO: I agree, Your Majesty. I don't understand why people try to cut each other's lives short for a piece of land which contains such and such resources or makes their country a little bit bigger. How long would we live if we died of natural causes? One hundred years at the most!

[*A young* SOLDIER *comes in and kowtows to the* QUEEN.]

SOLDIER: Your Majesty, reporting for duty from General Tran Can.

QUEEN: Soldier, you look so young! How old are you?

SOLDIER: Sixteen.

QUEEN: Tomorrow I'll transfer you to the Royal Guard. It's safer there.

SOLDIER: I can fight!

QUEEN: I know! But you are too young to die. Now, observe carefully the construction site and let me know when Co Hon come out of the ground.

SOLDIER: Yes, Your Majesty!

[*The* QUEEN *looks into the sky again and seems lost in her thoughts. Suddenly, like the other time, the soldiers guarding the fort fall on the ground and sleep. Moments later the* CO HON *wail eerily and appear. The young* SOLDIER *rushes back to the* QUEEN *and lets her know that the* CO HON *are coming out of the ground. The* SOLDIER, *followed by the* QUEEN *and the* ADVISOR, *returns in a hurry to the observing post. At this moment a deafening commotion is created by the ambushing unit's yelling and sound of arrows traveling through the air. The* QUEEN *discreetly shoots her special arrow without the* SOLDIER *and the advisor knowing it. The* CO HON *fall down and crawl away. The members of the ambushing team and* GENERAL TRAN CAN *come out of their hiding places and raise their arms in victory. Shortly afterward the soldiers guarding the fort wake up, and the members of the ambushing unit start talking to them.*]

QUEEN: How is the fort, soldier?

SOLDIER: It's still standing! But I don't know for sure what is going on on the ground. A strange vapor prevents me from seeing clearly.

QUEEN: Very good! Everything is fine so long as the fort didn't collapse.

[GENERAL TRAN CAN rushes in.]

GENERAL: The fire arrows worked very well, Your Majesty. At the impact of the special weapons, Co Hon fell down and disappeared. They left behind an unwholesome vapor which made some of our men cough or sneeze. But nothing was more serious than that.

QUEEN: Is the fort intact?

GENERAL: Yes!

QUEEN: Very well done, General! Now we have a better chance to defend ourselves. [*pause*] I wish the King and the three Princes were still alive to participate in this unforgettable event.

GENERAL: I wish Princess My Chau were here to share this excitement.

QUEEN: [*sighs*] I did let her know about this. But no sooner had I mentioned Co Hon, than her face turned pale. She looked so frightened and miserable that I didn't insist. Oh, what a daughter of mine! [*pause*] Tomorrow we'll have a big celebration for the completion of the stronghold.

[*Blackout*]

END OF SCENE FIVE

SCENE SIX

SETTING: The fort.

AT RISE: The QUEEN, GENERAL TRAN CAN, and ADVISOR HOANG DAO are onstage.

QUEEN: The fort has relieved me of so much anxiety. At least the three of us can afford some leisure time in the days ahead. I've thought of having a garden and planting all the flowers the King liked. He never got tired of looking at flowers. The King also liked fishing very much. A guard just told me about a lake full of fish, not too far from here. I wish my husband were still alive to devote some of his leisure time to his favorite hobbies. [pause] Do you like fishing, too, General?

GENERAL: No . . . Your Majesty? I don't think I can catch any fish. I did try though, as a boy. But I never caught one. My father told me that my soul was too heavy and that scared the fish away. However, I was pretty fast. I could easily catch big frogs.

QUEEN: [smiles] I doubt if either of us can catch any frogs, big or small, these days. How about you, Advisor? Do you have a heavy soul too?

ADVISOR HOANG DAO: Not really, Your Majesty. I used to get big fish from the river in front of my house. Sometimes I could even afford to give some good ones to friends. Once, as a boy, I was almost pulled into the river by a huge carp. Like the King, fishing is my favorite hobby.

QUEEN: I've been carried away by thoughts of having a garden and the King's favorite hobbies. I almost forgot to ask you something, General. Did you grant furloughs to our soldiers?

GENERAL: Yes! As a matter of fact, two-thirds of our standing army were allowed to visit with their families. When they return, the others will follow suit. Everywhere I go, I hear cheerful talk about going home.

QUEEN: Glad to hear that! [pause] By the way, did you notice any good young men around?

ADVISOR HOANG DAO: I've tried hard to find a suitor for the Princess. But so far my search has been fruitless. The young men I've talked to don't have all the qualities of a good leader Your Majesty wants. I'll try harder.

GENERAL: The other evening, during the celebration of the completion of the fort, I introduced to the Princess some young, potentially good military leaders. But Her Grace was indifferent to them. It seemed she didn't care for military people.

QUEEN: What an irony! Born to warrior parents, but she doesn't like warriors. [She sighs.] Well, the three of us are getting old. The Princess needs a capable husband to help her keep the Chinese out of our country. Keep searching, will you?

GENERAL AND ADVISOR HOANG DAO: Yes, Your Majesty!

[*Frantic sounds of drums and gongs are heard.*]

GENERAL: Sentries on duty at the top of the stronghold are sounding the alert. There must be trouble!

ADVISOR HOANG DAO: The Chinese are coming, I guess.

QUEEN: Not so soon!

[*A* SOLDIER *rushes in.*]

SOLDIER: The Chinese are approaching our positions in great numbers, Your, Majesty!

QUEEN: General, Advisor, go ahead and supervise the defense! I'll join both of you shortly! [*The* GENERAL, *the* ADVISOR, *and the* SOLDIER *exit.*]

QUEEN: Golden Turtle, it's about time for me to test the power of your claw again. I hope I can protect this nation without any more bloodshed on either side. [*The* QUEEN *takes down from the wall the bow and the quiver containing several arrows and chooses the arrow with the turtle claw on it. She goes to the window, looks out of it for a moment, then shoots the special arrow. Suddenly, battle cries, sounds of drums and trumpets, and the neighing of war horses stop dead. The* QUEEN *sighs a sigh of relief.*] Thanks, Golden Turtle! It's worked just as well as before.

[*The* GENERAL *and the* ADVISOR *come in.*]

GENERAL: A miracle has just happened, Your Majesty! As soon as the enemy was ready to launch the attack against our fort, foot soldiers crumpled to the ground and horsemen fell off their mounts.

ADVISOR HOANG DAO: Now they're lying there helpless!

QUEEN: I've never known a happier day! The will of Heaven is clear! No more bloodshed! General, Advisor, go out of the stronghold and tell the Chinese in person that they should go home as soon as they regain the movement of their limbs. Make sure to warn them that if they return, we won't tolerate it.

GENERAL AND ADVISOR HOANG DAO: Yes, Your Majesty! [*They exit.*]

QUEEN: What a joyful day! Now I can let most of our warriors go home. I hope the Chinese will leave us alone from now on.

[*Blackout*]

END OF SCENE SIX

SCENE SEVEN

SETTING: The fort.

AT RISE: The QUEEN walks back and forth with a perplexed look on her face. The PRINCESS comes in.

QUEEN: Shut the door behind you. [*The* PRINCESS *shuts the door.*] And take the bow and the quiver down from the wall.

[*The* PRINCESS *takes down the bow and the quiver and hands them to the* QUEEN.]

PRINCESS: What for, mother?

QUEEN: I want to teach you how to shoot an arrow.

PRINCESS: For heaven's sake! You're not going to send me to the battlefield, are you?

QUEEN: No! But you must learn how to use a bow and arrow.

PRINCESS: Oh mother! You puzzle me!

QUEEN: I'll explain to you later. But now your business is to learn how to shoot an arrow.

PRINCESS: Oh, why should I have to go through all this?

QUEEN: Stop complaining and listen to my instruction carefully.

PRINCESS: Yes . . .

QUEEN: Put your right leg a step forward. [*The* PRINCESS *puts her right leg forward.*] Hold the bow firmly in your hand. [*The* PRINCESS *holds the bow near one of its ends.*] Not like that! You have to hold it right in the middle. . . . That's better! When you pull the string, you have to lean backward a bit to add the weight of your body to the strength of your left arm.

[*The* PRINCESS *tries to follow the instruction.*]

PRINCESS: The string is so tough! It hurts my fingers!

QUEEN: You'll get used to it! Go ahead and pull the string and release it a few times as if you were shooting real arrows.

PRINCESS: [*clumsily executes the order*] I don't think I can hit a water buffalo standing still just ten steps in front of me!

QUEEN: It looks like it! But it doesn't matter. You won't need to hit a water buffalo or anybody. [*pause*] Now you need to practice with real arrows.

[*The* QUEEN *shows the* PRINCESS *how to adjust an arrow to the bow and its string. Shortly afterward the* PRINCESS *absent-mindedly points the ar-*

row at the QUEEN. *Immediately the* QUEEN *pushes the tip of the arrow away and raises her voice.*] You never point an arrow at anyone unless you intend to kill that person!

PRINCESS: Sorry, mother!

[*With the help of the* QUEEN *the* PRINCESS *shoots a few arrows out of the window.*]

QUEEN: Now sit down and listen to me carefully.

[*The* PRINCESS *sits down and looks worried.*]

PRINCESS: I'll listen to you carefully.
QUEEN: You know that I've grown older and older and you are my only child which war hasn't taken from me.
PRINCESS: Yes.
QUEEN: You are the only one to whom I must entrust the survival of this nation.
PRINCESS: Mother, you scare me! I can't even kill an ant! How can you expect me to become a leader of men?
QUEEN: [*sighs*] I know! I know! But I have no other choice.
PRINCESS: Yes, you do! Uncle Tran Can and Uncle Hoang Dao have served you well all along. The sound of war cries numbs me. And I couldn't make heads or tails of those administrative discussions you wanted me to attend. Please, mother!
QUEEN: Listen! General Tran Can and Advisor Hoang Dao are dedicated associates and trustworthy friends. But both are like me, very old! Our days are numbered. To whom else would you want me to entrust a secret on which the future of this nation depends?
PRINCESS: I don't know! Uncle Tran Can and Uncle Hoang Dao can help you find that one.
QUEEN: They've been trying, very hard. But they didn't come up with anyone suitable yet. Listen! You are my only child left. It is your destiny to take on the responsibility.
PRINCESS: What do you want me to do?
QUEEN: You don't have to lead men into bloody battles or engage in complicated administrative tasks. What I need from you is to keep a weapon secret, and if need be, use it to save lives.
PRINCESS: Why should I need a weapon without going to war? And what kind of weapon can, instead of killing, save lives?

QUEEN: Yes! There is such a weapon. That is why I want only you to know about its existence. I must tell you now before advanced old age or sudden sickness confuses me and makes me give foolish orders. Now listen carefully! I'll make the story short. The other day, all the Chinese in front of the fort were immobilized, thanks to this weapon. And it is the same one which prevented Co Hon from destroying our stronghold.

PRINCESS: [almost cries] I don't think I am capable of such a responsibility, mother!

QUEEN: [raises her voice] Do as I command!

PRINCESS: [starts acting like a somnambulant] Yes.

QUEEN: [takes down a sword from the wall] Place your hand on this sword . . . [The PRINCESS places her hand on the sword.] And repeat after me.

PRINCESS: Yes.

QUEEN: I swear . . .

PRINCESS: I swear . . .

QUEEN: I would die by the sword . . .

PRINCESS: I will die by the sword . . .

QUEEN If I reveal the secret weapon to anyone . . .

PRINCESS: If I revealed the secret weapon to anyone . . .

QUEEN: Who would undermine the security of this nation.

PRINCESS: Who would undermine the security of this nation.

QUEEN: Good!

PRINCESS: May I go now?

QUEEN: No! I haven't shown you the secret weapon yet. Hand me the quiver.

PRINCESS: Yes.

[The PRINCESS gives the QUEEN the quiver.]

QUEEN: [takes the special arrow out of the quiver] Look at this arrow carefully! See this turtle claw?

PRINCESS: Yes.

QUEEN: It is fixed firmly to the tip of the arrow. You just shoot it at the enemy troops, and they will all be paralyzed. The arrow will return to the quiver by itself.

[The QUEEN hands the special arrow to the PRINCESS. She looks at it while tears comes into her eyes. Blackout]

END OF SCENE SEVEN

ACT II
SCENE ONE

SETTING: The Chinese Imperial Palace.

AT RISE: The Chinese EMPEROR and ADVISOR TRUONG LUONG are onstage.

EMPEROR: Our spies in Vietnam have discovered nothing about the secret weapon that immobilized our invading army. They humiliated us, and we couldn't do anything to get back at them. How long shall we wait? How long can we afford the secession of that southern province without worrying about the others? They may follow suit soon. Oh, Vietnam is a pain in my neck and a thorn in my side! Do you have any idea how to get hold of their secret weapon, Advisor?

TRUONG LUONG: Your Majesty, the best way to secure the secret weapon, I believe, is to have someone infiltrate the Vietnamese Royal Family.

EMPEROR: Can a servant or a maid do the job?

TRUONG LUONG: I don't think so.

EMPEROR: Why?

TRUONG LUONG: Because no Queen would reveal such a secret to such a lowly member of the household.

EMPEROR: Who then?

TRUONG LUONG: The Prince.

EMPEROR: You mean Prince Trong Thuy, my only son?

TRUONG LUONG: Yes.

EMPEROR: Why should it be him?

TRUONG LUONG: The Prince is the right man for the job.

EMPEROR: What do you mean?

TRUONG LUONG: The Vietnamese Queen has only one daughter, and she is of marriageable age. First, we should propose a permanent peace to Vietnam, and then as a guarantee of good faith on our part, we'll ask the Vietnamese Queen to let her only daughter marry the Prince. And as another show of good faith, the Prince will stay in Vietnam as long as the Vietnamese Queen wishes. While staying there, the Prince will figure out a way to obtain the secret weapon.

EMPEROR: An excellent idea!

TRUONG LUONG: I am afraid the Prince won't like the idea.

EMPEROR: Don't worry about that! I've brought him up in the traditional way. He always obeys me as his father and sovereign, without any hesitation.

He'll carry out the mission, no matter what. I've instilled in him that Vietnam is just another province of China and that the Vietnamese Queen is accountable, as a traitor, for the rebellion of that southern province. I've also taught him that if one couldn't crush the enemy by force, then one should resort to deceit to protect Imperial interests.

TRUONG LUONG: Then the plan will have every chance of working. The Vietnamese Queen is difficult to handle, but her daughter may not be. I doubt if any girl can resist such a charming Prince as Prince Trong Thuy. If Your Majesty wishes, I'll disguise myself as the Prince's only attendant and follow His Highness to Vietnam.

EMPEROR: Good! You've always served me well. I made no mistake by choosing you as my chief advisor. You'll accompany my son on this mission. He needs someone like you in that remote and unpredictable land. He was born as a kind boy, too kind to make an accomplished emperor. I want this occasion to toughen up his character. I expect you ˙ ⌣ help him in that respect. He needs guidance to complete the learning process so that one day he can succeed me to rule the empire well. Problems may also come up during his stay in Vietnam, and he'll need your experience to solve them. You'll be well rewarded when the mission is accomplished.

TRUONG LUONG: Thank Your Majesty very much! You've already rewarded me with your trust. I'll do my best to make the mission a complete success.

EMPEROR: Go ahead and send the peace initiative and marriage proposal to Vietnam. Then tell the treasurer to provide you with enough diamonds, gold, ivory, gingseng, and mother-of-pearl for the bride price. You can go now. I'll instruct the Prince about the mission in person.

[Blackout]

END OF SCENE ONE

SCENE TWO

SETTING: The fort.

AT RISE: The PRINCESS is onstage, doing needlework. The QUEEN comes in.

QUEEN: Daughter, I've just received a peace initiative from China. The Chinese Emperor also asked me to give your hand to his only son, Prince Trong Thuy. It's about time for you to get married. I want the marriage to go well. So there'll be possible permanent peace between our two countries.

PRINCESS: China is far away, and I don't know anybody there, mother.

QUEEN: Don't worry about that! You don't have to follow the Prince to China. As a guarantee of good faith, the Chinese Emperor has informed me that I can keep the Prince here as long as I want.

PRINCESS: Chinese girls are pretty—and I am ugly! I don't think the Prince will like me.

QUEEN: Don't worry about that, either! I regret that I couldn't make you a good leader. But in beauty you can compete with any girl, Chinese or Vietnamese.

PRINCESS: Why didn't you tell me that?

QUEEN: Because all along I've tried to build leadership qualities in you. I didn't want you to look in the other way by telling you that you were pretty—very pretty, indeed! I also forbade others to tell you so. Beauty pleases but doesn't lead. Now it is obvious that you can't lead. You've admitted it yourself. But at least you can make a pleasant and agreeable companion to give peace a chance.

PRINCESS: I'll do my best.

QUEEN: Glad to hear that! We have the magic turtle claw. But it is only with a good relationship between China and Vietnam, strengthened by this marriage, that our people have the chance to live in peace. War has been going on for so long. The secret weapon can't prevent sudden Chinese raids on the border towns because I am not there to shoot the arrow. For the same reason,I can't protect the Vietnamese fishing industry from Chinese warships on the high seas. Moreover, only a lasting peace can promote a productive trade and exchange of cultural interests between our two countries.

PRINCESS: I'll do what I can to make the Prince happy.

QUEEN: We all should try to end this continuous war. To tell the truth, I am not without suspicion concerning the Chinese Emperor's intention. He may fear, I suppose, that we'll use the secret weapon to attack his country. I don't know for sure whether he is sincere or not; but one way or another, war has been going on for so long. Our people, especially those at the border towns, have been miserable. We have to give peace any possible chance we can; and if things go wrong, we'll have the turtle claw to rely on. [*pause*] By the way, the Prince is well educated, intelligent, considerate, and very handsome!

[*The* PRINCESS's *eyelashes flutter, but she does not say anything.* Blackout]

END OF SCENE TWO

SCENE THREE

SETTING: The fort.

AT RISE: The PRINCE and the PRINCESS dance together to the sound of a flute, through intercom. They show signs of a couple deeply in love with each other. Knocks heard at the door.

PRINCE: Come in!

[A GUARD *comes in.*]

GUARD: Your personal attendant requests an audience with you, Your Majesty.
PRINCE: Tell him to come back some other time.
PRINCESS: Honey, it's the third time he's requested to see you.
PRINCE: He can wait.
PRINCESS: He may have some personal problems. And only you can help him.
PRINCE: He is too smart to have any problems. I'll go to see him.
PRINCESS: You don't have t go anywhere. Guard, tell him he can see the Prince right here. [*to the* PRINCE] I'm going to do some needlework. Don't hurry! Take your time talking to him.

[*The* PRINCESS *opens the imaginary door between the two chambers, sits down on a chair, and starts doing needlework. Soon, two* CO HON *appear and dance. While dancing, one of them hypnotizes the* PRINCESS *and leads her to the bed. As she lies down and falls asleep, the two* CO HON *disappear. Moments later the Chinese advisor,* TRUONG LUONG, *comes in.*]

PRINCE: [*tries to smile*] Do you have any news from China?
TRUONG LUONG: We don't have any news, Your Highness. I am sorry to disturb you. Please forgive me. I'm just trying to do the job the Emperor has entrusted to me.
PRINCE: What job? Oh, the secret weapon!
TRUONG LUONG: Yes! We've been here for more than six months, but you haven't made any moves. Now you are reluctant to see me. At times I don't see you for days. Lately you've fallen in love, deeply, with the one you should consider your enemy. What shall I say when I see the Emperor again?
PRINCE: I am in a difficult dilemma.
TRUONG LUONG: What dilemma, may I ask, Your Highness? Do you forget that the Vietnamese Queen is an obstacle to our national unity?
PRINCE: I've changed my mind about that.
TRUONG LUONG: Why? Please tell me why, Your Highness!

PRINCE: In Vietnam people don't speak the same language or wear the same clothes as in China. Vietnam is definitely not a province of China. The Queen is very reasonable. I agree with her that the well-being of a nation doesn't depend on the size of its territory but on the peaceful existence of its inhabitants. She is also right to say that a piece of conquered land brings more suffering because it causes endless war.

TRUONG LUONG: Your Highness, don't you remember your duty to your father and Emperor?

PRINCE: I do! As a son, I must show my filial devotion toward my father; and as a subject, I must fulfill my promise to my Emperor.

TRUONG LUONG: What then, Your Highness?

PRINCE: That's why I'm facing a dire dilemma. I need time to make the right choice. Thanks for your concern. You may leave now.

TRUONG LUONG: Please remember your duty to your father and Emperor!

[*The advisor bows to the* PRINCE *and exits.*]

PRINCE: It hurts me to think of using my wife as a means to carry out my father's scheme, but what else can I do? Who knows more about the Queen's secret weapon than her only daughter? And if the Queen liked someone else more, that one would have already married the Princess before my father's proposal. [*He stops talking and starts walking back and forth. Suddenly he taps his head with his hand.*] I've found the solution to my quandary! The Queen has told me that it will make no difference to her who will really govern Vietnam, the Princess or I, after her. For this reason I won't really betray the Princess's trust and the Queen's kindness by complying with my father's order. Of course, I'll prevent the Emperor from using the weapon to attack other countries, especially Vietnam. I'll try my best to obtain the secret weapon. But I'll give it to my father only when he promises to live peacefully with his neighbors. I have to carry out this resolution right now. [*He opens the imaginary door between the two chambers, goes to the* PRINCESS, *who has fallen asleep over her needlework.*] Wake up, sleepyhead!

PRINCESS: For what? I am too sleepy to talk! Give me a kiss, so I can go back to sleep!

PRINCE: Not before you do me a favor.

[A CO HON *is seen upstage briefly.*]

PRINCESS: Any favor you want, big or small! But it has to be followed by a kiss!

PRINCE: What is the weapon which immobilized my father's army?

PRINCESS: Oh, just an ordinary arrow with a turtle claw fixed to its tip! It is right there, in the quiver on the wall! Now the kiss!

[He kisses her and she falls back to sleep. Quickly he removes the quiver from the wall and takes the special arrow out. He then deftly uses the wax from a burning candle nearby and makes a mock turtle claw from it. As soon as he removes the real turtle claw from the arrow and replaces it with the mock one, the real claw disappears from his hand.]

PRINCE: *[looks at his empty hand]* The claw has disappeared from my hand! I've passed the point of no return! The only thing I should do now is to send a secret message home. The Emperor will make up some excuse for the Queen to let me go back to China. Oh Heavens! Why all this trouble while the Princess loves and trusts me with all her heart. I have to go away from her, and what uncertainty is lying ahead! *[He kneels down in agony.]*

[Blackout]

END OF SCENE THREE

SCENE FOUR

SETTING: The fort.

AT RISE: The QUEEN is alone, holding a piece of paper in her hand. The PRINCE and the PRINCESS come in. They bow to the QUEEN.

QUEEN: Sorry to inform you that the Emperor has fallen very ill! He wants to see you as soon as possible. Here is the message.

[The QUEEN hands the PRINCE the piece of paper and he reads it quickly.]

PRINCE: I am also your son. My going back to China depends on your consent as well.

QUEEN: You could have gone home anytime you wished. Now that the Emperor is seriously ill, it is your duty to be with him.

PRINCE: Thanks!

QUEEN: If you need anything for the trip just let me know. I'll send General Tran Can to China to wish the Emperor a speedy recovery. In the meantime, I'll leave the two of you alone. *[The QUEEN exits.]*

PRINCESS: May I go with you?

PRINCE: I can't take you this time. I must get home as quickly as possible. And the road to China on horseback is very rough.

PRINCESS: How long will you stay in China?

PRINCE: It depends on the condition of my father.

PRINCESS: Will you come back as soon as your father gets well?

PRINCE: I will! And nothing can separate us again.

PRINCESS: I don't know why it worries me so much to see you go.

PRINCE: Don't worry! Nothing can destroy the bonds between us. [*pause*] By the way, I have something for you. Wait a moment! [*He exits and comes back shortly afterward with a white coat in his hand.*] This is made of white swan feathers. It's for you.

PRINCESS: Winter hasn't come yet. Why do you give it to me now?

PRINCE: For a special reason. Sometimes events get out of our control. In case you have to leave the fort in a hurry because of danger, drop the feathers of the coat along the way. Later on I can follow the white trail and find you.

PRINCESS: It's a lovely coat! I hope nothing will happen while you are away. I want to keep the coat forever.

PRINCE: But if need be, please promise me you'll follow my instruction.

PRINCESS: I will! But can you promise me one thing, too?

PRINCE: Anything you wish.

PRINCESS: Back in China, please don't look at Chinese girls or talk to them.

PRINCE: I promise! But why?

PRINCESS: Because they are pretty!

PRINCE: Don't worry about that! No Chinese girls are prettier than you, inside and out.

PRINCESS: Will your parents like me?

PRINCE: Of course! They will!

PRINCESS: How do you know for sure?

PRINCE: Because you are the only one I love.

[*She draws him closer to her and holds his face in her hands. She looks at him intensely, trying to memorize every feature of his face. Suddenly she breaks down.*]

PRINCESS: Oh, I won't know what to do with myself without you!

[*Blackout*]

END OF SCENE FOUR

SCENE FIVE

SETTING: The Chinese Imperial Palace.

AT RISE: The Chinese EMPEROR is onstage.

EMPEROR: It's been more than six months since the Prince left for Vietnam. Not a single day have I not thought of my son. Sometimes late into the night I couldn't go to sleep, worrying about his well-being in that remote and hostile land. Because of national interests I had to send my only son on this mission, but the heart of a father has revolted against such a decision. In order to toughen his character, I've always acted toward him as a severe, demanding, and aloof ruler, but at the bottom of my heart I love him dearly. He is my hope, my pride, and my future! Oh, sometimes I want to hug him, but I refrain from doing so for fear of revealing the true feelings of a father. He is too gentle! I must project the image of a strict Emperor for my son to imitate. I don't want the future Emperor to let feelings interfere with decisions which involve the empire's interests. Now the advanced dispatch from frontier guards has informed me that he'll be here anytime. My precious son will be home! I can't wait to see him. He must have accomplished his mission.

[Knocks heard at the door. The PRINCE and the Chinese advisor come in. They kowtow to the EMPEROR.]

PRINCE: Father, I tender you all my love and gratitude.

EMPEROR: Heaven bless both of you. You may be seated now.

[The PRINCE and the Chinese advisor get up and take their seats.]

EMPEROR: Was your mission successful?

PRINCE: I found out the secret weapon. But I couldn't bring it home, Father.

EMPEROR: Why not?

PRINCE: It was an ordinary arrow with a magic turtle claw fixed to its tip. As soon as I removed the claw from the tip of the arrow, it disappeared from my hand.

EMPEROR: So, they don't have the magic weapon anymore?

PRINCE: No! Instead, the Vietnamese Queen has a mock turtle claw in wax fixed to the same arrow.

EMPEROR: Glad to hear that! That gives her a false sense of security. Now we can attack Vietnam anytime we want.

PRINCE: Please spare Vietnam, Father!

EMPEROR: Why? Tell me why!

PRINCE: Because I love my wife!

EMPEROR: I chose your wife for you! How is it that you love her?

PRINCE: My heart tells me that the Vietnamese Princess is the one and only woman who deserves to be my wife.

EMPEROR: Oh ho! The heir to the Chinese Empire talked to his Emperor about his heart! Oh, I am so proud of my designated successor! Son, son, where is your brain, the brain that I've so painfully educated?

PRINCE: Father, I've carefully thought over the situation. The Vietnamese Queen has a genuinely peaceful attitude toward us. She didn't come to China to attack us with her magic weapon. She also told me that it would make no difference to her whether I or the Princess would govern Vietnam after her abdication. You have no need to attack our friendly neighbor.

EMPEROR: Vietnam is a friendly neighbor! Oh, you really disappoint me! Did I tell you that I wanted to get rid not only of that so-called Vietnamese Queen and her lieutenants but also of all the structures that have made Vietnam a separate country from China? You seem to have forgotten all about that! I also told you that when a province has left its Motherland, a good leader must bring it back by all means. It doesn't make any difference that you'll be King of Vietnam. You'll be the Emperor of all the provinces, including that black sheep which defies the central government.

PRINCE: Vietnam isn't a Chinese province. The Vietnamese don't speak Chinese. They wear their own clothes and have their own customs.

EMPEROR: [raises his voice] Enough of that! I want to invade Vietnam right now while they are still complaisant in their false security. I'll direct the conquering army in person. My decision is final! Advisor, come with me. I want to discuss the immediate expedition in detail with you. [The EMPEROR and the advisor exit.]

PRINCE: Oh My Chau, what can I do now? The last time we looked at each other, I saw trust in your eyes. And your unsuspecting look followed me all my journey home. Now, my betrayal is complete with my inability to convince my father. [He stands confused, shaking his head.]

[Blackout]

END OF SCENE FIVE

SCENE SIX

SETTING: The seashore near the Royal Palace, where the QUEEN first met the GOLDEN TURTLE.

AT RISE: The QUEEN and the PRINCESS are onstage. A trail of white swan feathers is behind them. The pandemonium made by war cries, war horses, etc. . . . from the pursuing army is heard. The CO HON appear. Upon seeing them, the PRINCESS hides behind the QUEEN.

PRINCESS: Co Hon, mother!

QUEEN: Yes, I see them! Do you recognize the one who stands apart from the rest?

PRINCESS: No!

QUEEN: *It's your brother! The one whose body we couldn't bury.*

PRINCESS: Oh, I recognize him now! My brother Dai Lan! He is crying, mother!

QUEEN: My son, the bravest of the brave, is crying!

[*The pandemonium made by the pursuing army grows louder and louder. The* CO HON, *except* PRINCE DAI LAN, *start dancing. While dancing, they urge the* QUEEN *and the* PRINCESS *to join them.*]

QUEEN: General Tran Can and Advisor Hoang Dao must have perished. Despite old age, they, with a handful of faithful soldiers, tried to cover our retreat. I used a shortcut through the territory I knew very well to avoid their pursuit. But no matter how hard I tried, we couldn't get away from them. I wanted to escape so later on I could reorganize the armed forces to fight back. Now, behind us is the relentless enemy and in front of us spreads the impassable sea. Sorry, daughter! I can't protect you any longer.

[*The* GOLDEN TURTLE *comes out of the sea and shouts to the* CO HON *to go away. They disappear.*]

QUEEN: Oh Golden Turtle! It is you! I had so much trust in your claw. Now I have no more standing army to fight back. My country will fall under Chinese rule again. Why did you play such a trick on me?

GOLDEN TURTLE: I didn't, dear Queen! Please look at the trail of white swan feathers behind you.

[*The* QUEEN *turns around and sees the white trail.*]

QUEEN: [*shouts to the* PRINCESS] Traitor! [*She draws her dagger and wants to kill the* PRINCESS, *but the* GOLDEN TURTLE *quickly intervenes.*]

GOLDEN TURTLE: Please spare the Princess's life! Because of the Co Hon she couldn't keep the secret of the claw, but she loves you dearly. As for her husband, he has for you all his respect and loyalty.

[*The* QUEEN *calms down and puts the dagger back into its sheath.* PRINCE TRUONG THUY *appears, kneels down in front of the* QUEEN, *and presents his sword to her.*]

PRINCE: Your Majesty, I deserve death!

[*The* QUEEN *takes the sword and then gives it back to the* PRINCE.]

QUEEN: Son, no matter what you've done, I forgive you. [*pause*] Take good care of your wife. As for me, I am not going to let my enemy take me alive.

[*The Chinese* EMPEROR, *followed by* AVISOR TRUONG LUONG *and a group of soldiers, comes onstage. Upon seeing his son kneeling in front of the* QUEEN, *he stops short, and for a moment he becomes speechless. The* PRINCE *gets up and faces the* EMPEROR.]

EMPEROR: [*shouts to his soldiers*] Kill them all, including him!

[*He points to the* PRINCE. *Immediately* TRUONG LUONG *waves to the soldiers to restrain them from carrying out the* EMPEROR's *order.*]

TRUONG LUONG: Please listen to me, Your Highness! The Prince is still very young! He deserves leniency. . . .

EMPEROR: What could I have expected from such a wayward weakling?

TRUONG LUONG: The Prince is your only child. And he is very loyal to you as a subject . . .

EMPEROR: Loyal to me! How could you say that? Did you see him, the future Emperor, kneel down to our arch enemy?

TRUONG LUONG: Yes! But the Prince may be under the influence of infatuation, and he needs time to think it over. If we get rid of the cause of his infatuation, he'll return to his former self . . .

EMPEROR: You mean that . . . that . . .

[*He points to the* PRINCESS.]

TRUONG LUONG: Yes, Your Highness.

PRINCE: [*draws his sword*] Father, if you give orders to kill her, I'll kill myself!

EMPEROR: You . . . you . . . will kill . . . yourself . . . for . . . for her? [*The* EMPEROR *is almost choked with rage.*]

PRINCE: Yes!

TRUONG LUONG: Please, Your Highness! Definitely the Prince is under the influence of infatuation. He needs help. . . .

PRINCE: I am not under the influence of any infatuation! And I don't need any help!

TRUONG LUONG: Then why are you behaving like that, Prince?

PRINCE: Because I love her!

TRUONG LUONG: I understand that she is pretty. But Your Grace can have a thousand Chinese girls as pretty as she.

PRINCE: Physical beauty isn't the only thing she has. Besides, I already betrayed her once! I don't want to do that again!

[TRUONG LUONG *turns to the* EMPEROR *and whispers something to him. The two of them then talk to each other in a low voice. The* CO HON *reappear and dance again. While dancing, they motion to the* QUEEN, *the* PRINCESS, *and the* PRINCE *to join them.*]

EMPEROR: Vietnamese . . . Vietnamese Queen, . . . I . . . I'll spare your life if you . . . you tell my son that . . . you . . . you don't want him to be your son-in-law any longer. . . .

QUEEN: My life is always mine! I am in full control of it! Nobody can spare it for me. And the Prince is always my son-in-law!

EMPEROR: I'll give you a moment to think it over. The alternative is death!

QUEEN: I've lived as a free person. I'll die as a free person. You waste your time!

EMPEROR: So you want to die instead of complying with my order?

QUEEN: Yes!

EMPEROR: [*shouts to his soldiers*] Kill her! [*He points at the* QUEEN. *As the soldiers move forward and the* PRINCE *rushes to the* QUEEN's *side to protect her, the* GOLDEN TURTLE *waves its leg. All of the Chinese are frozen, except the movements of their eyes indicate that they are conscious of what is going on.*]

GOLDEN TURTLE: [*to the* QUEEN, *the* PRINCESS, *and the* PRINCE] *It's not in my power to turn back the tides to change the fate of a nation. But I can bring the three of you to a distant island where you'll be safe. Let's go now!*

[*Before joining the departing group, the* PRINCE *turns around and faces his father.*]

PRINCE: Father, enjoy your conquered empire without me!

[*The* CO HON, *disappointed, stop dancing. Tears come into the* EMPEROR's *eyes.*]

END OF PLAY

Bondage

A play in one act by
DAVID HENRY HWANG

CHARACTERS

TERRI, late-twenties, female
MARK, early-thirties, male

PLACE: An S & M parlor on the outskirts of Los Angeles

TIME: Present

"Bondage" was commissioned by the Actors Theatre of Louisville (Jon Jory, Producing Director), where it opened March 1, 1992, at the 16th annual Humana Festival of New American Plays, on a double bill entitled "2 Acts of Love," with the following cast:

MARK	B. D. Wong
TERRI	Kathryn Layng

Directed by Oskar Eustis. Scenery by Paul Owen; Lighting by Mary Louise Geiger; Costumes by Laura A. Patterson; Stage Manager, Debra Acquavella.

[*A room in a fantasy bondage parlor.* TERRI, *a dominatrix, paces with her whip in hand before* MARK, *who is chained to the wall. Both their faces are covered by full face masks and hoods to disguise their identities.*]

MARK: What am I today?

TERRI: Today—you're a man. A Chinese man. But don't bother with that accent crap. I find it demeaning.

MARK: A Chinese man. All right. And who are you?

TERRI: Me? I'm—I'm a blonde woman. Can you remember that?

MARK: I feel . . . very vulnerable.

TERRI: You should. I pick these roles for a reason, you know. [*She unchains him.*] We'll call you Wong. Mark Wong. And me—I'm Tifanny Walker. [*pause*] I've seen you looking at me. From behind the windows of your— engineering laboratory. Behind your—horn-rimmed glasses. Why don't you come right out and try to pick me up? Whisper something offensive into my ear. Or aren't you man enough?

MARK: I've been trying to approach you. In my own fashion.

TERRI: How do you expect to get anywhere at that rate? Don't you see the jocks, the football stars, the cowboys who come 'round every day with their tongues hanging out? This is America, you know. If you don't assert yourself, you'll end up at sixty-five worshipping a Polaroid you happened to snap of me at a high school picnic.

MARK: But—you're a blonde. I'm—Chinese. It's not so easy to know whether it's OK for me to love you.

TERRI: C'mon, this is the 1990s! I'm no figment of the past. For a Chinese man to love a white woman—what could be wrong about that?

MARK: That's . . . great! You really feel that way? Then, let me just declare it to your face. I—

TERRI: Of course—

MARK: —love—

TERRI: It's not real likely I'm gonna love you.

[*pause*]

MARK: But . . . you said—

TERRI: I said I'm not a figment of the past. But I'm also not some crusading figure from the future. It's only 199_, you know. I'm a normal girl. With regular ideas. Regular for a blonde, of course.

MARK: What's that supposed to mean?

TERRI: It means I'm not prejudiced—in principle. Of course, I don't notice the color of a man's skin. Except—I can't help but notice. I've got eyes, don't I? [*pause*] I'm sure you're a very nice person . . . Mark. And I really appreciate your helping me study for the . . . physics midterm. But I'm just not—what can I say? I'm just not attracted to you.

MARK: Because I'm Chinese.

TERRI: Oh no, oh heavens, no. I would never be prejudiced against an Oriental. They have such . . . strong family structures . . . hard working . . . they hit the books with real gusto . . . makes my mother green with envy. But, I guess . . . how excited can I get about a boy who fulfills my mother's fantasies? The reason most mothers admire boys like you is 'cause they didn't bother to marry someone like that themselves. No, I'm looking for a man more like my father—someone I can regret in later life.

MARK: So you're not attracted to me because I'm Chinese. Like I said before.

TERRI: Why are you Orientals so relentlessly logical? [*She backs him up around the room.*]

MARK: Well, for your information, . . . it doesn't—it doesn't hurt that you're not in love with me.

TERRI: Why not?

MARK: Because I never said that I loved you, either!

[*They stop in their tracks.*]

TERRI: You didn't?

MARK: Nope, nope, nope.

TERRI: That's bullshit. I was here, you know. I heard you open yourself up to ridicule and humiliation. I have a very good ear for that kind of thing. [*cracks her whip*] So goddamn it—admit it—you said you love me!

MARK: I did not! If I don't tell the truth, you'll be angry with me.

TERRI: I'm already angry with you now for lying! Is this some nasty scheme to maneuver yourself into a no-win situation? God, you masochists make life confusing.

MARK: I came close. I said, "I love—," but then you cut me off.

TERRI: That's my prerogative. I'm the dominatrix.

MARK: I never finished the sentence. Maybe I was going to say, "I love . . . the smell of fresh-baked apple pie in the afternoon."

TERRI: That's a goddamn lie!

MARK: Can you prove it? You cut me off. In mid-sentence.

TERRI: It does . . . sound like something I would do. Damn. I'm always too eager to assert my superiority. It's one of the occupational hazards of my profession. [*pause*] So I fucked up. I turned total victory into personal embarrassment. God, I'm having a rotten day.

MARK: Terri—

TERRI: Mistress Terri!

MARK: Mistress Terri, I—I didn't mean to upset you. It's OK. I wasn't really going to say I loved apple pie. Now,—you can whip me for lying to you. How's that?

TERRI: I'm not about to start taking charity from my submissives, thank you. That's one good way to get laughed out of the profession. [*pause*] Sorry, I just—need a moment. Wouldn't it be nice if they'd put coffeemakers in here?

MARK: Look—do what you want. I'm a Mexican man, and you're an Indonesian—whatever.

TERRI: What went wrong—was I just going through the motions?

[MARK *kneels behind her, places his hands gently on her shoulders.*]

MARK: You feeling OK today?

TERRI: Of course I am! It just . . . hurts a girl's confidence to stumble like that when I was in my strongest position, with you at your weakest.

MARK: Why were you in such a strong position?

TERRI: Well, I was—a blonde!

MARK: And why was I in such a weak one?

TERRI: Oh, c'mon—you were . . . an Oriental man. Easy target. It's the kind of role I choose when I feel like phoning in the performance. Shit! Now, look—I'm giving away trade secrets.

MARK: Asian. An Asian man.

TERRI: Sorry. I didn't know political correctness had suddenly arrived at S and M parlors.

MARK: It never hurts to practice good manners. You're saying I wasn't sexy?

TERRI: Well . . . I mean . . . a girl likes a little excitement sometimes.

MARK: OK, OK . . . look, let's just pretend . . . pretend that I did say "I love you." You know, to get us over this hump.

TERRI: Now, we're pretending something happened in a fantasy when it actually didn't? I think this is getting a little esoteric.

MARK: Terri, look at us! Everything we do is pretend! That's exactly the point! We play out these roles until one of us gets the upper hand!

TERRI: You mean, until *I* get the upper hand.

MARK: Well, in practice, that's how it's always—

TERRI: I like power.

MARK: So do I.

TERRI: You'll never win.

MARK: There's a first time for everything.

TERRI: You're the exception that proves the rule.

MARK: So prove it. C'mon! And—oh—try not break down again in the middle of the fantasy.

TERRI: Fuck you!

MARK: It sort of—you know—breaks the mood?

TERRI: I'm sorry! I had a very bad morning. I've been working long hours—

MARK: Don't! Don't start talking about your life on my time!

TERRI: OK, you don't need to keep—

MARK: Sometimes, I really wonder why I have to be the one reminding you of the house rules at this late date.

TERRI: I didn't mean to, all right? These aren't the easiest relationships in the world, you know!

MARK: A man comes in, he plops down good money . . .

TERRI: I'm not in the mood to hear about your financial problems.

MARK: Nor I your personal ones! This is a fantasy palace, so goddamn it, start fantasizing!

TERRI: I have a good mind to take off my mask and show you who I really am.

MARK: You do that, and you know I'll never come here again.

TERRI: Ooooh—scary! What—do you imagine I might actually have some real feelings for you?

MARK: I don't imagine anything but what I pay you to make me imagine! Now, pick up that whip, start barking orders, and let's get back to investigating the burning social issues of our day!

TERRI: [*practically in tears*] You little maggot! You said you loved me . . Mark Wong!

MARK: Maybe. Why aren't I sexy enough for you?

TERRI: I told you—a girl likes a little excitement.

MARK: Maybe I'm—someone completely different from who you imagine. Someone . . . with a touch of evil. Who doesn't study for exams.

TERRI: Oh—like you get A's regardless? 'Cuz you're such a brain?

MARK: I have a terrible average in school. D-minus.

TERRI: I thought all you people were genetically programmed to score in the high 90s. What are you—a mutant?

MARK: I hang out with a very dangerous element. We smoke in spite of the surgeon general's warning. I own a cheap little motorcycle that I keep tuned in perfect condition. Why don't I take you up to the lake at midnight and show you some tricks with a switchblade? [*He plays with the handle of her whip.*] Don't you find this all . . . a lot more interesting?

TERRI: I . . . I'm not sure.

MARK: I'm used to getting what I want.

TERRI: I mean . . . I wasn't planning on getting involved with someone this greasy.

MARK: I'm not greasy. I'm dangerous! And right now, I've got my eye set on you.

TERRI: You sound like some old movie from the 50s.

MARK: I'm classic. What's so bad about—?

TERRI: Oh, wait! I almost forgot! You're Chinese, aren't you?

MARK: Well, my name *is* Mark Wong, but—

TERRI: Oh, well . . . I'm certainly not going to go out with a member of the Chinese mafia!

MARK: The Chinese—what? Wait!

TERRI: Of course! Those pathetic imitations of B-movie delinquents, that cheap Hong Kong swagger.

MARK: Did I say anything about the Chinese mafia?

TERRI: You don't have to—you're Chinese, aren't you? What are you going to do now? Rape me? With your friends? 'Cuz I've seen movies, and you Chinatown pipsqueaks never seem to be able to get a white woman of her own free will. And even when you take her by force, it still requires more than one of you to get the job done. Personally, I think it's all just an excuse to feel up your buddies.

MARK: Wait! Stop! Cut! I said I was vaguely bad—

TERRI: Yeah, corrupting the moral fiber of this nation with evil foreign influences—

MARK: Vaguely bad does not make me a hitman for the Tong!

TERRI: Then what are you? A Vietcong? Mmmm—big improvement. I'm really gonna wanna sleep with you now!

MARK: No—that's even more evil!

TERRI: Imprison our hometown boys neck-high in leech-filled waters—

MARK: No, no! Less evil! Less—

TERRI: Will you make up your goddamn mind? Indecision in a sadomasochist is a sign of poor mental health.

MARK: I'm not a Chinese gangster, not a Vietcong . . .

TERRI: Then you're a nerd. Like I said—

MARK: No! I'm . . .

TERRI: . . . we're waiting . . .

MARK: I'm . . . I'm neither!

[*pause*]

TERRI: You know, buddy, I can't create a fantasy session solely out of negative images.

MARK: Isn't there something in between? Just delinquent enough to be sexy without also being responsible for the deaths of a few hundred thousand U.S. servicemen?

[TERRI *gets up and paces about, dragging her whip behind her.*]

TERRI: Look, this is a nice American fantasy parlor. We deal in basic, mainstream images. You want something kinky, maybe you should try one of those specialty houses catering to wealthy European degenerates.

MARK: How about Bruce Lee? Would you find me sexy if I was Bruce Lee?

TERRI: You mean, like, "Hiiii-ya! I wuv you." [*pause*] Any other ideas? Or do you admit no woman could love you, Mark Wong?

[MARK *assumes a doggy-position.*]

MARK: I'm defeated. I'm humiliated. I'm whipped to the bone.

TERRI: Well, don't complain you didn't get your money's worth. Perhaps now I'll mount you—little pony—you'd like that wouldn't you?

MARK: Wait! You haven't humiliated me completely.

TERRI: I'll be happy to finish the job—just open that zipper.

MARK: I still never said that I loved you, remember?

[*pause*]

TERRI: I think that's an incredibly technical objection this late in the game.

MARK: All's fair in love and bondage! I did you a favor—I ignored your mistake—well, now I'm taking back the loan.

TERRI: You are really asking for it, buddy . . .

MARK: After all, I'm not a masochist—no matter how this looks. Sure, I let you beat me, treat me as less than a man—

TERRI: When you're lucky . . .

MARK: But I do not say "I love you!" Not without a fight! To say "I love you" is the ultimate humiliation. A woman like you looks on a declaration of love as an invitation to loot and pillage.

TERRI: I always pry those words from your lips sooner or later and you know it.

MARK: Not today—you won't today!

TERRI: Oh, look—he's putting up his widdle fight. Sometimes I've asked myself, "Why is it so easy to get Mark to say he loves me? Could it be . . . because deep inside—he actually does?"

MARK: Love you? That's—slanderous!

TERRI: Just trying to make sense of your behavior.

MARK: Well, stop it! I refuse to be made sense of—by you or anyone else! Maybe . . . maybe you *wish* I was really in love with you, could that be it?

TERRI: Oh, eat me!

MARK: 'Cuz the idea certainly never entered *my* head.

TERRI: Oh—even when you scream out your love for me?

MARK: That's what we call—a fantasy . . . Mistress.

TERRI: Yeah—*your* fantasy.

MARK: The point is, you haven't beaten me down. Not yet. You may even be surprised sometime to see that I've humiliated you. I'll reject *you* for loving me. And maybe, then, I'll mount *you*—pony.

TERRI: [*bursts out laughing*] You can't dominate me. I'm a trained professional.

MARK: So? I've been your client more than a year now. Maybe I've picked up a trick or two.

TERRI: I'm at this six hours a day, six days a week. Your time is probably squandered in some less rewarding profession.

MARK: Maybe I've been practicing in my spare time.

TERRI: With your employees at some pathetic office? Tsst! They're paid to humiliate themselves before you. But me, I'm paid to humiliate you. And I still believe in the American work ethic. [*She cracks her whip.*]

TERRI: So—enough talking everything to death! I may love power, but I haven't yet stooped to practicing psychiatry, thank you. OK, you're a—a white man and me—I'm a Black woman!

MARK: African American.

TERRI: Excuse me—are you telling me what I should call myself? Is this another of our rights you're dying to take away?

MARK: Not me. The Reverend Jesse Jackson . . . he thinks African American is the proper—

TERRI: Who?

MARK: Jesse—I'm sorry, is this a joke?

TERRI: You're not laughing, so I guess it's not. Tell me—the way you talk . . . could you be . . . a liberal?

MARK: Uh, yes, if you speak in categories, but—

TERRI: Um. Well, then that explains it.

MARK: Explains what?

TERRI: Why I notice you eyeing me up every time I wander towards the bar.

MARK: Let me be frank. I . . . saw you standing here, and thought to myself, "That looks like a very intelligent woman."

[*She laughs.*]

MARK: Sorry. Did I—say something?

TERRI: What do they do? Issue you boys a handbook?

MARK: What?

TERRI: You know, for all you white liberals who do your hunting a little off the beaten track?

MARK: Now, look here—

TERRI: 'Cuz you've all got the same line. You always start talking about our "minds," then give us this *look* like we're supposed to be grateful—"Aren't you surprised?" "Ain't I sensitive?" "Wouldn't you like to oil up your body and dance naked to James Brown?"

MARK: I can't believe . . . you're accusing *me* of—

TERRI: Then again, what else should I have expected at a PLO fundraiser? So many white liberals, a girl can't leave the room without one or two sticking to her backside.

MARK: Listen—all I said was I find you attractive. If you can't deal with that, then maybe . . . maybe *you're* the one who's prejudiced.

TERRI: White people—whenever they don't get what they want, they always start screaming "reverse racism."

MARK: Would you be so . . . derisive if I was a Black man?

TERRI: You mean, an African American?

MARK: Your African American brothers aren't afraid to date white women, are they? No, in fact, I hear they treat them better than they do their own sisters, doesn't that bother you even a bit?

TERRI: And what makes you such an expert on Black men? Read a book by some other whitey?

MARK: Hey—I saw *Jungle Fever.*

TERRI: For your urban anthropology class?

MARK: Don't get off the subject. Of you and me. And the dilemma I know you're facing. Your own men, they take you for granted, don't they? I think you should be a little more open-minded, unless you wanna end up like the 40 percent of Black women over 30 who're never even gonna get married in their lifetimes.

[*Silence*]

TERRI: Who the fuck do you think you are? Trying to intimidate me into holding your pasty-white hand? Trying to drive a wedge through our community?

MARK: No, I'm just saying, look at the plain, basic—

TERRI: You say you're attracted to my intelligence? I saw you checking out a lot more than my eyes.

MARK: Well, you do seem . . . sensuous.

TERRI: Ah. Sensuous. I can respect a man who tells the truth.

MARK: That's a . . . very tight outfit you've got on.

TERRI: Slinky, perhaps?

MARK: And when you talk to me, your lips . . .

TERRI: They're full and round—without the aid of collagen.

MARK: And—the way you walked across the room . . .

TERRI: Like a panther? Sleek and sassy. Prowling—

MARK: Through the wild.

TERRI: Don't you mean, the jungle?

MARK: Yes, the . . . Wait, no! I see where you're going!

TERRI: Big deal, I was sniffing your tracks ten miles back. I'm so wild, right? The hot sun blazing. Drums beating in the distance. Pounding, pounding . . .

MARK: That's not fair—!

TERRI: Pounding that Zulu beat.

MARK: You're putting words into my mouth . . .

TERRI: No, I'm just pulling them out, liberal. [She cracks the whip, driving him back.] What good is that handbook now? Did you forget? Forget you're only supposed to talk about my mind? Forget that a liberal must never ever reveal what's really on his?

MARK: I'm sorry. I'm sorry . . . Mistress!

TERRI: On your knees, Liberal! [She runs the heel of her boot over the length of his body.] You wanted to have a little fun, didn't you? With a wild dark woman whose passions drown out all her inhibitions. [She pushes him onto his back, puts the heel to his lips.] I'll give you passion. Here's your passion.

MARK: I didn't mean to offend you.

TERRI: No, you just couldn't help it. C'mon—suck it. Like the lily-white baby boy you are.

[He fellates her heel.]

TERRI: That statistic about Black women never getting married? What'd you do—study up for today's session? You thought you could get the best of me—admit it, naughty man, or I'll have to spank your little butt purple.

MARK: I didn't study—honest!

TERRI: You hold to that story? Then Mama has no choice but to give you what you want—roll over! [He rolls onto his stomach.]

TERRI: You actually thought you could get ahead of me on current events! [She whips his rear over the next sequence.]

MARK: No, I mean—that statistic—it was just—

TERRI: Just *what?*

MARK: Just street knowledge!

TERRI: Street knowledge? Where do you hang out—the Census Bureau? Liar! [*She pokes at his body with the handle of her whip.*] Don't you know you'll never defeat me? This is your game—to play all the races—but me—I've already become all races. You came to the wrong place, sucker. Inside this costume live the intimate experiences of ethnic groups that haven't even been born. [*pause*] Get up. I'm left sickened by that little attempt to assert your will. We'll have to come up with something really good for such an infraction.

MARK: Can I—can I become Chinese again?

TERRI: What is your problem? It's not our practice to take requests from the customers.

MARK: I—don't want you to make things easy on me. I want to go back to what you call a position of weakness. I want you to pull the ropes tight!

TERRI: [*laughs*] It's a terrible problem with masochists, really. You don't know whether being cruel is actually the ultimate kindness. You wanna be the lowest of the low? Then beg for it.

[*He remains in a supplicant position for this ritual, as she casually tends to her chores.*]

MARK: I desire to be the lowest of men.

TERRI: Why?

MARK: Because my existence is an embarrassment to all women.

TERRI: And why is that?

MARK: Because my mind is dirty, filled with hateful thoughts against them. Threats my weakling body can never make good on—but I give my intentions away at every turn—my lustful gaze can't help but give offense.

TERRI: Is that why you desire punishment?

MARK: Yes. I desire punishment.

TERRI: But you'll never dominate your mistress, will you? [*pause*] Will you?! [*She cracks her whip.*] All right. Have it your way. I think there's an idea brewing in that tiny brain of yours. You saw me stumble earlier tonight— then, you felt a thrill of exhilaration—however short-lived—with your 40 percent statistic. All of a sudden, your hopes are raised, aren't they? God, it pisses me off more than anything to see hope in a man's eyes. It's always the final step before rape. [*pause*] It's time to nip hope in the bud. You'll be your Chinese man, and me—I'll be an Asian woman, too. [*pause*] Have you been staring at me across the office—Mark Wong?

MARK: Who? Me?

TERRI: I don't see anyone else in the room.

MARK: I have to admit—

TERRI: What?

MARK: You are . . . very attractive.

TERRI: It's good to admit these things. Don't you feel a lot better already? You've been staring at me, haven't you?

MARK: Maybe . . .

TERRI: No, you don't mean "maybe."

MARK: My eyes can't help but notice . . .

TERRI: You mean, "Yes, sir, that's my baby." The only other Asian American in this office.

MARK: It does seem like we might have something in common.

TERRI: Like what?

MARK: Like—where'd your parents come from?

TERRI: Mom's from Chicago, Dad's from Stockton.

MARK: Oh.

TERRI: You didn't expect me to say "Hong Kong" or "Hiroshima," did you?

MARK: No, I mean—

TERRI: Because that would be a stereotype. Why—are *you* a foreigner?

MARK: No.

TERRI: I didn't necessarily think so—

MARK: I was born right here in Los Angeles!

TERRI: But when you ask a question like that, I'm not sure.

MARK: Queen of Angels Hospital!

TERRI: Mmmm. What else do you imagine we might have in common?

MARK: Well, do you ever . . . feel like people are pigeonholing you? Like they assume things?

TERRI: What kinds of things?

MARK: Like you're probably a whiz at math and science? Or else a Vietcong?

TERRI: No! I was editor of the paper in high school, and the literary journal in college.

MARK: Look, maybe we're getting off on the wrong foot, here.

TERRI: Actually, there *is* one group of people that does categorize me, now that you mention it.

MARK: So you *do* understand.

TERRI: Asian men. [*pause*] Asian men who just assume because we shared space in a genetic pond millions of years ago that I'm suddenly their property when I walk into a room. Or an office. [*pause*] Now get this straight. I'm not interested in you, OK? In fact, I'm generally not attracted to Asian men. I don't have anything against them personally, I just don't date them as a species.

MARK: Don't you think that's a little prejudiced? That you're not interested in me because of my race? And it's even your own? I met this Black girl a few minutes ago—she seems to support *her* brothers.

TERRI: Well, her brothers are probably a lot cuter than mine. Look, it's a free country. Why don't you do the same? Date a Caucasian woman.

MARK: I tried that too . . . a couple of women back.

TERRI: I'll tell you why you don't. Because you Asian men are all alike—you're looking for someone who reminds you of your mothers. Who'll smile at the lousiest jokes and spoon rice into your bowl while you just sit and grunt. Well, I'm not about to date any man who reminds me even slightly of my father.

MARK: But a blonde rejected me because I *didn't* remind her of her father.

TERRI: Of course you didn't! You're Asian!

MARK: And now, you won't date me because I *do* remind you of yours?

TERRI: Of course you do! You're Asian!

[*pause*]

MARK: How—how can I win here?

TERRI: It's simple. You can't. Have you ever heard of historical karma? That's the notion that cultures have pasts that eventually catch up with them. For instance, white Americans were evil enough to bring Africans here in chains—now, they should pay for that legacy. Similarly, Asian men have oppressed their women for centuries. Now, they're paying for their crime by being passed over for dates in favor of white men. It's a beautiful way to look at history, when you think about it.

MARK: Why should my love life suffer for crimes I didn't even commit? I'm an American!

TERRI: C'mon—you don't expect me to buck the wheel of destiny, do you? This is the 1990s—every successful Asian woman walks in on the arm of a white man.

MARK: But—but what about Italian men? Or Latinos? Do you like them?

TERRI: I find them attractive enough, yes.

MARK: Well, what about their cultures? Aren't they sexist?

TERRI: Why do you stereotype people like that? If pressed, I would characterize them as macho.

MARK: Macho? And Asian men aren't?

TERRI: No—you're just sexist.

MARK: What's the difference?

TERRI: The—I dunno. Macho is . . . sexier, that's all. You've never been known as the most assertive of men.

MARK: How can we be not assertive enough and too oppressive all at the same time?

TERRI: It's one of the miracles of your psychology. Is it any wonder no one wants to date you?

MARK: Aaargh! You can't reject me on such faulty reasoning!

TERRI: I can reject you for any reason I want. That's one of the things which makes courtship so exciting. [*pause*] It seems obvious now, the way you feel about me, doesn't it?

MARK: It does not!

TERRI: C'mon—whether Black, blonde, or Asian—I think the answer is the same. You . . . what?

MARK: I . . . find you attractive . . .

TERRI: Give it up! You feel something—something that's driving you crazy.

MARK: All right! You win! I love you!

TERRI: Really? You do? Why, young man—I had no idea! [*pause*] I'm sorry . . . but I could never return your affections, you being so very unlovable and all. In fact, your feelings offend me. And so I have no choice but to punish you.

MARK: I understand. You win again. [*He heads for the shackles.*]

TERRI: Say it again. Like you mean it.

MARK: You win! I admit it!

TERRI: Not that—the other part!

MARK: You mean, I love you? Mistress Terri, I love you.

TERRI: No! More believable! The last thing anyone wants is an apathetic slave!

MARK: But I *do* love you! More than any woman—

TERRI: Or man?

MARK: Or anything—any creature—any impulse . . . in my own body—more than any part of my body . . . that's how much I love you.

[*pause*]

TERRI: You're still not doing it right, damn it!

MARK: I'm screaming it like I always do—I was almost getting poetic, there . . .

TERRI: Shut up! It's just not good enough. *You're* not good enough. I won't be left unsatisfied. Come here.

MARK: But—

TERRI: You wanna know a secret? It doesn't matter what you say—there's one thing that always makes your words ring false—one thing that lets me know you're itching to oppress me.

MARK: Wha—what do you mean?

TERRI: I don't think you want to hear it. But maybe . . . maybe I want to tell you anyway.

MARK: Tell me! I can take the punishment.

TERRI: What sickens me most . . . is that you feel compelled to play these kinds of parlor games with me.

MARK: What—what the hell are you—?!

TERRI: I mean, how can you even talk about love? When you can't approach me like a normal human being? When you have to hide behind masks and take on these ridiculous roles?

MARK: You're patronizing me! Don't! Get those chains on me!

TERRI: Patronizing? No, I've *been* patronizing you. Today, I can't even keep up the charade! I mean, your entire approach here—it lets me know—

MARK: I don't have to stand for this!

TERRI: That you're afraid of any woman unless you're sure you've got her under control!

MARK: This is totally against all the rules of the house!

TERRI: Rules, schmules! The rules say I'm supposed to grind you under my heel! They leave the details to me—sadism is an art, not a science. So—beg for more! Beg me to tell you about yourself!

[*Panicked,* MARK *heads for the wall and tries to insert his own wrists into the shackles.*]

MARK: No! If I'm—If I'm defeated, I must accept my punishment fair and square.

TERRI: You're square all right. Get your arms out of there! Stand like a man! Beg me to tell you who you are.

MARK: If I obey, will you reward me by denying my request?

TERRI: Who knows? Out of generosity, I might suddenly decide to grant it.

MARK: If you're determined to tell me either way, why should I bother to beg?

TERRI: For your own enjoyment.

MARK: I refuse! You've never done something like this before!

TERRI: That's why I'm so good at my job. I don't allow cruelty to drift into routine. Now, beg!

MARK: Please, Mistress Terri . . . will you . . . will you tell me who I really am?

TERRI: You want to know—you wanna know bad, don't you?

MARK: No!

TERRI: In the language of sadomasochism, "no" almost always means "yes."

MARK: No, no, no!

TERRI: You are an eager one, aren't you?

MARK: I just don't like you making assumptions about me! Do you think I'm some kind of emotional weakling, coming in here because I can't face the real world of women?

TERRI: That would be a fairly good description of all our clients.

MARK: Maybe I'm a lot more clever than you think! Do you ever go out there? Do you know the opportunities for pain and humiliation that lurk outside these walls?

TERRI: Well, I . . . I *do* buy groceries, you know.

MARK: The rules out there are set up so we're all bound to lose.

TERRI: And the rules in here are so much better?

MARK: The rules here . . . protect me from harm. Out there—I walk around with my face exposed. In here, when I'm rejected, beaten down, humiliated—it's not me. I have no identifying features, and so . . . I'm no longer human. [*pause*] And that's why I'm not pathetic to come here. Because someday, I'm going to beat you. And on that day, my skin will have become so thick, I'll be impenetrable to harm. I won't need a mask to keep my face hidden. I'll have lost myself in the armor. [*He places his wrists into the wall shackles.*] OK—I bent to your will. You defeated me again. So strap me up. Punish me.

TERRI: But why . . . why all these fantasies about race?

MARK: Please, enough!

TERRI: I mean, what race *are* you, anyway?

MARK: You know, maybe we should just talk about *your* real life, how would you like that?

[*pause*]

TERRI: Is that what you want?

MARK: No . . .

TERRI: Is that a "no" no, or a "yes" no?

MARK: Yes. No. Goddamn it, I paid for my punishment, just give it to me!

[*She tosses away her whip and begins to strap him up.*]

MARK: What are you doing?

TERRI: Punishment is, by definition, something the victim does not appreciate. The fact that you express such a strong preference for the whip practically compels me not to use it. [*pause*] I think I'd prefer . . . to kill you with kindness. [*She begins kissing the length of his body.*]

MARK: Please! This isn't . . . what I want!

TERRI: Are you certain? Maybe . . . I feel something for you. After all, you've made me so very angry. Maybe . . . you're a white man, I'm a white woman—there's nothing mysterious—no racial considerations whatsoever.

MARK: That's . . . too easy! There's no reason you wouldn't love me under those conditions.

TERRI: Are you crazy? I can think of a couple dozen off the top of my head. You don't have to be an ethnic minority to have a sucky love life.

MARK: But there's no . . . natural barrier between us!

TERRI: Baby, you haven't dated many white women as a white man lately. I think it's time to change all that. [*Pause.* TERRI *steps away.*] So—Mark . . . Walker. Mark Walker—how long has it been? Since anyone's given you a rubdown like that?

MARK: [*after a pause*] I usually . . . avoid these kinds of situations . . .

TERRI: Why are you so afraid?

MARK: My fright is reasonable. Given the conditions out there.

TERRI: What conditions? Do you have, for instance, problems with . . . interracial love?

MARK: Whatever gave you that idea?

TERRI: Well, you . . . remind me of a man I see sometimes . . . who belongs to all races . . . and none at all. I've never met anyone like him before.

MARK: I'm a white man! Why wouldn't I have problems? The world is changing so fast around me—you can't even tell whose country it is any more. I can't hardly open my mouth without wondering if I'm offending, if I'm secretly revealing to everyone but myself . . . some hatred, some hidden desire to strike back . . . breeding within my body. [*pause*]

If only there were some certainty—whatever it might be—OK, let the feminists rule the place! We'll call it the United States of Amazonia! Or the Japanese! Or the gays! If I could only figure out who's in charge, then I'd know where I stand. But this constant flux—who can endure it? I'd rather crawl into a protected room where I know what to expect—painful though that place may be. [*pause*]

I mean . . . we're heading towards the millennium. Last time, people ran fearing the end of the world. They hid their bodies from the storms that would inevitably follow. Casual gestures were taken as signs of betrayal and accusation. Most sensed that the righteous would somehow be separated from the wicked. But no one knew on which side of such a division they themselves might fall.

[*Silence*]

TERRI: You want to hear about yourself. You've been begging for it so long—
in so many ways.

MARK: How do you know I just said anything truthful? What makes you so
sure I'm really a white man?

TERRI: Oh, I'm not. After all these months, I wouldn't even care to guess.
When you say you're Egyptian, Italian, Spanish, Mayan—you seem to be
the real thing. So what if we just say . . . [*Pause. She releases him.*] You're a
man, and you're frightened, and you've been ill-used in love. You've come
to doubt any trace of your own judgment. You cling to the hope that power
over a woman will blunt her ability to harm you, while all the time you're
tormented by the growing fear that your hunger will never be satisfied with
the milk of cruelty. [*pause*] I know. I've been in your place.

MARK: You . . . you've been a man? What are you saying?

TERRI: You tell me. Fight back. Tell me about me. And make me love every
second of it.

MARK: All right. Yes.

TERRI: Yes . . . WHO?

MARK: Yes, Mistress Terri!

TERRI: Yes—who?

MARK: Yes . . . whoever you are . . . a woman who's tried hard to hate men for
what they've done to her but who . . . can't quite convince herself.

[*She pushes him to the floor.*]

TERRI: Is that what you think? [*beat*] Tell me more . . .

MARK: You went out—into the world . . . I dunno, after college maybe—I think
you went to college . . .

TERRI: Doesn't matter.

MARK: But the world—it didn't turn out the way you planned . . . rejection
hung in the air all around you—in the workplace, in movies, in the casual
joking of the population. The painful struggle . . . to be accepted as a spirit
among others . . . only to find yourself constantly weighed and measured by
those outward bits of yourself so easily grasped, too easily understood.
Maybe you were harassed at work—maybe even raped—I don't know.

TERRI: It doesn't matter. The specifics never matter.

MARK: So you found your way here—somehow—back of the *Hollywood Star*—
something—roomsfull of men begging to be punished for the way they act
out there—wanting you to even the score—and you decided—that this was
a world you could call your own.

TERRI: And so, I learned what it feels like to be a man. To labor breathlessly, accumulating power while all the time it's dawning how tiring, what a burden, how utterly numbing—it is actually to possess. The touch of power is cold like metal. It chafes the skin, but you know nothing better to hold to your breast. So you travel down this blind road of hunger—constantly victimizing yourself in the person of others—until you despair of ever again feeling warm or safe—until you forget such possibilities exist. Until they become sentimental relics of a weaker man's delusions. And driven by your need, you slowly destroy yourself. [*She starts to remove her gloves.*] Unless, one day, you choose to try something completely different.

MARK: What are you doing? Wait!

TERRI: It's a new game, Mark. A new ethnic game. The kind you like.

MARK: We can't play—without costumes.

TERRI: Oh, but it's the wildest inter-racial fantasy of all. It's called . . . two hearts meeting in a bondage parlor on the outskirts of Encino. With skins—more alike than not. [*She tosses her gloves away.*] Haven't we met before? I'm certain we have. You were the one who came into my chamber wanting to play all the races.

MARK: Why are you doing this to me? I'm the customer here!

TERRI: No, you're time is up. Or haven't you kept your eyes on the clock? At least I know I'm not leaving you bored.

MARK: Then . . . shouldn't I be going?

TERRI: If you like. But I'm certain we've met before. I found it so interesting, so different, your fantasy. And I've always been a good student, a diligent employee. My daddy raised me to take pride in all of America's service professions. So I started to . . . try and understand all the races I never thought of as my own. Then, what happened?

MARK: You're asking me?

TERRI: C'mon—let me start you off. I have a box in my closet—[*She runs her bare hands up and down his body as he speaks.*]

MARK: In which you keep all the research you've done . . . for me. Every clipping, magazine article, ethnic journals, transcripts from Phil Donahue. Blacks against Jews in Crown Heights—your eyes went straight to the headlines. The rise of neo-Nazism in Marseilles and Orange County. And then, further—the mass-murderer in Canada who said, "The feminists made me do it." You became a collector of all the rejection and rage in this world. [*pause*] Am I on the right track?

TERRI: Is that what you've been doing?

MARK: And that box—that box is overflowing now. Books are piled high to the hems of your dresses, clippings slide out from beneath the door. And you

... you looked at it ... maybe this morning ... and you realized your box was ... full. And so you began to stumble. You started to feel there was nothing more here for you.

TERRI: If you say it, it must be true.

MARK: Is it?

TERRI: [*She starts to unlace her thigh-high boots.*] I'm prepared to turn in my uniform and start again from here.

MARK: You're quitting your job?

TERRI: The masks don't work. The leather is pointless. I'm giving notice as we speak.

MARK: But—what if I'm wrong?

TERRI: I'm afraid I'll have to take that chance.

MARK: No, you can't just—what about your hatred of men? Are you really going to just throw it all away when it's served you so well?

TERRI: I've been a man. I've been a woman. I've been colorful and colorless. And now, I'm tired of hating myself.

[*pause*]

MARK: And what about me?

TERRI: That's something you'll have to decide.

MARK: I'm not sure I can leave you. Not after all this time.

TERRI: Then stay. And strip. As lovers often do. [*As* TERRI *removes her costume,* MARK *turns and looks away.*]

MARK: I worry when I think about the coming millennium—because it feels like all labels have to be re-written, all assumptions re-examined, all associations re-defined. The rules that governed behavior in the last era are crumbling, but those of the time to come have yet to be written. And there is a struggle brewing over the shape of these changing words, a struggle that begins here, now, in our hearts, in our shuttered rooms, in the lightning decisions that appear from nowhere.

[TERRI *has stripped off everything but her hood. Beneath her costume she wears a simple bra and panties.* MARK *turns to look at her.*]

MARK: I think you're very beautiful.

TERRI: Even without the metal and leather?

MARK: You look ... soft and warm and gentle to the touch.

TERRI: I'm about to remove my hood. I'm giving you fair warning.

MARK: There's ... only one thing I never managed to achieve here. I never managed to defeat you.

TERRI: You understand me. Shouldn't I be a lot more frightened? But—the customer is always right. So come over here. This is my final command to you.

MARK: Yes, Mistress Terri.

TERRI: Take off my hood. You want to—admit it.

MARK: Yes. I want to.

TERRI: The moment you remove this hood, I'll be completely exposed, while you remain fully covered. And you'll have your victory by the rules of our engagement, while I—I'll fly off over the combat zone. [TERRI *places* MARK'*s left hand on her hood.*] So congratulations. And good-bye.

[*With his right hand,* MARK *undoes his own hood instead. It comes off. He is an Asian man.*]

TERRI: You disobeyed me.

MARK: I love you.

[*She removes her own hood. She's a Caucasian woman.*]

TERRI: I think you're very beautiful, too.

[MARK *starts to remove the rest of his costume.*]

TERRI: At a moment like this, I can't help but wonder, was it all so terribly necessary? Did we have to wander so far afield to reach a point which comes, when it does at last, so naturally?

MARK: I was afraid. I was an Asian man.

TERRI: And I was a woman, of any description.

MARK: Why are we talking as if those facts were behind us?

TERRI: Well, we have determined to move beyond the world of fantasy . . . haven't we?

[MARK'*s costume is off. He stands in simple boxer shorts. They cross the stage toward one another.*]

MARK: But tell the truth—would you have dated me? If I'd come to you first like this?

TERRI: Who knows? Anything's possible. This is the 1990s.

[MARK *touches her hair. They gaze at each other's faces, as lights fade to black.*]

CURTAIN

The Conversion of Ka'ahumanu

by
VICTORIA NALANI KNEUBUHL

CAST OF CHARACTERS

SYBIL MOSELY BINGHAM (30s, Caucasian)

LUCY GOODALE THURSTON (30s, Caucasian)

KA'AHUMANU (40s Hawaiian)

HANNAH GRIMES (20s Hapa haole [Hawaiian/Caucasian])

PALI (20s Hawaiian)

THE SET:
1. Downstage center: a free open space (playing area)
2. Downstage right: a simple set to suggest the parlor of the mission house (MH). No backdrop, but simple set pieces; a table with benches and a few chairs, one of which should be a Boston rocker.
3. Behind the playing area: On a slightly raised platform is a lauhala mat with pillows, perhaps a small Western table. This may be backed by a simple panel to suggest the wall of a hale pili (grass house). This is KA'AHUMANU's house (KH).

4. Downstage left: a lauhala mat covered with a small Chinese rug, a table behind it with a pretty candelabra, a nice chair, as well as cushions on the mat. This is HANNAH GRIMES's house (HH).

The Conversion of Ka'ahumanu *was first presented by Kumu Kahua Theatre at Tenny Theatre, Honolulu, on September 1, 1988. Professor Juli Burk served as dramaturg. The production was directed by Dale Daigle, with the following cast:*

SYBIL BINGHAM	*Katherine Lepani*
LUCY THURSTON	*Jana Lindan*
KA'AHUMANU	*Leonelle Anderson Akana*
HANNAH GRIMES	*Kehaunani Koenig*
PALI	*Nark*

Set design: Joseph D. Dodd; light design; Dale Daigle; costumes: Victoria Nalani Kneubuhl.

―――――――――

ACT I
SCENE ONE

[*Spot to* SYBIL *in the playing area.*]

SYBIL: In 1815, I, Sybil Mosely, felt the calling of our Lord and Saviour Jesus Christ. I confessed my faith before the congregation and now cling to the bosom of the church. Though I am a sinner, I now have hope that God will call me his own and receive me at his right hand.

[*Spot to* LUCY *in the playing area.*]

LUCY: In 1815, I, Lucy Goodale, was washed in the blood of our Lord Jesus. My family rejoiced in my pious calling. I do now truly believe and trust that dear redeemer who tasted death for us all.

SYBIL: In 1819, I am of low spirits. A kindred spirit to whom I was dearly attached has now departed from my life to serve God in another part of the world. I know not where my life is going or what the Lord would have me do. I feel many days of loneliness and sorrow. The joy I once felt at teaching these young girls slowly drains away, and I feel heavy with a weight I can neither understand nor overcome. I read of women who do mission work among the heathen peoples of this earth. I envy them; that they have a purpose and service to God. I pray that one day I might find such a purpose.

LUCY: In 1819, my mother died. My dear sister, Persis, was married and left our father's home. My mother, gone! Persis, gone! Wonder not when I say, that I more than ever felt myself an orphan. My solitary chamber witnesses my grief as I walk from side to side. My pillow is watered with tears. I apply to the fountain of all grace and consolation for support. I devote my life to the will of the supreme.

SYBIL: My prayers were heard! Today I go to Goshen, Connecticut, to meet one who is perhaps of the same heart and mind as I. A young man about to embark on a life of mission work in the Sandwich Islands seeks a companion for this noble cause. God will guide me.

LUCY: My cousin William visited me today. He gave me information that a mission to the Sandwich Islands was to sail in four-to-six weeks. He dwelt upon it with interest and feeling. Imagine my surprise to hear him say, "Will Lucy, by becoming connected with a missionary, now an entire stranger, attach herself to this small band of pilgrims and bring the word of the gospel to a land of darkness?" Now I feel the need of guidance! Oh, that my sister were here!

[SYBIL *and* LUCY *move together.*]

SYBIL: On October 11, 1819, I was joined in Holy Matrimony to the Reverend Hiram Bingham.

LUCY: On October 12, 1819, I was joined in Holy Matrimony to the Reverend Asa Thurston.

SYBIL: On October 23, 1819, we set sail as members of a pioneer company of missionaries to the Sandwich Islands.

LUCY: Like Rebecca, we have said, "I will go."

[SYBIL *and* LUCY *wave goodbye as if on a ship. The lights dim and* LUCY *steps out of the light.*]

SCENE TWO

[*A spot to* KA'AHUMANU *in the playing area.*]

KA'AHUMANU: Here is why I, Ka'ahumanu, Kuhina nui and widow of Kamehameha have done these things. For many years now we have seen these haole, these foreign men among us. We know that they break the kapu laws. Do the Gods come to punish them? No! Some of the women have gone to the ships and have eaten with these haole men. Do the Gods come to punish them? No! So why should it be that they will come to punish us at all? I think these beliefs are nothing, false. And here is another thing. We know where the punishment comes from. It does not come from Gods. It comes from men. It comes from the priests who grow greedy for power. And who is it who hates most this kapu law of eating? We, women of the ali'i. We do not want a lowly place any more, and the men of the priesthood will see this! [*She laughs*] You should have seen the fear in their faces when we sat to eat. Hewahewa made a great prayer to the Gods. Liholiho, the king, approached the women's table. Many of the faces in the crowd became as white as the full moon. Liholiho sat with us to eat. He ate and the people waited in silence, waited for the terrible wrath of the Gods . . . which never came! Then a great cry rose from the women " `Ai noa, `ai noa! The kapu laws are ended! The Gods are false."

[*Blackout*]

SCENE THREE

[*The sound of a rough sea.* SYBIL *enters.*]

SYBIL: What can I say to you my sisters this morning? I can tell you. Could your eye glance across the great water and catch this little bark ascending and descending the mountainous waves which contain your dear sister, your hands would be involuntarily extended for her relief and your cry would be to save her. The sea runs very high, while the wind runs through the naked rigging as you may have heard it in a November's day, through the leafless trees of a majestic forest. The dashing of the waves on deck, the frequent falling of something below, the violent motion of the vessel, going up and then down, would seem to conspire to terrify and distress. Yet, I feel my mind calm as if by a winter's fire in my own land. Is this not the mercy of God?

[LUCY *moves into the light. She is somewhat nervous.*]

SYBIL: Lucy, what are you doing out here?
LUCY: I felt so sick shut up in there!
SYBIL: It's very rough.
LUCY: How long have we been at sea?
SYBIL: About 60 days.
LUCY: And still not half-way there.

SYBIL: Lucy, are you all right?

LUCY: I'm frightened by the sea today.

SYBIL: [placing her arm around her] You are safe.

LUCY: What do you think will really happen to us, Sybil?

SYBIL: I don't know, Lucy.

LUCY: [building] You know anything, anything could happen to us out here in the sea, in the middle of nowhere. No one would know and no one would care. Why did I come here?

SYBIL: God called you.

LUCY: Suppose they don't want us in their islands? Suppose they aren't friendly? The sailors say . . .

SYBIL: Don't listen to what the sailors say!

LUCY: I hate the ocean and I hate this ship? [she sinks down]

SYBIL: Now we must lean on Him. Give all your thoughts and all your fears to Him.

LUCY: I'm trying.

SYBIL: And think on the poor heathen, Lucy, whose immortal souls languish in darkness. Who will give them the Bible and tell them of the Saviour if not us? Think of the Hawaiian people who will enjoy that grace because someone such as Lucy Thurston was willing to say "I will go."

[Blackout]

SCENE FOUR

[Lights to HH. HANNAH sits playing with a ribbon. PALI enters from the playing area.]

PALI: Hannah, Hannah, have you heard?

HANNAH: What?

PALI: A war!

HANNAH: What are you talking about?

PALI: On Hawai'i.

HANNAH: Get in here and be quiet.

PALI: Why?

HANNAH: My father is drinking with some haole men. When they get drunk, they might come looking for me.

PALI: I'm glad my father isn't a haole.

HANNAH: Hah! You don't even know who your father is.

PALI: I do so!

HANNAH: Who then, who? . . . See? You don't know.

PALI: Well, at least I'm not chased around by haole men.

HANNAH: Because you aren't as pretty as me.

PALI: No, because I'm not hapa haole. I don't look like them.

HANNAH: They aren't so bad. It's only when they're sick with rum.

PALI: Are haole men better than a kanaka?

HANNAH: I never went with a kanaka. My father would beat me until I couldn't walk. Besides, now I'm Davis's woman.

PALI: Will you have another baby with him?

HANNAH: Shut up, Pali. You're nothing but a chicken, clucking gossip all over the village. Now, tell me of this battle.

PALI: No, you told me to shut up. You think I'm stupid?

HANNAH: All right, I'm sorry. Tell me.

PALI: No!

HANNAH: Come on, Pali. Look, I'll give you this pretty ribbon, see? Everyone will envy you.

PALI: What should I do with it?

HANNAH: Tie it up in your hair. See how pretty it is?

PALI: Where did you get this?

HANNAH: I have a lot of them.

PALI: You're lucky.

HANNAH: Now tell me.

PALI: It's because of the free eating and the defying of the kapu. The chief, Kekuaokalani, and his followers don't like the old Gods going. He doesn't like the way Ka'ahumanu has begun to burn the images in the temples. He will fight with Ka'ahumanu and Liholiho.

HANNAH: My father said this would happen.

PALI: What do you think of the kapu?

HANNAH: Lies!

PALI: How do you know?

HANNAH: I know! There are no such foolish beliefs in other places. I have heard the talk of foreigners.

PALI: And there is never any punishment?

HANNAH: No! And be quiet! I told you, I don't want them to hear us.

PALI: Blood will be spilled.

HANNAH: It's a foolish war. A fight over nothing.

PALI: Everyone knows Ka'ahumanu will win.

HANNAH: I don't care, my life won't change.

[Lights down]

SCENE FIVE

[*Lights to KH. KA'AHUMANU sits on her mats.*]

KA'AHUMANU: I knew our lives would change forever. I knew that when I did this thing. There was blood spilled. Turmoil rose among the people. Kekuaokalani moved his forces out of Ka'awaloa. We met them at Kuamo'o. We had guns, that is why we won. From Kamehameha, I learned to strike swiftly and with strength. But my heart weeps for the death of Kekuaokalani and his faithful woman, Manono, who fought by his side. Now the old Gods have lost their power, and will go. [*Pause*] Have I done right? Or have I done great evil? I took down what I knew to be false, but will I, Ka'ahumanu, be able to guide these islands, be able to guide the people? The people now have no Gods, only the ali'i. How will I steer the canoe?

[*Enter* PALI]

PALI: My Ali'i.
KA'AHUMANU: Ah, Pali, my pua. You are well?
PALI: Yes, thank you. [*Pause*] A ship has come.
KA'AHUMANU: [*sighs*] Many ships come. Too many.
PALI: This one brings white men and—
KA'AHUMANU: They all bring white men.
PALI: And haole women! And they say they are bringing a new God!
KA'AHUMANU: Women?
PALI: [*excited*] `Ae!
KA'AHUMANU: This is a new sight. Perhaps I will come to see them—after I go fishing. You will come fishing with me?
PALI: Well, if it is your wish.
KA'AHUMANU: No, I can see your mind is filled with wondering about these haole women. Go and satisfy this longing.
PALI: Oh, thank you, thank you. I will tell you everything that I see.

[*Lights down on KH. Lights up on the playing area.*]

SCENE SIX

[*Lights to* SYBIL *and* LUCY *in the playing area.*]

SYBIL: Lucy! Come you can see them!
LUCY: There are hundreds, maybe thousands of them.

SYBIL: They look so dark. It's hard to see in this blinding light.

LUCY: They'll be closer in a minute.

SYBIL: How beautiful the mountains are.

LUCY: My feet won't know how to walk on solid ground again.

SYBIL: Look! Now they're closer. I see a man waving to us.

LUCY: Where?

SYBIL: In that canoe. Next to the woman holding coconuts.

LUCY: Where? Oh, there! [*Pause*] Oh Sybil, those are not coconuts!

SYBIL: No? Oh, my, no.

LUCY: Look at them!

SYBIL: Hundreds of them—   ·

LUCY: All of them—

SYBIL AND LUCY: Naked!

LUCY: [*terribly nervous*] What shall we do?

SYBIL: [*also nervous*] Compose ourselves. We must compose ourselves.

LUCY: What? They're getting closer.

SYBIL: Now, we must try to act naturally.

LUCY: Naturally? Yes, we must. But it's disgusting. Even the men.

SYBIL: Well, don't look! There I mean.

LUCY: Where? Where shall we look?

SYBIL: Lower your eyes and wave politely.

[LUCY *and* SYBIL *lower their eyes and wave politely.* LUCY *speaks straight to audience.*]

LUCY: I had never conceived in my life that I would ever see such a sight. To describe the dress and demeanor of these creatures I would have to make use of uncouth and indelicate language. To the civilized eye their covering is revoltingly scanty, to say the least. I have never felt such shame or embarrassment as when I first beheld these children of nature.

SYBIL: I saw them first as a swarming mass of dark savages, and even as I looked into their eyes I asked myself, can they be human? But the answer came to me: Yes! God made these people, they have immortal souls, yes they are human and can be brought to know and love our Saviour.

LUCY: Some of the women are grotesquely large.

SYBIL: Mountainous!

LUCY: Some chiefesses have Western cloth wrapped about them.

SYBIL: In something which resembles a Roman toga.

LUCY: . . . But is thoroughly immodest.

SYBIL AND LUCY: [*holding hands*] Here we will begin God's work.

[LUCY and SYBIL *freeze*. HANNAH and PALI *enter. They walk around the women as if examining objects.* LUCY and SYBIL *remain frozen.*]

HANNAH: Look how they cover up their bodies so!
PALI: Auē!
HANNAH: Look at this white hand.
PALI: What puny bodies! What sickly pink skin!
HANNAH: [*lifting up a dress*] Their legs are like sticks.
PALI: They look all pinched up in the middle . . .
HANNAH: . . . And wide at the top.
PALI: Their eyes are so small.
HANNAH: They have no smiles.
PALI: I'm sure it's because they are so thin and sickly.
HANNAH: Maybe they would improve with bathing in the sea, and lying about in the sun. [*She takes* PALI *aside*] Now we have learned something. This is just why many haole men who come to these islands go so crazy over our women. It is because haole women are so revoltingly ugly. How could a man find any desire for such a creature? Auwe! It must be hard for them to get children. I pity them, poor things. I will send them some food.

[SYBIL and LUCY *come to life. They approach* HANNAH and PALI, *offering them their hands.*]

SYBIL: Aloha.
PALI: [*shaking hands*] Aloha.
LUCY: [*to* HANNAH] Aloha.   SYBIL: [*to* PALI] Aloha.
PALI: Aloha.   HANNAH: Aloha.
LUCY: Aloha.
HANNAH: Aloha.

[KA'AHUMANU *enters regally, with an air of disdain.* SYBIL and LUCY *timidly approach her.*]

SYBIL: [*offering her hand*] Aloha, Your Majesty.

[KA'AHUMANU *haughtily extends her baby finger.*]

LUCY: [*stepping back, afraid*] Aloha . . .
SYBIL: [*haltingly*] Your, um, Majesty, we bring a message of hope.
KA'AHUMANU: Oh?
LUCY: Of Jesus.
SYBIL: The one true God, the blessed Jehovah—

KA'AHUMANU: [*insistent*] We don't need a new God. Why do you wear so much clothes?

SYBIL: This is the way ladies of America dress.

LUCY: Proper ladies.

KA'AHUMANU: [*fingering their clothes*] I wish to try such clothes. You will make one for me.

SYBIL: Yes, I think we could.

KA'AHUMANU: I will send you cloth.

LUCY: Perhaps you yourself would like to learn to sew.

KA'AHUMANU: Sew?

SYBIL: Yes, it is how we make clothes.

KA'AHUMANU: No! I want you to make it for me.

LUCY: [*flustered*] Oh! Yes! We know, I mean, I only thought that—

KA'AHUMANU: Why do you come to these islands? What do you want?

LUCY: Want?

KA'AHUMANU: Yes. Is it sandalwood? Whale oil? Your men come for women? What do you want?

SYBIL: [*quickly*] We don't want anything like that.

LUCY: Oh, no.

SYBIL: We want to bring you the good news of our Lord and Saviour Jesus Christ.

KA'AHUMANU: The news of Jesus Christ?

LUCY: Yes.

KA'AHUMANU: Why should I care for news of someone I don't even know?

SYBIL: Well he is God. The blessed son of—

KA'AHUMANU: I do not wish to hear of a God! We have finished with Gods. Pau! I have destroyed many images, burned many heiau. I have forbidden the worship in the old temples. And the king has spoken these things to the people: We want no Gods. The Gods brought only sorrow and unhappiness to our people. We will not have that again. Let us speak of other things.

[*A silence*]

LUCY: Our God is different. He—

[KA'AHUMANU *glares at* LUCY.]

SYBIL: [*loud whisper*] Lucy, please!

KA'AHUMANU: I want clothes which are yellow. I will send yellow cloth.

SYBIL: Yes, we will be happy to do this. You must also come so that we can measure you.

KA'AHUMANU: Measure?

LUCY: So we can cut.

KA'AHUMANU: Cut?

SYBIL: To make your clothes.

KA'AHUMANU: Yes, then I will come. [*to* SYBIL] You have a kind face, but very sad.

SYBIL: [*shyly*] Thank you. When you come, perhaps we will talk a little more.

KA'AHUMANU: Paha, perhaps.

SYBIL: So we may come to know each others ways.

KA'AHUMANU: Paha.

[*Exit the Hawaiian women.* LUCY *and* SYBIL *join hands.*]

LUCY AND SYBIL: Here we will begin God's work.

SCENE SEVEN

[LUCY *and* SYBIL *move into the Mission House area. They immediately begin to dust, sweep, and go through other actions of housekeeping, as they repeat phrases in Hawaiian.*]

LUCY: Aloha.

SYBIL: Aloha kakahiaka.

LUCY: Aloha awakea.

SYBIL: Aloha àuinalā.

LUCY: Aloha ahiahi.

SYBIL: Pehea `oe?

LUCY: Maika'i, pehea `oe?

SYBIL: `Ano māluhiluhi au.

[HANNAH *and* PALI *enter the playing area as they speak.* SYBIL *and* LUCY *continue to go through the motions of housework while mumbling to themselves in Hawaiian.*]

PALI: But why do you think she likes me, Hannah?

HANNAH: I don't know.

PALI: I know she likes you because you are pretty and smart.

HANNAH: [*laughing*] And because I know all of the gossip amongst the foreigners.

PALI: But why should she pick me?

HANNAH: I don't know. She just picks her favorites. Shall we look in at the mikanele?

PALI: Yes.

[HANNAH *and* PALI *look in at the mission women.* SYBIL *is dusting while* LUCY *sews.*]

PALI: Look at them. They're always busy.
HANNAH: Till their faces make water.
PALI: Why do they do that?
HANNAH: It's their way. [*She calls out.*] Aloha e, Mrs. Bingham, Mrs. Thurston.

[SYBIL *and* LUCY *stop. They come to meet* HANNAH *and* PALI.]

SYBIL: Good day, Hannah.
HANNAH: Good day.
SYBIL: Where are you going?
HANNAH: To the house of Ka'ahumanu. [*to* LUCY] Are you making a sail?
LUCY: A sail?
HANNAH: Yes, like the sailors, with a needle, in and out.
LUCY: Why no, this is how we sew. How we make dresses.
HANNAH: [*excited*] Are you making a dress? I would like to have a dress!
SYBIL: No, Hannah, she's just fixing a tear in her apron.
HANNAH: You tore your beautiful clothes? How?
LUCY: A fight in the village this morning.
PALI: You got into a fight?!
SYBIL: Oh, no! She was helping someone.
LUCY: A man was being beaten for no reason that I could see.
HANNAH: There is always fighting in the village.
LUCY: This man had funny marks on his forehead and around his eyes.
PALI: A kauā. That's why he was beaten.
HANNAH: We despise them. That is why they are marked.
SYBIL: Why?
HANNAH: I don't know. They're not allowed to live among us. In the old days, they sometimes served as a sacrifice at the heiau. They are filthy people.
LUCY: They don't look any different.
PALI: That is why they are marked. So people may know them.
SYBIL: I don't understand why—
HANNAH: I don't know why. They are just no better than animals. There are many who try to pretend they don't belong to the kauā. Some of them try to give away their babies to others so the children will grow up unrecognized. I knew a girl who had a baby by a kauwa once. If that happened to me, I would kill it!

SYBIL: [*turning away*] How disgusting.

HANNAH: They are disgusting.

PALI: That is how their blood is hated.

SYBIL: I don't want to hear this talk.

LUCY: Please, we must go now. We have work to do.

[SYBIL *is obviously disturbed.* HANNAH *and* PALI *think nothing of the conversation and turn to leave.* PALI *turns back to talk to* LUCY.]

PALI: This man, he was old?

LUCY: [*not very nicely*] Somewhat; he had a limp.

PALI: A bad leg? [LUCY *nods*] Was he killed?

LUCY: No, he managed to get away.

PALI: [*with sympathy*] Ah!

LUCY: Do you—

HANNAH: Come on Pali!

PALI: [*leaves fast*] Aloha!

SCENE EIGHT

[PALI *runs to meet* HANNAH *at KH.* KA'AHUMANU *signals them to come.*]

HANNAH: Aloha e, Kuhina nui.

KA'AHUMANU: `Ae, aloha nō. You have brought Pali, I see.

HANNAH: Yes.

KA'AHUMANU: Come Pali, my pua, you comb my hair.

PALI: Yes.

KA'AHUMANU: You have been well?

PALI: Yes, thank you.

HANNAH: We stopped in to look at the mikanele.

KA'AHUMANU: What were they doing?

HANNAH: Running around, taking off dirt.

KA'AHUMANU: They always do that!

HANNAH: I don't know why they won't get someone else to do the work for them.

PALI: Perhaps it is kapu in America.

HANNAH: No, it isn't.

PALI: How do you know, Hannah?

HANNAH: Because Davis told me! [*more slowly*] Once, a long time ago.

[*long pause*]

KAʻAHUMANU: What was his sickness?

HANNAH: I don't know. My father said he died because he drank too much rum.

PALI: You must be lonely for him.

KAʻAHUMANU: You have a kind heart, Pali.

HANNAH: Not very. He was never mean to me, but he was too old. He always smelled like rum. It was my father who made me go with him for a mate. He was as old as my father.

PALI: That is not what I would like.

KAʻAHUMANU: [slyly] Well, I hear other eyes are turned your way Hannah Grimes.

PALI: Who Hannah? Tell me who!

KAʻAHUMANU: A younger man whose body speaks for itself when Hannah is near.

PALI: Who is it, Hannah?

KAʻAHUMANU: It will be good for you to go with a younger man, Hannah. The canoe will fit the halau. [They laugh] I prefer one who is close to me in years.

HANNAH: I like the way he touches me, and he does not smell of rum. He likes to laugh.

KAʻAHUMANU: Jones is better to look at than Davis.

PALI: Is it Jones? The haole, the American consul?

HANNAH: Yes, you clucking hen!

PALI: Many women desire him.

KAʻAHUMANU: But it is Hannah he desires.

[The Hawaiian women begin to play cards as they speak. LUCY and SYBIL enter with a basket. They see the women engaged in a card game and sit on a bench, staring forward. KAʻAHUMANU acknowledges them by a nod of her head, but makes no move to speak to them.]

KAʻAHUMANU: When will you find a man for such pleasure, Pali?

PALI: I don't want one now, maybe later.

HANNAH: [sassy] Maybe you've never been with a man.

PALI: Maybe.

HANNAH: Why?

PALI: Because I didn't find one I wanted.

HANNAH: Or one who wanted you!

KAʻAHUMANU: [to PALI] Pali has her own wisdom, Hannah. It is not good to be with a man you don't want. Go and tell the mikanele they may join us in cards.

PALI: [going to LUCY and SYBIL] KAʻAHUMANU says you may join our game if you wish.

SYBIL: I'm sorry we can't play.

PALI: Well I will show you. I'm very good. I won a dollar from a sailor this morning.

LUCY: American ladies do not play cards.

PALI: You must wait then.

KA'AHUMANU: Well?

PALI: They said American ladies may not play cards.

KA'AHUMANU: Aloha `ino!

HANNAH: No wonder they never look happy. What is the pleasure in their lives?

PALI: Many people say the men of the mikanele brought these women only to be cooks and cabin boys to them.

KA'AHUMANU: They should learn to throw off their terrible kapu as we did.

[*Lights dim on the card game.* LUCY *is obviously uncomfortable.*]

LUCY: Sybil?

SYBIL: Yes?

LUCY: I, I want to tell you, something . . .

SYBIL: Tell me what?

LUCY: I feel something. I, I mean I found something.

SYBIL: What is it, Lucy?

LUCY: It's, it's, well, in my—

SYBIL: Yes? . . . Lucy?

LUCY: Nothing, it's nothing. I'm so silly. I'm sorry.

SYBIL: Are you sure?

LUCY: [*irritated*] Aren't they finished yet?

SYBIL: Not yet.

LUCY: Well, this is very rude!

SYBIL: It's only rude to us who think it rude to keep people waiting.

LUCY: It *is* rude to keep people waiting!

SYBIL: She is used to doing as she pleases.

LUCY: It's her heathen manners.

[PALI *is out of the game. She rises and goes to* LUCY *and* SYBIL.]

PALI: They are almost finished. Then you will be called.

SYBIL: Thank you.

[PALI *remains and begins to look over* LUCY'S *clothing and bonnet. She picks and pulls at* LUCY'S *clothing, not in a malicious way, but solely out of curiosity.* LUCY *becomes increasingly irritated.* PALI *looks at her sympathetically and begins to lomilomi* LUCY'S *shoulders. Lights go to* KA'AHU-MANU, *who watches* PALI *and* LUCY. LUCY'S *irritation reaches a pitch. Lashing out,* LUCY *violently pushes* PALI *away from her more than once.*]

LUCY: DON'T TOUCH ME!! TAKE YOUR FILTHY HEATHEN HANDS OFF ME!!

SYBIL: Sister Thurston!

[PALI *is stunned and frightened. She runs away.* KA'AHUMANU *strides over.*]

KA'AHUMANU: Why did you do that?

SYBIL: She was frightened. Please forgive her.

LUCY: I, I'm sorry. I just forgot myself.

HANNAH: Pali is a favorite.

LUCY: I'm very sorry.

KA'AHUMANU: [*sternly, moving to mat*] Come over here, now.

SYBIL: Sister Thurston and I have brought something to show you.

KA'AHUMANU: Yes?

SYBIL: [*taking out writing implements*] It is writing.

LUCY: [*taking out a book*] . . . And reading.

KA'AHUMANU: It is the palapala that haole men know?

HANNAH: You know these things?

LUCY: Yes, we do.

SYBIL: In America, many women know these things. We want to teach them to you.

HANNAH: [*excited*] And me? You will show me?

SYBIL: Why, yes, Hannah, if you would like to learn.

KA'AHUMANU: Show me.

SYBIL: [*writing*] We will start with your name, Ka'ahumanu, and yours Hannah. [*She gives them the pens and paper.*] Now try to copy every mark.

KA'AHUMANU: Help me.

SYBIL: [SYBIL *guides her hand.*] There, that is your name.

KA'AHUMANU: Again.

LUCY: Hannah, that is very quick of you.

KA'AHUMANU: [*looking at* HANNAH'S] Her's is better. Guide my hand again.

SYBIL: K,A,A,H,U,M,A,N,U.

KA'AHUMANU: Hannah, put away the cards, we will do this now.

SYBIL: Perhaps I could come back tomorrow and begin a lesson.

KA'AHUMANU: [*looking at her, almost yelling*] Not tomorrow, NOW!

[SYBIL *and* LUCY *give each other a frightened look as lights fade to black.*]

[*Lights to* HANNAH *on the playing area.*]

HANNAH: Many times I have watched the ships sail in and out of the port of Honolulu, and many times the question came to my mind. Who made this great world? Why are people different? Why are there different ways of talking? What does the world look like away from here, far away? These women of the mikanele are the first women of my father's people I have ever seen. They are very different. They work all the time and do not seem to care very much for play or laughter. But there is a way they do things which I like. There is a place for everything in their houses, and it is clean and quiet. There is a fresh feeling. It is a feeling of peace, without the yelling of drunken men and the smell of rum. There is a gentle kindness about Mrs. Bingham. And they know how to read and write! To know the palapala is to know many things. Their talk is of a kind God, Jesus. A God to whom women may speak, and a God who will let us in his temple.

[*Fadeout*]

SCENE NINE

[*Lights to the MH.* LUCY *sits sewing.* SYBIL *enters from the playing area with a basket.*]

LUCY: Will this heat ever stop?
SYBIL: The eternal summer?
LUCY: It's so oppressive.
SYBIL: I wish it would rain.
LUCY: Yes. [*Pause*] Some women came while you were gone.
SYBIL: Did they come in?
LUCY: No, I wouldn't let them.
SYBIL: Why not?
LUCY: They were sick.
SYBIL: Did you tell the doctor?
LUCY: I told them that the doctor couldn't help them.
SYBIL: Lucy, why?
LUCY: Because he couldn't. It was the venereal distemper.
SYBIL: I see.
LUCY: They had sores. Open running sores.

SYBIL: I'm sorry I wasn't here.

LUCY: One was in a great deal of pain, I could tell.

SYBIL: We see more of them every day.

LUCY: She cried to me, Sybil. Begged me for a medicine to make her well. I told her to go away, there is no medicine. Sometimes I feel as though I couldn't stand to see another face like that—like I won't be able to stand to see another face in pain.

SYBIL: This is the gift of men who call themselves Christians and have no knowledge of what that word truly means. Men come to these islands for pleasure, without the love of Christ in their hearts. They are killing them, Lucy. For their own pleasure and their own lust, they are killing these people. They thought Cook was a God? Perhaps he was their angel of death.

LUCY: Perhaps God is punishing these people for their sins of idolatry.

SYBIL: [*bowing her head*] We are all sinners, sister.

LUCY: Yes.

SYBIL: It is our job to bring the word of light.

LUCY: Yes.

SYBIL: And to minister to the needs of these people. But how will we, with so few doctors among us, ever be able to stay the hand of death which every day tightens it's grip on the people?

[KA'AHUMANU *approaches.*]

LUCY: Aloha, Your Majesty.

KA'AHUMANU: Aloha.

LUCY: Come in and be seated.

SYBIL: How are you today?

KA'AHUMANU: I am well.

LUCY: Shall we begin the lesson?

KA'AHUMANU: Yes, let's read.

SYBIL: I must ask you . . .

KA'AHUMANU: Yes?

SYBIL: [*uncomfortable*] This sickness that so many women have from the sailors—

KA'AHUMANU: You don't have this in America?

LUCY: Yes, but . . .

SYBIL: [*boldly*] Yes . . . But, well there are good women and there are bad women, and the good women do not do the things which cause this sickness.

KA'AHUMANU: No?

LUCY: NO!

KA'AHUMANU: Then how is it that they get children?

SYBIL: By getting married!

KA'AHUMANU: [*amused*] Binamuwahine, that is not what gives you a child.

LUCY: What we mean is—

SYBIL: We think something should be done . . .

LUCY: . . . To stop these women.

SYBIL: They spread the disease.

KA'AHUMANU: It is haole men who brought this here.

SYBIL: Yes, but these women who go to the ships, they . . . Well, they make it worse.

KA'AHUMANU: [*considering*] Perhaps I should make them kapu. All women and men who have this sickness may only go with each other.

LUCY: I don't think—

KA'AHUMANU: We can mark each person who has the sickness.

SYBIL: Perhaps it would be better to forbid people to do . . . what they do . . .

LUCY: . . . If they are not married.

KA'AHUMANU: Why?

SYBIL: Because it is a sin.

KA'AHUMANU: You don't like it?

LUCY: Certainly not!

SYBIL: It's only for those who are married.

LUCY: Only so they may have children.

KA'AHUMANU: [*amazed*] You don't do it for the great pleasure of it?

LUCY AND SYBIL: NO!

KA'AHUMANU: Auwe! You poor ladies! What do you have to make you happy?

SYBIL: We think it is wrong to do without a Christian marriage.

KA'AHUMANU: Why do you think this?

LUCY: God has said it in his holy commandments.

KA'AHUMANU: Oh, him!

SYBIL: [*defensive*] If your people followed this commandment, the sickness would not spread through your people. God is the only refuge, the only safe harbor.

KA'AHUMANU: These laws you speak of, I will think on them. Perhaps it is a good thing, as the palapala is a good thing. But, I will have no more Gods! There will be no more priests to make me a slave to their power. I have spoken. We will have the lesson now.

SYBIL: [*after a pause*] Very well, let us read.

KA'AHUMANU: I will read this that I like. "Where unto shall we liken the kingdom of God? Or with what shall we compare it? It is the grain of mustard seed, which when it is sown in the earth is less than all the seeds that be in the earth: But when it is sown, it groweth up, and becometh greater than all the herbs, and shooteth out great branches so that all the birds of the air may lodge under the shadow of it."

SCENE TEN

[Enter HANNAH, *distressed.]*

HANNAH: *[going to* SYBIL] Please, you will help me?

SYBIL: Hannah, what is it?

HANNAH: I just put Charlotte in your cellar.

LUCY: Why should you put your sister in the cellar?

SYBIL: Why does she need to hide?

HANNAH: He sold her. My son of a bitch father got drunk again and sold her to Captain Wills of a whaling ship, because he got drunk and lost at cards. He said he couldn't pay right away, but Wills just smiled back. "'Sure you can,' he says. 'Give me Charlotte. I'll take her up north and bring her back when the ship has a belly full of oil. I'll take good care of her, just for me, no one else.'" My father just looked at him and laughed. He called Charlotte and told her that she must now go with this stranger for many months at sea. *[Pause]* Charlotte is such a good girl, Mrs. Bingham. Hannah, she said, Hannah, what will he do with me? She is only 13.

KA'AHUMANU: The son of a bitch bastard.

HANNAH: I hate this way of being treated. I am sick of it. It is like we're nothing but hogs in the yard to sell. What can I do?

SYBIL: She's safe here, Hannah. There should be laws so that such things are forbidden.

LUCY: Yes, laws to protect women and children!

SYBIL: Hannah, if this trouble comes to you or your sisters again, you must come here. Reverend Bingham will stand up for you or any other woman who is forced to such a thing.

LUCY: And so will Reverend Thurston, Hannah.

SYBIL: Perhaps we should pray for your father, Hannah.

HANNAH: HIM!?

SYBIL: He needs your prayers.

LUCY: His heart is dark.

HANNAH: *[emotionally]* He is no good.

SYBIL: That is why he needs your prayers.

HANNAH: [*obediently*] Yes.

SYBIL: [*to* KA'AHUMANU] Will you join our prayers?

[KA'AHUMANU *shakes her head, no.*]

SYBIL: Hannah, please lead us in prayer.

HANNAH: Me?

SYBIL: `Ae.

HANNAH: Please, Jesus, come to my father's sick heart. Make him well again. Make him see the bad things he does to me and my sisters, how he hurts us and makes us suffer. Make him turn away from the evil things he does so his soul will be saved from the place of fires. We ask these things in Jesus name, Amene.

KA'AHUMANU: [*to* SYBIL] Why do you wish good things for a bad man?

SYBIL: It is the Christian way.

KA'AHUMANU: Why?

SYBIL: We feel that it is those who do bad things that most need our prayers. That with the help of God they might change their ways.

[*Pause*]

KA'AHUMANU: Perhaps I will hear more of these laws of which you speak. You will advise me.

SYBIL: On this matter, you must speak to Reverend Bingham.

KA'AHUMANU: Why? You have a wisdom I like better.

LUCY: We are not suited to advise you about laws.

KA'AHUMANU: But you told me about them.

LUCY: Yes, but we can't advise you. That would be politics.

SYBIL: You see, as ladies it is not a part of our sphere.

LUCY: The home is our world.

SYBIL: We must not make laws.

KA'AHUMANU: You will not make laws, but you will obey them?

SYBIL: We will.

KA'AHUMANU: I feel as if I'm walking through a forest of hao. Come Hannah, I wish to go. Your sister will be safe here. If anyone goes near her, they'll face my anger. Aloha.

LUCY: Aloha.

SYBIL: Aloha nō.

[KA'AHUMANU *and* HANNAH *move to the playing area.*]

SCENE ELEVEN

KA'AHUMANU: What do you think of these things, Hannah? Laws, and a marriage to only one man.

HANNAH: It would have been good if there was a law that would keep Charlotte safe.

KA'AHUMANU: Or a marriage that would have kept Jones from leaving you?

HANNAH: You know?

KA'AHUMANU: `Ae.

HANNAH: I suppose the whole village knows.

KA'AHUMANU: It's likely. He's gone for good?

HANNAH: Do we ever know if they're gone for good?

KA'AHUMANU: He went to America?

HANNAH: If I had been his Christian wife, he would have taken me.

KA'AHUMANU: You would wish to be as the haole women with a man?

HANNAH: Perhaps.

KA'AHUMANU: Their God is a man, and their men are Gods.

HANNAH: Perhaps it is their love.

KA'AHUMANU: It's easier to love a man than a God, Hannah.

HANNAH: `A`ole maopopo ia'u.

[They enter KH and sit.]

KA'AHUMANU: I watched Kamehameha. I saw all the women bow down to him like a God. Do you know why he loved me? [HANNAH *shakes her head, no*] Because, he knew I was powerful and did not fear him. [*She laughs*] My own father, Ke'eaumoku told him, "You have only one person to truly fear in your kingdom. Only one person to take away your rule—your own woman, Ka'ahumanu. For if she chose to rise up against you, the people love her so much they would follow." So you see, I stood on the same mountain, looked into the same valley, and when I looked at him, I saw a man, not a God.

HANNAH: And what did he see?

KA'AHUMANU: [*after a pause*] That would be for him to say, Hannah.

HANNAH: You don't like this idea of Christian marriage?

KA'AHUMANU: I don't care about it. In the old days, if women and men desired each other they joined; if that left, they parted.

HANNAH: But the old days go.

KA'AHUMANU: Yes, and tomorrow comes with more foreigners and their ideas and their ships and their desires.

HANNAH: Desire. Is that what rules us? I hardly know my own. But the mikanele, they have given me a new kind of desire. A longing to know the things in books and the world outside of here and the ways of God.

KA'AHUMANU: You believe this God?

HANNAH: Yes, because he is full of mercy.

KA'AHUMANU: But he keeps a terrible place of fires.

HANNAH: That's for the wicked.

KA'AHUMANU: Who is wicked?

HANNAH: Those who don't believe.

KA'AHUMANU: And those who do?

HANNAH: Life everlasting. Where everything is happiness and good.

KA'AHUMANU: Happiness and good, those are things we need before we die, Hannah.

HANNAH: This life is for tears and sorrow.

[*Cross-fade to playing area.* KA'AHUMANU *moves into the free space.*]

KA'AHUMANU: Is this what they teach her? Or is it because of her lover she is sad? Our islands are in the midst of storm, blown every which way by the white men who come here. Laws, these ladies speak of laws, and perhaps their laws are good. The old laws, many of them were foolish and unjust. But perhaps it is good to have the laws which protect the people from harm. As in the old days, if the people see their ali'i doing good things, they will continue to love and follow us. It would be easy to take this new God and make him steer our canoe through this time, but I can't do it. [*Cross-fade back to KH as* KA'AHUMANU *goes back to her space*] I can't trust this haole God.

HANNAH: I know in the days of the kapu, when our hearts were dark, we worshipped the hungry Gods. The Gods who must be fed with plants and animals and, most terrible, with human flesh that they might live. Men died that the Gods might live. But now comes a time of light. A new God who is so full of love that he sends his son to die for men, that they might live.

[*Blackout. Lights to the MH with* SYBIL *and* LUCY.]

SCENE TWELVE

LUCY: I don't see why you have to chide me for it!

SYBIL: I'm not chiding you, Lucy. I'm simply suggesting—

LUCY: You look down on me for it!

SYBIL: I do not, Sister Thurston.

LUCY: Perhaps you think my feelings don't become a minister's wife. . . .

SYBIL: I would never suggest that you weren't a good wife.

LUCY: . . . As a missionary.

SYBIL: Lucy, please. I was at fault to mention it.

LUCY: [*cooling*] Well, I'm not like you, Mrs. Bingham. I have never been free with my natural affection.

SYBIL: I'm sure if only you would open your heart, unafraid, you would soon find room for them.

LUCY: I have tried, Sybil. I have. I have told myself that they're people, that they have immortal souls, that I ought to love them as my neighbors at home, but I can't escape the feelings that come over me when I see them in their depravity. I can control the way I look before them, but I can't help the revulsion I feel. I can't bear to be touched by them, by those dark, dirty hands. And I hate the way I am stared at by those great dark eyes. I hate those eyes that stare at me like some animal. I even sometimes feel sickened if there are too many of them in here.

SYBIL: Our work must be selfless, Lucy.

LUCY: It's wicked, I know, but it's true, Sybil. I would change it if I could, but these feelings are beyond my control. But I have made a promise, a promise to God. I promised him that it would never make me falter in my work here in these islands. I can't love these people, but I will work to raise them to a state of Christian civilization. I suppose now you will think me a most unworthy person.

SYBIL: No, I will think no such thing. God gives us our trials, and we must bear them.

LUCY: [*breaking*] I can't! No! I just don't have the strength!

SYBIL: Lucy! What's wrong?

LUCY: [*regaining some composure*] I don't know how to tell you. I'm so ashamed.

SYBIL: What is it, Lucy?

LUCY: I've found a hard thing, a lump in my breast.

SYBIL: [*after a pause*] Have you told Dr. Judd?

LUCY: How can I?

[*Blackout. Lights to the playing area, where* HANNAH *meets* PALI.]

SCENE THIRTEEN

PALI: Where have you been, Hannah? In the house of the mikanele, night and day?

HANNAH: Why don't you come, too?

PALI: I think they hate us.

HANNAH: That's not true!

PALI: I think it is. They're not good for us. They're teachings are false and evil. They don't allow you any of the joys you knew before. Come, Hannah, return to the way you were before. Be happy again.

HANNAH: If they hate us, why would they come to teach us?

PALI: I don't know, it's a trick. . . .

HANNAH: A trick?

PALI: . . . To make us miserable like them.

HANNAH: They're not miserable.

PALI: Soon your life will leave you, Hannah, and you'll be like them.

HANNAH: No, Pali, they teach me to know more about life. They make new thoughts in my head which weren't there before, and now I may think of many new and wonderful things. I have knowledge and I will have more of it. Before, I was just a pretty thing that men wanted, but now I have a new world of thoughts that is kapu to everyone but myself.

PALI: These things you learn could be lies.

HANNAH: They're not.

PALI: I still say that haole woman hate us!!

[*Blackout*]

END ACT I

ACT II

SCENE ONE

[SYBIL, LUCY, AND HANNAH *are at the MH.* HANNAH *now wears a dress like the mission women.* SYBIL *quizzes* HANNAH *from a book.*]

SYBIL: Now, HANNAH, "What is sin?"

HANNAH: Sin is any want of conformity to, or transgression of, the law of God.

SYBIL: "What is the sin by where our first parents fell?"

HANNAH: The sin by where our first parents fell was the eating of the forbidden fruit.

SYBIL: "What is the misery of the estate wherein man fell?"

HANNAH: This one is still hard.

SYBIL: Baptism requires study and diligence. Now try again. "What is the misery of the estate wherein man fell?"

HANNAH: [*hesitant*] All mankind, by their fall, lost communion with God, are under his wrath and curse, and so made liable to all miseries in this life, to death itself, and to the pains of hell forever.

SYBIL: "Did God leave all men to perish in the estate of sin and misery?"

HANNAH: No, God, out of his mere good pleasure, has elected some to everlasting life and will bring these chosen to an estate of salvation by a redeemer, the Lord Jesus Christ.

[*Enter* PALI]

PALI: Excuse me, please.

LUCY: Yes?

PALI: The doctor wishes you in the village right away. There is some trouble.

LUCY: Trouble?

PALI: Many people have come down from the mountains where they cut the sandalwood. There is a great sickness among them.

SYBIL: No.

PALI: [*holding a note*] He asked you to bring these things.

LUCY: [*grabs the note*] Let me have that. [*to* SYBIL] They are powders from his medical supplies.

SYBIL: You get them, Lucy. Hannah, you will study until I return.

HANNAH: `Ae.

[*Exit* LUCY *and* SYBIL]

PALI: What are you doing, Hannah?

HANNAH: Learning the word of God so I may have baptism.

PALI: Oh.

HANNAH: "What does every sin deserve? Every sin deserves God's wrath and curse, both in this life and that which is to come."

PALI: Do you believe this, Hannah?

HANNAH: [*haltingly*] Yes, I want to be baptized.

PALI: Why?

HANNAH: So I can go to heaven.

PALI: This god allows the kanaka in his heaven?

HANNAH: Yes.

PALI: Even women?

HANNAH: Yes, we are all equal in God's sight.

PALI: Then why aren't we equal on earth?

HANNAH: Be quiet, Pali.

PALI: How many haoles do you know who treat us like one of their own? How many of the ali'i treat commoners as they do each other?

HANNAH: You don't know what you're talking about.

PALI: [building] No, you don't know Hannah! Things are different for you because you're hapa haole. They treat you so, bring you into their home as a friend because they think you are half like them. You're not like me! You've always had many more things for your comfort in life. You don't know what it is to be poor, and you don't know what it's like to be below everyone else. So don't say your stupid words to me Hannah!

HANNAH: [after a pause, softly] Pali, what is it? Why are you so angry with me? You could come here too if you wanted.

PALI: I'm sorry Hannah. Forgive my words. I don't mean to hurt you.

[Exit PALI]

SCENE TWO

[Lights to the playing area. LUCY sits; SYBIL stands behind her.]

LUCY: The greed of men has caused many deaths. Men come from foreign lands wanting iliahi, the scented sandalwood. They bring Western goods and teach the chiefs to covet these things.

SYBIL: They ply them with liquor until they are drunk . . .

LUCY: Sell them useless things . . .

SYBIL: Never worth half of what they charge . . .

LUCY: The chiefs pay in sandalwood. . . .

SYBIL: The makainana must go to cut the wood. . . .

LUCY: Holes, the size of ships are dug. . . .

SYBIL: The commoners must fill them with wood . . .

LUCY: Piculs.

SYBIL: One hundred thirty-three and one-third pounds, one picul.

LUCY: The wood grows high in the mountains. . . .

SYBIL: Many leave their fields unattended . . .

LUCY: Kalo rots. . . .

SYBIL: The sweet potatoes are eaten by worms . . .

LUCY: Men, women, mothers with their children go . . .

SYBIL: Today, many died . . .

LUCY: Tomorrow many more . . .

SYBIL: The people stayed too long. The winds blew too cold. The rain came too hard . . .

LUCY: Not enough food . . .

SYBIL: Exposed to nature's elements . . .

LUCY: Not enough to keep warm . . .

SYBIL: They came down from the green hills cryi...g, for the dead they left behind . . .

LUCY: All for what? . . .

SYBIL: So a few foreigners could increase their wealth . . .

LUCY: Buy lace for their wives . . .

SYBIL: Crystal for their tables . . .

LUCY: Stallions for their sons . . .

SYBIL: [*coming forward*] My dear sisters, if you could only see with what misery and death the foundations of wealthy lives in America, comfortable and safe, are built on! These were once a thriving people. The white men who come here for profits from sandalwood, profits from whale oil, or for the pleasure of women I am ashamed to call my countrymen. If you had seen what I saw today, men, women, and children dying, I'm sure you would not hesitate to lay down your beautiful silk dresses, your colored ribbons, your lace gloves, and all the finery that surrounds you, to take up a Christian vow of service and poverty so that you would never again prosper by the deaths of others.

SCENE THREE

[*Lights to* KA'AHUMANU *and* HANNAH *at KH.*]

KA'AHUMANU: Many chiefs have accepted this new God.

HANNAH: Yes.

KA'AHUMANU: Kaumuali'i wished I would believe, also, Keōpūolani.

HANNAH: Why don't you?

KA'AHUMANU: Some things I like. I think it is good that with this god, women may speak to him. In the old days, only the kahuna spoke to God at the heiau. And I like to see that women may teach things about this God, such as Mrs. Bingham teaches. But some things I don't like. I'm afraid that this God would have too much power. That too many things would change. There is something about the mikanele that I do not trust, something which I can't name.

HANNAH: They have been kind teachers to us.

KA'AHUMANU: And they seem to care for the people.

HANNAH: They do many things for us.

KA'AHUMANU: [*bewildered*] Yes. [*Pause*] You know, Hannah, when I was younger, I felt so strong. That is the good thing about youth, to feel strong in body and purpose. I was not afraid. I saw something to do, and I did it. But everything is changed with the coming of foreigners. Their wealth, ships, guns, these things change everything. They have made the power of the chiefs weak. I make a law against the sale of rum. A ship comes full of men eager for drink. If the captain does not like the kapu, he says, "Sell us rum or we'll fire our cannon on your town." Or perhaps he sends an angry mob to fight and make trouble. What am I to do? Keep the law and have destruction? If we engage him in battle, more and more ships with guns will come from his country. Should I relent and give him rum? This makes the chiefs look weak. What will I do? In former days, I did not hesitate to act. My mind did not trouble me. The way was clear. I was not afraid to do away with what I knew to be false or to take up what I wished. But now . . .

HANNAH: Everything has changed so much. I know.

KA'AHUMANU: `Ae, the chiefs pass. All the old ones, my counselors and friends, Keopuolani, gone. My own Kaumuali'i, gone! Kalanimoku grows so old. His strength fades. Our people die. I feel as if I am surrounded by darkness . . .

[*The lights go very soft, to a spot on* KA'AHUMANU *alone. She chants a kanikau, a mourning chant.*]

KA'AHUMANU:

> `Elua no wahi e mehana ai
> O ke ahi lalaku i ke hale
> O ka lua o ke ahi, o ka lua kapa
> I ka lua poli o ka hoa e mehana'i e
> Eia lā, aia lā, eia lā e

[*She lies on the mat.* HANNAH *covers her with a quilt and exits.* VOICES *speak from the darkness, rising to confusion and chaos.*]

VOICE 1: Why did you destroy the old ones?
VOICE 2: Why?
VOICE 3: Why?
VOICE 4: Why?
VOICE 1: Your people are dying!
VOICE 2: Why?
VOICE 3: Do something!
VOICE 4: Can't you do anything?
VOICE 1: Too many haole.
VOICE 2: Another warship . . .
VOICE 3: Another government . . .

VOICE 4: Give us sandalwood. . . .

VOICE 1: Women. Where are the women?! . . .

VOICE 2: And rum, more rum . . .

VOICE 3: Call for a warship. These chiefs can't tell us what to do. . . .

VOICE 4: I'll do what I like. This isn't America . . .

VOICE 1: England . . .

VOICE 2: France . . .

VOICE 3: These aren't civilized human beings.

VOICE 4: Take care of your own people.

VOICE 1: Take care!

VOICE 2: Can't you do anything?

VOICE 3: There's too much sickness. . . .

VOICE 4: I need some land. . . .

VOICE 1: Send for a warship. I want to be paid!

VOICE 2: These are only native chiefs. . . .

VOICE 3: Stupid savages!

KAʻAHUMANU: Why is it so hot?

VOICE 4: There aren't enough children anymore.

VOICE 1: Why did you leave the old Gods?

VOICE 2: Can't you do something?

KAʻAHUMANU: It's too hot.

VOICE 3: What does every sin deserve?

VOICE 4: Everyone will die!

VOICE 1: Die!

VOICE 2: It's too hot!

VOICE 3: Why can't you do anything??

VOICE 4: Why?

ALL VOICES: We're dying!! We're all dying. Do something.

SCENE FOUR

[*Enter* LUCY *and* SYBIL. *They begin to bathe* KAʻAHUMANU's *face with damp cloths and tend her as if she is ill.*]

LUCY: Is she improved?

SYBIL: Not much, her fever is still very high.

LUCY: You should rest.

SYBIL: I'm fine. It's you I worry over.

LUCY: You've been here all day. You could become ill yourself.

SYBIL: I've had a little sleep.

[PALI *has softly entered.*]

PALI: Will she die?

SYBIL: [*frightened*] No, she won't die!

PALI: Put her in the stream.

SYBIL: No, Pali, it could make her much worse.

PALI: She'll burn up inside.

LUCY: Such a stupid belief.

[*Exit* PALI, *quickly.*]

SYBIL: Sister Thurston.

LUCY: I know, I spoke too sharply.

SYBIL: People listen to those whom they feel to be kindhearted.

LUCY: It always happens when I feel tired.

SYBIL: [*urgently*] Perhaps you should go back to the mission and get Reverend
    Bingham and the doctor.

LUCY: Is she going?

SYBIL: I don't know. I can't tell if the fever is breaking or if she's falling into a
    worse state.

LUCY: I'll hurry.

[*Exit* LUCY]

KA'AHUMANU: [*mumbling*] No, no. I'm too hot. Go! Go! Go away . . . I won't
    go there . . . No . . . no . . . [*she opens her eyes slowly and looks at* SYBIL.] Bi-
    namuwahine!

SYBIL: [*smiling*] Yes, I'm here.

KA'AHUMANU: I'm very sick?

SYBIL: Yes.

KA'AHUMANU: I had a terrible dream. I saw that place.

SYBIL: What place?

KA'AHUMANU: The place of fires. [*She tries to sit up.*]

SYBIL: You must lie down.

KA'AHUMANU: It was a terrible place. I saw my people burning. It was so hot,
    great rivers of lava.

SYBIL: It's all right. You're here now.

KA'AHUMANU: You're so kind to bring me back from that place.

SYBIL: It is the love of Jesus that has brought me here.

KA'AHUMANU: It is Jesus who saves us from this place?

SYBIL: He is the light of the world. It is only through him that we are saved.

KA'AHUMANU: Perhaps now, Binamuwahine, I will try one these prayers to Jesus.
SYBIL: Now?
KA'AHUMANU: Yes, now, hurry.
SYBIL: Reverend Bingham will be here soon. Maybe you wish to pray with him.
KA'AHUMANU: No, it's you I wish to share my first prayer with.
SYBIL: [touched] Very well, we will pray as Jesus taught us to pray, saying: "Our
    father who art in heaven."
KA'AHUMANU: "Our father who art in heaven . . ."

[The lights fade as they continue the Lord's Prayer.]

SCENE FIVE

[Lights to HANNAH, reading in her house.]

HANNAH: "I opened to my beloved, but my beloved had withdrawn himself and
    was gone. My soul failed me when he spake: I sought him, but I could not
    find him. I called him but he gave no answer. The watchman that went about
    the city found me; they smote me, they wounded me, the keepers of the
    walls took away my veil from me. I charge you, O daughters of Jerusalem, if
    ye find my beloved, that ye tell him: I am sick of love."

[Lights to the MH. KA'AHUMANU, SYBIL, and LUCY sit. KA'AHUMANU
now wears a Mu'umu'u. HANNAH enters, depressed.]

SYBIL: Good morning, Hannah.
HANNAH: Aloha, Binamuwahine. [to KA'AHUMANU] Pehea oe, kupuna?
KA'AHUMANU: Maika'i.
SYBIL: Are you troubled, Hannah?
HANNAH: No.
SYBIL: Don't feel bad, Hannah. Reverend Bingham says you may try the ex-
    amination in another month. Someday you will be baptized.
HANNAH: It's all right.
SYBIL: Let's continue our work. You may begin reading with Matthew 13.
KA'AHUMANU: [haltingly] "And he spake in many parables to them . . . saying
    behold a sower . . . went forth to sow: and when he sowed, . . . some seeds
    fell by the wayside, and the fowls came and . . . devoured them up."
SYBIL: Hannah, please continue.

[HANNAH is daydreaming.]

SYBIL: Hannah.
HANNAH: I'm sorry.

SYBIL: Please continue.

HANNAH: I don't know the place.

SYBIL: You must pay attention, Hannah. Matthew 13, verse 5.

HANNAH: "Some fell upon a stony place where they had not much earth: and forthwith they sprung because they had no deepness of earth . . ."

SYBIL: What is wrong with you today, Hannah?

[HANNAH *says nothing, but looks at her book unhappily.*]

KA'AHUMANU: Jones, he came back.

SYBIL: I see.

KA'AHUMANU: He wants Hannah for his wahine.

HANNAH: I told him that I would not come to his bed unless we made a Christian marriage.

SYBIL: You are very right, Hannah. God's love and acceptance of you as one of his own requires your virtue.

HANNAH: He speaks so nicely to me. He says he loves me.

SYBIL: If he won't marry you, Hannah, it's not love, but only a bodily desire for you.

HANNAH: If only I could turn my thoughts away from him. I'm trying very hard.

SYBIL: Yes, I know, but you must learn to turn away from what is wicked, no matter how sweetly it calls you.

HANNAH: Can such kindnesses be wicked?

SYBIL: Yes, it is very clear.

KA'AHUMANU: I will read now! "And when the sun was up they were scorched and because they had no root, they withered away."

SYBIL: Hannah.

HANNAH: "And some fell among thorns; and the thorns sprung up and choked them . . ."

[*Offstage we hear* LUCY *calling to* SYBIL.]

LUCY: [*Offstage*] Sybil, please, come! Hurry!

[SYBIL *exits.* LUCY *and* SYBIL *return helping in* PALI, *who has been badly beaten. Her face is black and blue, blood comes from the corner of her mouth.*]

SYBIL: How did this happen? . . .

HANNAH: Pali!

KA'AHUMANU: Who did this to you?

LUCY: I found her outside like this. A lady came by and spat at her.

SYBIL: Why?

LUCY: She called her that name.

SYBIL: What name?

LUCY: Kauā.

SYBIL: She's badly hurt. Lay her down on the mat.

[PALI *cries out in pain.*]

PALI: I must go away.

SYBIL: You're in no state to go anywhere.

LUCY: What if those people find you again?

KA'AHUMANU: He kauā'oe?

PALI: [*defiantly*] `Ae!

HANNAH: Kūkapilau!

SYBIL: Hannah, don't speak like that to her!

KA'AHUMANU: But she is kauā!

SYBIL: Stop calling her that! She's a person, just like everyone else.

PALI: I don't care anymore. I'm tired of always be `ng afraid that someone will find out. My father gave me to a family when I was a baby. He wanted me to grow without the shame. He's been giving this woman food, kapa, pigs, to keep me. He lived poorly so that I might have life. It was him you saw being beaten once in the village. Last night he came to find me, to tell me that my real mother is very ill and wishes once more to see me. Others of the woman's family saw him and forced her to tell the truth. That's why you've found me this way, but I don't care anymore! My father is a better man than any in the village whether he has the marks of a kauā or not! He has given everything for me. I would rather stand by him than any other person! Even you, KA'AHUMANU!

LUCY: Be quiet now.

PALI: That woman only liked the food I brought to her table.

HANNAH: I must go, now.

PALI: I know you will hate me now, Hannah.

SYBIL: Hannah doesn't hate you. [*silence*] Hannah, where is your Christian charity?

HANNAH: [*coldly*] I will *try* not to hate you.

LUCY: Perhaps we should move her to the bed in the cellar.

SYBIL: Wait until the doctor looks at her.

KA'AHUMANU: You will keep her here?

SYBIL: Yes, we will.

KA'AHUMANU: She will be a filthy thing in your house.
LUCY: She needs our help.

[PALI *cries out in pain.*]

KA'AHUMANU: Come, Hannah, let's go.

[*Exit* KA'AHUMANU *and* HANNAH]

SCENE SIX

[KA'AHUMANU *and* HANNAH *walk to KH.*]

KA'AHUMANU: How could she lie and deceive me?
HANNAH: She has been in my house many times.
KA'AHUMANU: I treated her as one of my own. She should be punished for such lies.
HANNAH: Perhaps she is already.
KA'AHUMANU: My own favorite.

[*They arrive at* KA'AHUMANU's *house.*]

KA'AHUMANU: Have you seen Jones?
HANNAH: Only to talk.
KA'AHUMANU: And what does Jones say to you?
HANNAH: That he loves me and wishes me to share his bed.
KA'AHUMANU: You wish this?
HANNAH: Yes, but I don't go.
KA'AHUMANU: Ah.
HANNAH: He comes every day to my house. Every day he asks me.
KA'AHUMANU: Tell him not to come.
HANNAH: You think it's wrong?
KA'AHUMANU: The laws of Jehovah say it's wrong.
HANNAH: [*confused*] I tell him I can't sin, but he says I think too much about sin. He says that the mikanele worship God in a poison way. He says that God will love us no matter what we do, and if we don't harm others, we don't sin. He says he loves me better than any woman.
KA'AHUMANU: Then why doesn't he make a marriage with you? Isn't that the way of his people?
HANNAH: [*defensively*] You said yourself that you thought it took more than words to keep a man.
KA'AHUMANU: [*peevishly*] Perhaps my thoughts were wrong.

[Enter SYBIL]

SYBIL: I've come to ask you to have pity on Pali.

KA'AHUMANU: She's dishonored and deceived me. I chose her for my favorite. I gave her my affection.

SYBIL: She only tried to live a life like others.

KA'AHUMANU: She comes from a filthy race.

SYBIL: Why? Why do you think these people to be so terrible? Have they done great wrongs?

KA'AHUMANU: They are what they are.

SYBIL: Then think for a moment, Your Majesty, what if you were to find yourself in such a station in life?

KA'AHUMANU: Me! I am ali'i.

SYBIL: And what if your own father had suffered to give you a better life. Wouldn't you try to make the most of that life?

KA'AHUMANU: [*after a pause*] Perhaps.

SYBIL: And, think, if you were this person who looked to her chiefess as the one who should guide and protect you, what would you hope this chiefess would do?

KA'AHUMANU: You think I should change the way these people are treated, is that it?

SYBIL: [*exhausted*] I'm not one to advise the Kuhina nui, but I'll tell you what I know from the holy scriptures: "... and now abideth faith, hope, and love, these three, but the greatest of these is love."

[Silence]

KA'AHUMANU: Let's take some tea.

SYBIL: No, I must go. I have so much work.

KA'AHUMANU: No, you will stay. You look tired. You lie down. I myself will lomilomi.

SYBIL: Thank you, but—

KA'AHUMANU: No! You have cared for me when I was sick. Now, I will care for you.

SYBIL: Well, perhaps I will try it. [*She lies down.*]

HANNAH: You've never tried it?

SYBIL: No, I haven't, Hannah.

HANNAH: It's very good. Your body will relax and make itself well.

[SYBIL *lies on the mat and* KA'AHUMANU *begins to massage her.*]

KA'AHUMANU: Before you came we spoke of Jones.

SYBIL: Oh?

KA'AHUMANU: He wants Hannah to come to him.

SYBIL: Of course, you won't go, Hannah.

HANNAH: [*repeating*] Of course, I won't go.

KA'AHUMANU: She thinks he loves her.

SYBIL: Christian marriage is how a man proves his love.

HANNAH: All your life you will only have one husband?

SYBIL: Yes, only if a husband dies can a woman take another husband.

KA'AHUMANU: You have only had one?

SYBIL: Yes. [*Pause*] Although, once, a long time ago, I was engaged to another man.

HANNAH: Engaged?

SYBIL: [*now very relaxed*] That's when a man and a woman promise that they will marry each other.

KA'AHUMANU: A promise.

SYBIL: Then others know they are taken.

HANNAH: What was his name?

SYBIL: His name?

HANNAH: Yes.

SYBIL: [*smiling, relaxed*] Levi, Mr. Levi Parsons.

HANNAH: [*to* KA'AHUMANU] What's happening?

KA'AHUMANU: Her body and thoughts relax.

HANNAH: He was handsome, this man, Parsons?

SYBIL: Yes, he was. Like summer.

HANNAH: [*to* KA'AHUMANU, *delighted surprise*] I've never heard her talk like this before!

KA'AHUMANU: [*whispers back*] Auē! Her body is like a shoreline of rocks.

SYBIL: It was summertime when I met him. So beautiful. We'd walk and walk, and talk about everything.

HANNAH: Where is he?

SYBIL: He was so kind, and I was so lonely.

HANNAH: Where is he?

SYBIL: Gone.

HANNAH: Where?

SYBIL: To be a missionary.

HANNAH: [*surprised*] He is one of the mikanele?

SYBIL: Not here, in Turkey. Far away. They said he couldn't take a wife. The man must go single.

HANNAH: He left you.

SYBIL: It was our duty to part.

HANNAH: But he, . . . but you loved him, didn't you?

SYBIL: Summer. We were so close. Many times I've wished . . .

HANNAH: You've wished?

SYBIL: Yes, I have wished it so.

[SYBIL *stops abruptly. She sits up and looks around in a panic.*] I have to go!

KA'AHUMANU: [*trying to put her gently down*] No, Binamuwahine, you mustn't get up so fast, you are too deep.

SYBIL: [*jumping up, almost yelling*] I tell you, I have to go!!

[*Lights down on KH. SYBIL runs to the MH. She opens a drawer and snatches up a small hand mirror. She begins to softy touch her face and lips.*]

SYBIL: Please, remember me the way I was, not this old woman I've become.

[HANNAH *has approached. Unseen, she watches SYBIL for a moment.*]

HANNAH: Binamuwahine are you—

[SYBIL *wheels around and sees HANNAH. She throws the mirror into the drawer and slams it shut. She quickly turns on HANNAH.*]

SYBIL: [*intense, sternly*] You must choose, Hannah! Between a sensual pleasure of the flesh and what you know to be your Christian duty to God!

HANNAH: Please, you've been my teacher and my friend—

SYBIL: [*loudly*] Choose!

HANNAH: NO!

[HANNAH *runs from the MH to her own space. SYBIL moves into the playing area. There is a spot on each. HANNAH reads from her Bible.*]

HANNAH: "I sleep, but my heart waketh; it is the voice of my beloved that knocketh, saying, open to me, my sister, my love."

SYBIL: [*to audience*] She came to our own bosom to be instructed. Mature and meditative, her mind seemed instinctively prepared to receive instruction. . . .

HANNAH: "I am my beloved's and my beloved is mine: he feedeth among the lilies."

SYBIL: More intelligent, more attractive, more refined; she was our joy. The crown of our school. Rising to a new life, thoroughly instructed in a new system of morals, we even dared to believe that she loved the truth: but the test came. . . .

HANNAH: "I am my beloved's and his desire is towards me."

SYBIL: Official power and wealth, combined, turned the scale. Yet her conscience was so ill at ease. She was on the very point of resisting when she
found she had not the strength.

HANNAH: "Many waters cannot quench love, neither can the floods drown it:
if a man give all the substance of his house for love . . ."

SYBIL: Here is one of the keenest trials of a mission teacher. We plant a vineyard, when we look that it should put forth grapes, it brings wild grapes.

HANNAH: "Come my beloved, let us go forth into the field."

SYBIL: I loved her as a child of my own brother or sister.

HANNAH: "Set me as a seal upon thine heart."

SYBIL AND HANNAH: [*They face each other.*] "O that my head were waters, and
mine eyes a fountain of tears, that I might weep for the slain daughters of
my people."

[*Lights to* KA'AHUMANU, *who looks at* SYBIL.]

KA'AHUMANU: Faith, Hope, and Love, but the greatest of these is Love.

SCENE SEVEN

[*Spot to the playing area.* PALI *enters the light.*]

PALI: There was, when I was younger, a woman who came to live in the hale
nearby who was with child. She was a strange woman, with dark looks and
knotted fingers. I knew she did not want her baby because many times I saw
her gather plants to make a baby go away. But the baby wouldn't go away,
and it grew inside her anyway. She had the baby in the dark, by herself, and
when we went to see it, she told us to leave, that the baby was sick and would
not live. [*Short pause*] One night, when there was no moon, I saw her steal
out with the child all wrapped up. I followed her into the forest. She went
far into the night and into the uplands where no one lives but the mountain
spirits and the ghosts. I thought the baby had died, and she had come to
bury it. I thought perhaps its sickness had made it unbearable to look at, and
she wanted no one to see it, even in death. She stopped at a place that was
quiet and hidden. I watched her put the white bundle in the ground. She
began to walk very quickly back and forth, looking at the bundle. Then she
would turn away and pull at her fingers. Over and over again she did this,
until, finally, she turned and ran. Muttering under her breath, she ran away,
and I watched her disappear like a thin ribbon into the night. And there in
the forest I began to feel sorry for her. I felt sorry that she had lost her baby

and could now see that she now suffered from terrible loss and grief. And I walked away from that place, looking through the black branches at the sky. I had gone some distance when I heard the first sound. It was like a small cry, so small I thought it was the far away cry of an owl. But it came again, louder, and a little louder, and louder, and I knew. She would leave her child while it still had life! The soft crying moved through me. I was sick. I ran back. I ran as fast as I could, toward the sound, but there was nothing there. I heard it again and ran, but nothing. And again and again I would hear and run, searching and searching, and find nothing. For what seemed like hours, I tried, but I could not find it again. Exhausted, I sat down and wept. I cried for everything: for the baby, for myself, my father, for all those like me in the world who had been cast aside and now suffered. I do not know how long I sat there so alone and abandoned and without hope. When all of a sudden it came to me, it was as if loving hands had laid a kihei on my shoulders. Comfort washed over me, and I was quiet. And in the quiet, I heard the voice, the voice of a baby, clear and strong, crying in the night. I stood and walked straight to it. I gathered up the small life I was meant to save. I had made a new life—not from my body, but from a thrown away life that no one wanted. I took the baby far away to a kind woman I knew would care for a child. I had given a new life. And now, that is what the mikanele have given to me, a new life from one that was unwanted, thrown away, and treated like so much rubbish.

[*Cross-fade to the MH.* Pali *moves into that space, where she picks up the tea service and serves* Sybil *and* Lucy *tea.*]

PALI: I have made you some tea.
LUCY: Thank you, Pali.
SYBIL: You are so kind to us.
PALI: No, it is you who have given me kindness.
SYBIL: Do you like it here at the Mission, Pali?
PALI: Yes, Here, I hide nothing.
SYBIL: We have talked it over and would like to know if you will stay and work for us.
PALI: Stay?
LUCY: You will have duties.
SYBIL: We need some help very much. . . .
LUCY: But don't expect pay, we have no money . . .
SYBIL: . . . But can give you food, shelter, clothing . . .
LUCY: And your father may come to visit you here.

PALI: You don't care what I am?

SYBIL: We know what you are: kind, honest, and hardworking.

LUCY: We do expect you to study the way of our God.

PALI: Because of your kindness, I will learn the way of God and make him mine.

SYBIL: The doctor says you have mended nicely.

PALI: `Ae. You will let me wash the tea things?

SYBIL: Well, that's a good start, Pali.

[*Exit* PALI *with the tea service*]

SYBIL: And what does the doctor say of you, sister?

LUCY: He said we must wait. He said some of these things go away by themselves.

SYBIL: But, if . . .

LUCY: If it doesn't? He will have to operate.

SYBIL: Oh. [*pause*] It's past the time that the queen said she would call.

LUCY: I feel so tired.

SYBIL: Go and rest, Lucy.

LUCY: But the lesson.

SYBIL: I'll do it.

LUCY: I do feel strangely. I think I will take this time to rest, if you don't mind.

SYBIL: Please.

[*Exit* LUCY. *After a beat,* KA'AHUMANU *enters.*]

SYBIL: You've come for your lesson.

KA'AHUMANU: I've brought you some fish.

SYBIL: Thank you so much.

KA'AHUMANU: And some poi; fresh, as you like it.

SYBIL: You'll spoil me.

KA'AHUMANU: If good things aren't for good people, then who are they for?

SYBIL: Well, I guess, I don't know.

KA'AHUMANU: [*sitting*] I've thought more about the church.

SYBIL: You wish to join us?

KA'AHUMANU: I have some thoughts.

SYBIL: [*after a silence*] Do you wish to share them with me?

KA'AHUMANU: I don't wish to make you feel bad.

SYBIL: Make me feel bad? I will listen if—

KA'AHUMANU: But how will you listen? With what ears will you hear and what tongue will you speak? Your own or that of the mission? I wish for you to listen.

SYBIL: [*makes the connection*] I will hear your mana'o.

KA'AHUMANU: There are many things which I am glad to receive from this new God. Jesus Christ, he is a kind God.

SYBIL: Yes.

KA'AHUMANU: He shows us a way of mercy. . . . Such as the way you treat Pali.

SYBIL: Yes.

KA'AHUMANU: This is something the great Gods in the temples did not teach us. And women may speak to this God, and teach about this God as you do.

SYBIL: That is one of the unusual duties of a mission wife.

KA'AHUMANU: Nevertheless, it is done.

SYBIL: Yes.

KA'AHUMANU: You do many good things for the people.

SYBIL: We want to do good.

KA'AHUMANU: But my heart still holds itself back from your God. You see, I remember the old days. The Gods ruled over us in ways I did not like. So when I saw a chance, I took them down. I did away with them. But this new God, your God; I have seen what happens to those who choose him. He has a strong hold on their hearts. I know if I take this God, the people will follow.

SYBIL: As they have always followed you.

KA'AHUMANU: But I would never be able to change the beliefs of the people once this God took hold.

SYBIL: He is strength.

KA'AHUMANU: He is the God of white men.

SYBIL: Yes.

KA'AHUMANU: And it seems that the haole wish to be God over all. I will never be able to stop them here. There are too many ships, too many guns, too many diseases. If I take up this God perhaps there will be some good, some peace. Other nations will see that we believe in the same God and not think us ignorant savages. I know all the names foreigners have for us, but some will want to protect a Christian people from wrong.

SYBIL: It is a good thought.

KA'AHUMANU: We may be a dying people.

SYBIL: There is still hope that your people will revive themselves. Do not give up that hope.

KA'AHUMANU: You have shown me great kindness, but for some others of your race, I wonder. Will they ever lose their contempt, and will they ever cease to feel that they must be lords over us?

SYBIL: I don't know.

KA'AHUMANU: Our ways are so different.

SYBIL: Yes.

KA'AHUMANU: Perhaps we will never be able to meet without one ruling over another. [*Pause*] We frightened the very heart of your haole world. Even as I can frighten the very heart of you, Binamuwahine.

SYBIL: Yes.

KA'AHUMANU: The big wave comes, and how will I steer the canoe?

SCENE EIGHT

[*Lights to* LUCY *as she stands in the playing area.*]

LUCY: The doctor informed me that the tumor was rapidly altering. It approached the surface, exhibiting a dark spot. He said should it become an open ulcer, the whole system would be overcome with its malignancy. He advised immediate operation, warning me that my system would not tolerate any drug to deaden the pain. I agreed to proceed. That night, after everyone had retired, I walked for many hours, back and forth in the yard. Depraved, diseased, and helpless, I yield myself up entirely to the will of the holy one. Cold daylight. The doctor now informs me all is in readiness. [LUCY *walks into the MH, with a cross-fade*] The chair, the white porcelain wash basins, the dozens of fresh, clean towels, the shiny medical instruments, the strings for tying my arteries, shiny needles to sew up my flesh. I sink into the chair wishing it would swallow me away. The doctor shows me how I must hold my left arm, how to press my feet against the foot of the chair. He looks at me, "Have you made up your mind to have it cut out?" "Yes sir." "Are you ready now?" "Yes sir." My shawl is removed exhibiting my left arm. My breast and side are perfectly bare. I see the knife in the doctor's hand. "I am going to begin now." "Yes sir." Then comes a gash long and deep, first on one side of my breast and then on another. Deep sickness seizes me, deprives me of my breakfast. This is followed by extreme faintness. My sufferings are no longer local. Agony spreads through my whole system. I feel every inch of me failing. Every glimpse I have of the doctor is only his hand covered to the wrist with blood. It seems like hours that I feel my flesh cut away. I am beneath his hand, cutting, cutting out the entire breast, cutting out the glands, cutting under my arm, tying up the arteries, sewing up the wound. I know it is vanity, but I feel grateful that God has preserved what small dignity I now have. During the whole operation he has granted that I do not lose control of my voice or person. [*Long pause*] Kindly, the doctor tells me, "There is not one in a thousand who could have borne it as you have done." [*Pause*] Many dangers still lie ahead of me. I am greatly debilitated and often see duplicates of everything my eye beholds. Now, when all is done, a hollowness falls over me.

[*Lights rise a bit, and* SYBIL *enters.* PALI *stands apart watching them.*]

LUCY: [*reaching for* SYBIL's *hand*] Sister.
SYBIL: How are you, Lucy?
LUCY: I don't know.
SYBIL: You're still weak.
LUCY: Yes.
SYBIL: Is there any pain?
LUCY: Yes, and a kind of emptiness.
SYBIL: The doctor says I must change the dressing.
LUCY: Oh.
SYBIL: [*cautiously*] I hope that—
LUCY: I know now I'll be nothing but a shame to my husband.
SYBIL: Lucy, don't say that.
LUCY: Everyone knows. That's the first thing that people will think of when they see. I'll be a shame to him.
SYBIL: Don't think such things.
LUCY: You know it's true.
SYBIL: You must thank God for your life.
LUCY: [*no conviction*] Yes, I must.
SYBIL: Lucy, I have to change the dressing.
LUCY: Yes.
SYBIL: [*nervous*] Does it look, I mean is it—
LUCY: It's not a pretty sight. I'm sorry, Sybil.
SYBIL: Oh.
LUCY: There's also an odor, not pleasant.
SYBIL: I see, well, I must change it.
LUCY: I'm sorry, Sybil.

[SYBIL *approaches her. She begins to undo* LUCY's *dress.* SYBIL *is obviously in great distress over having to do the task. She several times turns away and then goes back to the work. Her anxiety builds. She becomes visibly nauseated. She struggles with the feeling, but finally turns away.*]

SYBIL: God forgive me, Lucy.

[*Silence*]

SYBIL: I can't do it. I can't.

LUCY: I'm sorry.

SYBIL: No, it's I who am sorry and ashamed.

LUCY: Is it very hard to see?

SYBIL: Yes, for me. I want so much to help you, but—

LUCY: It's all right, Sybil.

SYBIL: I've tended the sick so many times, I don't understand these feelings. . . .

LUCY: You must get the doctor to do it.

SYBIL: It frightens me.

LUCY: It won't happen to you, Sybil.

SYBIL: You were right, anything could happen to us here. [*Pause*] I'm so sorry.

LUCY: Don't say anymore, please, just get the doctor to see to it.

[*Exit* SYBIL. PALI, *who has been watching, slowly comes forward. A soft spot rises in KH.* KA'AHUMANU *rises, an observer to this scene.* PALI *goes to* LUCY.]

PALI: I wish to do this for you, Mrs. Thurston.

LUCY: Pali?

PALI: Yes, I wish to help you.

LUCY: You may feel sickened.

PALI: No. Tell me what to do.

[*Silence*]

[*firmly*] You will tell me what to do, and I will do it.

LUCY: First, you must remove the old dressings.

PALI: Yes.

LUCY: Then, you must wash the wound with . . . Pali?

PALI: `Ae?

LUCY: [*taking her hand*] I will remember this kindness all my days.

[*Lights fade on the MH for a beat, then slowly rise.* KA'AHUMANU *enters the MH.* PALI *is pinning up the hem of a white dress.* PALI *and* KA'AHU-MANU *look at each other.* SYBIL *enters and sees them.*]

SYBIL: Good morning.

KA'AHUMANU: Ah, good morning.

SYBIL: So you are resolved to study for baptism?

KA'AHUMANU: Yes.

SYBIL: Pali will be baptized this Sunday.

KA'AHUMANU: She will?

SYBIL: Yes, she has studied very hard.

[*Enter* LUCY, *arm in a sling*]

LUCY: The Christian path is not the easy one.

SYBIL: But the one which brings salvation.

PALI: I need a needle.

LUCY: You may sit here and sew.

PALI: Perhaps I'm not wanted.

[*Silence*]

KA'AHUMANU: You know these questions for the baptism, Pali?

PALI: `Ae.

KA'AHUMANU: Then you will sit beside me and help me.

PALI: [*sitting*] `Ae.

[SYBIL *gives* PALI *a catechism book and one to* KA'AHUMANU.]

SYBIL: Pali, you will begin the lesson by asking the questions.

PALI: Me? You wish me to ask the questions to—

SYBIL: Yes, you.

PALI: Here is the first question: "What is sin?"

KA'AHUMANU: [*reading back slowly*] "Sin is any want of conformity to or . . ."

PALI: ". . . or transgression of—"

KA'AHUMANU: "Or transgression of the law of God."

PALI: "What is the sin by where our first parents fell?"

KA'AHUMANU: "The sin by where our first parents fell, . . ." You read it first to me, Pali, my pua.

PALI: `Ae. "The sin by where our first parents fell was the eating of the forbidden fruit."

[*At the reading of the questions, the lights start a slow fade to black. Lights to* KA'AHUMANU *and* HANNAH, *who meet on the playing area.* HANNAH *is once again dressed in a kikepa instead of a Western dress.*]

HANNAH: Aloha, nō.

KA'AHUMANU: Aloha. Hannah. I hear from the village that you've chosen to live with Jones.

HANNAH: Yes, but what will you choose, my ali'i?

KA'AHUMANU: Why did you do it, Hannah?

HANNAH: I thought this new God, this new way of being, would fill me up full of happiness and purpose, as I thought it did the mikanele, and for a time, it did. But the happiness went farther and farther away, something to wait for after death, and I remembered what you once said to me. That happiness was a thing we need while we are alive. Come away from them, don't join them in their thought that everything which gives pleasure is bad. Come back to the way things were before.

KA'AHUMANU: You know things will never be as they were! The world changes before our eyes everyday, and we must change or be lost. Besides, we cannot go back to the way things were before. I will put aside those old ways because the people need a new way for the new world which comes to us. We will have laws. We will be Christian people.

HANNAH: This can never be my way. I will believe there is another way.

KA'AHUMANU: What way is that?

HANNAH: I don't know. I only know that I can't follow the ways of their God, although I know many of their ways to be good. It is something inside that will not be closed off, and this is what will happen to me if I listen to them.

KA'AHUMANU: Our lives take us on different journeys then, Hannah.

HANNAH: `Ae.

KA'AHUMANU: [embracing HANNAH] Aloha, my pua.

HANNAH: You will tell Mrs. Bingham something for me?

KA'AHUMANU: What is it?

HANNAH: [leaving] Tell her that it is summertime!

KA'AHUMANU: [alone] Aloha, my pua, and may the old Gods watch over your life.

[Exit HANNAH. KA'AHUMANU moves to a single spot of light downstage center.]

KA'AHUMANU: [straight out] Yes, I have listened to you my brothers. Now hear my thoughts. The foreigners are among us. Many more will come. Beware, some will come like the hoards of caterpillars, hiding their hunger to devastate the land as we know it, until the time when all the Hawaiian people may be trodden underfoot. We have seen this greed already with the sandalwood trade. We must fight now with our quick thoughts and our grasp of foreign ways. To think too long on the ways of the past is to ignore the hungry sharks that swim among us. I do not look to the past with contempt, but seek to preserve the ways that were good, uniting them with what is good of this new world, that comes to us, now.

[Blackout]

THE END

Cleveland Raining

a play in two acts
with a Prologue and Epilogue
by
SUNG RNO

He cannot see her happiness,
hidden in a thicket of blanket
and shining hair.
On the grass beside their straw mat,
a black umbrella,
blooming like an ancient flower,
betrays their recent arrival.
Suspicious of so much sunshine,
they keep expecting rain.

—CATHY SONG, "MAGIC ISLAND"

We must talk now. Fear
Is fear. But we abandon one another.

—GEORGE OPPEN, "LEVIATHAN"

Originally produced by East West Players in Los Angeles, Tim Dang, Artistic Director.

CHARACTERS

JIMMY "RODIN" KIM, *a Korean-American man in his late 20s. A failed artist. Walks with a noticeable limp.*

MARI KIM, *his younger sister, a medical student in her early 20s. A healer.*

MICK, *a mechanic of sorts, late 20s. A native Ohioan, non-Asian.*

STORM, *a woman involved in a motorcycle accident, late 20s. An Asian American woman who rejects everything "Asian."*

SETTING: The KIM family lives in a country house in Ohio, about a hundred miles south of Cleveland. The action is divided around the KIM's garage (a converted barn) and their front porch. The Volkswagen in the garage should be the most real object on stage. Everything else should be fluid, ephemeral, barely real.

TIME: An apocalyptic time.

PROLOGUE
SCENE ONE

JIMMY:	MARI:
Fork.	When I was a baby
Spoon.	my *Ahppah* had to
Knife.	feed me by himself
Brush.	*Uhmmah* wasn't around so he
Bread.	would come home early
Water.	from the clinic to make
Paint.	me lunch and at first he
Brush.	had trouble making
Mother.	the rice because he
Pencil.	had to make it soft
Brushfork.	like porridge for me
Forkbrush.	I would stare up at
Mother.	the reflection of me in
Motherbrush.	his glasses and he would
Paper.	never look at me, but
Knifepencil.	stare at the pot as the
Knifer.	rice got cooked,
Forker.	sometimes I caught him
Fuck.	looking at me and I—
[*Pause.*]	[*Pause.*]
Eatdrinkshit.	would smile at him he
Chew . . . chew.	would tell me that I
Eatdrinkshit.	looked just like *Uhmmah*

Chew . . . chew.	he wished we were
Brush.	still in Korea he
Dripping.	wouldn't say it just think
Knifeshitdrink.	it but I didn't
Dripping.	figure all of this out
Pencil. Mother.	until later, much later.

END OF SCENE ONE

SCENE TWO

[MARI, *alone in the light.*]

MARI: My mother, my *Uhmmah*, my painter, she painted a still life of a bowl of cherries and she captured the color just right. I could stare at that painting for hours. She had caught them at that exact instant when it would only be a matter of hours before they would start smelling too sweet, like wine. If I stared at that painting my body would move . . . the inside would move a little left of the outer . . . like when the earth shakes slightly, you feel disoriented. Then one day I couldn't stand just looking at the picture anymore and I had to lick the surface with my tongue to taste the cherries, but the taste wasn't there. My tongue got cut, there was the taste of blood. And still, the taste wasn't there.

END OF SCENE TWO

END OF PROLOGUE

ACT I

SCENE ONE

[*Late morning—the garage, a converted barn. Tools, used car-parts are scattered on the floor. To the left is a Volkswagen bug, battered and rusty, resting on blocks. Beyond the wall are cornfields and trees in the distant horizon.*]

[*Lights come up on* JIMMY *sleeping in the Volkswagen.* MARI *sits next to him, slowly wrapping a bandage around her arm.* JIMMY *tosses and turns.* MARI *stops wrapping the bandage, stares at her brother.*]

[*Long silence.*]

MARI: *Oppah.* [*Pause.*] Jimmy. [*Pause.*] *Rodin.*
JIMMY: [*Waking.*] What?
MARI: Help me.

[*He gives her his finger. She ties the bandage. He gets up and starts putting on clothes, shaving, etc.*]

MARI: [*Pause.*] I couldn't find him.
JIMMY: Yeah?
MARI: I went driving for an hour.
JIMMY: He'll come back.
MARI: You think? [*He doesn't answer.*] While I was driving I saw this accident on the road. This woman riding a motorcycle hit this pickup truck. I got out of my car to help, but she wouldn't let me touch her. She's screaming at me like I was the one who hit her. Tries to tear my hair out. She wants to kill the driver in the pickup, but she can't move, so she starts throwing parts of her bike at me. She hits me with this— [*She points to an exhaust pipe on the ground.*] Finally the ambulance came and took them both away.
JIMMY: Women shouldn't be out on the road. [*He cuts himself shaving.*] Shit! [*He puts tissue paper on the cut.*]
MARI: I saw her face so clearly as she flew over her bike. Like I've known her my whole life.

And this is the crazy thing: she hit her own grandmother.
JIMMY: Weirder things have happened.
MARI: Like what?
JIMMY: She could have hit her lover. Or her boss. Her minister. See, the possibilities are endless. I'm hungry. [JIMMY *looks at* MARI *expectantly.*] I thought maybe you had fixed something.
MARI: Think again.

[JIMMY *pulls out a jar of kimchee from the car, and a bottle of beer. He opens the jar and starts eating with a pair of chopsticks.*]

JIMMY: You want some?
MARI: No thanks. I'll never understand how you can eat kimchee on an empty stomach.
JIMMY: Kimchee is the one distinctive dish that Koreans have. There is no other dish in the world that comes close to it.
MARI: Sauerkraut.
JIMMY: Sauerkraut is for a baseball game, on top of a hot dog. Kimchee is more . . . spiritual.

MARI: And that's why you eat it?

JIMMY: I eat it because I'm lazy.

MARI: Shouldn't you be at work.

JIMMY: Oh . . . I was meaning to tell you . . . I quit.

Don't look at me like that.

Look, I'm unpacking a crate of tomatoes. I'm being the model worker. Then this lady comes up to me. Asks me where the bananas are. *Bananas.*

MARI: So what?

JIMMY: She was calling me a racial slur.

MARI: Chink is a slur. Gook is a slur. *Banana* is . . . a fruit.

JIMMY: What does it mean to you?

MARI: It means white on the inside, yellow on the outside.

JIMMY: It means *assimilated.* That's a fucking slur, if I've ever heard one.

MARI: You were in the fruit section.

JIMMY: It was her tone. She didn't just ask me for the bananas. She asked me for the *bananas.* You see? So I just get real quiet with her, just stare her in the eyes, and I say, "I don't know, ma'am, we don't serve people like you," and I throw a tomato in her face. Right in the eye.

MARI: You got fired.

JIMMY: Fired, quit—it's semantics.

MARI: Bullshit.

JIMMY: The only bullshit around here is that a big flood is about to come and no one seems to be aware of it.

MARI: The flood.

JIMMY: For a whole year I've been dreaming about the same thing, this Volks-wagen.

MARI: I know.

JIMMY: It was in my head, every night—I couldn't get rid of it. It scared me at first, but then I saw the power of it. This dream was a vision of some kind. Instead of resisting it, I opened myself up to it. And then—

MARI: I bet you expect me to bring in the money.

JIMMY: And then, I walk into this junkyard and I see it. It's the exact one that showed up in my dreams, sky blue, rust in all the right places. So I have to buy it, now don't I? But in these dreams I'm floating. You and I are floating. In this car, this very Volkswagen right here. There's enough kimchee and beer to last us forever. It's raining and raining. Everything gets covered up. Ohio becomes one big lake.

MARI: One big lake.

JIMMY: That's right. You have no imagination, that's your problem.

MARI: It's always an escape for you. You have to be running.

JIMMY: I'm not the one who blew out of this house. I'm still here.

MARI: You don't ever worry about him?

JIMMY: Of course I do. But I don't have to see him in front of me sipping his tea, reading his newspaper, to know what's happening with him.

MARI: That's a cop-out.

JIMMY: You believe what you want to believe. I just don't see how driving all over the interstate changes anything. He's probably not even in the area. Maybe he left us so that we could be free. Free to concentrate on more important things. The rain. The flood.

MARI: Why do you keep talking about this flood?

JIMMY: It's going to happen. I can feel it.

MARI: What you're feeling is all that kimchee you ate.

JIMMY: It'll be a mission of mercy. It'll take people in need. For instance, those two women in the accident.

MARI: You're not a prophet. You're a fired stock boy. You're someone who names himself after a sculptor and then . . .

JIMMY: Then what?

MARI: [Beat.] And you don't even care that he's been gone for almost a week now—no trace, nothing, zip, nada, zero. Why do I have to be the one who looks for him?

JIMMY: No one told you to look for him.

MARI: No one told you to dream about Volkswagens.

JIMMY: I'm happy about my Volkswagen. Are you happy about what you do?

MARI: I'm not supposed to be happy. The unwritten law of all Korean families: the youngest sibling takes care of everyone else's shit.

JIMMY: You exaggerate.

[MARI exits, bumping into MICK as he enters.]

[MICK is awkward and pushy at the same time. He wears overalls with his name "MICK" written into the fabric over his chest. He stands in the doorway for a moment.]

MICK: Hello.

JIMMY: Yes.

MICK: Are you Jimmy Roadin?

JIMMY: Rodin.

MICK: I hope I didn't come at a bad time.

JIMMY: No. That's just my sister.

MICK: What seems to be the problem?

JIMMY: She doesn't understand me.

MICK: I meant about the car.

JIMMY: Right. I need some work on the engine.

MICK: This VW here? Well, it's a beaut alright. Want to make it bigger? More power?

JIMMY: That wouldn't hurt, for what I need it for. But I need more than that.

MICK: More?

JIMMY: It has to be waterproof.

MICK: Uh-huh.

JIMMY: I need it to float actually.

MICK: Why, you taking it out onto Lake Erie or something? Ha-ha . . .

JIMMY: Yes.

MICK: Oh yeah? What the hell for?

JIMMY: For the big flood that's coming.

MICK: I'm sorry, am I at the right place?

JIMMY: I don't know, are you?

MICK: [*Checking his notebook.*] Yes, I am. Now let me get this straight. You want to make a boat out of a Volkswagen? What the hell for? And why a Volkswagen?

JIMMY: It was a vision, a vision that I've been dreaming about for a year.

MICK: Like a ghost.

JIMMY: Don't you know what I'm talking about? When you're a kid, you just wish things, like—

MICK: Like wishing the world was made of ice cream.

JIMMY: Yeah, or you think—

MICK: You're trapped on a island with some gorgeous, stacked babe—

JIMMY: But then you wake up and it's not there anymore—

MICK: Your sheet's soaking wet. [*Beat.*] You're talking about all those ideas you have when you're a little kid. I don't have those no more. But I understand where you're comin' from. Where do you want to go with this thing?

JIMMY: We'll have to see when the rains come. Maybe up north.

MICK: You mean, Cleveland?

JIMMY: If we have to.

MICK: Now I know you're crazy. And how long you figure to be on this thing?

JIMMY: A few months maybe.

MICK: You have a sail?

JIMMY: No.

MICK: Should never trust a machine without having a backup. That's why we got two hands, two legs. In case you lose one, you got an extra. What kind of fuel you using?

JIMMY: I'd like to build a fusion device. That way we can use the water as fuel.

MICK: What do you know about fusion?

JIMMY: I have some books.

MICK: A book don't tell you jack.

JIMMY: My father was a doctor. He taught us things.

MICK: So it's in your blood.

JIMMY: You're a mechanic, right?

MICK: And a damned good one. Don't get me wrong. I want to help you. I just don't work like you do. I block things out of my head. But I live the idea of making a VW float. What'd you say, we were gonna float over Lake *Ohio*?

JIMMY: Why not?

MICK: I like that. Yes, very much. You're payin' me, right?

JIMMY: Are you scared?

MICK: Scared? There ain't too much in this world that I'm scared of. Except a few things. Certain vegetables mainly. But why are you doing this?

JIMMY: Think of those people who climbed Mount Everest. Why do they go to all that trouble? People want to know how it *feels* to be on top of that damned thing.

MICK: I don't like heights. Shit, if I want to be on top of something, it's not going to be some damned *rock*.

JIMMY: If you were to climb a mountain, why would you do it?

MICK: But I wouldn't.

JIMMY: What if there was a mountain in front of you and you absolutely had no choice? What if you had no choice about it?

Answer the question.

MICK: I told you, I don't know.

JIMMY: Use your imagination.

MICK: Like we used to do in nursery school? Like that?

JIMMY: Yes. Like that.

[MICK *sits down. He closes his eyes.*]

MICK: Alright . . . Imagine it. Jesus. Okay . . . I can see the mountain . . . a big mountain . . . a tall mountain. Trees on it, the whole nine yards. And birds, they're shitting on me and everything. Are you satisfied?

JIMMY: Walk towards it.

MICK: I'm walking . . .

JIMMY: What do you see?

MICK: Corn . . . lots of corn.

JIMMY: What else?

MICK: Cows. [*Sniffs.*] Manure. I'm still walking towards it; there it is, I mean, it's miles away, you want me to start flapping my arms? [*He stops.*] Jesus. [*He opens his eyes.*] What are you doing to me?

JIMMY: Nothing.

MICK: You were leading me into the corn.

JIMMY: So what?

MICK: I don't like corn. Do you?

JIMMY: I don't know. . . . I eat it.

MICK: Yeah, but do you go crazy about it? Do you hang out with it?

JIMMY: Corn tastes good. It's a vegetable. It doesn't hurt anybody.

MICK: But man, I hate it. I hate corn. The sight of it makes me nauseous.

JIMMY: So don't eat it.

MICK: It sticks in me. It doesn't come out when I eat it. So every time I see it I feel like I'm eating it again.

JIMMY: It's just a plant, man. Ignore it.

MICK: You can't ignore it out here! It's like ignoring an ocean when you're swimming in it! It's a fact of life, it's there every day, every morning you wake up, staring you in the eyes.

So when I closed my eyes, you know what I saw? The stalks of corn—they started breeding, like fish—they started swimming and then there was like a school of them—and they were breeding like faster than you could even count—until there was like a whole fucking ocean of corn, a whole fucking country of corn—and I can't stand corn!

I've just been fooling myself. I thought I could condition myself, you know to like, or at least to get along with it. But it doesn't work that way.

Shit. The world just isn't the way we want it, is it?

JIMMY: No.

MICK: It's a sign. I can see that. A sign for change. When do we leave?

END OF SCENE ONE

SCENE TWO

[MARI *is reading a thick medical book while sitting on the porch.* MICK *sits a small distance away from her. He wipes his face with a dirty rag. Silence, then . . .*]

MICK: You don't mind me sitting here, do you?

MARI: No.

MICK: That's good. Because this is a mighty nice spot to be sitting. I can understand why you like it.

MARI: I'm glad.

MICK: Your brother's a little strange, ain't he?

MARI: Strange?

MICK: He's building an ark. Out of a Volkswagen.

MARI: He likes to keep busy.

MICK: Well, he's no Noah. [*Beat.*] Maybe you're weird too; what do you do?

MARI: I'm studying to be a doctor.

MICK: You've got the temperament of a doctor.

MARI: What do you mean by that?

MICK: By what?

MARI: "You have the temperament of a doctor." What the hell is that supposed to mean? I'm not just a cold, heartless scientist.

MICK: I never said you were.

MARI: You insinuated it.

MICK: Sorry.

MARI: You know, I used to play the piano. But then . . . my hands . . . didn't behave the way they used to. So I stopped playing.

MICK: What happened to your hands?

MARI: I had . . . an accident.

MICK: I don't generally like doctors. But you're different somehow.

MARI: Because I'm a woman? An Asian woman?

MICK: I can tell you really don't even like it. I don't like what doctors do. They open you up. They stick things into your body. [*Beat.*] So are you coming too?

MARI: Where?

MICK: To Cleveland.

MARI: Who's going to Cleveland?

MICK: Your brother.

MARI: I don't travel with my brother.

MICK: Why not?

MARI: That car isn't going anywhere.

MICK: You're a skeptic.

MARI: Skeptic?

MICK: Yea.

MARI: I'm a realist.

MICK: But life isn't real, you know. It just doesn't work that way.

For instance, my truck fell on me once. I was under it and the jack slipped. By the time the tow truck came I felt like me and the truck had fused, like I had melted with that engine and that steering column. They lifted all that metal off of me and part of me was still trapped in my old Ford.

MARI: Why are you telling me this?

MICK: To show you the possibilities out there.

MARI: Look. There's not a cloud in the sky.

MICK: You have beautiful eyes. Has anyone ever told you that?

END OF SCENE TWO

SCENE THREE

[*On the porch.* MARI *begins to read from her book.*]

MARI: [*Opening the book and reading.*] "The cadaver should not be mistaken for a real live person. A cadaver is only a receptacle, a tool, a construction that houses something else, something once living. It is something similar to an empty house. The people who once lived there have all moved somewhere else: to another city, another country. The cadaver is an empty space, four walls, a ceiling: and silence. There should be no attachment to the house itself, not even to the people who have left."

[*She closes the book, pulls out her diary. She scribbles for a few moments, then turns back to her previous entry. She reads, the lights and sounds "reliving" this dream.*]

This was my dream last night. I'm driving down the interstate and it's overcast. I can see the highway stretching over the plains for miles, but I look to my right and I see a farm, cows grazing, but past all of this I see trees stretched out across the sky, the stalks of wheat are like porridge like hair like someone's belly and then it seems like I can see even further, that past the fields, past the farms, I see . . . water . . . and waves and I can smell the salt the heat the taste of that sea.

I feel like turning the car into that wetness, that abyss. Only there's the shoulder, there's the guardrail, so I ignore it, I keep driving, I keep my eyes on the road. But I can't stop looking over there, into that invisible lake in the side of my vision, so finally . . . I do it . . . I turn I take a sharp turn I'm turning and—

Then I'm flipping . . . through the air . . . flying and flipping . . . over the barrier, up and over, there's the totally pure moment of silence, and then it's all noise: concrete, glass, the car the air the metal breaking, all of it breaking, and I'm bleeding, I'm in pain, I'm hurt, but I can't tell you, I can't tell you how happy I feel.

[*Lights come up on* JIMMY *and* MICK *working on the engine.* MARI *walks around them and talks; they do not acknowledge her.*]

All this dreaming. It upsets me. First my brother, now me. This dreaming. I fear the car because maybe . . . he's right. Maybe there's no hope. Maybe it all has to come down . . . the house, the memories, the keepsakes . . . maybe, maybe, it all has to go. I can't believe that.

[*Addressing* JIMMY.] Our father, fast becoming a memory. I try to keep him alive. I put hundreds, thousands, of miles on my car trying to find some trace of him. I write letters to distant relatives. But no. Nothing.

Explanation? Is that what I seek. No. Something different. Something more than the facts.

[*To* MICK.] And these strangers that come into our lives. What to do with them? What way of expressing ourselves can be sufficient? How to make it into a neat appetizer to serve on a dish? So silly. So stupid.

[*Lights fade on the garage as—*STORM *walks up to the "porch" area, dressed in motorcycle gear; one of* STORM's *legs is bleeding noticeably. She has the dazed look of a survivor.* MARI *crosses over to porch, sits down as she was before.*]

STORM: Hi.
MARI: Hi. Can I help you?
STORM: What?
MARI: I said, can I help you?
STORM: Do you think you can help me?
MARI: It depends on what your problem is.

Wait. This morning. You were in the accident. You were on the bike.
STORM: Bike? My bike's back home isn't it? [*Parenthetical statements are as if to her Grandmother:*] (ALL SAFE AND SOUND, LIKE NOTHING EVER HAPPENED TO IT!)
MARI: Of course . . . it is.
STORM: No, there's nothing wrong with my bike. (LAY OFF! JUST FOR A MOMENT!)

MARI: Excuse me?

STORM: [*picking up* MARI's *book*] What's this? *Gray's Anatomy.* Studying to be a doctor are you? Well, I've always admired doctors. (HEY I'M ABOUT TO ASK HER, DON'T WORRY.)

MARI: Who do you keep talking to?

STORM: Oh, just my Granny. She's telling me that I should quit beating around the bush. (NO THANK YOU! NO! I SAID NO!)

MARI: Granny?

STORM: My Grandmother. She's just asking me if I want a whiskey shot and I said no. She's bugging me, because it seems that my bike isn't safe and sound at home. You haven't seen it around here have you?

MARI: No, I'm afraid I haven't.

STORM: (I TRIED, OKAY? SHE SAID SHE HASN'T SEEN IT!) Well, thanks for the chitchat. I best be going.

MARI: You shouldn't be walking around like that. Your leg . . .

STORM: It's just a scratch.

MARI: I think I should take you to the hospital.

STORM: I need to find my bike first. See, I just kind of lost it.

[STORM *loses her balance.* MARI *holds her.*]

MARI: Maybe you should just rest inside for a little while.

STORM: No, I don't like being inside of things. Hospitals, houses, buildings, you name it . . . relationships . . . I can't stand them. Let me just sit here for a little bit, then I'll be on my way. [*She sits in* MARI's *chair.*] (I KNOW IT'S NOT POLITE, BUT IT'S ONLY FOR A MOMENT.) Jesus, she can be such a pain in the ass sometimes.

MARI: I really think you should be in a hospital.

STORM: I don't believe in them. Like I said, I admire doctors, but hospitals: they're like tombs. Big fluorescent tombs. [*She inhales the air.*] What's that smell?

MARI: My brother likes to eat kimchee.

STORM: Kimchee?

MARI: You don't know what that is?

STORM: No.

MARI: You're Asian aren't you?

STORM: I'm what?

MARI: Asian.

STORM: You mean, like a boat person? No, I'm American.

MARI: But your parents must have been Asian. . . .

STORM: You've got a lot of nerve assuming all that. I never knew my parents, okay? I've lived with Granny all my life. She's not really my Granny, she just likes people to call her that. No, it wasn't kimchee I was smelling, it was some WD–40. My favorite machine lubricant.

MARI: My brother's working on his car.

STORM: What about *your* parents?

MARI: They don't live here anymore.

STORM: (HEY! I'M JUST TALKING HERE ALRIGHT?) She's very weird about guests. She thinks if a guest comes you have to treat them like royalty. And if you go over to someone else's house, forget it, you'd better behave like you're in a museum.

MARI: You always talk to her like that?

STORM: We're very close.

Well, it was nice meeting you. Hope you find someone who does know what kimchee is. [*She gets up, her leg can't support her weight and she sits back down again.*] Do you mind if I rest here for just a little bit?

MARI: Why don't you just stay for awhile? I can put you in my brother's old room.

STORM: No, this is fine. I like being outdoors.

MARI: But what if it rains?

STORM: It's not going to rain for a long time.

MARI: I like you already.

STORM: Is it okay if I call you Doc?

MARI: Just don't treat me like one. And what should I call you?

STORM: My name is Storm.

END OF SCENE THREE

SCENE FOUR

[*Nighttime, garage.* MICK *is sleeping near the car. A lone spot on* JIMMY, *who speaks as if trying to explain something to himself.*]

JIMMY: Didn't always get these things in my head. Used to follow the rules. Listened to my father, did most of what he said. He gave me medical books to read. We got along fine. Then I decided to take up hunting. I went out on a day when it was wet. The sky grey, almost black. I kept walking even though I was getting lost. The rain starts coming down. It rolls down my face and it feels like I'm crying. Then I am crying. I can't really tell. It's all mixed together. I lean against a tree and I look up and this is crazy, there's this huge pencil in the sky. It's huge, monstrous. Big and yellow, the size of a tree. It's coming straight towards me, the eraser side down. Like it wants to rub me out. I said, this fucking pencil is not going to get me and I point my gun at it, only it's slippery and I feel it slipping. I hear it go off. I'm standing in a puddle. I look down and the rain is red. I'm not crying anymore. My foot's sinking deeper and deeper into this puddle. Can't move. Can't think. The rain comes down harder. I try to yell out. I can't hear myself. I'm drowned out by the wind. And I'm just this tree in a storm, the bark all stripped away. Just a naked piece of wood.

That's when I changed my name from Kim to Rodin. Kim means gold in Korean, but doesn't mean a damn thing in English. It's abstract, a word like "algebra" or "mutation." I wanted a name that meant something to me. Now Rodin was perfect, I thought. Jimmy R. Had a gangster ring to it. Someone who lived by his wits. And I had a battle wound to back it up. No one was going to mess with me.

[A *light comes up on* MARI, *who approaches* JIMMY *slowly. She is meant to be a figure of his imagination, his conscience.*]

MARI: And who was messing with you big brother?
JIMMY: Who let you in here?
MARI: I live here, don't I? Answer the question. Who was messing with you?
JIMMY: Everyone. The kids at school, my teachers. My father.
MARI: And so you took on the name of Rodin. The French sculptor. Silly, don't you think?
JIMMY: I did what I could.
MARI: Because . . . as I remember it, you were never an artist. You failed at it. I have a vivid memory of you coming back from school, angry about how no one understood you, how life was just shit . . . and then you went up into the attic and started getting Mom's old painting things.
JIMMY: Do we have to go through this?
MARI: And you were wearing this oversized painting shirt and you had an easel set up; you looked just like a painter should look I guess, although I've never met a real live painter; I mean, there was Mom, but I never knew her. And you tried and tried and tried to paint something, anything, but then what did you do?
JIMMY: I burned it all.
MARI: Even *Ummah's* things.
JIMMY: Yes.
MARI: And then what did you do?

JIMMY: I don't remember.

MARI: And then what did you do?

JIMMY: I told you, I don't . . .

MARI: What? [*Emphatically.*]

JIMMY: I stepped on your fingers.

> [MARI *stares at him with a look of victory. He bows his head. Light out on* MARI. JIMMY *holds his head in his hands.* MICK *stirs in his sleep, wakes up.*]

MICK: Jimmy R? You alright?

JIMMY: I'm fine.

MICK: [*Pause.*] I want to ask you something. Why do you live in this barn?

JIMMY: Convenience. And I don't want to drive my sister insane.

MICK: You guys could just live apart.

JIMMY: No, we need to be together. But a little apart.

MICK: I've been thinking. About Noah. Now the reason that old guy got on his boat was that the world was too corrupt and sinful, right? After the flood, then Noah and God should have had a clean slate to work with. Things should have gotten better. And they might have, for just a short time. But then the same old shit started happening: the same greed, the same corruption. The harlots . . .

JIMMY: Harlots?

MICK: Yeah, all of that shit. So my question is: why go to all that trouble when you end up at the very same place that you started from?

JIMMY: I look at it like motor oil. You have to change it constantly. Does the engine get any better? No. It's maintenance. Having a flood every now and then is a form of maintenance.

MICK: Jimmy R, you don't have to put everything into car talk for me to understand. [*Pause.*] Are you going to take animals?

JIMMY: Animals?

MICK: Like Noah did. Two of every kind: two rabbits, two sparrows, two pigs, two cattle . . .

JIMMY: We don't have to be like Noah.

MICK: We might get lonely, you know?

> My leg hurts. I can't sleep when my leg hurts. A good sign, though. My leg only acts up when it rains.

JIMMY: What happened to your leg?

MICK: I was under this pickup truck and it fell on me. Fucked my leg up really bad. I was lucky it didn't kill me. I actually didn't feel that much pain. I kind of liked being under that truck. You want to know a secret? [*Beat.*] I got . . . kind of turned on being under that truck.

JIMMY: Turned on?

MICK: Yeah, like . . . I got hard. I've never told anyone that before.

JIMMY: I don't know what to say. Did you come?

MICK: No! Jesus, that's sick.

JIMMY: Sorry.

MICK: I cared very deeply for that truck. When it's wet, my leg acts up. Probably the metal in there feeling like it has to rust. It has a mind of its own.

JIMMY: I have something like that too. With my foot. It happened a long time ago. A hunting accident.

MICK: You don't look like a hunter.

JIMMY: It was dark. This flash storm. It started raining. The gun was wet, it just slipped in my hands. That's all it did, really. Just slipped in my hands. You know, metal and water, they just don't mix.

MICK: And then what happened?

JIMMY: My sister came out. I think that's the day she realized she could be a great doctor. Because you see, there was no one else in the house. My father . . . he was gone. He was away at the clinic.

MICK: It was bad?

JIMMY: There was some blood. It didn't hurt though. That always surprised me.

END OF SCENE FOUR

SCENE FIVE

[*On the porch, night.* STORM *is sleeping on a makeshift "bed," made from a lawn chair.* MARI *sits next to her, watching over her. She opens her diary again.*]

MARI: [*Reading while writing.*] Someone's sticking their face into the crib. I'm sleeping. I feel someone's lips. Soft. Warm. There's that smell that I remember but I don't know from where. I open my eyes, my baby eyes, and I see my brother's face. He looks sad, he looks scared. Why are you scared, *Oppah?* Someone's shouting in the other room. Someone's crying. I'm crying. [*Stops writing.*] If that someone is me, then who is the other someone? [*To* STORM.] Can you tell me? A simple sign would do. I've been driving for over a week now. Still no sign of him. Driving so much my callouses have callouses. I dream in interstate miles, in state highways that bump and jerk through my head while I try to sleep. And still no sign.

Memory is my only weapon, my only hope. My friends tell me to move on, to leave this place. They don't understand. Escape doesn't always solve things. You can't just leave the pieces behind and expect everything to be fine. The past finds you. What you've done before, comes to your door today and tomorrow. Look at my mother and father. They leave their country, Korea; they come here, they make a better place. They think that they can just pick up where they left off. Just lift the needle off that record player, put another disc on, let the needle drop back down again. But see, the music has changed. You need different ears here. In this corn country, this state where flat is a color, and grey is a song.

Are you getting all of this? Because I see you Storm. You look like me. We have the same hair, the same eyes. Similar, not that different. Then I think I know you. I don't really, of course. But I think I do. And that gives me a strange kind of hope, a feeling that I can stay.

[JIMMY *appears (not at all dreamlike), in his pajamas, his hair a mess. He and* MARI *stare at each other for a moment.* JIMMY *looks at* STORM.]

JIMMY: Who's this?
MARI: The motorcycle woman.
JIMMY: This isn't a hospital.
MARI: It's not a garage either.
JIMMY: What's her name?
MARI: Storm.
JIMMY: She almost looks Korean.
MARI: She's not.
JIMMY: How do you know?
MARI: A name like "Storm"?
JIMMY: You never know these days. I mean, she could be our mother for all we know.
MARI: That's not funny. Why are you up, anyway?
JIMMY: Mick just kept telling me his crazy stories. He fucks trucks.
MARI: He's definitely not normal.
JIMMY: Well, who is these days? [*Pause.*] When you go driving . . . what do you see?
MARI: Sometimes . . . when there's no one else around . . . I close my eyes, I swear, I can feel him.
JIMMY: That's dangerous. You could get yourself killed.
MARI: I even take my hands off the steering wheel. Then the car seems like it's floating.

And I slow down. I can feel him right there. And knowing this keeps me warm for the next few hours as I drive and drive.

JIMMY: Nothing I've done even approaches that. How can you just sit there and tell me a story like that? So calm. It doesn't even affect you . . . [*Agitatedly.*]

MARI: But it does affect me. That's why I told you.

[JIMMY *leaves. Lights dim for a second,* MARI *falls asleep, then the lights brighten: morning, a new day.* STORM *opens her eyes. She wakes* MARI.]

STORM: I'm not Korean. [*Pause.*] Did you hear me?

MARI: You were eavesdropping?

STORM: I can't help my ears from hearing things. Just leave me out of all this ethnic bullshit. Any word about my bike?

MARI: It's in the shop.

STORM: You gave my bike to *mechanics?* Who the hell gave you permission to do that? Mechanics are the worst! They're worse than dentists. At least a dentist doesn't have the radio on, playing for-shit-music, some blonde bimbo up on the wall, while he's got a drill stuck in your mouth. A dentist would never do that.

How come you know so much about the crash? You ain't the one who hit me are you?

MARI: You hit a truck. I was there watching it unfold in front of me like some awful flower. I watched you fly through the air.

STORM: How's the other person . . . the one who hit me.

MARI: She's in the hospital. I wanted to tell you—

STORM: She still knocked out?

MARI: She's unconscious, yes.

STORM: Serves her right.

MARI: You shouldn't say that.

STORM: It's the goddamned truth. She was looking dead at me wasn't she? She should have stopped.

MARI: It was no one's fault really.

STORM: I know what happened. That bitch shouldn't be out on the road.

MARI: Storm, she's your grand—

STORM: She sure took a mean hit. It was me against that truck . . . and I won. God I hate four-wheeled vehicles.

MARI: Did you hear me? Your grandmother is in the hospital.

STORM: Granny? You didn't go and call home did you? You didn't go and tell her I got into an accident?

MARI: No—

STORM: That's good. Shit, you scared me. God, you don't want my grandmother getting mixed up in any of this. She would just skin me alive. My Granny is not someone you want to fuck with. No. I'd rather be stuck in a bar with some horny mechanics than deal with Granny when she's mad.

She always did things her own way. She had her own way of telling *Little Red Riding Hood*. Little Red wasn't a namby-pamby, lavender and lace type, in her version; no, she saw the wolf for who he was right off. So when she asks the wolf, "My what big eyes you have, Granny," and the wolf answers back, "The better to see you with," Little Red doesn't miss a beat—she grabs the wolf by the throat, jabs her fingers in the wolf's eyes. Then she drags him out of bed and beats the living shit out of him. That's the way my grandmother told Mother Goose.

MARI: My father always said that Korean stories made more sense than American ones. They were more realistic he said.

STORM: I'm not Korean.

MARI: Okay.

STORM: No one ever told me who my parents were. I don't need to know. Look, I've taken enough of your time. [*She tries to get up, winces in pain, sits down again.*] Shit! [*Pause.*] You know, in *Little Red Riding Hood* . . . the grandmother—she doesn't make it does she?

END OF SCENE FIVE

SCENE SIX

[*Garage. Morning.* JIMMY *and* MICK *are having breakfast.* JIMMY *eats his usual kimchee/beer/rice combo;* MICK *is eating a bowl of cereal. Suddenly* MICK *has a revelation.*]

MICK: Amino acids! I finally figured out how we can take the animals. We just take the essential amino acids along and then whenever we feel like it, we can regenerate the animals: we can build them up from their DNA structure.

JIMMY: What do you know about amino acids?

MICK: I just read about them. Your sister is probably more knowledgeable in this area. Maybe we can ask her.

JIMMY: You ask her.

MICK: She's your sister.

JIMMY: She wouldn't listen to me.

MICK: No? Why is it that you don't seem to like each other?

JIMMY: I like my sister.

MICK: She doesn't like you.

JIMMY: She doesn't have to, she's my sister.

Come on, let's get to work.

MICK: So no amino acids?

JIMMY: Where did you get this idea anyway?

MICK: I was in the supermarket checkout line. It was a long line, so I picked up this magazine on display there. This article was about how some scientist believed that life started from this primordial soup, this pool of broth that had DNA, amino acids, just the basic building blocks, and then life just kind of happened when electricity hit it. That's what they believe anyway.

I couldn't finish the article because this stock boy was throwing vegetables at everyone and nearly caused a race riot.

JIMMY: I have a better idea. I've been thinking about how this engine should be powered. We need a special kind of fuel. Fusion, gas, none of it will work. This has been a mystery to me, because this mechanical element ties in with the spiritual element of the journey. And finally it hit me, the lightbulb went off in my brain: *emotional loss*.

MICK: Emotional loss?

JIMMY: Yeah. It runs on emotional loss.

MICK: How?

JIMMY: I'm leaving that to you.

MICK: Does that mean we're going to be depressed on this whole trip?

JIMMY: It just means . . . look, it's all based on entropy. Harnessing the energy of emotional breakdown. It makes sense if you think about it.

MICK: How do you expect me to do any of this? Tell me that. Emotional loss. And why is everything so destructive with you? I think it's all that foul cabbage you eat. It warps your brain.

JIMMY: What do you think that primordial soup tasted like, Mick?

MICK: I don't know.

JIMMY: I bet it tasted good.

MICK: Yeah? Like minestrone?

JIMMY: Clam chowder.

MICK: Red or white?

JIMMY: Red.

MICK: You're making me hungry. I finally placed your face. You used to work at the supermarket. You were that crazy stock boy. What was that all about anyway.

JIMMY: You really want to know?
MICK: Please.
JIMMY: Bananas.
MICK: Bananas?
JIMMY: Yeah, bananas.
MICK: I see.

END OF SCENE SIX

SCENE SEVEN

[*Porch.* MARI *has set up a makeshift hospital bed. She has just finished putting a fresh bandage on* STORM's *leg.*]

STORM: [*Grimacing.*] I need something.
MARI: You sure?
STORM: Yeah. It hurts . . .
MARI: Take these.

[STORM *swallows some pills, with water.*]

STORM: Thanks.
MARI: Just sit back and sleep for awhile.
STORM: You'll tell me if my bike happens along, won't you?
MARI: Of course.
STORM: Thanks.

[STORM *slowly falls asleep.* MARI *stares at her. She opens her medical book again.*]

MARI: [*Reading.*] "The medical student must learn to suppress the desire to ask too many questions. As a doctor there is a great danger in becoming too emotionally involved with one's patient. Empathy can only create a dangerous situation for the doctor. It will cloud the doctor's thought processes. It will in some cases lead to disaster."

[MARI *shuts the book. She takes out a matchbook and lights the medical book on fire. As the book catches fire, she kisses* STORM *very lightly on the forehead. She watches the book burn.* MICK *enters.*]

MICK: Your book is on fire.
MARI: I know.
MICK: Don't you want to put it out?

MARI: Let it burn. It makes me feel good.

MICK: I see why you and Jimmy are related. He needs your help. He's beginning to crack.

MARI: Crack?

MICK: He's got some crazy idea for his engine now. [*Seeing* STORM.] Who's that?

MARI: A friend.

MICK: She looks like you.

MARI: How?

MICK: Well . . . it's just . . . I didn't mean it like . . . forget it.

MARI: Why do you think my brother is cracking?

MICK: He's making it run off of emotional loss.

MARI: Sounds like my brother.

MICK: Are all Koreans like you?

MARI: Are all mechanics like you?

MICK: No, I'm serious. I remember I used to watch that TV show, you know the one with Hawkeye and Klinger, that crazy cross-dresser . . .

MARI: M*A*S*H?

MICK: That's it, and in that show, you people always seemed so, so—

MARI: So what?

MICK: *Nice.*

MARI: Nice?

MICK: Yeah, nice.

MARI: My parents were *from* Korea. I was born here. Just so you know.

MICK: Oh get off your high horse. My grandparents were from Germany. You don't see me having crazy dreams, burning my books, building boats out of Volkswagens.

MARI: Let's drop the subject.

MICK: It's dropped.

MARI: I hear you really like cars.

MICK: Sure I like them. I prefer trucks actually.

MARI: I hear you *really* like them.

MICK: I'm a mechanic, what do you expect? [*Moving to the fire.*] Do you mind if I put this out? [*He puts the fire out somewhat gingerly.*]

MARI: If you have so many doubts, why are you going on this trip?

MICK: I thought if I went along with him, I would learn something. I thought I could become . . . a better person.

MARI: And are you?

MICK: I don't know yet.

MARI: It's still not raining.

MICK: Oh, it's going to rain.

MARI: You're certain about this?

MICK: My leg's been hurting. It always knows when rain is coming.

MARI: Should I trust your leg?

MICK: My legs are very trustworthy. I have metal in mine.

MARI: You're a tin man. Are you looking for a heart?

MICK: Are you Dorothy?

MARI: I don't have any red shoes. And I don't live in Kansas. [*They laugh.*] I once thought the only thing that mattered was my music. I practiced day in and day out. I thought I was above everyone else. I was a musician, an artist. Then I lost my gift suddenly. It was like a curtain fell from eyes. I suddenly saw that my brother didn't talk to my father and vice versa. I saw that I had never known my mother.

I saw I saw I saw.

I saw that my brother had a talent for hurting everybody around him, most of all himself. And so I tried to do something different: I tried to become a doctor.

And the crazy thing is, my brother was responsible for all of that.

MICK: How do you mean?

MARI: He . . . just did things. An idea would come into his head and he wouldn't stop and think about it, he would just go ahead and act it out.

MICK: Internal combustion. The process by which a car burns fuel. The hydrogen bonds in the gasoline are destroyed, releasing energy.

That's your brother alright.

MARI: And what about the rest of us?

MICK: I guess we're the fuel.

END OF SCENE SEVEN

SCENE EIGHT

[*Focus switches back and forth between garage and porch. First: Garage. Later in the day. JIMMY is under the car. MICK is pacing around the car, clearly upset.*]

MICK: You told her. I can't believe you told her. That was a secret. That was like a code of honor, between men. And you broke that.

JIMMY: [*Sliding out from under car.*] What are you talking about?

MICK: Your sister. You told her.

JIMMY: About what?

MICK: Bessie.

JIMMY: Bessie?

MICK: My truck.

JIMMY: I did not.

MICK: Then why was she insinuating things? She was saying, "Mick, you like trucks don't you? You *really* like trucks." It was like she thought I was some kind of a pervert.

JIMMY: I didn't tell her anything.

MICK: Who else did then? The fucking mailman? You were the only one I told.

JIMMY: Okay, I may have made an offhand *remark*.

MICK: Like what?

JIMMY: Oh, I don't know, something like, like, uh . . .

MICK: I'm listening.

JIMMY: Like . . . uh . . . like—

MICK: LIKE WHAT?

JIMMY: Like: "Mick fucks trucks."

MICK: "Like: 'Mick fucks trucks'?" I can't believe—that's not even true! I told you I never did that! How could you tell her that?

JIMMY: I'm sorry.

MICK: Now your sister's going to tell her friends, their friends are going to tell their friends, and pretty soon the TV crews will be here, waving their cameras in my face.

JIMMY: It was just a figure of speech.

MICK: "Mick fucks trucks," is *not a figure of speech!*

I trusted you too. [*He picks up the jar of kimchee, threatens to heave it.*]

JIMMY: Put it down.

MICK: No! [MICK *opens the jar, but takes one eye-opening whiff* . . .] Oh my God . . . [JIMMY *takes the jar away. He starts eating.*]

JIMMY: Look, I'll even set things straight with my sister. I'll do it right now. [*He goes to the "door". Yells to* MARI *offstage.*] Hey Mari! Mick does not fuck trucks! [*To* MICK.] There? Is that better? [MICK *stands to the side, still angry.*] You know what I think? You're afraid.

MICK: [*Shows his fingernails, which are black.*] See that? That's built-in grease. Doesn't wash out. Ever. I am a real mechanic. So don't give me any bullshit about me being scared. I could make your engine run off of fucking yogurt if I wanted to.

JIMMY: [*Beat.*] Really?

[*Lights cross-fade to porch scene.* STORM *and* MARI.]

STORM: I had a very strange dream. As I was flying through the air over my bike, the windshield on that pickup truck, it became different, something soft, like skin, and so when I hit it, it didn't hurt, and when I looked up I saw the face of the person driving the car . . . and it was you.

MARI: Me?

STORM: What does that mean?

MARI: You've gone through a very traumatic event. [*Pause.*] I have some bad news. I got a call from the hospital today. The other person in the accident . . . she passed away.

STORM: Oh.

MARI: I thought you would like to know.

STORM: I'm glad . . . you told me. Did this other person suffer?

MARI: I don't think so.

STORM: It's funny, isn't it. I was the one on the motorcycle. She was in a truck. I was the one who should have died.

MARI: No one should have died.

STORM: There's always a victim in an accident.

MARI: You're a victim too.

STORM: I always survive, Doc. How about you?

MARI: I survive too.

STORM: You have to. You're the doctor.

MARI: Please, call me Mari.

STORM: Okay, Mari, when can I walk?

MARI: Soon. Hopefully.

STORM: That smell this morning . . . that was kimchee, wasn't it?

MARI: Yes.

STORM: I like it.

[*Lights cross-fade to garage scene.* MICK *has fashioned a large funnel on top of the engine.* JIMMY *looks at it.*]

JIMMY: What the hell is that supposed to be?

MICK: You wanted an emotional loss engine, well, here it is.

JIMMY: How does it work?

MICK: You just stick things into this funnel, and then it runs.

JIMMY: You sure?

MICK: Let's put something into it and try it out.

[*They look around the garage. They look at each other.*]

JIMMY: I don't really have anything. How about you?

MICK: It's your car, you should provide the fuel.

JIMMY: I don't have anything.

MICK: Nothing?

JIMMY: Just memories.

MICK: You have to have something.

JIMMY: Like what?

MICK: A photograph, a book, something.

JIMMY: I used to have some paintings. But I burned them.

MICK: What about your sister? Does she have something we could use?

JIMMY: She wouldn't give me anything like that.

MICK: How about this jar of kimchee?

JIMMY: No.

MICK: Just a piece?

JIMMY: No.

MICK: Why are you being so difficult?

JIMMY: Because . . . I'm a difficult person.

END OF SCENE EIGHT

SCENE NINE

[*Light and sound suggests a dream, or an awful memory. We see* MARI *kneeling on the ground,* JIMMY *standing above her. They are younger, both in their teens.*]

JIMMY: I said, put your hands out on the floor.

MARI: But why?

JIMMY: Because I said so.

MARI: You're going to hurt me.

JIMMY: I am not.

MARI: Then why do I have to put my hands out?

JIMMY: You have to trust me.

MARI: Trust?

JIMMY: Yes.

[*She places her hands on the ground. With a swift movement,* JIMMY *steps on them.* MARI *yells out in pain.*]

JIMMY: Be quiet.

MARI: You said I should trust you.

JIMMY: One day, you'll understand.
MARI: I hate you.
JIMMY: I'm sorry.
MARI: You don't want me to play the piano, is that it?
JIMMY: I don't want you to leave me.
MARI: My hands hurt.
JIMMY: Let me hold them.
MARI: Don't touch me.

END OF SCENE NINE

SCENE TEN

[*Night, on the porch.* STORM *is having a nightmare. Her words come out with very little control on her part.*]

STORM: [*Feverishly.*] Memory without a woman man life no meaning is is is without time meaning makes it with no lack loss the sky is so damn bright, where people, steep drop plunge down farewell good-bye only the woman no mother grandmother? Not dead, everyone dead yes, dead, yes, this shaking ground I walk every step a sinking please forgive don't forget old car driving now, flowers in the window little girl peeking over window broken glass everywhere so many faces. In the storm. Faceless. You got no face, no eyes. Burn my lips, break them.

Grandma?

Halmuni?

[*It begins to rain.*]

END OF SCENE TEN

END OF ACT I

ACT II
SCENE ONE

[*Early morning. The garage is now the central part of the stage. In the dim morning light we can see* JIMMY *and* MICK *asleep on the floor of the garage. The door bangs open noisily.* MARI *walks in, her clothes drenched and covered with mud. Her hands are covered in bright colors, like paints.*]

JIMMY: [*Barely awake.*] Mari?

MARI: Yeah?

JIMMY: It's raining.

MARI: Just a little.

JIMMY: No, a lot, it's raining a lot.

MARI: I was sitting out there. In the field. I wanted to listen to my thoughts. It was raining after all. Just like you said. And then I noticed that the dirt out there was oozing these—colors—this clay that had all these colors—I dropped my hands into it, this red and yellow and green—it's as if they were alive.

But where did they come from?

JIMMY: Why are you looking at me?

MARI: I wanted to just find some ground I could attach myself to. And then this happened. I like these colors. Don't you?

JIMMY: I can't see them.

MARI: These colors—they remind me of those pictures that Mom did.

JIMMY: What pictures?

MARI: Those oil paintings. The cherries.

JIMMY: No—you must have dreamed that—I don't remember that. Your memory is too active—it makes things up.

MARI: I thought I saw him this morning. I thought I saw him shooting through this intersection, so I followed him, but he ran a red light and—

JIMMY: And what?

MARI: Then I saw Storm. I saw the accident. [*Beat.*] In that dream when you are up on the water . . . what happens then?

JIMMY: We . . . wait.

MARI: For what?

JIMMY: For things to change. For life to start fresh.

MARI: And how will that happen?

JIMMY: It will happen. On its own.

MARI: You still don't know where you're going?

JIMMY: The dream doesn't say.

MARI: I'm not asking the dream, I'm asking you.

I think you know. You just don't want to tell your little sister.

JIMMY: You know that's not true.

[MICK *enters.*]

MICK: Have you ever taken a pee that gives you a whole new feeling about life?

END OF SCENE ONE

SCENE TWO

[*Morning.* MARI *has fashioned a makeshift "table" around which she and* MICK *sit. A small kerosene lamp burns. They are drinking coffee.* JIMMY *is hammering away at the engine.*]

MARI: I thought you were a mechanic.

MICK: I already did the hard part. I built the engine.

MARI: It looks like a big wok.

MICK: He wanted an engine that runs off of loss. I tried to do what I could. But there's no fuel he said.

MARI: No fuel?

MICK: What does the word amino acid do for you?

MARI: It gives me hives. It makes me think of medical school and all those exams.

MICK: You've given it up?

MARI: For now.

MICK: That's a shame. We could benefit from your knowledge. I thought you could do some of the scientific work. You know, amino acids, DNA . . .

[STORM *comes in.*]

STORM: What does a person have to do around here to get a fucking cup of coffee?

MARI: Are you sure you should be up?

STORM: The rain was keeping me up anyway. [*Seeing* JIMMY.] You her brother? [JIMMY *nods.*] What's your name?

JIMMY: Jimmy R.

STORM: What does the R stand for?

JIMMY: Nothing.

MARI: It stands for Rodin.

STORM: That is so cool. Like Godzilla's arch enemy, right?

JIMMY: No.

STORM: Then who?

MARI: The sculptor.

STORM: Oh yeah? You an artist? [*Pause.*] I go by Storm.

MICK: As in the rain and thunder?

STORM: Yeah.

MICK: Hmm. The best kind.

STORM: Who's that?

JIMMY: That's Mick. He's a mechanic.

STORM: I can see that. What are you doing to that car?

MICK: We've modified the engine—we've made it run off of feelings. Because of the flood.

STORM: What are you talking about?

JIMMY: We're taking a trip.

STORM: Where to?

JIMMY: Don't know yet.

STORM: Sounds kind of dumb.

JIMMY: Haven't you ever just gone out on the road for a long ride?

STORM: Sure, but driving a car is like watching television.

JIMMY: I prefer horses, personally.

MARI: Horses?

STORM: With horses there's too much shit. A bike's the best thing.

MICK: What kind of bike you ride?

STORM: It's black, like my eyes.

MICK: Big engine?

STORM: Feels like an F–16 when you ride it.

MICK: Well, is it a Honda? A Harley-Davidson?

STORM: It's a smooth ride, you understand? You forget the bike's even there.

JIMMY AND MICK: Must be a Honda.

STORM: I keep the chrome polished so that if I look down at the exhaust pipes when I'm on the road I can see the sky and trees, everything around me, re-flected right there. My personal video unit.

JIMMY: You just said you hate television.

STORM: Not if it's my own show.

MICK: I own a pickup myself. . . .

STORM: [Not listening.] And I've got these special mirrors on them so when I look back at the drivers I've just passed, I can see their faces. . . .

MICK: It runs great. Pretty useful too.

STORM: I can tell if a couple's been fighting or even if they've just had a roll in the backseat.

MICK: If I roll the windows down I can get a great sense of speed actually.

STORM: Is it fast? Do you take it out and let 'er rip?

MICK: No . . . actually . . . speed scares me.

STORM: It's a damned *Sony* that you're driving. You imagine you're in some kind of *sitcom* while the cornfields race by at 17 miles per hour?

MICK: I thought you women like men who take their time.

STORM: For some things, yeah, but when it comes to driving, or leaving, it's best to just get the hell out!

But where are you going?

JIMMY: We need to survive. That's what's important.

STORM: Survive what?

JIMMY: This flood.

STORM: Flood?

MARI: The flood.

JIMMY: There's a flood coming; haven't you noticed?

STORM: It's raining, sure, but there's no flood coming.

MICK: How do you know?

STORM: I just know. Anybody who's been on a farm for awhile knows how *nature* behaves. Don't you know anything, Jiffy-Lube?

MICK: For me, a farm means shit. You wake up in the morning, you smell it, you go to bed at night, it's still there. And you got all your varieties: pig, horse, cow.

STORM: You scared of shit too?

MICK: I suppose you aren't scared of anything?

STORM: Actually, everything scares me. Except mechanics. They just make me laugh. [*She laughs.*]

MARI: You're feeling better.

STORM: I feel like I'm better. I don't have any bruises on my body or nothing. I feel like my body's good as new.

JIMMY: No one ever really gets healed. The wounds only get buried.

STORM: Your brother thinks he's one of those prophets in the Bible.

MICK: He is a prophet.

STORM: The question is, is he false or true?

JIMMY: I don't lie.

STORM: Have you seen my bike in any of your visions?

JIMMY: No.

STORM: Then what kind of prophet are you? How about you, Goodwrench?

MICK: No, I haven't seen your bike.

STORM: You sure?

MICK: I *am* a mechanic.

JIMMY: This is a rain that will not be able to stop. It will just keep coming and coming. We will not be able to control the water. We will be overwhelmed and cleansed.

I've been having these dreams for a year now. Dreams of rain, of Volkswagens floating. This flood that wipes this town, this house clean. I know it's going to happen. It has to happen. Doesn't it? You feel that don't you?

STORM: You know how I know this isn't going to be a real flood?

JIMMY: How?

STORM: There are no colors.

MICK: Colors?

STORM: When there's a real flood I see colors in the sky, or in the water, somewhere. I haven't seen any colors so far.

JIMMY: Who taught you all of this?

STORM: My grandmother.

JIMMY: Isn't she—

MARI: Jimmy!

STORM: Isn't she what?

JIMMY: Old?

STORM: She'd still kick the shit out of you.

MICK: You people are giving me the chills. All this dreaming and signs and floods. It's raining outside, we're making this Volkswagen float—what's the goddamn problem? Why can't you guys just let yourself be amazed?

STORM: It's not about being amazed. It's about seeing. That's all anyone can do with the weather. All those weathermen with their computers and satellites—it just comes down to seeing. Open your eyes.

JIMMY: That's funny. You talking about seeing. As far as I can tell, you don't see things either. You just see what you want to see.

STORM: Like what?

JIMMY: The way you behave.

STORM: How do I behave?

JIMMY: You pretend to be someone else.

STORM: Pretend to be who?

JIMMY: Someone else.

STORM: I know who I am.

JIMMY: I don't think you do.

STORM: And you know?

JIMMY: I think I know.

STORM: Tell me.

JIMMY: Look at yourself.

STORM: What about it?

JIMMY: You look like us.

STORM: I don't look like you.

JIMMY: You do.

STORM: Mick, do I look like him?

MICK: I don't know, he's a guy and you're a woman and—

STORM: Shut up! Mari, tell your brother he's out of line here.

MARI: Jimmy, . . .

JIMMY: But I'm right.

MARI: That's not the point.

JIMMY: If that's not the point, then what is?

MARI: You shouldn't go around saying things like that. It's none of your business.

JIMMY: I can't believe you're falling for her game. It's all an act. The bike. The attitude. She's a fucking banana in a leather jacket!

MARI: Jimmy, what's your problem?

JIMMY: Who said there was a problem?

MARI: I say there's a problem when you're rude to my friends. Apologize to her.

JIMMY: What?

[MARI *picks up the exhaust pipe.*]

MARI: Apologize!

JIMMY: Storm, I'm sorry.

STORM: [*Seeing the exhaust pipe*] Wait a minute. This belonged to my bike. Oh, Jesus. Mari.

[STORM *picks up the pipe.*]

MARI: I can explain*, this morning—

STORM: [*overlapping*] *She's gone, isn't she? I hit her . . . and I was going fast . . . and . . . I didn't mean to hit her . . . you know? I didn't mean to. God. Shit. God. Shit. This belonged to my bike. What am I going to do?

MARI: Storm . . . I tried to tell you.

STORM: I know.

[MARI *holds her.*]

[JIMMY *takes the exhaust pipe from* STORM *and puts it in the "engine." The engine turns over, then dies. They all stare at the car.*]

END OF SCENE TWO

SCENE THREE

[MARI *is trying to wash her hands clean of the paint.* MICK *talks to her.*]

MICK: I really admire you.

MARI: What's to admire?

MICK: You're just so open   . about everything. You aren't scared.

MARI: I am scared. I just don't let it bother me. Anyway, what are you so scared about? I've never met a mechanic like you. You're a bundle of nerves. Most mechanics I know are about as sensitive as a wrench.

MICK: I just have a lot of fears.

MARI: Like what?

MICK: Corn, mainly.

MARI: That's it?

MICK: It's a big one. You don't know what it's like to wake up every morning and see all that yellow and green staring you in the face.

After we had a pile of it we would have to husk it all afternoon. Then we'd eat it for the next week. Every meal. I thought my skin would turn yellow. We gave the leftovers to the pigs and then that was another problem.

MARI: What problem?

MICK: All the corn, mixed with the pig's shit. One time I went out there into the fields with a friend of mine. And I got lost. No escape. My chest started to hurt. I couldn't breathe. My friend just left me there. All alone.

MARI: I was wondering if there was something else to your fear for corn. Whether it was the farm itself.

MICK: It's the corn, I tell you. Look around you, it's everywhere. If you close your eyes, you can still see it, you can still smell it. It's not a mystery—you don't need to have a vision to understand—there's just so much fucking yellow and green out here, it gets to you, you know, it just gets to you.

MARI: There's only one way to conquer your fears. You have to attack them. Stop running.

MICK: Yeah?

MARI: Just stop running.

END OF SCENE THREE

SCENE FOUR

[*Later that day.* MARI *and* STORM *sit in the car and talk.*]

STORM: I wanted to talk to her one last time. I thought I would just find my bike and go talk to her. Now I don't have her. I don't have anyone. Not even my bike.

MARI: Stop blaming yourself.

STORM: She drives too fast. I always told her that. And her eyesight was going on her.

MARI: It was an accident.

STORM: No, it wasn't, I must be doing something wrong in my life. I believe in fate. And punishment. I've done something wrong to deserve this. Maybe your brother's right. I'm escaping something. What's that on your hands?

MARI: It's paint.

STORM: Those colors.

MARI: I know.

STORM: Maybe there will be a flood.

MARI: I hope not.

STORM: A flood? Is that what I need? Something to cleanse me?

MARI: There's not going to be any flood.

STORM: But those colors.

MARI: This is just paint.

STORM: Where did it come from?

MARI: The ground.

STORM: You're kidding.

MARI: No.

STORM: That's even worse.

MARI: Why?

STORM: Color from the ground—that means the Earth is upset—she's bleeding.

MARI: Upset about what?

STORM: Us. She's upset about us.

MARI: But I didn't even do anything. She should be upset at my father. Or my brother, or cars, or machines, or hospitals. Not me. I haven't done anything to anyone.

END OF SCENE FOUR

SCENE FIVE

[MARI *is handing* JIMMY *tools as he works under the car.*]

JIMMY: Hex wrench. [MARI *hands him a wrench.*] No, the bigger one. [*She hands him another one.*] Does this mean you're coming?

MARI: I guess so.

JIMMY: You could be happier about it.

MARI: Now that would be lying wouldn't it? [*Beat.*] You think we'll find him?

JIMMY: For the millionth time, I've told you: this isn't about him. We just need to get the hell out of here. We're following his example.

Can you give me some more light?

MARI: When you stepped on my hands . . . did you know what you were doing?

JIMMY: Of course not.

MARI: Sometimes I could kill you for that.

JIMMY: I know.

MARI: I don't know why I don't.

JIMMY: I don't know either.

MARI: I burned my medical books.

JIMMY: That's stupid.

MARI: I don't want to be a doctor anymore.

JIMMY: What are you going to be?

MARI: A professional healer.

JIMMY: Like a faith healer?

MARI: No.

JIMMY: A therapist?

MARI: No. A healer. It's a new kind of job. Nothing destructive about it. No engines. No blood. No money. Just healing.

JIMMY: [*Wiping his hands.*] It's done. We can leave. I just have to wait.

MARI: For what?

JIMMY: The water. It has to come up to a certain level.

END OF SCENE FIVE

SCENE SIX

[JIMMY *stares out at the sky.*]

JIMMY: We have nothing. Our family was a ghost family. It looked and felt like a family. But it really wasn't there. It was this faded photograph. Black and white. Smudged. Grainy.

If you looked too closely at the faces in it, you could see that everything was blurry. The shots were taken in Korea. The lens moved. A little. Or someone was in a hurry. Time, we never had any time.

Everyone was working so hard. We were in such a rush to move on. To leave. To make it to the next day. That brighter next day. But we never looked hard at the day we had. And the photographs would get blurrier . . . and blurrier. Until finally all you had was dream pictures . . . faces that were ghosts.

[MARI *and* STORM *enter, drenched, clearly happy.*]

MARI: [*Singing.*] It's raining, it's pouring . . .

STORM: The old man is snoring.

MARI: Hey big brother, are you snoring?

JIMMY: What's gotten into you?

MARI: We're just happy. And we found something.

STORM: Someone.

JIMMY: Who?

STORM: Jack. Jack Daniels. [*She pulls out a bottle of whiskey.*] Want a sip?

JIMMY: No thanks.

STORM: Where's that lug-nut friend of yours?

JIMMY: He went out. Something about corn.

STORM: Oh God. Where'd you find him anyway?

JIMMY: Yellow pages.

STORM: What'd you look under, "Emotionally Disturbed Mechanics"?

MARI: You like him, don't you?

STORM: Too much of an oil-can.

MARI: He's a tin man.

STORM: Looking for corn.

MARI: You hungry?

STORM: Starved.

MARI: Jimmy, what do we have?

JIMMY: Just the usual.

MARI: Okay. Storm, how do you feel about rice and kimchee?

STORM: Hey, I'll try anything. I need to prove to JR here that I'm open to Korean food I guess.

[MARI *sets the table with three bowls, serves food.*]

JIMMY: [*To* STORM.] So it's still raining, isn't it?

STORM: Heavily.

MARI: I think it's letting up.

STORM: We washed Mari's hands.

JIMMY: How'd you do it?

MARI: The rain.

JIMMY: See, this is a magical rain.

MARI: Some people call it acid rain.

[JIMMY *starts to eat.*]

STORM: Don't you people say grace first?

JIMMY: [*Stopping.*] Uhh, sure.

STORM: Lord, bless this house, these people in it. Bless this rain that it may bring us food and happiness. Bless those who have left us, bless those of us left . . . who must deal with their pain. Amen.

MARI: That was beautiful.

STORM: This is spicy.

MARI: You like it?

STORM: I do.

MARI: [*To* JIMMY.] See, maybe she's Korean after all.

STORM: You guys are really hung up on being Korean aren't you? It's like bikers. We look down on the rest of the world. All the station wagons, the trucks, the mini-vans. We know that deep down we're better than everyone else.

MARI: I don't think we're better than anyone else.

JIMMY: But there's a bond there. A secret code.

MARI: Storm says I should come along.

STORM: It's like one big fucking family.

MARI: Jimmy, my hands are clean. Don't they look nice? I just realized something when I looked at my hands in the rain. These hands of mine are strong. They endured a lot of things. They can still do things. Can still make things.

[MICK *comes in from the rain, covered with mud and brightly colored paint.*]

JIMMY: Mick. Where did you go?

MICK: [*Breathless.*] I was trying to get used to it. It's about time I faced up to all that corn, I told myself. Just like Mari said.

JIMMY: Mari?

MICK: So I waded into it as far as I could go. Pretty soon I felt lost. The same old feelings. Disoriented. Yellow and green on all sides of me, like I was held captive. Then I see the colors. Oozing out of the ground. So I start digging. These colors start flying with the dirt. They splatter all over the corn. Now it's not just yellow and green. It's red and blue and white and black. I can't stand it. It's too much. This is making me so happy—goddamn it—and then I find this.

[MICK *pulls a muddy oil painting from his jacket that had been rolled up. It appears to be an old still life. He unrolls it and shows them.*]

STORM: It's a painting. One of your's Jimmy?

[MARI *takes the painting in her hands.*]

MARI: A year becomes a minute becomes a second becomes a lifetime.

JIMMY: You found all of this out there?

MARI: This was a painting that I would write long entries in my diary about. I would try to know my mother through this painting. And all along it was just laying out there under all that mud. All that corn. I thought I had only dreamed about it, but it's real. Why didn't you ever tell me?

JIMMY: Tell you what?

MARI: That you had this?

JIMMY: I don't know how it got there.

MARI: Yes you do.

JIMMY: I don't know.

MARI: I'm going out there. [*Beat.*] I want to see if it really is flooding.

END OF SCENE SIX

SCENE SEVEN

[*Sometime later that night.* STORM *stands at doorway looking out.* MICK *testing the batteries of the car.* JIMMY *sits, stonefaced, staring at* MICK.]

MICK: Maybe someone should go look for her. Jimmy?

JIMMY: The water is going to come up soon.

STORM: It's true, it is raining a lot more than I had thought.

JIMMY: You never get everything to work out. Just some things.

STORM: You think she's cc...ing back?

JIMMY: Yeah. She probably will.

Is the water getting higher?

STORM: It's high.

END OF SCENE SEVEN

SCENE EIGHT

[*Later, that same night.* STORM, MICK, *and* JIMMY *are sleeping.* MARI *walks back in.* JIMMY *opens his eyes.*]

JIMMY: Hi!

MARI: I walked all through the fields, up and down the road. You know, walking is much better than driving. You can think about things. You really see things. The rain falling. The water beading to the stalks of corn. The feel of the drops as they run down your face, walking through water.

JIMMY: [*Getting up.*] You should sit down.

MARI: No. You sit. [JIMMY *sits.*] Now talk.

JIMMY: Talk?

MARI: Yes.

JIMMY: You want me to start from the beginning?

MARI: That would help.

JIMMY: I don't know where to start.

MARI: Anywhere. Start anywhere.

JIMMY: Okay. This is my first memory. I see myself as a little kid running in from the back and knocking over her easel, spilling the paints everywhere. Instead of getting upset . . .

Is this what you want?

MARI: Don't stop.

JIMMY: Instead of getting upset, she looks at the mess I made on the canvas and says, "Son, you're a born artist." I said, "Mom, why are you leaving us? Where are you going?" She couldn't explain, she said. She tried, but she stopped. Her face is wet. She goes and kisses my baby sister.

Mari. You.

I didn't understand. "Mom, you're coming back, aren't you? You are, aren't you?" The door shuts. I hear the car drive away. My father doesn't look at me. Only Mari looks at me. She doesn't know what's happened. And I think, isn't that the best thing? Why should she know any of this?

MARI: No, why should she? She's the baby sister after all. She should just be cute, the baby of the family.

We're a family of leavers, aren't we? We leave Korea. Then we leave each other.

And Dad?

JIMMY: He just took off. I think he was just sick of seeing me everyday. I was a walking monument to his failures.

MARI: Why didn't he come talk to me?

JIMMY: He was ashamed.

MARI: Ashamed?

JIMMY: He wanted to do things for you. But he thought maybe you and I were better off together. And he knew that he had to leave. For his own good.

MARI: Did you talk to him?

JIMMY: No. He did leave me something though. This note. [*He unfolds a piece of paper.*] "Remember to forget."

MARI: Remember to forget? That's all it says? I've been driving for miles and
 miles so that I can get a note that says "Remember to forget"?
JIMMY: I drove him away. He saw what happened.
MARI: Saw what happen?
JIMMY: The hunting accident.
MARI: That was years ago.
JIMMY: So what, it seems like it just happened yesterday. It wasn't an accident.
MARI: What was it then?

[*Silence.*]

JIMMY: You think I really went out to hunt? I don't like hunting. I don't like killing
 things. He saw the whole thing. He knew all along that I was lying about it.
MARI: So he didn't forgive you for that?
JIMMY: No.
MARI: Jimmy, it's not your fault. It's just like you saw it in your head. The Volk-
 swagen. The flood. Because that's the beauty of dreams. They're based on
 hope. They're based on maybe things changing from what they are today.
 From what they really are. You see yourself doing things you wouldn't do.
 You see a strange face. A car floating. Rain. [*Beat.*] Jimmy, they left because
 they could. Mom and Dad left because . . . they could.

[*Water starts to seep across the floor of the garage.* MICK *and* STORM
wake up.]

MARI: [*To* JIMMY.] You should be happy. All your dreams have come true. But
 I need to follow the family tradition. I have to leave too.
JIMMY: You can't do that.
MARI: Yes, Jimmy, I can. And I am. This family . . . it needs to be put to rest.
 It's an idea that's had its day. Now we need to do something new.
STORM: Mari, you need company?
MARI: Love some.
STORM: What about you Mick?
MICK: I'm not going anywhere.

[MARI *gives him the painting.*]

MARI: Here, you can use this for your engine.
JIMMY: No, you keep it.
MARI: I don't want it. This has nothing to do with me anymore. Your dreams
 are not my dreams.
JIMMY: You're my sister. All we have is each other. We should hang on to that.

MARI: *Oppah. Jimmy.*
JIMMY: I'm sorry.
MARI: Yeah. [*To* STORM.] Storm?
STORM: I'm ready.

[*They exit. Long silence.* JIMMY *walks around the floor for awhile. He looks into the engine. He picks up the painting. He goes to the car and opens the canvas in front of him. He stares at the painting.*

MICK *opens the jar of kimchee. He starts eating a piece. He starts eating another piece. He sits down next to* JIMMY.

Long silence. MICK *continues to chew and eat.* JIMMY *takes the painting and places it in the engine. It roars to life, glowing with a surreal and bright light.* JIMMY *and* MICK *look at each other. They smile. They get into the car. The engine revs. Blackout.*]

END OF SCENE EIGHT

END OF ACT II

EPILOGUE

[*As in the opening scene of the Prologue.* MARI *and* JIMMY *begin to speak, sometimes simultaneously, sometimes as echoes of each other.*]

MARI:	JIMMY:
The stories really matter don't they? I still have my memories.	A brush. You start with a brush.
And they live in me, like those wild flowers you see by the road. Those flowers survive even the most vicious storms.	Paint. Rich and black.
	See how it thickens near the brush? You have to control it.
You see them by the road, their colors get more bright in the rain. The water makes—	

the colors seem more
vivid when the brush is
wet—

from the rain and the petals
drip with what has newly fallen
to the earth, small drops—

of paint, which are to be
avoided in the beginning
if at all—

Possible. And you look out past
the road, the fields, you see
the infinite line of the land
against the clouds.
Uhm-mah. Uhm-mah,
play with me,
put your brush down
put your brush down.

Possible. Watch the
canvas carefully, imagine
it as more than that,
add depth to it,
wrap the cloth around
your eye, and paint
all the colors you see.
From violet to red.

[*They freeze. The lights fade.*]

END OF EPILOGUE

END OF PLAY

Breaking Glass

a play in two acts
by
DMAE ROBERTS

CHARACTERS

MEI JEN, the mother. She is a 42-year-old Chinese woman, a beautiful, strong-willed, controlling, and at times delightful, matriarch of the family. She often talks of war-torn Taiwan and the hard times. She has a strong sense of survival and is very, very clever. She now works at a plywood mill and has carpal tunnel syndrome. She dreams of having a Chinese restaurant, a dream no one else in the family shares.

RICKI, the Amerasian daughter. She secretly writes poems while working at the same mill as her mother. She is 22 years old and struggling to leave home and finish her last two years of college. Her mother keeps her at home with guilt and by convincing her that she can achieve her dreams if she works and saves money. She has difficulty in believing in herself or her dreams.

JIMMY, the Amerasian son. He is socially withdrawn and non-communicative. He is working a seasonal job at the cannery and is studying to be a welder. He spends his time doing chores on the farm or piecing together miniature stained glass windows. He is an attractive young man who is younger than his 20 years.

BUDDY, the father. He is a 42-year-old Caucasian man who looks older. He works as a salesman to support the family and often is away. He is an easygoing country boy who is not in good health. He smokes all day, even though he has asthma and is overweight. He is torn between his natural optimism, his wish to live an easy life, and a sense of failure. He swings between being outgoing and upbeat and withdrawing into depression and heaviness.

MONICA, the friend. She is a Caucasian woman who is the same age as Ricki and who works at the mill as a janitor. She is pretty, very good natured, and friendly.

THE TIME: 1977, two weeks during a hot July.

THE PLACE: a dilapidated country house outside of Junction City, a small rural mill town in Oregon.

———

This play is dedicated to Kirby Roberts

———

ACT I
SCENE ONE

[*Light fades up on* RICKI. *She is wiping a clear drinking glass with a towel. She holds it up in front of her. A fragile piece of music plays softly in the background.*]

RICKI: Wait for the light. The light. How it glistens.
How it keeps you from seeing clearly, cleanly.
The pathway through the glass stopped by the glass.
Mesmerized. Quieted. She holds it as far as her arms
will reach. She holds it, trying to be part of the light,

hoping it will go through her and connect her
to something far and unattainable.
There is still water there as diamond shapes
slide slowly down her hand. Coolness soothes her,
captures her. She watches as it trickles
till it becomes absorbed. It stops. Stops.

[*Lights up on* MEI JEN *sitting quietly, almost sadly at the dinner table.*]

RICKI: Looks again at the light through the prism, turning
the glass one direction, then another.
This goes on. Could go on. Were it not for the voice.
MEI: [*calling out, almost automatically*] What you doing! So slow. Finish it up!
RICKI: Striking fear in her, she drops the glass. [*A crash*]
She drops it. And the voice returns much stronger.
Louder. Then a cloud forms over her,
pressing her down again. The weight is heavy,
and she doesn't know if it will ever leave.
MEI: [*no emotion*] Stupid. Why you drop it! Stupid girl! I got to do everything.
Stupid Girl!
RICKI: If it will ever leave . . .

[*Light shifts to next scene.*]

SCENE TWO

[*Dinner time. Lights up on the interior of a lower middle class house. The
house is not dirty but messy. The furniture is well worn and used. It is an
impressionistic representation of a house. There is a sense of walls closing
in and very little space. Upstage there is a small dining area, with a swing-
ing door leading to the kitchen. The dining area has a buffet, a table, and
four chairs. A door opens to a tiny front porch area. There are crates,
boxes, and a rusty washing machine outside.* RICKI *is outside, sitting on
the porch. She is writing in her journal.*]

MEI: [*calling out urgently*] Ricki! Ricki-ahhh! [MEI JEN *enters from the swing-
ing kitchen door.*] Ricki! Come here. Help me!
RICKI: [*writing*] "This goes on. Could go on. Were it not for the voice . . ."
MEI: Ricki-ahhh!

[RICKI *enters the house and takes off her shoes.*]

RICKI: All right. You don't have to yell—

MEI: Ricki, help me pick the peas. It just grow and grow. You know what they worth in store?

RICKI: Uhm-hm . . .

MEI: At least two, maybe three dollar a pound. See what I do for you! [RICKI *starts peeling.*] No, no. Pick from this end, then peel it off.

RICKI: Okay.

MEI: Ahhh. [MEI JEN *stops and shakes her hand.*] Darn Cupple Tun.

RICKI: I wish you'd file for disability. The mill really screwed up your hands.

MEI: No, I only been working a couple of years. Got to save for retirement. Good job—

RICKI: No, it isn't.

MEI: The pay's good.

RICKI: Not that good. If you don't get carpal tunnel. Or emphysema. Or go deaf from the noise—

MEI: You young. Quit after you save some money for college. Don't want to be hippie like all you friends.

RICKI: My friends aren't hippies, all right?

MEI: You always go out with your friends. Do what you want.

RICKI: I'm twenty-two years old, for God's sake.

MEI: Then come home. Stay in you room. Writing. Writing. Always writing something . . . Then you want to leave again. You Chinese. Family should work together. No Chinese restaurant in Junction City. We could make lots of money . . .

RICKI: That's your dream, not mine.

[MEI JEN *flashes her a look.*]

MEI: You rather be broke like last Spring? Come to your mother beg her for money.

RICKI: I asked for a loan.

MEI: 'Cos you waste you money—

RICKI: [*overlap*] For school!

MEI: Here you don't pay much rent, save money. Come/go as you please. What you want. [*silence*] Ricki, look at you mother. I had nothing when I was in Taiwan. Now I got you. You brother. This house. You daddy never do anything. I do all my self.

RICKI: I know. It's just . . . I want more.

MEI: When I was you age in Taiwan, I made lots of money before I meet you

Daddy. I had two houses. I work in the army base PX and got good tips. [*a secret*] If I got education like you, I could be doctor/lawyer.

RICKI: I'm sure you could—

MEI: You can be anything you want. You could be President of the United States of America if you want—

RICKI: [*laughs*] Don't think so.

MEI: It's true. [*believes in the American Dream*] You a good, smart girl. You can do anything in this country. Just got to work hard. I say someday, "That's my daughter, President Ricki Donnelly!" I think that sound pretty good, huh?

RICKI: You're funny, Ma . . .

MEI: Not too funny for you . . . [*tries to tickle her stomach.*]

RICKI: Hey, stop that . . . [*She can't help laughing.*]

MEI: Still got to lose a little bit more weight right there—

RICKI: Ma!

MEI: Okay, okay . . . I like it when you laugh.

RICKI: I hate it when you do that.

MEI: Ricki, don't quit right now. Save money. Then you can go back to school. Do what you want.

RICKI: I'm going back in September.

MEI: You could go back to community college.

RICKI: I need to get my degree from the university.

MEI: Stay home. We take care of you.

RICKI: You should have let me leave home after high school—

MEI: [*overlap*] What you mean "let you"?

RICKI: [*overlap*] —then I might have handled things better.

MEI: [*overlap*] I never keep you—

RICKI: [*overlap*] Let's not fight— [*overlap*] I really want to be a writer—

MEI: [*overlap*] Can't make no livin' doin' that. I told you, be a doctor/lawyer—

RICKI: [*overlap*] Ma, you have to have money! [*beat*] And you have to be a certain kind of person—I'm from Junction City for God's sake. Home of the Scandinavian Festival. At the U of O, I met people who knew more than I did. About everything. Sometimes, I feel so stupid—

MEI: You need more protein.

RICKI: Ma, I'm afraid. God, I don't want to get fat again.

MEI: I make good food for you. Work at mill, eat anything you want.

RICKI: Ma, I think about food all the time. More since I've been here.

MEI: You work at the mill, dance like me, wear a girdle, you won't get fat. I you mother, I know.

RICKI: Ma! [*gives up*] Forget it.

[*another silence*]

MEI: Where you brother?

RICKI: Outside.

MEI: What he do out there, I don't know. Been makin' those space movie sounds. I think he koo-koo in the head.

RICKI: He's not crazy.

MEI: No, but hard to talk to.

[MEI JEN *goes to the door and calls out, not harshly.*]

MEI: Jimmy-ahhh! Jimmy! You come inside! Stop chasing the ducks around!

RICKI: I wish you wouldn't yell.

MEI: You always criticize.

[JIMMY *enters the house. He is almost animalistic, dirty from doing farmwork, wearing tattered jeans, windbreaker, boots, and a hard hat. He takes off his boots at the entryway.*]

MEI: [*She is used to ordering him around, but there is no animosity.*] Take the hat off. Don't like you wearing space hat in house.

[JIMMY *sits at a table with bits of broken glass and pieces them together. A subtle light change.* JIMMY *is entering his dreamworld.*]

MEI: [*almost whispering*] He's playing again . . .

RICKI: [*She too is quiet.*] Ma, please . . .

MEI: He don't got girlfriend.

RICKI: He's got time . . .

MEI: No friends. Don't even talk . . .

RICKI: Because of those damn school kids. And it'd help if you wouldn't yell at him. He's very sensitive . . .

MEI: I don't yell! You koo-koo, too!

RICKI: I'm outta here—

MEI: Where you going?

RICKI: For a drive. To the movies. I don't know.

MEI: Stay for dinner first.

RICKI: I'm not hungry.

MEI: I cook something special for you. You daddy say he be home tonight—

RICKI: Ma . . .

MEI: Whole family be here tonight. Stay. Talk to you brother. Please?

RICKI: He doesn't want to talk to anyone.

MEI: Try. Just try for you mother, okay? Stay?

RICKI: Okay. Okay.

MEI: I go cook.

[MEI JEN *smiles. She exits.* RICKI *sits by* JIMMY.]

RICKI: Hey Jimmy . . . how's my handsome brother?

JIMMY: Mmmph.

RICKI: What's the matter, you can't even say "hi" to me?

JIMMY: Hi.

RICKI: So what you workin' on?

JIMMY: Glass.

RICKI: I know glass. But what are you making?

JIMMY: Something to hang in a window.

RICKI: It's beautiful. Will you make one for me?

JIMMY: Maybe.

RICKI: Great! [*Silence.* RICKI *knows that* JIMMY *has become more withdrawn since she left.*] So . . . how was welding class today?

JIMMY: Mmmmph.

RICKI: [*trying to make him laugh*] That good, huh?

JIMMY: I'm tryin' to concentrate here.

RICKI: Geez, Jimmy. We used to be able to talk—[*another silence.* RICKI *tries again.*] Can I help? At least let me glue one piece, okay?

JIMMY: It's not glue.

RICKI: Whatever.

JIMMY: It's solder.

RICKI: Okay.

JIMMY: Hot.

RICKI: I'll be careful.

JIMMY: It's hot. [JIMMY *hands her the soldering iron.*]

RICKI: Show me how to do it.

JIMMY: [*with authority*] Keep the soldering iron moving carefully along the line. If you hold it still too long, the glass could break. It could be danger-ous. Please be careful . . .

RICKI: Okay. Oh, man, this is great.

JIMMY: Keep it moving!

RICKI: This is so cool. No wonder you like it. Beautiful. I bet you could sell these things.

JIMMY: Nah, I'm not good enough.

RICKI: I think so.

JIMMY: It's hard work. There're lotsa people better than me.

RICKI: Well, I'd buy this. For ten dollars.

JIMMY: No, it's worth a lot more than that. It's expensive.

RICKI: Twenty dollars.

JIMMY: No, I'm not selling—

RICKI: Thirty dollars.

JIMMY: You stop that?!

RICKI: Okay. Ya' know I was just playing. . . . But I really think you could make a living at this.

[MEI JEN *enters with food in Chinese dishes and sets it on the table.*]

MEI: Make living at what.

RICKI: Glass-making. Jimmy's really good at it.

MEI: Ahh. That's just silly stuff! [*exits into the kitchen.*]

RICKI: That's Ma.

JIMMY: She can't help it.

RICKI: [*imitation of* MEI JEN] "Ahh, that's just silly stuff!" [JIMMY *laughs a little.* RICKI *is encouraged.*] Hey, you want to see a movie later? We could go see *Star Wars* again.

JIMMY: Maybe.

RICKI: After dinner. Okay?

JIMMY: Mmmm . . .

RICKI: Save room for popcorn.

JIMMY: And M&M's?

RICKI: Yeah! M&M's!

[MEI JEN *enters with more food as* BUDDY *enters the house.*]

BUDDY: Phew, it's hot out there.

RICKI: Hi, Daddy . . .

BUDDY: Hi there.

MEI: Ahhh! Off with the shoes!

BUDDY: Oh, give me a chance, woman. I just walked in the—

MEI: No dirty shoes in house. Japanese-style!

BUDDY: I know. I know. Japanese-style . . . What's for dinner?

MEI: Pork chop and vegetables. Egg for Ricki 'cos she a vegebel.

RICKI: Vegetarian!

BUDDY: Girl, when're you gonna get off that kick?

RICKI: It's wrong to kill animals. I could never eat the meat we killed here.

BUDDY: People need meat to live.

RICKI: I really don't wanta have this conversation every time I eat.

MEI: You leave you daughter alone. Go wash for supper.

BUDDY: Okay. Okay. I just hope she doesn't make herself sick. . . . [exits]

MEI: Ricki, you set the table.

[MEI JEN exits. RICKI sets the table.]

RICKI: Great. Now I'm doing chores . . .

[MEI JEN enters.]

MEI: I hear that.

RICKI: You hear everything.

MEI: That's right. I hear everything. And I smell everything. So don't go smoking that dope stuff. I smell everything

RICKI: And don't forget you know everything too.

MEI: That's right. Dinner ready. Everybody eat. Come on. Everybody to the table.

BUDDY: [offstage] Just hold on woman. I'm still washin' up!

MEI: You hold on. Jimmy, hurry up! Jimmy. He never pay attention to me.

RICKI: That's because you're always yelling.

MEI: I hear that.

RICKI: Come on, Jimmy, we'll go to the movie after dinner.

[JIMMY sits by RICKI.]

MEI: Going to movie? Good. Get brother out of the house. Good. Buddy, hurry
up!

[BUDDY enters.]

BUDDY: Hold your horses. I'm a-comin'. I'm a-comin'.

[They sit. MEI JEN serves everyone. MEI JEN and RICKI eat with chopsticks. JIMMY and BUDDY eat with forks and knives.]

MEI: Here Ricki, have some egg—

RICKI: I wish you would sit down.

MEI: You need protein. More egg. Here Jimmy, a big pork chop for you. Pork
chop for you Daddy from Harold the pig.

RICKI: God, that's Harold?

MEI: Almost 400 pounds. Good pig—

RICKI: Jeez . . .

MEI: More rice for Ricki.

RICKI: I'd like more vegetables.

MEI: Rice good for you.

RICKI: So are vegetables.

MEI: Take more egg.

RICKI: [*attacks*] Ma, please sit down and eat.

BUDDY: [*rescues*] Confound it, woman, sit down at the table. You're makin' us all nervous.

MEI: Okay, okay. Everybody got food? Okay. I eat.

[*They eat in silence. A big moment of silence, except for the sound of eating.*]

RICKI: Daddy, pass me the soy sauce please?

BUDDY: Salt's better for you.

RICKI: I like soy sauce.

MEI: Why you not eat the egg?

RICKI: It's kinda greasy.

MEI: You call my food greasy!

RICKI: I told you I don't want to gain weight—

BUDDY: A little extra cushioning never hurt nobody—

RICKI: Daddy!

MEI: So picky! When I was girl, no food. No meat. Just rice. Sometimes have to wash the white worm from the rice—

RICKI: Great. Now I'm going to be sick—

MEI: Always so hungry. You lucky you got food on the table—

RICKI: Ma, please—

BUDDY: Mei Jen, no more war stories. Okay? [*silence*] Well, I made the month's quota so far, and the week ain't over.

RICKI: That's good, Daddy.

BUDDY: Yep. I think my luck is turning. It was slow-goin' there for awhile. But things are a-changin' . . . I think it's gonna change for all of us. I can feel it . . . [*another big silence*] So Ricki, how was work today?

RICKI: Pretty awful. They made me clean under the dryer presses again. I think it's dangerous.

BUDDY: Well, you be careful. Don't let them push you around—

MEI: Oh what you know? You never work at mill.

BUDDY: Ricki's right. It can be dangerous.

MEI: You just sit on your butt all day and talk, talk, salesman talk. Leave Ricki alone.

BUDDY: What the hell are you harpin' about?

RICKI: Please don't get started.

BUDDY: I work hard. It's not easy selling Wynn's oil products. I'm keeping a roof over our heads, ain't I?

MEI: I got roof in first place. Who made money for down payment on house? You got to be on farm in country. What kind of farm is this?

BUDDY: It was good for the kids.

MEI: Good for you. The kids hate the country. Ask Ricki.

RICKI: Oh God . . .

MEI: You already tell me you hate this place.

RICKI: Let's just eat, okay?

BUDDY: Ricki Sue, you really hate it out here? That much? Ricki?

RICKI: Yeah, I hate it. I didn't want to move out here. I hate the country. I hate being trapped on this highway with no place to go. I hate having scrub brush for a backyard. I hate the field mice and the rats. I hate the poor pigs—poor Harold the pig—

MEI: You like the baby ducks.

RICKI: Yes, I like the baby ducks.

BUDDY: But you hate it here. I guess I knew that. [A *change comes over his face.*]

MEI: Kids miserable and all you fault. Look at Jimmy. He don't say nothing. Dumb in school—

RICKI: Ma!

MEI: Got bad grades. Not good like you. Now I got you job. You make money. Lose weight. Not pretty like me when I was you age. But okay now.

RICKI: Hey! I have an idea. Let's change the subject.

[JIMMY *holds his plate and licks it clean. He is unaware of their stares, and even enjoys this action. This stops all possible conversation.*]

MEI: Look at what he do . . . He don't even know how to eat like human be-ing. Who taught him that. [*to* BUDDY] You taught him that?

BUDDY: Jimmy, don't lick your plate anymore, son.

MEI: Oh that'll do it. Sure. He won't do that anymore. What are you good for anyway? Never home except to eat and sleep. Look at this house. Every-thing fall apart. The washing machine. The sink plugged up—

BUDDY: Maybe if you'd stop harpin' on me every chance you get, I'd want to get something done—

RICKI: Come on Jimmy. Let's go to the movies.

MEI: See, you drive you kids out.

RICKI: Come on Jimmy—

[*They put on their shoes.*]

BUDDY: What the hell are you startin' in on me for? Cain't I eat my meal in peace? All I want is some peace and quiet when I get home—

MEI: [*overlapping*] Peace/Quiet?! You just want to eat!

RICKI: Let's split.

MEI: [*overlapping*] What you good for anyway?

RICKI: [*overlapping*] Warp speed ahead! To *Star Wars*!

BUDDY: Get off my back!

MEI: You get off back.

JIMMY: [*overlapping*] Fwoooosh!

BUDDY: Oh kiss my ass—

MEI: Tell your mother to!

[RICKI *and* JIMMY *exit.* MEI JEN *and* BUDDY *freeze. Lights dim.* BUDDY *moves to front porch area as* MEI JEN *clears table and puts on a robe. It is more a lounging robe than an actual bathrobe. Sound of a Hank Williams tune plays in background.* BUDDY *sings quietly and lights a cigarette as they begin next scene. It's a warm, sultry summer night.*]

BUDDY: [*singing*] "I'm so lonesome I could cry . . ."

SCENE THREE

[*Later that night.* MEI JEN *sits at the table, shaking a colander of seeds. There is a lulling effect to the shaking. When she isn't in conflict, her sadness is visible. She can't be alone or have too much time to reflect, or she will feel that sadness.*]

MEI: [*calling out*] Buddy, what you doin? Buddy?

BUDDY: I'm out here, Mei Jen.

MEI: What you doin' out there?

BUDDY: Just watchin' the cars go by.

MEI: What?

BUDDY: Just watchin' the cars.

MEI: That's stupid. Come inside; it bad for your asthma.

BUDDY: How can fresh air be bad?

MEI: Why you want to watch cars?

BUDDY: It helps me think.

MEI: Think about what?

BUDDY: Just let me sit and think.

[MEI JEN *comes to the screen and thinks for a moment.*]

MEI: What there to think about, Buddy?

[*He puts out his cigarette.*]

BUDDY: Nothin', dear, nothin'.

[BUDDY *enters house. Maybe he will help her and keep her company.*]

MEI: Come help me do seed, huh?
BUDDY: Too tired . . .

[BUDDY *sits in easy chair and reads newspaper.* MEI JEN *crosses to table and shakes the seeds in the colander. There is more anger in the shaking.*]

MEI: Good seed this year. Make nice garden. Next year bigger, if you rototill bigger spot.
BUDDY: It's big enough now. What are you going to do with all the vegetables you already have?
MEI: Freeze them.
BUDDY: In what?
MEI: In freezer.
BUDDY: The refrigerator freezer is already full.
MEI: [*drops the bomb*] In big freezer we gonna buy. On sale at Sears.
BUDDY: How much is that gonna cost?
MEI: Only need $75 more. Freeze vegetables. Now you have more sales, maybe we can afford freezer, huh?
BUDDY: [*looks at her for the first time*] So you did hear me.
MEI: Look at these good seeds. Next year vegetable even better with new freezer. What you think, Buddy?
BUDDY: We'll see, Mei Jen. We'll see . . . Why don't you sit down here with me . . .
MEI: I gotta do the seeds.
BUDDY: Suit yourself.

[*silence*]

MEI: Can we go see Mrs. Lin in Camas, Washington, on Saturday?
BUDDY: We just went a couple of weeks ago.
MEI: A month. A whole month. I don't have no other Taiwanese friend. Got to talk to someone . . .
BUDDY: Okay. Don't get worked up. Okay . . .

[MEI JEN *stops a moment to shake her hands.*]

MEI: So tired. Work since little girl. When it will stop. When.

BUDDY: You wouldn't know what to do if you didn't work.

[*A hurt look comes over her face.*]

MEI: When I was little girl, I dream of easy life with maid to clean up house. Take trips all over the world. I always want to take cruise on the *Princess* love boat—never happen.

BUDDY: Never's a long time.

MEI: Long time for me. I had so many pretty dresses in Taiwan. Pretty Chinese dresses. Remember?

BUDDY: You sure were pretty. Heck, you still are.

MEI: Dance all night when I met you. Cha-cha-cha. Rumba. Jitterbug. Swing dance.

BUDDY: You sure like to dance.

MEI: You talk nice voice. So I dance with you. Bring me nice presents. Real gentleman. No try no funny stuff. So I go with you. Thought you were good military man—

BUDDY: Mei Jen, I was just a sergeant, for God's sake. How could I wait till I was thirty-five to quit? It would have killed me.

MEI: You forty-two now. Could have had good pension now. [*to herself*] I wouldn't have to work. [*to* BUDDY] Mrs. Lin in Camas, Washington, say Mr. Lin retired from Taiwanese military. They got good house. Military take good care. Take good care— [*Her face changes to joy.*] Oh look! S and H green stamps!

BUDDY: Wondered how long it would take for you to notice 'em.

MEI: Only need one page more for the new toaster-oven!

[*She licks stamps and puts in booklet.*]

MEI: New toaster-oven! You good man, Buddy. Lazy, but good.

BUDDY: If I'm so lazy, why am I so tired? . . .

MEI: You good man. Remember when I was in hospital with Ricki for three days, you sat by my bed till I wake up . . .

BUDDY: I remember, and I said, "Look Mei Jen . . . a little baby girl." What'd you want to call her?

MEI: Beauty. Like Sleeping Beauty story.

BUDDY: Not a normal name. I wanted to call her Ola Sue, after my mother.

MEI: And you thought that better? All you mama ever do is cry. Cry when she sad. Cry when she happy. Drive me crazy.

BUDDY: Mama never meant any harm.

MEI: You mama never like me. Thought I not good enough for you. Drive me
to nervous breakdown. Criticize, criticize. Not good enough for her Buddy.
BUDDY: Let me read the paper, Mei Jen . . .
MEI: You promised me lots of promises, Buddy.
BUDDY: Not now . . .

[BUDDY *starts to fall asleep.*]

MEI: You said, "We gonna give her lots of things I never had. Anything you
want. The world our oyster!" "Really?" I said. "I like oysters. Oyster got pearl
inside." I like pearls! You called Ricki our China Pearl. You tell me you take
care of me. I can count on that.
BUDDY: I'm only a man, Mei Jen. I tried the best I could . . .

[*He falls asleep.* MEI JEN *knows he's asleep, but she keeps talking anyway.*]

MEI: I said, "We gonna have good life, huh, Buddy . . ." good life . . . not like
when I little girl . . . always hungry . . . have bomb fall everywhere . . . Who
would ever know you don't like to work. . . . We could have had nice Chinese restaurant. Make good money. When I'm gonna be happy? When?

[*Lights dim on* BUDDY. MEI JEN *falls asleep. Light change.* MEI JEN
opens her eyes to find RICKI *dressed in a waitress apron and hat.*]

RICKI: [*sings*]
            "You can get anything you want,
              at Mei Jen's Chinese restaurant . . ."
Hello, I'm Ricki, and I'll be your hostess—slash—waitress—slash book-
keeper for a delightful evening of dining pleasure at Mei Jen's Famous Chinese Restaurant right here in the heart of downtown Junction City—right
next to the A&W and across the street from the Dairy Queen. Here in Junction City, we have one of everything. One root beer place, one ice cream
palace, one family owned grocery story, and one—count it—one—Chinese
restaurant owned and operated by the one—count it—one interracial Asian
family in town—the Donnelly's!

[*Applause.* MEI JEN *is delighted. She claps, too. It's almost like "This is
Your Life!"*]

And now let's introduce the family—slash—staff of Mei Jen's Famous Chinese Restaurant, beginning with Buddy Donnelly!

[BUDDY *enters in a workman's hat, wheeling in a dolly cart.*]

BUDDY: Hi. I'm Buddy Donnelly, and you won't be seeing too much of me unless somethin's wrong. I work behind the scenes here at Mei Jen's, and I
kinda like it that way. Save the spotlight for Mei . . .

MEI: That's right, Buddy!

RICKI: Tell them what you do, Daddy!

BUDDY: Well, I order all the food and restaurant supplies, pick 'em up, that
kinda thing. Then I take stock and do the inventory. Stuff I just love to do.
It's my life's work makin' that little woman happy. She's my China Pearl,
the star of my favorite TV show, the light of my life. Anything to make her
dreams come true—that's my motto! As long as Mei's happy, we're all
happy here at the Donnelly's! We're just so durn happy, I can't tell you!

MEI: I'm happy, too, Buddy!

RICKI: Thank you, Daddy! And now here's another member of the family—
slash—staff at Mei Jen's Chinese Restaurant—Jimmy Donnelly!

[JIMMY *appears in sun glasses, holding a towel and plate.*]

JIMMY: I'm the dishwasher. [JIMMY *flips the plate in the air and catches it. He
is a cool, collected and hip* JIMMY.] Hey!

RICKI: And what else do you do, Jimmy!

JIMMY: Ya' wants ta know what else I do?

RICKI: Yes, Jimmy!

JIMMY: Ya' wants ta know what else I do at the cool-est, grooviest, swingin-est
place in town?

RICKI: Tell us, Jimmy!

JIMMY: I'm the busboy . . . Heyyyy . . .

RICKI: Wow! Is he cool or what?

[MEI JEN *applauds.*]

MEI: That's my son!

RICKI: Mommy! You better get ready for your entrance.

MEI: Thank you, Ricki. I'm so proud of you.

RICKI: I know, mommy! I love you, too!

[BUDDY *and* JIMMY *take a blanket from the couch and hold it so* MEI JEN
can dress behind it.]

RICKI: And now without any further ado, right here in her happiest of her
dreams—the star of Mei Jen's Famous Chinese Restaurant. We bring you
the fabulous, the beautiful, the ever-youthful and energetic mother—
slash—owner—the incredible and charming—mother of the year and this

century, and all centuries from her to maternity! The one and only—MEEIIII JEEEENN!!!

[*They release the blanket and* MEI JEN *appears in a Chinese dress. She struts sexily to the sound of a lavish big band rumba number. There is massive applause. All the family members join in clapping. She is speaking perfect English.*]

MEI: Thank you. Thank you. I love you all so much. I want to thank my family—slash—staff for making my dream come true—because it could never have been possible without them.

RICKI/JIMMY/BUDDY: That's right!

[JIMMY *and* BUDDY *exit.*]

MEI: Here at Mei Jen's Restaurant, I not only cook you the finest Asian dishes you're likely to find on this good earth, but they are made with special vegetables picked with my own two hands. Why? Because I love you, that's why! At Mei Jen's Chinese Restaurant, you not only get . . .

BUDDY: Chow Mein!

JIMMY: Chop Suey!

RICKI: Egg Foo Young!

MEI: —all that American-style Chinese food—but you met ME!

RICKI/JIMMY/BUDDY: Mei Jen!!!

MEI: —and lots and lots of love! So why wait? Everybody's welcome! Come, eat, and be happy. Join us, and be part of the family at MEI JEN'S FAMOUS CHINESE RESTAURANT!!!

[*Applause.* MEI JEN *smiles, bows, blows kisses.* RICKI *holds up the blanket. Music ends.* RICKI *is left in a single light.*]

RICKI: And there you have it, folks. You saw it here first. The realization of the Asian-American dream. Where every person has a place and there's a place for every person. You just have to say "yes"—it's that easy!

[RICKI *rumbas out in silence. Light returns to* MEI JEN *awakening in her robe. She crosses to the Buddha altar, rings the bell three times, and rubs the beads in her hands.*]

MEI: Na myo ho reng ge kyo . . . Na myo ho ren ge kyo . . . Buddha say everything gonna be all right . . . gonna be all right . . . Please Gwa Nim Posa, make my dream come true . . .

[*Light dims.* MEI JEN *bows. Light change, then sound of male voices.*]

SCENE FOUR

[*Early morning the next day.*]

VOICE 1: Hey you, Jimmy Chink!
VOICE 2: Hey nip eyes! Come out and fight! Hey Chink!

[RICKI *rushes out with a baseball bat.* JIMMY *looks out the window.*]

RICKI: Shut up, you fucking asshole racist rednecks. Shut the fuck up! Fucking asshole cowards!!! I'm callin' the cops!

[*She swings the bat at objects outside. Crates. Washing machine . . . while
the voices overlap with her words.*]

VOICE 1: What're you scared of Charlie Chan! Your sister do your fightin' for
ya? Ow' what a sexy mama!
VOICE 2: Jimmy Chink! Jimmy Chink!

[*Sound of truck speeding off.* JIMMY *comes outside.*]

RICKI: Asshole cowards! Come back here so I can fucking kill you!
JIMMY: They're gone.
RICKI: How fucking dare they! This isn't high school! Grow the fuck up you
racist fucking idiots!!!
JIMMY: You can stop now.

[RICKI *is exhausted by her anger and her effort. She collapses onto the
ground. She is having trouble breathing.*]

RICKI: [*takes a breath with each word*] Idiot. Racist. Cowards . . .
JIMMY: You okay?
RICKI: Catch—my—breath. [*She takes a breath and calms down.*] When I get
upset, sometimes it's hard to breathe . . .
JIMMY: Better see a doctor.
RICKI: Why did you just take it. Why didn't you fight them?
JIMMY: What for?
RICKI: Jimmy. Wait. Don't go chase the animals. Come here . . .
JIMMY: You're too upset. I gotta feed the ducks.
RICKI: You'll just chase them around. Maybe hurt them. Like you did your
pony—
JIMMY: He broke outta the fence—
RICKI: You kept riding him after you were too big.
JIMMY: I didn't hurt him!

RICKI: I'm sorry. Come here. Help me clean up this mess. [*She indicates the boxes strewn all around the yard.*] You have to fold these up anyway for the dump, don't ya'? [JIMMY *shrugs. They work together a moment, taking the boxes apart and folding them.*] How can you stand this, Jimmy? Those kids. This house. Doing all the chores.

JIMMY: I don't care.

RICKI: Why don't you move out with me? Maybe we can share an apartment in Eugene.

JIMMY: Ma says you couldn't make it out there. That's why you're back.

RICKI: She's wrong. I can make it.

JIMMY: They why're you here?

RICKI: Money. School. Ma. I don't know . . . I made a lot of friends in Eugene. We'd take trips together to the coast or the lake, just for the hell of it. Freedom, Jimmy. A whole new world! Then I made myself lose a bunch of weight. And all of a sudden there were these boys who liked me. Thought I was pretty. First I went out a lot because it was fun, and I felt like a totally different person. Not me. Better. Then I couldn't stop.

JIMMY: Sex.

RICKI: [*surprised*] Yeah. What do you know about sex?

JIMMY: The movies at school. The guys in the locker room talkin'.

RICKI: Talking. Some friends are your true friends, and some only like you if you do what they want you to, Jimmy.

JIMMY: I don't ever want friends.

RICKI: Family's like that, too. Ma only likes you if you do what she says.

JIMMY: I don't wanta talk about it anymore.

[*a beat*]

RICKI: Where are they anyway?

JIMMY: Visiting.

RICKI: Don't tell me. Mrs. Lin in Camas, Washington. [*imitating* MEI JEN] "Her daughter is good to her mother. Her daughter treat her mother better than you . . ." [JIMMY *laughs.* RICKI, *still doing her mother*] "Oh, Buddy-ahhh! Mrs. Lin got big house. How come we no got big house, Buddy? Huh? Huh?" [RICKI *eggs on* JIMMY, *as her mother, hoping he will respond as the father.*] "Where my big house with the two-stories and the big staircase and the good furniture with the plastic on it. Huh, Buddy? Where's my new car and swimming pool and my baby elephant. I like baby elephants!"

JIMMY: [*as* BUDDY] "Ahh, lay off woman . . . I'm workin' hard—"

RICKI: "Who you callin' woman?"

JIMMY: "What you harpin' on now? Cain't ah have no peace and quiet here?"

RICKI: "No peace/quiet. No peace/quiet as long as you live in my house! Buddy—ahhhh!"

[RICKI *takes the cardboard and makes a roof over herself and* JIMMY.]

JIMMY: "It's mah house too! Dab nab it!"

[JIMMY *takes the cardboard and holds it over his own head.*]

RICKI: "Hey, what you doin' to my house!"

JIMMY: "Leggo of mah house!"

[RICKI *takes the cardboard and puts it over her head.*]

RICKI: "Hey you, Buddy!"

JIMMY: "Ah said leggo of mah house, durn woman!"

RICKI: "I got roof in first place. You good for nothin' Buddy!"

JIMMY: "Well, kiss mah ass!"

RICKI: "You tell you mother to!"

[JIMMY *sticks his rear out.* RICKI *kicks it.*]

JIMMY: [*as himself*] Hey! That hurt!

RICKI: "Too bad. I make all the money here. I cook all the food. Nobody respect me."

JIMMY: I don't want ta play anymore.

RICKI: "Everybody selfish. I do everything! What you do for me, huh?"

JIMMY: Stop now.

RICKI: "You all a bunch of lousy failures! You all take, take, take. Never give me anything! Nobody good enough. Not you. Not Buddy. Not Ricki!"

[JIMMY *puts his hands on* RICKI's *shoulders and gently shakes her.*]

JIMMY: I said stop it.

RICKI: "I'm not good enough. Not good enough."

JIMMY: Please. Ricki. Stop!

[*a moment*]

RICKI: [*crying*] God, Jimmy. I'm losin' it. I've got to get out of here. Oh, God . . .

JIMMY: You know when Kirk was on the planet of Indians and he had amnesia and fell in love and his wife died? Remember what Spock said to Kirk when he was so upset?

RICKI: What

JIMMY: [*touches his fingertips to her forehead in vulcan mind meld*] Forget. Forget . . .

[RICKI *looks at* JIMMY *a moment. He hugs her.* MEI JEN *enters carrying groceries. They stand up.*]

MEI: Jimmy, go help you Daddy with the groceries. Look, Ricki, Mrs. Lin in Camas, Washington's, daughter gave me this big box of cookies. Look pretty good, huh?

RICKI: Beautiful, Ma.

MEI: Hey, how come you not ready for work?

[JIMMY *exits. Ricki puts on a flannel shirt, her leather mill gloves, and leather tool apron.* MEI JEN *puts on a pair of soft cotton work gloves. They cross to next scene.*]

RICKI: I guess because I love it so much . . .

SCENE FIVE

The Mill Poem

[*Sound of factory machines, deafening at first, then fades under.* RICKI *and* MEI JEN *face each other. They are working in sync, but there is a strong tension between them. This poem should be fast and intense and reflect what it's like to work under this kind of physical pressure.*]

MEI: First you take the veneer, then shake loose.
They hurry, stick it to the dryer teeth.
Hurry, take the second sheet, stick it to the teeth.
Hurry, take another sheet, shake it loose,
feed the dryer quick before the teeth shut down.
Whoosh! Goes the wood into the dryer.
One, two three . . . Shake the splinters from your fingers.
Shake the hands before they sleep.
Hurry. Hurry. Hurry.
Before it start again—hurry!

RICKI: Out comes the veneer.
Hot, very hot onto the belt.
Very hot.
Fast, it comes out fast, so you pull the gloves on tight.
Grab the wood, lift it high, slide it onto the cart.

Stack it nice 'cos the foreman's always watching,
always watching to see the edges line—
edges line up nice, line up neat.
Grab the next piece, stacking quickly, stacking neatly
so the corners all match up.
Shake your hands if you have time.
Pull the splinters from your fingers, off your arms,
if you have the time.
Then back, go back to the belt.
Grabbing. Grabbing. Pulling.
Because it never stops.
never stops till it breaks down.
Never stops till you screw up.
And they know it was you—
you who screwed up because the foreman's always watching.
Always watching, and it doesn't stop—never stops—

MEI: First, you take the wood, shake it loose—
RICKI: Grab the dry veneer, sail into the cart—
MEI: Stick it to the teeth, before it grabs the wood—
RICKI: Then the dryer spits it out—
MEI: Feed it to the dryer—
RICKI: Before you screw up—
MEI: Whoosh!!! Goes the wood!
RICKI: And it doesn't stop—
MEI: Doesn't stop till you screw up—
RICKI: 'Cos the foreman's always watching—
MEI: The foreman's always watching, and you start it all again.
RICKI: And you start it all again, and THAT'S THE MILL POEM!

[*Lights fade to next scene.*]

SCENE SIX

[*Afternoon, a few days later.* JIMMY *enters outside area.*]

MEI: [*offstage*] Jimmy—Jimmy-ahhh! Come to the garden and help me. Jimmy!

[JIMMY *enters the house.* RICKI *enters outside area with* MONICA.]

RICKI: I just need to change my clothes and get this sawdust off me.
MONICA: Okay.

[*They enter the house.*]

RICKI: Excuse the mess. Pretty tacky, huh? You want anything to drink, Monica?

MONICA: Some water would be nice.

RICKI: Okay. I'll be back.

[RICKI *exits.* MONICA *wanders to the stained glass table.* JIMMY *enters.*]

JIMMY: That's mine!

MONICA: Oh, I'm sorry. I didn't know. [JIMMY *covers the tablecloth.*] I'm really very sorry.

[RICKI *enters with glass of water.*]

RICKI: Jimmy. Monica from work. Monica, my handsome brother, Jimmy. We're goin' to see a movie in Eugene. Want to come?

MONICA: We're seeing *Robin and Marian* with Sean Connery and Audrey Hepburn. It's supposed to be very romantic.

JIMMY: Nah, I don't think so.

RICKI: Jimmy likes science fiction movies.

MONICA: We could see *Star Wars* . . .

RICKI: That'll be the seventh or eighth time?

[*She exits. Silence.*]

MONICA: You know we went to school together. The same year even. You don't remember me, do you?

JIMMY: No.

MONICA: That's because I was in the retard class. That's what the kids called it. It was really "special ed." But the kids called us retards . . . You didn't though. Because the kids made fun of you, too. Mostly that ugly Greg Swensen . . . yuck!!! He thought he was cute, but he was really ugly . . . and that other guy, the weasel guy, Chuckie—what was his name? Chuckie . . .

JIMMY: Lemhouse.

MONICA: Yeah, Chuckie the mouse, Lemhouse . . . What a funny name . . . You know, they were the dopey ones. They were mean guys, huh?

JIMMY: Yeah. Swensen threw my books into the toilet once.

MONICA: Your schoolbooks?

JIMMY: Schoolbooks. Library books. My parents got mad because they had to buy me new ones and pay back the library.

MONICA: It wasn't your fault.

JIMMY: They thought I did it.

MONICA: You didn't tell them?

JIMMY: What's the use?

MONICA: It's not right, Jimmy. Swensen should have got in trouble.

JIMMY: Would've done somethin' else.

MONICA: I saw them throw food on you once in the cafeteria. I felt really bad, but I couldn't do anything. They made fun of me, too. They called me "retread." They thought it was so funny . . . I'm so glad I'm not in high school anymore. Aren't you?

JIMMY: Yeah.

MONICA: I'm working at the mill with Ricki. You know that, I guess. On clean up. The bathrooms. The lunchroom. I sweep around the mill. It's a very dirty place, but I don't mind. What do you do?

JIMMY: I push the carts at the cannery right now. Been going to welding school . . .

MONICA: Do you like it?

JIMMY: Nah . . .

MONICA: What do you like?

JIMMY: This.

MONICA: What is it?

JIMMY: Show you. See I take some colored glass and piece 'em together to make a pattern. Like this. [*picks up another piece of glass*] See?

MONICA: That's beautiful. What is it?

JIMMY: Look closer.

MONICA: A tiger face. That's pretty . . .

JIMMY: Tigers aren't pretty.

MONICA: Then handsome. A very handsome tiger. But there's something missing. The eyes.

JIMMY: Just need a couple more pieces of glass. Then it'll be perfect. There. See? When it's done, it'll be perfect.

MONICA: Oh yeah, it will be . . . I don't think I've seen anything as beautiful. [RICKI *enters. She has changed into a black leotard and shorts. She looks very attractive.*] Ricki, you look good.

RICKI: [*does a dance step*] Maybe we'll go to a disco after the movie. Jimmy, sure you don't want to go?

MONICA: We could see *Star Wars* if you want . . .

JIMMY: Nah . . .

MONICA: Are you sure?

RICKI: I was just kiddin' about the disco. Come on, Jimmy.

MONICA: Yeah, come with us.

JIMMY: I gotta do the chores.

MEI: [*offstage*] Jimmy-ahh! Come outside and help me in the garden!

RICKI: Let's go, Monica.

MONICA: Maybe we could go to a movie another time, Jimmy . . .

[MEI JEN *enters.*]

RICKI: Bye.

MONICA: Bye, Jimmy . . .

MEI: You dressed up.

RICKI: Goin' to the movies. Ma, you know Monica from work . . .

MONICA: Hi, Mrs. Donnelly.

MEI: Hello. Are you coming home for dinner?

RICKI: Don't think so—

MEI: Why not.

RICKI: Because I'm going to the movies—

MEI: Don't eat junk food. Come home for dinner.

RICKI: I'll get a salad.

MEI: No protein. I make you fried shrimp.

RICKI: I'll be fine.

MEI: When you be home?

RICKI: Don't know. Bye, Ma . . .

MONICA: Good-bye . . .

[*They exit.*]

MEI: What kind of daughter is she? [*calls out*] Jimmy! Jimmy, what you doing! Come help me rototill the garden! [JIMMY *enters outside area.*] Ricki
going to movies again! Look like she taking that poor girl from work. Koo-
koo, that's what they call her. She pretty, but real slow. Poor, poor girl . . .
People make fun, and she don't even know.

JIMMY: Who cares?

MEI: Hey, you like her . . . Maybe you gonna marry her. Maybe good idea, huh?

JIMMY: Cut it out!

MEI: You better watch out, maybe she want to marry you! What wrong with
that?

JIMMY: Cut it out!

MEI: You old enough to get married—

JIMMY: I am not!

MEI: [*singing*] Jimmy gonna marry a koo-koo girl!!!

JIMMY: I said stop it!

MEI: Jimmy gonna—

JIMMY: Stop it!

MEI: [*realizes she needs to soften with him. She takes his arm and strokes him on the shoulder*] Okay, okay. You know you mother love you . . . You a good son, Jimmy. A good son . . . Chinese mothers love their sons. Remember that, Jimmy. I always take care of you . . .

[JIMMY *seems calmer.* MEI JEN *exits. Light change.* JIMMY *enters the house.*]

SCENE SEVEN

[*Later that day.* BUDDY *is fixing small television set on dining table.*]

BUDDY: [*singing*]

> "Will the circle be unbroken . . .
> By and by, oh by and by . . .
> There's a better world awaitin'
> In the sky, Lord, in the sky . . ."

[JIMMY *enters.*]

BUDDY: Hey, son. Take a look at the repair manual, and read me the section on the vertical hold knob . . . Come on Jimmy, I kinda have my hands full. Jimmy Jay, you hear me? What're you waiting for? Fall to set in? Damn wires are so small . . . Jimmy Jay!

JIMMY: What page?

BUDDY: Where the marker is . . .

JIMMY: First make sure—the au-the ax-something-knob is turned to a clock-wise—pos-i-tion . . . Then insert—the a-ligned pairs of wire cable-connec-tors to the—

BUDDY: Son, didn't that high school of yours teach you how to read properly? What the hell did they graduate you for? My God, Jimmy . . .

JIMMY: Who wants to read anyway.

[JIMMY *is deeply embarrassed. He's been caught and wants to escape.*]

BUDDY: Wait son. Your grades weren't that good, but you used to read better than this. What happened?

JIMMY: I can read. Jus' not out loud. Okay?

BUDDY: Well, that's good.

JIMMY: Can I go now?

BUDDY: Sit down. Talk to me boy . . .

JIMMY: 'bout what?

BUDDY: How are you doing at welding school? [*silence*] You do go to welding
    school?

JIMMY: Yeah . . .

BUDDY: Good.

JIMMY: Jus' not every day.

BUDDY: What?

JIMMY: I go when we weld. I don't go when we got tests.

BUDDY: Ah, Jimmy . . .

[BUDDY *takes out a pack of cigarettes.*]

JIMMY: Can I go now?

BUDDY: We have ta talk, son.

JIMMY: Then don't smoke. Hurts my eyes.

BUDDY: All right already. [*Puts away cigarettes.* JIMMY *sits not looking at*
    BUDDY. *The more* BUDDY *tries to reach him, the more* JIMMY *feels perse-*
    cuted.] Dammit, Jimmy, what are we gonna do with you? Answer me, son.
    How you gonna pass the class if you can't take the tests?

JIMMY: Cheat?

BUDDY: That's no answer, Jimmy Jay. [*silence*] Don't you want anything out
    of life, son?

JIMMY: I don't care.

BUDDY: There must be something. You're always working on that pile of bro-
    ken glass over there.

JIMMY: Don't!

BUDDY: Then you do care about something, huh? That's a step, son. You know
    what your grandpa Jay used to do when I was a boy? If you had an ailment of
    any kind, he'd take a fresh young twig from a peach tree. And he'd ask you
    where you hurt. Then he'd cut notches in the twig. The more notches, the
    more the healin' power. That's what we gotta do, Jimmy. Cut some notches to
    heal you where ya' hurt, son. 'Cos you gotta care, or you curl up and die . . .

JIMMY: Grandpa Jay didn't like Black people.

BUDDY: No, that's not true. He was just an Oklahoma boy.

JIMMY: He called them niggers.

BUDDY: Yes, he did. But it wasn't outta hate. He just came from another time,
    Jimmy.

JIMMY: Like the kids at school.

BUDDY: You don't know how many times I went to see the principal to try to
    get those kids off your back. He just said it was harmless name-calling.

JIMMY: Nip. Jap. Chink. Slant-eyes—

BUDDY: All right already! You don't have to repeat them.

JIMMY: Are we done yet?

BUDDY: No! Dammit! I gotta think! I tried to get you to fight back. If you whupped them, they would have left you alone. They were just country kids, Jimmy. All they know here is white people. If you could have just got one of them. Just one . . . [*a beat*] I guess we should never have moved out here 'cos they weren't ready for us . . . [*a beat*] Let me take a look at this glass here . . . Hey, it kinda looks like Tony the Tiger!

JIMMY: No, just a tiger.

BUDDY: Well, it's good. Damn good. Maybe you could sell it. You could make a livin' that way. Maybe sell it at the Saturday market in Eugene—

JIMMY: I don't wanta sell it.

BUDDY: Why not?

JIMMY: It's mine.

BUDDY: Jimmy, what am I gonna do with you?

[*silence*]

JIMMY: Can I go now?

BUDDY: It's that bad, huh? Talkin' to me?

JIMMY: Please. I wanta go do the chores.

BUDDY: Son, I just wanta look out for you. Don't tell me it's too late, Jimmy Jay . . .

[*silence*]

BUDDY: Please, son . . .

JIMMY: I have to go.

[JIMMY *exits the door running.*]

BUDDY: Jimmy! Dammit.

[BUDDY *goes to the buffet and picks up a photograph of his parents.* BUDDY *puts the photo down and looks at a picture of himself and* MEI JEN. *He sits at the table and puts his head down onto his arms.* MEI JEN *enters with a small box of vegetables and a letter.*]

MEI: Buddy, we got the letter from the bank. There's a mistake you gotta take care of. Buddy? You hear me? [*She crosses to* BUDDY, *puts the vegetables down, and hands him the letter.*] They made the mistake. Look at how much they say we got. You gotta call the bank now and tell them they made the mistake.

BUDDY: What?

MEI: Look, Buddy, we got more money than this.

BUDDY: Oh lordy.

MEI: Call them now. You know they don't understand what I say. Call them and fix it, please?

BUDDY: Honey, please, come here . . . sit down.

MEI: Look, it say we got $800 missing. Fix it, Buddy.

BUDDY: There's somethin' I been puttin' off tellin' you. Please, darlin' sit down . . . [*She sits.*] I wanted to be able to tell you this when it was quiet. When we were gettin' along. When you would say to me—"Buddy, I understand—I understand why you did it, Buddy. And it's okay . . ."

MEI: What you talkin' about?

BUDDY: You know I don't lie to you, Mei Jen. You do know that—

MEI: What, Buddy, what?

BUDDY: I took that money out of our bank account to pay for some insurance.

MEI: You took my money last month and not tell me?

BUDDY: For the kids—to make sure they have something when we're not around.

MEI: And not tell me? You say you would never do that again. You always just take, take my money and not tell me!

BUDDY: Mei Jen. I wish I could've told you. But I'm not sorry. Not after what I found out about Jimmy Jay. The boy can barely read. What's he gonna do when we're not around?

MEI: You never worry before. You the one move us out here. You the one who gave away our money in Reno to no-good friend. Want to get-rich-quick! Sell land in desert! He take off with all the money—

BUDDY: Please let this go. I've paid enough.

MEI: No, not pay till I get nice house. Not pay till we don't have to worry about money all the time!

BUDDY: I can't keep goin' through this same old broken record—Lordy, Mei Jen, haven't I done anything right by you?

[*silence*]

MEI: You got the TV on the table. Take off for dinner, Buddy. Don't leave it like you leave everything!

BUDDY: I don't got the strength for this anymore . . .

MEI: Don't ever touch my money again! [*She exits into kitchen.* BUDDY *clears the tools and sets the TV in the livingroom while* MEI JEN *continues talking offstage.*] He the one who make us miserable. [*in Chinese*] Jei shir wode chen! Take my money, and now all of a sudden he gotta help Jimmy—gotta help the kids—I gotta do everything myself! Why you can't help me, why! Never gonna do this to me again. Open new bank account tomorrow!

BUDDY: I just don't got the strength for this, Mei . . .

[BUDDY *gathers up his salesman briefcase and exits out the front door. Lights cross-fade to next scene.*]

SCENE EIGHT

[*After dinner that night. Sound of weird space music fades up and out. JIMMY appears in a futuristic, colorful light. Holding a spaceship model, he makes sound effects as he moves through his own world.*]

JIMMY: "FWOOSHHHH!!! Stardate 4051 point 378 dash 2. Commander Kurt of the *World Vessel Ulysses* circling the globe of a new class M planet, undiscovered by prior expeditions! Fwooosh!!! The *Ulysses* was hailed by an urgent distress call that has since disappeared. While searching for signs of intelligent life, my crew and I encounter an eerie noise off the starboard side . . ."

[RICKI *appears in space helmet.*]

RICKI: "Commander!"

JIMMY: "Yes, Lieutenant Smart!"

RICKI: "I have readings of an energy source emanating from outside the ship!"

JIMMY: "Lieutenant Smart, have you any idea what it is?"

RICKI: "No, sir, I haven't seen anything like it. The computer has no possible—"

JIMMY: "Fwooosh!"

RICKI: "Wait—The bio-scan indicates it is a life form—an energy-sucking entity which appears to grow larger the more the ship resists its strange pull."

JIMMY: "Plan of action, Lieutenant?"

RICKI: "For the time being, do not repel it until further study. It appears to be growing larger, sir, the more we strengthen our force field."

JIMMY: "Then lower the force field, dammit!"

RICKI: "Lowering, sir . . ."

JIMMY: "Status, Lieutenant?"

RICKI: "Stable at the moment. Sir, we're being signaled—"

JIMMY: "From the planet?"

RICKI: "No sir, from the entity."

JIMMY: "The entity? Can we communicate with it?"

RICKI: "I'm attempting the all-purpose translators . . . There doesn't seem to be a link with any known language in this solar system—I'll try another code—It's not working!" [*Sound of strange music. Eerie lights.* MEI JEN *appears, dressed in sexy alien unitard.*] "Captain, I am getting strange readings in the anti-matter grid. I'm afraid the ship is going to blow—"

MEI: "Greetings Earth-things!"

RICKI: "The signals are stabilizing, but only a little, sir!"

JIMMY: "Lieutenant, run a scan!"

RICKI: "Checking, sir!"

MEI: "You have no need to fear. I have come to welcome you to my world."

JIMMY: "You live on that planet?"

MEI: "Did I not just say that?"

RICKI: "I'm not getting any life readings as we understand them, sir. The energy fluctuations are too erratic to be considered a legitimate organic life form."

JIMMY: "What do you want from us?"

MEI: "Nothing dear things. Nothing. I came to greet you and show you a good time around Rumba!"

[*Rumba music plays. She does a short dance.*]

JIMMY: "What was that?"

RICKI: "I believe it's the name of her planet, sir."

JIMMY: "What is?"

RICKI: "Rumba."

[*Rumba music plays.* MEI JEN *does another short dance.*]

MEI: "Very good, Smart-thing. You shall be the first visitor to our oh-so humble planet!"

[MEI JEN *points her finger at* RICKI, *who disappears in the light.*]

JIMMY: "I demand to know what you have done to my first officer!"

MEI: "Demand? How dare you presume to demand. Just for that no milk and cookies for you, Commander-thing . . . Cha-cha, beam me back to Rumba!"

[*Rumba music plays.* MEI JEN *claps her hands and disappears.*]

JIMMY: "Ensign Rune, locate Lieutenant Smart on the planet surface!"

[MONICA *appears. Light changes to normal.*]

MONICA: "Aye-aye, Commander!" [*silence*] "Sir, I'm running a scan on the planet. We found the Lieutenant on the southern part of the planet." [*silence*]

"Sir, should we send a rescue team? Sir, awaiting your orders . . ." Jimmy? It's okay, Jimmy, this is really fun to pretend. This is fun. Okay, Jimmy? Okay?

[*silence*]

JIMMY: "I'm Commander Kurt of the *World Vessel Ulysses* to you, Ensign Rune! Join me in the transit room. I'll lead the rescue team!"
MONICA: "Aye, aye, Commander!"

[JIMMY *and* MONICA *exit, whooshing past* RICKI.]

RICKI: Right on, Jimmy!

[RICKI *looks ecstatic. She turns on the small radio on the porch. Sound of a 70s rock song blasts on and* RICKI *dances to it.* RICKI *dances as if there were no one else on earth. It is a dance of elation one does in front of the mirror when no one else is watching.* MEI JEN *appears at the doorway in her robe. She turns the music off.*]

MEI: What's the matter. You drunk?

[RICKI *stops and enters the house. She pulls her journal from her backpack and starts writing in it.* MEI JEN *turns on the record player, then sits at the dining table playing solitaire. Sound of a Chinese opera song.*]

RICKI: Could you turn that down a little?
MEI: You don't like Chinese music?
RICKI: Just a little quieter.
MEI: If you don't like it, I don't want to play it—Go ahead. Shut if off. [MEI JEN *waits. No response from* RICKI. MEI JEN *turns off the music.*] You daddy left. Not even tell me. I left food on the table for you. Fried tofu. Shrimp. Vegetables.
RICKI: I'm not hungry.
MEI: So picky. Pick, pick at my food. Too greasy. Too salty. No meat. What's the matter with you?
RICKI: Monica and I grabbed something in town—
MEI: No-good junk food—
RICKI: Salad. A great big salad. I'm not hungry. Let's drop it. Okay?

[*beat*]

MEI: Ricki, get me some Pepto Bismol. Stomach not feel so good . . .
RICKI: I think there's one on the buffet . . .
MEI: You get it for me.

RICKI: It's right next to you on the—

MEI: Please?

RICKI: O.K. [RICKI *closes her journal. She crosses to the buffet, gets and hands the Pepto Bismol to* MEI JEN, *who drinks it straight from the bottle.*] You really should use a spoon—

MEI: Don't criticize. [*a pained look*] My stomach upset. I got headache. My hands hurt . . . Life is so complicated, Ricki.

RICKI: Ma, you worry yourself sick. That's why you're so cranky—

MEI: Who say I'm cranky!

RICKI: No one. Sheesh . . . [*heads for her bedroom*] I'm going to bed.

MEI: Why you going out with that koo-koo girl?

RICKI: What?

MEI: That koo-koo girl from work. She got something wrong with her. Everybody say so.

RICKI: Her name is Monica.

MEI: She real slow—

RICKI: But I've never met anyone as sweet and empathetic—

MEI: What's that mean?

RICKI: She feels for other people.

MEI: But she's koo-koo—

RICKI: [*overlapping*] Stop saying that! God, how can you be prejudiced after the way those people treat you at the mill—

MEI: [*overlapping*] What you mean—

RICKI: [*overlapping*] Never mind.

MEI: [*overlapping*] No. I want to know what you mean.

RICKI: [*overlapping*] Nothing—

MEI: [*overlapping*] What!?

RICKI: The real old farts—they're very condescending.

MEI: What that mean?

RICKI: They talk down to you. Like a child.

MEI: They just want to make sure I understand.

RICKI: I heard them tell chink jokes in the lunchroom.

MEI: What's that—

RICKI: Jokes about Chinese people.

MEI: Who make fun of me?

RICKI: Olson, Jensen, and Sweeney.

MEI: Sweeney the Shop Steward? What they say?

RICKI: They kind of imitated the way you talk—

MEI: [*overlapping*] There's nothing wrong with the way I talk—

RICKI: [*overlapping*] That's right! They're stupid jerks, and that's why you shouldn't listen to what they say about Monica—

MEI: [*overlapping*] I not the same as Monica. I go talk to Sweeney tomorrow.

RICKI: [*overlapping*] He's a jerk. Why the hell would you trust them over me?

MEI: [*overlapping*] Because you think you got education, you smarter than me.

RICKI: [*starting to leave*] Okay—believe all those creeps at work. Believe whatever the hell you want!

MEI: They hard-working people. Not like you and you daddy! He hurt me so bad . . . Now you want to hurt me too!

RICKI: I don't want to hurt you!

MEI: I dig in garden for you. [*She shows her hands.*] To give you fresh vegetable! And this the way you treat me . . .

RICKI: Why do you do this?!

MEI: Ungrateful—

RICKI: I don't ask you to—

MEI: Selfish daughter! All I do for you—

RICKI: [*overlapping*] Don't do things for me! I never asked you to—

MEI: [*overlapping*] I you mother! You treat me with respect!

RICKI: I hate you trying to run my life—

MEI: [*overlapping*] You hate it so much, why don't you go! Go be broke. Who got you job, huh?

RICKI: [*overlapping*] You tricked me. Tell me to stay here so I can save money. Two months later you tell me to pay rent. You're trying to trap me here—

MEI: Then move out!

RICKI: I—just—want—to—

MEI: Move out and go drinking and have sex with all your friends all night long—

RICKI: [*overlapping*] What?

MEI: You probably had abortion already! I saw you pills in dresser drawer—

RICKI: You went in my room?!

MEI: You been having sex—

RICKI: You have no right—

MEI: This my house! I do what I want!

RICKI: It's—my—life!

MEI: I gave you life!

RICKI: I—have to—get out!

MEI: Ungrateful. Selfish. Not even eat my food. Not good enough for you Miss Ricki! You come back here 'cos you failure.

RICKI: I am not a failure!

MEI: I try take care of you.

RICKI: I am not a failure!

MEI: [overlapping] Won't even eat the food I make with my own hands—

RICKI: [overlapping] You want me to eat! Here! [grabs food with hands stuff into her mouth] Here! You happy? Does this make you happy?

MEI: [horrified] I don't deserve to be shit on like this—

RICKI: [overlapping] Here let me eat some more! [stuffs more food in her face] Then I can be big and fat and never leave you! You want me to be just like Daddy and Jimmy so I won't ever have a fucking life of my own!

MEI: [total loss of control, speaking at the same time.] What you doin' to my food! I GAVE YOU LIFE! STOP IT!!! [Now she is crying.] My own daughter hate me . . .

RICKI: I can't hate you. You're my mother . . .

MEI: No one ever love me! Not even my own mother. Ever love me.

RICKI: I just need to breathe . . .

[MEI JEN continues to cry to herself. It is a sad, solemn wail. JIMMY and MONICA enter the outside area.]

RICKI: Jimmy, I'm sorry to leave you like this . . . I'm—sorry—I have to go . . .

JIMMY: Uh-hmmm . . .

[RICKI exits.]

MONICA: [She looks toward the house and then back to JIMMY.] I guess I should go home. I had a good time, Jimmy.

JIMMY: Yeah . . .

MONICA: Can I give you my phone number? [JIMMY nods. MONICA writes it down on a movie stub.] Maybe we can go out sometime?

JIMMY: Okay . . .

MONICA: Don't be sad . . .

[MONICA kisses him on the cheek. She hands JIMMY something wrapped in tissue paper and runs off. JIMMY sits on the porch. He unwraps the tissue. Two pieces of glass.]

JIMMY: Done. Eyes for the tiger! Done!

[MEI JEN stops crying. She looks up. Lights fade slowly.]

END OF ACT I

ACT II
SCENE ONE

[*Later that night.* RICKI *is outside. She has a jacket wrapped around her shoulders. She looks up at the sky, then sits on the steps of the front porch. Delicate, quiet music plays.*]

RICKI: She has always been a light sleeper.
Listening to the sound of crinkling paper
in the closet, the sound of tiny feet
scurrying across the ceiling. This kept her awake,
kept her alert, so sleep was never deep,
never long.

For many years, she lived with a mouse in her
bedroom closet. Afraid to open the door
during the day because at night she'd hear
the crinkling. Afraid to look out of her
bedroom window, fearing a big rat
would be peaking in, standing on its
hind legs pulling in toward the light.

So when the light shut off, the only safe place
to look wasn't out, but up, up at the stars
late at night. Then her problems seemed
so small. Because around each star, were planets
and perhaps, too, people who might also
be looking up toward her wondering
at the same time. Wondering.
Wondering.

Sometimes the moon shined so bright, it glowed
cool on her face as she tried to sleep. Drifting.
And as she counted the stars and learned to name them,
she found comfort
                        and a sense of belonging.
And in reaching out,
                        she learned to sleep more deeply,

more safely,

more at peace . . .

Still learning.

[*Lights cross-fade to next scene.*]

SCENE TWO

[*Lights fade up. It is before dawn and still dark. There is a light coming from behind the kitchen door.* RICKI *enters quietly. She is trying to sneak into the house without being heard. She slowly crosses toward her bedroom when she hears* BUDDY *singing in the kitchen. She stops a moment to listen.*]

BUDDY:

> "Amazing grace, how sweet the sound
> that saved a wretch like me . . .
> I once was lost, but now am found,
> was blind, but now I see . . ."

BUDDY: [*enters holding a skillet and a pancake turner*] Hey, Sleeping Beauty . . . [RICKI *looks awkwardly at* BUDDY.] Hey, how 'bout some flapjacks? Your ma's still in asleep. What d'ya say. Join me for breakfast?

RICKI: No, I'm just getting my work clothes—

BUDDY: [*overlapping*] Come on . . . It gives us a chance to catch up on things, just the two of us . . .

RICKI: I can't stay.

BUDDY: Gotta eat.

RICKI: Okay. Just one. But no butter—

BUDDY: Good, goin', girl. Be back with some coffee.

[*She sits at the table. He exits into kitchen.*]

BUDDY: [*offstage*] How is it?

RICKI: Good, Daddy.

BUDDY: [*enters with coffeepot*] It's the buttermilk. Here's a fresh cup, courtesy of the new Mr. Coffee . . .

RICKI: You got one of those?

BUDDY: Salesman of the month bonus prize.

RICKI: That why you're in a good mood?

BUDDY: Life's too short to be frettin' and worryin' all the time. [*sits*] Now what's this about movin'?

RICKI: I've gotta get outta here. We've never fought like that before, Daddy. It scares me.

BUDDY: Lord knows, your ma ain't exactly the easiest person to get along with—

RICKI: Oh really?

BUDDY: —but she does love you, Ricki Sue.

RICKI: Love. Me.

BUDDY: Your ma . . . just . . . grabs too hard most of the time. She ends up losing what she had. Lord knows, I've wanted to leave a few times.

RICKI: You should have—

BUDDY: [overlapping] We couldn't do that to you kids.

RICKI: You should have put us in an orphanage.

BUDDY: What kind of talk is that?

RICKI: We're not a normal family—

BUDDY: Well, who the hell is?

RICKI: I should never have come back. I can't fight like that again. Maybe you're used to it, Daddy, but it feels like something in me dies when I get that mad . . .

BUDDY: Yeah . . . Remember when your ma and I had that big fight in Reno?

RICKI: Which one?

BUDDY: And I told you to pack up your clothes, we were leaving. Do you remember that? And you just stared at me.

RICKI: I was ten years old. You were asking me to make a choice. I couldn't.

BUDDY: I saw that in your eyes. [a beat] Ricki, how could I leave her? Who would read for her? Send out the bills. Hell, I'm scared every time she drives that car.

RICKI: I know.

BUDDY: Family's family, Ricki Sue. Bad times and good times.

RICKI: Mostly bad . . .

BUDDY: She's not feelin' good these days.

RICKI: Then she should see a doctor and a psychiatrist while she's at it.

BUDDY: For God's sake, at least you know your mother! Her mother sold her to the highest bidder to be a maid. Have a little compassion, Ricki . . .

RICKI: Compassion.

BUDDY: What's wrong with you?

RICKI: It's not my fault.

BUDDY: Nobody said it was. Lord, it's like talkin' to a signpost and taking the wrong road home!

[Silence. BUDDY softens.]

BUDDY: I know this isn't the life you dream of. It's not mine or your mother's. I don't even know if Jimmy Jay has any dreams . . . But you gotta make the best of it, Ricki. You think I'm a failure just like your ma does. Well, these are the cards we've been dealt. It's the best I can do. I know I eat too much. I smoke too much. Been away when your ma starts gettin' crazy . . . But I've tried to be there when I could. Remember the Easter outfits I bought you every year?

RICKI: [*She loved the Easter outfits.*] White dress. Little white gloves. Green shoes and purse . . .

BUDDY: We went fishin' in the summer. Had fun.

RICKI: I hated putting the worm on the hook.

BUDDY: So I did it. When you moved out. Who helped ya? I tried Ricki. It's different with a father and daughter. I never got mad at you when you didn't invite me to that banquet.

RICKI: What banquet?

BUDDY: The father-daughter one at the high school.

RICKI: You knew?

BUDDY: I figured you had your reasons.

RICKI: Daddy . . . [RICKI *is speechless.*]

BUDDY: Back in Tahlequah, things were simple. Your grandpa Jay had two hundred acres of some of the richest farm land. His daddy before him had eight hundred. It was beautiful, Ricki. We milked the cows right about this time o'mornin'. Lots of chickens. Sometimes the Oklahoma heat got so bad—I remember it got to 114 one day—can you believe that? 114. Sometimes it was so bad Mama and I had to spray the chickens with water to keep them from dying. Yeah . . . You know I'd walk to school. It was just a one-room schoolhouse. Sometimes rode my horse when it was snowin'. In the summer, all the kids would go the swimmin' hole. All the relatives would have picnics with all the trimmins'. Barbecues . . . Everybody knew each other. It was a damn good place to live . . .

RICKI: [*finally*] What do you want from me?

BUDDY: I never moved us out here to make you miserable. I thought we had a chance to be happy. I was so happy then—[A *pained look comes over his face.*] Why the hell does everyone have to blame me for everything—

RICKI: [*She rises from the table.*] Daddy, it's time to leave.

BUDDY: At least wait a month. Then you can save up enough for a decent place.

RICKI: I have to go.

BUDDY: A couple of weeks.

RICKI: I need to go—I'm afraid if I don't I'll never leave—

BUDDY: You can't find a place that fast, can you?

RICKI: [*caving in*] Well, no . . .

BUDDY: Take a bit of time. Get something you can afford. I'll help you move again. Ease into it Ricki. It'll be easier for her . . . for all of us.

RICKI: No matter what I do, everyone pulls me back . . . I can't get anywhere . . .

BUDDY: Please, Ricki. We can't handle an abrupt change right now.

RICKI: When then?

BUDDY: Do you hate us that much?

RICKI: I don't hate anybody . . . But when am I going to get to . . . All right then. Two weeks. No more.

[MEI JEN *enters in her robe.*]

MEI: [*quietly*] Two weeks for what.

BUDDY: Your daughter's gonna wait a little before movin' out so she can find a good place.

MEI: She want to go. Should go now.

BUDDY: Now Mei Jen. Be nice.

MEI: Why? She the one who insult me.

BUDDY: Ricki?

RICKI: Ma, I'm sorry. I didn't mean it. [*a moment*] I'm sorry I hurt your feelings.

[*Silence as* MEI JEN *inspects* RICKI'S *face.*]

MEI: [*gently*] You stay for couple of weeks. Save money for a nice place.

RICKI: But you promise not to go in my bedroom again?

MEI: [*defensive*] Why I gotta promise—

BUDDY: Mei Jen . . .

MEI: Sure. I stay outa your room. No problem.

RICKI: And you'll treat me like an adult? Not a child.

BUDDY: Of course she will. Right Mei?

MEI: Sure.

RICKI: And you can't make me eat when I don't wanta eat.

MEI: That makes no sense—

BUDDY: We're just worried about you Ricki—

RICKI: Daddy!

BUDDY: We gotta let her run her own life, Mei.

MEI: Okay. I don't make you eat. Except for dinner. You promise to come home for dinner every night.

RICKI: Can't. I'm going on swing shift soon.

MEI: You always tricky one. Okay. Dinner on weekend?

RICKI: Sure. Till I go.

MEI: Now I gotta get ready for work. . . . [MEI JEN *exits into bedroom.*]

BUDDY: Now that wasn't so bad, was it? [*He looks out the front door. Gradual light change.*] Sun's breakin' through . . . I love the dawn. Always packed with new hope.

RICKI: Why are you still together?

BUDDY: Your mother and I love each other. That's the only answer I got . . .

RICKI: Okay.

[*He turns to her. She needs to know this.*]

BUDDY: Ricki, you'll always be taken care of. I know it's hard workin' your way through school. You'll be the first one in the family with a college degree. I'm proud of ya'. Damn proud.

RICKI: You are?

BUDDY: [*toasts her with his coffee cup*] Here's lookin' at another Shakespeare!

RICKI: No way.

BUDDY: Then you'll be Ricki Donnelly.

[*Light fades as we hear* BUDDY *voiceover singing the last phrases of* "Amazing Grace."]

VOICEOVER:

"I once was lost, but now am found
Was blind, but now can see. . . ."

[*Then the sound of roller rink music.*]

SCENE THREE

[*That evening.* MONICA *enters, skating.*]

MONICA: [*singing*]

"You put your whole self in,
you put your whole self out,
you put your whole self in
and you shake it all about . . ."

[*calling out*] Come on Jimmy . . .

[JIMMY *enters, carrying skates. He sits on bench and takes his shoes off.*]

MONICA: [*singing*]

"You do the hokey pokey,
and you shake yourself around,
That's what it's all about . . . Woo-Woo!"

[*She laughs and sits next to him.*]

MONICA: Can I help you with that?

JIMMY: No.

MONICA: Are you mad about something?

JIMMY: No.

MONICA: Oh . . . [*silence*] Maybe coming here wasn't such a good idea. Skating's pretty dumb, huh?

JIMMY: No. I just don't know how.

MONICA: Oh. Neither do I. We can both fall down together then.

JIMMY: I don't want to fall down. People'll look at me.

MONICA: You mean like Olaf the big football star over there?

JIMMY: He's here?

MONICA: Yeah. Over there. And he just fell on his butt. See?

JIMMY: Yeah . . . He looks pretty silly . . .

MONICA: Everybody falls down sometime Jimmy. Even the football guys . . . So it's okay. Nobody's going to care because they're tryin' to stay on their feet. Okay, Jimmy?

JIMMY: Okay. [*a big moment for him*] Monica?

MONICA: Yes?

JIMMY: [*slowly*] I'm glad you like me.

MONICA: Me, too, Jimmy. You're a nice guy . . . and handsome, too.

JIMMY: [*surprised and delighted*] Me?

MONICA: Oh yes! You look like a movie star.

JIMMY: [*more delight*] I do not.

MONICA: You do. I remember the girls looking at you in school.

JIMMY: What girls?

MONICA: Just girls.

JIMMY: Really?

MONICA: You mean you never noticed?

JIMMY: I thought they just wanted to make fun at me. Anybody who looks at me I think just wants ta make fun of me.

MONICA: [*takes his hand*] No, Jimmy. Not anymore . . .

[*She kisses him right on the lips for good amount of time.* JIMMY *is almost in shock.*]

VOICEOVER: All skate!!!

MONICA: Now hurry up and tie your shoes. I want to skate and fall on my butt!
[MONICA *skates and waits for* JIMMY *to follow. He tries and almost falls just as he reaches her.*] Last one around the rink has to buy ice cream cones!

JIMMY: Here I go! Ahhhh!

MONICA: Yay, Jimmy!

[*They exit skating. Sound of music fades as light cross-fades.*]

SCENE FOUR

[*A few days later at dinnertime.* MEI JEN *is kneeling at the Buddha temple, chanting and rubbing beads together. She rings bell three times. She chants.*]

MEI: Na myo ho reng ge kyo . . . Na myo ho reng ge kyo . . . Na myo ho reng ge kyo . . . [JIMMY *enters the living room. He tries to sneak out the front door.*] Jimmy! Don't go outside. Come here. Let me look at you. Turn around.

JIMMY: What for?

MEI: You getting so stubborn. Just like your sister. I want to see you . . . You look good. You a good-looking boy, Jimmy, you know that? All you got to do is smile . . . like this . . . [*She smiles.*] Come on, now you do it. Smile. What's a matter, someone got all your teeth?

JIMMY: I don't feel like smiling right now.

MEI: Did you shave?

JIMMY: What for?

MEI: Go shave. Now.

JIMMY: Why?

MEI: Because I say so . . . Please Jimmy, do it for you mother . . . okay? [BUDDY *enters with a bag of groceries and a cake box. He is smoking.*] You got the cake?

BUDDY: I got the cake.

MEI: German chocolate?

BUDDY: German chocolate.

MEI: You favorite Jimmy. Now please go shave, okay? [JIMMY *exits to his bedroom.* BUDDY *starts to set the groceries on the dining table.*] Ahhhh! Take them into the kitchen. I gotta set the table. Ahhh . . . you're getting ashes everywhere.

BUDDY: Alright already! Alright! Quit rushin' me, woman!

[BUDDY *exits into kitchen.* MEI JEN *takes off her robe and looks at herself in mirror.*]

MEI: I can still wear my Chinese dresses. [BUDDY *enters and whistles.*] Shoosh!

BUDDY: There's my China doll!

MEI: Oh you shush up!

BUDDY: Well, you look—

MEI: I cut up more vegetable. Jimmy! Hurry get out here. Whatsa matter, you die in there? [JIMMY *enters with tissue paper on his face. He has cut himself shaving.*] Oh, look at you!

JIMMY: I hate shaving.

MEI: Buddy, fix up his face. I want him to look good.

JIMMY: Why?

MEI: I told you.

JIMMY: No, you didn't.

MEI: I invite a Chinese girl to meet you.

JIMMY: What?

MEI: You dumb or something? Friend of Mrs. Lin in Camas, Washington, has a nice daughter. I invite her here to meet you. Maybe be your wife. What you think of that?

JIMMY: I think it stinks.

MEI: She real nice. Mrs. Lin say so. Buddy, fix him up.

[*She exits into kitchen.* BUDDY *crosses to* JIMMY *to wipe off his face.*]

JIMMY: I'm not meeting anyone.

BUDDY: Your ma just gets carried away. Let's just make the best of it, okay?

[BUDDY *takes the cigarette out of his mouth to cough.*]

JIMMY: Could you put out your cigarette? The smoke's hurting my eyes.

BUDDY: Oh, for God's sake, cain't a man smoke in peace!

MEI: [*offstage*] Buddy! Help me!

BUDDY: Oh for God's sake, quit your yappin', woman!

[BUDDY *exits into kitchen.* JIMMY *heads for the front door as* RICKI *enters.*]

RICKI: Whoa, Jimmy! What's going on! Ma left me a message at work. Said I should come right home after my shift. She made it sound like an emergency.

[MEI JEN *enters.*]

MEI: Ricki. Good. You home. Hurry get dressed for dinner.

RICKI: Ma, why did you call me at work?

MEI: We're having special dinner. Hurry up.

RICKI: You called me home for dinner? I was going to look at some apartments—

MEI: Friend for Jimmy coming over—

RICKI: Really? That's great! [*She looks at* JIMMY.] So Monica's coming over?

MEI: What Monica. I got Chinese girl for Jimmy.

RICKI: What?

MEI: Chinese girl, that's what. Why everybody gotta ask "what" in this family? Nobody got ears anymore? Go get dressed. Then help you daddy in the kitchen. I think he catching the bad cold.

BUDDY: [*enters*] No, it's just the asthma acting up.

RICKI: Daddy, maybe you should lie down a bit.

MEI: I need him help me.

BUDDY: I'm fine, really . . .

RICKI: Are you sure?

BUDDY: Hey, I'm still alive and kickin'. That's all that counts.

RICKI: Really, Daddy, go rest. I'll help Ma with this crazy dinner scheme.

MEI: What crazy dinner scheme?

RICKI: Inviting a Chinese girl here for Jimmy. [*to* JIMMY] Did she even tell you about this?

JIMMY: No.

MEI: I tell him.

JIMMY: Just now you did. You didn't even ask me.

MEI: So what. You would have tooken off. Now you stay.

RICKI: That's not fair.

MEI: What you know?

RICKI: Jimmy likes Monica. And she likes him. Why can't you accept that?

MEI: Why can't you mind your own business?

BUDDY: Who's Monica?

RICKI: A girl at work Jimmy's been seeing.

MEI: You been seeing her?

RICKI: Yes!

MEI: Who I talkin' to, huh? Jimmy, you been seeing that koo-koo girl behind my back?

RICKI: MONICA!

JIMMY: Yes. And it's none of your business.

RICKI: Right on, Jimmy!

MEI: Then you stop after you meet Connie.

BUDDY: Who's Connie?

MEI: Friend of Mrs. Lin in Camas, Washington. I told you I don't know how many times!

RICKI: You have no right to stop Jimmy from seeing Monica—

MEI: You stop munching in. I not talking to you. Jimmy. No Monica. You hear? I don't want no two-timer in this house!

RICKI: How can you do this to your own son?

BUDDY: Ricki's right, Mei Jen. If Jimmy likes this girl—

MEI: You the one who ask me what we gonna do for Jimmy. What do you do but criticize. Everybody in this family tell me I'm wrong!

BUDDY: But, honey, this isn't right. [*He coughs again.*] Oh Lordy, I don't got the strength to fight you, Mei—

MEI: [*overlapping*] Buddy, you take your asthma medicine?

BUDDY: [*overlapping*] Yeah, yeah . . . Lordy . . .

MEI: [*overlapping*] Maybe I get you some more?

BUDDY: [*overlapping*] No, no, I'm fine . . . I just . . .

RICKI: Daddy, you better go lie down . . .

BUDDY: Okay, okay, maybe you're right . . . Wake me when it's time for dinner . . .

MEI: Ricki right. You go to sleep for while, Buddy. Go rest. We have good dinner for when you wake up . . .

BUDDY: Mei Jen, go easy on the boy. It's just dinner for God's sake, okay? [BUDDY *exits.*]

MEI: Jimmy. Go put another shirt on. There's blood on your collar from where you shaved. Jimmy, please, do it for you mother. Come on, Connie gonna be here soon. Go . . .

[JIMMY *exits grudgingly.*]

RICKI: Ma, please, let's talk about this thing with Jimmy—

MEI: [*overlapping*] I don't got time—

RICKI: [*overlapping*] It's not right to force this on him—

MEI: [*overlapping*] I just try to help—

RICKI: [*overlapping*] But Jimmy has a chance with Monica—

MEI: [*overlapping*] Maybe he like Connie—

RICKI: [*overlapping*] I know you're doing this because you care—

MEI: [*overlapping*] That's right—

RICKI: [*overlapping*] But it's not right to—

MEI: [*overlapping*] You think you know him better than I do—

RICKI: [*overlapping*] I'm just asking you to help him—

MEI: [*overlapping*] I am helping—

RICKI: [*overlapping*] —grow up—

MEI: [*overlapping*] What you talking?

RICKI: He has a chance, Ma. A real chance with Monica.

MEI: How do you know he won't like Connie? How do you know? [*Something about* MEI JEN'*s tone stops* RICKI.] Why you never help me. All I ask is you help once in awhile.

RICKI: We can't live here forever.

MEI: We could have had nice Chinese restaurant. All work as team. Wouldn't have to work at mill. But nobody help me. You daddy. Or you. What am I supposed to do, huh, Ricki?

RICKI: Ma, that's your dream—

MEI: You love everybody else but me, don't you?

RICKI: No.

MEI: Everybody always better. Jimmy. You Daddy. You friends. Even that Monica. Everybody come first with you. What about you mother. When I come first Ricki, huh? When?

RICKI: I do love you . . .

MEI: No, you just criticize me. You use those big American words to tell me I'm dumb. I just wanted good thing for you and Jimmy. How you know that Connie wouldn't be good for family—for Jimmy—maybe she help me more than you, Ricki. Help me make Chinese restaurant. Who knows.

[MEI JEN *exits into kitchen.* JIMMY *enters in a different shirt.*]

JIMMY: I'm not marrying Connie. I don't care what she says.

RICKI: Ma's just being crazy. I'm sure Connie doesn't want to be here either.

MEI: [*offstage*] Jimmy, go wake up you daddy. He sleep long enough.

RICKI: Ma, he needs his rest. I'll help you in the kitchen. Don't worry, I'll talk to her . . . [RICKI *exits into kitchen.* RICKI *offstage*] What do you want me to do?

MEI: [*offstage*] Wash up the cabbage and chop it up—

JIMMY: I'm not marrying Connie!

[JIMMY *crosses to front door.* MEI JEN *enters.*]

MEI: [*quietly*] You know why you sister movin' out of the house? She argue too much, that's why. That's what happens when you argue too much. You get kicked out of the house.

JIMMY: I don't think so.

MEI: What you say?

JIMMY: She's leaving because she hates it here.

MEI: She going 'cos I kick her out. That's what happen when you argue. Remember that. Now go wake up you daddy. Go. I don't want him sleepy when Connie get here.

[JIMMY *crosses to bedroom.*]

MEI: Jimmy. You mother only care about you. I take care of you all my life . . .

[JIMMY *exits.*]

MEI: Ricki, you done with the cabbage?
RICKI: [offstage] You don't have to shout. Yes, I'm done with the—
MEI: Open up can of bamboo shoots and mushrooms—
RICKI: [offstage] Yes, Master . . .
JIMMY: [enters] He won't wake up.
MEI: What you mean?
JIMMY: He just keeps sleeping. He won't wake up.
MEI: I go. He hard to hear sometimes.

[She exits. JIMMY sits on the couch. MEI JEN screams.]

MEI: [offstage] Buddy? Buddy? Buddy—AAHHHH!!!
RICKI: [enters.] What the hell was that?
MEI: [enters.] You daddy! You daddy!
RICKI: What!
MEI: You daddy!

[RICKI runs to the bedroom. MEI JEN crumples to floor.]

MEI: Buddy! Buddy! Why you do this to me? Why you do this?!
RICKI: [offstage] Jimmy, call the fire department! Tell them to get somebody
  here!

[JIMMY crosses to phone and dials.]

MEI: Ahh, you daddy dead . . . why . . . why . . . you daddy dead . . . Buddha
  why you do this . . . why . . . [in Chinese] Wei shemma, wei shemma, Gwa
  Nim Posa . . . Aiiyaa . . .
JIMMY: [to the phone, overlapping] Yes, please come here. . . . We need help. . . .
  Donnelly . . . Buddy Donnelly . . . we live off of Highway 99 East . . . yes . . .
MEI: [overlapping] Bu yow sweijow . . . bu yow . . . I not want him to go to sleep
  . . . I not want . . . I not want him to sleep . . .
JIMMY: [hangs up phone.] They're coming now . . .

[RICKI enters]

RICKI: [to MEI JEN] He won't breathe. I can't get him to breathe . . .

[MEI JEN looks up at her.]

RICKI: Ma, I tried. I tried to get him to breathe.
MEI: It's you fault.
RICKI: No.
MEI: You make him go to sleep. [points to RICKI] You fault you daddy dead!

RICKI: No . . . O God . . . no . . . [RICKI *runs from the living room. Lights fade low until* RICKI *is in a single light.*]

SCENE FIVE

[*The funeral.* BUDDY *enters and places a black shawl around* RICKI'S *shoulders. Sound of* BUDDY *humming* "Amazing Grace."]

RICKI: Black has always been her favorite color.
She liked it for its slimming effect. The drama
of the color fit her many moods.
So she always wore black when she could.

[BUDDY *kisses her on the cheek, then exits.*]

RICKI: Always writing. Writing. Always writing.
Her hands were tired from filling out forms. Useless
information. Then so many choices.
The color of the casket. How many flowers.
Leave his glasses on or not. Get
a reverend. How? He was a Baptist
who never went to church. She who'd never even
been to a funeral now took care of everything.
All. Everything in its place.

They said his heart stopped beating. Stopped because
he couldn't breathe anymore. Suffocated.
Now she sat under the canvas tent,
Looking, looking at all the pretty flowers.
She knew the minister was doing the best he could,
not really knowing the family. Not knowing.
Then came her turn—her turn to speak. She glanced
at all the shadows also dressed in black.
She was ashamed she knew so few—the faces.
Friends he had, she never knew. His friends.

Words failed her though she tried to speak.
She wanted to say she knew him, that wasn't true.
After he died, she had to clean out his wallet.
She found two pictures inside—of her and her brother.
One as children—later together in high school.
Wanted to say she loved him, couldn't say it then.

And if he still lived. She couldn't say it yet.
Not to his face. His worried, heavy face.
She just couldn't . . .

["Amazing Grace" ends. RICKI exits to living room as light fades on BUDDY. Cut to the loud sound of vacuuming. It cuts off to reveal RICKI vacuuming in the living room.]

SCENE SIX

[A week after the funeral. Lights on in the house. The house is cleaner. Outside JIMMY is picking up trash. MEI JEN in her robe enters from the bedroom. She sits on the couch and watches TV. RICKI turns off the vacuum and puts it away.]

MEI: House look real good, Ricki. You a good girl.

RICKI: Do you want anything Ma. Maybe some rice soup?

MEI: No, not right now. Maybe glass of ice tea. So hot . . .

RICKI: Sure. Tea coming right up. [RICKI exits into kitchen. MEI JEN changes channels then turns the TV off.] Here you go . . .

MEI: You take care of me good. Everything. The funeral. The house. I very lucky mother.

RICKI: How's your hands today?

MEI: (shakes her right hand) Oh, not bad . . .

RICKI: I just want you to feel better, Ma . . . I don't think you should go back to work.

MEI: I'm fine. Gotta go back soon.

RICKI: Ma, please don't take this the wrong way—Geez, I don't know how to say this—

MEI: What, Ricki.

RICKI: I know this has been hard on you. I know you really loved daddy, but why did you blame me?

MEI: Blame you?

RICKI: When daddy died, you said it was my fault.

MEI: I was upset, Ricki. Don't be sad 'cos you mama was koo-koo in the head. It not you fault. Don't worry.

RICKI: You mean it?

MEI: You a good girl. Look at all you do for me. You stay here, take care of house, just like when you lived here before. It's good, huh, Ricki? [beat] You know I love you. I proud of you. You know that?

RICKI: Oh Ma . . .

MEI: [*she strokes* RICKI's *head*] A good girl. Very, very proud of my good daughter . . .

[RICKI *hugs her mother very tightly. This is the closest they have ever been.*]

RICKI: Mama . . .

MEI: Everything gonna be okay. I save up money for my restaurant and everything gonna be okay. I know you don't want to work at mill for long, but maybe you can work a little while longer, stay here and be family. We need you, Ricki. Jimmy and me need you. You stay a little while longer, okay?

RICKI: [*feeling the tug again*] Ma . . .

MEI: Ricki, don't leave you mother now. Everything will be okay. I promise. Maybe soon I have enough for the restaurant. I know you don't want to work there, but Jimmy could. Maybe Connie might move here . . .

RICKI: Connie?

MEI: I talk to Mrs. Lin. Connie need job.

[RICKI *releases from her hug.*]

RICKI: Ma, what are you talking about?

MEI: I got dream, too, Ricki. Maybe we can both make dream come true. Me—my restaurant. You—go to school. We all work together like family.

RICKI: Do you know how much money it would take—

MEI: Twenty thousand dollars. I got over half already.

RICKI: Half?

MEI: I been saving. You daddy never knew. [*beat*] He would have spent or given it away, Ricki.

MEI: Ma, I asked you for a loan for school—

MEI: And I got you job at mill.

RICKI: Ma, it's important for me to get a degree. I'm afraid if I don't go back, I never—

MEI: Just a little while, Ricki—we need you. Got funeral bills to pay now. You daddy not here to work—he not here . . .

RICKI: Don't get upset, Ma. Please don't get upset.

MEI: Okay. Okay. [*beat*] You want to put on some country music for me? You daddy liked country music.

RICKI: Sure. [RICKI *turns on the record player. An instrumental country song plays.*] Well, I'm going to do the dishes . . .

MEI: Okay, Ricki . . . Ricki?

RICKI: Yes.

MEI: You a good girl.

[RICKI *exits into kitchen. Outside,* MONICA *enters. She is holding a bas-ket of fruit.*]

MONICA: Hi Jimmy . . .
JIMMY: Hi . . .
MONICA: How are you?
JIMMY: Ummm.
MONICA: I was at the funeral.
JIMMY: You were?
MONICA: Yeah. Way in the back. And when you went to the cemetery, I just hung around behind the trees.
JIMMY: Why?
MONICA: I didn't want to . . . get in the way . . . I'm very sorry about your father. I wish I had met him. . . . Jimmy, do you think you want to talk sometime?
JIMMY: I don't feel anything.
MONICA: About your dad?
JIMMY: Nothing.
MONICA: Why?
JIMMY: I don't know.
MONICA: Not even sad?
JIMMY: I don't think so . . . What am I supposed to feel?
MONICA: It's a terrible thing to lose your father, Jimmy.
JIMMY: Alive and kickin'.
MONICA: What's that?
JIMMY: Whenever you asked him how he felt, he would always say he was alive and kickin' . . . I used to tell him to quit smoking around me . . . he'd get mad—"Cain't a man smoke in peace!"
MONICA: You don't have to feel bad about that Jimmy.
JIMMY: I feel . . .
MONICA: You know what Spock said to Kirk when he felt bad?
JIMMY: I can't forget.
MONICA: "Maybe just for a little while . . ."

[JIMMY *reaches for her hand.* MEI JEN *is at the front door.*]

MEI: Jimmy, who you talking to?
MONICA: It's me, Mrs. Donnelly. I brought you some fruit.
MEI: Oh, that very nice . . . very pretty. You don't have to do that, Monica. Why don't you ask her to come in, Jimmy?

[*They both enter the house.*]

JIMMY: You have to take your shoes off.

MONICA: Oh . . .

MEI: Come in, Monica. Jimmy, get Monica something to drink. Make some
ice tea.

JIMMY: Do you like ice tea?

MONICA: Yes, I do. Very much.

MEI: Get Monica ice tea. And turn the music off, okay Jimmy?

MONICA: Thanks, Jimmy.

[JIMMY *turns the music off and exits to kitchen.*]

MEI: So you like my boy?

MONICA: Yes, I do.

MEI: He not feeling too good since his daddy die. He never say much. He move
real slow. Everything real slow with Jimmy now.

MONICA: I'd like to help out if I can . . .

MEI: You mean that?

MONICA: Yes, I do, Mrs. Donnelly.

MEI: Maybe you be good friend for my son.

[RICKI *enters from bedroom at the same time* JIMMY *enters from kitchen.*]

RICKI: Monica. Hi.

MONICA: Hello. [JIMMY *hands* MONICA *the tea.*] Thank you, Jimmy.

MEI: Monica bring us the fruit basket. Real pretty, huh, Ricki?

RICKI: Yeah, they look great, Ma. Thanks, Monica. So, you're all visiting here.
This is great—

[*Phone rings.*]

RICKI: I'll get it. [*picks up phone*] Hello? Yeah, this is her . . .

MONICA: Everybody misses you at work. Did you get all the flowers they sent?

MEI: Very nice . . . so many pretty flowers.

MONICA: Everybody's really sorry at work, Mrs. Donnelly. They hope you feel
better real soon. . . .

MEI: You a good girl, Monica.

MONICA: Well, I should be getting ready for work. Thank you for the tea.
[MONICA *crosses to the front door.* JIMMY *follows.*]

MEI: You come back and visit anytime.

MONICA: Thank you, Mrs. Donnelly. [MONICA *and* JIMMY *exit.*]

RICKI: [*still on phone*] You're kidding me! Omigod! Oh man! I can't believe this. Thank you, Mr. Rasmussen. Thank you. Goodbye . . . [RICKI *hangs up the phone.*]

MEI: What is it?

RICKI: Ma. Everything's going to be okay. God, thank you, Daddy. Thank you! That was daddy's lawyer on the phone. Who knew he had a lawyer?

MEI: Mr. Rasmussen. We made the will long time ago with him.

RICKI: Well, he says that daddy named Jimmy and me as beneficiaries to his life insurance.

MEI: Life insurance?

RICKI: He left us six thousand bucks!

MEI: That's what he wanted. For you kids—

RICKI: Do you know what that means? It means I can go to school in September. It means we could pay the funeral expenses. That'll still leave Jimmy and me two thousand each. [*She crosses to* MEI JEN *and takes her hand.*] Ma, we can both have our dreams. You won't have to spend any money on the funeral, and you can keep your money for the restaurant. And I can finish school. Daddy was thinking of us, Ma. He was thinking of us!

MEI: Yes, that your money. That's what you daddy wanted for you kids. That good.

RICKI: [*hugs* MEI JEN] I have to tell Jimmy. Jimmy!

[RICKI *exits out the front.* MEI JEN *sits quietly. Sound of altar bell ringing three times as lights fade to low.*]

SCENE SEVEN

[*Four days later.* MEI JEN *is talking offstage. She is on the phone in the living room, talking in Chinese.* MONICA *enters and knocks on the front door.*]

MEI: [*offstage*] Kuhee gei wo chen . . . shir . . . howla . . . Connie . . . Wo kuhee kaige fanguar. Hen pyou lyan. Wo zow lowban! Aiiyo . . . [*translation: Could give me money. Yes. That's good, Connie. I could open a restaurant. A beautiful one. I could be boss!*]

MONICA: Hello, Mrs. Donnelly.

MEI: Oh. Come in, Monica . . . [*to phone*] Wo yo zola. Howla, Connie. Howla. Tzai jen. [*translation: I have to go now. That's good, Connie. Goodbye . . . She hangs up phone.*] Monica, nice to see you. Jimmy and Ricki not here.

MONICA: Oh.

MEI: But I think they comin' back. You come and sit for awhile . . . [MONICA *enters the house.*] Here, sit at the table with me and pick the peas . . . you know how? I show you . . .

MONICA: You look better, Mrs. Donnelly.

MEI: Feelin' better. I was just talking with my Taiwanese friend. She comin' down to help me. We gonna maybe open a restaurant together.

MONICA: That's exciting.

MEI: A Chinese restaurant right here in Junction City.

MONICA: Very exciting.

MEI: She gonna come down. Talk about it. You ever work in a restaurant?

MONICA: I tried to work at the Dairy Queen. But I wasn't fast enough. Everybody was yelling all the time. It made me nervous.

MEI: Oh. Not good. I'm gonna get Jimmy to work as busboy. He'd be good at that.

MONICA: I thought Jimmy was going to welding school.

MEI: He don't like welding. Work at restaurant, maybe he start talking to people. He don't like strangers much.

MONICA: It would be good for Jimmy to meet more people.

MEI: You a good friend to him, huh Monica?

MONICA: I like him very much.

MEI: Maybe you want to marry him?

MONICA: [*laughs*] Mrs. Donnelly . . .

MEI: Well, you know how people treat Chinese marrying Americans here. Don't like mixing blood . . . Now if Jimmy marry another Chinese girl, I don't think they treat him so bad.

MONICA: I don't know—

MEI: You a good friend. You want Jimmy be happy, right?

MONICA: Sure.

MEI: His daddy die. Now I need him here. Ricki always want to leave. But Jimmy always stay here and take care of me in old age. That make sense. See? If you want Jimmy be happy, then you be friend, Monica. Good friend.

MONICA: Mrs. Donnelly, I like Jimmy.

MEI: That's right. And you want him be happy.

MONICA: Of course.

MEI: My friend who's coming to see me. Connie. Nice Chinese girl. Maybe she marry Jimmy. What you think.

MONICA: Does Jimmy like her?

MEI: Monica, you good girl. I don't want see you hurt. You want to do good for Jimmy, don't you?

MONICA: I don't understand.

MEI: Monica, you can still be friends. [*beat*] You always welcome my house. [*beat*] Maybe come to opening of my restaurant. That sound good?

MONICA: I think I should go now . . .

MEI: [*takes* MONICA's *hand*] You a good girl. I like you, Monica. I just lookin' out for you . . . and for Jimmy.

[JIMMY *enters outside area.* MONICA *exits the house.*]

MONICA: Jimmy. [*She takes a moment before speaking.*] I have to go now. I want you to be happy. I want to do good for you, Jimmy. And I want you to be happy. Goodbye.

JIMMY: Monica . . .

MONICA: We can always be friends. I will always like you, Jimmy. [MONICA *runs off.* JIMMY *is stunned.*]

MEI: [*calling*] Jimmy, is that you? Come inside and help me pick the peas . . .

[JIMMY *enters the house and sits by* MEI JEN.]

MEI: Monica just here. She a nice girl. Said she would talk to you later. Where you been? Jimmy, what's the matter? Talk to you mother.

JIMMY: What about.

MEI: I got good news for you. Connie comin' to help me with the restaurant. We need to do somethin' now you daddy gone. Maybe in six months, we can be in business. You be done with the cannery then. Don't need to work with stinky vegetables anymore.

[RICKI *enters the outside area. She walks slowly toward the door and listens awhile.*]

MEI: We can have our own business. How's that? I gotta still work day shift. That's okay 'cos dinnertime when everybody come anyway. Connie can work as waitress, keep books. I think it gonna be good, Jimmy—gonna be good. You know you mother love you, Jimmy. We only got each other now, don't we? I take care of you. Always take care of you.

[RICKI *enters and lets the screen door slam behind her. There is a low burning intensity to her.*]

RICKI: Sorry.

MEI: Oh good you home. ⌐ ⌐nna have snow peas for supper. You favorite.

RICKI: What's this about Connie.

MEI: I also thawing out some shrimp. You like shrimp.

RICKI: What about Connie?

MEI: She drivin' down from Camas, Washington, in a couple of days.

RICKI: What for.

MEI: Visit. Never got to visit before. 'Cos . . . [*changes subject*] You want to help pick the peas?

RICKI: Sure. I'll help. [RICKI *stands next to* MEI JEN.]

MEI: Maybe you better go sit down. You look tired.

RICKI: So what's this about Connie being a waitress? You starting your restaurant?

MEI: Maybe later on. Not right away. After you go back to school.

RICKI: When? In September?

MEI: Maybe . .

RICKI: Or later? After September?

MEI: I don't know. Maybe. Whenever you go back to school—

RICKI: Well that won't be in September. Know why? Of course you know why. Jimmy knows why. Only I don't. You want to tell me why I can't go back to school?

MEI: I thought you want to go back—

RICKI: Why do you tell me one thing, and then do the opposite? Why do you tell me you love me, when you don't? I really thought you would change. But you don't care about me or Jimmy or that daddy's dead—you just care about one thing—tell her, Jimmy. Tell her what she cares about—

MEI: What she talkin' about—

RICKI: Tell her, Jimmy!

JIMMY: NO!

RICKI: Tell her!!!

JIMMY: NO!!! Leave me alone.

MEI: Now you upset you brother.

RICKI: Didn't we at least deserve to be told?

MEI: This no way to treat you mother, Ricki.

RICKI: I know you're scared. But couldn't you have at least told us! Just one sentence. One single sentence! *Ricki, I took your daddy's insurance money!* Do you know what it feels like to be sitting at that lawyer's office and have him explain how your own mother took your inheritance? To have this stranger looking at us, saying how sorry he is, but he's going ahead with your request to be the only beneficiary to daddy's insurance. Our names are on the policy, but your name is in the will. So you're entitled to whatever he left.

MEI: You have no right to accuse me.

RICKI: Daddy wanted that money for Jimmy and me. He believed in me. That was my money, Mother. My money to be somebody. And you took it.

MEI: You still have job.

RICKI: We were going to pay for the funeral. We weren't going to take all of it.

MEI: It's my money. You children get everything when I'm gone. I a widow now. I need the money—

RICKI: You said it was ours. You said that's what daddy wanted for us.

MEI: You daddy take it from my bank account to get the insurance.

RICKI: You lied to us.

MEI: I take care of you all you life. I you mother.

RICKI: And it doesn't matter what daddy wanted—

MEI: You love you daddy so much, why you let him die?

[silence]

RICKI: You're not going to kill me, like you killed him. That's why he smoked so much. That's why he couldn't breathe. You're the one who killed him! YOU KEEP PEOPLE FROM BREATHING! [RICKI exits to bedroom.]

MEI: How dare you! You have no right!

JIMMY: Will you guys please cut it out . . . I'm tired of all this yelling . . .

MEI: Ungrateful. Selfish.

JIMMY: It hurts my ears!

MEI: Other mothers have good daughters, good Chinese daughters who take care of them. Not me!

RICKI: [enters with suitcase] Other mothers love their children.

JIMMY: Stop it!

MEI: Who the one make sure we have food? I take care of you. No one ever take care of me. It was my money!

JIMMY: I just want to be left alone. Why can't anyone leave me alone!

[JIMMY starts to exit outside. MEI JEN starts to faint. She grabs hold of him.]

MEI: No, don't leave me, Jimmy. Everybody leave me, I die!

RICKI: Jimmy. If you stay here. You won't ever have a life.

JIMMY: You know I can't go anywhere.

RICKI: She'll make you work in that restaurant. You'll be her servant forever. You'll never be able to leave.

MEI: All you know is what Ricki wants. Get out of my house. Get out!

JIMMY: I want to be left alone!

MEI: Jimmy, don't leave you mother. No husband. No daughter. Nothing. Don't leave me!

RICKI: Jimmy, don't you see what she's doing?

JIMMY: You're upsetting her. Why can't you both stop?! Why do you keep doing this?

MEI: [*to* RICKI] Get out. Never come back to my house again!

JIMMY: Both of you stop!

RICKI: Jimmy, if you don't come with me now—

MEI: [*overlapping*] He not! He not!

JIMMY: I can't take any more of this!

RICKI: Jimmy. I don't know if I can ever come back for you—

JIMMY: Don't ask me—

MEI: No listen to her! She just want to turn you against me. She no good. No good!

RICKI: Jimmy! Please!

JIMMY: [*crosses away from them*] Why won't it stop? Won't it ever stop?!

MEI: You try to poison Jimmy against me! Get out of here!

JIMMY: I don't want to hear it—

RICKI: I hear! I hear that voice screaming at me, screeching at me! Never out of my head—

MEI: No good! No good! You not my daughter!

RICKI: Jimmy! I'm asking you—

JIMMY: Don't do this to me—

RICKI: She kills everyone!!!

MEI: Don't ever come back! Don't ever—

[JIMMY *picks up the stained glass and throws it down.* RICKI *and* MEI JEN *stare at him.*]

JIMMY: Done! Are you happy! I'm DONE!!!

[*Lights dim as* JIMMY *crumples to the floor.*]

RICKI'S FINAL POEM

[*Music transition.* RICKI *reaches slowly to* JIMMY *and helps him to his feet.* MEI JEN *slowly moves away till she is in shadow.*]

RICKI: To crack, to break, to split or divide.
  To rip open, to sever,
  a very crisp sound—like ripping silk . . .

I was done. Finished. Gone.

I—left you.

Left you alone with the heaviness I once felt.
My handsome brother.
Till each year you drift further and farther
Till the boy I once played with in the snow
no longer exists.
And the glass no longer shines
except here.
Just when I think I've left you behind,
you are still here.

I hold the light
to find my way.

I wait
to come out—to see—to breathe.
For you and still for me.
I hold the light
and I wait.

Come, please, come with me . . .

Into the light.

[*Lights fade.*]

END OF PLAY

Junk Bonds

a play in two acts

by

LUCY WANG

Originally produced by HOME for Contemporary Theatre and Art, Randy Rollison, Artistic Director.

Original Resident Theatre production by Capital Repertory Company, Albany, NY, Margaret Mancinelli-Cahill, Artistic Director; Mark Dalton, General Manager.

Junk Bonds won the Katherine and Lee Chilcote Foundation Award for Best New Play in the Cleveland Public Theatre New Play Festival, 1995.

Junk Bonds won an award from the Kennedy Center Fund for New American Plays, a project of the John F. Kennedy Center for the Performing Arts with support from American Express Company in cooperation with the President's Committee on the Arts and the Humanities.

CAST OF CHARACTERS

DIANA: Chinese American. Mid-to-late 20s. Nick-
         named D.K. for "Don't Know." Sharp, ambi-
         tious, idealistic. New bond trader.

CONNOR: Early 30s. Nicknamed JAMMER. Totally win-

ning. Loves pranks, funniest trader on the
desk, most lovable, snappy dresser.

BILL: Late 20s to early 30s. Nicknamed the KING.
Head trader, boyish but likable, former body-
building champion. Cheap functional dresser,
wears tube socks with suits. Not an MBA or
Ivy Leaguer. Professes to champion common
man.

JEFFERSON: Early 40s. Nicknamed CUFFLINKS. Most corporate of the traders, obsessed with preserv-
ing his youth while privately resenting Wall
Street's preoccupation with youth. Can be
African American.

KENT: Early-to-mid 40s. Ex-Marine, charismatic.

SQUAWK BOX: SQUAWK BOX looks like a normal phone with
speakers except that it allows the sales force
across the country and overseas to communicate to a trader instantaneously. Voice is am-
plified, sounds like a loud speaker or public
announcement system. SQUAWK BOX is a
collection of different voices, male and female, not one person.

HIRO WATANABE: HIRO is pronounced Hero. Early 30s, from
Japan. Stylish, but understated.

SCENES: New York, New York, decade of disclosure. Sets needn't be elaborate
or costly.

*The HOME for Contemporary Theatre production was performed in the round,
using the stage as a boxing ring, microphone as squawk box, and red plexiglass
floor to signify blood. The Cleveland Public Theatre production was also performed in the round, but designed as a football stadium. At Capital Rep, the play
was performed 3/4 and the set was very stylistic and angular, abstracting elements of a trading floor. In all productions, each character had 2 phones with 25
ft cords and rolling chairs.*

    *The squawk box is like a public announcement system. They look like regular
phones and have speakers for amplification. They are essential in disseminating
information as quickly and efficiently as possible. For example, if a salesperson
in London wants a simple bid, she can use the squawk box to call a trader. It's*

*instantaneous, and once the trader gives a bid, every Tapir employee in the world
knows where that bond is trading at the moment—if the squawk box speaker is
turned on (comes with volume dial).*

Trading screens look like little TVs.

ACT I:	TRUTH
Scene One	An office, November.
Scene Two	Trading floor, January.
Scene Three	Trading floor, February.
Scene Four	Trading floor, March.
Scene Five	Trading floor, April.
Scene Six	Ballroom, following week in April.
ACT II:	DARE
Scene One	Trading floor, September.
Scene Two	Trading floor, October.
Scene Three	Trading floor, the next Friday.
Scene Four	Trading floor, following February.
Scene Five	Trading floor, April.
Scene Six	Trading floor, May.

*Monologues originally created for HOME production. They can be said simul-
taneously or improvised upon to serve as filler when trading.*

========

KENT MONOLOGUE

Kent here. I'm fine. Tapir's making a lot of money today. A fuck of a lot of
money. Hear the roar of the trading floor? The time to invest is now. Year
end, we're reporting record earnings. That's right, we're taking over. Number
one. When the news hits the Street, you'll kick yourself for missing the gravy
train. That's what happens when you hire the best. Sign of a truly gifted
managing director is one who's not afraid of hiring someone smarter than
himself. I'm telling you, bunch of anal-retentive Einsteins. All that raw energy and hunger. They glow in the dark. Makes me proud. As I was saying,
calculate the compound interest. Daily. Low risk, high reward. You won't
find a sweeter deal. Virtually guaranteed. S-E-C approved. I'd be happy to
discuss details with you. I love meeting people, all kinds. Ever been to Le
Cirque? Or if you prefer, spend the weekend with my family at Martha's

Vineyard. Beautiful country; it's God's country. Nine guest rooms. Use the Lear jet. No pressure. Think it over, let me know. [*click*] Where's Chrysler at today? Boeing? Pfizer? OK, keep me posted. [*click*] Bill, your position? Desk long or short? I expect major-league profits. Who you betting on in the Superbowl? Think so? One thousand dollars says you're wrong. Step up to the plate, it's for charity. Keep producing, gotta hop. [*click*] Jefferson, you in or out in the football pool? I can't stress enough the importance of giving to the less fortunate. Only time of the year I ask this of my boys. Thanks. [*click*] Sunny skies, Ralph. We got a few bites. Big bites. Don't worry, I got it covered, no turbulence in sight. Go ahead, sink a couple more holes-in-one at Maidstone. I mean if you can't love life, what's the point of being chairman? Oh yeah, your wife called here, asking questions. That's what I told her. Cannot be disturbed, and you'll call her back first chance. Enjoy. [*click*] Jammer, you in the football charity pool? Jamming. Great. Think about American buffaloes. [*click*] I'd like to make reservations for two at 7:30. My usual out-of-the way table. Far away from the crowds. [*click*] So Boeing up or down? Ok, great. [*click, as if to secretary*] Tell my boys to make some fucking money and report their position. Now. A man's got a right to know if his future is long or short.

BILL MONOLOGUE

Who needs the King? Ginnie Mae nines are perfect for the Teachers Retirement Fund. I'll let five go at a bargain. Done. [*click*] This is the King. Hey, Don, how's it hanging? Ready to pump it up? King of Fixed Income is pure fucking muscle. Almost. Less than 6 percent body fat. Who do you think is fucking bigger in real life? Schwarzenegger or Van Damme? Stallone or Seagal. Oops, gotta hop. [*click*] Tell your account the option adjusted spread is incredible; you can't lose. Thumbs up. [*click*] Scotty, where is rong bond? I'll buy two. Done. [*click*] So, Jammer, you pork her yet? Let's go skiing in Lake Tahoe this winter, just you and me and ski bunnies. Is it really necessary to sleep in luxury? OK, I'll cough up the extra bucks. Get back to me. [*click*] Kent, when you going to invite me to God's country? I promise I'll behave. Actually I wasn't going to join the football pool this year, $1000 is steep. I know it's for charity, but isn't that what social workers do? Alright, Kent, I'll play. Yes, Kent, we're making fuckwads of money. [*click*] Who needs the King? Trade of the day goes like this. You sell 50 Fannie tens and buy 50 Ginnie tens. Pick up 40 basis points in yield for a few extra bucks. Cheap swap. That's right, tell Cufflinks it was your account's idea. [*click*] Talk to me about that trade. How many sellers? Buyers? Oh, I want two tix to the Rangers game tomorrow night. As close to that supermodel chick as possible. I bet a buck on the Rangers. Just a buck. [click] Who needs the King? For GM Pension Fund, I'll pay 97 and a half. Done, I buy 25 from GM. [click] This is the King. Oh, it's you. Not my fault if an account wants to swap out of Fannies, Cufflinks. Didn't say you couldn't make money; of course you can. Gotta hop. [click] Talk to me about that trade. Buyer want more? How many more? OK, I'll sell him seven, tick higher. Done. [click] Scotty, throw me the football. I'm the fucking captain. [click] Forgot to tell you. Want two tix to "Les Miz" anytime next week. For my parents; I want front seats. [singing] "I'm master of the house." Gotta hop [click] What are the Feds doing now? What does this mean for me, the King of Fixed Income?

BILL MONOLOGUE, MARKET UP

This is the King here. How many buyers? One buyer for 50 million? You shitting me? OK, I'm next. Gotta jump. [Click] Scotty, where are T bills? Seven years? Long bonds? I'll buy 25 seven-years and 25 long bonds. Done. [click] OK, Fed watcher, tell me what's happening. Fed hiking interest rates? Prime rate? Thanks for the scoop, dirtbag. [click] Hey Don, need a favor. Ask your accounts if they know who's hoarding Ginnie Mae elevens. Maybe your account's selling behind our backs. Looks like someone's trying to squeeze the Street. Be fucking discreet. [click] You got the King. Yeah I'll buy 10 million Ginnie nines at 95–22. Done. [click] Katie, tell Teachers to sell me some fucking bonds. I'm a major buyer here. Major buyer. Double commission. [click] Not a good seller. Market's soaring, you fuckwad. OK, I offer you two at 98. Told you I'm not a seller. OK, we're done. Gotta hop. [click] Unemployment will be highest ever? I dunno, but thanks anyways. Yeah, yeah, I'll warn the desk. [click] King. Can't talk, Steve, market's hopping like catfish. Later. [click] Where the fuck are long bonds, Scotty. Yes, I sell you 25! Done. [click] King! Guess what—just made ten grand turning around long bonds. I am whippersnapping machine. Gotta hop. [click] Where's stocks? Buy me thousand shares of Boeing. Put it in my account. [click] I'll lift that cheap offer for Ginnie eights. Yeah, I'll buy more; shoot 'em in. How many sellers? Two? Only two brain donors today. OK, total of six, we're done. Gotta hop. [click] Talk to me about that trade. Very strong bid. Buyer wants more? Desperate to cover, huh? We talking CMO collateral? Sure I'll be happy to castrate. Sell you ten at the high and mighty price of one-oh-one! Yeah, buy be a cocktail at High Steaks. [click] Who needs the King?

BILL MONOLOGUE, MARKET DOWN

Who needs the King? Quick, I'm very busy. Not a buyer. Give you a shitty bid of 92 even for a pair of those Ginnie Mae seven and halves. We're done? Sorry fucking account. Gotta hop. [*click*] I'll sell ten of those. Yeah, done. How many buyers? Three? Must be covering. [*click*] Scotty, where are 7-years? I sell you 25. Done. [*click*] Don, I'm a very good seller. Ask your accounts what they're seeing where. Thanks I owe you. [*click*] Talk to me about that trade. Who's the asshole flooding the Street with Ginnie nines? Shit take his license away, he's depressing the market. Gotta hop. [*click*] You got the King. I'll sell five Ginnie tens. Bargain-basement prices. Triple commish. [*click*] King. Can't jabber, dad, later. [*click*] Talk to me, how many sellers? Four, with two more behind? Shit, bunch of field mice. [*click*] King. Not a good buyer. I bid a lousy 91 for those bonds. I'm the cover? Thanks, Katie. [*click*] Yeah, I'll sell 20. Who's the brain donor today? Done. Gotta hop. [*click*] What's happening? Treasury auction, only five bidders? How fucking weak. [*click*] Scotty bid me 30 long bonds? I sell you 30. Done. [*click*] King. Yeah, so I think your account should buy Ginnie Mae eights and sell Fannie nines. Pick up 25 basis points in yield like that. An incredible swap. I'll sell you the eights real cheap. Ask Cufflinks for his bid and get back to me. Remember, your account can't go wrong. Cannot. [*click*] Now who needs the King? Oh, it's you Kent, yes I'm making money. Staying real short. I'll ask. Yeah, the desk's short. [*click*] I'm a strong seller. Sell you five. How many buyers? Just one. Cool. Gotta hop. [*click*] I'll lift that offer for Ginnie nine and halves. I'll buy eight at that unbelievable low price. Only four? OK we're done. Leave my bid in for five, two ticks lower though. [*click*] King here. Great. We'll do the swap. I sell you Ginnie eights at 92. Double commission; just buy me a steak later. [*click*] Yo, Don, what paper they seeing? That's what they've heard, huh? From who?

JEFFERSON MONOLOGUE

Jefferson the Third. I sell you ten Freddies eights at 92–8. Done. [*click*] Talk to me about that trade. Seller has more? I don't want any, thanks. [*click*] Hi, sweetie, can't talk now. OK, I'll ask. [*click*] No, I don't think swapping 50 Fannies for 50 Ginnies is a smart trade. Account pays up for diddly squat. I recommend swapping coupons. Depends if your account thinks interest rates going up or going down. Ask 'em what they think, call me back. [*click*] OK, Bill, what nonsense have you been feeding the salesfarce? I'll make money either way so level with me. [*click*] Scotty where are ten-year Treasuries? I buy five. Done. [*click*] So, Jammer, how's your love life? Pork her yet? See how happy I am? You should get married. Yeah, I think ostrich meat has potential. Gotta hop. [*click*] Talk to me about that trade. How many buyers? Just one. Wow. Must be for a CMO. Keep me posted. OK, meet you for drinks Thursday. [*click*] Kent, I always like the wrong teams, week after week. But since I know how much charity means to you, count on my $1000 contribution. [*click*] Yeah I'll bid in the Fannie Mae auction today. Shoot. 92, 93–21, 95–01, and 96–30. That's all. Gotta hop. [*click*] What's happening with those Freddies? No, can't sell him any. Someone's hoarding. His balls are going to be squeezed dry at the end of the month. By the way, my wife wants tix to David Bowie concert. Done? Thanks a lot. She worships him so much it's embarrassing. Gotta hop. [*click*] Scotty, over here, I can still throw a mean pass. [*click*] Tapir. For your account I buy 15 at 96. Done. [*click*] Hey Alex, D.K.'s bringing me some more ginseng and other Chinese goodies. I'll sell you some. We'll beat these crybabies yet. The King is dead. [*click*] Hey who's dumping those precious Fannies? Four sellers, two buyers. Is that all? [*click*] Dirtbag, get me a car tonight. Send us some California rolls and those yellow pickles. Thanks. [*click*] Jefferson the Third. Didn't win any bonds today. Oh well. Always tomorrow. Gotta hop.

CONNOR MONOLOGUE

Jammer. Gnome eights, I sell you 10 at 93 double commission. Done. [*click*] Scotty, where are Treasuries; five years? OK, I buy seven. Done. [*click*] Talk to me about that trade. How many buyers? Sellers? Just one. Is that Semen Brothers? Gotta jam. [*click*] Love life's fine. Why you ask, Cufflinks? I'll get to her, don't worry. Stop living vicariously through me, Cufflinks. Sure you're happy. Not healthy to covet being somebody else. A sin. What about my ostrich idea? [*click*] Kent, no problem. One thousand dollars it is. You know I'm going to win. I'm lucky that way. Pick a charity? Chosen. Given any thought to my ostrich farm? You really think I can make more money off of buffalo? Jammer's jamming big time. [*click*] Scotty, throw me the football. High pass. [*click*] Lake Tahoe? Sounds fucking fun. Not sure I can take the time off. Sure you can afford it, Scrooge? D.K. will check air fares and ski lodges. I love my fucking trainee. Obedient and cheerful. Gotta hop. [*click*] Jammer. Swap of the day, dwarf nines for my Midget tens. Option adjusted spread is fucking panoramic. At my prices you pick up 52 basis points in yield—52 pick up. That reminds me, gotta hop. [*click*] Atlantic City this weekend. We'll count cards. Rake profits. Monopoly. We'll take my Vette. [*click*] Talk to me about that trade. Seller has a lot more to go. How much more? Put me behind him. I'm a seller. [*click*] Gotta introduce you to my new trainee, D.K. She remembers everything. Great mammories. Regular yellow pages. Gotta hop. [*click*] I'm a buyer of those gnome seven and halves. Shoot 'em in. That all? I buy four at 91–2. Brain donor. [*click*] High Steaks tonight. Surf and turf. Done. [*click*] I'd like to make reservations for six humans at 7. Jammer. [*click*] Rainʋʋw Room. Chicks melt all over you like ice cream. Win win. [*click*] Talk to me about that 50 million going down. Two sellers, six buyers all lined up. What do they know that I don't? Truth or Dare, pal.

DIANA MONOLOGUE

D.K., Jammer's partner. Yeah we should meet. Tonight, tomorrow, whenever's convenient. Gotta hop. [*click*] People's Savings ought to buy these gnome eights. A steal at 93. Double commission for you. Rich. Strong sellers. Thanks. Tell Jammer I helped. [*click*] Talk to me about that trade. Four buyers. Buyers wanted more, both of them? [*click*] Scotty, where are 7-year Treasuries? We'll sell you five. Done. [*click*] D.K. here. Love life? Do I strike you as feminine? Ex-boyfriend said I was a man trapped in a woman's body. So I dumped him like a man. Fuck him. Gotta hop, Jammer's calling. [*click*] I'm no good at ballroom dancing. I've nothing to wear to the Rainbow Room. OK, I'll check. [*click*] Hi, need to check air fares to Lake Tahoe from New York? For two big boys. Market's moving, gotta hop. [*click*] Talk to us about that trade. We'll hit that bid for dwarves at 96–12. Sell you six. Buyer wants two more? Too bad. We're done. [*click*] Jefferson, what's the fucking rush? You're not going to die tomorrow are you? How many do you take a day? OK, I'll order more. [*click*] Mom, will you send me more of those Chinese herbs? The ones for longevity and youth. Not for me. For this weird dude on the desk. Send it quick. He thinks his days are numbered. Thanks. Can't talk now. Gotta hop. [*click*] D.K. here. I sell you 12 Midget tens at 98 and a half. You gouged 'em, what guts. Triple commission. [*click*] Andy, I'd like two tix to see "Mostly Mozart." Trying to impress this French guy. He's an artiste, paints triangles. Nothing but triangles. I don't get it, maybe Mozart can help. Thanks. Gotta hop. [*click*] I'd like to order. Tapir. Five rare bacon cheeseburgers and ten diet cokes. I know it's early but we're all hung over. [*click*] Talk to me about the 50 million. Two sellers? Maybe three? Buyers? Going up or down? What do you mean you don't know? Get me your boss. [*click*] We're buyers, folks.

HIRO MONOLOGUE

Scotty, where is long bond? I buy eight. Done, Hiro. [*click*] Samurai. Tell your account gnome nines offer excellent return. Very cheap. OK, I sell you five at 96. Double commission. Gotta hop. [*click*] Hiro Watanabe. Konnichiwa. Paperwork too slow. No good. I move from Tokyo. Deserve better. You promised. Yes I see, but I cannot wait much longer. [*click*] Andy, talk to me about that trade. How many sellers? Only one; buyer wants more? Then I'm next. I'm a strong seller too. OK, I sell you ten Midgets. [*click*] Where is Nikkei today? Dollar yen? Deutsche marks? Thank you. Gotta hop. [*click*] Samurai. Hiro. Most profitable for your account to buy dwarf tens and sell Midget tens. Pick up 37 basis points in yield. Little risk. Get back to me. [*click*] Talk to me about that trade. Fifty million going down? One buyer, four sellers. Buyer want more? Yes, I see. No, I'm not a seller. Market moving up. Maybe later. [*click*] Hiro. OK, I meet you and your account to explain my total return analysis. I prefer kobe steaks and ama-ebi. Very good for you. Ask Jefferson, he's a big health nut. Makes me laugh. Gotta hop. [*click*] Samurai. Hiro. We swap 20 dwarf tens for 20 Midget tens. Double commission. Your pleasure. [*click*] Scotty where are Treasuries? Seven years? I sell you five. Done. [*click*] Andy get me two tickets to Rangers game. Front seats. Call me a car, too. Thank you. [*click*] Hiro. What Japanese stocks do I recommend your account buy? Depends on goals of portfolio. This portfolio manager a field mouse or a tapir? Yes, I see. I suggest we discuss over three-pound lobster. Sake fine. But I also like 25-year-old scotch. [*click*] Hiro. I buy three non-gnome seven and halves at 91–02. [*click*] Samurai. Ten mobile home eleven and a quarters, I bid one-oh-two. Done, I own all ten. [*click*] Hiro Watanabe. Hi, how are you? I'm very busy. America is a very busy country. Too busy. People here don't understand me. Who I am. Who I am not.

ACT I

SCENE ONE

SETTING: A November morning. Takes place in an office, a boardroom, or the trading floor.

AT RISE: Lights fade up, landing us in the middle of a job interview between KENT and DIANA.

KENT: So you want to be a bond trader—
DIANA: More than anything—
KENT: Why?
DIANA: I think it's the only job left where you really win when you're right. Where you get to run your own business with the capital and power of a big, safe, muscular institution.

KENT: What about the money? You must be in it for the precious gold metals. Otherwise, the occupation ain't worth the price—

DIANA: Sure, money's important to live, but I can't trade just for the money.

KENT: Why not? Profit turns you off, makes you feel downright dirty and cheap?

DIANA: No, of course not. Not yet.

KENT: You're one of them closet liberals who wants to tax the light out of day.

DIANA: No. Alright if I must confess, I love money as much as you do.

KENT: No kidding. How much money do you want to make?

DIANA: You mean starting out?

KENT: Whenever.

DIANA: I'm flexible, very flexible.

KENT: Give me a total. What do you hope to earn over your entire lifetime?

DIANA: A lot.

KENT: What's a lot? Give me a round number. A whole round number.

DIANA: One number?

KENT: Be honest. Honesty is an open-door policy.

DIANA: I don't know, say 450 million?

KENT: Is that before or after taxes? With or without early retirement? I bet you expect to make partner too.

DIANA: Naturally.

KENT: You're awfully optimistic, aren't you? I should warn you very, very few people go on to make partner. You might never make it.

DIANA: I understand the odds are against me. But if what you're really saying is it's outright impossible for women to ever become partners, then—

KENT: Hell, no. I was only stressing Tapir's management hierarchy is extremely flat.

DIANA: Well just because I might not hit the bull's-eye doesn't mean I won't take dead aim. I mean, as long as I know it's possible, I can hope, right?

KENT: Seems fair enough. Sure, hoard as much hope as you need.

DIANA: We can never get enough hope.

KENT: It's tax free. Diana, I'm prepared to offer you a starting salary of sixty thousand with a minimum five thousand dollar bonus.

DIANA: I'm hired just like that? Don't you want to check my references? Review my transcript?

KENT: I do have one overriding concern that could be a major deal breaker—

DIANA: I can pass any drug test fair and square—

KENT: Would you say you have a generous sense of humor? A high tolerance for diversity of wit?

DIANA: Believe me, I can laugh at anything—

KENT: Super, just between you and me, I'm afraid the trading floor is too high pressure for the typical woman.

DIANA: Kent, that's so sexist—

KENT: Exactly. I am so relieved you feel the same way I do because as the first female bond trader on our floor, you have to be the perfect example.

DIANA: I'm the first? I feel honored—

KENT: You can't flood my office with tears every time you hear a nasty four-letter word. Or every time one of my guys flirts with you, or commits a faux pas. Pioneers persevere. Think of the Marines.

DIANA: [*Gives Marine salute, Latin for Always Faithful*] "Semper Fi."

KENT: It's for your own good. My men wouldn't respect you. Still capable?

DIANA: I've climbed this far—

KENT: Congratulations, when can you start?

DIANA: May I give you my answer in a couple of weeks?

KENT: Two weeks! Jesus, a few minutes ago, you told me you wanted to be a bond trader. More than anything else in the world.

DIANA: I do—

KENT: [*snaps his fingers with rhythm*] Well, then, hop. Successful bond traders make multimillion-dollar decisions in a snap. Hit, lift, and hop in seconds.

DIANA: I know, but what about my other job offers?

KENT: If we're not your first choice, then you don't deserve my hot bid. But if you need more silver, tell you what, I'll throw in an extra five thousand dollar signing bonus and cover all your moving expenses if you say yes today.

DIANA: Really.

KENT: Fill or kill. Can you handle the pressure?

DIANA: Give me two days—

KENT: Perhaps I've miscalculated, overestimated—

DIANA: Tomorrow?

KENT: I'm taking a tremendous risk hiring you, if you don't pay off—

DIANA: I will, Kent. But considering I'm going to be the one and only female trader, will you guarantee me a trading position in writing?

KENT: Absolutely not a problem.

DIANA: Raise my starting salary to 70 grand and I'll start work a week after graduation.

KENT: It's a done deal. Welcome aboard, Diana. I promise you won't be sorry.

DIANA: Thank you.

[*Blackout*]

END OF SCENE ONE

SCENE TWO

SETTING: Early morning, January. A large yet claustrophobic trading floor at Tapir, Inc. Traders boxed in by high tech: trading screens, two phones apiece, squawk boxes, computers. Taped somewhere prominently is a list divided into two columns with names under the headings "Hung like a Field Mouse" and "Hung like a Tapir." Names on the list should be a mix of topical, well-known national and local newsmakers. JEFFERSON has many bottles of pills and juices on his desk.

AT RISE: Lights fade up to traders talking all at once, using monologues to improvise, glued to fluorescent flickering screens, on the phones and actively trading.

CONNOR: [*into his phone to a broker*] Don't needledick me! Fucking brain donor, I'm putting you in the goddamn box! No more trades until I fucking say so! [*slams phone*]
BILL: [*cupping his phone*] Jammer, that was your sixth phone this week. The King is gonna have to bill you for that one. Company orders.
CONNOR: Fuck you, numb nuts. Take your goddamn Benjy.

[CONNOR *pulls out a $100 bill, throws it over to* BILL; BILL *walks over to* CONNOR]

BILL: Get it? I'm going to *bill* you.
CONNOR: What do you want? You got your title. Your money.
JEFFERSON: Your youth, your future.
BILL: Yeah I know, but I promised Kent the desk would act more corporate.
CONNOR: Go play ball in heavy traffic. Go chase some parked cars.
BILL: That's it. Come on, Cufflinks, it's time to tune the radio.
JEFFERSON: Bill, I'm making a market here. And my name is Jefferson the Third.
BILL: Yo, hark, I said I hate this rap muzak. Much too provocative.
JEFFERSON: And Kent thought you were going to be a superior manager.

[JEFFERSON *hangs up reluctantly and pins* CONNOR's *arm behind his back.* BILL *tweaks and turns* CONNOR's *nipple like a radio knob.* CONNOR *struggles. Action of tuning the radio throughout the play is very fast*]

BILL: Too much static on this station. Does anyone hear any music?
CONNOR: Where's the assistant trader you promised me?

BILL: Cufflinks, did you hear anything? Quick, find me a golden oldie.

JEFFERSON: It's Jefferson the Third. And no I can't seem to hear a thing. Modulate, Jammer, please, I gotta hop.

BILL: Two things I can't stand—muzak and talk radio.

CONNOR: Yes wise master, king of all bonds junky and cheesy, you're hung like a tapir, and I, your feudal serf, am hung like a field mouse.

BILL: Finally, a good tune loud and clear.

[BILL *and* JEFFERSON *release* CONNOR]

JEFFERSON: No offense intended. OK, Jammer? Just following our fearless leader. You know how it is. You got to talk the talk, walk the walk. It's double or nothing. [*picks up phone and resumes trading*]

BILL: Hey Jammer, I betcha four dollars Rocky Balboa's a bigger tapir than James Zero Coupon Bond.

CONNOR: Dickless wonders. Field mice. [*reacting to screen or market news*] Yikes! Ream me.

JEFFERSON: What's down? You can tell me.

CONNOR: [*distrustful of* JEFFERSON] My hair's falling out over this shit. What elixir ya got for old-fashioned hair, Cufflinks?

JEFFERSON: [*hands* CONNOR *a bottle*] Try Horsetail, it's rich in silica. Strengthens fingernails, hair, and fractured bones. Also good for the eyes, ear, nose, throat, and— [*points to* CONNOR's *crotch*] glandular disorders.

CONNOR: Pegasus is too succulent for me, pal. But nothing's too rich for boy wonder, master of *succulent*. [*tosses it to* BILL]

BILL: Cufflinks, why do you bother trying to outlive the King? [BILL *tosses pills to* JEFFERSON]

JEFFERSON: God helps those who help themselves. And my name's Jefferson the Third.

[DIANA *enters*]

DIANA: Hi, you guys, I'm Diana. Your new mortgage bond trader. Where should I sit? What do I trade?

CONNOR: Somebody come claim your exotic stripper.

DIANA: Oh no, I'm not *that* much fun.

CONNOR: Too bad, I am.

JEFFERSON: If you're healthy, you're fun.

CONNOR: [*offers his back for massage*] Ah, Lotus Blossom, give me the mysteries of the Far East.

DIANA: I'm here to trade bonds. Kent hired me.

CONNOR: Kent who?

DIANA: The managing director. Your boss?

JEFFERSON: No way. Kent knows women are distractions.

BILL: Major distractions.

CONNOR: Kent would have consulted Bill first.

JEFFERSON: Then Bill would've asked for our permission. Right, Bill?

BILL: [*dodges into his phone*] Someone need the King?

JEFFERSON: Sales desk is over there. Women make good salesmen on account of their fair gender and miniskirts.

CONNOR: Such pleasant personalities. Friendly smiles. Hot legs. What do you think, Bill?

BILL: Pretty for an Oriental.

DIANA: I'm Asian American.

BILL: Now don't get delirious; every woman at Tapir is a looker.

CONNOR: Good looks makes us rich crooks.

JEFFERSON: We are the *fixed* income department.

DIANA: [*timidly*] I can be mean if I really have to.

BILL: Miss, do you know you're talking to a fearsome bodybuilder?

JEFFERSON: Show her your muscles, Bill. [BILL *flexes*, DIANA *laughs*, CONNOR *sees trade flashing*]

CONNOR: [*dives into the phone to a broker*] Talk to me about that trade. Is that Semen Brothers buying all the dwarf eights? What d'ya mean it's confidential? You want out of the penalty box or what? [*slams the phone*]

BILL: Miss, do you want to become him? A human earthquake?

DIANA: If that's what it takes.

BILL: Are you one of those women who hates their father? Who constantly needs to prove something to men to overcompensate for this feeling that no matter what you do, you're just not good enough?

DIANA: Of course not.

BILL: Then give me your father's phone number. We wanna ask him a few questions.

DIANA: What for? [*softer*] You can't, he doesn't speak English.

CONNOR: I bet a Lincoln Gloria Steinem hated her father.

BILL: I bet a Washington she has hairy armpits.

CONNOR: One dollar won't even buy you a new pair of tube socks, King Kong.

BILL: Fill or kill, Jammer.

CONNOR: Miz, show us your armpits. Unbutton your shirt.

DIANA: Are you serious?

JEFFERSON: Whoa boys, settle down. We ask politely. *Please* unbutton your shirt.

[KENT *enters as they surround* DIANA]

KENT: So glad you've charmed the Stooges so quickly, Diana. Did my man Bill explain the ideology behind Tapir, Inc.?

BILL: Kent, we were just introducing ourselves.

KENT: Show her our mascot, Bill.

JEFFERSON: Have you ever seen a tapir up close?

CONNOR: You got to have big fuzzy balls.

BILL: [*shows* DIANA *photo*] My hammer, myself. Look at what's touching the ground. It's his manliness.

DIANA: Oh my God. Is this for real?

BILL: You can go *pet* him at the Bronx Zoo. Better scurry over there; tapirs are endangered species.

KENT: Was this what you expected? Now do you see our bottom line?

DIANA: Maybe I should have been a lawyer.

JEFFERSON: Boring. You'd hate yourself.

KENT: If you need anything, I'm certain Bill will take good care of you. Plus my office is always open. I mean it, Diana, please don't hesitate.

DIANA: Actually, Kent, I could use a chair.

KENT: Bill, really, you promised if I made you head trader, you'd gang-bang the mighty buck.

BILL: Yes, sir, bang bang shebang.

KENT: Mr. Bodybuilder swore he'd flex those big fresh muscles, bench-press and bully—

BILL: Kent, you promised to give me more time—

KENT: Time? Prisoners serve time.

BILL: OK, OK, you win, just like we planned—

JEFFERSON: Planned?!

CONNOR: Figures he's a traitor. Performance pays.

BILL: —she'll rotate on the desk somewhere.

KENT: Somewhere?

BILL: OK, somewhere between Jefferson and Connor.

CONNOR/JEFFERSON: What?

KENT: Splendid, everything's settled. Bill, find this good woman of Szechwan a chair. With my help, Bill, you'll make partner yet.

BILL: Appreciate ya' Kent.

KENT: Hang tough, Diana. My office is over there if you want to talk, ask questions, shoot the shit.

DIANA: Thanks. I'd like very much to pick your brain.

KENT: Anytime. But later. Meantime, everybody keep banging. Gotta hop. [KENT *exits*]

BILL: You won yourself a parking spot, but that's it.

DIANA: You think Kent pays me to babysit?

JEFFERSON: Maybe, but I'd go ask him.

DIANA: [*bluffing*] Alright, I will.

CONNOR: Don't even think about tattling. Don't you fucking dare.

BILL: You'd be better off joining the IRA. The fucking army. In times of woe, remember, the IRA needs you!

DIANA: Then again, patience is a virtue.

JEFFERSON: Yeah, so I've heard.

CONNOR: Now and then, some smartass claims a trader made a trade at a certain price, a price *no* trader in his right mind would ever agree to, you know what I mean. Never ever.

DIANA: Of course. Buy low, sell high.

JEFFERSON: Either a trader knows a trade or he doesn't.

CONNOR: The trader *doesn't know* the trade. Not in a million years. He D.K.'s it.

BILL: That's right. This whole desk doesn't know you, do we, guys? We D.K. you. D.K.!

DIANA: You guys, the trend's your friend.

BILL: Wanna bet? D.K.!

CONNOR: D.K.!

JEFFERSON: D.K.!

BILL: We all D.K. you!

DIANA: If you'll excuse me, I'll be right back with my chair. Relax, guys, I promise you're gonna love me. [DIANA *exits*]

CONNOR: King Midas needs a tune-up real bad.

JEFFERSON: [*to* BILL] Tell me, Stalin, has the fat lady sung yet?

BILL: C'mon, I was going to tell you guys about Miz Bruce Lee. Later—today. It isn't easy when you care about you guys as much as I do.

JEFFERSON: [*rummages through his things*] Those dials look awfully greasy. Squeaky too. [*pulls out a pair of pliers, opens and closes*] Will pliers do?

BILL: I know, let's call her dad and ask if he has ping pong balls.

JEFFERSON: Like we need a snoozer.

[CONNOR *and* JEFFERSON *advance towards* BILL]

BILL: You can't touch management! Eat cake.

[CONNOR *and* JEFFERSON *tune* BILL's *radio*]

CONNOR: Way out of alignment.

BILL: I got a crisp Ulysses that says overhead is Miz Sai-gone in two months. I'll give two-to-one odds.

CONNOR: A hundred bucks says I pork her by year-end too.

JEFFERSON: You mean poke her with your pine nuts.

SQUAWK BOX: Bill? Bill? I got 50 Ginnie Mae tens to go.

[CONNOR *and* JEFFERSON *release* BILL *and resume trading.* BILL *rushes to pick up squawk box, gets shaving cream on him*]

BILL: Who needs the King? Pick me up on the inside. [*hangs up squawk box phone and wipes his face*] Fucking A. You guys are fucking lucky I'm such a regular guy. For that, Jammer, all bets are off.

CONNOR: Chicken gizzard.

JEFFERSON: Watch your position, Jammer. Five Gnome seven-and-halves getting lifted at 92—

CONNOR: Yahoo, I'm whippersnapping major cash flow!

JEFFERSON: You robber baron, that seems like an awfully high price to pay.

CONNOR: Pure gravy. Twenty bucks says long bond closes down from yesterday.

JEFFERSON: Ten bucks, couple pieces of tropical fruit, and you're on.

CONNOR: [*takes a bite out of a cheeseburger*] Taste my profit. Mushroom gravy.

JEFFERSON: Cut it out, Jammer, don't you know you're supposed to eat bran muffins at this hour?

CONNOR: Need the protein to quiet a hangover.

JEFFERSON: You're making me ravenous. [*pops a pill*]

CONNOR: [*recited like a rhyme*] The bubble bunch. When I'm not eating breakfast, I'm eating lunch.

[*Blackout*]

END OF SCENE TWO

SCENE THREE

SETTING: Trading floor, February.

AT RISE: DIANA is sandwiched between JEFFERSON and CONNOR, wearing a suit, with a bow tie. CONNOR slams his phone and bumps into DIANA.

DIANA: So, Jefferson, how did you decide to sell 50 million bonds at 97–30?

CONNOR: Something rotten has come between us, Cufflinks, and it ain't Denmark.

JEFFERSON: [*hands* DIANA *a bottle*] Here, D.K., have some Gota Kola, it's a memory herb. Stimulates circulation to the brain, increases learning ability.

DIANA: You can't ignore me forever.

JEFFERSON: Wanna bet?

CONNOR: [*picks up phone, talks to a broker*] Midget 8, 93 bid 94 ask. You know what I'm up to, right? [*He's daring someone to pick the right price, a one-point spread equals a one thousand dollar difference, which must be multiplied by the millions traded.*]

SQUAWK BOX: Jammer, bid five million mobile home ten-and-a-quarters.

CONNOR: Gotta hop. Walking brain donor calling. [*hangs up phone with broker, picks up squawk box phone*] Jammer, here, what zip code do these mobile homes reside in?

SQUAWK BOX: The beautiful Sooner state where you just can't say no.

CONNOR: [*cupping phone*] When was the last natural disaster to strike Oklahoma? Jefferson, you're from Texas, what do you know about dust bowls?

JEFFERSON: For your information, Jammer, all cowboys don't look alike.

CONNOR: Would you quit your strapping bronco stories? Just call weather service and ask about the tornado watch.

[DIANA *gets an idea and surreptitiously calls around*]

JEFFERSON: Shit, Jammer, I'm busy at the rodeo.

CONNOR: Be a bollweevil. [*into squawk box phone*] Your wife was pretty fucking insatiable last night, Cufflinks. Not healthy for you to work so much. I bid a whopping 93.

[JEFFERSON *gives* CONNOR *the finger*]

SQUAWK BOX: These are *ten*-and-a quarters, Jammer.

CONNOR: [*into squawk box phone*] Hey, bed wetter, you're as worthless as the mobile home paper you peddle. Tornadoes love trailer parks. One act of God, I lose, the bonds are cashed in at par. You get your beefy fat commission either way.

SQUAWK BOX: Go fuck yourself, midget. At 93 you skin my customer alive.

[DIANA *tries to get* CONNOR's *attention*]

CONNOR: [*into squawk box phone*] Eat me, scrotum. [CONNOR *slams squawk box*]

KENT: [*Voiceover over squawk box*] Bill? Is everything under control?

BILL: Jammer, stifle it. The whole country can hear you.

SQUAWK BOX—LONDON OFFICE: London hears you loud and clear.

SQUAWK BOX—TOKYO OFFICE: Tokyo hears you too.

JEFFERSON: [*taps* CONNOR] Jammer, Andy just called on *my* phone, someone's lifting your offer for Midget eights.

CONNOR: Shit. That wasn't a real market. [*into phone to broker*] You were supposed to protect me, scumbucket! I quoted you a market wide as a diesel truck. What do you mean you had to take a leak? [*slams* JEFFERSON's *phone*]

KENT: [*into squawk box*] Bill, what's all this banging going on? Pick me up on the inside. [*into phone to* BILL] Order Jammer to give Don a decent bid on those mobile homes.

BILL: Aye aye, boss. [*to* CONNOR] Jammer, upgrade Don's bid or he'll sic Kent on us.

JEFFERSON: On you, Bill. We're always covering for you.

CONNOR: Yeah, when am I gonna get some real help around here?

DIANA: Jammer, I got a—

CONNOR: D.K.!

JEFFERSON: Ask Kent. He knows how to bang. None of this fucking bullshit.

BILL: You want your radio tuned, Cufflinks?

DIANA: [*into squawk box*] Don, upgrade Jammer's bid to one-oh-one and seven-eighths.

DON: [*V.O. squawk box*] Done. Sold ya five, woman.

CONNOR: Who said you could trade my position? [*grabs* DIANA]

DIANA: Jammer, I already sold the bonds at one-oh-two and an eighth. Pretty good for crap. Aren't you going to thank me for locking in a quarter profit?

CONNOR: [*releases* DIANA] You got big tits for an Asian girl.

DIANA: And you got such a big mouth for such a small dick.

JEFFERSON: Ouch! She just called you numb nuts.

DIANA: Now are we gonna trade or what?

JEFFERSON: [*into squawk box phone; weight to approximate actress's weight*] Salesfarce, the mortgage desk is pleased to announce the arrival of a new baby tapir. Female, approximately 110 pounds, 6 ounces, black hair, answers to the name D.K.

BILL: Jammer, I found you a devoted slave. Show the King some gratitude.

CONNOR: The test ain't over. What's the average life of my paper?

[*Q and A are fired very quickly*]

DIANA: Five-to-seven years.

CONNOR: Durable goods up or down tomorrow?

DIANA: Down is my prediction.

CONNOR: Shape of yield curve? [*outlines shape of his kind of woman*]

DIANA: [*concedes the uphill road ahead*] Steep. Very steep.

CONNOR: Explain negative convexity.

DIANA: It's what happens when I put in my contacts backwards.

JEFFERSON: Witty.

CONNOR: Nit*wit*, I call the jokes around here.

DIANA: It's the problem of adverse changes in duration for a mortgage-backed security, relative to the move in interest rates, which happen to be *rising*. [*acknowledging* CONNOR's *increased interest in her*]

JEFFERSON: Impressive.

CONNOR: Let's get one thing straight, yellowtail. You freshly grated MBAs all think you're hot shit, but you're nothing but cold diarrhea.

DIANA: I understand I have to eat cold shit.

CONNOR: Exactly. With a smile.

DIANA: It's just temporary. Like temporary insanity. It comes but it goes.

CONNOR: Jefferson, tell D.K. what you started at.

JEFFERSON: Lousy 21 grand. Bill started at 26. Just because we didn't have MBAs.

BILL: And went to public schools.

JEFFERSON: How much they paying you?

DIANA: Can't tell, company policy, page 12.

BILL: She makes 70 peanuts.

CONNOR: [*shows her W-2 stub*] Chump change, pal.

DIANA: Seven hundred fifty thousand dollars? Wow, some bonus.

JEFFERSON: That doesn't include his high falutin' salary.

CONNOR: Bill took home 13 million dollars last year and he still dresses like a used car salesman.

BILL: Jammer! I represent the common man. Someone has to. And I don't need no fucking Harvard MBA to succeed either.

CONNOR: Common man nothing, jealous quantoid, facts are facts. You fell short so they rejected you.

DIANA: [*to* CONNOR, *surprised*] You have an MBA? From Harvard?

CONNOR: You know, my parents ask me that very same question. [*beat*] I've set my sights on a world record profit for my product. And a 14 million dollar bonus.

BILL: [*feeling threatened*] Dream on, Jammer. Kings always outrank pawns. [*to* DIANA] In every language.

JEFFERSON: Don't forget about me, guys. I work here, too, you know. Lot longer than you two field mice.

BILL: Jefferson took home a cool million-dollar bonus.

JEFFERSON: One million dollars is a tidy sum. Show your seasoned trader some fucking respect.

CONNOR: Jump as high as you can before gravity kicks in and kills you. Are you a pouncer?

DIANA: A panther. Thirteen million dollars . . . Bill, show me the way.

BILL: Fuck me.

JEFFERSON: Look at D.K. lick her chops like some rabid raccoon.

CONNOR: Now what do you think of your 70 Gs?

DIANA: Stale bread crumbs.

CONNOR: You're overhead. We have to deduct you from our profits. So overhead listens, never speaks unless asked. Overhead fetches coffee, orders lunch, places bets. Overhead makes copies, write tickets. [*drops a pen, bends over to pick it up*] Now do you still like my butt? [*flirting begins*]

DIANA: I'll manage.

CONNOR: I'm a leg man myself.

DIANA: [*shows off her legs*] I shave.

CONNOR: Just so we understand each other. [CONNOR *tries to touch her legs; she pulls away*]

DIANA: We have to maintain industry standards.

CONNOR: [*grabs the list of "Hung like" and shows* DIANA] You see this list? Scribble your name under "Hung like a Field Mouse."

DIANA: How do you *know* Ronald Reagan and James Bond are hung like tapirs?

CONNOR: Some truths are self-evident.

DIANA: That explains Margaret Thatcher.

CONNOR: You can aspire to join her.

DIANA: What about Hillary Rodham Clinton? She sure can trade.

CONNOR: No fucking way. Circumstantial evidence. Anyone would look like a tapir next to corn-fed Bill. Ready, guys? [*cues the other guys to imitate President Bill Clinton*] Special report, we interrupt this program to give you this special report.

CONNOR, BILL, JEFFERSON: "I feel your pain. I feel your pain."

DIANA: [*smiling*] Yes, sir. There you go, Jammer.

CONNOR: [*grabs list*] You wrote in "Don't Know"? Clever. But where's my fucking lunch, Don't Know?

DIANA: What do you want?

CONNOR: Bacon cheeseburger rare, cheese fries, and a coke. You fly, I buy.

DIANA: [*picks up phone*] Where do you want to order from?

JEFFERSON: [*hands* DIANA *a menu*] Order from Harry's. Get me an organic vegetable plate and fresh-squeezed orange juice.

BILL: Hey, nobody asked me. I want spaghetti with meatballs, garlic bread, and an iced capuccino with cinnamon sprinkles. [*throws* CONNOR *a package of tube socks*] Jammer, catch. That oughta more than cover my share.

CONNOR: Bed wetter.

DIANA: [*into phone*] Harry's? I'd like to order take-out . . . yes, yes, and a tuna fish salad and iced tea.

BILL: Tuna fish! Jammer, Cufflinks, it's time to tune her radio. Tune the radio.

JEFFERSON: Bill, really, she's a *chick fillet.*

BILL: [*retrieves crumpled memo*] Didn't you read the latest memo on sexual harassment? As of yesterday, Tapir does not discriminate.

DIANA: [*into phone*] Fifteen minutes? That'll be fine. [*hangs up*]

BILL: My stereo receiver is in desperate need of some fine tuning. [CONNOR *and* JEFFERSON *grab her*]

DIANA: If you let me go, I'll treat.

BILL: [*his hand gets dangerously close to* DIANA's *breast, but does not touch*] I'm not used to these big knobs. Knobs you can really hold onto. Girls are so much fun.

CONNOR: The electrical impulses.

JEFFERSON: Simply shocking.

DIANA: Let me go! I'll scream.

BILL: Muffle her.

[JEFFERSON *covers* DIANA's *mouth.* BILL *retrieves scissors*]

JEFFERSON: Shut your eyes, pretend it's a quick nightmare.

BILL: [*twists her bow tie like a radio knob, his ear against her chest*] I'm turning, turning, but I can't hear any music. Complete cacophony.

DIANA: [*speaking with her mouth covered*] Animal.

BILL: [*snips off her bow tie,* DIANA *is released*] This is the sissy method of tuning radios. Gotcha didn't we?

DIANA: Misogynist.

BILL: You wanted to be a trader.

CONNOR: We did you a favor. It's an ugly bow tie.

JEFFERSON: Women think bow ties make them men.

[CONNOR *goes through* DIANA's *briefcase, picks up a book.* DIANA *tries to stop* CONNOR]

DIANA: What are you doing?

JEFFERSON: The trading floor is no place for secrets.

BILL: Women who perspire to be men have problems with intimacy.

CONNOR: "To be or not to be . . ." [*beat*] Willie Shakespeare, too creamy, clogs the arteries. [CONNOR *throws book in the trash*]

DIANA: I'm gonna get you back. All of you.

CONNOR: Yes! Can't wait. I'll help you outwit them.

BILL: You mad, D.K.? You gonna cry? Gonna quit?

JEFFERSON: Go shopping? Try a new diet?

DIANA: Hell no. I'm not afraid of you.

BILL: Guess she doesn't like us anymore.

JEFFERSON: Maybe we better check her pulse.

BILL: This is why it's no fun to have a woman on your team. Can't take a fucking prank.

CONNOR: I'm starving. Where's my fucking lunch?

DIANA: I'm going!

CONNOR: [*hands* DIANA *a cigar*] A Cuban cigar for your troubles.

JEFFERSON: Aw D.K., we're really a bunch of nice—

BILL: Hungry—

JEFFERSON: Carnivores.

CONNOR: The kind you take home to mom and dad.

BILL: Tapirs.

[*The men growl as* DIANA *exits. Fade out*]

END OF SCENE THREE

SCENE FOUR

SETTING: Trading floor, March, around 5:30 PM.

AT RISE: End of a highly profitable trading day. DIANA, BILL, JEFFERSON, and CONNOR are ecstatic.

JEFFERSON: We sure banged the buck today. I'm going to purchase me a Mercedes convertible.

BILL: Buttfucking incredible. I'm up 200 grand on the day. Time for hot chicks and ouzo. How's bayou, Jammer? Shall we summer again in Southampton?

CONNOR: Slam festival. D.K., we're fucking awesome.

BILL: Show us how we whippersnapper major cash flow. Please, Jammer.

CONNOR: For the King of Fixed Income. [*bangs his groin against the back of a chair or desk, or against wall*] Was it as good for you as it was for me?

DIANA: You guys are so barbaric.

JEFFERSON: What are you going to buy, D.K.?

DIANA: I need so much that I don't know where to start.

CONNOR: Yup, she wants to slam dunk like us.

[BILL *passes out cigars, hesitates briefly before giving one to* DIANA]

BILL: Reward yourself with the black market.

CONNOR: No one else will.

BILL: D.K., give yours to your boyfriend, or your whatchacallit, "domestic partner."

DIANA: What do you mean?

BILL: You got a pork chop?

DIANA: I date a bay of pigs.

BILL: How come I never meet your alleged pork chops?

DIANA: Simple, they wouldn't like you.

BILL: That's what I mean.

CONNOR: All the heavy hitters inhale.

DIANA: Show me how to smoke.

[CONNOR *clips off the end and lights the cigar for her*]

CONNOR: Look at her suck on it. Snowpea can't wait to get cancer.

JEFFERSON: D.K., remember to bring me some ginseng and those funky Chinese herbs that preserve youth, increase potency, and prolong life.

DIANA: Then why do you smoke?

JEFFERSON: The key is to always cover yourself. When I drink alcohol, I order a cocktail with fruit juice. This way I break even.

SQUAWK BOX: Mortgage desk, please extinguish your cigars immediately. Tapir is a smoke-free environment.

[*Everyone extinguishes cigars*]

DIANA: [*relieved*] Great cigar, but the law's the law.

BILL: I make 13 million dollars. Those alfalfa sprouts have no respect.

CONNOR: Let's brand those cows. Tune some radios.

BILL: [*retrieves extinguished cigars*] And we will. Tonight. We'll take over our city. Start off with three-pound steaks and lobsters, couple bottles of Amarone. Play a few rounds of Truth or Dare. Pick up some hot chick fillets with front-row basketball tickets.

JEFFERSON: Can't pull an all-nighter. Turns you into a raisin over night. Raisins are boxed and shelved. Besides, I want to see my wife and kid.

BILL: Cufflinks here is pussywhipped.

JEFFERSON: Hey, every time you guys take a leak, you're shaking hands with the unemployed. We'll see who comes in grinning tomorrow.

BILL: Let's split.

CONNOR: I haven't finished checking my trades.

BILL: The King demands we storm the city.

DIANA: I'll go out with you.

BILL: Why are you here at my firm? Why don't you go back wherever you came from? Why me?

DIANA: I'm from America.

CONNOR: [*wiping and blowing his trading ledger*] Shit! Market bounced all over the place, but no fucking way I sold bonds this cheap. [*shows* DIANA]

DIANA: Simple, Wrong handle. D.K. it.

CONNOR: I already OK'd it, *on tape twice.*

JEFFERSON: Quantos, amigo?

CONNOR: Sixty grand I'll have to swallow in a single gulp.

BILL: Damn it, Jammer, you constipate me.

CONNOR: See this brown spot? What I think happened here is D.K. spilled some coffee on my ledger but I OK'd it because I trusted her numbers.

DIANA: Impossible. I never forage on or over your ledger. Ask Jefferson.

JEFFERSON: Oh no, as far as I'm concerned, you both exceed the recommended daily allowance for caffeine.

CONNOR: Snowpea, I'm not blaming you, Heaven knows we need our double espresso. It's not like Kent's going to fire us over 60 K.

BILL: That's why you can't trade with a chick fillet. Sooner or later she sends you up in flames. [*to* DIANA] Fucking Beatrice.

DIANA: [*feels persecuted, sighs, grabs* CONNOR's *ledger, picks up phone, calls a broker*] We got a problem with your fingerprints on it. Know that trade for 58 million dwarf nines? Wrong handle, it's 97 not 96. Why did Jammer OK the trade? Probably isn't used to my writing yet.

JEFFERSON: She's becoming one of us. Kafka's metamorphosis. One big giant cockroach coming up.

DIANA: [*into phone*] We're supposed to protect Jammer, not gouge him, you brain-dead beat off. Name's D.K. and I D.K. you. Sixty grand is a lot to digest, but you can't exploit a fucking trainee. That's unethical. No we won't split the difference. You can't talk to Jammer 'cuz you're in the goddamned box. Well, fuck you too.

CONNOR: Good with details. Very diplomatic. I think I'll keep her.

DIANA: [*still into phone*] How much did you make in commissions off us last year, you bloodsucking leech? And your bonus? Of course we'll throw you some juicy T-bone steaks tomorrow. You're welcome. One more thing. Call us a couple limos for the whole night, fully stocked. Sure, join us if you want to play. [*hangs up. everyone is still watching her.*] Do I look like your mother? C'mon, guys, tidy up!

BILL: You shouldn't pick up our bad habits. Makes you unfeminine. Beastly. Really, what would your pork chop say?

DIANA: We're tapirs first.

CONNOR: You were great, *partner.*

DIANA: I'm still trembling. Do you think I was too harsh?

JEFFERSON: [*holds up and offers tea bag*] Hawthorne tea unjangles the nerves.

DIANA: I need a cigar. For later. [CONNOR *gives* DIANA *one*] You have to bang to win, right?

CONNOR: [*extends a hand that shakes*] You'll get used to the shaking. *Movers shake.* First thing tomorrow we'll transfer your name to "Hung like a Tapir." Iron Maggie could use a female comrade.

BILL: Don't you miss being a woman? You one of them Lesbos?

DIANA: Bill, I understand your terror. Once upon a time there was a husband and a wife who lived the life of luxury in China. But when kid number two arrives and it's a girl, they're supposed to fucking kill her. Instead they trade their lives, servants and all, wholesale for America. For what? To become manual laborers in some stinking rubber factory. When I see their hands— red, raw, and ugly—I wish we had never melted in this fucking country. So you see, Bill, I *am* that flash of horror you wear so well.

JEFFERSON: Wow, that's gotta be tough.

CONNOR: My trainee's fucking intense.

BILL: OK, she's in. But you have to open your own doors.

DIANA: [*picks up phone because turret is flashing*] Yeah? Car 124 in five minutes. Thanks. [*hangs up*] We ready to hop, guys?

BILL: Almost.

JEFFERSON: Let's not get too sauced guys. Sales of single family homes comes out tomorrow.

CONNOR: I betcha a buck sales went up by at least 10 percent.

JEFFERSON: One dollar? You're so *long* on the American dream.

CONNOR: You heard my woman. The American dream is a soaking wet dream. But then you wake up and everything dries instantly. Every day you wake up in a scorching desert.

BILL: Horatio Fellatio.

CONNOR: [*hands out brochures to* BILL *and* JEFFERSON] That's why I say we purchase an ostrich farm together.

BILL: Oh no, not this pitch again. Roast it, Jammer.

JEFFERSON: Ostrich is healthier than red meat, lean and mean. Wave of the future.

CONNOR: We'll make a killing on ostrich boots alone. Eight hundred percent return.

DIANA: [*points to ledger*] You owe me some precious trade secrets for this.

CONNOR: [*pushes* DIANA *in her chair as if it's a car*] Picture yourself zooming along in your Ferrari, your Alaskan Samoyed next to you, suddenly you're waving to this gorgeous hunk in the next lane.

DIANA: [*thrilled*] Yeah? Then what?

JEFFERSON: [BILL *and* JEFFERSON *wave and smile*] He's waving back, grinning—

BILL: [JEFFERSON *and* BILL *blow kisses*] Blowing you kisses,

CONNOR: Begging you to pull over and *possess* him.

DIANA: What's he look like?

BILL: Like one of us.

CONNOR: Who do you want?

DIANA: [*laughing, but engaged by this vision*] Right. I won't know if he likes me for me, my car, or my dog.

JEFFERSON: So what? You own him. You have what he covets. Lucrative investments. Freedom, happiness, beauty.

BILL: Relish your new powers. Nobody ever stops us, or tells us what to do.

CONNOR: Nobody. It's so exhilarating.

[*Men spin* DIANA *around in a chair. Blackout*]

END OF SCENE FOUR

SCENE FIVE

SETTING: Trading floor, April, early morning.

AT RISE: BILL, JEFFERSON, CONNOR, and DIANA nervously await employment data and are happy to learn they bet right. Everyone works at a frenetic pace, juggling phones, buying and selling, to reflect an extremely volatile day.

SQUAWK BOX: U.S. nonfarm payroll employment increases by two hundred fifty six thousand, reversing the drop reported last month!

JEFFERSON: Yahoo! Market's skyrocketing. Ride 'em high, cowboys.

CONNOR: No fucking way! Now I bet you wish you had some kickass ostrich boots.

BILL: Watch your position, guys. Don't try to be heroes.

SQUAWK BOX: Jammer, I need a bid on 75 Midget nine-and-halves.

CONNOR: D.K., what do you think?

DIANA: I bid 97 tops.

CONNOR: You still throw like a girl, Snowpea. [*into squawk box*] I'll pay 98.

SQUAWK BOX: You own 75 million at 98.

CONNOR: [*into squawk box*] Salesfarce, double commission for anyone who can sell these bonds at 98 and a quarter.

DIANA: Jammer, I think you're asking for too big a spread. The fundamentals don't support a real recovery. We got to look at the *quality* of jobs, not just the raw numbers. Everyone knows the decrease in quality of jobs spells more unemployment.

BILL: Careful, Jammer. Either she's with you or she's against you.

CONNOR: D.K., did I give you permission to speak? Yammer all you want after five. I'll explain it all over dinner.

SQUAWK BOX: Jammer, I buy ten of those Midgets at 98 and a quarter with double commission.

CONNOR: [*into squawk box*] Thank you kindly, sir. And congratulations. You've just taught D.K. a valuable lesson in arbitrage.

DIANA: We still have 65 million to go. If we narrow the spread, we'll sell 'em faster—

CONNOR: Smile, Snowpea. I'm taking you to the Rainbow Room tonight. In my Corvette. Celebrate our record 460 million dollar profit. Pick you up at seven.

DIANA: I can't. I have a date.

JEFFERSON: I'd yield to temptation, D.K. You might bite into a forkful of inside information.

CONNOR: World is divided into two kinds of people. People who read history. People who make history. I'm not going to sit around reading financial statement tonight. I got women to pleasure.

DIANA: Then let me go over your profit and loss statements.

CONNOR: I thought you said you were getting laid tonight.

DIANA: I have time to do both.

JEFFERSON: Ambidextree-ous.

DIANA: What happens when Teachers Pension Fund buys a Fannie Mae from us at 96 and two hours later, Teachers wants to sell it back and we say we'll only pay 95—

[CONNOR, JEFFERSON, *and* BILL *reply on top of each other*]

CONNOR: "Sorry, market's moved. Left town. No forwarding address."

JEFFERSON: "It's not the heat, it's the volatility."

BILL: "I'm not a buyer."

JEFFERSON: "I'm not a seller."

DIANA: But is it ethical? Won't we lose valuable long-term relationships?

BILL: Hey, depreciation kicks ass soon as I drive my new Beamer off the lot—

CONNOR: You want an unending relationship, get pregnant.

JEFFERSON: [*into phone with a broker, finishing a trade*] Yes, Andy! An easy 27 grand. Have to love it when opportunities are so ripe and sweet I can smell 'em. Most the time my lucky breaks are like magnolia blossoms, soon as I pluck the white flower, the petals brown. That's why this little piggie wants to celebrate while he can. A juicy porterhouse steak with Roquefort cheese! Andy, reservations at High Steaks tonight. Of course, your treat. Is my name Rockefella?

BILL: I'm in! Be prepared for this evening's more dastardly Truth or Dare. I've got some real whoppers, D.K., Jammer. The MBAs against the BAs.

DIANA: I can't make it. I have a hot date, remember?

BILL: Sure you do. A bay of pigs.

JEFFERSON: Congratulations. Hope he's worth the money.

BILL: Bring *her* along, the sow.

DIANA: I happen to like this guy. He's French.

CONNOR: Monsieur Wee Wee.

SQUAWK BOX: Jammer, D.K., please bid 40 million dwarf seven-and-halves.

CONNOR: Date a real man. [*into squawk box*] I'll pay 92 for those lovely deformed bonds.

SQUAWK BOX: Firemen pension thanks you in all your grandeur!

CONNOR: D.K., time to really jam.

DIANA: [*into squawk box*] Sales force, have we got a terrific deal for you—

SQUAWK BOX: Folks, more news on the March employment report. The figures show a dramatic increase in corporate downsizing, automation, and the low-paying labor force, along with continued decreases in manufacturing. The average work week has doubled. Despite the steep drop in prime earnings, average wage is rising to offset escalating CPI.

[*Everyone resumes frenetic pace*]

BILL: Shit! Inflation's plunging bond prices. Watch the market tank.

JEFFERSON: Rain dance. Duck for cover.

CONNOR: Fuck, why do people panic at the same time?

JEFFERSON: Wonders of technology.

BILL: Lettuce-picking is still a decent job in my book.

CONNOR: Go ahead, D.K., slam dunk, tell me you're smarter.

DIANA: [*into squawk box*] Sales force, we're a little long 15-year paper. Triple commission for anyone who can move the first 100 million. [*to* CONNOR] Why don't you believe I'm on your side? Why can't I do our profit and loss?

CONNOR: I know you're just praying for me to have a heart attack so you can take over my position.

DIANA: You're being absolutely ridiculous. Paranoid.

CONNOR: Then why is it you won't hang out with me more?

DIANA: Because we already see each other sixty, seventy hours a week.

CONNOR: You're using me. Admit it.

DIANA: Is that why you constantly humiliate me in front of everyone?

CONNOR: I'm soft and squishy inside too, you know. Once a trader reveals his secrets, he becomes a disposable diaper. [*into squawk box*] Salesfarce, we really need your help moving paper. [*softly*] Me and [*louder*] D.K. bid a little too agressively so we're prepared to let some beautiful bonds go at obscenely low prices. Call us direct to negotiate.

DIANA: Alright, we can hang out more. Shoot some pool or something.

CONNOR: [*elated, hits speed dial*] I'd like to make reservations for two humans. At seven. Merci, Jean Claude, à bientôt.

JEFFERSON: Make sure the bed wetter pays.

CONNOR: Listen, D.K., you're almost ready to trade on your own. I swear, real soon I'm gonna ask Kent to give you a sizeable position. You're only a tick or two away. Almost there, D.K. Super close.

KENT: [*V.O. over squawk box*] Bill, how long is Tapir's mortgage desk? Pick me up on the inside.

BILL: [*into squawk box*] In a sec, Kent. We're banging.

KENT: [*V.O. over squawk box*] How long, Bill? Shorten it up, we need to speak NOW.

BILL: [*into phone*] Yo Kent, what do you want?

KENT: [*V.O.*] Latest rumor on the street is President's about to declare a global crisis. Two hundred of the world's largest firms are going under . . . expected to auction billions of assets next week. How long is our desk?

BILL: Holy shit. Let me check and relay. [*hangs up*]

KENT: [*V.O.*] Bill, keep it under your Stetson. One whiff of this, we got a nuclear meltdown.

BILL: Yo, tapirs, no more purchases. Kent heard a rumor that some companies are going bankrupt, dumping assets, the usual. Cufflinks, your position?

JEFFERSON: I'm comfortably short. You'll back us when the sales force belly-aches?

BILL: A King always champions his commoners. Jammer, D.K.?

CONNOR: [lying] All under control. Yourself?

BILL: Shit, I need to be much shorter. Everybody, jam as fast as you fucking can. Always plenty of time to panic.

SQUAWK BOX: Bill, Jefferson, Jammer, People's Savings wants to sell you their portfolio. First bid 100 million Ginnie Mae elevens.

CONNOR: Why is my name last?

BILL: [into squawk box phone] I'm not a buyer. Salesfarce, the desk is a strong seller of all paper. Christmas fire sale.

JEFFERSON: Fire? Scare the hell out of 'em, King Kong.

SQUAWK BOX: I need a bid, Bill. Jefferson quick, bid me 65 Fannie Mae nines.

JEFFERSON: How low can we bid and still be respectable? That is a modern art.

BILL: We're fucked.

SQUAWK BOX: Jammer, please bid 35 Midget tens.

CONNOR: D.K., say I'm taking a dump and you don't know where anything trades.

DIANA: I know what to bid.

CONNOR: We must let it trade away, can't you see?

DIANA: What about my dignity?

CONNOR: Nothing a few cocktails can't revive. I'll buy.

SQUAWK BOX: Jammer? I need a bid, pronto.

JEFFERSON: It's called job preservation. Perfectly legal. Got nothing to be ashamed of. Human instinct.

CONNOR: [hands DIANA squawk box phone] Team player.

DIANA: [into squawk box] Jammer stepped off the desk.

SQUAWK BOX: D.K., give me a bid on 35 Midget tens.

DIANA: [into squawk box] I can't. [beat] I'm stupid. [hangs up]

SQUAWK BOX: Christ! Bill, People's Savings wants to know if you've heard of anything about corporate restructuring.

BILL: [into squawk box] Nada. Fucking bullshit.

SQUAWK BOX: Got my bid on those 100 Ginnie elevens? People's Savings is waiting.

BILL: [into squawk box] I pass. Advise them to wait until durable goods to-morrow.

SQUAWK BOX: Fuck you. Fuck durable goods. Durable goods means diddly squat and you know it better than me.

CONNOR: [*into squawk box*] Fuck People's!

[*Blackout*]

END OF SCENE FIVE

SCENE SIX

SETTING: Fancy restaurant/ballroom, April.

AT RISE: DIANA and CONNOR are enjoying life.

DIANA: Ever get scared that if we bet wrong, we could lose everything? The firm, our jobs, people's life savings?

CONNOR: Responsibility's awesome. Precisely why we're highly compensated, keeps us healthy and bullish.

DIANA: I'm so nervous I can barely sleep through the night.

CONNOR: Relax, everyone knows you shouldn't gamble what you can't lose. If you wanna play the markets, you gotta embrace the dangers. It's not like we force anyone to hand over their money. People like us get hired and fired with a drop of a tick. Over in one thirty-seconds.

DIANA: Still, it seems to me that millions of people depend on our expertise—

CONNOR: Oh yeah, the whole world's trying to make a killing off us so they can retire rich. Can't we talk about something else for a change? Something that has nothing to do with bonds or interest rates?

DIANA: Sure, how 'bout them Rangers?

CONNOR: Have you ever been really deep in love? So deep you feel yourself drowning?

DIANA: Connor—you tell me to ask questions after five, but after five you're grilling me.

CONNOR: As partners, we have to bond, build trust. Or else it proves you're just exploiting me.

DIANA: I swear I'm not.

CONNOR: You know, a lot of babes are into me, a whole spectrum of chick fil-lets, because I know how to relish life. Even homos tell me I'm sexy. Don't you think that carries a ton of weight? I mean everybody knows how particular homos are about looks.

DIANA: No question you're a hunk.

CONNOR: Great because I need a date this Saturday night. Pick you up at eight. Wear silk. Now let's tango.

[*They dance.* CONNOR *leads to a tango*]

DIANA: Listen, Connor, I've struggled long and hard to get where I am. And look at me, I'm still nowhere. That's why we can't date. I need to work even harder so maybe I can succeed like you.

CONNOR: Hold me close, I'll fly you there first class—

DIANA: I want to be your partner, not your fast food chick fillet—

CONNOR: The beauty is we can be both. All this pressure to succeed and produce, it divides us into desperate lonely selves. Can't you see—we need each other.

DIANA: Kent promised me once I mastered the art of finance, I'd trade millions and billions.

CONNOR: I often wish I could quit. Don't you?

DIANA: No. I just started, I love my job. It's a dream come true.

CONNOR: You shitting me? Is that all you dream about—spreads, yield curves, basis points, important bullshit, but bullshit.

DIANA: I can picture myself retiring in the South of France or on the Italian or Spanish Riviera. I'm not that picky.

CONNOR: Aha, you're normal like the rest of us! With my help, you're gonna end up there. You're making rapid progress; everybody admires how fast—

DIANA: People only admire you when you dare to go where they expect you to fail. When I wanted to become President of the United States, people admired me for my naiveté because they knew I could never, I wasn't born here. My second dream was to win a few Academy Awards—people applauded, what courage, what strength. Then I saw A *Chorus Line*. Dance Ten, Looks Three. Whatever the score, I would always be too Chinese. That's why I can't blow it, Connor. I can't lose another dream with a blink of an eye. Especially trading. The only place where for a couple of seconds, it doesn't matter where you were born, what you look like. We're all the same over the phone.

CONNOR: God, you're deep, must be why my man Kent hired you. You move me too. So I propose every time you do something for me, like be my date, I answer one of your questions. Risk-free swap.

DIANA: Nothing physically demanding? How can I be sure you won't use personal information against me? Are you ever going to let me trade huge blocks, or are you just hoping to tweak my breasts?

CONNOR: All I want is some jocularity to relieve the pressure, make up for paradise lost.

DIANA: Anything risk-free sounds too risque to me. What if me and you, you know—

CONNOR: [*dips* DIANA, *threatens to drop her*] Fall? No problemo, if we're professionals, and I think we both are.

DIANA: [*attempting to lead in the tango*] But are we equal?

[*Blackout*]

END OF SCENE SIX

END OF ACT I

ACT II

SCENE ONE

SETTING: Trading floor, September, late afternoon.

AT RISE: DIANA and JEFFERSON write tickets. CONNOR calculates the day's profit and loss. BILL hams it up with a reporter on the phone.

BILL: [*into the phone with a reporter*] Today's sharp sell-off in the mortgage markets is not justified by the fundamentals. People just don't trust the Feds anymore. The Feds got an agenda just like you and me. So investors are bearish. Everyone's scrambling to interpret the hieroglyphics from Washington. Too many people hung up on "gainful employment." What is *gain*ful employment? A job used to be a job. A job used to mean economic security. Now it has to be an excellent adventure. I mean I agree, who wants to pick grapes when you can be a swashbuckling bond trader? But if it's grapes or nothing, you join AA. So of course, the figures look too robust for a nation of unemployed actors. Go figure. [*pause*] My name? [*beat*] OK, you can quote me, my name's Ted . . . Nugent. [*hangs up*]

JEFFERSON: How much you up, Jammer? Fifty, sixty grand?

BILL: I'm up 155 grand on the day.

CONNOR: We're up 92.

DIANA: We are? You sure? Amazing. Show me.

CONNOR: [*to* DIANA] Yeah sure, over dinner.

JEFFERSON: Shit, I'm only up 76.

CONNOR: We're fucking geniuses.

BILL: Excellent. I can't wait to tell Kent what well-endowed tapirs we all are.

JEFFERSON: Then let's head over to High Steaks for a bawdy, high protein, red corpuscle celebration.

BILL: Yeah, let's see who can collect the most phone numbers from hot chick fillets.

CONNOR: Count me out.

DIANA: Me too. Rain check. Gotta hop.

JEFFERSON: Why, where are you two going?

DIANA: Nowhere. Home.

BILL: Jammer, it's no fun without you.

CONNOR: I feel nauseous. Canceled my hot date.

JEFFERSON: I'm a lot of fun too. You just don't get my kind of fun.

BILL: Jammer makes us do outrageous things. Jammer, whippersnapper for us.

JAMMER: Later. Gotta hop.

BILL: For the King of Fixed Income.

CONNOR: [bangs with much less energy than before] There's got to be a better release.

JEFFERSON: Sex and yoga.

CONNOR: I'm wiped. This volatility is killing me.

JEFFERSON: Shoot, grab some old-fashioned R & R. You've been such a pill lately, I should know.

CONNOR: I do need a real vacation.

BILL: You have my permission to get laid and tan; consider it next year's Christmas gift.

JEFFERSON: Yeah, why don't you? I bet D.K can trade your position. Right, D.K.?

DIANA: Sure. Love to.

CONNOR: I know I deserve to lie on the sand and do nothing. I made a record 460 million dollar profit this year. But no one understands my market. Plus I've got some really elaborate hedges that need careful watching and reversing.

JEFFERSON: I'll help watch D.K. for you. Free of charge.

DIANA: I promise to be lucrative. Just show me what to cover.

CONNOR: Just waiting for my Lear jet to crash, aren't you?

BILL: What happened to our honeymooners? You didn't pork each other, did you?

DIANA: Haven't you heard? Asians are the most loyal bunch of bananas.

BILL: It's true, Jammer, lifetime loyalty is the secret to Japan's success. It's in all those books.

JEFFERSON: [flipping through his calendar] Shit, Jammer, look, it's been 15 months since you went skiing in Vail. You have to rejuvenate yourself. Do it for the firm. If you run into trouble and Kent finds out you've been trading under the influence of burnout . . . [motions off with the head]

BILL: [slightly threatened] OK that's it. I have to report our P & L to Kent and I'm telling him you're going on vacation. That's a direct order.

CONNOR: Okay already, I'll go.

JEFFERSON: Listen, I'm hungry. Andy's waiting for us downstairs.

BILL: I'll meet you at High Steaks.

[BILL *and* JEFFERSON *exit*]

DIANA: Jammer, where did you come up with 92 grand? I kept a record of all our trades today and I can't find any 92 grand.

CONNOR: Got any aspirin? [*goes through her purse*] I have a huge headache. [*beat*] Let me see your work. [*looks at her ledger quickly*] Your closing prices are all wrong.

DIANA: All of them? Again? You're kidding.

CONNOR: Concentrate harder, don't scribble like some secretary. I'm breaking the *Guinness Book of World Records* and you're playing Bartleby the Scrivener. "I would prefer not to."

DIANA: Where did you close the Midget nine and halves?

CONNOR: Up a quarter from yesterday.

DIANA: But the market plummeted today. Isn't it possible that our position lost 50 grand today? Considering the roller-coaster ride, we did good. Fifty grand is nothing. Chump change. Tomorrow, clear skies, up 100.

CONNOR: [*hands* DIANA The Wall Street Journal] Find me a quote on a Midget.

DIANA: I know, it doesn't exist.

CONNOR: You're gifted; you're remarkable. I even told Kent you deserve a raise yesterday.

DIANA: Really? How much?

CONNOR: Too much. [*snatches his* Journal *back*] As I was saying, my market is so fucking esoteric. Nobody really knows where my product trades. My product moves mysteriously, like a sensuous woman. How can I go on vacation when you're so clueless?

DIANA: Of course you can go on vacation. Just don't be so afraid to share the magic.

CONNOR: D.K., please go away with me. Let's escape from all this. We'll feel our way through Florence, Paris, Mount Kilimanjaro, . . . anywhere.

DIANA: [*tempted*] Jammer are you serious—

CONNOR: I know you wanna travel. Name your destination.

DIANA: Is this another test of my loyalty, timing how long it takes me to pounce? To admit I want to trade your position more than anything.

CONNOR: I don't understand. You'd rather trade my crappy bonds than discover the real world? Aren't you sick and tired of a life imprisoned by junk? Junk mail, junk food, junk bonds. We're goddamn junkies.

DIANA: I know I get super excited trading and how my energy can be scary. But you have nothing to worry about. Nothing.

CONNOR: I know you love me. I love you, too. A true deep love.

DIANA: Really? O, Connor, I think you're saying that 'cuz we've both been feeling lonely and depressed lately. Take Prozac. It's normal.

CONNOR: Chicks don't understand what I do for a living, so how can they fathom who I am. Hell, my mom thinks I'm some gerbil racing around in an orange jacket, screaming and flapping, "Bonds? Peanuts? Popcorn? Bonds?" But you, D.K., day in day out, side by side, you see me, I see you. We see each other so much so well.

DIANA: You're right, we do spend too much time together.

CONNOR: Didn't we have fun sailing in Southampton? Driving around in my red Corvette.

DIANA: Sure, who wouldn't—fun is fun.

CONNOR: Pick any tropical island. We'll uncover buried treasure in between making passionate love. My treat.

[*They kiss*]

DIANA: Stop; this is a horrible idea.

CONNOR: What a wicked witch you are. Frigid too. You seemed so real to me, D.K. Don't you ever long to hold something natural? Flesh that's soft and smooth as a baby's butt?

DIANA: Reality is a pedophile. [*beat*] Sure, I dream of falling in love, but how can I rush into romantic intimacy, Connor, knowing you're my boss?

CONNOR: I think of us more like partners.

DIANA: Then give me a chance to prove myself. One week. If I'm profitable, maybe Kent will give me a new position. What are you afraid of? That I might make more money than you? In five lousy days? Please.

CONNOR: Open your eyes, D.K. Shop around. Chicks get locked into the short end of the yield curve.

DIANA: Is that your excuse? Or your only way of staying on top?

CONNOR: Harsh. You MBA women are all alike. Glue your eyes 'n ears to the screens and the phones. That's where the green is. You promise not to record every trade for posterity, I promise to get us in the Hall of Fame.

DIANA: What about sharing your stellar trading strategies?

CONNOR: Swear you'll call me first if you have any trouble whatsoever.

DIANA: Connor, of course I love you, after all we've been through. If you really love me, you should trust me. Show me today's profit. Then yesterday's, the

day before yesterday, the day before that, and so on. Do you still love me? I
mean, really?

CONNOR: Hey, I took you in as my partner when nobody else wanted you. Now
everyone accepts you as a part of the A-team, but without me, Snowpea,
you'd still be an outlier.

DIANA: No doubt I plan to make big bucks to show you proper gratitude.
That's why I need your computer password and your P & L statements.

CONNOR: I'm going to make a list of do's and don'ts for you. At the end of the
day, call Simon and compare closing prices. Then have Dave input the
prices in the computer. It will save you time and free you to concentrate on
trading.

DIANA: Whatever. Thank you, Jammer. But will you please—

CONNOR: I'll call you collect several times during the day.

DIANA: A sign of true love.

CONNOR: We'll rally over dinner tonight, steak au poivre, langostino, Amarone—

DIANA: I can't, I have plans. Maybe once I'm trading my own position—

CONNOR: Oh lighten up. I blundered. You were right, Snowpea. I can't possibly love you. You're my fucking trainee. Goddamn overhead. You should
trust me after all we've been through. [*beat*] Now get your *boss* some more
tickets.

DIANA: Yes, Jammer.

[DIANA *exits.* CONNOR *picks up the phone and dials a restaurant*]

CONNOR: Yes, Antoine, I'd like to make reservations for two Humans at eight
PM. Merci beaucoup. Ça va bien. [CONNOR *hangs up and retrieves* DIANA's
records of trades] Two humans. Trusting. [CONNOR *rips* DIANA's *records,
dumps them in the wastebasket, and urinates on them*] Great fucking story,
but . . . "I would prefer not to. I would prefer not to."

[*Blackout*]

END OF SCENE ONE

SCENE TWO

SETTING: Trading floor, October.

AT RISE: JEFFERSON, BILL, and DIANA are calculating profit and loss. KENT is
hovering.

JEFFERSON: Personally, I think it's overblown gas. Indigestion. The new gasoline taxes mixed in with anxiety over the free trade agreement have totally freaked the markets out.

BILL: If we don't make fucking megabucks, we're going to be replaced by cheap Mexicans. Or worse.

JEFFERSON: Robots and rednecks.

KENT: So how much are we up or down on the week? C'mon folks, I thought we were fucking math majors. Einsteins.

JEFFERSON: I'm up 56 grand.

KENT: For the entire week? Shit, we should have all gone on vacation.

BILL: Why the fucking rush?

KENT: Because management rushes and tackles. Wake up, Bill. Rushing is what top management tackles best.

BILL: I'm down 37. I also had to spend a lot of time rushing around this week, with Jammer gone and all.

KENT: Well, D.K.? And your bottom line is?

DIANA: Depends. Bill?

BILL: Go ahead, slam dunk.

DIANA: I'm up 88, I think.

JEFFERSON: Eighty-eight? Congratulations, way to go.

BILL: How humiliating. Beaten by a chick fillet.

KENT: Super, D.K.; what do you say I buy you a drink to celebrate and you catch me up on your fantastic progress.

DIANA: I'd love to.

KENT: Fabulous. Bring me a copy of your work and let's hop.

DIANA: I can't, I mean, shouldn't we wait until Jammer doublechecks my ledger?

KENT: What the hell for?

DIANA: I promised.

KENT: If this is your way of bracing me for a loss, D.K., I want to know now. Not later. Because if you have something to confess later, I'm kicking your sweet ass over to Trinity Church. Women do not get special treatment.

DIANA: I didn't lose money.

KENT: You sure? Then why consult loverboy?

DIANA: Ninety-nine percent certain that I'm up 88 grand.

KENT: Bill, please tell me why D.K. is trading a half-billion dollar position if she only *thinks* she can add and subtract. If she can't tell the difference between a jackpot and a jackass.

BILL: Looks like 88 to me, Kent. Jammer gave her all these rules, like how a Midget 9 always trades a certain spread over a seven-year Treasury note, and we were going to straighten things out with him when he got back. Can't it wait a few more days? We owe Jammer a decent vacation. He's such a funny guy. Cracks me up, buys me lunch.

KENT: Why don't we just call him? Fax him an urgent note?

BILL: As your manager I thought of that, but you see, it's hard to do this over the phone.

DIANA: We don't exactly have his number.

KENT: Oh you must know where he is.

DIANA: He mentioned the sand on Saint Thomas.

JEFFERSON: Jammer was calling nonstop. Collect.

DIANA: Dickering over prices. Driving me berserk.

BILL: We couldn't get anything done. So I ordered him to stop calling.

KENT: And he stopped, like that?

BILL: For once he listened to me.

JEFFERSON: Can you imagine?

DIANA: We never got around to asking him for his number.

JEFFERSON: We were more concerned for his mental health.

BILL: He accepted my authority.

KENT: I can't fucking believe my ears. Is it fair to say none of you know what to think? Or is it you guys don't think at all?

DIANA: I don't think Jammer's rules apply, but he's my partner. My good friend.

BILL: He's our brother.

JEFFERSON: Crazy brother.

KENT: Bill, how much profit do you think Tapir's mortgage desk generated this year?

BILL: A billion.

KENT: How much of that do you think you've each contributed? Not all at once now.

[*There is a pause before* BILL, JEFFERSON, *and* DIANA *answer simultaneously*]

BILL: Eighty percent.

JEFFERSON: Fifty.

DIANA: Twenty-five.

KENT: How would you recalculate the percentages, Bill, if your future depended on these estimates?

BILL: Jesus, Kent, the market crashed on everyone today. We agreed to meet some traders from Semen Brothers half an hour ago. To plot strategy and defense. We should all go and mine truth. Before the market drowns us in our own blood.

KENT: I want an accurate P and L. I don't care if it takes you all night.

BILL: Normally I'd agree with you 100 percent, but the market is too slippery—

JEFFERSON: It's crucial we find out what paper they're seeing and how much. For the long run.

DIANA: Then I should go too.

JEFFERSON: Relax. We promise to relay all the gossip on the Street.

KENT: As head trader, Bill, I do expect you to shoulder more responsibility.

BILL: Shit, Kent, all these fucking expectations are killing me. Do this, do that, *and* make fucking tons of money. D.K.'s a big chick. She beat us fair and square today.

DIANA: Go ahead. Save me a seat in case.

KENT: Alright, go.But I want a total figure by nine AM.

[JEFFERSON *and* BILL *exit*]

KENT: You and Jammer have grossed 460 million dollars worth of profit this year. Close to half a billion dollars. Broken a record. I'm mighty proud of you two.

DIANA: Thanks, Kent.

KENT: How much did you personally contribute to that 460 million, if you had to guess?

DIANA: Kent, I can't really say because—

KENT: You have no guts?

DIANA: Because I'm a team player.

KENT: Jammer called me this morning. Said Semen Brothers offered him triple his salary. I can't match it. So he quit. Ancient history. But I figure I saved Tapir thousands and thousands of dollars because I have half the winning team that booked record earnings. You're a big Hollywood producer, stars everywhere. Isn't that right? Reassure me, D.K. Tell me I made a damn smart decision.

DIANA: No way he quit. He'd tell me first.

KENT: Why? Are you two lovers?

DIANA: No, but still . . . he has to pick up his effects and say good-bye.

KENT: Oh really? You can't even reach him. Nobody has his number. How well does anyone know anyone else, D.K.? What do you know about me? I don't know jackshit about you, where you live, whether you're happy here.

DIANA: You were a hippie Democrat, an ex-Marine. You voted for Gene Mc-Carthy and drove a school bus. Now your wife collects art and you summer at Martha's Vineyard. As for me, what do you want to know—

KENT: I can't help but wonder who you are, D.K. I mean, less than a year ago, you said you wanted to make 450 million over your entire lifetime, and today with Jammer, you've hit 460. Eureka! So you must be capable of risking millions and millions of Tapir's dollars, without constant supervision? Without your boyfriend Connor?

DIANA: Definitely. Definitely have to say I'm a good trader.

KENT: Terrific, from now on you won the 15-year position. I'm also giving you a raise.

DIANA: Great. How much?

KENT: Depends. How much of that 460 million is yours? Show me your 88 grand.

DIANA: I promised to wait until Jammer got back.

KENT: Jammer jammed you. He's not coming back.

DIANA: Prove Jammer really quit.

KENT: The definition of an ex-trader is one who tries to cover up a loss. There's no appeal, no nothing. Just out. O-U-T. D.K., there is no record 460 million dollar profit, is there?

DIANA: Of course there is. Jammer will explain. He's a genius.

KENT: Either you know how to trade or you don't. Either you want to trade or you don't. Either you want to work here or you don't. Choose. In or out. No more blinking.

DIANA: [*reluctantly decides to come clean*] I studied the entire year's P and L printouts, backwards and forwards. I cannot find any 460 million dollar profit. So far.

KENT: When were you going to tell me? What was the magic number that signaled management?

DIANA: I made a fuck of a lot of money this week; how do you think I feel?

KENT: Violated. Sodomized.

DIANA: The morning printouts were fucking linguini, couldn't find the clams. Always mismarked and tangled. So at night, I rummaged through Jammer's desk, searching for his computer password, couldn't find it anywhere. Then one evening Jefferson helped me. Did you know he's a computer hack?

KENT: What's the bottom line?

DIANA: It goes way back, long before you hired me.

KENT: Give me a range.

DIANA: We never should have accessed his computer files. Jammer must know what he's doing. Isn't that why you pay him 750 thousand dollars and me 70? That's conviction. Who am I to doubt his judgment? Bill's right, why should anyone fucking believe me? I stand to gain if Jammer leaves.

KENT: [*shocked, disappointed but contained*] Bill knows too? The entire desk knows?

DIANA: Of course I told Bill. I panicked. Bill said traders often underreport income to save some money to cover losses. Losses are spread out over time like chunky peanut butter.

KENT: Of all people.

DIANA: You once traded futures and options; you know the incredible pressure. No one likes to lose money. We're only human.

KENT:I expected more from Bill. More from you.

DIANA: I must give Jammer the same chance he gave me.

KENT: Spare me. What's clear is Jammer was going to pin you with this fraud and call it beginner's luck. Isn't that why he seduced you? Maneuvered another job and skipped the country? I hired you, D.K.

DIANA: Bill said if it were some gross amount like the national deficit, we would notify you immediately.

KENT: How much?

DIANA: Ask Bill, he's the King.

KENT: Not for very much longer. D.K., a man's got a right to know if his future is long or short.

DIANA: I calculated a total loss of 150 million. It doesn't hurt to go over the numbers one more time. Something has to turn up.

KENT: Is a 150 million dollars a nice round even figure with all those pretty smiley faces.

DIANA: It's not like Tapir's going to go out of business tomorrow over a bucket of clams. We're a risk-taking firm. We're tapirs, not field mice.

KENT: Listen, sweetie, the rumor on the street is Tapir is cash rich. Tapir is a galaxy of supernovas. Several companies are offering to buy all or part of us. It's a dream come true. But the truth is we're not doing as well as everyone thinks. Govvies took a bloodbath. Corporates are sinking. And now this 150 million dollar surprise. [*more to himself*] How long can we keep this secret? Now who can we get to buy us? Now I know how it feels to be a farmer. My plans are fucking ruined. Overnight.

DIANA: Let's not race to conclusions. We don't know what the truth is yet.

KENT: Give me one solid reason why I shouldn't fire you. Guilty by association.

DIANA: I'm not a fucking criminal, Kent. Innocent before proven guilty.

KENT: Good point. Let's keep everything under our hats. But if I ever find out you dipped your hands in the honeypot, you can kiss your dolce vita good-bye.

DIANA: You won't, because I didn't. I made fuckwads of money, I swear.

KENT: You mean those phantom profits? Please don't make me laugh. Maybe you are an awesome producer, but you had better show me proof. Proof beyond a reasonable doubt, because in this business an indictment stings forever. What ever happened to the whole truth and nothing but the truth?

DIANA: What happened to the truth shall set you free? To the truth shall be an absolute defense.

[*Fadeout as* DIANA *searches for P & L documents*]

END OF SCENE TWO

SCENE THREE

SETTING: Trading floor, next Friday, early evening.

AT RISE:DIANA is writing tickets and calculating P & L after the market has closed. Everyone else has gone home. CONNOR enters.

CONNOR: And here's Jammer!

DIANA: What are you doing here? Why didn't you call? You better leave before Kent sees you. You and me together. Please hide.

CONNOR: Tell me you missed me. I missed you. I couldn't wait until Monday to see your face.

DIANA: Stop diminishing me. I can't like you anymore. Now.

CONNOR: You rupture some arteries?

DIANA: I'm up on the day, but it doesn't matter, does it?

CONNOR: Today's your last day. I came to pick you up.

DIANA: [*distressed*] Am I fired?

CONNOR: I got us new jobs over at Semen Brothers. Generous dental plans too.

DIANA: Triple your salary?

CONNOR: And double yours! Shit, I wanted it to be a surprise. You don't look too happy—

DIANA: Are you for fucking real? Kent told me you quit.

CONNOR: Does that mean the bed wetter refuses to match our offers? He sounded flexible the last time I spoke to him.

DIANA: Why did you tell Kent before me?

CONNOR: [*hands her gift box*] I told you, it was my surprise. Here, got you a present. Impressed? [*puts scarf on her*] Your hair rustling in my brand new Porsche Turbo as we drive into sunsets and skylines. That's why I bought you a scarf; you have no excuse. I'm giving you a ride home. Ready? [*dangles keys*]

DIANA: I'm staying here.

CONNOR: D.K., you're masochistic. What's wrong with more money, more position?

DIANA: Nothing, if it's mine.

CONNOR: That's right, maybe now that you've got a room of your own, I can be your special late night entertainment. Where should we celebrate? Sparks?

DIANA: Jammer, I can't go anywhere with you. If you had confided in me about the 150 million, maybe everything would still be OK. Maybe.

CONNOR: You fucking bitch. D.K., you fucking vulture.

DIANA: So it's really true. It isn't a simple misunderstanding.

CONNOR: You couldn't wait to betray me. How much did you sell me out for? Kent triple your salary in exchange for your testimony?

DIANA: Where's your guilt? Kent almost fired me and sent me to jail. Defending your sorry ass has cost me my reputation and my bonus.

CONNOR: Oh. Well if this is really about your bonus, D.K.—then I can forgive you. I know you're no match against Kent—yet. Kent is pond scum, he scammed you. He'd scam us at bonus time too. But no need to cry or panic, because I saved you. I found us superior jobs. We can walk out richer and happier. Just say yes and the whole world changes. A new rainbow shines for us out there. Just say yes, please.

DIANA: [*throws lottery tickets on the desk*] I've been playing Lotto just in case. Like you, I picked losing numbers.

CONNOR: That's so sweet.

DIANA: Don't you care about all those people who might have lost their life savings? You're so calm.

CONNOR: Sure I care, but I'm not going to die over money. Christ, Diana, I thought you were more spiritual than that. Plus, you act like it's your money we lost. Like it's my fault I wasn't born a cash cow. The sad truth is everybody loses something valuable, eventually. The big L humbles us all.

DIANA: Why does Jefferson know your computer password and I don't?

CONNOR: How the hell do I know? Fucking bastard snooped over my shoulder. He's just dying to take over the desk. Same as you.

DIANA: No.

CONNOR: You act so damn high and mighty. I'd understand if we were playing football. Then it'd be your legs breaking. Your head exploding. Your body getting all smashed up. But this ain't football, D.K.

DIANA: Kent said he plans to press charges.

CONNOR: You know everyone will think we're in this together. The way I make you laugh so much, everyone naturally thinks we bone each other.

DIANA: But we don't.

CONNOR: After all, I cut a package deal for two.

[KENT *enters*]

KENT: I almost tripled your salary, Jammer. If only you hadn't been so ambitious. You had to go for platinum. Gold wasn't good enough. Record 460 million.

CONNOR: Damned straight we kicked ass. Tapir's no longer some second-rate bucket shop. I did everything you wanted and more—your 22 million dollar bonus, MVP of the year, and early retirement. Everything you asked for, Kent, I made it happen. Me. Aren't you going to say thank you?

KENT: Sure thing, Connor. Mucho gracias.

DIANA: Wait a minute, was all this planned?

CONNOR: Relax, Kent, we know you're not going to lose any of your money. You're free to leave too. And we all know you were planning to retire in God's country soon.

KENT: Yeah sure, Connor, we all are. Except now we'll have to sell the firm because of you.

DIANA: Kent said several firms have submitted offers.

CONNOR: No shit. Sell high, we can all retire in the South of France.

KENT: You mean South America.

CONNOR: I'm sorry, Kent, I really am. The market crashed on me. What was I supposed to do—kill myself? I was taking my losses one spoonful at a time. Like layaway. You both act like I did it on purpose.

KENT: You have some goddamn nerve to demand I triple your salary.

DIANA: Did he ask you to double mine?

KENT: [*nodding*] That's why your're still a suspect.

CONNOR: Kent, you're a partner. If you sell the firm now, you walk out with a killing. You can buy another firm. Move to Woodstock. Start a new film festival.

KENT: My reputation will take a beating.

CONNOR: Change your name. What's in a name?

KENT: Jammer, call Semen Brothers. Tell them you've decided to stay here. Or I'll press charges.

CONNOR: You're absolutely right, Kent. I got carried away. But only because I was scared. Scared to fail in your eyes. Look at my eyes. Full of sorrow. You're like a father to me, and you only have one father in life. I'll stay right here and we'll make it all back. We owe it to you.

DIANA: We?

CONNOR: Me and D.K. came from fucking poor families. It's not our fault. Blame the environment. How can we see and not want? It's inhuman.

DIANA: Touching, Jammer, but false. My father's a neurosurgeon at Mount Sinai.

CONNOR: You fucking bitch.

DIANA: Nobody was going to ridicule my father on the squawk box. Asking a brain surgeon if he had ping pong balls.

KENT: I don't care about personal shit as long as you produce. Even a cow knows that. D.K., call the police.

CONNOR: No need to get physical, Kent. Sure I'll call Ed. If you're sure that's what you want. [dials] Hi, is this superman, Ed? Yeah, Ed, the deal's off. I've decided to stay. Me and D.K. I know a deal's a deal, but listen, Kent coughed up more money, you understand. [After CONNOR talks for a few, KENT looks to see what line CONNOR is on and reaches for an empty phone to eavesdrop. CONNOR speeds up his delivery] Of course I still hope to work together someday soon. No problem. I'm swamped too. Bye. [CONNOR hangs up just as KENT gets on the line] Ed had to hop.

KENT: How did Ed take the news?

CONNOR: Like a true gentleman. Ed sends his love.

KENT: It's been too long since I've seen Ed. [hangs up]

KENT: You will refund us for last year's bonus.

CONNOR: No, I'm afraid I can't do that, Kent. You see I bought this ostrich farm, a ski house in Vail, and a Porsche. I'm sure you understand—didn't you already say you spent your 22 million? Because, you know, Kent, if you didn't, you can still be a partner in my ostrich farm.

DIANA: What is going on? What am I doing here?

KENT: I'll press charges. See you in court, buddy.

CONNOR: [approaches KENT to compare profiles] Good move, Kent. I've always wanted to be newsworthy and famous. And you're so photogenic. Much more so than me. Right, D.K.?

KENT: I'm curious, Jammer, what role did little D.K. play in your scam?

DIANA: Please, Connor.

CONNOR: Now who's shaking? Think you know me so fucking well, D.K.? You're nothing. D.K. has nothing to do with anything because she's nothing. Zero times any number is still zero.

DIANA: Thanks, Jammer.

KENT: Clean out your desk. D.K., make sure he only takes personal items.

DIANA: Kent, it wasn't necessary to lie to me.

KENT: But I didn't lie. Jammer, did you quit? Or did you get axed?

CONNOR: I quit.

KENT: My powers to foresee the future are simply amazing.

CONNOR: You have no fucking heart, Kent. You were a trader before you sold out. You know that everybody loses. What I did is perfectly human. Sooner or later, we're all casualties. You should be thanking me for making you so goddamn rich.

KENT: No appeal. [exits]

CONNOR: What are you staring at? You act like nobody ever bleeds.

DIANA: Were you going to stick me with that loss? Were you ever going to tell me?

CONNOR: I protected you. Can't you get that through your head?

DIANA: I want the truth.

CONNOR: You turned me in. What is truth but self-improvement?

DIANA: Truth is some Jackson Pollack painting, all splattered across an innocent canvas.

CONNOR: [confused, makes a face reacting to DIANA's comment] Ask yourself why you trust an ex-hippie to look out for your best interests. Is that so bright? Didn't Kent double-cross you? He lied to both of us. You lied to me, too—about your dad.

DIANA: That was way before we became buddies. You could have bothered to ask.

CONNOR: Guess you're right, Snowpea. Truth is a painting. The oil never dries. A few brush strokes here, splash of color there, complete different picture.

DIANA: I almost went away with you.

CONNOR: You still can. Don't forget, I'm giving you your dream of a lifetime. A job that surpasses all this shit. Colossal upside potential. You're gonna despise yourself in the morning when you wake up here, making cow chips instead of blue chips. What did Kent ever give you?

DIANA: Respect. Opportunity. Position. I can't be partners with someone I can't believe in, or recognize.

CONNOR: Big fucking deal. Look to your left, look to your right. Everyone lies, cheats, and steals, given the opportunity. We can't help it. Human nature is evil. It's very well-documented in the Bible.

DIANA: And you said you loved me. I don't know how to feel about you anymore.

CONNOR: It can't be love until someone's heart is broken. [beat] But if you have any business sense, D.K., you know it's in both our best interest to stay friends, the 15-year market being such an enigma. We get together, discuss the market, spot the trends over a bloody steak, vintage Amarone. Play another stimulating round of Truth or Dare.

DIANA: Yes, the usual. But what for? Without trust there is nowhere to go.

CONNOR: Trust is a fucking dinosaur. [*imitates his father, showing how his father played with him*] My father used to pick me up and throw me in the air. He bounced me way up high. Sometimes he'd pretend I was a missile. Sometimes a plane. Zoom zoom zoom. "UFOs sighted." "Say hi to the UFOs, Connor." "Oh no, UFOs have decided to take us hostage and torture us." "Prepare for crash landing." He'd twirl me in the air, dip me abruptly, threatening to drop me. "Sudden turbulence." "Dangerous air pocket." I giggled and smiled high up in the air because it's thrilling to touch the ceiling. Because my father loves me. My father will protect me. Father and son soaring high in the sky together. What could be more beautiful? I loved him so much. But he drops me. He fucking *drops* me.

DIANA: I don't fucking believe you anymore. Tell me, why should I?

CONNOR: Luckily he dropped me on a soft mattress. Otherwise I'd be fucking dead.

DIANA: You never cease to amaze me.

CONNOR: My father shook his index finger at me and said, "NEVER EVER TRUST ANYONE COMPLETELY."

DIANA: Great, Connor, so the only way to protect yourself is to fuck over everyone else. How fucking mature.

CONNOR: My own father drops me from the ceiling. In my own bedroom. He kept laughing and laughing like I was some goddamned joke.

DIANA: I'm terribly sorry, Jammer, I really am. But mostly I pity you. Because without something to believe in or hope for, you might as well be dead.

[*Blackout*]

END OF SCENE THREE

SCENE FOUR

SETTING: Trading floor, the following February.

AT RISE: JEFFERSON, BILL, and DIANA are trading.

KENT: [*V.O. squawk box*] Tapir is proud to announce that we have a new partner in the ever-changing global economy, Samurai Brothers. As you may know Samurai Brothers is a premiere investment banking house headquartered in Tokyo. Samurai Brothers, like Tapir, Inc., recognizes the importance of international markets and has agreed to join forces. Samurai is committed to Tapir's future, a very lucrative future. So committed they've already pumped 750 million dollars in us—750 million dollars! Let's give a warm welcome to Samurai Brothers.

BILL: What the fuck! Japs are taking over?

KENT: [V.O., *squawk box*] I repeat, this is not a hostile takeover. We courted Samurai Brothers to enable us to penetrate Japanese and Japanese-driven markets. Think of it as a friendly joint venture. A marriage of convenience. However, we will be changing our name to Samurai Brothers.

BILL: If the name changes, it's a takeover.

JEFFERSON: Why are we the last to know?

KENT: [V.O., *squawk box*] I'd also like you to join me in welcoming Hiro Watanabe. Hiro was an excellent long bond trader from Samurai's Tokyo office. He will be joining the mortgage desk. Temporarily.

DIANA: What? Have you know about this all along, Bill?

BILL: I'm fucking pissed myself. Don't you guys trust me?

DIANA and JEFFERSON: No.

BILL: Jammer would crack a funny joke right about now. He's the funniest and scariest person I know. Tense moments like this, I kinda miss Jammer.

DIANA: Send him a love note.

JEFFERSON: He'd tune your fucking radio.

BILL: Bet he's making tons of money.

JEFFERSON: No shit, Sherlock, he's why the Japanese own our big American butts.

BILL: You should have gone over with him. We should have all gone with him.

JEFFERSON: Maybe it's not too late.

DIANA: Why is it people who lose incredible amounts of money somehow still manage to find ungodly sums of money? It should be a crime.

JEFFERSON: "Hell hath no fury like a woman scorned."

BILL: Cufflinks, I owe you five bucks. They were intimate.

JEFFERSON: Ssh. Quiet. Here they come. We promised Kent never to mention his name.

[KENT *and* HIRO *enter.* BILL, JEFFERSON, *and* DIANA *pretend to be busy on the phone*]

KENT: Folks, I'd like to introduce you to Hiro Watanabe.

HIRO: Good morning, I am Hiro Watanabe.

DIANA: *Ohayo Gazaimasu.* [*NOTE: The "u" in* Gazaimasu *is virtually silent*] My name's Diana but everyone calls me D.K.

HIRO: *Ohayo Gazaimasu.* Wonderful, you speak Japanese.

DIANA: [*gestures "a little"*] *Skoshi skoshi.*

HIRO: Nice to meet you. You Chinese?

DIANA: I know. Born in the wrong country.

KENT: D.K. trades 15-year.

HIRO: Yes, I see. Pleased to make your acquaintance. Good luck.

JEFFERSON: I'm Jefferson the Third. Like the American president, but no relation. Welcome. I trade Fannies and Freddies. [JEFFERSON *and* HIRO *shake hands*]

HIRO: Yes, I see. Hello. How are you? Pleased to meet your acquaintance. Best wishes.

KENT: And this is Bill, the head trader of the mortgage desk. Trades Ginnies.

HIRO: It is my pleasure, Bill. [HIRO *and* BILL *shake hands*]

BILL: No, my pressure. You may be a Hiro in Japan, but in America, Hero is a sandwich, and I am the King of Fixed Income.

HIRO: Yes, I see. No joke, it's all true, what I heard about you.

KENT: [*to* HIRO] He's joking. An American joke.

DIANA: Where will Hiro sit? What will Hiro trade?

BILL: I don't need Hiro. It doesn't take a fucking Hiro to trade bonds.

JEFFERSON: I don't need him either because my markets are too slow . . . [*covering*]; Hiro would be bored to death.

HIRO: Yes I see Hiro not wanted. Everybody afraid of Hiro. But fear quite unnecessary. Hiro will be very fair man. Treat Hiro right, you will go far. Very far.

KENT: Eventually, Hiro. I was thinking, D.K., that you wouldn't mind training Hiro.

DIANA: We agreed I should trade solo to quantify my net worth.

HIRO: Yes, I agree. Better I not work for this woman. I am extremely capable myself. Deserve excellent managerial position.

KENT: Of course you do, Hiro. In fact we all do. This is only temporary. Markets change so rapidly around here, even Bill has trouble keeping track. Isn't that right, Bill?

BILL: Do you have to keep dredging that up? I said I was sorry.

KENT: Samurai and Tapir are still negotiating the gritty details. Soon as we iron out those wrinkles, we'll all get something bigger and better.

HIRO: Paperwork almost finished. Is that a promise?

BILL: Kent promises everyone.

KENT: Patience, Hiro.

DIANA: Hey, if he doesn't want to learn from me, I don't want to teach him.

KENT: Cheer up, D.K., he's probably just trying to save face. You know that trick. After you train Hiro, I promise I'll promote you to a sexier product and make you a vice president. Besides, Hiro might help you turn the position around. Big money.

DIANA: I guess this means we're partners, Hiro. "It's going to be a bumpy bumpy ride."

HIRO: I know. Will *not* be my pleasure either. But I see absolutely necessary in the short run.

KENT: What troupers! Glad that's resolved. [*hinting to* BILL *to be busy*] I was explaining to Hiro that our mortgage desk is the busiest and most profitable desk on the whole floor. Aren't you busy? Because you're so busy, I'm going to introduce Hiro to the rest of the floor.

BILL: That's right. We got to jam some bonds. Yankee bonds. C'mon Jefferson, D.K., time to whippersnapper major cash flow.

HIRO: Bye bye. I'll see you all later, won't I?

[BILL, JEFFERSON, *and* DIANA *act busy*]

KENT: Let me introduce you to the corporate desk.

[KENT *and* HIRO *exit. When they are out of sight,* BILL, JEFFERSON, *and* DIANA *stop acting busy*]

BILL: Sayonara! Why does he keep repeating "Yes, I see." What does he see? What will he see. What the hell can he see?

DIANA: Watch it.

JEFFERSON: America is going out of business. Closed. For sale.

BILL: Why oh why can't Johnny read or write? Add or subtract?

JEFFERSON: It's those damned free trade agreements and illegal immigrants. Look at California.

BILL: Hey, D.K., I don't understand the appeal of Sumo wrestling. Can you explain?

DIANA: Wrong nationality, remember?

JEFFERSON: So sensitive. He's just teasing.

DIANA: If we want to keep our jobs, we better behave.

JEFFERSON: She has a point. We've just been taken over; who knows what happens next.

BILL: It's your job, D.K., to tune Cato's radio. He's your trainee. Your slave. Use him well.

JEFFERSON: How's it feel to graduate?

DIANA: Depends. Where am I going?

BILL: As the King, I say you show him who's boss. Show us you got what it takes.

DIANA: I can't. Kent's keeping very close tabs on me.

BILL: He's watching me, too, but I'm no jellyfish.

DIANA: Cufflinks, you're safe, you do it.

JEFFERSON: Oh no, I think you should show him who's in charge together. You two need to make up.

DIANA: Why me? I'm just a chick fillet.

BILL: Even chicks have to preserve the pecking order.

JEFFERSON: I'm counting on you guys. After all, you're America's youth.

BILL: The Battle of Midway has begun. What are you thinking, D.K.?

DIANA: For 750 million dollars, we ought to cooperate.

BILL: I'm going to keep my eye on you, D.K. Either you're a bona fide American, or you're another goddamned foreigner. Choose.

[*Blackout*]

END OF SCENE FOUR

SCENE FIVE

SETTING: Trading floor, April.

AT RISE: JEFFERSON, BILL, DIANA are throwing away their shaving cream cans, nipple toys, and other prankster possessions. Chinese money cat (one raised paw) has been placed on the desk in response to a memo request: "Please no more cursing." HIRO is seated with DIANA.

BILL: How dare the Japanese tell us to clean our fucking mouths. Cut down on our pranks. How are we supposed to release the fucking pressure, chained to our fucking desks.

HIRO: [*opens money cat*] Please deposit 75 cents, Bill. You cursed three times.

JEFFERSON: Isn't civilization fun? The money pays for our Christmas party.

BILL: This is a direct attack on me.

HIRO: Could be. I suggest you be more careful.

BILL: What's that supposed to mean, Cato?

HIRO: Japan is the land of the *rising* sun, and soon I will rise like the sun.

BILL: That's it. I'm going to set your sun where it don't shine.

JEFFERSON: Hey hey, chill. Don't fuck up, Bill. Or I just might have to succeed you.

[HIRO *motions* JEFFERSON *to deposit 25 cents in money cat*]

DIANA: Kent has asked us many times to act more corporate.

BILL: Swearing is a fundamental American right.

JEFFERSON: We can say "fu-kayed" instead. Sounds French.

[HIRO *doesn't buy it, points to the cat*]

DIANA: *Allez vous faire foutre!* Sounds so classy but I just told you to fuck off. [*deposits 25 cents*]

HIRO: I teach Japanese curse words if everybody like. Kusotaré.

DIANA/JEFFERSON: Kusotaré.

HIRO: Means shithead.

HIRO/DIANA/JEFFERSON: [*all looking at* BILL] Kusotaré.

HIRO: Bakayarō.

DIANA/JEFFERSON: Bakayarō.

HIRO: Means stupid asshole.

HIRO/DIANA/JEFFERSON: [*all looking at* BILL] Bakayarō.

BILL: There ain't nothing like an American "fuck." [*deposits 25 cents into money cat*]

DIANA: [*deposits quarter into money cat*] Fuck is so perfect and complete.

HIRO: [*deposits quarter for every obscenity*] Yes, I see very true. Fuck fuck here, fuck fuck there. Everywhere, everybody say fuck fuck. So much fun. Gets expensive.

JEFFERSON: Save it for extreme emergencies.

BILL: This is payback for World War II.

JEFFERSON: I can't stand the after-hours strategy meetings. Hiro, why do your people believe in consensus so much?

HIRO: I think it is good to make everybody happy. Don't you think it's worth a try?

BILL: [*honestly*] What kind of camera do you recommend I buy, Hiro?

HIRO: Cheap one. Since you so cheap.

JEFFERSON: He got you there.

DIANA: If you hate this place so much, why don't you quit?

BILL: And give up? Did John Wayne fucking quit at Iwo Jima? [*into squawk box phone*] Salesfarce, Uncle Sam needs you. We're living under enemy occupation. I ask all of you to call your customers on behalf of the Stars and Stripes and ask them to buy a bond today. Any bond. Every bond goes toward buying us back from the foreigners.

JEFFERSON: [*reluctantly, into squawk box phone*] A bond for Uncle Sam and Fay Wray.

BILL: D.K., your turn at bat.

DIANA: Red, white, and blue are my favorite colors.

BILL: I have a question, D.K. When you're watching the Olympics and a Chinese guy comes up against an American, who do you root for?

DIANA: I am a full-fledged American. I weighed 55 pounds when I became a citizen. I was practically born here.

JEFFERSON: Practically.

DIANA: OK, so I can't be president, but it's a lousy job.

HIRO: Hiro curious too. Who would you root for? The Chinese or the American.

DIANA: My American citizenship papers are irreplaceable. Do you know what that means?

HIRO: Means she votes American.

BILL: Now what if a Chinese American guy is competing against a regular American guy? Who do you pick then?

DIANA: I don't have anything to prove to you.

BILL: Bullshit, I've never met a woman who didn't have something to prove.

JEFFERSON: Me neither.

HIRO: Yes, me too. Women all the same everywhere. Such a tragedy.

BILL: Who do you root for to win?

DIANA: I don't know, the best person.

HIRO: Honestly?

BILL: Say the two are equally talented, equally cute, equally likable, then who?

DIANA: Then it doesn't matter, does it?

BILL: Answer my question.

DIANA: I want both to win.

BILL: One winner, one loser.

DIANA: I'm not choosing.

HIRO: You must choose. Pick Chinese American.

BILL: Why don't you two go back to wherever it is you came from?

DIANA: I'm from America. You want your radio tuned? Cufflinks, help me change the King's public station.

HIRO: Yes, things must change very soon.

JEFFERSON: Pipe down, everybody. We all need to breathe deeply and rechannel our hostilities. One for all, all for one, the four Tapirs, right?

HIRO: Four Samurais! Long live four samurais! [HIRO *draws imaginary sword with pen and slices the air several strokes*]

DIANA: Hiro, would you mind getting some coffees for the desk? Please. Let me give you some money.

HIRO: No I buy. How about something good to eat? Maybe chili dogs and cheese fries. [*exits*]

BILL: You make me puke with those manners. Why you so goddamn sweet to Cato? Giving him all our trade secrets for free. Learning a few Japanese phrases. *Skoshi skoshi.*

DIANA: [*into squawk box phone*] Salesfarce, Uncle Sam needs you to stand up for bald eagles and social security. Triple commission offered all day on all bonds. [*hangs up squawk box. To* BILL *and* JEFFERSON] Satisfied? Home run?

BILL: I never once heard you call him Cato. I never once saw you tune his radio.

DIANA: Sure I have. Plenty of times.

BILL: If there were no witnesses, it didn't happen.

JEFFERSON: How about you, Bill? Have you tuned Hiro's radio?

BILL: *Moi?*

JEFFERSON: We follow our fearless leader. Lead us to the promised land, Bill.

DIANA: Isn't it enough that he was expecting something much better?

JEFFERSON: We've all been down that dirt road how many times?

BILL: Traitor.

[HIRO *enters, carrying four cups of coffee, shows* DIANA *which is which, takes his and orders her to serve. Reluctantly, she serves and the guys chuckle*]

HIRO: Two regular, one light, one black. Come on, come on, Diana, please . . . I can't.

BILL: [*takes his coffee from* DIANA] Fucking tune his radio, D.K.!

DIANA: You're the King, you do it.

JEFFERSON: [*takes his coffee from* DIANA] Scissors are in the top drawer.

DIANA: He doesn't understand our pranks are really tokens of affection.

HIRO: [*oblivious to others, into his phone*] I speak and understand English perfectly. Hello? Hello? Moshi moshi.

BILL: Isn't this what your women's movement is about? You bust our balls, you scratch for our position, but when you finally crawl on top, you don't know what the fuck to do? You just want to sit and bitch.

JEFFERSON: We haven't got all fucking day. We got positions to watch, you know.

HIRO: Oi, oi, oi, please, fill or kill your orders, quickly, I'm very busy too. OK!

[*This drives* DIANA *and* BILL]

BILL: We do it together. D.K., you grab the scissors.

JEFFERSON: You better cry for help, HIRO. American custom.

[BILL *grabs hold of* HIRO; DIANA *gets scissors*]

HIRO: [*unaware*] Only if that would please you. Help! Help. I'm being attacked by very ugly Americans.

BILL: Pretend you're going to castrate him!

[HIRO *crosses his legs*]

HIRO: Please let go of me. You will be very sorry because I am Hiro Watanabe. Tell them, Jefferson. *Namenna-yo!*

JEFFERSON: I can't hear any music.

BILL: Change the fucking radio station, D.K. I don't speak Japanese. Not the Spanish station either. [DIANA *snips* HIRO's *tie and tunes his radio*] Rock and roll [BILL *lets* HIRO *go*]

DIANA: You happy now?

BILL: Encore!

JEFFERSON: Isn't it cathartic, Hiro?

DIANA: It means you're one of us—

HIRO: Never—

JEFFERSON: Releases all this bad karma. Now we can all be friends again.

HIRO: No, never. I am not afraid of you. Soon you will all be very sorry because I am Hiro Watanabe.

BILL: He thinks he's a Hiro. What's his name, D.K.? Remind him.

DIANA: Excuse me, but I have to trade. [*picks up squawk box*] Salesfarce, we are a strong seller. Please call me on the inside for a custom-tailored deal.

HIRO: That was my favorite tie.

DIANA: It's just a tie.

HIRO: I demand real apology.

BILL: [*to* JEFFERSON] Who we betting on?

DIANA: I did you a favor, Hiro. It was hurting your neck; you couldn't breathe.

JEFFERSON: [*to* BILL] Always bet on the winner.

HIRO: I trusted you. I thought we were friends. Both of us, we have same face.

DIANA: It hasn't got a damn thing to do with your people or my people. It's about respect.

HIRO: Diana—let me explain who I am—

DIANA: No, here I am, doing my best to get you up to speed and you treat me like your geisha girl. So from now on, you're my good-for-nothing piece-of-shit trainee. When I dish, you shit, you say yum yum and ask for seconds. You smile too. You got it?

HIRO: Yum Yum. So ugly. I think not, D.K. I did not come to America to eat shit. Sometimes I have to wonder why I even bother to come to America

. . . *Koji Oji-san* promise me great prosperity. If everybody so anti-Japanese, why Kent invite *Koji Oji-san* to buy him out. American values, all sliced up like pieces of stale bread.

DIANA: *Koji Oji-san?* Are you referring to the President of Samurai Brothers?

HIRO: But of course I am.

DIANA: [*mumbling to herself*] I thought his name was Koji Suzuki . . . *Oji-san* . . . [*realizes*] Does that mean Koji Suzuki is your—

HIRO: SSH, please be more quiet.

DIANA: Pack up, Hiro, we gotta hop.

HIRO: Are you not scared I'll seek revenge? Too late, Miss Diana—

DIANA: Not if you want exactly what they have. I make Tapir fuckwads of money. I'm profitable, I'm honest, so where's my reward? Why shouldn't I have what they have? And why shouldn't you?

[*Blackout*]

END OF SCENE FIVE

SCENE SIX

SETTING: Trading floor. May. First thing in the morning.

AT RISE: KENT enters with a small box for DIANA.

KENT: Congratulations, Miss Vice President. Just a token of our deepest appreciation. A reminder we all think you're terrific.

DIANA: [*opens box*] Wow! A scarf with our company logo. Tapirs. How versatile. Thanks.

KENT: I even took the liberty of ordering you new business cards.

JEFFERSON: Welcome to the club, sport.

BILL: Now you wait around 5, 10, 15 years to make partner. Like me. Maybe.

DIANA: Listen, Hiro is perfectly capable of trading the 15-year position by himself. I'm ready to move on to bigger and better.

KENT: Is that right, Hiro?

HIRO: Of course it is, Kent. Please.

KENT: Well D.K., I know I promised you a sexier product with wider spreads, irresistible angles. The smell of arbitrage wafting through the air like hickory smoked bacon.

DIANA: Sizzling bacon.

KENT: Certainly you should have been promoted long ago. Entirely Jammer's fault. Fact remains sometimes lightning strikes same place twice.

DIANA: Oh no, don't tell me I'm stuck trading the same thing, fucking gnomes and nongnomes. [*off* KENT] You mean this scarf is some sort of consolation prize? Do I at least get a raise?

KENT: Sure do, 10 percent.

DIANA: Kent, you swore—

KENT: Chin up, D.K., you got your whole life ahead of you. You never know, bulls might storm the capital tomorrow. Desk doing well, Bill?

BILL: Banging harder than ever. Staging my comeback. The King lives on.

KENT: Wonderful. Folks, I'm outta here! The Japanese bought out my contract.

HIRO: *Yosh!* Sake for everyone.

KENT: The Japanese are very generous people. I bet you didn't know that.

BILL: Kent, is this another prank to punish me for Jammer? You want me to admit I fucked up on the squawk box? It's unjust to blame me for everything.

KENT: Shit, you know, it sears me to know how unfair life is. But, folks, markets keep changing on us. Creative destruction is a simple fact of life. Samurai promised us that as long as our return on equity was better than 20 percent, we'd have no interference from them. But Tapir failed to live up to great expectations.

JEFFERSON: No fucking way we lost.

BILL: Rematch.

DIANA: How much?

KENT: It appears Tapir fell short by about 150 million. What we get taking risks. For being a full service firm. Now I understand why everybody's so damn conservative. Even reactionary.

BILL: Please, 150, that's chump change.

KENT: Twenty percent. That was the deal.

HIRO: Deal's a deal. No more, no less.

JEFFERSON: No shit.

KENT: No such thing as friendly takeover. Oxymoron. Sure wish I could do more for everyone. You know how it is. My hands are tied. Out of my control.

BILL: Where you going? We'll follow. Hire us away.

KENT: Really wish I could but I'm moving to Montana.

HIRO: Oh really? You know, Japan is approximately the size of the Montana.

JEFFERSON: Fascinating, Hiro. Kent, what's in Montana?

KENT: "*Oro y plata.*" Gold and Silver. That's the state motto.

BILL: We can open a bucket shop there and fly fish in the slow afternoons.

DIANA: What's going to happen to us? To me?

HIRO: Time to explain, Kent.

KENT: Don't be so impulsive. Management is by nature brimming with optimists. That's what you all must be with Hiro as your new managing director.

HIRO: Thank God finally official. Paperwork finished. Many times I almost quit.

KENT: Yes. Now the mess is all yours.

BILL: What the fuck, Kent? When did this all happen? Cash me out. I resign.

HIRO: *Yosh.* Finally!

BILL: If you force me to stay, I'll lose money on purpose. Hiro, please buy me out.

HIRO: Oh no, my English never good enough for you. Speak to my new head trader, Mister Jefferson.

JEFFERSON: *Arigato, Hiro-san.*

HIRO: *Dōmo itashimashité.*

DIANA: Congratulations, Jeffer-san. Did you know?

JEFFERSON: [*gesturing "a little"*] *Skoshi skoshi.*

BILL: Why didn't you say something? Such a liar. After all I've done for you.

JEFFERSON: [*imitating* BILL *from* Scene 2] "I was going to tell you later—today." Bill, D.K., I'm certain we can work something out. After all what are colleagues for?

BILL: I fucking quit.

HIRO: Oh no, I'm afraid Samurai Brothers owns your signed contract. Very expensive to hire brilliant lawyer, but totally up to you— [*off* BILL] Come on, Bill, don't sweat, I still let you trade Ginnies.

DIANA: I can't fucking believe this. I'm sick of being the lowest-paid trader on the desk. Why shouldn't I be compensated for my dashed hopes? You all are.

KENT: Now now, D.K. you're overreacting. You'd be crazy to leave. Soon as you step out that door, your phones stop ringing. Left with busy signals and no answer. Every business is the same. Fungible. Except nobody pays you like we do and markets always come back with a vengeance.

JEFFERSON: But then again, no one can blame you for quitting. I just know everyone will miss you, especially me.

[*Everyone nods*]

HIRO: Bill, D.K., what will you two do all day? Eat cheese and drink beer?

BILL: You got me. Everybody I know's got to work.

DIANA: Who said I was quitting?

KENT: Naturally we all thought . . . isn't that where you were leading?

BILL: It's perfectly understandable . . .

DIANA: Hiro, allow me to shed a lot of light on that 150 million dollar surprise. Floodlights. Everyone will melt like ice cream. Tell your Uncle Koji to call a top management meeting, it's an emergency.

KENT: Koji Suzuki's your uncle?

HIRO: What shall I say is the emergency exactly?

DIANA: Extortion. Coverup. Front page exposé.

KENT: Shit, D.K., it's brutal out there. Think real hard about your future. You'd be crazy to sue. Massive layoffs and restructuring. Do you want everyone to get sacked?

DIANA: Of course not. Triple my salary, guarantee my bonus, and guarantee me a position trading with Bill.

BILL: Wait a fucking minute. I'm not sharing my prestige and position.

HIRO: Kent, D.K., I demand to know what the hell is going on.

KENT: Hiro-san, I had no idea D.K. was such a disgruntled employee.

DIANA: Hiro, you will get deported for being embroiled in scandal. If you're lucky. Otherwise it's jail. American jail.

KENT: [in a tough manner] Oh please, D.K., who do you think you're kidding, arbitration would side with us. Tapir bet too heavily on high risk, high return. Happens now and then.

JEFFERSON: No question, every lawyer, every judge will rule against you. It may take a while, but we'll win.

DIANA: Montana's really far away. Count the miles, Kent.

BILL: Hey, you guys, do something, my future's at stake too.

KENT: Calm down, D.K. Man is by nature a rational being.

DIANA: Don't bet on it.

KENT: Hiro-san, may I share a few private moments with you?

DIANA: Fill or kill. You said yourself, only prisoners serve time.

[KENT whispers a few things to HIRO while DIANA packs some things into her briefcase. DIANA overhears]

HIRO: Is that so? Fucking serious? Bakayarō! Kent, you really disturb me!

KENT: She's bluffing.

DIANA: You hope. And we all know what happens to our fucking hopes.

HIRO: I don't think so, Kent. American legal system not pretty. Really not necessary for Samurai Brothers to go on prime time TV.

JEFFERSON: Economy's so damn slow right now we can't afford to lose any more business.

HIRO: I just arrived in America.

KENT: And I already sold my penthouse.

HIRO: OK, OK, we settle like true samurai, we triple your salary. Guarantee you bonus and position with Bill—

BILL: No fucking way, dude, you're supposed to protect my interests; I'm stunned—

HIRO: American women, so demanding—

KENT: I'm certain you'll still make gazillions, Bill. Can't you see we got problems to solve?

JEFFERSON: We start layoffs Friday. Oops, shit! Sorry, Hiro-san—

BILL: I still get my minimum, right?

HIRO: A contract's a contract.

BILL: Alright, I'm staying, but only for the money. Not for the glamour, or the hot chicks.

KENT: Sensational, everything's settled. Good luck, everybody. I know you'll be fine, born to bang. God, I love the Japanese. You will too. Wonderful bunch of people. Take good care of them, Hiro-san.

HIRO: Thank you, Kent, I will.

JEFFERSON: Best wishes.

BILL: Maybe someday we can open a bucket shop and fly fish in the slow afternoons.

KENT: Marvelous resilience. Keep a stiff upper lip. Think of the Marines.

HIRO: OK, OK, party's over. Come on, come on. Everybody back to work.

JEFFERSON: That's right, Bill. Let's jam. [*sits in* BILL'*s chair*]

HIRO: D.K., first I go buy some breakfast, then later you come to my office, draw up official contracts—

[HIRO *exits*]

DIANA: *Oro y plata.* [*picks up squawk box*] Salesfarce, D.K. here. From now on I'll be co-trading Ginnie Maes.

KENT: You're lucky I'm sick of the godammned business. I can't fucking believe you almost spilled our precious secret to them. Where's your company pride, D.K.?

DIANA: Our new owners, whoever they may be, deserve the truth. To know exactly what and who they're buying.

KENT: Is this little victory worth it? You should be ashamed of yourself, selling us out so cheap to the opposition—

DIANA: Drop the bullshit, Kent. Hiro told me you practically begged Koji to buy us.

KENT: Who do you think are, D.K.? The Red Cross? As managing director, my responsibility is to the firm. Shit, D.K., did you expect me to liquidate Tapir and call *60 Minutes?* My duty. If I didn't find a buyer quick, the whole firm would be out on the street, begging for work.

DIANA: Kent, you told me honesty was an open-door policy—

KENT: And you think you're going to make partner, honestly—

DIANA: That's why I asked for a solid position; I could have demanded a huge payoff. But I just can't accept that there isn't a way to win without losing your self.

KENT: Please, you'll end up like I did, bankrupt, driving a dilapidated school bus, wondering if you're the only buffoon left observing the speed limit—

DIANA: No risk, no reward. [*sees a trade flash, grabs a phone, talks to broker*] Talk to me, how many buyers?

KENT: Well, I better hop. Takes a long time to get to Montana. Gold and silver.

DIANA: Good luck. *Semper fi.* [KENT *exits.* DIANA *resumes talking into phone to broker*] I'm in; I sell 7.

BILL: Whatcha doing that for? You gotta clear your trades with me. C'mon, move over, D.K., give a man some space—[*elbows for more room*]

DIANA: If I were you, Bill, I'd focus on the flashing green lights because you never know—Tomorrow yen down, dollar up.

[*Blackout*]

END OF SCENE SIX

END OF PLAY

Kimchee and Chitlins

a play in two acts
by
ELIZABETH WONG

Originally produced at Victory Gardens Theatre in Chicago and subsequently produced at West Coast Ensemble in Los Angeles.

CHARACTERS
One woman, eight-person chorus
(three women, five men, multiracial, multiple roles)

SUZIE SEETO	a television reporter
MARK THOMPSON	the news director
TARA SULLIVAN	the television anchor

A BLACK CHORUS
(three actors)

THE REVEREND LONNIE CARTER	an activist
BARBER JAMES "SMOKEMAN" BROWN	a barber
NURSE RUTH BETTY	a nurse

A KOREAN CHORUS
(three actors)

GROCER KEY CHUN MAK   a store owner
SOOMI MAK, the niece   the store cashier
WILLIE MAK, the nephew   a store worker

In addition, actors double in the following:

MATILDA DUVET, a Haitian woman, played by SUZIE SEETO

HAITIAN MAN, played by BARBER BROWN

BLACK MAN WITH EYEPATCH, played by REVEREND CARTER

BLACK BOY WITH SCARS, a gangbanger, played by BARBER BROWN

MEDIATOR, played by MARK THOMPSON

THE JUDGE IN HIS SARTORIAL SPLENDOR, played by MARK THOMPSON

POLICEMAN IN RIOT GEAR, played by MARK THOMPSON

PACK OF REPORTERS, played by CHORUS

KOREAN CHURCH WOMAN, played by SOOMI MAK

KOREAN MAN WITH WHITE APRON, played by WILLIE MAK

A PAKISTANI NEWS VENDOR, played by GROCER MAK

OFFSTAGE VOICE/STAGE MANAGER, played by WILLIE MAK

GENERAL NOTE: All roles of authority must be played by the Caucasian male, MARK THOMPSON. All characters, *including* MARK *and* TARA, must be on stage to witness the action at all times.

TIME: The Present.

PLACE: New York City.

PRODUCTION NOTES

SET: *The world of the play must be symbolic and not literal. It must reflect the humor of the play, or be humorous in some way. Color choices should be bold. Most importantly, designs must provide a "home" on stage for the Chorus. Multi-layered platforms allow for fluidity of motion and quick changes of locale.*

The play can support many interpretations. It may be all white and look like a model for a theatre set or a replica of a television studio. It might also be a cartoon, drawn with bright "Looney Tune" colors. Literal interpretations are the weakest choices. Brick, mortar, windows, doors, storefronts, sidewalks must be avoided.

COSTUMES: *Bright "team" colors for each Chorus, or clothing of a symbolic nature. Pastels and greys must be avoided. Clothes for Suzie, Mark, and Tara must be professional, crisp, and stylish.*

PROPS: *All props, except for Soomi's sign, must be mimed. Absolutely no trash, trash cans, and no wonga basket.*

LIGHTS: *Must be bright. Comedies don't work well in the dark.*

SOUND: *No underscoring, no musical bridges. No drums. Cartoon sound effects are fine. Any sounds are better made by the Chorus.*

ACCENTS: *There must be distinctions in accent—Haitian from Jamaican, Korean from Japanese and from Chinese. The Chorus must develop various shades of inflection; shouting must be kept at a minimum.*

ACT I

AT RISE: SUZIE SEETO looks longingly at the anchor chair.

VOICE: [*Offstage, heavily miked.*] Two minutes to air. Two minutes.

[A CHORUS, *composed of the* BLACK CHORUS *and the* KOREAN CHORUS, *appear behind her.*]

SUZIE SEETO: The first time I ever saw an African American, it was *no big deal.*
KOREAN CHORUS: Ha! She was petrified.
BLACK CHORUS: She was calm. She was nonplussed. She was *smoooooth* as silk.
SUZIE SEETO: [*To* BLACK CHORUS.] Thank you. [*To audience.*] I was five. Maybe I was six.
CHORUS: [ALL.] You were eight.
SUZIE SEETO: I was objective.
KOREAN CHORUS: You cried like a baby. Waaaaaaa!
SUZIE SEETO: [*To* KOREAN CHORUS.] Do you mind?

BLACK CHORUS: She smiled.

KOREAN CHORUS: She was scared.

SUZIE SEETO: I was not.

BLACK CHORUS: She was friendly.

KOREAN CHORUS: She rolled up that car window, lickety split! Practically snipped off the man's nose.

SUZIE SEETO: I said, "Touch your hair, mister?" It was *sooooo* soft.

BLACK CHORUS: Then, the colored man said . . .

KOREAN CHORUS: "Here, you go, lil' darlin'. Go on, take it. Wants some Pez?"

SUZIE SEETO: [*As a child.*] Oooooh, it's Donald Duck! I've got Mickey, and Minnie, and Popeye, but not Donald Duck." [*As herself.*] Naturally, I took it.

BLACK CHORUS: "Thank you very much for the Pez," you said. You were very polite.

SUZIE SEETO: Yes, I was.

KOREAN CHORUS: Not! She screamed. She quaked. She squished down, down, down deep in that late-model Dodge. "Make the boogeyman go away," you said. "Make the boogeyman, go away."

CHORUS: [ALL, *whispering.*] Make the boogeyman go away. Make the boogeyman go away. Make the boogeyman go away.

SUZIE SEETO: [*To* CHORUS.] Get lost.

CHORUS: [ALL, *whispering.*] Make the boogeyman go away.

SUZIE SEETO: [*To audience.*] Look, I know I'm not perfect. I'm just an average Joe. You've got to take your opportunities as they come, right? But don't you think for one minute, I got my job, or my promotion through affirmative action. That's a dead notion. Everybody knows that. And . . . I didn't get it by sleeping with the boss.

[SUZIE *steps aside, and with sweeping gesture, reveals* MARK THOMP-SON *reading a newspaper.*]

CHORUS: [ALL.] That's him. Over there. Behind the headlines. [*Eying* THOMP-SON'*s physique.*] Not bad!

MARK THOMPSON: Mark Thompson, news director. Suzie now anchors the six and eleven o'clock news. We are a local oh-and-oh, that's owned-and-oper-ated affiliate, in a major news market. When I hired her, she was a fresh and innocent cub reporter straight out of J-school, cute little run in her stock-ing, just like Mary Tyler Moore. One big story, then boom. The girl is in the anchor seat. Anything can happen in the news business.

CHORUS: Some screw up, get sacked. Muck up, move out. Foul up, get fired. And some?

[TARA SULLIVAN *appears. She takes her seat in the anchor chair.*]

TARA: And some? Get promoted.

BLACK CHORUS: [*Whisper.*] KOREAN CHORUS: [*Whisper.*]
Make the boogeyman go away. *Ton ton macoute. Ton ton macoute.*

SUZIE SEETO: Hey, anything can happen in the news business. More power to you, I say. Parlay *gaffes* into gains. *Faux pas* into the seat of power. [*short pause.*] Sometimes, the boogeyman comes at night. I mean, well, sometimes, I do feel guilty about my success. But look at me, I'm young, I'm moving up, I've got the world on a string, dancing to my tune at six and eleven. [*refers to the anchor chair.*] Sometimes, yes, I do feel guilty. But mostly? I don't.

CHORUS: [ALL.] The newsroom. Same time, last year.

[*The newsroom.* TARA *gets up and gives a note to* SUZIE.]

TARA: The assignment desk asked me to give you this.

SUZIE SEETO: Jesus, the desk.

TARA: We girls have to stick together.

SUZIE SEETO: Thanks. I owe you one.

TARA: [*Watches* SUZIE *dash off to her assignment.*] Don't mention it.

[*In the street. Flatbush Avenue and Church Street.*]

SUZIE SEETO: With only ten minutes to air. Finally, my crew and I arrive at the New Way Grocery Store, fresh from being hopelessly *lost* in the bowels of Brooklyn. Those morons on the desk. [*To unseen cameraman.*] Can you make out these directions? My point exactly. [*To self.*] Okay. I've got ten minutes. [*Surveying the scene.*] Some fifty black people on this side, and three Koreans on that side. And . . . What's that in the middle?

CHORUS: [ALL.] What in the world is it?

SUZIE SEETO: Oh, it's a wonga!

[MARK *and* TARA *watch from the newsroom.*]

MARK THOMPSON: What's a wonga?

TARA: What's a wonga?

KOREAN CHORUS: What's a wonga?

BLACK CHORUS: Don't look at us! Hell if we know.

SUZIE SEETO: It's Haitian. You know, voodoo. [*Aside.*] I learned a few things on my last vacation.

CHORUS: [*Mysteriously.*] Wonga, wonga, wonga. Vooodooo!

[*The newsroom.*]

MARK THOMPSON: Nice live shot, Suzie, fine work, and you said you didn't want the assignment. No story is beneath a good reporter.

[SUZIE *returns to newsroom from the field.*]

SUZIE SEETO: Face it, Mark. It's the only kind of story you ever send me out on. If it's got Asians, Latinos, blacks, Jews, women . . . and/or cute fluffy animals, I'm your man. Why is that, Mark?

MARK THOMPSON: Yup, bad day. What's the matter, Suzie? You seem a little miffed. Have a dumpling?

SUZIE SEETO: No, thanks. Please, this is serious. Don't kid with me. I'm not in the *mood*.

MARK THOMPSON: I never kid about *food*. *Food* is a serious subject. Have you noticed that every major relationship you have or ever will have . . . was and is solidified, destroyed, or reconfigured at the dinner table. Now get out of my office, or grab a chopstick.

SUZIE SEETO: Look at this. The desk got the location wrong, wrong, wrong. [*Grabs chopsticks.*] Let me have that.

MARK THOMPSON: I tell them more plum sauce. They never get it right. Give me back my chopsticks.

SUZIE SEETO:	MARK THOMPSON:
I want some justice.	I want my plum sauce.
I don't want to anchor the five o'clock.	I want an antacid.
I don't want a raise.	You are a pain in the ass.
I want retribution. Yes!	I want you out of my office, yes!
Divine vengeance!	Get out of my office.

[*She breaks the chopstick in two, unbeknownst to him.*]

SUZIE SEETO: Mark, compared to where I've been, Dante's trip to purgatory was a joyride. I want someone's head on a plate with a kaiser roll.

MARK THOMPSON: Oh, stop blaming the assignment desk. Next time, get yourself a map of the city. Get out . . . and give me my chopsticks.

SUZIE SEETO: Get a map yourself. You don't know this city from one end of your elbow up to your fine white ass.

MARK THOMPSON: I beg your pardon. I'm a man who blushes.

SUZIE SEETO: Mark, I had ten minutes to air. That's just not enough time to do a good job. Who do you think I am, Lois Lane? I want to lodge a formal complaint.

MARK THOMPSON: Look, Suzie, you'll go where we tell you to go. If it were up to me, you'd be *on* the space shuttle, I mean, *covering* the space shuttle. I know you're disappointed. But you *handled* it, like a pro. I expect no less.

SUZIE SEETO: You bet I *handled* it, and it wasn't easy. [*She hands him his chopsticks and starts to exit for the street.*]

MARK THOMPSON: Can I ask you something?

SUZIE SEETO: [*Almost in the street.*] What?

MARK THOMPSON: [*To audience.*] Do I really have a fine white ass?

[*Meanwhile, in the street.*]

GROCER MAK: [*Looks into basket.*] E-guh-mwa-ya? (What is this?)

SUZIE SEETO: I wish I spoke Korean.

CHORUS: [ALL, *mysteriously.*] Chicken heads. Lizard skins. Feathers from the sacrifice. Chicken heads. Lizard skins. Feathers from the sacrifice.

GROCER MAK: E-guh-mwa-ya?

CHORUS: [ALL, *in the round.*] Lizard heart. Soomi's lost bracelet. Willie's lost watch.

GROCER MAK: Hey, this looks like my hair.

CHORUS: [ALL, *whispering.*] Your soft black hair.

GROCER MAK: Can't be, I'm not losing any hair! No grey, either!

CHORUS: [ALL.] Don't be too sure.

GROCER MAK: E-guh-mwa-ya?

CHORUS: [ALL, *in the round.*] The tip of the index finger. Index finger. Index finger. All shriveled up.

SUZIE SEETO: That's it. Excuse me, pardon me, coming through. Watch the skirt!

CHORUS: [ALL, *sotto voce.*] Wonga, wonga, wonga. Voodoooooo . . .

SUZIE SEETO: I survey the sea of black faces.

BLACK CHORUS: Who do you talk to? How do you choose? Do you pick them? Or, do they pick you?

KOREAN CHORUS: Talk to me. Don't talk to me. Talk to her. Talk to him. Don't talk at all.

SUZIE SEETO: [*Approaches the* BLACK CHORUS.] Are you in charge?

BLACK CHORUS: No, we're not.

SUZIE SEETO: Do you know who is?

BLACK CHORUS: [*In rotation, different persona.*] No, I don't. No, not me. I don't know. No, I don't. No, not me. I don't know.

[*Meanwhile, from the newsroom.*]

MARK THOMPSON: Nine minutes, Suzie!

SUZIE SEETO: [*Still in the street.*] I pick . . . YOU!

NURSE RUTH BETTY: Go away, Korean girl!

SUZIE SEETO: Ooops! Try again.

BLACK CHORUS: [*In rotation.*] No, I don't. No, not me. I don't know. [*Together.*] This is a grassroots movement.

SUZIE SEETO: Look, I don't know why you are hiding, but if you are an organizer of this protest, please step forward. Or will all non-organizers, please step backward. Don't be shy.

NURSE RUTH BETTY: [*Left standing in front.*] Send her back! Tell teevee to give us an African-American reporter. Go away, Korean girl!

SUZIE SEETO: Boy, I'd like to pop her one.

BARBER BROWN: Ruth Betty, she's not Korean, she's Chinese. She's Suzie Wong, the teevee reporter.

SUZIE SEETO: That's Seeto. S-e-e-t-o. You're getting me confused with that actress in that old movie.

CHORUS: [ALL.] *The World of Suzie Wong.* A good-time girl with a heart of gold. Good movie. William Holden looked great!

BARBER BROWN: Right! I like that old movie.

SUZIE SEETO: What's going down?

BARBER BROWN: Down as in the direction of gravity? Or down as in, what's happening?

SUZIE SEETO: I get your point, sorry. I mean, can you tell me what's going on?

BARBER BROWN: Only if you, you know, point that camera in some other direction.

SUZIE SEETO: Camera shy?

BARBER BROWN: It's just . . . I'm a little uncomfortable being here, you know, cameras and all. I'm not political in any way, just a businessman out for a little stroll . . . is that camera on?

SUZIE SEETO: What's your name?

BARBER BROWN: James Brown. Not related. I own and operate the best barbershop in all Flatbush, if not all Brooklyn. Baldy Brown's Sartorial Hair *Saloon.* I'm working on an advertising slogan, Wild West theme. "We shoot your hair off your head."

NURSE RUTH BETTY: Hey, Smoke! The protest, remember? You promised to do the protest, Smokeman. The fire's burning. Don't wait to put on your pj's.

BARBER BROWN: [*To* NURSE.] Hey, do you mind? [*To* SUZIE.] That's so tired. Something happens to a man in a crisis situation, and people won't let you live it down, know what I mean?

SUZIE SEETO: I have a feeling there's a story behind that name.

BARBER BROWN: I'd rather not talk about it. Is that camera on? Could you have them . . . I really don't want to be, you know, bad for business. See that big guy, the one who needs a better barber? He's your man. Point your camera in that direction.

SUZIE SEETO: Thank you. Thank you very much.

MARK THOMPSON: Eight minutes, Suzie.

SUZIE SEETO: [To MARK, *calling back*.] All right. Eight minutes.

NURSE RUTH BETTY: Hey, wait a minute! Hey, reporter! You can talk to me. This is a grassroots movement here. For months, I have been calling you news media on the telephone. We've been boycotting for months. How come . . .

REVEREND CARTER: [*Takes over, interrupting*.] Are we going to forget what those Korean bloodsuckers did to our sister Matilda Duvet? I ask you, what are we going to do about it?

BLACK CHORUS: [*As a group, no individuals*.] Boycott, let it rot! Boycott, let it rot!

REVEREND CARTER: That's right!

SUZIE SEETO: [*To audience*.] At last! The leader of the pack.

BLACK CHORUS: [*Speak and move in the polyrhythm of the "fraternity step."*] Boycott, let it rot! Boycott, let it rot!

REVEREND CARTER: [*Joins in*.] Boycott, let it rot!

BLACK CHORUS: Boycott, let it rot! Boycott, let it rot! Boycott, let it rot! [*The* KOREAN CHORUS *has been watching the* BLACK CHORUS *until* . . .]

WILLIE MAK: Call the police. Yes, better do it now. Call the police. 911! [*To* BLACK CHORUS.] You better go! The police are coming. They'll be here. I said, the police are coming.

REVEREND CARTER: Call all you want, yellow man! They won't come.

WILLIE MAK: Yes, they will. You'll see.

GROCER MAK: [*To* KOREAN CHORUS.] Willie, Soomi, come on. Let's go inside.

REVEREND CARTER: Where are you going, Korean coward?!

GROCER MAK: I was in the Korean army.

NURSE RUTH BETTY: Is that guy speaking English? Sounds like gibberish to me? What's the matter? Can't you speak English?

BLACK CHORUS: Speak English! Speak English!

KOREAN CHORUS: You speak English! You speak English!

SUZIE SEETO: Incredible. Just incredible. [*To unseen cameraman*.] Are you getting these pictures? Go around and get another angle.

REVEREND CARTER: Get your filthy Korean trash off our streets!

SUZIE SEETO: [*To unseen cameraman.*] Oh, oh! Let's move. Do you want to get clobbered? Move your butt. But don't drop that camera! Okay. Deep breath. What am I going to do next?

REVEREND CARTER: [*Overlapping.*] What are we going to do with Korean garbage?

[*Playwright's Note: The* BLACK CHORUS *hurls words, not actual trash.*]

BLACK CHORUS: Sit on it. Wreck it. Toss it. Off the street, off the street! Sit on it. Wreck it. Toss it. Off the street, off the street!

[*The* KOREAN CHORUS *must only respond to words. No gathering up trash.*]

GROCER MAK: Hey! Hey, get away from my trash! Now I'm hopping mad! Get off my garbage! Leave my garbage alone! This is my trash! This is my garbage! My trash! My garbage!

REVEREND CARTER: Matilda Duvet is in a coma. And that Korean is responsible.

[SOOMI MAK *steps from the* KOREAN CHORUS.]

SOOMI MAK: Forget the trash, Uncle.

GROCER MAK: Willie, help your sister.

WILLIE MAK: Let's go inside, Uncle. The police will come soon. Let's go inside, and pray to God for peace.

GROCER MAK: Why, Willie? Why do they do this?

SOOMI MAK: It's America. It's called *boy*cotting.

GROCER MAK: Leave your *boy*friends out of this, Soomi. I don't care. I fight them. I fight them. Do you hear me, you devils? I fight you until I am dead!

BLACK CHORUS: Speak English! Speak English!

GROCER MAK: [*To audience.*] Huh? I am speaking English. [*To* KOREAN CHORUS.] What's the matter with them? I am speaking English.

REVEREND CARTER: That's right, go away, Korean monkey.

SUZIE SEETO: Did I hear that right? [*Runs over to him.*] Excuse me, sir, did you call that man a monkey?

REVEREND CARTER: I call a spade a spade. Matilda Duvet is in a coma. And that Korean is responsible.

SUZIE SEETO: I can't believe he said that. I wish he'd say that again for the camera.

REVEREND CARTER: [*Happily obliges.*] Go back to Korea, Korean monkey!

SUZIE SEETO: [*Sotto voce, to audience.*] Perfect.

MARK THOMPSON: Five minutes, Suzie.

SUZIE SEETO: What are you? Three-quarter cuckoo, one-half Big Ben?

MARK THOMPSON: Suzie.

SUZIE SEETO: Okay. Okay. I said,okay! Okay, five minutes.

BLACK CHORUS: We don't want your apples!

SUZIE SEETO: Please, I have to get through. Let me through. Thanks. Watch the skirt.

BLACK CHORUS: We don't want your limes! We don't want your cantaloupes! We don't want your apples. We don't want your kiiiiwiiiii!

SUZIE SEETO: Coming through.

BLACK CHORUS: We want black-eyed peas. We want collard greens. We want hog maws and chitlins and sweet potato pie. Black-eyed peas. Collard greens. Sweet potato pie.

SUZIE SEETO: [*To* WILLIE.] Please, sir, are you the owner of this store?

WILLIE MAK: Who, me? Not me, lady. He's the owner.

MARK THOMPSON: Three minutes, Suzie.

SOOMI MAK: Uncle, talk to the reporter.

GROCER MAK: No.

WILLIE MAK: Why, Uncle?

GROCER MAK: Because. Tell her, no!

SOOMI MAK: [*To* SUZIE.] It's because his English stinks.

WILLIE MAK: Soomi, be quiet. [*To* SUZIE.] It's true. It really stinks.

SUZIE SEETO: Please, I've got to talk to you.

SOOMI MAK: Talk to her, Uncle. Maybe she can help. She's teevee.

GROCER MAK: She can take out the trash. [*He hands her the wonga.*]

WILLIE MAK: Someone left it in front of the store.

SUZIE SEETO: Oh God, not the wonga! [*She starts a game of "hot potato" among the* CHORUS.]

MARK THOMPSON: Two minutes, Suzie.

KOREAN CHORUS: *Ton ton macoute.* It's evil.

BLACK CHORUS: *Ton ton macoute.* It's mean.

SUZIE SEETO: Hey, this is no time for kiddie games. I hate hot potato.

BARBER BROWN: Got your name on it, Rev! Catch!

KOREAN CHORUS: It's stinky.

REVEREND CARTER: Back to you, Suzie.

CHORUS: *Ton ton macoute* is THE BOOGEYMAN!

SUZIE SEETO: [*Holds the basket. Trancelike, childlike.*] The boogeyman is coming to get me. The boogeyman comes at night. He takes little girls and little boys. The boogeyman is here. I'm afraid, Mommy. I'm afraid. Don't let the boogeyman take me away.

MARK THOMPSON: One minute, Suzie.

TARA: [*Overlapping.*] One minute, Suzie. *Plenty o' time.*

SUZIE SEETO: [*Startled, drops the basket.*] Oooops, it's dropped! [*The* CHORUS *is shocked. An audible breath.*]

MARK THOMPSON: Looks like there's a curse on the street.

SUZIE SEETO: I didn't mean to . . . really I didn't.

BLACK CHORUS: A curse on our street. My street!

KOREAN CHORUS: A curse on our neighborhood. My neighborhood!

SUZIE SEETO:Hey, so I'm clumsy. Sue me.

CHORUS, MARK, AND TARA: A curse on the whole fucking world!

SUZIE SEETO: Oh, great! That's just great. Okay, I can handle this. Mark, tell the desk, I'm ready for the toss. [*To audience.*] Thank you, Tara. Yes, that's right. I'm standing here in front of the New Way Grocery Store. As you can see, all the fruit and produce usually out front of this green grocery has been put away as nearly fifty people—mostly African Americans and other blacks—have congregated here for a protest against this store.

BLACK CHORUS: Boycott, let it rot! Boycott, let it rot! Boycott, let it rot!

SUZIE SEETO: [*Overlapping.*] I'm sorry, Tara, your question is a little hard to hear as many of the protesters are shouting anti-Korean slogans. I have here one—

[NURSE RUTH BETTY *steps up to be interviewed.*]

SUZIE SEETO: [*To* NURSE.] Can you step aside? Step aside, please.

[*The* REVEREND *steps up alongside* SUZIE, *replaces* NURSE RUTH BETTY.]

SUZIE SEETO: [*To* REVEREND.] Excuse me, sir. What's your name?

REVEREND CARTER: Reverend Lonnie Olson Carter.

SUZIE SEETO: Reverend Carter, are you one of the organizers of this protest?

REVEREND CARTER: No, Suzie, I'm not. This is a grassroots movement. But I can tell you that those people over there are taking advantage of our captivity in America to become rich.

NURSE RUTH BETTY: I could have said that.

REVEREND CARTER: The only solution I see is the Koreans should leave the black community *en masse.* Who asked them to come? Go back to Korea!

SUZIE SEETO: Could you repeat that?

REVEREND CARTER: Korean monkeys, go back to Korea!

[*In the newsroom.*]

MARK THOMPSON: I don't believe it. He actually said it.

SUZIE SEETO: [*To audience.*] You heard it live. [SUZIE *joins her boss. The* CHORUSES *stand by.*]

MARK THOMPSON: That's incredible. He actually called that guy a Korean monkey. Amazing, just amazing. It's like the '60s all over again, but in reverse. I don't mean to sound relieved. But, I mean, this time, the white man isn't part of the lynch party. It's all so strange.

SUZIE SEETO: How so?

MARK THOMPSON: Not being the bad guy for once. Whitey always gets the bad rap.

SUZIE SEETO: I just love it when you try to be hip. It's so deliciously awkward.

MARK THOMPSON: So who's the preacher?

SUZIE SEETO: I checked, he's a reverend, all right. Storefront preacher.

CHORUS: [ALL, *sotto voce.*] The Reverend is the white man's dream. The Reverend is a white man's nightmare.

SUZIE SEETO: I just want to know why we didn't get on it earlier. I heard on the street, people have been calling the station for months.

MARK THOMPSON: Is that right?

SUZIE SEETO: Why didn't we get on it earlier?

MARK THOMPSON: You're on it now. That's what matters. You just do your job. It's hot stuff.

SUZIE SEETO: Got that right. Whosoever said "sticks and stones" . . . didn't live in the twentieth century.

MARK THOMPSON: Got that right. Good work, Suzie. Keep it up. It's on the budget for tomorrow. I want a full one-and-fifteen package. This is good stuff. I like it.

SUZIE SEETO: Aren't you the bluebird of happiness? Like a kid with his hand down the front of his pants.

MARK THOMPSON: Nothing like a good story.

SUZIE SEETO: You should get a life outside the newsroom.

CHORUS: [ALL.] Look who's calling the kettle black.

SUZIE SEETO: [*to* CHORUS.] Hey!

CHORUS: [ALL.] You eat at work, sleep at work. You fornicate—with co-workers.

MARK THOMPSON: [*To* CHORUS.] Changing the subject. [*To* SUZIE.] Suzie, look, I know you didn't want this story. But aren't you glad you listened to Papa Bear? Good, I'm glad you see it my way. I have a feeling about this one. Could be big. Could be real big.

SUZIE SEETO: Mark, the think is . . . I've gotten these phone calls. You should hear what people are saying.

MARK THOMPSON: Oh, just ignore it. Who cares what they're saying.

BLACK CHORUS: [*On the phone.*] Those uppity blacks. See what happens when you give them an inch. They take a mile. Give them a hand, they want your arm. Those niggers. Those coons. Those black devils. What more do they want?

SUZIE SEETO: It's open season on African Americans, thanks to me. I can't believe people in this day and age are still using the word "tar baby."

MARK THOMPSON: You didn't force that reverend to say what he said. He said it of his own volition. Loud and clear. Hatred, Suzie, is color-blind. [*The* CHORUS *groans loudly. To* CHORUS.] Hey, give me some credit. I was for the ERA. I read about the march from Selma to Birmingham. I voted for a woman, for Christ' sake. I cry at weddings. Look, Suzie, all the affiliates are chasing down *your* story. Fast and dirty. That's the nature of the beast.

SUZIE SEETO: It's true, I did the best I could—given the time constraints, nobody could do better. I don't know what I'm complaining about.

BLACK CHORUS: [*Kindly.*] Do better, Suzie. You can do better.

MARK THOMPSON: Get back out there, track it down. Find out why, and all that good Journalism 101. And close the door. And don't get lost this time.

[*The barbershop. The* KOREAN CHORUS *witnesses the action, but it does not participate.*]

KOREAN CHORUS: In the barbershop, Nurse Ruth Betty, a local resident, tells Suzie the truth about Koreans.

NURSE RUTH BETTY: Five years. I been going to that New Way Grocery Story, ever since it opened. That's five years.

BARBER BROWN: Used to be a dump. Sitting empty, collecting dust for a decade. Sit down, Suzie. Be comfortable. That's my best chair.

NURSE RUTH BETTY: Ooooo, Baldy Brown done taught his son to be a gentleman. Smokeman, you are too cute.

BARBER BROWN: What did I tell you?

NURSE RUTH BETTY: Oh, don't worry. I'm not gonna tell the reporter your secret.

SUZIE SEETO: You were saying about the New Way Grocery Store.

NURSE RUTH BETTY: As I was saying, I live only four blocks away, so naturally I pick up a few things here and there on a regular basis. But no more. I've had it. Do you think Mister Key Chun Mak ever said "boo" to me in five years. I walk past that store every day on my way to work.

KOREAN CHORUS: Ruth Betty is a nurse practitioner. She works in the neighborhood clinic. It is very busy there.

NURSE RUTH BETTY: Yeah, I used to think all you Orientals were polite.

BARBER BROWN: Now, Ruthie, that's just a misguided stereotype.

NURSE RUTH BETTY: Smokeman, you do sound like your father. Lord bless him.

SUZIE SEETO: Not even a hello, Miss Ruth?

NURSE RUTH BETTY: Not even.

SUZIE SEETO: And that's why you are making that picket sign?

BARBER BROWN: Picket signs, collectin' money for photocopies, phone calls. Buzz, buzz, buzz.

NURSE RUTH BETTY: Laugh all you want. But I got you here, didn't I? And I got Smokey here to politicize even if it was just one day. But it's a step, right? I've been putting money into that Korean man's pocket for five years, and he can't even look me in the eye when I open my purse. Once, I held out my five dollars, good honest money, and he refused to take it from my black hand. Do I look like I have a social disease?

BARBER BROWN: Yeah, it's called social *work*. Ruth Betty, I don't know when you have time for it all. Your sorry boyfriend hangs his nappy head in here, moaning and whining, bein' pitiful. "Where's Ruth, ohhh Ruth, ohhh Ruth"—wantin' me to shave your name on the back of his sorry head.

NURSE RUTH BETTY: [*To* BARBER.] You hush up. [*To* SUZIE.] I'm tellin' you, I put the money down on the counter. And Mister Mak, he scoops it right up without so much as a blink. I'm telling you, the man is afraid to touch my black hand, and I always have a perfect manicure. Rude. Downright rude.

BARBER BROWN: All right. I've made all the protest signs I'm going to make. Here it is. I don't know why, Suzie, I agreed to do this. I have customers, a business to run. As my old man . . .

NURSE RUTH BETTY: Bless him.

BARBER BROWN: As my father would have said, "Awake and sing, ye who dwell in the dust." Communicate with this. [*He shows his sign.*] Suzie, ever think about dreads? How about braiding?

NURSE RUTH BETTY: Smokeman, your consciousness needs raising, my brother. Look at that. Those words are too small. What kind of sorry sign is this? I need a microscope to read them words. You are a flunky from Protestin' 101.

BARBER BROWN: Suzie, my brother is the college man. I'm just a good-looking businessman. And I'm shy.

SUZIE SEETO: But not modest.

BARBER BROWN: Right. You catch on quick.

NURSE RUTH BETTY: I'm telling you straight, Smokeman. The house is on fire. Wake up, and run out naked. Don't wait to put on your pj's.

BARBER BROWN: That's enough, Ruth. We don't have to get personal. Suzie don't need to know about my pj's. She isn't here to listen to your gossip or our debate. Let's just say, we agree to disagree.

NURSE RUTH BETTY: You know what, Smokey? I think, I think you like Koreans. Why is that, Smokey?

BARBER BROWN: People are people. There's good and there's bad.

NURSE RUTH BETTY: That sounds just like your poor misguided father. Bless him. Old Baldy was always right out in front singing "We Shall Overcome."

BARBER BROWN: Hey! That grocer gets his haircut in here. That's all I have to know; that's all I need to know. I don't care if he lives outside the neighborhood. I don't care if he don't take money from my black hand. He puts money in this place.

[A *flashback*. GROCER MAK *sits in barber's chair*.]

BARBER BROWN: You know, Makie. You should really update your look. How about a little fade, you know. Fade. Short like all along the sides. I invented that look, you know.

GROCER MAK: [*Gruffly.*] No, no fade. I'm sexy enough.

BARBER BROWN: Women love it!

GROCER MAK: Yeah? Work for you?

BARBER BROWN: That's a low blow, my man. I'm just shy, that's all. [*They laugh.*] Sure you don't want to change your mind about that fade? Didn't think so. By the way, Makie, that vegetable stuff you gave me worked like a charm. Cleared me right up. Thanks, man.

GROCER MAK: Kimchee not just dead cabbage, kimchee is the heart of Korea. When I eat it, my homesickness says "Adios."

BARBER BROWN: Well, it sure stunk up my house. Worse than the East River *and* the subway on a hot sunny day.

GROCER MAK: When I was a boy, my mother cut up Chinese cabbage, garlic, ginger, put in chili pepper, salt. That's kimchee. The trick is to pickle it for a long time. Put in pot, airtight, wrap old shirt around it, bury it in ground. When I eat it, it reminds me of when I was a boy sitting with Mother in warm kitchen, trying to remember where in hell we buried last year's kimchee.

BARBER BROWN: Tilt your head. Well, all I know is I can breath free.

GROCER MAK: Yes, kimchee is like wonder drug. Also, puts hair on chest. [*They laugh.*]

BARBER BROWN: Maybe you could show me how to do up some of that kimchee. I got a big backyard.

GROCER MAK: Forget it. Comes in jar.

BARBER BROWN: Well, I had this idea, see. I was eating your kimchee. I was sneezing my head off. Then for no reason, I put some of that kimchee into my chitlins, and wouldn't you know, it tasted good, AND it cleared up my sinuses. So, I got to thinking, I mean, you could sell the stuff in your store. In the food-to-go section *or* in your pharmaceutical department. Kimchee and Chitlins. The wonder *food* or the wonder *drug*.

GROCER MAK: Okay! [*Beat.*] What is chitlins?

BARBER BROWN: What is chitlins? Next time you come in, I'll make you a mess of chitlins on a sweet soft bed of kimchee. I might even enter it into some kind of Betty Crocker cookbook contest. [*Haircut completed, he hands* GROCER *a mirror.*] Killer!

GROCER MAK: Okay! [*Gives him the thumbs-up. They separate and speak to the audience directly.*]

BARBER BROWN: That was the last time Makie was in my chair. Almost two months ago, I think it was. Now, I toss and turn. Can't sleep at all since this thing started.

GROCER MAK: Soomi cuts my hair. She does a terrible job. I don't sleep good. I get up and sit in a chair, stare at nothing until morning comes.

BARBER BROWN: I'm losing money being out on the picket line.

GROCER MAK: Yesterday, I make twelve dollars. How can I keep my store open?

[*The newsroom.* SUZIE *eyes the anchor seat. Fondles it.* TARA *enters, watches her.* SUZIE *is unaware of* TARA. TARA *is not a sexpot. She's all business.*]

TARA: Dream all you want, Suzie. That chair is mine. And, I know what it takes to keep it. Talent isn't enough, my friend. I've got plenty of talent. But I've discovered a good blow job really cuts to the chase. I have the mink kneepads to prove it. Look at you, all your idealism shining bright in your eyes. Go on, try it out. Sit in it. That's right. Do you really think they'll let you sit there? You just sail in here fresh and innocent out of J-school, you little yapping Chihuahua. I paid my dues. I did my time in shitholes, hauling my own equipment around, doing my own makeup—gofer, researcher, weathergirl. And you think you got it over me? Look where I am. I'm on top. And I'm going to stay on top. I'm young, I'm beautiful, I've got the world dancing to my tune at six and eleven. You can nip and yip at my ankles all you want, but that's as close as you'll ever get because *Connie Chung, you ain't.* Not if I can help it.

KOREAN CHORUS: Suzie called the Reverend Carter on the matter of Matilda Duvet thirty-eight times.

BLACK CHORUS: Suzie is persistent.

MARK THOMPSON: They meet at the barbershop.

NURSE RUTH BETTY: Speaking of folks who live outside the neighborhood.

[*Enter the* REVEREND.]

BARBER BROWN: Now here is a man who knows how to make his protest signs.

REVEREND CARTER: Crosstown traffic was murderous. Hello . . . ah . . . ?

NURSE RUTH BETTY: Ruth Betty, the nurse with the two first names.

REVEREND CARTER: Of course, you do. And good day to you. And to you . . .

BARBER BROWN: James Brown. Not related. Can't sing.

SUZIE SEETO: Reverend, if we could get started. I'm in a bit of a crunch. Time wise. About Matilda Duvet . . .

NURSE RUTH BETTY: Reverend, now you look here at this sorry sign.

REVEREND CARTER: Too much white space.

NURSE RUTH BETTY: See?

REVEREND CARTER: Be bold, brother. Fill up that *white* space, with some *black* letters.

NURSE RUTH BETTY: Amen.

BARBER BROWN: How about a little trim, Rev? You know, you really need to use a different brand of relaxer.

REVEREND CARTER: Some other time, young man.

NURSE RUTH BETTY: Better tend to the reporter, Reverend. She looks like she's going to barbecue me alive with all her questions. [*To* BARBER.] Come on. We got more signs to make for tonight.

BARBER BROWN: I got writers' cramp.

NURSE RUTH BETTY: Come on.

[SUZIE *and the* REVEREND *converse. The* KOREAN CHORUS *observes from afar.*]

SUZIE SEETO: Reverend, thank you for meeting me here. I know you are busy—maybe you were even in the mayor's office?

REVEREND CARTER: We are trying to get our case to the mayor, that's true. But I'm always happy to accommodate the press when I can, especially if she is as pretty as you.

SUZIE SEETO: I've been to the hospital, checked the records. Matilda Duvet was treated and released, according to the nursing supervisor. How do you explain it?

REVEREND CARTER: The records are wrong.

KOREAN CHORUS: [*Sotto voce, but urgently.*] Don't let him slip away. Chase him with a question.

SUZIE SEETO: Well, I'm confused. Matilda Duvet is not listed as ever being hospitalized for being in a coma, as you and your protesters claim.

KOREAN CHORUS: Chase him with a question.

REVEREND CARTER: Well, Suzie. That may well be. But it doesn't change the fact that those people in that store, those Koreans, attacked a black woman. They've been insulting black people ever since they opened their store.

KOREAN CHORUS: Chase him with a question.

SUZIE SEETO: Did you witness the alleged attack?

REVEREND CARTER: Nothing alleged about it, Suzie. I talked to Matilda myself.

SUZIE SEETO: I'd like to talk to her. I want to hear her side. You know I'll be fair and impartial.

REVEREND CARTER: I know no such thing. I'm sorry. I can't help you.

SUZIE SEETO: Reverend Carter, no one's been able to find her. She's given no interviews. She hasn't been seen in public. Can't you help me out?

REVEREND CARTER: Look here. It's simple. The woman was carrying a shopping bag.

KOREAN CHORUS: A plastic bag with red stripes, blue stripes, white stripes.

REVEREND CARTER: Come here, Jimmy. You are Matilda Duvet. Hold your arm like this. Like you was holding a colorful plastic handbag.

BARBER BROWN: Uh uh, no way, not me. Those are not my colors. I'm a winter.

KOREAN CHORUS: It's not his style.

REVEREND CARTER: [*To* BARBER.] You are Matilda Duvet. You are going home after a long day sweeping and cleaning for some uptown peoples.

KOREAN CHORUS: Matilda meets a friend on the street. It's Ruth Betty, the nurse practitioner!

NURSE RUTH BETTY: You look tired, Tildy. How's your feet?

BARBER BROWN: [*As* MATILDA, *falsetto.*] "My dogs are barking today. Gonna stop in New Way, then go on home."

NURSE RUTH BETTY: I heard your sister from Port-au-Prince is visiting.

BARBER BROWN: "More like she is escaping. Things are pretty bad back home in Haiti. My sister's husband . . . poof, disappeared."

NURSE RUTH BETTY: I'm sorry to hear about your sister's husband. It's too sad for words. You must make her a good dinner to take away her troubles.

BARBER BROWN: "Woy! *Mez Ami!* [Oh my! My friend!] Truly there's going to be good cooking in the house tonight. *Banan peze, ri ak pwa kole.*"

SUZIE SEETO: Sounds tasty.

KOREAN CHORUS: It is. Fried pressed bananas, also rice and beans.

BARBER BROWN: "Ooooh yes, and don't forget the *poule*, with *bejine* and *zonyons*."

SUZIE SEETO: That's chicken, with eggplant and onions.

BLACK CHORUS: [*Surprised.*] Very good.

SUZIE SEETO: It's like a Chinese dish my mother makes. I love to eat.

KOREAN CHORUS: Matilda Duvet turns the corner, and goes into the New Way Grocery Store.

REVEREND CARTER: "I Key Chun Mak. Store owner. Two time alleady today, I catch shopliftahs. Stupid things—candy, potato chips, cig-a-lettes. How come dey never steal tofu?"

KOREAN CHORUS: Makie was a civil servant in his own country. Now he is stacking cans of soup. Vegetable soup. Tomato soup. Miso soup. Cup of Soup.

NURSE RUTH BETTY: "I'm Willie Mak."

KOREAN CHORUS: The son of the cousin of the brother of the owner. In other words, a nephew. He's goes to a Christian church. He works for less than minimum wage. He's cheap labor. He's family.

NURSE RUTH BETTY: But I don't got nothing to do in this scene, so I be Soomi Mak. [*Aside.*] I have a double role. Because there are not enough us of up here. [*To* SUZIE.] "Like I was saying, I Soomi Mak and I am in high skoo. My uncle work me like a dog. I am behind da cash registah."

KOREAN CHORUS: Ruth Betty as Soomi is thinking . . .

NURSE RUTH BETTY: [*As* SOOMI.] "Saaaay, dat woman. She rook bery suspic'us."

BARBER BROWN: [*As* MATILDA.] "That's because I can't decide. Which eggplant, which onion? The okra looks a little limp. Put it back. Pick it up. Put it back."

REVEREND CARTER: [*As the* GROCER.] "Do I know her? Dey all rook arike to me. All those brack monkeys rook arike to me."

BARBER BROWN: "Looks a little soggy. Put it back. What about this one? Pick it up. Put it back. Looks like mold. Put it back. Here's one with a little leaf. Pick it up. No, not good. Put it back. Pick up, put back. Pick up. Put back."

KOREAN CHORUS: All right, already! Go on with your story!

BARBER BROWN: "Those Korean's eyes follow me everywhere I go. I feel eyes on me."

REVEREND CARTER: "Many peepole comprain today. How come dis? Why not that? I want dis. You wanta Pepsi? Go get it yourself."

BARBER BROWN: "They think I'm a thief. They think I don't work. He follows me, makes me nervous."

NURSE RUTH BETTY: "Watch her, Uncle. She is touching ehberyting with her dirty hands."

BARBER BROWN: "I'm sick and tired of them thinking I'm a thief. I'm sick and tired of them thinking I don't work."

REVEREND CARTER: "I'm sick and tired of razy peepole. No, you cannot pay me latah. Pay now. I'm sick and tired of peepole coming into store with anglee faces, anglee fists. I sick of brack peepole."

NURSE RUTH BETTY: "I sick and tired of tloublemakahs with anglee faces, anglee fists. Gif me back dat candy bar. I sick and tired of brack peepole."

BARBER BROWN: "Nothing good here. I tink I go."

NURSE RUTH BETTY: "Uncle! Uncle! Stop her! She stole someting! That rady stole someting!"

REVEREND CARTER: "Where you going?"

BARBER BROWN: "I'm going to another store."

REVEREND CARTER: "Let me see what's in your bag. I want to rook inside your bag."

BARBER BROWN: "No."

REVEREND CARTER: "Let me see inside your bag."

BARBER BROWN: "No, I tell you, no! Let go of my bag!" [*They have a tug of war with the shopping bag.*]

REVEREND CARTER: "I'm sick and tired of peepole who talkin' too fast. I'm sick and tired of working so hard. Five A.M. to one A.M. I sick and tired of peepole yelring at me. Of peepole who do not understand even when I speakin' Englrish. I sick and tired of being sick and tired."

NURSE RUTH BETTY: "Watch out! She's going to lrun!"

REVEREND CARTER: "No, you don't!" [*The* REVEREND *pulls back his fist to strike the* BARBER. *The* KOREAN CHORUS *gasps, as does* SUZIE.]

BARBER BROWN: Rev. Hey, Rev! You can be yourself now. Rev? Hey! Snap to.

REVEREND CARTER: [*Snapping to.*] And that's it. That's what Matilda Duvet told me. And that's why we are protesting this Korean store, until the day we shut them down.

[GROCER MAK *steps out from the* KOREAN CHORUS.]

GROCER MAK: Lies!

SUZIE SEETO: That's not how it happened?

GROCER MAK: That's not how it happened.

KOREAN CHORUS: That's not what happened at all.

GROCER MAK: You talk to me. You will see the truth.

REVEREND CARTER: Look, Suzie, we want respect. That's all. And that's everything.

GROCER MAK: You talk to me, Miss Seeto. You will see the truth.

CHORUS: [ALL, *including* SUZIE.] But first, a word from our sponsor!

[*The newsroom.* MARK *addresses the audience.*]

MARK THOMPSON: The first time I met an Asian person, well, it was after I got kicked out of college. My father pulled a few strings, got me a job in a mid-market teevee station. So, with promises of employment, I took off to see the world for a year. There was this girl in Thailand. She had a cheese grater and a bar of fragrant soap.

CHORUS: [ALL.] Uh huh.

MARK THOMPSON: She laid me down on a rubber mat, poured water all over me, grabbed my wrists, and started moving me around. I got sudsy all over.

CHORUS: [ALL.] Ooooooo.

MARK THOMPSON: Usually, she gets paid. But this one she said was free, on the house. Asked me to come back even. I've been hooked on Oriental women ever since.

CHORUS: [ALL.] Oh, brother.

TARA: Well, that explains everything.

MARK THOMPSON: So you must be wondering. But I make it a policy *never* to fraternize with employees, contrary to rumor. Naturally, I like Suzie. But there's nothing exotic, nothing Asian about her. I mean, I'm a Buddhist, for Christ's sake. Tell you the truth, I'm more Oriental than she is.

BLACK CHORUS: We're sorry. We are experiencing technical difficulties. Please stay tuned.

SUZIE SEETO: [*Addresses the audience.*] I hate covering minority issues. But don't get me wrong, I love my job. Not many people can say that, but I can. I have loved journalism ever since Clark Kent, Lois Lane, and the *Daily Planet.* A comic book isn't the sturdiest foundation on which to build a career, but . . . When I was ten, all my friends were crazy about Superboy. And Superboy was crazy about that redhead, Lana Lang. SuperMAN obviously had better taste. He was in love with a brunette! So, I figured if Lois Lane, news reporter, a brunette, could land a super MAN—hence, ergo, presto, one Suzie Seeto, news reporter.

CHORUS: Comic books, however, do lie.

SUZIE SEETO: Twenty years later, I still can't find that super *guy*, but I sure got the super *job.*

CHORUS: We believe in facts.

SUZIE SEETO: That's right. I believe in facts. Gather up enough facts, and they add up to a decision, an action, even a revelation. I'm not in this business for the glamour or the money.

CHORUS: We're in it to make a difference.

SUZIE SEETO: That's right. I'm in it to make a difference. To ensure fairness and civility in the world.

CHORUS: Fairness and civility.

SUZIE SEETO: I believe that, with all my heart.

BLACK CHORUS: Thank you for your patience. And now, our regularly scheduled program continues in progress.

[*Inside the New Way store.* SOOMI MAK *and* GROCER MAK *are posed in the last image of the black version. The* BLACK CHORUS *observes from afar.*]

WILLIE MAK: So you see, Miss Seeto, it's impossible. It couldn't happen the way they say. How could my uncle do this thing they say he did? First of all, my uncle wasn't even here. Soomi was here.

SOOMI MAK: I was at the cash register. Willie was in the back room.

WILLIE MAK: Soomi was here, behind the cash register. Right, Soomi? No, take it back. You play the black lady. Uncle, come here. Uncle, you be Soomi.

GROCER MAK: Huh?

WILLIE MAK: Switch. Trade . . . you stand behind counter. Get behind the . . . that's right.

BLACK CHORUS: And I thought we were confusing.

WILLIE MAK: No, no. It's very simple. You'll see. So, okay, so you, Soomi, you are the big black lady wearing . . .

SOOMI MAK: . . . A big floppy hat.

WILLIE MAK: That's right.

BLACK CHORUS: And dark shades. Don't forget the shades.

WILLIE MAK: Oh yes, sunglasses.

SOOMI MAK: I come in. No, first comes two customers. They are from a gang, you know. Lots of big muscles, and a bandana on his head. The other one, he wears big pants.

WILLIE MAK: "Yo, yo, yo. How 'bout some service?"

GROCER MAK: [*To* SOOMI.] "I needs a quarter. Please, please, please."

WILLIE MAK: "I don't got all day. Gimme some of that. What? You got a problem. I tole you I don't smoke this shit. Don't go messing wit me. I want that, yeah, to the left, no the next one ovah, yeah, that's it. That's better."

GROCER MAK: "Don't be looking at my face. The man beat me up for nuthin'. What right does he have, putting me in jail for sittin' on my own stoop, saying I look suspicious in my own neighborhood?"

WILLIE MAK: "Check this." [*Opens coat.*] "Got myself a .38. Yeah, I'm not gonna go down, that's for sure. I'm gonna make it to my sixteenth birthday. Yeah. Brothers killing brothers, that's bullshit."

GROCER MAK: "Listen, listen, listen. Come closer. You keep knockin' a man down and he stays down. Ain't that right? And I'm down, man. I'm as down as a man can git and still be on this earth."

WILLIE MAK: "You can't knock a man for trying to survive. Hear what I'm sayin'?" [*Beat.*] "Put that shit on my tab, Chinaman. Later."

GROCER MAK: "Yeah, later."

SOOMI MAK: Whew, I am so glad when they leave.

WILLIE MAK: So now the lady comes in.

SOOMI MAK: I come in. I play her. I'm Matilda Duvet.

WILLIE MAK: Right. Then Soomi says . . . Uncle, your turn. Pay attention!

GROCER MAK: [*As* SOOMI, *falsetto.*] "Auh suh o sae yo."

BLACK CHORUS: A formal greeting. It means hello.

SOOMI MAK: [*As* MATILDA.] "I go to ze apples. I pick one up. It tis red. It looks okay. Maybe not. I put it down. I pick one up. No good. Forget it. I go to the lemons. Tese look nice. I take one, two, three. No, I put them down. Pick one up, put it down. Pick it up, put it down. Pick up, put down. Pick up, put down. Up, down. Pick up. Put down. Tiss looks nice."

WILLIE MAK: I see a black lady. I'm playing me, Willie Mak. I am carrying a broom. My uncle, who is Soomi, dropped a sack of flour. A mess is all over the place.

GROCER MAK: [*As himself.*] You stupid girl. Girls are so clumsy.

SUZIE SEETO: What did he say?

WILLIE MAK: He said Soomi is so cl . . .

SOOMI MAK: [*As herself.*] . . . clever! Soomi is very clever. And a very good worker.

GROCER MAK: You will see, Miss Seeto. Willie explain it. Explain it, Willie.

SOOMI MAK: Willie explain it. Willie is always right.

WILLIE MAK: My English is better than yours. At least, I study.

BLACK CHORUS: Soomi gets bad grades in school. She wants to be a material girl, but she doesn't have the clothes. [*Finger snap.*]

SOOMI MAK: "How much are ze limes?"

WILLIE MAK: "What?" I said. Just like that. The lady has very big accent.

SOOMI MAK: "Idiot boy! Mi dogs are barkin', and you are makin' me stand here when I am sooo tired. I caun't tink."

BLACK CHORUS: Matilda has had a long day. She is worried about her sister; her husband has disappeared.

SOOMI MAK: "Why don't you speak English? I've been here in dis countree tee years, and see how good my English is? Lime, lemon, how much? Lime, lemon. See? How much? How much?"

WILLIE MAK: Oh. One for one dollar.

SUZIE SEETO: One for one dollar!

BLACK CHORUS: It's expensive to live in New York.

SUZIE SEETO: But one for one dollar!

WILLIE MAK: So, okay. I make a mistake.

BLACK CHORUS: He means three for one dollar.

WILLIE MAK: Hey, I make a mistake. Now, the lady gets very upset.

SOOMI MAK: "Take back your lime." [*She mimes a wicked toss at* WILLIE MAK.]

WILLIE MAK: Hey, stop!

SOOMI MAK: "Haf anothah lime. And anothah. Haf a lemon."

SUZIE SEETO: Nice fast ball.

BLACK CHORUS: Low and inside.

SOOMI MAK: "Take zat."

WILLIE MAK: Calm down, lady.

SOOMI MAK: "Haf a lemon and a lime."

BLACK CHORUS: Curve ball, with a sexy swerve.

SOOMI MAK: "Haf two lemons and two limes."

BLACK CHORUS: Lefty! Lefty! Lefty! [*The* BLACK CHORUS *does* "*the wave.*"]

WILLIE MAK: Here. Here. You take lime. You want lime. It's free. Take it. [WILLIE *offers her the fruit. He puts his hand on her shoulder, encouraging her to take it.*]

SOOMI MAK: [*Screams.*] Don't touch me! Stop it! Stop it! Don't touch me.!"

WILLIE MAK: I'm not touching you, lady. Please, please. I'm not touching you.

SOOMI MAK: "Get away from me."

WILLIE MAK: We don't want any trouble. Please. [*Beat.*] Then Soomi comes over. Uncle! Come here.

GROCER MAK: Oh? My turn. [GROCER MAK *scurries over. He carries a broom.*]

SOOMI MAK: "What are you going to do wid zat broom? Get it away from me."

GROCER MAK: [*As* SOOMI.] "What is she saying! I don't understand her."

SOOMI MAK: "Get away from me with zat broom."

GROCER MAK: [*Still* SOOMI.] "Here. Here. I put broom down. Okay. Calm down. Now, you take it. Here I put the lime in your bag. Okay? Okay? I put two limes in your bag."

WILLIE MAK: Okay, Soomi, don't give her the whole store! Now, all is calm. So, I turn around, and Soomi turns around. Uncle, turn around.

GROCER MAK: Oh.

SUZIE SEETO: And when you look back to see if the lady has gone . . .

WILLIE MAK: That's right.

SOOMI MAK: That's right.

SUZIE SEETO: Turns out the lady isn't gone.

WILLIE MAK: Next minute we know, she's on the floor. Fall on floor, Soomi. No, not you, Uncle. Soomi falls on floor.

SUZIE SEETO: She is lying on the floor in the middle of the store.

WILLIE MAK: Like wet noodle.

GROCER MAK: Enough of this silly game! I am no more Soomi, now I am me, Key Chun Mak. You see, Miss, I think maybe the lady . . . she . . . aiiiii. Willie, help me . . . *huh mal hal ju mul la yo.* (I don't know how to say it.)

SOOMI MAK: What *don't* you know how to say, Uncle?

GROCER MAK: Stupid girl. Maybe the lady, she, ah . . .

WILLIE MAK: Had a heart attack.

GROCER MAK: No . . . ah . . .

WILLIE MAK: . . . went crazy nuts insane?

SOOMI MAK: Maybe she fainted?

GROCER MAK: Yes, fainted. Tell her, Willie. The black lady fainted.

SOOMI MAK: What makes Willie so great?

WILLIE MAK: Soomi, be quiet. My uncle says the black lady fainted.

SUZIE SEETO: That's possible. She might have fainted.

GROCER MAK: Yes, she fell down, fainted. [*Short pause, as* SUZIE *considers the story.*]

BLACK CHORUS: Check your notes, Suzie. Chase him with a question.

SUZIE SEETO: Mr. Mak, you said you weren't in the store when the incident happened. Exactly where were you?

GROCER MAK: Yes, this you can check it.

BLACK CHORUS: Chase him with a question.

SOOMI MAK: He's a pretty vain guy, my uncle.

WILLIE MAK: Soomi!

SOOMI MAK: He went to get his haircut. To look nice for his girlfriend.

WILLIE MAK: Soomi!

SOOMI MAK: My aunt Yunjin is in South Korea. But her parents are stuck in the North, so she doesn't want to leave. Isn't that convenient? So now, like, I have to slave in this store for ZIP!

WILLIE MAK: Soomi! Suzie doesn't want to hear.

SOOMI MAK: Well, it's true.

WILLIE MAK: Just because it's true, doesn't mean it needs to be said. [*To*

Suzie.] He works hard to make enough to send for his wife. But he's a man, you know . . .

Soomi Mak: My uncle is a male chauvinist pig!

Willie Mak: Suzie, where is the police? How come they don't come?

Chorus: [All.] Don't touch that dial! We'll be right back, after these brief commercial messages.

Tara: [*Does one.*] Whenever you see black people, do you lock your doors? Do you cross the street? Do you ever get a churning unsettled feeling? Do black folks make you nervous? If you want to ease that queasy feeling . . . if you want to get along with black people, like I do, just say, "Hey, bro, whas'up" and give 'em a high five. And all your fears will disappear . . . like magic. [Suzie, Soomi, *and* Ruth *do one.*]

Suzie Seeto: My mother marched into my room. I was about Soomi's age.

Soomi Mak: I was in the girls' room, combing my hair.

Nurse Ruth Betty: Tangles. Ouch. Don't pull so hard, Nana.

Suzie Seeto: And she threw out my platform shoes. Why do you wear these things? Mother asked. Because, Mom, I like being taller.

Soomi Mak: There was a girl, a classmate of mine, Stacy Skowronski. [Tara *combs her hair.*]

Nurse Ruth Betty: Straight hair. All the boys flocked around the girls with straight hair.

Suzie Seeto: Then Mom took away my eyeliner. Why do you wear so much? Because, Mom, it makes my eyes look bigger.

Soomi Mak: Stacy was combing her long blonde hair. Her hair was like gold.

Nurse Ruth Betty: Hair like Diana Ross. So I marched myself down to the Nubian Princess House of Beauty and sat myself down. I looked at the magazines. All those perky noses and blue eyes, and I wondered if it was true.

Suzie Seeto: Next, she took my curling iron. So I looked her straight in the eye and formulated a question.

Soomi Mak: Stacy was at the mirror, combing with long smooth strokes. "Stacy?" I said.

Tara: "Yes?"

Soomi, Suzie, and Ruth: "Is it true what they say, blondes have more fun?"

Soomi Mak: Stacy stopped combing her hair. She paused. She thought about it. A very serious expression came over her blue eyes. And then she said . . .

Tara" "Uh huh. Yes. Yes, they do."

Soomi Mak: I'm gonna be *screwed up* for years.

Suzie Seeto: Give me that peroxide.

Nurse Ruth Betty: Fuck that shit.

[GROCER MAK *and the* BARBER *address audience.*]

GROCER MAK: I get along with black people.

BARBER BROWN: People are people. My father, Baldy Brown, told me that. People are people.

GROCER MAK: I show them respect plenty.

BARBER BROWN: My own brother, an uptown Wall Street man, don't come around much. What he want with his barber brother anyway. Sometimes he treats me like I was dirt.

GROCER MAK: Plenty of respect. I don't look in their eyes. I don't touch them in false sign of friendly greeting. This is our way. This is the Korean way.

BARBER BROWN: I could been a Wall Street man. When I was a kid, I wanted to make some paper money, so I could buy Park Place. My brother got all the good properties, and I needed to transact, and fast. So, I get Pop's big scissors and snip, snip, snip. Made me some quick cash.

GROCER MAK: To be honest, I don't have many black people as my friends. [*Grunts.*] I am too busy for friends. Wake up at five A.M., work until one A.M. Do it all over again next day. Seven days a week. Even Sunday.

BARBER BROWN: Next thing I know, my uncle sees red. Shoutin', "Oh no. Oh no. What you doin' with my Sunday paper, boy?" I said, "Uncle Joe, I don't care about your stupid newspaper, I gotta buy Park Place." Boom, he whacks me good. Then he gets on all fours, muttering "Jackie Robinson, Jackie Robinson," and he starts putting the pieces of the newspaper back together, trying to read about Jackie Robinson retirin'.

GROCER MAK: The only happiness I have is on Sunday when June massages my feet and tells me not to worry about anything. June has a beauty mark, right here on her cheek, in the shape of a small strawberry. When she laughs, this little berry dips into her smile. I like that. Sometimes she insists and pours me a glass of Soju. She says, "Here, drink this. You need it." The Soju wipes away my tears.

BARBER BROWN: Aunt Natalie wipes the tears from my face. "Don't you mind, Uncle Joe." Then, I'll never forget this moment, Aunt Natalie hands me the big scissors and says, "Lil' Jimmy, will you cut my hair?" She undoes her bun; her shiny black hair falls straight to the middle of her back.

GROCER MAK: The Soju goes to my head and makes me think about my wife still in Korea. Are you shocked? Sure, I have a girlfriend. My wife is far away, and my girlfriend she lives upstairs. I miss my wife, but she is so stubborn. She does not want to leave her family. She wants me to save up enough to bring her whole clan to America. This I am trying to do, but sometimes the loneliness I feel . . .

[*Back in the newsroom.*]

MARK THOMPSON: Suzie!

BARBER BROWN: At first, the family said, "What is this Korean girl doing in Harlem?" My uncle said Aunt Natalie was his first real girlfriend. They met at the Fighting Tiger Bar in Pusan (Poo-san). Uncle Joe says it was love at first sight. I stopped crying. I cut her hair just like she told me. Her long black hairs tickled my bare feet as they fell to the floor.

MARK THOMPSON: Suzie, you are late! You have one-half hour. Go! Go! Go! What do I run here? An old folks' home?

SUZIE SEETO: I'll be at the editing bay.

MARK THOMPSON: Get in there! That's my girl.

[*The editing room.* SUZIE *reviews her taped interviews.*]

SUZIE SEETO: Okay. What's the time code on the establishing shots? Never mind, I got it in front of my nose. Can I have a fast forward to . . . somewhere about 5:50?

[*The street in front of the New Way Grocery Store. The* BLACK CHORUS *and* KOREAN CHORUS *move erratically, as if in fast-forward motion.*]

BLACK CHORUS: [*High-pitched, fast-forward.*] Boycott,letitrot! Boycott, letitrot! Boycott,letitrot!

SUZIE SEETO: Great. Let's take it from here and go about six seconds.

BLACK CHORUS: [*Silently, mouthing the words.*] Boycott, let it rot! Boycott, let it rot! Boycott, let it rot!

SUZIE SEETO: That's it. Now, how about some natural sound over that?

BLACK CHORUS: [*More fraternity stepping.*] Boycott, let it rot! Boycott, let it rot! Boycott, let it rot! Boycott, let it rot!

SUZIE SEETO: That's it. That'll be the establishing shot. Okay, can I have 6:12 for a closer look? Give me another five seconds of that. [*The* BLACK CHORUS *scurries downstage, continuing the protest. The* KOREAN CHORUS *remains behind.*]

BLACK CHORUS: We want respect! We want respect! We want respect!

SUZIE SEETO: Great. That's what I want. Now, skip to . . . somewhere around 6:12:45. The Korean grocery owner, no, wait. First a general shot of the Koreans, and their reaction. About 6:08, just before this Grocer stuff. I need a reaction shot. [*The* KOREAN CHORUS *scurries downstage, joins the* BLACK CHORUS. *The* KOREANS *pose—their faces are frozen in a frown.*] That looks good. What do you think, Tommy? Yeah. I think that's nice. Let's do that, and now let's cut to the interview with . . . ah . . . what's his name, here it is, the Reverend. The bite I'm looking for starts with ". . . no longer . . ." and ends with ". . . force them out of business."

REVEREND CARTER: No longer are we forced to shop with people who do not look like us. Those Koreans don't respect us. Now, they can no longer disrespect us. We'll force them to respect us. We'll force them out of business. [*Beat.*] This is a grassroots movement, Suzie. We are here because we are tired of Korean disrespect towards African Americans right in our own neighborhoods. [*He freezes.*]

SUZIE SEETO: Hold it there. Okay, so let's keep that bite. But I want to dump out after . . . "force them to respect us."

REVEREND CARTER: [*Backtracking.*] . . . ssenisub fo tuo meht ecrof ll'eW.us tcepser ot meht ecrof ll'eW . . .

SUZIE SEETO: There.

REVEREND CARTER: We'll force them to respect us. We'll force them out of business.

SUZIE SEETO: Stop! And out. Great. Thank you. Now, can I have the grocery owner, please?

GROCER MAK: [*Garbled, like a piece of film off its sprocket.*] Why are they do-do-doing this to me? All my bl-bl-blood, all my sw-sw-sweat is in this st-st-store.

SUZIE SEETO: Oh . . . fudge! What do you think? Do you think we can use it? Never mind, we'll look for something else. How about 6:45:17?

GROCER MAK: This is America-ca-ca! What kind of America-ca-ca is this?

[MARK *enters the editing room.*]

MARK THOMPSON: That sounds terrible. Don't use it.

SUZIE SEETO: Yes sir, I'll rework it.

MARK THOMPSON: Good. And Suzie, you now have twelve minutes.

SUZIE SEETO: [*Calmly.*] Plenty of time. [*Panicked.*] So okay, well . . . let's keep the picture anyway. I'll do a voice over. Problem solved. Now, let's see what follows, maybe I can use something from Willie Mak, the guy's nephew.

WILLIE MAK: [*Also garbled, slow motion.*] Poqiwuer bladkj ieowowut yruie rewqy ouior cneiowpcustomers away. They act like animals. They act like animals.

SUZIE SEETO: [*Joins* WILLIE *for the interview. Mimes microphone in hand.*] Willie? Ruieow fjapwoiur rueiwoqp ur woiwur ywurei?

WILLIE MAK: Yes, I yyriewjbnm. I yrnfmdhewm.

SUZIE SEETO: But do you urie alskh vnuriwqe?

WILLIE MAK: It's true laksjdf yuiop lksj.

SUZIE SEETO: And does your uncle sdflkouios werosi suio?

WILLIE MAK: My uncle is very asdffdsfj ouedb utsoie sicklikswe animals. They are like animals. They act like animals.

SUZIE SEETO: [*Sits back down.*] This is not my day. [*Sighs.*] All right. I'll bridge this with . . . I don't know what. Let's keep looking for something I can use.

[NURSE RUTH BETTY *addresses the audience.*]

NURSE RUTH BETTY: [*Silently mouths the words.*] Don't Buy Here! Don't Buy Here! Don't Buy Here!

SUZIE SEETO: Natural sound over this, please.

NURSE RUTH BETTY: Don't Buy Here. Don't Buy Here. Don't buy here.

SUZIE SEETO: Thank you. Please make sure we doublecheck with graphics on her name. She's got two first names. Thank you. Now, let's try to get something of the Koreans.

MARK THOMPSON: Ten more minutes, Suzie.

NURSE RUTH BETTY: I been asking the bank for three years now. I need a loan so I can start my own shop in my own neighborhood. I want to get out of working for other people, start working for myself. Back in North Carolina, where I'm from, all my people think I'm crazy. A woman alone owning a business.

SUZIE SEETO: Yeah, yeah, yeah . . . let's skip that.

NURSE RUTH BETTY: [*Insistently.*] They say I'm a bad risk. They say, you don't have the proper collateral. I've been trying to get a loan, but no one will give me one.

SUZIE SEETO: Didn't I say, let's get through this part?

NURSE RUTH BETTY: [*Insistently.*] But I tell them, I have ideas. A special children's clinic. A place to go for inoculations, general preventative maintenance, classes on baby care. Our neighborhood's got a need. I could do it too, if someone would just give me a boost up.

SUZIE SEETO: Hey, what's the idea? I'm working a deadline here. A little fast-forward, if you please.

NURSE RUTH BETTY: [*Practically shouting.*] I'm just asking for a hand, not a handout. The answer is always no. I say, "black businesses for black communities."

SUZIE SEETO: [*Overlapping, shouting.*] Hey, what gives? We're not using this. I like it, but I'm already over and I don't have a bite from the Korean side. Cut out Ruth Betty.

BLACK CHORUS: Say what?

SUZIE SEETO: It's really a side issue.

BLACK CHORUS: It's the central issue. Put Ruth Betty back in.

NURSE RUTH BETTY: Why are you cutting me out?

SUZIE SEETO: I'm slotted for a one minute–fifteen package. This is no time for an economics lesson.

BLACK CHORUS: But she's telling it like it is. She's giving the story balance, context, motive.

NURSE RUTH BETTY: I've been trying for years to get a loan from the bank. The answer is always no! How come those people get loans? How come? You know very well why. I got dreams too. What about my dreams?

REVEREND CARTER: Black businesses for black people.

NURSE RUTH BETTY: [To REVEREND.] I can handle this, thank you. [To SUZIE.] I say, "black businesses for black people."

REVEREND CARTER: You have a responsibility and an obligation to remind racist America just how racist it is.

KOREAN CHORUS: What about us? She doesn't have a comment from us. What about our dreams? What about our side of the story.

BLACK CHORUS: Who can understand you anyway, with your bad accent!

KOREAN CHORUS: Says who!

BLACK CHORUS: Says we, that's who!

KOREAN CHORUS: Oh yeah?

BLACK CHORUS: Yeah.

KOREAN CHORUS: Oh yeah?

SUZIE SEETO: Hey, I don't have time to argue. I've only got limited resources; namely, one minute and fifteen seconds to tell the story. I promise to do an in-depth investigation, get all the angles, later.

NURSE RUTH BETTY: But . . .

MARK THOMPSON: Suzie, you got two minutes. What are you doing in there?

SUZIE SEETO: You hear that? I'm being paged. I'm needed on the set. I've got to go.

NURSE RUTH BETTY: We knew you would side with them. They all stick together.

KOREAN CHORUS: Help us, Suzie. We have to stick together.

BLACK CHORUS: [Softly.] Bias. Unfair. Bias. Unfair. Bias.

SOOMI MAK: Please help us, Miss Seeto.

WILLIE MAK: Please help us.

GROCER MAK: We understand each other, yes?

REVEREND CARTER: Bias. Unfair. Bias. [Whispers.] Racist.

SUZIE SEETO: [Pause.] All right, let's use the "blacks for black business" portion of her interview. Tell Tara I have to take a set question on the Korean position. I repeat, Tara has to ask me a question on the Korean side.

MARK THOMPSON: Suzie! Get your fan tan fanny on the set! One minute.

SUZIE SEETO: One minute to spare. Not bad, no problem. Okay, let's go, let's go. We're outta here. Where's my copy? How's my hair?

BLACK CHORUS: Suzie, as always, looked calm and collected.

KOREAN CHORUS: She looks very good on the set.

[*The newsroom.* TARA *is in the anchor seat.* SUZIE *is seated next to her. Silently, the* CHORUS *reenacts.* SUZIE*'s taped report.*]

TARA: . . . our reporter Suzie Seeto was there . . .

SUZIE SEETO: Here's a couple of set questions. Don't forget to ask this one about the Koreans. [*The* CHORUS *moves, as if the tape is on.*]

TARA: No problem. Good job on this Flatbush story.

SUZIE SEETO: Thanks. Fast and dirty. The morons on the desk gave me the wrong directions and I had only ten minutes to . . .

TARA: Uh, we're coming back. [*The tape ends.*]

SUZIE SEETO: Oh. I'll tell you about it later.

TARA: Well, what a confusing story.

SUZIE SEETO: Yes, it's difficult, but the Koreans—

TARA: [*Cuts her off.*] Excellent job, Suzie, on a complicated story that grows more complicated by the minute. Up next, our very own Kevin Alexander will preview the weekend weather. We'll have more on that and other top stories of the day when we return. [CHORUS *looks at* SUZIE, TARA.] Ooops!

CHORUS: Accidents will happen.

SUZIE SEETO: I can't believe it. I can't believe it. That ignorant no-talent ditzy blonde.

[MARK *enters.*]

MARK THOMPSON: Who's got no talent? And that piece you just did was terrible. What happened to the Korean position?

SUZIE SEETO: Tara, the Goddess of the Airwaves, was supposed to ask me a question, so's I can get in the Korean side of the story.

MARK THOMPSON: So . . .

SUZIE SEETO: So I'm waiting, and waiting, and still waiting, and . . . she tosses to a fucking commercial. Mark, I want her head . . . and I want her job.

KOREAN CHORUS: Immediately after the broadcast. The station is deluged with phone calls.

[*The* CHORUS *is on the phone.*]

BLACK CHORUS: That's it girl. Be impartial like that all the time.

KOREAN CHORUS: You screwed us.

SUZIE SEETO: Tara, you screwed me, good.

TARA: I don't know what you mean?

BLACK CHORUS: We're gonna give you an N.double-A.C.P award.

KOREAN CHORUS: You are no friend to Korean people.

TARA: I had to make a judgment call. Barri was giving me a countdown to the commercial. I guess we ran over. I'm sorry:

SUZIE SEETO: You did it on purpose, and you know it.

TARA: You are hallucinating.

BLACK CHORUS: You are beautiful.

KOREAN CHORUS: You stink.

BLACK CHORUS: You're gonna get profiles in *Essence* <u>and</u> *Ebony*.

SUZIE SEETO: I thought you were my friend. All that sisterhood crap.

BLACK CHORUS: Sistah! Sistah!

SUZIE SEETO: I could strangle you.

TARA: Don't you touch me.

BLACK CHORUS: We could kiss you.

KOREAN CHORUS: We could kill you.

GROCER MAK: I'm ashamed of you.

REVEREND CARTER: I'm proud of you.

SUZIE SEETO: You were giving me a blow job all along.

TARA: How dare you. You rank beginner.

KOREAN CHORUS: You traitor!

SUZIE SEETO: You traitor!

BLACK CHORUS: Girlfriend!

TARA: Get a hold of yourself, Suzie. You really aren't ready for the anchor seat, my dear. You just don't have the composure. If you can't stand the heat, stay out of the newsroom.

KOREAN CHORUS: You screwed us. You fucked us. You buried us like kimchee.

BLACK CHORUS: You helped us. You treated us right. You told the truth.

TARA: You'll never amount to anything in this business.

KOREAN CHORUS: Traitor!

BLACK CHORUS: Girlfriend!

TARA: Bitch.

KOREAN CHORUS: You screwed us. You fucked us. You buried us like kimchee.

BLACK CHORUS: You helped us. You treated us right. You told the truth.

TARA: You'll never amount to anything in this business.

SUZIE SEETO: No more! Please! I'm tired. [*Short pause.*] The mayor's press conference is tomorrow, and I'll have the walls of Jericho under my eyes. [MARK *approaches her.*] What?

MARK THOMPSON: Suzie, I know you had a hard day. Maybe you'd like to . . . I know a quiet little place where the bartender frosts the mugs, pours big tall ones. Little rubber sharks perched on the rim. Come on, let me buy you a drink.

SUZIE SEETO: Are you? Are you asking me out? On a date?

MARK THOMPSON: Oh, god. I feel like I'm back in high school. It's not what you think, Suzie.

SUZIE SEETO: Oh, god.

MARK THOMPSON: Let me help. I'd like to help. Jesus, you are beautiful.

SUZIE SEETO: Mark, this is too much for me. I'm from Canton, *Ohio*, for Christ's sake.

MARK THOMPSON: Well, welcome to the big city. [*He holds out his hand to her. She looks at him. Slow blackout.*]

END OF ACT I

ACT II

AT RISE: Both CHORUSES address the audience, as SUZIE and the REVEREND sit in a cafe.

BLACK CHORUS: Warning! The following may contain material that may not be suited for . . .

KOREAN CHORUS: If this had been an actual emergency . . .

BLACK CHORUS:	KOREAN CHORUS:
Warning! The following may not be suited for . . .	If this had been an actual emergency . . .

TARA AND MARK: The world is a bigger place than where we are.

CHORUS: [ALL, *sotto voce.*] The world is a bigger place than where we are.

[*In the cafe.*]

REVEREND CARTER: Suzie, if you wouldn't mind, I'd like to sit with my back to the wall. To keep an eye on the door.

SUZIE SEETO: Post-traumatic stress syndrome? That's a joke.

REVEREND CARTER: Survival techniques for life in the jungle. That's not a joke. Well, Suzie, I hear from you more times in one day. My wife's beginning to wonder.

SUZIE SEETO: It's my job. I'm sorry if I'm such a pest.

REVEREND CARTER: What do you need, Suzie? Whatever you want, you can have it.

SUZIE SEETO: Reverend, I want to talk to Matilda Duvet. I need to talk to her. I know she can clear everything up.

REVEREND CARTER: Is that right?

SUZIE SEETO: I think you are hiding her. I think you've been keeping her sequestered. Look, I have an obligation to talk to her. You have an obligation to the truth.

REVEREND CARTER: Suzie, you want to talk about truth? Today, I buried three black boys, barely teenagers.

SUZIE SEETO: I didn't hear anything about it.

REVEREND CARTER: I'm sure you didn't. The boys pulling the trigger were black, and the victims were black. No, I'm sure you didn't hear about it. But it's everyday to me. Nothing delayed about this stress. One of those boys was a close friend of my son's.

SUZIE SEETO: I'm sorry. I didn't mean to be insensitive.

REVEREND CARTER: No, I know you didn't. Well, let's dispense with the small talk. I have something you want, and I'm willing to give it to you.

SUZIE SEETO: An exclusive with Matilda Duvet?

REVEREND CARTER: No one else will have it but you, I guarantee.

SUZIE SEETO: One on one. No one else.

REVEREND CARTER: Just you and the truth.

SUZIE SEETO: Great! Great, that's just great. I can't believe it.

REVEREND CARTER: You help us, I help you. That's the way it works.

SUZIE SEETO: The way it works.

REVEREND CARTER: We like to repay the people who work with us.

SUZIE SEETO: You want to repay me.

REVEREND CARTER: Let's just say you showed your true color.

SUZIE SEETO: My true color. I see.

REVEREND CARTER: Besides, Matilda Duvet, what she knows or doesn't know, what happened or didn't happen . . . that's irrelevant now. The ball is rolling. What this story is now . . . well, it's bigger than Matilda Duvet. Keep up the good work, Suzie! [*He pushes a piece of paper towards her.*]

MARK THOMPSON: [*From the newsroom.*] Suzie! Don't take shortcuts. Find another source.

SUZIE SEETO: Reverend, thank you, but . . .

MARK THOMPSON: People might get the wrong impression.

SUZIE SEETO: People might get the wrong impression. No, I can't be owing you any favors. I know Matilda Duvet is the key to all of this, but I'll have to find her on my own, without your help. I can't be bought.

REVEREND CARTER: You reporters have an overinflated sense of ethics. I don't think you can be bought for a simple slip of paper.

SUZIE SEETO: You don't have me in your pocket, sir. I'm fair and impartial. I need Matilda Duvet to get to the bottom of it, but I won't accept favors.

MARK THOMPSON: The appearance of wrongdoing . . .

CHORUS: . . . is as dangerous as the deed.

SUZIE SEETO: I'll find Matilda Duvet somehow, on my own.

REVEREND CARTER: Suit yourself . . . if that's what you want. I know a dozen reporters who might be interested in this piece of paper.

SUZIE SEETO: Look, I've got you guys thinking I'm in bed with you. I've got Koreans who think I'm a traitor to the yellow race. I've got a knife in my back from someone I thought was a friend. I'm getting love notes from my boss, and on top of that, I think you are a racist.

REVEREND CARTER: [Laughs.] Suzie, Suzie, Suzie. [Still chuckling.] A black man in America can never be a racist. To be a racist, you have to have power. And that, I most certainly do not have. I may be bigoted. I may be prejudiced. But I am not a racist.

SUZIE SEETO: [Nods, puts out her hand to say good-bye.] See you at the courthouse tomorrow. [He pulls out the paper, holds it out to her. SUZIE debates.]

MARK THOMPSON: Don't do it, Suzie. [She takes the paper anyway.]

[Meanwhile, in the street.]

BLACK CHORUS: White court, black injustice. White court, black injustice . . .

[The New Way Grocery Store. A POLICEMAN IN RIOT GEAR sets up a blue barricade, which reads: DO NOT CROSS. The POLICEMAN has a Brooklyn accent.]

SUZIE SEETO: I am coming to you, live, from outside the New Way Grocery Store. A judge this afternoon ruled in favor of the owner of this Korean store, who filed for an injunction to keep protesters away. I see the store owner. Mr. Key Chun Mak. You had a successful day in court, how . . . [GROCER MAK grunts, waves her away.] Uh, Mr. Mak, we're live and coming to you from the New Way Grocery Store. The owner is right here, Mr. Mak, could I speak with you for a moment?

GROCER MAK: No! [He walks away from her.]

SUZIE SEETO: I'm on live. Today is a good day for you, isn't it, Mr. Mak? Today, the judge ruled in your favor.

SOOMI MAK: We're pretty happy about the decision.

GROCER MAK: Soomi!

WILLIE MAK: Every time you are on teevee, more of them come everyday.

GROCER MAK: *Gae-sek-ki! Gae-sek-ki-dul! Ggam-doong-e!*

SUZIE SEETO: That was Key Chun Mak, store owner. Things are understandably tense here. Some 200 protesters are marching from the courthouse, and they plan to hold a rally right in front of the store.

BLACK CHORUS: White court, black injustice. White court, black injustice.

SUZIE SEETO: Here they are. [*The* BLACK CHORUS *to one side, the* KOREAN CHORUS *on the other—a face-off.*]

BLACK CHORUS: White court, black injustice. White court, black injustice. White court, black injustice. White court, black injustice . . . [*Etc.*]

SUZIE SEETO: [*Quietly, overlapping with* CHORUS.] The protesters are disappointed by the judge's decision, but they say it is no surprise. What?

TARA: Speak up, Suzie. We can't hear you.

BLACK CHORUS: White court, black injustice. White court, black injustice. White court, black injustice. White court, black injustice . . . [*Etc.*]

SUZIE SEETO: I said, they say they can't trust the courts to uphold their civil rights. And so they've taken their complaints to the streets. [*Quietly.*] The judge has ruled that the protesters must stay fifty feet from police lines.

TARA: Suzie, we can't hear you. Please speak up, Suzie.

SUZIE SEETO: What? Oh, I said the judge said stay back *fifty feet* from the store.

POLICEMAN IN RIOT GEAR: *Fifty feet!* Let's go. Let's move. That means you too. [*To audience.*] Oh, it's Nancy Kwan.

SUZIE SEETO: Do I look like I sell pearl cream?

POLICEMAN IN RIOT GEAR: Poor kid, she's scared out of her mind. You'd never know it, but I can always tell. Her fingers twitch like Morse code. She's thinking she's too close to the action.

SUZIE SEETO: I shouldn't have had so much coffee.

POLICEMAN IN RIOT GEAR: But she's also thinking she's got a job to do.

SUZIE SEETO: Got that right, officer. I'm gonna stay right here.

POLICEMAN IN RIOT GEAR: [*To audience.*] All reporters think they are invincible. You always see them running across police lines, drawing sniper fire like bullets just bounce off. Her job is her bulletproof vest. Wear the job, and nothing can hurt you. You know what I'm talking? Emotional armor. I know. I've got it on too.

SUZIE SEETO: I'm going to stay right here.

POLICEMAN IN RIOT GEAR: Suit yourself. All right, judge said get back. Fifty feet. Fifty feet from the sidewalk! Let's go. Everybody move. I said, move!

SUZIE SEETO: Nobody moved.

BLACK CHORUS: Korean monkey!

KOREAN CHORUS: Black monkey!

BLACK CHORUS: Go back to Korea!

KOREAN CHORUS: Go back to Africa!

BLACK CHORUS: Black nigger.

KOREAN CHORUS: Yellow nigger.

BLACK CHORUS:	KOREAN CHORUS:
Well, you know what I mean.	Did we say that right?

POLICEMAN IN RIOT GEAR: All right. Keep it moving. Keep the sidewalk moving.

KOREAN CHORUS: The Reverend Carter prepares to be interviewed.

REVEREND CARTER: I clear my throat. [SUZIE *acknowledges the* REVEREND.]

BARBER BROWN: Stand aside, Ruthie, can't you see Suzie is going to interview the Reverend?

SUZIE SEETO: That's how it stands now. I'm Suzie Seeto. Back to you in the newsroom.

REVEREND CARTER: Suzie, I'm hurt.

SUZIE SEETO: Reverend, I'm not your personal publicist.

REVEREND CARTER: But you always get my best side.

SUZIE SEETO: Reverend, I'm not in your camp, their camp, any camp. I'm trying to be fair and impartial, just the facts, okay?

REVEREND CARTER: No one wants to interview me, and now you? *Et tu,* Suzie?

SUZIE SEETO: I think you said plenty at the courthouse.

CHORUS: He caused quite a commotion.

REVEREND CARTER: [*Proudly.*] I did.

SUZIE SEETO: He was dragged out of court by police.

CHORUS: It was quite a sight.

REVEREND CARTER: [*Proudly.*] It was.

[*The* JUDGE IN HIS SARTORIAL SPLENDOR *addresses the audience.*]

JUDGE IN HIS SARTORIAL SPLENDOR: Reverend Carter, you do not further the cause of justice with your outbursts and grandstanding. I won't tolerate it in my court.

REVEREND CARTER: [*To* JUDGE.] Then I'll take it to the streets! I'll take it to the court of public opinion. That man sitting there is no judge, he is the devil. The devil incarnate!

JUDGE IN HIS SARTORIAL SPLENDOR: That's quite enough, Mr. Carter.

REVEREND CARTER: It's never enough, you racist! I said, racist! You are a devil racist!

JUDGE IN HIS SARTORIAL SPLENDOR: You are in contempt, mister.

REVEREND CARTER: Got that right! You got that right! Contempt for institutionalized racism.

JUDGE IN HIS SARTORIAL SPLENDOR: I'm not going to dignify this. Bailiff, have that man ejected from my court. I will not tolerate disrespect! [*The* CHORUS *surround and descend upon the* REVEREND *like a* PACK OF REPORTERS.]

REVEREND CARTER: White America tells us things have gotten better. I'm telling you, Rise Up Black Man! Rise up and come down to the New Way Grocery Store and claim your dignity and self-respect. And after we shut those Koreans down, white racist America is next!

SUZIE SEETO: That caused a feeding frenzy among my fellow colleagues. Reporters descended on the Reverend and shoved microphones and recording devices in his face.

PACK OF REPORTERS: What do you think? How do you feel? Question!

REVEREND CARTER: We rioted back in the 1960s, and we'll riot again. There will be a race riot if something doesn't change! But let's call it a rebellion, shall we? Black America, rise up and have a Boston Tea Party!

PACK OF REPORTERS: How did you? Will you ever? What if? Question!

REVEREND CARTER: Innocent black children are doping up, dropping out, dying young—and why is that? Because all their lives they're ashamed of being black. I'm telling you the truth; racist America has stripped us of our dignity.

PACK OF REPORTERS: How can it be? What is your evidence? Question!

REVEREND CARTER: That devil judge! He dragged me out of court like an animal. I'm a man, a human being. He dragged me out of court because he didn't want to hear the truth.

PACK OF REPORTERS: How about? Can it be? What if? Question! How did you? Will you ever? What if? Question! Question! Question!

SUZIE SEETO: Question! Reverend Carter, I have a question. Are you doing this to advance your career as an activist?

REVEREND CARTER: Suzie, are you doing this story to advance your career as a journalist?

[*Meanwhile, in the newsroom.*]

SUZIE SEETO: I can't believe you killed the story. I just used a little bit of what he said.

MARK THOMPSON: Are you saying every reporter in town is in on a conspiracy of silence? No one else saw fit to give the Reverend fifteen seconds of airtime. No one dignified his comments, except you. Why is that? Maybe you have a predisposition for the darker hues of the color spectrum? Is that why you won't have dinner with me? Am I too white for you?

SUZIE SEETO: You? You are too Asian for me.

MARK THOMPSON: Well, now, that's very telling.

SUZIE SEETO: Mark, that was a good story. A good overall view, with a little context thrown in for good measure. I'm not making it up, Mark. Everybody mobbed him. He was the focal point of the whole story.

MARK THOMPSON: Matilda Duvet and what happened at the grocery store was the focal point of that hearing, Suzie. Court injunction. Cover that, not some rabid reverend.

SUZIE SEETO: But, listen, Mark . . .

MARK THOMPSON: But what? Calling for a race riot, I'd say, was self-serving and inflammatory. This station isn't going to be irresponsible, or accused of adding more fuel to the fire. Suzie, that guy is a racist.

SUZIE SEETO: People of color can't be racist. [*Quoting.*] "It implies power, which we don't have."

MARK THOMPSON: What WE don't have is a little good judgment. How about exercising yours every once in a while. [*Softening.*] Maybe we should go to Joe Allen's and talk about this.

SUZIE SEETO: No, I'm not going to Joe Allen's. The Reverend may be a publicity stunt, as I pointed out in the piece, but as I also pointed out, he very eloquently explains why the boycott is happening. It was a chance for once to put the WHY into a story.

MARK THOMPSON: I find it hard to believe the Reverend is a representative sample of the popular majority of black sentiment. Do you like hamburgers?

SUZIE SEETO: Look, I don't want to inflame people. I don't want to contribute to the hate machine. But the truth, in this case, is inflammatory by nature. I'm not going to sanitize the news.

MARK THOMPSON: Are you saying NBC, CBS, ABC, CNN are laundering, bleaching the news. The *New York Times?*

SUZIE SEETO: Fuck the *New York Times*, and fuck that hamburger.

MARK THOMPSON: Suzie, sometimes reporters make value judgments in order to keep from giving every lunatic airtime. Yes, report what happens, but also consider the source. Listen, Suzie, listen to me carefully, don't do it again!

SUZIE SEETO: But . . .

MARK THOMPSON: Did this Reverend put some kind of voodoo spell on you? I will say it slowly. Do it again and you might as well pack up and go to Peoria. If the Reverend shows up at the mayor's office tomorrow, yes, I want to see you shoving your microphone up his . . . nose. But no, I don't necessarily want to hear what he has to say, okay? Got that?

SUZIE SEETO: Yes'um boss, I'll tote that bucket fer ya.

MARK THOMPSON: Do not disrespect my office. Disrespect has its consequences. You got that? [*Beat.*] Meanwhile, back in the street.

[*The street.* SUZIE *conducts interviews—Ping-pong style.*]

BLACK CHORUS: We want Koreans to put their money in black-owned banks.

SUZIE SEETO: Black-owned banks?

KOREAN CHORUS: We did that. We got no service.

SUZIE SEETO: You got no service?

BLACK CHORUS: We want Koreans to hire blacks to work in their stores.

SUZIE SEETO: Blacks working in Korean stores?

KOREAN CHORUS: We did that. They stole from us.

SUZIE SEETO: They stole from you?

BARBER BROWN: You paid them slave wages.

SUZIE SEETO: They did?

GROCER MAK: We paid them more than we paid ourselves.

SUZIE SEETO: You did?

BLACK CHORUS: White court, black injustice. White court, black injustice.

SUZIE SEETO: Live from Brooklyn. I'm Suzie Seeto. Back to you, Tara and Ted.

REVEREND CARTER: Cool it. Cool it. Hold it down. Teevee's off.

GROCER MAK: Go away, black devil! You get away from my store!

BARBER BROWN: Forget it, Makie. We're taking a break.

GROCER MAK: Huh?

BARBER BROWN: When the red light goes on, we go on and when the red light goes off . . . forget it, Makie. My throat is sore.

GROCER MAK: I am not a performing bear.

BARBER BROWN: I feel the same way. But one thing leads to another, and before you know it, you get swept up.

GROCER MAK: Swept up?

BARBER BROWN: Yeah, carried away. All the cameras and the excitement and the meetings, the feeling of being bigger than just a nobody barber.

NURSE RUTH BETTY: Come on, Smokeman. Everybody's meetin' on the corner.

[*The New Way Store.*]

SUZIE SEETO: Willie, aren't you glad the police are here?

WILLIE MAK: They don't do anything. Just stand there. [*Beat.*] I've been reading the Bible, and it says, an eye for an eye.

SUZIE SEETO: So I've heard.

WILLIE MAK: I . . . I bought a gun! I didn't want to do it. But look how it fits in my hand, isn't it nice?

SOOMI MAK: Willie's got a Bible in one hand and a gun in the other. Well, not me. I made a protest sign instead, just like them. I'm gonna use it next time, too. See if I don't. Willie don't even know how to use that stupid gun thing. But I know how to use this. [*Shakes her sign.*] Then teevee will see we mean business too. Don't I catch on fast? [*She holds up a sign. It reads:* YELLOW IS BEAUTIFUL!] I know a protest song too. Want to hear it?

CHORUS: [ALL.] No!

SOOMI MAK: [*Sings quickly.*] Glory, glory, hallelujah. Glory, glory, hallelujah. Glory, glory, hallelujah. His truth is marching . . .

POLICEMAN IN RIOT GEAR: [*Interrupts her.*] That's it. Everybody fifty feet. Move!

SOOMI MAK: [*Undeterred, defiantly.*] . . . on! . . .

POLICEMAN IN RIOT GEAR: You too! Everybody fifty feet away from the store. Fifty feet! Everybody fifty feet from the store. Fifty feet!

SUZIE SEETO: Thank you, Tara. The situation is pretty much the same as it was five minutes ago. Things get pretty quiet once the cameras go away, but protesters don't leave even when the media isn't around.

NURSE RUTH BETTY: Hey, we're on again. Come on, everybody. We're on.

BARBER BROWN: Wait, wait. [*He takes out his pick, combs his hair quickly.*] Okay.

REVEREND CARTER: Show time. [*The* BLACK CHORUS *mugs audience, freezes, smiling big.*]

KOREAN CHORUS: And now for the following editorials.

WILLIE MAK: [*Has his moment.*] In school, back in Korea, we learned about the melting pot. I want to *melt* into the melting pot. Not my sister Soomi, she was born here. She wants to pierce her nose and put a ring in there. She wants to shout, "I am here." But not me. I want to get along with everybody. Last year, I took the citizenship test. The test was so hard. So much brain work, you know. But I pass it. America is the place for me. I look around the courtroom to make the Pledge of Allegiance, and I see all the crying faces of happiness. We are all so different, but we all have crying faces of happiness. And now, I have a gun. My uncle won't let me buy bullets. He said, no bullets. But I have the freedom to bear arms. And if they throw one more rock or shove one more customer, I'm going to send all those motherfuckers to heaven.

TARA: [*Takes her turn.*] Actually, I like Suzie. We both came from the Midwest. We both like country music, and we both love our jobs. I'll never forget, we were at this great Thai place near 72nd and Columbus, and Mark was showing off, ordering our lunch in perfect Thailandese, whatever. The waiters were eating it up.

SUZIE SEETO: Mr. Asiaphile really does know his stuff. I think my mother would like him. What do you think?

TARA: Suzie was so funny, she kept talking about fly-fishing. Mark was so confused. He didn't know a yellow humpy from a black wooly worm.

SUZIE SEETO: So I'm showing Tara how to tie a Mickey Finn with a cellophane noodle.

TARA: Suzie puts down the Mickey Finn, she calls the waiter over. Then, she calmly hands back her chopsticks and orders—a *fork!*

SUZIE SEETO: Mark spits up his pot sticker, it goes sailing into the air, lands in Barbara Walters's soup.

TARA: Splash! [*They laugh.*] I guess you had to be there.

GROCER MAK: Soomi is a pain in the butt. Always asking me about our history.

BARBER BROWN: I been thinking about history. My history.

GROCER MAK: Korean history.

BARBER BROWN: African history. This whole protest has got me thinking about expanding the business into African tee shirts, bangles, Kente cloth, maybe get some caps in the colors of my people. Man, I do love my business.

GROCER MAK: You see, Soomi, Japanese people took your grandfather, made him a slave. Those black people, they think I don't understand them. But I understand. I know all about slaves. I met many black GI's in Korea during the war.

BARBER BROWN: Makie loves his business too. But it's about time I get off the fence. It's time to make a stand. Ruth Betty is right. I been hanging back too long. I just wish it wasn't Makie, that's all.

GROCER MAK: I know all about the Cotton Club. I know all about Dizzy Gillespie. I can dig it. Korean people know plenty about Harlem. Many black GI's marry Korean girls and take them home to Harlem. This I don't like. No, I don't like it. But no hard feeling.

BARBER BROWN: Maybe what we're doing is wrong. I don't want to make enemies. Oh, man, I don't know what's right anymore. I just don't know.

GROCER MAK: I don't want to make enemies. I came to America to be a businessman. To make for a better life. That is my dream. To be a free businessman in America, and make money!

CHORUS: The opinions expressed were not necessarily endorsed by the management. For rebuttals, please contact this station. Thank you.

[Back in the street.]

SUZIE SEETO: Right street, wrong address. Wrong street, right address. I should have gotten a map.

[Two black men—one is Haitian, the other wears an eyepatch—appear behind SUZIE. They follow her. Meanwhile, TARA is in the studio.]

TARA: We'll also be bringing you, live, from city hall, the mayor's first public address on the boycott. Our reporter on the scene, Suzie Seeto, will have live details of the mayor's press conference when we come back.

SUZIE SEETO: Not much time before the mayor's press conference. I can make it. *[Reciting, as if memorizing her notes.]* Haiti in the West Indies. Poorest nation in Western Hemisphere. Papa Doc became dictator 1957, died 1971. Created secret police called the *ton ton macoute*. Why are those guys slowing down when I slow down? Baby Doc overthrown 1986. Priest named Aristide, duly-elected president, ousted by military coup. The *ton ton macoute* still terrorizes the country. The *ton ton macoute* comes at night. I speed up, they speed up. Where's my mace?

HAITIAN MAN: I said, "Coochie, baby, come over to my house. I love you. *Ba'm ti fle(ur) ou. Ba'm ti fle(ur) ou.* Say no, to kung fu! Say yes, to love. Baby, I love you."

SUZIE SEETO: Hey. Why are you following me so close? Back off! Just back off. Back the fuck off!

BLACK MAN WITH EYEPATCH: Very uptight. You been living in New York too long.

HAITIAN MAN: Chill, baby! *[The men walk on, downstage. They must not interact with SUZIE, nor she with them.]*

SUZIE SEETO: I don't know what's come over me. What's the matter with me? *[Beat.]* Can I be . . . ? No, no way. NOT ME!

TARA: We've just gotten word from our camera crew, the mayor's press conference is starting a little early.

[MARK in the booth.]

MARK THOMPSON: Tell Tara, no live shot. Tell Tara, we have no Suzie. Tell Tara to kill, the . . . nix the . . . oh no.

TARA: . . . we're switching live to city hall to our reporter Suzie Seeto. Suzie, what's the atmosphere down there? Is the mayor going to call for a special mediator? Suzie?

MARK THOMPSON: Tell the remote to just feed us whatever's going on. Tell someone to find Suzie! Tell Tara to go to a commercial.

CHORUS: And now, ladies and gentlemen, live direct from the island, Matilda Duvet. [*In the round.*] And now, and now, and now, and now . . . [*Together.*] here's Matilda Duvet!!!

SUZIE SEETO: [*As* MATILDA. *She has a Haitian Creole accent. She must be seated, and relaxed by the Haitian sun.*] "Hi-tee! *l'union fait la force.*" (Haiti! Together we are strong.) "*Hi-tee, se yo bel payi eh moun yo tu.*" (Haiti is a beautiful country and the people are beautiful.) "*La vie ya ha-yeh pouli change.*" (Life will get better.) "*Mwen espere.*" (I hope.) [*Sighs.*] "*Hi-tee.*" (Haiti.) "Yes, I hope for a change. You see, I came from a poor, frightened, brutalized country. I came here of my own free will to make something of my life. I want to do it here in America. And this is the way I am greeted . . . poof, I'm a teef. Poof, I'm no good. [*Laughs.*] Poof, I'm a celebrity, and everybody's wanting to know me business." [*As herself,* SUZIE.] And then Matilda offers me tea, and I try to get her back to my questions. But she was one of those people, you know. She wasn't being dishonest, just difficult. I guess she didn't think my questions were very relevant. [*As* MATILDA.] "I have more important tings to worry my mind. Don't you have more important tings?" [*As* SUZIE.] But Miss Duvet, about the New Way Grocery Store? [*As* MATILDA.] "Aiiiii, what about it? The *ton ton macoute* came at night; they took my sister's husband. He got shipped off to the Dominican, a place I don't know, except it's far. A slave on a plantation, if he is alive. Miss, the world is a bigger place than where we are." [*As* SUZIE.] But Matilda, if we could just go over the events at the New Way Store, I'm sure we could clear up a lot of misunderstanding. [*As* MATILDA.] "Miss, you understand nothing. You go on about your own business. I'll go about mine. So much fuss." [*As* SUZIE.] So I left. I stood outside her doorway just . . . stunned. I mean, all that time, I thought . . . she was just . . . I mean facts. Facts illuminate the truth. And the truth will set you free. Right? Isn't that supposed to be the way it works? What just happened in there?

[TARA *at the anchor desk.*]

TARA: Suzie there now? [*Tapping her earpiece.*] Hello, are you there?

MARK THOMPSON: Tell Tara to stall. We don't have Suzie.

TARA: We are live with our remote camera crew at city hall, and the mayor is in the middle of his prepared remarks . . . let's listen to what he has to say.

[*The newsroom.* MARK *is fuming, hopping mad.*]

MARK THOMPSON: Suzie, I don't care if you got an exclusive with Elvis Presley. I am so angry I can barely speak.

SUZIE SEETO: It was an unfortunate judgment call, Mark. But . . .

MARK THOMPSON: I don't want to hear about it.

SUZIE SEETO: The crew got the major. But I got Matilda.

MARK THOMPSON: You got nothing. Matilda Duvet is a dead issue, Suzie. The story set sail, but you missed the boat.

SUZIE SEETO: I know I made a bad judgment call. I admit it. But Matilda Duvet, Mark. I'm the only one to have an exclusive with Matilda Duvet.

MARK THOMPSON: Exclusive nothing. She's a zero. I saw your video. Everyone in the front office saw your video.

SUZIE SEETO: But . . .

MARK THOMPSON: Suzie, you are suspended—one month, without pay! Consider yourself lucky!

BLACK CHORUS: Insubordination is rampant.

KOREAN CHORUS: What is the point of being the boss when your orders are followed, but not feared.

CHORUS: It's no fun being a tyrant anymore.

MARK THOMPSON: Damn. I hated doing that. But she deserved it.

TARA: [*Approaches* MARK.] You have tough decisions to make, Mark. You can't beat yourself up over it. She got off easy. It could have been worse. You put your own job on the line for her. You saved her from being fired. Want to go to lunch? Joe Allen's?

[SUZIE *and the* REVEREND *in a cafe.*]

SUZIE SEETO: So I'm suspended. One month, without pay. Reverend, you were right. I really barked up the wrong tree. Talking to Matilda didn't make one hoot of difference. Her truth, your truth, their truth. The Truth so help me God, the Truth and nothing but the Truth. The *Truth* will set you free.

REVEREND CARTER: I still believe that's *true*.

SUZIE SEETO: I don't know anymore. And I still don't know what happened in the store, and whatever DID happen isn't as important as what HAS happened. How did such a trivial event cause all *this*—boycott, court injunction, pain, suffering.

REVEREND CARTER: Don't forget media circus! [*They laugh.*] History, Suzie, has often been triggered by such trivial events. Someone in Montgomery, Alabama, orders a black woman to give up seat on a bus. Mahatma Gandhi created a free India all because he got thrown off a train.

SUZIE SEETO: I heard a rumor that an informal mediator session is being organized. Do you think the two sides will even sit in the same room?

REVEREND CARTER: People coming together to talk can only be a good thing, Suzie. Yes, if there is a mediation. I'll be there. I'm sure they'll try to keep me out of it. But I wouldn't miss it. [*Puts on an evangelical tone.*] "Even if I have to camp out on their doorstep and beat the drum."

SUZIE SEETO: You really are an actor, aren't you?

REVEREND CARTER: Well, Suzie, I did aspire once to the musical theatre, a long time ago. In trying to get our message across, I've found some theatrical tricks of the trade helpful in garnering attention to the cause. The welfare of my people, Suzie, that's what is important to me. Anyway, politics and theatre are the same thing in my mind. Magic and illusion. Do you know this one, Suzie? [*He sings a cappella.*] "Hello, young lovers, wherever you are. I hope your troubles are few . . ."

GROCER MAK: [*Sings.**]

> "Al ree rang, al ree rang, al rang ne yo o oh.
> Al ree rang, ko o ge ne ma kan da
> Na rul pa ree ko, ka she nun mem umm
> schem nee do mok ka saw, pa pyong nan da."

That's a Korean song. A Korean love song. When I hear it, it gives me a big feeling. Understand? I love that song. My wife, she loved that song. [*Gruffly.*] What was your question? Oh . . . I remember. The first time I ever saw an Oriental man in America. It was in the movies. I laughed my head off. Charlie Chan and his Number One Son. I was still in Korea at this time. I was still a young handsome man. I took my girl to the cinema to watch your American movies. Lots of your American GI's are there too, even black ones. That girl, now my wife, was young and okay looking. The lights go down. The movie starts. I tell my girl, "Hey, that guy. He's not Chinese. He's a white man. Eyes pulled back like this." [*Demonstrates.*] Who cares? I laugh anyway. This Charlie Chan cracks me up. But I'm telling you Chinese people are not so smart like this Charlie Chan. I'm telling you Korean people are smart. They should make this Charlie Chan *Korean.*

[*The New Way Grocery Store.*]

WILLIE MAK: It's true, Suzie. People at my church organized classes for Korean businessmen to get along with American people, except Uncle Makie doesn't want to go.

---

*A Korean folk song, "Al Ree Rang," also known as "The Mystery Hill Song."

SOOMI MAK: It's so silly. I don't want to go to charm school. People should take classes to get along with me. Why don't people take classes to learn about Korean culture? I say, "Let 'em eat *kimchee*." If Uncle Makie doesn't want to go, right on!

GROCER MAK: I don't want to be nice. Those people out there, they are not nice. Why should I? Ask her why she's here. Then tell her to go away.

WILLIE MAK: Uncle, Suzie came here to be our customer! No reporting, just buying food. Suzie, you be our customer. I'll practice on you.

SUZIE SEETO: Hello, I'm a customer.

WILLIE AND SOOMI MAK: Hello! Welcome to our store.

WILLIE MAK: Uncle?! Come on, try it.

SOOMI MAK: This I gotta see.

WILLIE MAK: Come on, Uncle. Try it.

GROCER MAK: [*Reluctantly.*] Yeah, welcome to store.

WILLIE MAK: Ah, hello, welcome to our store. May I help you find something? Do you need some assistance? Please let me know if there is anything I can do to make your shopping experience a pleasant one.

SOOMI MAK: Oh, brother.

WILLIE MAK: Practice. Be nice. Make change.

GROCER MAK: [*Gruffly.*] Your change.

SOOMI MAK: Put the change in her hand. Look her in the eyeballs. [GROCER MAK *puts change into* SUZIE's *hand.*]

WILLIE MAK: Now what, Uncle?

GROCER MAK: Please, thank you. Come again! [*All applaud, including* BLACK CHORUS. GROCER MAK *grumbles.*] Only children and Chinese say, "Please, thank you." Now buy something, or get out of my store. If you can't help us, then leave, please, thank you.

SUZIE SEETO: Mr. Mak, I hear some church groups on both sides are trying to organize a mediation, an informal get-together of blacks and Koreans? Nothing is set yet. I just heard a rumor.

GROCER MAK: Oh yeah? Well, maybe this get-together is good. Talk is good. Yes, a meeting would lay things on the table, give me hope for a solution. Yes, if there is such a meeting, I will go. Yes.

[SUZIE *interviews* RUTH BETTY.]

NURSE RUTH BETTY: Never eat it without hot sauce. You pour it on like maple syrup. A lot of hot sauce. Are you writing this down, Suzie? That's the key, lots of good Louisiana cajun hot sauce. When I was a child, nine years old, my grandfather was in the kitchen. I opened the kitchen door, and, oh my, the stink would hit you. "Oooo, who left the bathroom door open," I said. "Child, that is your dinner. Don't you go maligning your meal," Grandpa said. "Uh uh, I'm not gonna eat that. No sir." "You know, Ruthie, chitlins is our history. It come about because the slave master took the best part of the pig and left the slaves with the shit." "Life is like chitlins," he would say. "Someone gives you shit, but you make a banquet out of it." [*Beat.*] Is that the kind of story you were looking for? I don't know how you could use it in your report.

SUZIE SEETO: Ruth Betty, did you hear this rumor about a meeting between blacks and Koreans, the possibility of an informal mediator's session? Do you think getting the two sides together is a good idea?

NURSE RUTH BETTY: Might be better than all this shouting. Yes, it might bring some peace to the neighborhood. Putting things on the table, yes, might clear things up. I'm for it. I'm getting tired of it all. If there's a meetin', I'll be there. Yes.

[*Back in the newsroom.*]

MARK THOMPSON: Suzie, you are on suspension, remember? Go home, read a book. You are becoming a workaholic, do you know that? Get a life.

SUZIE SEETO: Mark, I know I'm on suspension. But, please. Take a look at my tapes.

MARK THOMPSON: If this is what you do on suspension, I hate to see what you are like on vacation. On second thought . . .

SUZIE SEETO: Mark, just stop it. That's enough, okay? What are you trying to do, ruin me? Suppose we get together, my reputation as a reporter would be impugned and maligned forever. No matter what I achieved, people would say Suzie got that job by boinking the boss. I can't live with that stigma.

MARK THOMPSON: Oh, now I'm a stigma.

SUZIE SEETO: No one, especially you, is going to diminish my accomplishments.

MARK THOMPSON: I know, I know. Yeah, I know. Suzie, I understand what you are saying intellectually. But emotionally, all I can say is . . . [*Rapidly, passionately.*] Paul Newman and Joanne Woodward, Alec Baldwin and Kim Basinger, Connie Chung and Maury Povitch!

SUZIE SEETO: Mark, please just look at my videos.

MARK THOMPSON: Okay, I'm looking, but it's personal, not professional. Okay?

SUZIE SEETO: Then forget it. I'll go home.

MARK THOMPSON: Okay, okay, have it your way. We're now on company time. Okay? [*Beat.*] Let's see what you've got.

CHORUS: As news director, Mark Thompson has the final say. He always has the final word. He decides what you see on teevee, and . . . what you don't.

MARK THOMPSON: The following happened over the course of a few months. Okay. Susie, let's see what you've got.

[SUZIE *and a* KOREAN CHURCH WOMAN.]

KOREAN CHURCH WOMAN: Forget it! To get a loan from an American bank? Not easy for Koreans, either. We don't like to talk about it because of potential tax problems, you know. But basically, Koreans are able to lend money to other Koreans. Usually, it's kept within the family, but also they come to the church, and we facilitate a loan from a pool of money we maintain for economic advancement, emergencies, things like that. The American system does not work for Koreans either.

MARK THOMPSON: Not interested. Next! Please.

[SUZIE *and* NURSE RUTH BETTY.]

SUZIE SEETO: Ruth Betty, I've been wondering . . . why do you have two first names?

NURSE RUTH BETTY: Now, that's the first intelligent question you asked. I have two first names because I have no last name. I reject that name. I won't even speak it. That name was the name of my great-great-grandmother's slave master. I don't know what my real family name is. I don't know what tribe I'm from. I don't have any family history. I'm *persona non grata.* And you can't get or give a better reason to boycott than that. Make America fulfill its promise to my great-grandmother, to my mother, and to me!

MARK THOMPSON: Next.

[SUZIE *and a* PAKISTANI NEWS VENDOR.]

PAKISTANI NEWS VENDOR: I been selling newspapers on the corner for a long time. Black people don't bother me. I am Pakistani. What is all the fuss? I guess black people don't know, Korean people are like that. They are rude to everybody.

MARK THOMPSON: Next! Next!

[SUZIE *and a* KOREAN MAN WITH APRON.]

KOREAN MAN WITH APRON: *Maketsu Halame kajeu esumneda.*

SUZIE SEETO: He says he owns a store in Harlem. Go on, Mr. Park, but slowly.

KOREAN MAN WITH APRON: *Koben nagee ahnsumneda. Yol scheme eel hameyan, ton holsu odesaeyo. Halame wchum hadagu mal tortutcheeyo.*

SUZIE SEETO: Uh, basically, he said he knew Harlem was dangerous, but he thought if he worked hard, he, uh, could have a good business.

KOREAN MAN WITH APRON: But, now, Miss Seeto, I think those people can starve. I say, let them shop in *hell*.

MARK THOMPSON: Nice to know, Suzie, you put your month's suspension to good use. Next time, try Russian or better yet, *Esperanto*. Next!

[SUZIE *with a* BLACK BOY WITH SCARS.]

BLACK BOY WITH SCARS: See this? And this? And one on my stomach, from here to here. For what? For nothing, that's what. I got a news flash. Those Koreans are bad. All that innocent victim shit. I was on my way to school, and this Korean dude comes up to me, starts diss'n brother, but hey, ain't my business, he's entitled to an opinion. But then, he goes cuckoo, pulls a knife, and before I know it . . . [*Makes slashing motions.*] Yeah, was in the hospital for a long time, months. Missed a lot of school. Shit. Really set me back, know what I'm saying? But, hey, I'm still here, right?

MARK THOMPSON: Is that it?

SUZIE SEETO: No, I saved the best for last.

MARK THOMPSON: I think I've seen enough, Suzie.

SUZIE SEETO: Mark, the more in-depth I get, the less interested you are? Why is that?

MARK THOMPSON: The news moves on, Suzie. The writing hand has writ, and moves on. Basically, a case of waning news value. I thought you hated doing these minority issues anyway. Well, now you can graduate on to bigger . . .

SUZIE SEETO: . . . whiter . . .

MARK THOMPSON: . . . more pressing issues.

SUZIE SEETO: Nothing is more pressing or more important to me than this issue. The race issue.

MARK THOMPSON: Aren't you being a little personal about this? We're a news operation, remember? Not a race relations seminar.

SUZIE SEETO: Please finish watching the tape.

MARK THOMPSON: I don't have time to look at any more. Time's up. I, for one, have to go back to work.

SUZIE SEETO: Please, Mark.

MARK THOMPSON: Suzie, I've bent over backwards for you.

SUZIE SEETO: Mark.

MARK THOMPSON: Suzie, I think you have consistently bent over ass-backwards to accommodate the African American, nigger-loving point of view. What color do you think you are, anyway?

SUZIE SEETO: Oliver, roll to 10:06:58. [*Beat.*] Thank you.

[*The mediator's office, a melee in progress.*]

CHORUS: Heads up! Duck! Look out! Duck! Watch out! Duck! Duck! Duck! Heads up! Duck! Look out! Duck! Watch out! Duck! Duck! Duck!

SUZIE SEETO: The two sides, so hopeful for a peaceful solution, ended up on the floor and in the aisles, taking pot shots at each other. As you can see, this first-ever meeting has degenerated into fist fighting and spilled out into the street. I'm Suzie Seeto, and, whoa, watch out, duck. I'm Suzie Seeto coming to you from the mediator's office.

MARK THOMPSON: That's good. Very good. Good work, Suzie. I'm very impressed. Why didn't I know about this mediator's session? It wasn't on the budget. You should have told us about it. But you were there, and that's what matters. You are back on the job. That's my girl. [*The tape is still rolling.*] What's this? Am I supposed to be looking at this? Suzie?

SUZIE SEETO: [*Still on camera, whispering.*] I'm on the corner of, I don't know where.

MARK THOMPSON: Suzie, what am I looking at?

SUZIE SEETO: I am about three blocks away from the mediator's office. As I told you earlier, the session ended badly, and the fighting has . . . I'm whispering because . . . look up ahead. See those boys. Oh my god. The baseball bat is going up. It's sending that kid skidding . . .

MARK THOMPSON: Wait a minute . . . what is this? Can we back up here.

SUZIE SEETO: . . . The baseball bat is going up. It's sending that kid skidding across the sidewalk. Hear that sound . . . that's the sound of the bat against the boy's head. I'm putting my minicam into my purse, because one of the boys is looking in my direction. Four black kids are beating the boy, he appears to be . . . Do you hear what they are saying? Filthy Korean dog bastard. We're going to send you back to Korea. Korean monkey. Go back to Korea. The boy on the ground is screaming. "I'm from Vietnam. I'm Vietnamese. I'm Vietnamese." I'm going to put my purse on the ground. I'm going to leave the camera going, but I have to call the police. [*Sounds of police sirens.*]

MARK THOMPSON: Hold it. Suzie? Suzie? Suzie, are you okay?

SUZIE SEETO: [*Nods, approaches* MARK, *no longer on tape.*] What luck, eh, Mark? Just happened to be a yellow person on the street doing my nigger-loving stories.

MARK THOMPSON: That was a real stupid comment, Suzie. I'm sorry. I was just so frustrated. Here, sit down. [*She does, and then she confides in him.*]

SUZIE SEETO: There was a girl from Taiwan. She was terrible at tetherball. She was awkward. Her accent was thick. She smelled like tiger balm ointment. I didn't want to be associated with her. She desperately wanted to be my friend, always hanging around me, trying to have lunch with me in the school cafeteria. "Just get away from me." Then one day, a substitute teacher mistook me—ME, the all-time tetherball champion—for that horribly awkward girl. That was the feeling I had that day. Standing there, watching those boys and that kid. I wasn't hating them. No, no . . . I was too busy, too preoccupied with disassociating myself from that squirming, weak, yellow boy on the ground. Coolly, I hid behind my profession, thoroughly brainwashed by my complete-and-utter certainty that I could not and would not be hurt . . . because I was NOT like that kid. Those black boys with their baseball bat shattered my beautiful delusion once and forever. For if I wasn't yellow, then what color did I think I was? . . .

CHORUS: [ALL, *sotto, but matter-of-factly.*] The boogeyman is here. Inside you. Inside me. The boogeyman takes little girls and little boys. Make the boogeyman go away. Make the boogeyman go away. Make the boogeyman go away.

[SUZIE *and the anchor seat.*]

VOICE: [*Offstage.*] Ten seconds everyone. Ten seconds.

CHORUS: [ALL.] Call it a hunch, or maybe just a good nose for news. Suzie's timing, as always, was impeccable.

SUZIE SEETO: A few days later, not long after the failed mediator's session, Grocer Key Chun Mak closed his store for the last time.

[SUZIE *goes into the street, to witness:*]

SOOMI MAK: I finished making the sign, Uncle.

GROCER MAK: [*Softly.*] Put it up. [*Beat.*] Let's go. [SOOMI's *sign reads:* FOR SALE.]

SUZIE SEETO: Soomi put her sign on the door. Willie brought the gates down. Mr. Mak put on the padlocks, and then he walked away. He never looked back.

[GROCER MAK *walks slowly, followed by* SOOMI *and* WILLIE. *The* BLACK CHORUS *watches silently.* BARBER BROWN *approaches* GROCER MAK.]

BARBER BROWN: Makie, I'm . . . I'm sorry. I feel real bad about all this. I remember the day you opened your store. You and Willie making all kinds of noise with those heavy shelves. [*Long pause. The men consider one another.*]

GROCER MAK: I thought you were my friend. Why didn't you teach me how to be a businessman in America?

BARBER BROWN: Why didn't you ask me for help?

GROCER MAK: Why didn't you help me to understand?

BARBER BROWN: Why didn't you help me understand?

GROCER MAK: You stay with your people. I stay with mine.

BARBER BROWN: [*Flatly.*] United we stand.

GROCER MAK: United we stand. Now, get out of my way. I'm going home. [*The* BARBER *stands aside. The* KOREANS *freeze.*]

SUZIE SEETO: Any comment, Reverend Carter?

REVEREND CARTER: [*Sadly.*] No, Suzie. No comment.

CHORUS: [ALL, *gather together, stand intermixed.*] We think reality is very depressing. We would like to offer you a more cheerful solution. [*Everybody goes backwards in time.*]

BARBER BROWN: Suzie look who's here. I can't believe it. What a coincidence. Hey, don't walk away, man. [BARBER *takes down the "For Sale" sign.*] Suzie, you tell this man. You tell this man. I didn't sleep for weeks during. I didn't sleep for weeks after. Then I realized, "Hey, I didn't even have this guy's phone number, man." I mean, we do business, act like friends, but we ain't. Come on, Makie, you never even invited me to your house. But hey!

GROCER MAK: It's too late.

BARBER BROWN: No, no it's not. I'm having a dinner. A few people over, nothing special. You should come. Yeah, I'm inviting you. Fact, check this out. I had to go two miles out of my way to find this. [*Holds up a jar of kimchee.*] My house is gonna smell like the East River and the subway on a hot sunny day. The stink is gonna wake up the whole neighborhood. Maybe the whole world.

GROCER MAK: Kimchee, good.

BARBER BROWN: And chitlins, good.

GROCER MAK: Us bachelors have got to stick together. [BARBER *and* GROCER *laugh.*]

[STAGE MANAGER *enters.*]

STAGE MANAGER: Five, four, three . . .

SUZIE SEETO: Just goes to show, the best stories are . . . the best stories are *invented.* [SUZIE *takes the anchor seat.*] Hello, I'm Suzie Seeto. Thank you for joining us. Here now, the news . . .

[*Lights out*]

THE END

A Language of Their Own

by
CHAY YEW

LEARNING CHINESE

A *spartan set.*

OSCAR, *a thirtysomething Asian male, speaks English with a slight unobtrusive accent.* MING, *twentysomething Asian male, speaks American English.*

In this series of monologues and dialogues, Oscar and Ming often speak to the audience, as if they were lawyers defending different points of view on the same case.

The playing and direction must never be obvious, sentimental, or heavy-handed. More is gained in subtext, subtlety, and interpreting the darker tones of the characters and the play's themes. The director may choose to employ a live musician in the production.

———

MING: I can never forget what he said to me.

OSCAR: I don't think we should see each other anymore.

MING: It wasn't unexpected. It had to happen the way things were going. Which was nowhere.

OSCAR: Of course, we can still be friends.

MING: Sure. Friends. If that's what you want.

OSCAR: That's not what I wanted. Not really. But it was all I could say. All I could do.

MING: Friends. A change of labels. From lovers to friends. It's the same person whom you have loved, made love to, thought about day in and day out. A person whose secrets, fears, and hopes were made known to you. Now that very same person is a friend. A person you have coffee with, a person you call when you want company to the theatre, the movies, and the bars. Lovers to friends. Label musical chairs.

OSCAR: We can call each other up. Have coffee. Go to the movies or something.

MING: Or something. Yes. We'll be friends.

OSCAR: Good friends.

MING: Sure. Whatever.

OSCAR: You know, this is not easy to say.

MING: Please, get on with it.

OSCAR: It's not working out. We've become two very different people.

MING: You just don't become different people overnight.

OSCAR: What I'm trying to say is that things haven't been quite the same.

MING: Let's not start this—

OSCAR: Especially—

MING: You always—

OSCAR: Since the test.

MING: The test. You always bring it up.

OSCAR: It's the truth.

MING: It's not true.

OSCAR: Of course, it's true. He has a life ahead of him, and my days have suddenly become numbered. Why should he give up what's his for me? What right do I have to ask that of him? Love? Surely, love, too, has its limits before it sours into impassivity, apathy, and hate.

MING: Listen, I want to take care of you.

OSCAR: You can't even take care of yourself.

MING: I love you.

OSCAR: Please don't.

MING: But I do.

OSCAR: I—know. Just don't. Okay?

MING: Why are you doing this then?

OSCAR: It's for the best.

MING: There's nothing I can say to—

OSCAR: Nothing at all. Please don't—

MING: What will I do?

OSCAR: I don't know.

MING: I'll move out.

OSCAR: You don't have to.

MING: It'll be easier.

OSCAR: You can wait until—

MING: Tomorrow.

OSCAR: You can stay until you find—

MING: I'll stay with a friend.

OSCAR: You really don't have to rush—

MING: I want to.

OSCAR: Then the silence.

MING: There's really nothing left to say. Even between friends.

OSCAR: He's angry. I'm upset. Maybe I was wrong to break it off. Some people like to rehearse their speeches, say the right things, use the right words, wear the right color-coordinated clothes, put on the right music—put on a Broadway production just to ease the pain. Maybe I should have rehearsed. Soft lighting might have helped. But what good will it do? I'm lousy at beating around the bush. Just say it. Straight to the point. The facts. Over and done. There's no easy way to end a relationship.

MING: Maybe this is what I really need. A fresh start. A fresh break.

OSCAR: He's probably depressed. I know, deep inside, this is for the best. It is. It is. I know it is.

MING: A thousand thoughts exploding in my mind. Moving. Packing. A new apartment. Maybe roommates. New phone number. Explaining to everyone why I'm moving out. Dating again. Loneliness.

OSCAR: I just want to say that you mean a lot—

MING: Don't.

OSCAR: The last four years were—

MING: Can you be an asshole and make this easier for me?

OSCAR: Do you want some tea? I—I'm having a cup.

MING: Yeah. The usual.

OSCAR: Cookie?'

MING: Uh-huh.

OSCAR: It won't be a moment.

MING: We were polite even when we broke up. We've always been so fucking polite to each other. Please. Thank you. You're welcome. After you. I guess we were both afraid to offend each other, to see each other in the real light, to lose one another. Now we have nothing to lose.

OSCAR: I see no reason to start a fight.

MING: We never fought. Maybe that's why. We should have fought regularly. About small things. About big things. Lay things out on the table. Express ourselves. Release the anger instead of bottling everything inside. Like every couple.

OSCAR: Like every American couple.

MING: Like every normal couple.

OSCAR: My father used to beat me with his fists, when I didn't get the perfect grade in school. Once I failed English. I was ten. I didn't understand my tenses—couldn't get them right—got them all mixed up—past, present, perfect, continuous. That night, with a whip in his hand and the test paper in another, my father caned me. And in a consuming rage, he struck me in the left eye. The next day, I went to school, half-blind. My left eye was covered with a patchy white cream. The pain didn't bother me. The embarrassed, silent looks from my friends did. Fighting and violence didn't solve a thing even if I got an A in my next English test. Now, I correct my father's English. Most of the time—deliberately.

MING: I want to fight.

OSCAR: I don't.

MING: Scream. Shout. Throw things.

OSCAR: Then we'll have to replace them.

MING: Talk. We should at least talk.

OSCAR: You know I'm no good at talking.

MING: You're not good in expressing your feelings.

OSCAR: Let's not bring this up again. You know that—

MING: Why not?

OSCAR: Because—

MING: Why the fuck not?

OSCAR: I don't like it when you are—

MING: Let's talk about this—

OSCAR: No.

MING: I want to.

OSCAR: You're getting ridiculous—

MING: I want to. I want to. I want to.

OSCAR: We were in the kitchen. Cooking dinner.

MING: Come on. Let's hear your stupid fucking reason again.

OSCAR: I was dicing tomatoes. I pretended I didn't hear a word.

MING: You're always like this. Always. When you don't want to talk, you just clam up. Keep quiet. I hate it. Hate it.

OSCAR: All I could think of was the image of a little boy with a patchy white cream on his left eye and his angry father. I kept dicing the tomatoes. Into smaller pieces.

MING: Did you hear me? I hate it when you do this.

OSCAR: He got carried away. He started talking. Loudly.

MING: I was yelling.

OSCAR: Screaming.

MING: I got frustrated. Angry. Trapped.

OSCAR: He threw things around when his words finally failed him. Pots. Pans. Dishes. Glasses. Tomatoes. From the kitchen counter. Into the air. Onto the kitchen floor. A mess. A loud mess.

MING: He kept silent. Not looking at me. Looking at the floor.

OSCAR: Dented pots. Pieces of glass shattered into a thousand pieces. Tomato slices all over the floor.

MING: Then he methodically cleaned the floor. Without a sound. Later, we never mentioned the incident again. Acted as if nothing happened.

OSCAR: It happened once. And never again. Fighting solves nothing.

MING: He's not good in expressing his feelings.

OSCAR: You know the reason.

MING: You're Chinese. You're supposed to be lousy in expressing yourself.

OSCAR: Words don't come easily.

MING: I'm a Chink too.

OSCAR: I wish you'd stop that.

MING: Stop what?

OSCAR: You know.

MING: Chink?

OSCAR: I hate it when you use that. It's—

MING: Offensive.

OSCAR: Self-debasing.

MING: Ooh. Big word.

OSCAR: Racist. Please don't use that word in front of me.

MING: Chink?

OSCAR: You're not really Chinese, anyway, so what would you know about—

MING: What do you mean by that?

OSCAR: Nothing.

MING: Tell me.

OSCAR: Forget it.

MING: Say it.

OSCAR: You're of a different type.

MING: Of Chinese? Meaning?

OSCAR: You're an ABC.

MING: Labels. Boxes. Categories.

OSCAR: American-born Chinese.

MING: So?

OSCAR: You know what I mean.

MING: I'm a banana. Another category.

OSCAR: Yellow on the outside. White on the inside.

MING: I can't order anything in a Chinese restaurant. I know what the food looks like. What it tastes like. But I just don't know what the fuck it is. What it is called. Of course, it doesn't help if I try describing it in English to the waiters. All I get is a dish that is completely different from what I want, and vile looks. It's as if I have committed some kind of cultural rape, a racial sacrilege. And if I try to order with the pathetic string of elementary Cantonese words every Caucasian tourist in Chinatown knows, they mutter and defiantly speak broken English to me. My Chinese is unbearable to them.

OSCAR: I always order for the two of us.

MING: He does that because I embarrass him.

OSCAR: I do that because you always order the same thing. I thought we'd order something different. That's all.

MING: I don't know when I stopped learning how to speak Chinese. Must be in grade school. Everyone at school spoke English beautifully and my English was always—well, unrefined, pidgin, tainted. The stuff Rex Harrison sang of in *My Fair Lady*. When I saw the movie, I felt I was Audrey Hepburn. More than anything else in the world, I wanted to be like her: delicate, refined, speaking perfectly and wearing a Cecil Beaton original. Since no one at home spoke English fluently, I would spend countless hours watching TV everyday. Repeating the same lines after Connie Chung and Mary Tyler Moore until I got the pronunciation, the rhythms, the expressions all down pat. My mother thought I was insane. But I finally did speak English just like everyone else, if not better. I think *My Fair Lady* was pivotal in my life. It taught me how to speak proper English, appreciate good clothes, and made me realize I was gay.

OSCAR: Let's not talk about this.

MING: About what?

OSCAR: About who's more Chinese and who isn't.

MING: There you go again. Changing the subject. Shying from confrontation.

OSCAR: I don't know why we stay together sometimes. He infuriates me. He's the complete antithesis of who and what I am. Yet I need him. Without him, I'm incomplete. Empty.

MING: I feel the same way. We're opposite poles.

OSCAR: The only thing that truly binds us together is being Chinese.

MING: The other thing that truly pits us against each other is being Chinese.

OSCAR: And he's always contradicting me.

MING: You never hold me.

OSCAR: In public, I don't.

MING: Kiss me.

OSCAR: Not here.

MING: Why not?

OSCAR: What I feel for you is private. Between us. Not some crude display for the rest of the world to see.

MING: I've often felt the urge to put my tongue into his mouth in public. To shock? For effect? I don't know.

OSCAR: For effect.

MING: You never said you loved me.

OSCAR: I have.

MING: When?

OSCAR: In my own little way.

MING: It's not enough.

OSCAR: I'm not the type who has to remind you of my feelings constantly.

MING: I need to hear it. Constantly. It makes me feel—wanted. Needed.

OSCAR: My father and mother have never said they loved me. My friends are the same. It's our way.

MING: Another excuse.

OSCAR: We show our affections through deeds. Through actions. When I got a Lego set for my seventh birthday, I knew I was very loved. All thirty-five dollars and seventy-six cents of love. That's why some people see the Chinese as materialistic. You know someone is well-loved when they're driving a Mercedes-Benz.

MING: I think I can live on that kind of love.

OSCAR: Sometimes I wish I can hug him freely. Touch him, hold him whenever I want to. Instinctively. And I need that touch too. The funny thing is that it's the same physical touch that repels me. Makes me uncomfortable. Awkward. Vulnerable.

MING: You're not demonstrative.

OSCAR: Being physically demonstrative is very difficult for me.

MING: How difficult can it be? You haven't tried. Come. [*Opens his arms out to* OSCAR.]

OSCAR: What?

MING: Come here.

OSCAR: This is stupid.

MING: Hold me.

OSCAR: I can't.

MING: Come on.

OSCAR: Stop it.

MING: Forget it. You are right as usual. It was stupid.

OSCAR: I don't know when was the last time I held my father, kissed my mother. It just isn't done. Sometimes I want to, especially when I see how my American friends behave towards their loved ones. Hugging and kissing. When I was young, I often wished that I was born into the Partridge Family or the Brady Bunch. They were always smiling, laughing, doing all those tactile kinds of things—

MING: Tactile—

OSCAR: As in touching—

MING: Why can't you use simple words? You always complicate—

OSCAR: As I was saying, when I see my parents, I automatically keep a respectful distance. Because it's a part of our upbringing and because it's expected. Are you physical with your parents?

MING: No.

OSCAR: So why are you singling me out for?

MING: My parents, in case you forgot, are not speaking to me.

OSCAR: That's not the point.

MING: That's precisely the point. I came out to them.

OSCAR: That was a very intelligent thing to do.

MING: I didn't want to lie to them. They are my parents, for Christ's sake.

OSCAR: Not anymore.

MING: At least I don't have to lie to my folks about having no time to date because I'm busy at work.

OSCAR: You should have understood where your parents were coming from. They may live here in the U.S. but their ways are still of China.

MING: Mine aren't.

OSCAR: This is one of the reasons why I'm so madly attracted to him. His questioning. His challenges. It's also one of the reasons why I sometimes feel compelled to swing an axe into his forehead every now and then.

MING: I hated his line of reasoning. It's so logical. So rational. No other way, except the right way. His way. Sometimes I think I'm fucking Mr. Spock.

OSCAR: We've known each other for some time now.

MING: We've been seeing each other for four years.

OSCAR: Four years, two months, three weeks, and four days to be exact. We were lovers.

MING: I always hated that word. "Lovers." It's so—

OSCAR: Committed.

MING: No.

OSCAR: Ambiguous.

MING: Yes.

OSCAR: What about companion?

MING: Roommate.

OSCAR: Boyfriend.

MING: Sex toy?

OSCAR: Husband and wife?

MING: Friends.

OSCAR: We lived together.

MING: Slept together.

OSCAR: Ate together.

MING: Watched TV together.

OSCAR: Spent countless weekends at Ikea. Rummaging through bins of turquoise plastic utensils we bought but never used.

MING: Spend countless hours at Tower Records. Buying CDs we never played.

OSCAR: Years of dancing in the living room on quiet afternoons.

MING: Years of wearing each other's underwear.

OSCAR: Years of tolerating each other's friends.

MING: Borrowing and stealing each other's vocabulary.

OSCAR: "Way cool."

MING: "Tactile."

OSCAR: Observing each other's idiosyncrasies change from cute little gestures to annoying habits.

MING: Years of loving each other.

OSCAR: And hating each other.

MING: Years of quietly sitting beside each other without having to exchange a word.

OSCAR: Him reading. And I watching him.

MING: We were the perfect couple.

OSCAR: We never quarrelled. Never fought.

MING: Sometimes we should have. But we never did.

OSCAR: I was very happy.

MING: I was—happy.

OSCAR: Then things change. Like they always do.

MING: He got sick.

OSCAR: AIDS.

MING: Sick.

OSCAR: I had the flu that wouldn't go away.

MING: The warning bells were ringing. Loudly. But I said, hey, you're just para-noid. Nothing a couple of aspirins can't do.

OSCAR: I felt tired.

MING: No night sweats. No lesions. No nothing. It's only a cold. Keep calm.

OSCAR: So I went to the doctor.

MING: Why? It's only a cold. Everyone gets a cold.

OSCAR: He gave me a whole slew of tests.

MING: It's a cold.

OSCAR: I tested positive.

MING: He was sick. Sick.

OSCAR: I tried to persuade him to take the test.

MING: I don't have a cold.

OSCAR: That's not the issue here.

MING: I'm not tired.

OSCAR: You have to find out—

MING: Do I look sick?

OSCAR: Go.

MING: I couldn't.

OSCAR: You must.

MING: Later.

OSCAR: Why are you so hesitant?

MING: Why don't you leave me alone?

OSCAR: Are you afraid that you might be—

MING: Sick.

OSCAR: HIV positive.

MING: Sick.

OSCAR: Positive.

MING: Sick is a better word.

OSCAR: But it has the same meaning.

MING: I don't know why you keep volleying, ramming the words AIDS and

HIV positive down my throat. It's like you're almost fucking proud to wear the label around your neck. I hate it. I hate it.

OSCAR: But it's the truth.

MING: He likes categorizing people. Boxing things into their rightful places. This is white. This is Asian. This is gay. This is straight. And this is what you're fucking supposed to do when you're in this category. He organizes people like he organizes his office.

OSCAR: It's just easier for me to deal with life this way. Okay?

MING: What if I'm positive?

OSCAR: We were always safe, weren't we?

MING: What if the condom tore?

OSCAR: Was the lubricant water-based?

MING: Were we ever irresponsible? Forgot about safe sex in the heat of passion or when we had too much to drink?

OSCAR: After persuading him.

MING: Nagging.

OSCAR: He finally went.

MING: Waiting for the results almost crippled me for a week. Kept me wondering—what if? What if?— I started to write a will. Who'd get the CDs? Who'd get my books? It's so morbid. I'm not even fucking thirty!

OSCAR: I did the same. What should I give him? What do you give someone you love after you die? Perhaps memories, photographs, strange obscure objects that have significant meaning—even those things get lost eventually. He tested negative.

MING: Thank God.

OSCAR: He only believed in God when it was convenient. Only when he wanted things. Like a car phone or a leather jacket.

MING: I suddenly felt free. Like I've been given wings. To fly.

OSCAR: I am happy for him. I am. Yet I felt a little left behind. A little betrayed.

MING: Then it got uncomfortable.

OSCAR: We got uncomfortable.

MING: We had nothing to say to each other.

OSCAR: If we did, the only word that lingered at the tip of our tongues was AIDS.

MING: If we didn't, we thought it. Loudly.

OSCAR: We stopped having sex. With each other.

MING: All of a sudden, I couldn't bear his touch.

OSCAR: We began spending strenuous hours in the apartment in our own different worlds.

MING: Sat beside each other without exchanging a word.

OSCAR: Me wanting to be closer.

MING: Me wanting to be as far away as possible.

OSCAR: And I knew.

MING: We avoided each other like the plague.

OSCAR: That was a poor choice of word.

MING: I didn't mean it.

OSCAR: Right.

MING: Really.

OSCAR: Thoughts swirl in my mind: Maybe his results were botched. Maybe the test didn't detect the virus. Did he infect me? Did he fuck around? I didn't.

MING: I thought the same thing.

OSCAR: Maybe it was someone else. Years ago. Before I met him.

MING: A quick moment.

OSCAR: A brief encounter with a hastily scribbled telephone number on a piece of paper as a souvenir.

MING: Or a harmless fling in Montreal with a Jean-Pierre, Jean-Luc, Jean-Claude, or Jean-something.

OSCAR: The summer vacation you took without me.

MING: You said it was healthy we took separate vacations. Expand our horizons, you said.

OSCAR: But I didn't say you could—

MING: Exactly.

OSCAR: I have been faithful since we started seeing each other.

MING: I slipped. Every now and then. So I'm human. Sometimes I wondered if I should have been the one who was sick.

OSCAR: We got further away from each other.

MING: Deliberately.

OSCAR: Naturally.

MING: It was then I realized that I wasn't strong. The sickness tested our relationship and I wasn't passing with flying colors like I ought to.

OSCAR: I became his obstacle, his wet blanket.

MING: I slept around more. A little more. Discreetly, of course.

OSCAR: He came back from work later than usual.

MING: Meetings.

OSCAR: I see. Do you want dinner?

MING: I had something to eat. Before I came home.

OSCAR: I see.

MING: I'm tired.

OSCAR: Long day?

MING: Yeah.

OSCAR: I see.

MING: I'm going to bed.

OSCAR: Good night.

MING: Yeah.

OSCAR: I can usually tolerate harmless indiscretions. I turn a blind eye. Pretend it doesn't happen. So why is it worrying me now?

MING: Jealousy?

OSCAR: Were his casual relationships more than physical? Was he getting emotionally involved with someone else?

MING: During this time, I slept around with many different men. But every time I was having sex, I only saw his face. Heard his urgent moans. Felt his smooth, hot body against mine. Then I'd stop. Get up and leave.

OSCAR: I—masturbated—thinking of him when we were both still—happy.

MING: You just don't turn me on anymore.

OSCAR: I gathered.

MING: I keep thinking of death when—

OSCAR: Please.

MING: I wanted to—

OSCAR: I know.

MING: I wanted to leave.

OSCAR: Then leave.

MING: But I can't.

OSCAR: Why not?

MING: Because I want to look after you.

OSCAR: You feel responsible.

MING: Perhaps.

OSCAR: Guilty.

MING: Maybe.

OSCAR: Afraid of what our friends are going to say if you leave?

MING: That, too. Yes.

OSCAR: Then I'll make it easier for the both of us.

MING: How?

OSCAR: I don't think we should see each other anymore.

MING: We'll be friends.

OSCAR: Good friends.

MING: It seems so long ago.

OSCAR: What seems so long ago?

MING: When we first met.

OSCAR: Yes. Doesn't it?

MING: Do you remember how it happened?

OSCAR: Some dinner party on Charles Street.

MING: I thought it was in the South End.

OSCAR: Some gay Asian party with lots of French hors d'oeuvres.

MING: Yellow creamy seafood droppings on water crackers that look like they should hang on an earlobe with a skimpy black dress, instead of dripping on the side of your mouth.

OSCAR: A typical Asian-Wanna-be-Caucasian-and-Caucasian-Wanna-be-an-Asian kind of party.

MING: Everyone at the party was frantically speaking in tongues.

OSCAR: Thai, Cantonese, Vietnamese, Tagalog, pig latin. And believe it or not, French.

MING: The Americans were looking rather bewildered. Sat there politely complimenting the host and deciphering what the hell they were eating. Nodding too frequently and sometimes a little too enthusiastically at anyone who wasn't white. Arching their eyebrows at everyone white as if to say, "Where am I?"

OSCAR: While all this was going on, I stood by the kitchen, looking at him across the room.

MING: Staring.

OSCAR: I wondered at that moment what it was like to kiss you.

MING: To see you naked.

OSCAR: To run my fingers down your chest.

MING: I wondered if you had a big cock.

OSCAR: But we never spoke to each other.

MING: Instead we talked to the people around us half-heartedly. Pretending to smile. Pretending to be engaged in conversation while we stole glances at each other every opportunity we got.

OSCAR: We couldn't get away.

MING: I was with friends.

OSCAR: I was with a date.

MING: And I desperately wanted to lose them.

OSCAR: I wanted to shoot my date fatally. I think that would garner a logical reason to excuse myself to walk towards him.

MING: It must be an ancient Chinese mating ritual. Never speaking to people you desire to have wild sex and a meaningful relationship with. That's why it was easier to pre-arrange marriages in the old days. You know, the ritual of binding feet is not an indication of the breeding of fine Chinese women. No, parents bind their daughters' feet so they can't run away from their pre-chosen spouses. They'd have to fucking hop like mad to run away. Right now, I'd love to bind his feet. Chinese S and M.

OSCAR: The Chinese can be shy.

MING: You should make the first move. Come over, accidentally spill a drink on me. Apologize profusely but never for once take your glance off me. Compliment me. Write your phone number on a paper napkin and slip it in my pocket.

OSCAR: You should have. After all, you were the whiter one. The more physically demonstrative one.

MING: Anyway, I got a call from him the next day.

OSCAR: I got his number from the host.

MING: We arranged to meet for dinner the following evening.

OSCAR: How about Ciao Bella on Newberry Street?

MING: Sure.

OSCAR: Dinner in a small Italian restaurant.

MING: At first, it was rather awkward.

OSCAR: So—did you enjoy the party?

MING: Yeah.

OSCAR: Trying to make polite conversation.

MING: We talked.

OSCAR: In circles.

MING: About the unpredictable New England weather.

OSCAR: About politics.

MING: About people whom we have in common. People we know. People we didn't want to know.

OSCAR: About Madonna's latest CD and its political significance on Asians in America.

MING: About his name. Oscar. Asians always pick out the most curious and most discarded English names from books and TV. Like Cornelius. Elmo. Wellington. They do it to assimilate into the American culture.

OSCAR: Oscar is easier to pronounce. I've had my Chinese name massacred all too frequently by strangers and friends. And his name? Ming. It's not even his real name. He picked up a Chinese name because he wanted to be in touch with his cultural roots. Picking up a name is not like picking up a culture.

MING: All the while, I was mentally undressing him.

OSCAR: All the while, I was wondering what it was like to stroke your cheek.

MING: I kept looking at you.

OSCAR: You were beautiful.

MING: Mature.

OSCAR: Intelligent.

MING: Polite.

OSCAR: Talkative.

MING: We ate.

OSCAR: And talked again.

MING: After dinner, we walked around for a while.

OSCAR: Peered into brightly-lit shop windows.

MING: Sat on steps of an old church in Copley Square.

OSCAR: Looking at young couples walking by.

MING: Looking at old couples on park benches.

OSCAR: Looking at each other.

MING: Then you asked me back. To your place.

OSCAR: Hope—I'm not—being too—

MING: No—

OSCAR: I'm not usually—

MING: I know—

OSCAR: I really—like you.

MING: I kept thinking: Will he respect me in the morning? Should I care whether he respects me?

OSCAR: My apartment is a mess. I should have vacuumed. Lemon Pledged. Something.

MING: Fuck, I'm wearing contact lenses. Maybe he's got some saline. What if he doesn't. Then I'm fucked.

OSCAR: I've got to get up early tomorrow. Work. What am I doing?

MING: If I go back to his apartment, he might think I'm a slut.

OSCAR: Is he a slut?

MING: It's not like this crosses my mind every time I go back with someone. But I kinda like him, and I really don't want to fuck this up because I want to—I want this to be right.

OSCAR: So we took a cab.

MING: Back to his apartment in Brookline.

OSCAR: And made love.

MING: On the staircase.

OSCAR: In the cold bedroom above.

MING: Yes.

OSCAR: Again and again.

MING: Yes.

OSCAR: Then you moved in.

MING: For four years.

OSCAR: We discovered new uses for the kitchen and the living room.

MING: Acted like children in museums on Sundays.

OSCAR: Read poetry in my large wooden bed by candlelight.

MING: Had breakfast in Union Park.

OSCAR: Secretly held hands on crowded Boston streets.

MING: You were always embarrassed to hold hands in public.

OSCAR: I wasn't.

MING: Instead you let me hold your finger.

OSCAR: Yes. Sometimes.

MING: Not your hand.

OSCAR: Sometimes my hand.

MING: Sometimes.

OSCAR: Holding hands on subway trains to Brookline after work.

MING: Chasing after trains that are never on time.

OSCAR: Do you know how many trains we sat on together?

MING: Seemed like thousands.

OSCAR: And I thought—in thousands more.

MING: Four years.

OSCAR: Four years.

[MING *goes over to* OSCAR, *and they kiss passionately.*]

OSCAR: Yes. [*Pause.*] Ming?

MING: Yes?

OSCAR: I—want to say—I—

MING: Yes.

OSCAR: I—I—eh—nothing. It's nothing.

[A *beat.*]

MING: [*Disappointed.*] I see. [*Pause.*] Then one night when I came home, you
    said—

OSCAR: I don't think we should see each other anymore.

MING: I didn't know what to say. I stood there as if someone had slapped me
    in the face.

OSCAR: I had to say it.

MING: I was hurt. Bruised. Stunned. I knew this was going to happen and I even thought about it. But when it really happens, it just takes your breath away. All the time, rehearsing, thinking, plotting, doesn't matter. It's the moment, that moment, that does.

OSCAR: Maybe I just wanted to say it before he did.

MING: I laid my brown coat and leather briefcase down on the wood floor.

OSCAR: It was very difficult for me as well. You know that, don't you?

MING: Let's not talk. Okay?

OSCAR: I want you to know—

MING: Shh—shh—

OSCAR: Okay.

MING: So I moved out.

OSCAR: Is this Donna Summer CD yours or mine?

MING: Yours. "La Traviata," "Turandot," "Carmen." All the classical stuff—yours.

OSCAR: Pet Shop Boys—

MING: Mine—

OSCAR: Pet Shop Boys—

MING: Mine—

OSCAR: Pet Shop Boys—

MING: Mine. All mine.

OSCAR: And this?

MING: Yours.

OSCAR: Mine.

MING: Uh-huh.

OSCAR: I don't know what I was feeling as I saw him pack his things away. Quietly and methodically. Breakables in one. Books in another. Perhaps he's right. I should express what I feel. Say what I think. But how can I express something when I don't know what I feel? I want to say "don't go" but I know I'm doing the right thing.

MING: The usual anger.

OSCAR: Silence.

MING: Sadness.

OSCAR: The process of lovers becoming friends.

MING: The process all civilized ex-lovers go through.

OSCAR: Here.

MING: What is it?

OSCAR: Satie.

MING: Take it.

OSCAR: It's yours.

MING: You've always liked it.

OSCAR: I couldn't.

MING: I want you to have it. You liked it more than I ever did.

OSCAR: Thanks.

MING: Books.

OSCAR: Underwear.

MING: Kitchen utensils.

OSCAR: Bed sheets.

MING: Toiletries.

OSCAR: All divided.

MING: All sorted into nice, little brown boxes.

OSCAR: Our lives in the past four years packed neatly in boxes.

MING: The room was empty.

OSCAR: Listen, I want us to be friends.

MING: Sure.

OSCAR: And if you need anything, please call.

MING: I know.

OSCAR: Anything at all. I insist.

MING: So fucking amiable.

OSCAR: He won't call.

MING: I won't call.

OSCAR: Call me when you're settled in.

MING: The first night I moved out, I got myself drunk with warm beer and quickly fell into the warm, sturdy arms of a handsome waiter.

OSCAR: I sat home and watched Seinfeld. Wondering if I had done the right thing. Wondering if he was all right. Wondering if I had made a very bad mistake. Wondering why everyone thought Seinfeld was funny. Wondering.

MING: I was thinking about you while making love to the waiter.

OSCAR: I watched TV until one. I didn't know what I was watching.

MING: I made love to this stranger who smelled of coffee and roast chicken the same way I made love to you. The exact order. The exact style. But the stranger's moans and whispers weren't yours.

OSCAR: How was he? Where was he? What was he doing?

MING: Three weeks later, I moved in with the waiter. His name is Robert.

OSCAR: Will he call? Shall I call? Call me.

MING: Robert's a head waiter in some fancy restaurant downtown.

OSCAR: After moping around for a month, I started dating again. At first I got in touch with a group of people who were HIV positive. In that group there was a whole different world of gay men, people who had different priorities than going to clubs or the gym. We met twice a week and talked about what and how things were like now that we're HIV positive. Personally, I don't see any difference. My pay is still the same. My lover is still gone. I don't club much anyway. The best analogy for being positive is losing your boyfriend. Losing a part of you you took for granted. You're still the same, but never whole, not completely. In the group, there was a new vocabulary, a new language, discussions on T-cells, AZT and PCP, vegetarian picnics on Sundays, jazz bowling on Tuesdays, and advanced macrame classes on Thursdays—but I soon tired of it. I just wondered what he was doing. How he was getting along.

MING: I fell in love with Robert. Sometimes I wondered if I was on the rebound. Or just emotionally needy.

OSCAR: Then I heard from some of my friends that he has been seen with a white guy in a bar. All over each other. Kissing, holding hands in public. Said he looked happy. Not happier, just happy.

MING: I heard he spends most of his time alone. It would be nice to hear he'd gotten out and started dating. Seeing other people. Or something. On the other hand, I think it would make me upset to know that he was dating someone else. I don't know what I think or feel anymore. I just don't want to think or feel. Just be. Be myself. I don't know who or what I am. Without him.

OSCAR: I started meeting people again. Being positive is one thing. Knowing that he's dating again and being happy is another.

MING: Six months flew by. And not a word.

OSCAR: Then one day when I got home from work, I saw a letter in his handwriting. He sent me a birthday card. But no present.

MING: He sent me a Christmas card. Typed. Very cordial. Detached. Like it was sent by a bank or an insurance company.

OSCAR: Then silence.

MING: Just the other day, I got a message on my phone machine.

OSCAR: Hi. It's—eh—me. Listen, I'm having a little party this Saturday and would like—you to come. Can you? It'd be great to catch up with you again. It's nothing fancy. Some of the old gang will be there. They'd love to see you. Really. I hope you can come. Bring your—friend—or any friend along. [Pause.] Bye.

MING: My heart started beating wildly.

OSCAR: Maybe I'm curious to see who replaced me.

MING: I started playing his message over and over again. Hearing his voice.

Trying to read between the lines. I was already coordinating my clothes for the party in my head.

OSCAR: I wondered if we'll be friendly and civil to each other. I wonder if he'd show up at all.

MING: I thought it'd be nice to see him again.

OSCAR: After all these months.

MING: I wanted to see his boyfriend.

OSCAR: And I, his.

MING: I wanted to see him.

OSCAR: Yes.

MING: The party was just that—a party. About forty people once again crammed into a Boston apartment, speaking wildly in tongues. Like an evangelical convention.

OSCAR: I saw him come into the apartment with his friend and I immediately ran into the kitchen. I don't know why. But I did. My cheeks were flushed red. I stood there, pretending to arrange food by color hues—orange with reds, blues with purples, on and on.

MING: Where could he be?

OSCAR: I came out. Finally. Excited and nervous. Carrying a fruit tray.

MING: Hi.

OSCAR: Hi.

MING: You look great.

OSCAR: You do, too.

MING: Like your new hairstyle.

OSCAR: Silence.

MING: This is Robert.

OSCAR: Hi.

MING: He's wearing that shirt I got him when we were on the Cape last year. I wonder if it's deliberate. Trying to guilt me or something.

OSCAR: Robert is very good-looking. I can see them both naked, making love on the kitchen floor. Our kitchen floor.

MING: Nice party.

OSCAR: What?

MING: Nice party.

OSCAR: Oh, thanks.

MING: I shouldn't look at him too much, otherwise Robert will get funny ideas and then we'll have another drama at home.

OSCAR: Let me get both of you a drink.

MING: Bet he knows what drink to get me without asking. Habits die hard.

OSCAR: I have this sudden urge to kiss him.

MING: He has no visible signs of being HIV positive.

OSCAR: Why is he looking at me that way?

MING: He is a little thinner. But still as handsome.

OSCAR: I wish Robert wasn't that good-looking. It would be easier for me to know that he's been sleeping with a troll.

MING: There were people I haven't seen in ages.

OSCAR: The party was large enough to get lost in, but small enough to know he's around somewhere.

MING: We were looking at each other again.

OSCAR: Across the room.

MING: But not directly. Fleeting glances.

OSCAR: Like the first time we met.

MING: I finally met his Asian friend through some old friends of mine. Quite a nice guy. Amusing in his own little way. I'm glad for the both of them. Or aren't I?

OSCAR: Robert is a nice man. Charming, personable, smart, good-looking. He must have some flaw. Maybe he has a small dick. He must have.

MING: I saw him slip into the bedroom. I'm sure he looked in my direction.

OSCAR: I don't know if I did it deliberately.

MING: I excused myself.

OSCAR: I hoped he'd seen me walk in here.

MING: There you are.

OSCAR: Here I am.

MING: I was looking for you.

OSCAR: Really?

MING: Yes.

OSCAR: I'm here.

MING: So you are. [Pause.] Everything's exactly the way it was.

OSCAR: Uh-huh.

MING: Nothing changed.

OSCAR: Why? Should it?

MING: No.

OSCAR: I don't know why I'm getting defensive.

MING: Maybe I should just hightail the fuck out of here.

OSCAR: You said you were looking for me?

MING: Yeah. I wanted to talk to you.

OSCAR: About what?

MING: Nothing in particular.

OSCAR: Just the usual pleasantries, then.

MING: What do ex-lovers talk about?

OSCAR: Are you happy with Robert?

MING: Do I want to talk about Robert and me?

OSCAR: Talk about us. How we used to be. How we still can be.

MING: Do I want to talk about his new friend? Do I want to talk about us? Do I want to talk?

OSCAR: I want to pin him down on the bed and rape him like a Sabine woman.

MING: A what woman?

OSCAR: Sabine.

MING: What's that?

OSCAR: It's—forget it.

MING: Tell me.

OSCAR: The moment's lost.

MING: Now what? Do I touch him?

OSCAR: Like the way you used to. Instinctively. Automatically. Without question or hesitation.

MING: Do I hold him? Hug him? Kiss him?

OSCAR: The harmless gestures we once took for granted. The casual and familiar actions that became second nature to us. These old habits now hold different meanings and interpretations. All of a sudden, we've become two awkward strangers in a cold room. Wrestling with a new, unspeakable language that only belongs to old lovers.

MING: So why are you here?

OSCAR: Because I want to.

MING: Is something wrong?

OSCAR: No.

MING: I know you.

OSCAR: So?

MING: Your health?

OSCAR: It's fine. My T's are up.

MING: Your what?

OSCAR: Nothing.

MING: Boyfriend?

OSCAR: No.

MING: Family? Not your father again?

OSCAR: No.

MING: Someone you want to avoid out there?

OSCAR: Maybe.

MING: I knew it. I shouldn't have come.

OSCAR: Forget it. I shouldn't have said anything.

MING: I knew coming here was a mistake.

OSCAR: I wanted you to come. You and Robert. Both of you.

MING: I know but it's just too soon.

OSCAR: It's not.

MING: I'll go. I'll get Robert and we'll both go.

OSCAR: Don't.

MING: I think it's—

OSCAR: Stay. I want you to stay.

MING: Assertion and aggression. Quite a change.

OSCAR: I want to tell him so many things. The things I've been thinking, feeling. But it's difficult.

MING: Seems so long ago.

OSCAR: What seems so long ago?

MING: My being in here.

OSCAR: Yes.

MING: The nights, the afternoons in here.

OSCAR: Making love.

MING: Smoking French cigarettes.

OSCAR: Lying next to each other. Not talking.

MING: Never wanting to leave the room except to take a quick leak.

OSCAR: Listening to Satie. Reading the Sunday papers together.

MING: Telling each other secrets.

OSCAR: Secrets he's now sharing with his new friend.

MING: I've run out of conversation. Out of words.

OSCAR: I want to kiss you. Gently on your soft lips.

MING: You know there are mornings when I wake up thinking I'm here. The bay windows, wood floors, candles, and the cat purring on top of me.

OSCAR: What does he mean by that?

MING: Why did I say that?

OSCAR: He wants me.

MING: He must think I'm flirting with him.

OSCAR: He's flirting with me.

MING: You should be out there.

OSCAR: Why?

MING: You're the host. You should be mingling, introducing people, asking if they want more food, drink, I don't know. Out there. Not here.

OSCAR: I want to be here. For a while, anyway.

MING: I'm getting aroused.

OSCAR: Come sit on the bed.

MING: Should I sit on the bed?

OSCAR: Sit.

MING: No. It's okay, I'll just stand.

OSCAR: Come on, sit.

MING: It'll be too awkward.

OSCAR: Sit.

MING: I wonder if Robert is looking for me.

OSCAR: Sit.

MING: I'll sit.

OSCAR: Thank you, God.

MING: I haven't seen these people in such a long time.

OSCAR: Sit closer.

MING: So many familiar faces.

OSCAR: Closer

[MING *sits closer to* OSCAR.]

MING: Am I sitting too close?

OSCAR: You should have called them.

MING: It isn't the same.

OSCAR: What do you mean?

MING: They're your friends.

OSCAR: His knee is touching mine. Oh, Jesus.

MING: I'm being too coy. Think about Robert. Think about what mother looks
     like naked. Think about what Jesus looks like naked.

OSCAR: Fuck, he's pulling away.

MING: I'm getting uncomfortable.

OSCAR: They were your friends too.

MING: Yeah, but you knew them longer.

OSCAR: That's not the point.

MING: After we broke up, it's natural they took your side.

OSCAR: That's ridiculous.

MING: They blame me, don't they?

OSCAR: Blame you for what?

MING: Us.

OSCAR: No.

MING: They blame me. I can see it in their eyes.

OSCAR: They like you.

MING: Sure.

OSCAR: They always ask about you.

MING: Gossips.

OSCAR: After all, I was the one responsible for the breakup, remember?

MING: Yes. You were.

OSCAR: I wish we didn't break up. If I could just make it right again. Wish I never did what I did. Wish it all never happened. And we're here together again.

MING: How's work?

OSCAR: Good. How's your work?

MING: The usual. Busy.

OSCAR: Did you and Robert fuck in the bathroom like we did?

MING: I'm going to Venice next week. On business.

OSCAR: We always wanted to go to Venice together. Gondolas in sleepy canals.

MING: He said he wanted to retire there.

OSCAR: We never did it, did we? Venice. Another regret. Now, he's probably going to Venice with Robert. Doing things we always wanted to do there.

MING: I'll be there for four days.

OSCAR: Venice should be very nice this time of the year.

MING: Wish you could come with me. Ask me.

OSCAR: We can walk across old bridges and make love in a small pensione in hot afternoons. Take me to Venice with you.

MING: I'm taking Robert with me.

OSCAR: I see. Good.

MING: Are you dating?

OSCAR: Yes and no.

MING: Which?

OSCAR: Yes, I'm dating. No, it's nothing serious.

MING: Anyone in particular?

OSCAR: Yes.

MING: Who?

OSCAR: A Filipino guy.

MING: He's here.

OSCAR: Yeah.

MING: What's his name?

OSCAR: His name is—why do you want to know?

MING: Just want to know.

OSCAR: His name is Daniel.

MING: Daniel. Hmm.

OSCAR: He's young.

MING: I've been replaced by someone younger.

OSCAR: He's nice.

MING: Good. I'm happy for you.

OSCAR: He's not you.

MING: Does he know?

OSCAR: About?

MING: You.

OSCAR: Yes.

MING: Quite a responsibility for someone so young.

OSCAR: We're only dating. Anyway, he manages.

MING: I see. How long have you been—

OSCAR: Dating? Oh, about three weeks. Your friend—

MING: Robert.

OSCAR: Yes. He's—very cute.

MING: He's nice.

OSCAR: He's white.

MING: So?

OSCAR: I thought you never dated white guys.

MING: Well, I am.

OSCAR: I see.

MING: A lot of Asian guys date white guys.

OSCAR: I know all too many.

MING: Is that a problem?

OSCAR: Asians only date white guys—

MING: Please don't—

OSCAR: To assimilate—

MING: That is not fair—

OSCAR: To emulate—

MING: I'm with Robert because I love—

OSCAR: Anyway, I always thought you only dated Asian guys.

MING: It was a phase.

OSCAR: Like homosexuality.

MING: No. Like it was the politically correct thing to do.

OSCAR: I see.

MING: Some Asians only date Asians because—

OSCAR: They found Asians attractive—

MING: And some—

OSCAR: A politically correct thing to do.

MING: You know what I mean—

OSCAR: Like us.

MING: No. Not like us. Can we not do this?

OSCAR: I've been rude. I shouldn't pry.

MING: I hope I'm making him jealous. He must still care if he's jealous.

OSCAR: He's—young.

MING: He's a year older than me.

OSCAR: A waiter?

MING: Head waiter.

OSCAR: Same thing.

MING: Once I wanted him to be aggressive, but that was then.

OSCAR: Which restaurant?

MING: Cafe Orpheus downtown. What does Daniel do?

OSCAR: A student. Majors in—

MING: Business.

OSCAR: Yes. Harvard.

MING: Like every foreign student from Asia.

OSCAR: Who's putting people into boxes now?

MING: Rich parents?

OSCAR: Yes. He's also a committee member of Act-Up.

MING: Really.

OSCAR: He's a radical queer Asian who lives and breathes Sondheim.

MING: He loves me, you know.

OSCAR: Who?

MING: Robert.

OSCAR: Why is he telling me this?

MING: Why am I telling him this?

OSCAR: I'm—happy for you. Really.

MING: Does—Daniel love you?

OSCAR: I think this is a little premature. I mean, we've only gone out a few times.

MING: Oh.

OSCAR: And we haven't had sex or anything.

MING: You kissed.

OSCAR: No.

MING: Am I prying?

OSCAR: I'm not in love with him.

MING: He's in love with him. God, I don't want to hear this.

OSCAR: I'm still in love with you. Tell him.

MING: Well, that put an end to my childish fantasies.

OSCAR: Tell him or he'll go away. Again.

MING: He's being silent again. It's so annoying.

OSCAR: For once, express yourself. Tell him about your feelings.

MING: He's probably thinking about his friend.

OSCAR: I'm not in love with him.

MING: Why not?

OSCAR: Must you ask?

MING: No.

OSCAR: Because—I still—

MING: What?

[Pause.]

OSCAR: *[Muttering.]* I still— *[Pause.]* —love you.

MING: I have to get back to the party.

OSCAR: I thought you always liked confrontations. Wanted me to express what I was feeling.

MING: I—have changed.

OSCAR: Become more Chinese?

MING: Maybe.

OSCAR: I should have said it earlier, I know.

MING: It's different now.

OSCAR: Yes, but—

MING: Why did you end our relationship then?

OSCAR: I thought it was for the best.

MING: Best for you?

OSCAR: Best for you.

MING: How do you know what's best for me?

OSCAR: It wouldn't be fair to you. Looking after me when I got sicker. I couldn't bear to see you hating me.

MING: I wouldn't.

OSCAR: You would. Because I would hate myself if I were in your place.

MING: Then you don't know me.

OSCAR: We lived together for four years. I know you all too well.

MING: How dare you make a selfish decision for the both of us without telling me?

OSCAR: It was for the best.

MING: Fuck you. What right do you—

OSCAR: It's past.

MING: Your decision hurt me.

OSCAR: I'm sorry.

MING: I was lost for weeks.

OSCAR: So was I.

MING: And that was supposed to make me feel better?

OSCAR: You could have asked me to stay.

MING: Asked you to stay?

OSCAR: But you didn't.

MING: I don't believe I'm having this conversation.

OSCAR: You don't remember what happened?

MING: I remember every single word.

OSCAR: I don't think we should see each other anymore.

MING: Every single word! I hear it in my head, at the back of my mind, every
single day! Like a scratched record playing on the same groove, over and
over again! And it hurts every time I hear it!

OSCAR: And you said nothing! [*Softly.*] You just stood there and listened to
me. Smiled and walked out of the room.

MING: And what should I have said?

OSCAR: You're the expressive one. You could have asked me to stay.

MING: Begged for you to stay.

OSCAR: No. Just ask. [*Pause.*] This isn't easy for me to say—but I want you
back in my life.

MING: As a friend.

OSCAR: More than a friend.

MING: Meaning?

OSCAR: We could start again. From the beginning.

MING: We can't.

OSCAR: Why not?

MING: You know why.

OSCAR: No.

MING: Because it's not the same anymore.

OSCAR: It can be.

MING: What makes you so sure I want to?

OSCAR: I don't know.

MING: We can't go back to the way things are, and make everything alright.
It's like learning Chinese. Once I started speaking English, I stopped learning how to speak and write Chinese. I dropped my culture for another. And
you can't go back. Only forward. And every now and then, you'll remember
a few phrases, a few words, the names of a few Chinese dishes. It sounds a

little vague, a little romantic. But the language escapes you because you'd let it go. It's like learning Chinese. Learning to be Chinese.

OSCAR: We can try and make it work this time.

MING: What if I'm not strong enough to be there for you when you're really sick?

OSCAR: I'll take that risk.

MING: It isn't fair to you.

OSCAR: I'll chance it.

MING: No!

OSCAR: Then we're just going to be friends.

MING: Yes.

OSCAR: Just friends.

MING: Yes.

OSCAR: It's not going to be easy.

MING: I know.

OSCAR: Watching you hold someone else the same way you held me.

MING: Yes.

OSCAR: Watching you hold his hand. His finger.

MING: Let me hold your finger. [*Holds* OSCAR's *index finger.*]

OSCAR: It hurts me deeply. To see you happy. To see you in love with someone else. I know it's wrong but I can't help it. I wish it could have been me.

MING: But I love Robert differently.

OSCAR: More. More than me?

MING: No. Differently.

OSCAR: I do want you to be happy. You know that, don't you?

MING: Yes.

OSCAR: It's just—

MING: Difficult.

OSCAR: You're very handsome.

MING: Thanks.

OSCAR: You are. [*Suddenly lurches towards* MING *in an attempt to kiss him.*]

MING: Don't.

OSCAR: They won't know.

MING: I don't want to.

OSCAR: I'm asking you now. Stay. Please stay.

MING: There are others involved now. [*Pause.*] No matter what happens, I'm always there for you.

OSCAR: We'll become friends then.

MING: Best friends.

OSCAR: Best friends.
MING: I wished it would have been different.
OSCAR: So do I.
MING: But it can't. [*Walks away.*]
OSCAR: I love you.

[MING *stops with his back to* OSCAR.]

MING: I love you too.

[*Pause.*]

OSCAR: Hold me.
MING: Okay. [*Goes to* OSCAR *and embraces him.*]
OSCAR: Close.
MING: Hmm.
OSCAR: Hold me close.
MING: Yeah.
OSCAR: Don't let go.
MING: Yeah.
OSCAR: Don't let go.
MING: I won't.
OSCAR: Don't let go.
MING: Shhh.
OSCAR: Don't let go. Don't let go. Don't let go.

[*Lights dim.*]

BROKEN ENGLISH

OSCAR *and* MING *as they were in the last act.*
Despite the numerous scenes in this act, this whole act should flow as fluidly as the prior act. In this act, all characters should physically remain on the set.

BECOMING FRIENDS

MING: I can never forget what he said to me.
OSCAR: Hold me.
MING: Don't let go.
OSCAR: It seemed like an eternity.
MING: Us holding each other.
OSCAR: After a while, we broke away.

MING: Then Robert and I quickly left the party.

OSCAR: I saw both of them walking away. They made a handsome couple. We looked like that once. A long time ago.

MING: Walking beside me, Robert's mute eyes wrestled uncomfortably with the question of where I had earlier disappeared to. I squeezed Robert's hand. Deliberately. As if I was squeezing all his doubts away. And he smiled. That Robert smile. It was as if I never left him.

OSCAR: I saw Daniel. Sitting on an overcrowded couch with his friends. Holding court. I lingered near the couch and managed to catch snippets of their heated conversation. Government spending on AIDS. Racism within the gay community. Relationships. Madonna. Suddenly, I wanted to shout. At Daniel. Fuck off. You don't know what the fuck you're babbling about. Shut up. Shut up. Fuck off. Shut up. Fuck off. Then my head began to ring. Pound. Felt faint. Thirsty. Weak. Couldn't breathe.

MING: I agreed to move to L.A. With Robert. He thought the move was best. For him. For me. For us.

OSCAR: He never called. Not once. When I finally called—months later—a dull, lifeless, middle-aged female voice told me the number has been disconnected.

MING: Our belongings were already packed into little brown boxes. Phones disconnected. Mail forwarded.

OSCAR: In desperate disbelief, I kept dialing the same seven numbers over and over again. But her obstinate, mechanical voice never wavered from her prepared text. She didn't give me a clue to where he's gone. A hint to what he's up to.

MING: Perhaps the reason why I wanted to go to Oscar's party was to revisit the apartment where I spent four years of my life. To see Oscar's face one last time. To say good-bye to him. But, I guess I didn't know the words to tell Oscar about leaving for L.A. About leaving him.

[ROBERT, *a Caucasian man in his late twenties, enters.*]

ROBERT: In three weeks we found ourselves in a quaint, sun-kissed Spanish stucco apartment overlooking the restless Pacific Ocean in a place called Venice.

SEEING US

MING: I see us
ROBERT: Paris in winter, hand in hand.
MING: I see us.

ROBERT: Walking along frigid banks of River Seine.
MING: I see us
ROBERT: Not saying a word
MING: Laughing.
ROBERT: I see us
MING: Lost
ROBERT: In narrow streets of Florence.
MING: I see us
ROBERT: Walking along old bridge Vecchio
MING: Listening to lonely arias in adagio
ROBERT: In awe of shadows
MING: Cast in paintings by Caravaggio.
ROBERT: I see you
MING: Looking at me
ROBERT: Not saying a word
MING: Smiling.
ROBERT: I see us
MING: Here in L.A.
ROBERT: Cooking pasta made like mom's
MING: Listening to a sad violin by Brahms.
ROBERT: I see you
MING: Not saying a word
ROBERT: Thinking.
MING: I see us
ROBERT: Taking hot showers together
MING: His hands on me
ROBERT: His mind far away.
MING: I see us
ROBERT: On a lone pier
MING: Old couples on park benches with nothing to say
ROBERT: Young lovers at play
MING: Doves taking to the air, flying far, far away.
ROBERT: I see you
MING: Not saying a word
ROBERT: Contemplating.
MING: I see us
ROBERT: Sitting on expensive furniture
MING: In vast showrooms
ROBERT: On rainy Saturday afternoons.

MING: I see us
ROBERT: Not saying a word
MING: Sighing.
ROBERT: I see us
MING: In the comfort of bed
ROBERT: Sunlight falling
MING: On bodies breathing.
ROBERT: I see you
MING: Silent
ROBERT: Not saying a word
MING: Frowning.
ROBERT: I see you
MING: Looking away
ROBERT: Not saying a word
MING: Wondering.
ROBERT: I see us.
MING: I see us.
ROBERT: I see us.
MING: I see us. [*Looks at* OSCAR.]

COMFORTABLE DISTANCES

[DANIEL, *an Asian man in his early twenties, enters.*]

DANIEL: I thought it was high time to move off-campus. It's one thing to bunk in with a hundred, heterosexual, horny, half-naked boys. It's another if I have to wait in line for the bathroom. Just to blow dry.

OSCAR: Of course—I suggested—that he should—move in with me.

DANIEL: He hinted that I move in. In so many words.

OSCAR: Danny—you can—you know—stay—move in—here—if you want.

DANIEL: You only have to read between the lines. If you want.

OSCAR: It was only proper. Given our circumstances. We were seeing each other.

DANIEL: Move in as roommates. Or move in as lovers?

OSCAR: I didn't know what to say.

DANIEL: Boyfriend wasn't ready. To make the leap.

OSCAR: I'm HIV positive. It's a different lifestyle.

DANIEL: Boyfriend has a disease. Called fear of commitment.

OSCAR: It's not about commitment. I love him—I do—I want to be with—want him—more than anything else in the world—I just don't want this to—come between—pry us apart—it'll strain—it's bad as it is—but living with someone who's positive—twenty-four hours a day—isn't easy—it's probably best—this way.

DANIEL: He thinks I'll leave. Like Ming. His ex.

OSCAR: So he went on a rampage looking for a place to call his own.

DANIEL: I don't need much.

OSCAR: A place which is quiet.

DANIEL: Comfortable.

OSCAR: Affordable.

DANIEL: Gay-friendly. Asian-friendly. Or just—friendly.

OSCAR: A Victorian brownstone building circa late 1800s.

DANIEL: No screaming children. No femmes with big hair.

OSCAR: Large bay windows with a view of trees. Like mine.

DANIEL: A stone's throw from the hairdressers, gay bars, and a trendy outdoor cafe.

OSCAR: Hardwood floors. [*Looks at* MING.] Exactly like the one Ming and I used to—eh—walk on.

DANIEL: Cute security men wielding thick batons.

OSCAR: Heat and air-conditioning.

DANIEL: The basic necessities for an urban queer.

OSCAR: I was almost relieved he said he wouldn't move in.

DANIEL: If I move in with him, and he's not ready, I'll be out on the streets. Back to square one. Looking for an apartment in three weeks. With my matching suitcases. Sans boyfriend.

OSCAR: I was actually a little offended when he said no.

DANIEL: Listen, I love him. Without a doubt. He's my first big love. But, to be practically honest, it's tres difficult to live with someone who's HIV positive. Tres, tres, tres high maintenance. You've got to watch your temper. Watch what you say. Be understanding. Be June Cleaver on a good hair day. And that's real tough when you feel more like Linda Blair with a chainsaw.

OSCAR: I mean, I want him here with me. But not all the time.

DANIEL: So I found a place close by.

OSCAR: He moved into a little apartment.

DANIEL: Across the street.

OSCAR: It's a comfortable distance.

SEEING OTHER PEOPLE

[ROBERT *goes to* MING *and hugs him from behind.* MING *shrugs him off.*]

MING: Don't—
ROBERT: What?
MING: You always do that—
ROBERT: I thought you always liked—
MING: I did—just don't—
ROBERT: Listen, I got us—
MING: Tickets—
ROBERT: "Otello"—
MING: "Otello"—
ROBERT: It's the opera everyone's raving—
MING: Well, good—
ROBERT: The critics love—
MING: Okay, okay—
ROBERT: And right before the—
MING: No—
ROBERT: Cocktails with Jason and Tim—
MING: Not again—
ROBERT: Can you be nice?—
MING: Listen—
ROBERT: They're people we should get to—
MING: Robert—
ROBERT: Tim is an important—
MING: Robert—
ROBERT: Let's not fight over this—
MING: We should—talk.
ROBERT: Fine. But we're still going to—
MING: About other things
ROBERT: I've been trying to bring you to operas, plays—
MING: I've been thinking—
ROBERT: Art exhibitions, books, magazines—
MING: I think—
ROBERT: And you always fight me—
MING: I think we should see other people.
ROBERT: What?
MING: I think—
ROBERT: Other people—
MING: You know—
ROBERT: See other people—
MING: Which means—

ROBERT: No.

[*Pause.*]

MING: No?
ROBERT: We are not seeing other people.
MING: I don't understand—
ROBERT: We're not—you can't—that's final—
MING: I don't think you—
ROBERT: Have you thought about this? Have you?
MING: Yes—
ROBERT: No, you haven't—
MING: Yes, I have—
ROBERT: Do you want to break up—
MING: No—
ROBERT: You want to leave—
MING: You're not listening—
ROBERT: This is exactly how my folks broke up—
MING: Let's not get into this again—
ROBERT: I wanted us to be different—
MING: Listen—
ROBERT: I can't believe this—
MING: We're not breaking up—
ROBERT: I thought we were perfect—happy—
MING: I'm not saying we should stop seeing—
ROBERT: No. Of course not.
MING: Nothing's going to change. Nothing.
ROBERT: Except you'll be seeing other people.
MING: It's not only me. You can—as well—
ROBERT: That's very generous.
MING: I think this will be good for us—
ROBERT: Good for you.
MING: For you. For us—
ROBERT: See other people. What's "see?"—
MING: You know what I mean—
ROBERT: To look?—
MING: Let's not—
ROBERT: Browse—stare—
MING: Robert—please—
ROBERT: Have coffee. Go to the movies. What?—

MING: Why are you doing this?—
ROBERT: To touch—to feel—to be with—
MING: To sleep with—to fuck with—okay?

[*Pause.*]

ROBERT: [*Softly.*] Why?
MING: I am—
ROBERT: Bored.
MING: No. I am—
ROBERT: Suffocated.
MING: Stop finishing my sentences.
ROBERT: What did I do?
MING: Nothing.
ROBERT: What didn't I do?
MING: It's not you. It's me. Listen, I'm doing this to—
ROBERT: Hurt me—
MING: Would you rather I lied to you? Cheated on you?
ROBERT: Yes.
MING: Nothing will change.
ROBERT: Yeah.
MING: Between us. Really.
ROBERT: Yeah. Sure.
MING: What would you rather I—
ROBERT: I don't know.
MING: Tell me.
ROBERT: See other people.
MING: Are you sure?
ROBERT: No.
MING: I don't want to do this if you're—
ROBERT: Don't. Please. Just do it. And be careful.
MING: I will.
ROBERT: Hold me.
MING: Yeah.

[ROBERT *stands immobile as* MING *walks towards him.* MING *hugs* ROBERT.]

ROBERT: Tight.
MING: Yeah.
ROBERT: I love you.

MING: More than anything else in the world.
ROBERT: More than anything else in the world.

A GLIMPSE OF US

ROBERT: I have this glimpse of us
Ming and me
Sitting on a park bench
Old and wrinkled
Together holding hands
Framed by naked, barren birch trees
Invisible light rain, among golden crimson leaves
Like the old couple in the park
The couple we saw years ago when we first met
And that image always lingered in corners of my
    mind

It haunted me, excited me, in so many ways

That old couple became a dream
A glowing, beckoning dream within arm's reach
A dream to be in love with that someone for
    eternity
That friend, that lover, that soul mate
That someone I've been dreaming of
Ming

That same dream became a nightmare
An unattainable, unfathomable dream
And with it, a crippling fear
A fear that hot love and passion may simmer to its
eventual cool
A fear that he may be uncertain, unsure, of his
    feelings, his touch, his affection, for me
A fear that he may find someone else, and I, like
    light rain, dissolve, disappear from mind
A fear that he may leave, like all others before
    him, and I, back where I started, in the
    lonesome dark

A fear that I may find deliberate ways, words,
    measures, unfair, unkind, uncalled for, to
    cling desperate onto loose seams of my
    fractured dream
A fear that we may never be that old couple in the
    park

I have this glimpse
Of us

LIVING ROOM

OSCAR: We spend all of our weekends at Ikea.

DANIEL: Not all. Every other weekend.

OSCAR: Glorious Ikea. The Swedish fix-it-yourself discount furniture megastore.

DANIEL: Possibly Sweden's biggest export since Abba and euthanasia.

OSCAR: He moved into a new apartment, and tastefully decorated it according to pages 56 to 59 of the Ikea catalogue.

DANIEL: I spared no expense.

OSCAR: Instant homes. Affordable prices. If only relationships came that way.

DANIEL: The concept of instant homes was appealing and accessible. But assembling the furniture was another issue.

OSCAR: Building a home takes time. Each piece of furniture in the room should evoke a memory, a time, and the people that surrounded it. Furniture is sentimental. Not mass produced and instant.

DANIEL: We would spend hours—

OSCAR: Hours—

DANIEL: Looking at living room upon living room. One was done in black leather and cold steel that said "single-gay-Asian-workaholic-accountant-in-late-thirties-unable-to-have-emotional-relationships-a.k.a.-you-know-who."

OSCAR: We were making our second round of the showrooms.

DANIEL: Another had a oak and pine theme—tres Heidi—dripping in Laura Ashley prints that screamed Republican virgin spinster or repressed male homosexual.

OSCAR: I was getting tired.

DANIEL: Then there's an Oriental rosewood and marble motif that told me to brew some Jasmine and call the girls over for some serious mahjong. Tres *Joy Luck Club.* ·

OSCAR: The place was getting crowded and hot.

DANIEL: And I still haven't made up my dizzy mind.

OSCAR: I felt achy.

DANIEL: Now, there's an interesting kitchen table. Tres Quaker.

OSCAR: Suddenly, I realized Danny was gone. Nowhere to be found.

DANIEL: Love that couch.

OSCAR: Crowds of people.

DANIEL: The fabric design is so cubist.

OSCAR: People pushing. Shoving.

DANIEL: It speaks to me.

OSCAR: I feel hot. Sweaty.

DANIEL: It'd look fabulous with my Picasso print.

OSCAR: People talking. Toddlers shrieking.

DANIEL: But do I really want to look at that couch every time I'm in the living room?

OSCAR: I was lost. In a maze of showrooms. Like a child.

DANIEL: When I turned to Boyfriend to ask for his opinion, I discovered he was missing.

OSCAR: I started getting panicky.

DANIEL: Fuck.

OSCAR: Worried.

DANIEL: I looked around for him.

OSCAR: Started to push my way through the crowd.

DANIEL: No sign of him anywhere.

OSCAR: People got upset. Angry.

DANIEL: Where the fuck is he? Shit.

OSCAR: Suddenly my strength left me. I had no choice but to sit on the floor. [Sits on the floor.]

DANIEL: I shouldn't have wandered. He shouldn't have wandered.

OSCAR: People looking at me. Concerned. Curious.

DANIEL: There was a crowd straight ahead.

OSCAR: Children laughing. Pointing their fingers at me.

DANIEL: Then I found him. Sitting in the middle of the floor. Looking like a desperate child who had lost his parents.

OSCAR: I wanted to die.

DANIEL: For a moment, I couldn't move. Couldn't push myself into the voyeuristic crowd to help him. Instead, I stood there. Paralyzed. With fascination. Watching him. Sitting on the floor. As if he were a stranger. Someone I didn't know. Someone I didn't care for. Someone I could leave behind in a moment's notice.

OSCAR: I started crying.

DANIEL: After a while, I broke through the crowd and moved towards him.
  [*Goes over to* OSCAR *and helps him up.* OSCAR *holds* DANIEL *tightly.*]

OSCAR: Danny?

DANIEL: Baby.

OSCAR: [*Scoldingly.*] Don't leave me.

DANIEL: It's okay. It's okay. Let's go home.

RANDY IN THE AFTERNOONS

MING: I receive Randy's message on my voice mail
I hear him say, "Same place at one"
I drive, in the blistering heat, as if given a
      command
I'm half-shaking with anticipation, half-annoyed at
      his barking message
I arrive, in a bathhouse, in Hollywood
I get myself a locker
I wrap myself with a white towel smelling faintly
      of bleach
I walk barefoot to our usual room, at the end of
      the floor
I see him there, lying on a narrow bed, with a
      half-open door
I see him, naked, stroking himself, smoking a
Marlborough
I think of Robert, most afternoons, in a bathhouse,
      in Hollywood

I'm greeted by Randy's hungry wet kisses
I feel his urgent tongue forcing down my throat
I flip his hot body over, grabbing his hairy legs
      tightly
I hoist them angrily into the air, his head buried
      in a soft pillow
I enter him forcefully, ignoring his welcoming
      whimpers
I fuck him ruthlessly, punishing him for his
      halting voice mail, thinking I'm his secretary
      in his office, his curt orders I shamelessly
      follow

I grab his hard dick, fucking him, slowly, gently
I feel his tight warmth, fucking him, sturdily,
    steadily
I hear him grunt in pain and sensation, fucking
    him, harder and harder, with abandon
I think about Oscar, wondering how he is, fucking
    him cruelly
I think about why I'm here, why I'm doing this,
    fucking him, feeling weak, feeling close
I think about the countless strangers I've made
    love to in this narrow room, fucking him,
    exploding, biting his neck, screaming
I think about Robert, most afternoons, in a
    bathhouse, in
    Hollywood

I see Randy, walking away, to the sound of roaring
    showers
I wonder if his wife knows about him, me, us
I think about my habit of meeting strangers in
    white towels, in the flickering, dim light of
    my room
I enjoy the welcome anonymity, the immediate
urge to possess these men, to make love to them
I bask in the comfort of their silence, making love
without uttering a word, leaving without a
    sound
I'm always struck by the immediate emptiness and
disappointment, once the love is made, once the
door is again shut
I notice how my cavalier, silent lovers seem to
    look like Oscar, how they smell like him, how
    they feel like him
I make love to them the way I made love to Oscar
I wonder if they like me, love me, need me
I wonder if they feel anything for me

I think this, as a nameless man in half light looks
    at me, nodding

I think this, as he drowns me in a sea of hot
kisses, his fingers, touching me, there
I think this, as he gets on his knees, his head
    against my aching groin, his warm mouth, there
I think this, my head arching back, against a wall,
    my eyes closed
I think of Robert, most afternoons, in a
bathhouse, in
    Hollywood

BREATHING ROOM

MING: So?
ROBERT: Look, I didn't plan it—
MING: Didn't plan it—
ROBERT: It was a spur of the moment thing—
MING: Spur of the moment—
ROBERT: I didn't plan it—I didn't think, okay? Look, I thought you were at
    the gym—
MING: You must think—
ROBERT: Otherwise I wouldn't have—
MING: What's your point?
ROBERT: Wait a minute.
MING: Who's the one fucking in our bedroom?—
ROBERT: Don't you fucking put the blame on me—Don't—
MING: On our bed? With what's his name—
ROBERT: Pran—
MING: Him. Again—
ROBERT: I didn't plan this—
MING: I think you did—
ROBERT: I didn't—it wasn't deliberate—it just—
MING: I don't care—
ROBERT: You were the one—
MING: Don't. You always use that against me—
ROBERT: See other people. You were the one who said—
MING: But didn't we agree—
ROBERT: Expand our horizons, you said—
MING: Didn't we agree we shouldn't do it in our apartment—
ROBERT: So I slipped—Oops—

MING: Slipped—

ROBERT: Now what do you want me to do? Beg? Beg for your forgiveness? What?—

MING: You broke our—

ROBERT: We were just watching TV and it just—

MING: It doesn't matter. I thought this arrangement would be a good thing—

ROBERT: I just went along with it—

MING: Willingly. You went along—

ROBERT: Get real. The real reason you're upset with me isn't that I'm on our bed fucking. You're upset I'm fucking Pran, isn't it? The guy I'm always with. Not like one of your one-night stands.

MING: I don't know what you're—

ROBERT: Let me put this in plain and simple English: You're jealous.

MING: Jealous? Of that little Vietnamese boat person? I don't give a—

ROBERT: Obviously you do.

MING: I don't.

ROBERT: You're upset because I keep seeing him. Spending time with him.

[ROBERT *tweaks* MING's *nipple.*]

MING: I'm not—stop it—

ROBERT: I keep seeing him. And you keep seeing other guys—

[ROBERT *plays with* MING's *hair.*]

MING: I said stop it—

ROBERT: Says something about you, doesn't it?—

MING: That's enough—

ROBERT: You just can't deal with the fact that Pran likes me—

[ROBERT *kisses* MING's *neck.*]

MING: He what?

ROBERT: He likes me.

[ROBERT *gently nibbles on* MING's *ear.*]

MING: Really?

ROBERT: Yeah. He likes me.

[ROBERT *touches* MING's *face.*]

MING: He likes you.

ROBERT: He likes me.

[ROBERT *flirtatiously touches* MING's *chest.*]

ROBERT: He likes me.

[ROBERT *sits on* MING's *lap.*]

ROBERT: He likes me.

[MING *suddenly lurches forward to* ROBERT *and slaps him hard in the face. He punches him twice. Suddenly, as if exhausted or shocked, he stops dumbfoundedly, staring blankly at* ROBERT. *On the ground,* ROBERT *winces in pain and surprise. When* MING *realizes what he has done, he reaches out for* ROBERT. ROBERT, *thinking* MING *is about to assault him again, shies away. Remorsefully,* MING *hugs* ROBERT *tightly. A beat later.*]

MING: I—love you—
ROBERT: Yeah. [*A beat.*] More than anything else in the world.

[ROBERT *looks longingly at* MING. MING *kisses* ROBERT. *Urgently,* ROBERT *responds.*]

THREE LITTLE WORDS

[OSCAR *looks at* MING.]

OSCAR: I love you.
DANIEL: Three little words.

[OSCAR *looks at* DANIEL.]

OSCAR: I love you.
DANIEL: He says to me.
OSCAR: I love you.
DANIEL: Every moment of the day.
OSCAR: I love you.
DANIEL: All the time.
OSCAR: I love you.
DANIEL: Unceasingly.
OSCAR: I love you.
DANIEL: His affection never wanting.
OSCAR: I love you.
DANIEL: He always touches me.
OSCAR: I love you.
DANIEL: Holds me. Hugs me. Kisses me.

OSCAR: I love you.

DANIEL: On crowded street corners. On subway trains. On kitchen floors.

OSCAR: I love you.

DANIEL: I hear it.

OSCAR: I love you.

DANIEL: He says. He whispers. He shouts.

OSCAR: I love you.

DANIEL: In the throes of love. Under duvet covers. Flat on my back.

OSCAR: I love you.

DANIEL: On the rinse cycle. With my mud mask. Aerobizing. To Whitney.

OSCAR: I love you.

DANIEL: I never tire of these words.

OSCAR: I love you.

DANIEL: Not really. Really.

OSCAR: I love you.

DANIEL: It's what I breathe for. What I live for. What I die for.

OSCAR: I love you.

DANIEL: It's—music—to my—you know—

OSCAR: I love you.

DANIEL: I never want him to—stop—not really—

OSCAR: I love you.

DANIEL: I wonder if he means it. What he says.

OSCAR: I love you.

DANIEL: I wonder if he's cheating on me. Hiding something.

OSCAR: I love you.

DANIEL: I wonder what "love" means—translated in Chinese.

OSCAR: I love you.

DANIEL: I wonder if that's his way. The way they do it in China or wherever he's from.

OSCAR: I love you.

DANIEL: It's delightful. Nice. It's driving me insane.

OSCAR: I love you.

DANIEL: I wish he'd stop. I thought all Asian men are typically quiet.

OSCAR: I love you.

DANIEL: Three little words.

OSCAR: I love you.

DANIEL: He says to me.

OSCAR: I love you.

DANIEL: All the time.

OSCAR: I love you.
DANIEL: Unceasingly.
OSCAR: I love you.
DANIEL: Cease it.

MORE THAN ANYTHING ELSE IN THE WORLD

[*At one corner of the stage,* OSCAR *wakes up with a start.*]

OSCAR: Danny? Danny? Danny! Danny! Danny!

[DANIEL *enters.*]

DANIEL: Yes?
OSCAR: Where were you?
DANIEL: Outside. I was—
OSCAR: Where were—
DANIEL: Here. I'm here.
OSCAR: Don't—don't do that—
DANIEL: I won't.
OSCAR: Don't leave—without—
DANIEL: Are you okay?
OSCAR: Don't ever do that again!

[*In another corner,* MING *and* ROBERT *attempt to make love.*]

MING: I'm sorry.
ROBERT: It's okay.
MING: I guess I'm just—
ROBERT: Yeah.
MING: I really want to—you know—
ROBERT: I know.
MING: Do you want to—?
ROBERT: No. It's okay.

[*In* OSCAR'S *corner.*]

DANIEL: Another bad dream?
OSCAR: Yes. Struggling. Fighting. Running.
DANIEL: Running from?
OSCAR: Just running. Like I was being chased.
DANIEL: Where?
OSCAR: Don't know. In some shopping mall.

DANIEL: Ikea?
OSCAR: No. You weren't in the dream.

[*In* MING's *corner.*]

MING: I'm sorry about—You get me so—
ROBERT: Upset.
MING: The things I want to say—
ROBERT: Comes out—
MING: Yes. Like this. The words—thoughts—it's—
ROBERT: Difficult.

[*In* OSCAR's *corner.*]

OSCAR: Funny. All my dreams. I'm always chasing or being chased.
DANIEL: Freudian.
OSCAR: Never once—flying.
DANIEL: You've never? It's a great feeling. You feel so free. Like a bird. Like a
    Maxi-pad commercial. It feels just like that.
OSCAR: I wish I could—[OSCAR *groans.*]

[*In* MING's *corner.* MING *slowly and delicately touches the bruise on*
ROBERT's *face.*]

MING: Does it—?
ROBERT: No.
MING: Really?
ROBERT: I'm fine.

[*In* OSCAR's *corner.*]

DANIEL: What's wrong?
OSCAR: I feel—
DANIEL: Sick?
OSCAR: Weak.
DANIEL: I'll call the doctor.
OSCAR: It's okay. Just queasy. Wiped out.

[*In* MING's *corner.*]

MING: It won't happen again. You know that. It won't happen again.
ROBERT: No. It won't.
MING: Promise.
ROBERT: Yeah.

[*In* OSCAR's *corner.* OSCAR *grimaces in pain. When* DANIEL *reaches for* OSCAR's *hand,* OSCAR *grabs* DANIEL's *finger. Holding it tightly.*]

DANIEL: Better?
OSCAR: No. But it'll be better.
DANIEL: Sure?
OSCAR: Sure.

[*A beat.*]

DANIEL: You're holding my finger.

[*In* MING's *corner.*]

MING: I—love you.
ROBERT: I love you too.
MING: More than anything else in the world.
ROBERT: More than anything else in the world.

[ROBERT *kisses* MING *tenderly.*]

FINE AND PERFECT

DANIEL: I know I'm not perfect. But you know what gets my dander up? It seems that Boyfriend always has the perfect reason to be upset. Throwing random tantrums because he's sick. And if I get into a hissy fit, especially during that time of the month, I'm Bette Davis serving din-dins on a silver platter. So maybe he has a better reason. But being Dear Abby all the time isn't easy.

ROBERT: I know what I want isn't easy. I know my dream of a perfect relationship is difficult to obtain. I know it's a fantasy to want the kind of life prescribed by Judith Krantz paperback novels and misty black and white movies. I know. But I know I can have it. I know we just have to try a little harder, Ming has to try a little harder. I know this relationship is what I want, it's what Ming wants. I know things aren't perfect now, but we'll be perfect, he'll be perfect.

DANIEL: Our tres sincere friends always mince up to me and ask me about Boyfriend. "How is he doing?" "Is the poor dear okay?" "Does he want to watch *My Fair Lady* again?" Like he's dying. Like he's Camille. Meanwhile, Boyfriend looks fine. Looks perfect. Not a hair out of place. Never felt better. Smiling like he's just got laid by Fabio. He's fine. Fine.

ROBERT: We're still in love. We're still in a relationship. We still go to the opera. We still have quiet dinners only at the best restaurants. We still spend long weekends with interesting people doing interesting things. We still take spontaneous exotic trips to faraway places where a word of English is never spoken. We're fine. Perfect. We are. We are.

DANIEL: So it's not perfect all the time. Sometimes life can be difficult with Boyfriend. It's hard to care for him. To be around him. His moods. Sometimes I wonder why I'm here. And sometimes I get a little emotional. Cry in the middle of the day. Wondering what it's like without Boyfriend. Don't know why. Sometimes I just blank. Get angry. Depressed. Sometimes I—I just—just—I'm fine. Really. Fine.

ROBERT: You see other people. You come home late. You kiss me. You buy me gifts. You go to bed. You sleep. You smell of someone's cologne. You give me things. You see other people. You give me money. You take me on trips. You see other people. You take me to expensive restaurants. You give me your credit card. You see other people. You know I love you. You know I'll never leave you. You see other people. You know I need you. You know I need what you give me. You know I need you more than you need me. You see other people. You know it's perfect.

DANIEL: Sometimes I'd spend a thoughtless hour or two with a nameless man. Slipping into another world that could have been Boyfriend's and mine. A world without AIDS or death. Just the two of us. Happy. Together. And after the passion between two strangers is spent, I'm back in the same living room with unsuspecting Boyfriend. Feeling a little guilty. A little renewed. A little hopeful. A little fine.

ROBERT: I wonder if my dream of a perfect relationship is just that. A dream, a stupid dream. I wonder if I will ever find that special someone. I wonder if that special someone is him. I wonder if I'll lose that special someone in the crowd if I stayed too long with him. I wonder if I'm always on his mind. I wonder if he wants me, needs me, loves me. I wonder if he feels the same way I do. I wonder if he sees through all my careless imperfections. I wonder if someone else can love him more than I can. I wonder if someone else can love me more than he can.

DANIEL: No one asks how I'm doing. Everyone assumes. That I'm fine. And I am. Fine. For a while. Fine. I try to be. I have to be. Fine. And, of course, after softening my luscious cheeks with Pearl Cream, I'll look better than fine. I knew this relationship was going to be hard. Going into it. And somehow I thought it'd be a little easier. Because Boyfriend's the one, you know. The only one for me. And that—keeps me going.

FOLIE-A-DEUX

[*In* MING's *corner.*]

ROBERT: It's for the best—
MING: Why?—
ROBERT: It's not working—
MING: You're in love with—
ROBERT: That's not the point—
MING: That Vietcong—
ROBERT: Don't—
MING: I thought you said we should talk—
ROBERT: I did but—
MING: Let's talk—
ROBERT: It's too late.

[*In* OSCAR's *corner.* OSCAR *slow dances with* DANIEL.]

DANIEL: Dancing.
OSCAR: Like we used to. In the living room.
DANIEL: Yes. I missed this.
OSCAR: Me, too. [*They kiss.*]

[*In* MING's *corner.*]

ROBERT: I'm going to stay with—
MING: That boat person—
ROBERT: You're so incredibly—
MING: You planned this, didn't you?
ROBERT: Racist—it's amazing that—
MING: Like you always did—scheming—plotting—
ROBERT: Is it so difficult to remember his—
MING: It slips my mind—
ROBERT: Pran—
MING: You always clam up when—
ROBERT: I don't want to talk about him—
MING: I want to—
ROBERT: Why? There's nothing to—
MING: I'm not asking for intimate—
ROBERT: Hey, I don't ask what you do—
MING: I'll tell you if you want to know.

[*In* OSCAR'*s corner.* OSCAR *and* DANIEL *dance. Suddenly,* OSCAR *winces in pain.*]

DANIEL: What's wrong?
OSCAR: Pain. Shooting pains.
DANIEL: Where—the pain— [OSCAR *falls to the ground.*]

[*In* MING'*s corner.*]

ROBERT: Drop it. You're acting like a child—
MING: You're so full of secrets.
ROBERT: I'm going. To Pran. I'm staying with him.

[*Overlapping with* MING *and* ROBERT.]

DANIEL: You've got to hold on.	MING: Maybe you like to finish his sentences too. Correct his English. Don't you think it's so cute when he calls? [*Mimics.*] "Hello, can I please speak to Robert?"
OSCAR: In my—stomach. DANIEL: Let me get your—	ROBERT: I'll leave his number on the table in case—
OSCAR: It won't help.	MING: No!
DANIEL: Here. OSCAR: No, It hurts.	

[*In* OSCAR'*s corner.*]

DANIEL: Think about something else. It'll help. Anything. I don't know.

[OSCAR *looks at* MING.]

OSCAR: Ming?

[MING *looks at* OSCAR. *They look at each other for the first time in this act. A beat later.*]

DANIEL: Daniel.

[OSCAR *turns his glance to* DANIEL. MING *looks at* ROBERT.]

OSCAR: What?

DANIEL: Nothing.

[*In* MING'*s corner.*]

MING: So what do you do with your evenings together? Practice English?—
ROBERT: Leave me alone—

[*In* OSCAR'*s corner.*]

OSCAR: You've got to help me.
DANIEL: Yes. Anything.
OSCAR: I need some—sleeping pills.
DANIEL: Sleep. I'll get you a Valium from—
OSCAR: No! Not one. A lot.

[*In* MING'*s corner.*]

MING: You love it, don't you? This white superiority—
ROBERT: He talks to me, asshole! With the few fucking English words he
knows! In his broken English unbearable to your ears! He fucking talks to
me! Not like you! I hate you!

[*In* OSCAR'*s corner.*]

DANIEL: It's not what—
OSCAR: I know.
DANIEL: We said—
OSCAR: Fight it to the end.
DANIEL: But now—
OSCAR: You're not fighting it. I am.

[*In* MING'*s corner.* MING *grabs* ROBERT *by the neck and passionately
kisses him.* ROBERT *responds.*]

MING: You love me. You need me.

[*In* OSCAR'*s corner.*]

DANIEL: What about me? What about me?
OSCAR: I don't care! [*Pause.*] I mean—
DANIEL: I know. Really.

[*In* MING'*s corner.* ROBERT *breaks away from* MING'*s kiss.*]

ROBERT: I don't love you.
MING: Leave then.

[MING *strikes* ROBERT *across the face. With a sudden burst of strength,* ROBERT *lunges for a surprised* MING. ROBERT *decks him hard.* MING *does not retaliate, numbly accepting each blow.*]

ROBERT: I'm sick of you. Sick of you hitting me. [*A beat.*] Oh my god. I've become you.

[*In* OSCAR's *corner.*]

OSCAR: I'm dying.
DANIEL: No. You have to fight—
OSCAR: You promised. Promised to do anything for me.
DANIEL: But not this—I don't know—
OSCAR: Please.
DANIEL: Oh god. I don't know. I don't know. I don't know.

A LANGUAGE OF THEIR OWN

ROBERT: In the beginning of our relationship, we learned
        each other's language
Like over-eager babies
Mouthing unintelligible gaggles and sounds
Unable to articulate
Clumsily tripping on words
Falling into abject frustration
But once we found the common language
Each action and deed, every word and sentence, was a
        joy,
and an excitement
A tingling of senses
A radiant discovery

Then, as if through osmosis, we used each other's
        words and expressions
Borrowing shamelessly and
Indeliberately incorporating them into our language
Speaking as one
Thinking as one
Feeling as one
And in the course, we invented new words

Gave existing words new meaning
Redefined and polished our language
Making it a special one of our own
One that we selfishly shared
One that no one could decipher or understand
One that we used in the comfort of each other's
    arms in quiet evenings

Then we tired of it
Lost interest
Got lazy
Became indifferent
Words gradually lost their meaning and significance
Like drunken dancers, we emphasized wrong accents
    in words
Sentences led to misinterpretations
Misinterpretations led to misunderstandings
Misunderstandings led to inevitable silence

In the end, we spoke different languages
MING: Even though, we wanted the same thing.

SAYING GOOD-BYES

DANIEL: I—don't want to do this.
OSCAR: I know.
DANIEL: Don't want you to—
OSCAR: Yes.
DANIEL: How—how are you feeling?
OSCAR: The same.
DANIEL: Is it—helping?
OSCAR: Slowly.
DANIEL: Good.
OSCAR: You knew it'd come to this—
DANIEL: Yes but—
OSCAR: Me leaving.
DANIEL: Leaving. Yes. I know.
OSCAR: If the hospital finds out—
DANIEL: I'll say I can't read English or something—
OSCAR: Say I did—

DANIEL: Misread the prescription on the bottle—

OSCAR: Say I wanted it—

DANIEL: I'll think of something.

OSCAR: We make a great team.

DANIEL: Yes. A great team.

OSCAR: Danny?

DANIEL: Yes?

OSCAR: I really appreciated everything—

DANIEL: I know.

OSCAR: Everything we did. Everything I put you through—

DANIEL: Do you love me?

OSCAR: What kind of question is that?

DANIEL: I don't know. Do you love me?

OSCAR: Of course. Yes.

DANIEL: I love you too.

OSCAR: I know. So what are you going to do? With yourself. Once I—go.

DANIEL: Well, there's a fire sale at Ikea in the Whitelands Mall. So if you can kick off within the next half hour—

OSCAR: You always make me laugh.

DANIEL: You won't if you knew I was charging that tres—that tres—

[*Pause.*]

OSCAR: Live.

DANIEL: What?

OSCAR: I want you to live.

DANIEL: Well, I don't feel much like it at the moment. Living. Live. [*A beat.*] I think I'm supposed to be the one to tell you that.

OSCAR: I'm sorry—

DANIEL: I want to say—say—I don't know what I want to say—there are so many things—and I can't—so many things but—

OSCAR: I know.

DANIEL: I want to grow old with you. I want to always hear your voice. I want to dance with you. Like we used to. Every night. To Satie.

OSCAR: Me too.

DANIEL: I want to—so many things.

OSCAR: I know. You knew this would come.

DANIEL: Don't leave me. Please.

OSCAR: I think I'll miss you very much. [*A beat.*] Why?

DANIEL: Why what?

OSCAR: Why did you get involved knowing that—
DANIEL: I think you know why.

[*A beat.*]

OSCAR: Say good-bye.
DANIEL: What?
OSCAR: It'll be easier.
DANIEL: I want to stay. With you.
OSCAR: Go.
DANIEL: Please.
OSCAR: I love you. [*A beat.*] Go.
DANIEL: No.
OSCAR: Go. Get a drink of water. Around the corner.
DANIEL: Why are you—
OSCAR: I need some time alone.
DANIEL: Why?
OSCAR: Remember. Live.

[DANIEL *looks at* OSCAR *for a long moment. Suddenly, he gets up and leaves. A beat later,* MING *comes into the room.*]

OSCAR: You are here.
MING: I never left.
OSCAR: Will you hold my hand?
MING: Yes.
OSCAR: It's getting a little colder.
MING: Do you want me to get you a blanket?
OSCAR: No. Hold my hand. Hold. Hold my finger.
MING: Your finger.
OSCAR: Yes. Like that. Yes. You used to hold it like that.
MING: Yes.
OSCAR: On trains. In streets.
MING: Listen—
OSCAR: Uh-huh—
MING: I'm sorry about how we—
OSCAR: Me too.
MING: I wish we could—
OSCAR: Yes. I wish—
MING: Wishing seems a little—
OSCAR: Never too late—

MING: You know I—

OSCAR: Yes. I love you too.

MING: Me too.

OSCAR: You know—I always saw your face—everywhere I turned—felt you were always with me—

MING: I wish—

OSCAR: Shh—I know—

MING: You okay?

OSCAR: Yes. Fading. Feel like I'm—

MING: What?

OSCAR: Flying.

MING: Flying?

OSCAR: Higher and higher—

MING: Don't.

OSCAR: Have to—got to—flying—it's so—

MING: Liberating?

[*A beat.*]

OSCAR: Let go.

MING: What?

OSCAR: Let go.

MING: Of your finger?

OSCAR: Yes.

MING: No.

OSCAR: Need to fly.

MING: Fly.

OSCAR: Yes.

MING: Fly.

OSCAR: Fly.

MING: You're free.

OSCAR: Yes. Free. Free. Free. I'm flying.

A CHURCH IN THE SOUTH END

MING: I heard he died alone in a sterile hospital room, overlooking the Charles River on a winter day.

DANIEL: After I took a drink at the water fountain, I stole back into Oscar's room and sat by his bed. He was breathing heavily. Choking. Mumbling. When I rested my hand on his—he suddenly grabbed my finger, as if by instinct. Holding it. Tightly. As if he knew it was me. Then he let go. He was gone.

MING: He's gone. That's what Daniel said. On the phone machine. Gone. Passed on. Whatever. We always have such nice words for terrible things. It was as if he was someone temporary. Someone we were never meant to have. To keep and to hold. Someone never meant to stay too long.

DANIEL: He was the first person I called. I just thought he should know. Ming would have wanted to be there. By his side.

MING: It was two years since I last saw Oscar. Two years. In a drafty bedroom upstairs. A rowdy party down below. Now, I'll never see his face again.

DANIEL: Later, I left him another message. Telling him where and when the service was going to be. In a church in the South End.

MING: I called back and said I'd be there.

DANIEL: We waited for about an hour before starting the service. But he never showed up.

MING: Of course—I would have been there—really—I would—if—but—I don't know—I wanted to but—I didn't—

DANIEL: When I got back to the apartment, there was a message on my machine. It was him. Saying that something has come up. Suddenly. Last minute. Couldn't make it. Hope it went well. That's what he said. Hope it went well.

MING: I remember telling him regardless of what happened, I would be there for him. I promised him. I did. And I would have, you know. Really. Now all I've said—it's just words. Empty words.

DANIEL: He didn't return my calls. The bastard would not return my calls.

MING: Daniel and I never really knew each other. All we could ever talk about was him. I didn't call him back.

DANIEL: I tried calling and calling. Leaving messages and—finally, I gave up. Perhaps, silence is best.

WHAT HE LOOKS LIKE

MING: I can never forget what he said to me.

OSCAR: Hold my finger.

MING: Like this?

OSCAR: Let go. Let go.

MING: I can't.

OSCAR: You have to.

MING: They say you always remember your first love.

OSCAR: You were mine too.

MING: I wanted to grow old with you.

OSCAR: Yes.

MING: Every day, the image of you grows dimmer in my mind. Like castles made of sand. With each oncoming tide, a little bit of the castle washes away. Until there's nothing left. I've forgotten what you look like.

OSCAR: It's okay.

MING: Forgotten what you smell like. What you sound like. What you taste like. I don't want to lose that.

OSCAR: You'll find new sounds. New smells.

DANIEL: I can never forget what he said to me.

OSCAR: Live.

DANIEL: Things haven't been the same without you.

OSCAR: How are you, Danny?

DANIEL: Okay.

OSCAR: Dating?

DANIEL: No. Organizing your things. Disconnecting your phone. Packing. Your things. Into little brown boxes. I hope you don't mind but I'm giving most of it away to the AIDS Project and Salvation Army.

OSCAR: I don't mind.

DANIEL: I'm going to keep a few things. A few things that remind me of us.

OSCAR: The grey scarf you bought me last fall.

DANIEL: It still smells of you.

OSCAR: The Donna Summer CDs.

DANIEL: And Satie. Don't forget Satie. We used to—

OSCAR: Yes. And some pieces of furniture that hold history. Our history.

DANIEL: Sometimes I see you sitting on them.

OSCAR: How have you been?

DANIEL: Good. [A beat.] I'm positive.

OSCAR: No.

DANIEL: But I'm keeping healthy. Making cardboard-tasting protein vegetable shakes. Bought a Cuisinart with your credit card at Neiman's.

OSCAR: You could have gotten it cheaper at K-Mart.

DANIEL: I spared no expense.

OSCAR: I thought we were safe.

DANIEL: We were. It's probably not you. Perhaps someone before. Someone after. I don't know. The point is I'm positive.

OSCAR: Oh, Danny.

DANIEL: I'll be fine.

OSCAR: I wish I could do something for you, like what you did—

DANIEL: I'll be fine. Really. [A *beat*.] I miss you. Very much.

OSCAR: Me too.

ROBERT: I can never forget what he said to me.

MING: I think we should—get together—meet—something—

ROBERT: Coffee?

MING: Yeah.

ROBERT: So—

MING: I have been thinking about you.

ROBERT: So have I.

MING: I want us to see each other again.

ROBERT: Uh-huh.

MING: You're not thrilled. You're seeing someone. Pran.

ROBERT: No. I am. Thrilled. I mean, I'm not seeing—it's all over with Pran. [A *beat*.] I just want it to be right, you know?

MING: Me, too. [A *beat*.] I've been getting help. With the—

ROBERT: Good. [*Pause.*] So—

MING: Coffee?

ROBERT: Dinner.

MING: Movie.

ROBERT: Revival?

MING: Sure. Sounds great.

[*Pause.*]

ROBERT: Listen.

MING: What?

ROBERT: I want to say—

MING: Yes?

ROBERT: I—I still—still—

[A *beat*.]

MING: I know. I know.

END

About the Contributors

JEANNIE BARROGA Barroga has been writing plays since 1981. She created the Playwright Forum in Palo Alto, California in 1983, and since 1986 has been the literary manager at TheatreWorks, a regional theater also located in Palo Alto. Her play *Eye of the Coconut* premiered in Seattle in 1987. Her play *Walls* was produced at the Asian American Theater Company in San Francisco in 1989 and is published in *Unbroken Thread: An Anthology of Plays by Asian American Women* (1993, ed. Roberta Uno). *Talk-Story* premiered at Theatre-Works in 1992. Her latest play, *Rita's Resources*, was produced at Pan Asian Repertory Theater in New York in 1995. Her work has also been presented on San Francisco Bay area cable television specials, and a book, *Two Plays*, was published in 1993.

LIA CHANG (cover photographer) A fourth-generation Chinese American born and raised in San Francisco, Lia Chang has worked extensively as an actress in film, television, and on the New York stage. As a portrait and performing arts photographer for KYODO News, her work has been widely published and exhibited. Her solo exhibit, "Asian Pacific Americans in the Workforce and the Arts," commissioned by APALA, was featured simultaneously in several locations in Washington, D.C. and New York City to commemorate Asian Pacific American Heritage Month in 1996.

PHILIP KAN GOTANDA Gotanda's plays include *The Wash, Fishhead Soup, Yankee Dawg You Die, Song of a Nisei Fisherman,* and *The Ballad of Yachiyo.* His work has been produced nationally at such theaters as the Asian American Theatre Company, Manhattan Theatre Club, Berkeley Repertory Theater, and East West Players. His many honors include a Guggenheim Foundation fellowship, the Lila Wallace–Readers' Digest Writer's Award, a National Endowment for the Arts fellowship, Gerbode and McKnight Foundation fellowships, and the Theatre Communications Group/National Endowment for the Arts Directing Fellowship. Gotanda has collaborated with composer Dan Kuramoto on a full-length spoken-word piece entitled *in the dominion of night* and in performance with a beat-retro jazz combo, "the new orientals." He wrote, directed, and is featured in *The Kiss,* a short film presented at the Sundance Film Festival, the Berlin and Edinburgh International Film Festivals, and the San Francisco International Film Festival, where it won the Golden Gate Award. He has also written and is directing an independent feature film, *Gioconda Smile.* Gotanda resides in San Francisco with his wife, Diane Emiko Takei, an actress, director, and producer. He is currently serving a PEW Charitable Trust–Theatre Communications Group National Theater Artist Grant residency at Berkeley Repertory Theater.

VELINA HASU HOUSTON Houston is an award-winning writer of plays, cinema, television, poetry, and critical essays. Her body of plays includes the internationally acclaimed *Tea, Kokoro, Asa Ga Kimashita, Necessities, The Matsuyama Mirror,* and many others including commissions from the Mark Taper Forum, the Asia Society, the Lila Wallace–Readers' Digest Foundation, and others. Her work has been presented at many venues in the U.S. and Japan, including the Old Globe Theatre, Manhattan Theatre Club, the Smithsonian Institution, A Contemporary Theatre, Negro Ensemble Company, and Nippon Hoso Kai. She has written film for Columbia Pictures, Sidney Poitier, PBS/KCET, and others; and she is chronicled in five U.S. and Japanese documentaries. Houston has edited one other drama anthology: *The Politics of Life* (Temple University Press, 1993). Her many awards for excellence in writing include two Rockefeller Foundation fellowships. A screenplay version of *Kokoro* has been optioned by Tina Chen. Houston is completing a novel based on her play *Tea,* an anthology of writings by Amerasians, and a book about film and multiethnic (mixed race) identity. She is an associate professor and director of the playwriting program at the University of Southern California School of Theatre. A Phi Beta Kappa, she holds a Master of Fine Arts from the University of California at Los Angeles and is completing her Ph.D. She resides in Santa Monica, California, with her children, Kiyoshi and Kuniko-Leilani.

HUYNH QUANG NHUONG Huynh's childhood in a village of the Central Highlands in Vietnam was evoked poignantly in his successful first book, *The Land I Lost* (1982). He has also written *Wandering Clouds* (1995). His plays include *South African Mother, Nostalgia,* and *Rain in the Mountains and Lightning at Sea* and have been presented at the Maplewood Barn Theatre (Columbia, Missouri), the Black Theatre Group (Berkeley), the Organic Theater company (Chicago), and elsewhere. His awards include a National Endowment for the Arts creative writing fellowship, the Friends of American Writers Award, and the Missouri Writers' Biennial Award. He received first prize in the Pamoja Theater Workshop's National Playwriting Contest (St. Louis), and first prize in the Lodi Arts Commission Drama Fest '94 (California). Huynh graduated from Saigon University with a degree in chemistry. He was permanently paralyzed by a gunshot wound while serving as an officer in the Vietnamese army. He emigrated to the United States in 1969. Huynh holds a Master of Arts in French and Comparative Literature from the University of Missouri.

DAVID HENRY HWANG This award-winning writer has created works for theater, opera, and film. Hwang is perhaps best known as the author of *M. Butterfly,* which ran two years on Broadway and won the 1988 Tony, Drama Desk, John Gassner, and Outer Critics' Circle Awards, as well as the 1991 Los Angeles Drama Critics' Circle Award. A film version, based on Hwang's screenplay, was released by Warner Brothers in 1993. He also penned the screenplay for *Golden Gate,* a feature film released in 1994 by the Samuel Golden Company. Some of his other plays include *FOB* (1981 OBIE Award), *The House of Sleeping Beauties* (1983), *Face Value* (1993), and *Trying Hard to Find Chinatown* (1996). His newest play, *Golden Child,* premiered in 1996 as a co-production of the South Coast Repertory and the New York Shakespeare Festival. Hwang's grants and awards include fellowships from the Guggenheim and Rockefeller Foundations, the Pew Charitable Trust, the New York State Council on the Arts, and the National Endowment for the Arts. Hwang graduated from Stanford University and attended the Yale School of Drama. He recently joined the staff of the nationally broadcast cable television show "Asian America" as an interviewer. He lives in New York City with his wife, actress Kathryn Layng, and their son, Noah.

VICTORIA NALANI KNEUBUHL Kneubuhl was born in Honolulu and is of Samoan, Hawaiian, and European-American ancestry. Among her many plays are *Tofa Samoa,* which was presented in 1994 at the Okinawa International Children's Theatre Festival, and *Ka'iulani,* which she co-authored and which has been produced in Edinburgh, Los Angeles, and Washington,

D.C. She holds a Master's degree in Drama and Theatre from the University of Hawaii at Manoa and recently received the Hawaii Award for Literature, the highest literary award in that state.

SUNG RNO Rno's poetry has appeared in *Caliban*, *APA Journal*, and in *Premonitions* (an anthology edited by Walter Yew), and his plays have been produced at East West Players, Asian American Theatre Center/Thick Description, Northwest Asian American Theater, Dance Theater Workshop, and Grinnell College. Workshop presentations include the HBO Writers' Showcase, the Mark Taper Forum, the Public Theater, the Seattle Group Theater, Pan Asian Repertory Theater, Theater Mu, Circle Repertory Theatre, and Brown University. He is the recipient of Van Lier Foundation playwriting fellowships through New York Theater Workshop and New Dramatists, first prize in the Seattle Multicultural Playwrights Festival, and commissions from the Mark Taper Forum and the Public Theater. Rno holds a Master of Fine Arts in poetry from Brown University, and he is a member of the Dramatists Guild. He lives in New York City, where he works as a copywriter.

DMAE ROBERTS Roberts is an Amerasian actor, producer, and playwright who resides in Portland, Oregon. Her thirteen-part radio series, *Legacies: Tales From America*, was broadcast nationwide on National Public Radio (NPR). Roberts has written and produced more than one hundred radio productions for NPR, and she is the recipient of the prestigious George Foster Peabody Award for her autobiographical radio docu-play *Mei, Mei, A Daughter's Song* (also broadcast on NPR). Her other plays include *Picasso in the Back Seat*, *Mei Mei* (based on her radio play), and *Janie Bigo*. Roberts has described *Breaking Glass* as a product of her interest in the "role of the inner life and its ability to help one survive, and her belief that a person's resilience is determined by family, culture, environment, and "the enigmatic qualities that make up a human personality." It explores, she has said, "the breaking points, the determinants that spark the individual will to survive."

ROBERTA UNO A director, writer, and producer, Uno is currently in residence at the Fine Arts Center at the University of Massachusetts at Amherst and is an associate professor in the university's Department of Theater. She founded the New WORLD Theater at the University in 1979 and has served as its artistic director ever since. Her directing credits include *Walls* by Jeannie Barroga, *Tea* by Velina Hasu Houston, *The Dance and the Railroad* by David Henry Hwang, *Miss Ida B. Wells* by Endesha Ida Mae Holland, *the bodies between us* by le thi diem thuy, *Flyin' West* by Pearl Cleage, *R.A.W.* (*'Cause I'm a Woman*) by Diana Son, *Combination Skin* by Lisa Jones, *A Dream of Canaries* by Diana Saenz, *Sneaky* by William Yellow Robe, and *Blues for Mr. Charlie* by James Baldwin. Uno is a member of the Society of Stage Directors and Choreographers. Recent publications include articles in the *Dramatist's Quarterly, Theatre Topics*, and *International Theatre Forum*. She is the editor of *Unbroken Thread: An Anthology of Plays by Asian American Women* (Amherst: University of Massachusetts Press, 1993) and co-editor with Kathy Perkins of *Contemporary Plays by Women of Color* (London: Routledge, 1996). She holds a Bachelor of Arts degree from Hampshire College, a Master of Arts in dramatic literature from Smith College, and a Master of Fine Arts in directing from the University of Massachusetts at Amherst.

LUCY WANG Wang's plays include *Bird's Nest Soup, Mah-Jongg, Trayf,* and *Number One Son.* Her plays, short stories, poems, essays, and articles have appeared in such publications as *Sistersong, New People,* and *Contemporary Women Playwrights.* Performances of her plays have been held at HOME for Contemporary Theatre, the Mark Taper Forum, Capital Repertory, Playwrights Preview Productions, the Asian American Theatre Company, and others. Wang's awards include a MacDowell Colony Fellowship, a Berrilla Kerr Foundation Grant, and the James Thurber Fellowship. Her plays have been finalists in the Cleveland Public Theatre's Festival of New Plays, the L. Arnold Weissberger Playwriting Competition, and others. She is a member of the HB Playwrights Studio (founded by Uta Hagen and Herbert Berghof) and of the Dramatists Guild.

ELIZABETH WONG Wong was a staff writer for the ABC sitcom, "All-American Girl." Her play, *Letters to a Student Revolutionary*, is published by Dramatic Publishing and is included in two anthologies, *Women on the Verge* (Applause Books) and *Unbroken Thread: An Anthology of Plays by Asian American Women* (ed. Roberta Uno, 1993). It was first produced Off-Broadway by Pan Asian Repertory Theatre, with subsequent productions in Philadelphia, Seattle, Los Angeles, and other cities. Wong's newest play, *China Doll*, has been workshopped at the Mark Taper Forum and the Denver Center Theatre. *Kimchee and Chitlins* premiered at the Victory Gardens Theatre (Chicago) and received its West Coast debut at West Coast Ensemble (Los Angeles). The play was featured in the Out in Front Festival at the Mark Taper Forum and was workshopped in New York and Chicago and has been produced in colleges and universities throughout the country. Wong has received fellowships from Yaddo, the Ucross Foundation, and Walt Disney Studios and has worked as a dramaturge at Actors Theatre of Louisville and as an editorial columnist for the *Los Angeles Times*. She lives in Los Angeles and teaches playwriting and sitcom writing at the University of California at Santa Barbara and at the University of Southern California. She is currently working on two commissioned plays and a screenplay.

CHAY YEW Yew is a writer and producer living in Los Angeles. Theatre Works in Singapore commissioned his first play, *As If He Hears*. Initially banned by the government of Singapore, it was finally produced in 1989. In 1990, to raise AIDS awareness in Singapore's schools and colleges, Yew wrote a video docudrama, *Someone I Used To Know*, broadcast on SBC Channel 12 in 1992. He wrote his second play, *Porcelain*, while artist-in-residence at Mu-Lan Theatre company in London. It premiered at the Etcetera Theatre in May 1992 and has since been produced in Los Angeles, San Francisco, Washington, D.C., Dallas, Chicago, and San Diego. Yew was awarded the 1993 London Fringe Award for Best Play for *Porcelain*. His short play, "Learning Chinese," was given a public reading at the Mark Taper Forum in 1993. Yew combined this play with the companion piece "Broken English." The result, *A Language of Their Own*, was given staged readings at Seattle's Intiman Theatre and New York City's Public Theatre and received its world premier production in 1994 at the Celebration Theatre in Los Angeles. *A Language of Their Own* has since been produced at East West Players. Yew is a member of the Dramatists Guild and is artistic director of the Asian Theatre Workshop of the Mark Taper Forum.

Also in the *Asian American History and Culture* series:

Sucheng Chan, ed., *Entry Denied: Exclusion and the Chinese Community in America, 1882–1943*, 1991

Gary Y. Okihiro, *Cane Fires: The Anti-Japanese Movement in Hawaii, 1865–1945*, 1991

Yen Le Espiritu, *Asian American Panethnicity: Bridging Institutions and Identities*, 1992

Karen Isaksen Leonard, *Making Ethnic Choices: California's Punjabi Mexican Americans*, 1992

Shirley Gok-lin Lim and Amy Ling, eds., *Reading the Literatures of Asian America*, 1992

Renqiu Yu, *To Save China, To Save Ourselves: The Chinese Hand Laundry Alliance of New York*, 1992

Velina Hasu Houston, ed., *The Politics of Life: Four Plays by Asian American Women*, 1993

William Wei, *The Asian American Movement*, 1993

Sucheng Chan, ed., *Hmong Means Free: Life in Laos and America*, 1994

Timothy P. Fong, *The First Suburban Chinatown: The Remaking of Monterey Park, California*, 1994

Chris Friday, *Organizing Asian American Labor: The Pacific Coast Canned-Salmon Industry, 1870–1942*, 1994

Paul Ong, Edna Bonacich, and Lucie Cheng, eds., *The New Asian Immigration in Los Angeles and Global Restructuring*, 1994

Carlos Bulosan, *The Cry and the Dedication*, edited and with an introduction by E. San Juan, Jr., 1995

Yen Le Espiritu, *Filipino American Lives*, 1995

Vincente L. Rafael, ed., *Discrepant Histories: Translocal Essays on Filipino Cultures*, 1995

E. San Juan, Jr., ed., *On Becoming Filipino: Selected Writings of Carlos Bulosan*, 1995

E. San Juan, Jr., *The Philippine Temptation: Dialectics of U.S.–Philippine Literary Relations*, 1996

Deepika Bahri and Mary Vasudeva, eds., *Between the Lines: South Asians and Postcoloniality*, 1996

Josephine Lee, *Performing Asian America: Race and Ethnicity on the Contemporary Stage*, 1997